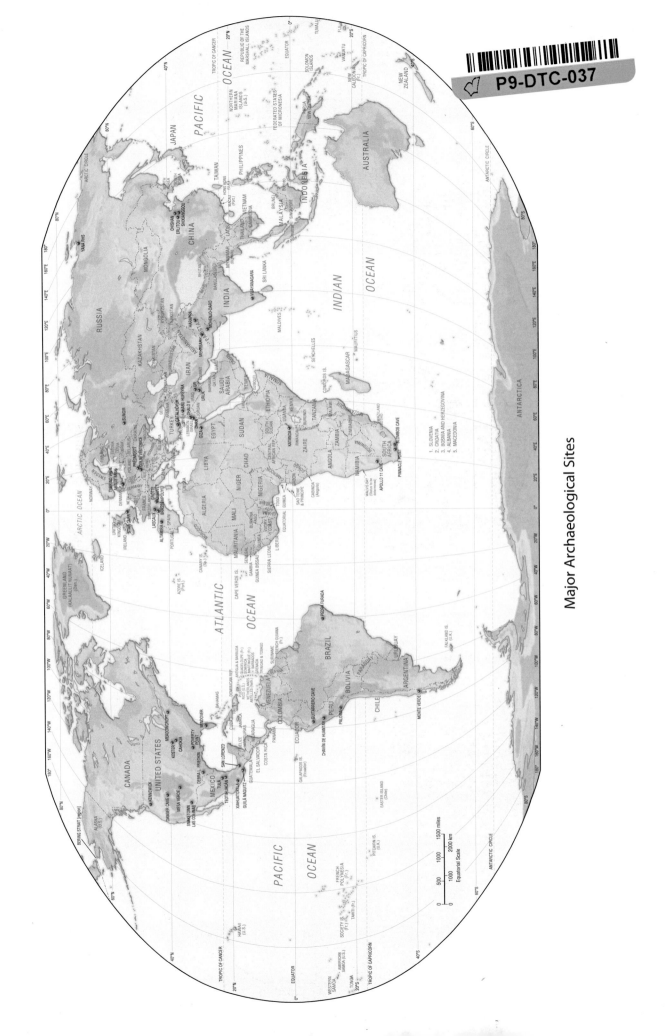

Major Archaeological Sites

UNDERSTANDING HUMANS

UNDERSTANDING HUMANS

Introduction to Physical Anthropology and Archaeology

Eleventh Edition

Barry Lewis

Professor Emeritus, University of Illinois at Urbana–Champaign

Robert Jurmain

Professor Emeritus, San Jose State University

Lynn Kilgore

University of Colorado, Boulder

WADSWORTH
CENGAGE Learning

Australia • Brazil • Japan • Korea • Mexico • Singapore
Spain • United Kingdom • United States

WADSWORTH
CENGAGE Learning™

Understanding Humans: Introduction to Physical Anthropology and Archaeology, **Eleventh Edition**
Barry Lewis, Robert Jurmain, and Lynn Kilgore

Executive Editor: Mark Kerr

Acquiring Sponsoring Editor: Erin Mitchell

Developmental Editor: Lin Gaylord

Assistant Editor: Mallory Ortberg

Media Editor: John Chell

Marketing Program Manager: Janay Pryor

Content Project Manager: Cheri Palmer

Art Director: Caryl Gorska

Manufacturing Planner: Judy Inouye

Rights Acquisitions Specialist: Dean Dauphinais

Design, Production Services, and Composition: Hespenheide Design

Photo Researcher: Patti Zeman, Hespenheide Design

Text Researcher: Ashley Liening

Copy Editor: Janet Greenblatt

Cover Designer: Hespenheide Design

Cover Image: © Rosino / www.flickr.com/photos/rosino

For product information and technology assistance, contact us at **Cengage Learning Customer & Sales Support, 1-800-354-9706**.

For permission to use material from this text or product, submit all requests online at **www.cengage.com/permissions**. Further permissions questions can be e-mailed to **permissionrequest@cengage.com**.

Library of Congress Control Number: 2011945172

ISBN-13: 978-1-111-83177-6
ISBN-10: 1-111-83177-7

Wadsworth
20 Davis Drive
Belmont, CA 94002-3098
USA

Cengage Learning is a leading provider of customized learning solutions with office locations around the globe, including Singapore, the United Kingdom, Australia, Mexico, Brazil, and Japan. Locate your local office at **www.cengage.com/global**.

Cengage Learning products are represented in Canada by Nelson Education, Ltd.

To learn more about Wadsworth, visit **www.cengage.com/wadsworth**

Purchase any of our products at your local college store or at our preferred online store **www.CengageBrain.com**.

Printed in the United States of America
4 5 6 7 16 15 14

Brief Contents

Anthropology

© Dr. Robert Clouse

Heredity and Evolution

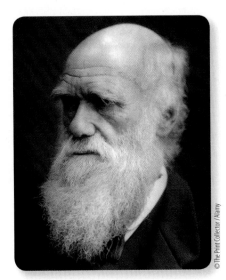

© The Print Collector / Alamy

© Louie Psihoyos / Corbis

Primates

© iStockphoto.com / Dmitry Rukhlenko

© Richard Mittleman / Gon2Foto / Alamy

Paleoanthropology/Fossil Hominins

Barry Lewis

© David Lordkipanidze

Harry Nelson

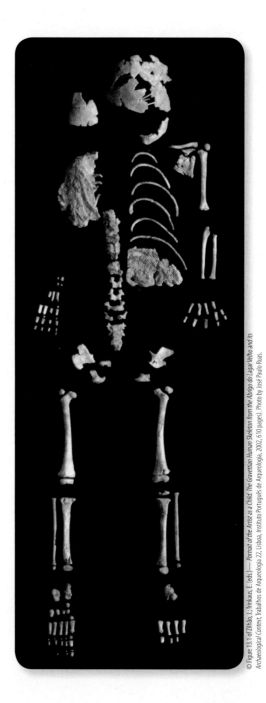

© Figure 13.1 of Zilhão, J.; Trinkaus, E. (eds.) — *Portrait of the Artist as a Child. The Gravettian Human Skeleton from the Abrigo do Lagar Velho and its Archaeological Context*, Trabalhos de Arqueologia 22, Lisboa, Instituto Português de Arqueologia, 2002, 610 pages). Photo by José Paulo Ruas.

Archaeology

William Turnbaugh

Dr. Robert Clouse

Preface

The study of human evolution and culture is a rapidly changing field. More researchers are working in more places around the world than ever before in human history. They are asking new questions and applying new methods and techniques in their search for the roots of the human past. The results are dynamic, exciting, and full of surprises as scientists continually reevaluate what we know about how and why our ancestors evolved biologically and culturally to produce us.

The eleventh edition of *Understanding Humans: Introduction to Physical Anthropology and Archaeology* addresses these new developments in an engaging manner and presents students with the most important aspects of the current understanding of human development. Working with the help of many constructive comments and suggestions from instructors and students who used the tenth edition in the classroom, we improved and updated its content, tightened up its coverage of key topics, enhanced the quality of its pictures and graphs, and held it to the same length as the tenth edition. Cengage Learning, our publisher, also worked hard to improve the quality of its production.

The new edition stays true to our long tradition of providing introductory students and their instructors with a current and comprehensive understanding of human biological and cultural development from an evolutionary point of view. As always, the most compelling justification for a new edition is simply that the story of the human past changes rapidly. New discoveries, fresh theories, and new methods and technologies force revisions, sometimes fundamental revisions, in the understanding of how the world around us works.

Although each edition of this text is committed to providing up-to-date subject content for students and their instructors, we authors are also teachers and even sometimes students ourselves. We know that instructional software, the Internet, multimedia, new teaching approaches, and a host of other factors (including technologically adept students!) are reshaping classrooms and the ways in which students and instructors engage the course material. To meet the pedagogical challenges of today's classrooms, we enhance each edition with in-chapter learning aids (see "In-Chapter Learning Aids," p. xvi) to help ensure that learning and teaching the course material continue to be positive and productive experiences.

What's New in the Eleventh Edition?

Much is new. Every chapter has been revised and updated to ensure that students are introduced to the most current and timely interpretations of human biocultural evolution. Chapter 1 sets the ball rolling with an important new chapter opener that makes the case for the relevance of the study of biocultural evolution to modern everyday life. The chapters on heredity and evolution (Chapters 2 through 5) were trimmed and updated, and more material was added on the mechanisms of evolution and examples of natural selection in action. Chapter 5 also includes the new section "What Are Fossils and How Do They Form?" supported by a new photo display. More material on social organization and a new archaeology section was added to the chapters on primates (Chapters 6 through 7).

The paleoanthropology chapters (Chapters 9 through 12) include more material and photos on Paleolithic tool traditions, a new transition from the Upper Paleolithic to the Holocene, and an expanded section on the history of race and modern examples. The first half of Chapter 9 has been reorganized so that the major topics flow in an order that students will find easier to understand. Up-to-date material on an important new species, *A. sediba*, is included, as well as a revised discussion of the earliest appearance of the genus *Homo*. Chapter 10 includes recalibrations of crucial dating for *H. erectus* finds from Dmanisi, Koobi Fora, and Ceprano. We also revised and updated interpretations of stone tool technologies of the earliest African immigrants (that is, defining where and with whom Oldowan and Acheulian industries are found and what they tell us about the behavioral capabilities of these hominins). The major changes to Chapters 11 and 12 rest on new molecular evidence as well as important new fossil and archaeological discoveries. These data reinforce recent theories concerning the origins of modern humans in Africa (Chapter 12), as well as the earlier dispersal of Neandertals and the interbreeding of Neandertals and modern humans outside of Africa (Chapter 11).

The chapters that deal with the human experience from the end of the Ice Age to the earliest civilizations (Chapters 13 through 15) have been thoroughly updated. In Chapter 13, we tightened up the discussion of competing theories for the earliest entry of humans into the New World. The weight of evidence supports the interpretation that the earliest North Americans entered the New World from northeastern Asia. In the discussion of the origins of agriculture

(Chapter 14), we expanded our coverage of Africa and East Asia and added more material on the many recent contributions based on plant microfossil (for example, phytolith) research and DNA analyses. In Chapter 15, which deals with the origins of the earliest civilizations, we updated the section "Why Did Civilizations Form?"; we also shortened and updated the Mesopotamian and Peruvian sections and expanded coverage of the earliest Chinese civilizations.

Finally, we added a new concluding chapter entitled "Biocultural Evolution and the Anthropocene," which returns to the theme of the relevance of biocultural evolution to modern everyday life. It draws important implications from the course of human evolution and heightens student awareness of the consequences that the extraordinary success of our species holds for the future of all living things and the earth itself.

Throughout this textbook, we streamlined the presentation of material in every chapter with a thorough editing to simplify explanations and added more headings to better define and focus on shorter text segments. We devoted considerable effort to improving the conversational tone of the text, as well as forging a stronger explanation of the biocultural approach that tells the story of where we came from, where we are going, and how we know this. Learning objectives have been added to the beginning of each chapter to help students identify and understand what important concepts and material they are expected to learn, and chapter summaries have been updated in bullet format for easier access. Finally, the photos and artwork have been substantially expanded and updated, not just to make the book more visually appealing, but also to provide a better sense of what physical anthropologists and archaeologists do and why they enjoy doing it! For those familiar with earlier editions, you'll notice that all the maps have been redrawn, as has much of the other artwork. In addition, many photos have been replaced with upgraded versions and new ones added.

In-Chapter Learning Aids

▶ **Learning Objectives**, at the beginning of each chapter, help students identify the important concepts and material they are expected to learn.

▶ A **running glossary** in the margins provides definitions of important terms on the page where the term is first introduced. A **full glossary** is provided at the back of the book.

▶ **At a Glance** features briefly summarize complex or controversial material in a visually understandable fashion.

▶ **Figures**, including numerous photographs, line drawings, and maps, most in full color, are carefully selected to clarify and support discussion in the text.

▶ **Critical Thinking Questions**, at the end of each chapter, have been completely revised to reinforce key concepts and encourage students to think critically about what they have read.

▶ **What's Important** tables that summarize the most significant fossil discoveries and archaeological sites are included at the end of relevant chapters to help students as they review the chapter material.

▶ **Full bibliographical citations** throughout the book provide sources from which the materials are drawn. This type of documentation guides students to published source materials and illustrates for them the proper use of referencing. All cited sources are listed in the comprehensive bibliography at the back of the book.

Acknowledgments

We wish to thank our colleagues who so carefully reviewed the text and gave us many helpful suggestions:

Anne Browning, University of Arizona; Richard Deutsch, John A. Logan College; Mark Mehrer, Northern Illinois University; Carol Morrow, Southeast Missouri State University; Bob Mucci, Indiana University; Jon Oplinger, University of Maine at Farmington.

In addition, we want to thank the team at Cengage Learning: Erin Mitchell, Lin Marshall Gaylord, Mallory Ortberg, John Chell, Caryl Gorska, and Cheri Palmer. Moreover, for their unflagging expertise and patience, we are grateful to our copy editor, Janet Greenblatt, our production coordinator, Gary Hespenheide, and his skilled staff at Hespenheide Design: Patti Zeman, Bridget Neumayr, and Randy Miyake.

To the many friends and colleagues who have generously provided photographs, comments, and criticism, we are greatly appreciative: Zeresenay Alemsegel, Lee Berger, Colin Betts, Jonathan Bloch, C. K. Brain, Günter Bräuer, Peter Brown, Joanna Casey, Chip Clark, Desmond Clark, Ron Clarke, Robert Clouse, Lisa Cordani-Stevenson, Raymond Dart, Louis de Bonis, Emanuelle de Merode, Jean DeRousseau, Tom Emerson, Dennis Etler, Andy Fortier, Diane France, Robert Franciscus, David Frayer, Glen Freimuth, Kathleen Galvin, Michael Hargrave, Eve Hargrave, David Haring, Nancy Hawkins, John Hodgkiss, Almut Hoffman, Ellen Ingmanson, Fred Jacobs, Don Johanson, Peter Jones, John Kappelman, Richard Kay, Kenneth Kelly, William Kimbel, Laura Kozuch, Arlene Kruse, Christopher Kunz, Richard Leakey, Linda Levitch, Hannah Lewis, Susan Lewis, Carol Lofton, David Lordkipanidze, Giorgio Manzi, Monte McCrossin, Russell Mittermeier, Lorna Moore, Stephen Nash, Gerald Newlands, John Oates, Bonnie Pedersen, David Pilbeam, Dolores Piperno, William Pratt, Judith Regensteiner, Debra Rich, Sastrohamijoyo Sartono, Jeffrey Schwartz, Eugenie Scott, Rose Sevick, Helaine Silverman, Elwyn Simons, Meredith Small, Fred Smith, Thierry Smith, Suzanne Spencer-Wood, Li Tianyuan, Philip Tobias, Erik Trinkaus, Shane Vanderford, Richard VanderHoek, Alan Walker, Dietrich Wegner, James Westgate, Randy White, Milford Wolpoff, and Xinzhi Wu.

November 2011
Barry Lewis
Robert Jurmain
Lynn Kilgore

Supplements

Understanding Humans: Introduction to Physical Anthropology and Archaeology, **Eleventh Edition**, comes with a strong supplements program to help instructors create an effective learning environment both inside and outside the classroom and to aid students in mastering the material.

Supplements for Instructors

Online Instructor's Manual with Test Bank   This online resource includes a sample syllabus and offers detailed chapter outlines, lecture suggestions, key terms, student activities, and Internet exercises. In addition, each chapter offers over 50 test questions, including multiple-choice, true-false, short-answer, and essay questions. Contact your local Cengage Learning sales representative for access.

PowerLecture™ with ExamView® for *Understanding Humans: Introduction to Physical Anthropology and Archaeology, Eleventh Edition*   This easy-to-use one-stop digital library and presentation tool includes the following book-specific resources as well as direct links to many of Wadsworth's highly valued electronic resources for anthropology:

▶ Ready-to-use Microsoft® PowerPoint® lecture slides with photos and graphics from the text, making it easy for the instructor to assemble, edit, publish, and present customized lectures.

▶ ExamView testing software, which provides all the test items from the text's test bank in electronic format, enabling the instructor to create customized tests of up to 250 items that can be delivered in print or online.

▶ The text's *Instructor's Resource Manual and Test Bank* in electronic format.

The Wadsworth Anthropology Video Library, Vol. 1–3   The Wadsworth Anthropology Video Library drives home the relevance of course topics through short, provocative clips of current and historical events. Perfect for enriching lectures and engaging students in discussion, many of the segments on this volume have been gathered from BBC Motion Gallery. Ask your Cengage Learning representative for a list of contents.

Supplements for Students

Companion website for *Understanding Humans: Introduction to Physical Anthropology and Archaeology,* **Eleventh Edition**   This companion website offers an in-depth and interactive study experience that will help students make their grade. Chapter resources include tutorial quizzes, glossary, flash cards, and more!

Classic and Contemporary Readings in Physical Anthropology   Edited by Mary K. Sandford and Eileen Jackson, this accessible reader presents primary articles with introductions and questions for discussion, helping students to better understand the nature of scientific inquiry. Students will read classic and contemporary articles on key topics, including the science of physical anthropology, evolution and heredity, primates, human evolution, and modern human variation.

Case Studies in Archaeology, edited by Jeffrey Quilter   These engaging accounts of cutting-edge archaeological techniques, issues, and solutions—as well as studies discussing the collection of material remains—range from site-specific excavations to types of archaeology practiced.

Lab Manual and Workbook for Physical Anthropology, Seventh Edition   Written by Diane L. France, this edition of the workbook and lab manual includes a new "Introduction to Science and Critical Thinking" that precedes the first chapter. Using hands-on exercises, this richly illustrated full-color lab manual balances the study of genetics, human osteology, anthropometry, and forensic anthropology with the study of primates and human evolution. In addition to providing hands-on lab assignments that apply the field's perspectives and techniques to real situations, this edition provides more explanatory information and sample exercises throughout the text to help make the concepts of physical anthropology easier to understand. Contact your Cengage sales representative to package with the text.

Virtual Laboratories for Physical Anthropology, CD-ROM, Fourth Edition, by John Kappelman   Through the use of video segments, interactive exercises, quizzes, 3-D animations, and sound and digital images, students can actively participate in 12 labs on their own terms—at home, in the library—at any time! Recent fossil discoveries are included, as well as exercises in behavior and archaeology and critical thinking and problem-solving activities. *Virtual Laboratories* includes weblinks, outstanding fossil images, exercises, and a post-lab self-quiz.

Genetics in Anthropology: Principles and Applications CD-ROM, Version 2.0, by Robert Jurmain and Lynn Kilgore This student CD-ROM expands on basic biological concepts covered in the book, focusing on biological inheritance (such as genes and DNA sequencing) and its applications to modern human populations. Interactive animations and simulations bring these important concepts to life so that students can fully understand the essential biological principles underlying human evolution. Also available are quizzes and interactive flash cards for further study.

Hominid Fossils: An Interactive Atlas CD-ROM, by James Ahern The interactive atlas CD-ROM includes over 75 key fossils important for a clear understanding of human evolution. The QuickTime Virtual Reality (QTVR) "object" movie format for each fossil enables students to have a near-authentic experience of working with these important finds by allowing them to rotate the fossil 360°. Unlike some VR media, QTVR objects are made using actual photographs of the real objects and thus better preserve details of color and texture. The fossils used are high-quality research casts and real fossils. The organization of the atlas is non-linear, with three levels and multiple paths, enabling students to see how the fossil fits into the map of human evolution in terms of geography, time, and evolution. The CD-ROM offers students an inviting, authentic learning environment, one that contains a dynamic quizzing feature that allows students to test their knowledge of fossil and species identification as well as providing more detailed information about the fossil record. Available at a discount with the text upon request.

Cengage Modules in Physical Anthropology series Each free-standing module is actually a complete text chapter, featuring the same quality of pedagogy and illustration contained in Cengage's physical anthropology texts.

Evolution of the Brain: Neuroanatomy, Development, and Paleontology, by Daniel D. White The human species is the only species that has ever created a symphony, written a poem, developed a mathematical equation, or studied its own origins. The biological structure that has enabled humans to perform these feats of intelligence is the human brain. This module explores the basics of neuroanatomy, brain development, lateralization, and sexual dimorphism and provides the fossil evidence for hominin brain evolution. This module in chapter-like print format can be packaged free with the text.

Human-Environment Interactions: New Directions in Human Ecology, by Kathy Galvin This module begins with a brief discussion of the history and core concepts of the field of human ecology, the study of how humans interact with the natural environment, before looking in depth at how the environment influences cultural practices (environmental determinism) as well as how aspects of culture, in turn, affect the environment. Human behavioral ecology is presented within the context of natural selection, examining how ecological factors influence the development of cultural and behavioral traits and how people subsist in different environments. The module concludes with a discussion of resilience and global change as a result of human-environment interactions. This module in chapter-like print format can be packaged free with the text.

Forensics Anthropology Module: A Brief Review, by Diane France The forensic application of physical anthropology is exploding in popularity. This module explores the myths and realities of the search for human remains in crime scenes, what can be expected from a forensic anthropology expert in the courtroom, some of the special challenges in responding to mass fatalities, and the issues a student should consider if considering a career in forensic anthropology. This module in chapter-like print format can be packaged free with the text.

Molecular Anthropology Module, by Leslie Knapp This module explores how molecular genetic methods are used to understand the organization and expression of genetic information in humans and nonhuman primates. Students will learn about the common laboratory methods used to study genetic variation and evolution in molecular anthropology. Examples are drawn from up-to-date research on human evolutionary origins and comparative primate genomics to demonstrate that scientific research is an ongoing process with theories frequently being questioned and reevaluated. Mitochondrial DNA and the human-chimp biological connection are also examined in this fascinating and timely module. This module in chapter-like print format can be packaged free with the text.

These resources are available to qualified adopters, and ordering options for student supplements are flexible. Please consult your local Cengage sales representative for more information or to evaluate examination copies of any of these resources or receive product demonstrations.

About the Authors

Barry Lewis

Barry Lewis received his Ph.D. from the University of Illinois at Urbana-Champaign, where he is Professor Emeritus of Anthropology. During his 27-year tenure at the University of Illinois, he taught courses on introductory archaeology, quantitative methods in archaeology, geographic information systems, and social science research methods. He has published extensively on the archaeology of late prehistoric Native American towns and villages in the southeastern United States. His recent research and publications focus on the archaeology and history of early modern South India.

Robert Jurmain

Robert Jurmain received an A.B. in anthropology from UCLA and a Ph.D. in biological anthropology from Harvard University. He taught at San Jose State University from 1975 to 2004 and is now Professor Emeritus there. During his teaching career, he taught courses in all major branches of physical anthropology, including osteology and human evolution, with the greatest concentration in general education teaching for introductory students. His areas of research interest include the skeletal biology of humans and non-human primates; paleopathology; and paleoanthropology. In addition to his three textbooks, which together have appeared in 28 editions, he is author of numerous articles in research journals as well as the book *Stories from the Skeleton: Behavioral Reconstruction in Human Osteology* (1999, Gordon & Breach Publishers).

Lynn Kilgore

Lynn Kilgore earned her Ph.D. from the University of Colorado, Boulder, where she currently is an adjunct Assistant Professor. Her primary research interests are osteology and paleopathology. She has taught numerous undergraduate and graduate courses in human osteology, primate behavior, human heredity and evolution, and general physical anthropology. Her research focuses on developmental defects, disease, and trauma in human and great ape skeletons.

Anthropology

CHAPTER 1

Introduction to Anthropology

© Dr. Robert Clouse

LEARNING OBJECTIVES

After you have mastered the material in this chapter, you will be able to:

▶ Explain and give examples of the relevance of anthropology to modern everyday life.

▶ Describe the concept of biocultural evolution and explain why it is an essential component of understanding human evolution.

▶ Define basic anthropological concepts and understand their relationship to the goals of anthropological research.

▶ Describe the main similarities and differences between physical anthropology and archaeology as approaches for understanding the human past.

▶ Explain the logic of the scientific method as it is applied in anthropological research.

Figure 1-1

We are complex products of both culture and biology. In many ways, the evolutionary history of modern humans left us better adapted to life as a hunter-gatherer than as a modern city dweller.

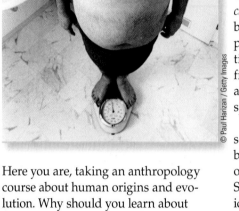

© Paul Harizan / Getty Images

evolution A change in the genetic structure of a population from one generation to the next. The term is also frequently used to refer to the appearance of a new species.

anthropology The field of inquiry that studies human culture and evolutionary aspects of human biology; includes cultural anthropology, archaeology, linguistics, and physical anthropology.

scientific method An approach to research whereby a problem is identified, a hypothesis (or hypothetical explanation) is stated, and that hypothesis is tested through the collection and analysis of data.

biocultural evolution The mutual, interactive evolution of human biology and culture; the concept that biology makes culture possible and that developing culture further influences the direction of biological evolution; a basic concept in understanding the unique components of human evolution.

culture All aspects of human adaptation, including technology, traditions, language, religion, and social roles. Culture is a set of learned behaviors; it is transmitted from one generation to the next through learning and not by biological or genetic means.

species A group of organisms that can interbreed to produce fertile offspring. Members of one species are reproductively isolated from members of all other species (i.e., they can't mate with them to produce fertile offspring).

Here you are, taking an anthropology course about human origins and evolution. Why should you learn about "stones and bones"? It's irrelevant to modern everyday life, right?

Think again.

In *Collapse: How Societies Choose to Fail or Succeed*, Jared Diamond says that he remains optimistic about the future because of the interconnectedness of modern societies: "Past societies lacked archaeologists and television" (Diamond, 2005, p. 525). His point is that we are much better prepared to face future challenges because, unlike our ancestors, so many of us know so much about how and why past societies developed and failed. We have the opportunity to learn from these mistakes and successes and, hopefully, to build a better, more sustainable, and brighter future for everyone.

On a more personal level, consider the recent rise of obesity as a serious health problem in many affluent countries. The underlying causes are complex, but the human biological past is one important factor (Bellisari, 2008). All but a tiny fraction of the existence of our species was spent as physically active hunter-gatherers whose everyday staple foods tended to be low in fat, sugar, and salt and high in fiber, going from nature to table with minimal processing. Few

twenty-first-century lifestyles are like that, but our bodies are well designed for our biological past, not our very different present (**Fig. 1-1**). The more that we understand our biological past, the better we will understand many modern health issues.

This and many other examples demonstrate that modern humans are cultural and biological beings whose present and future reflect their past. Humans are also probably unique among animals in the capacity to ask the question *why*. We *can* learn about our deep, rich past, and by doing so we gain the opportunity to profit from the experience. These qualities are fundamental motivations for the field of anthropology and for this book as an introduction to the biocultural perspective of human **evolution**.

Anthropology addresses the entire scope of the human experience and brings multiple perspectives to bear on the study of what it is to be human. Such a broad focus encompasses all topics related to behavior, including social relationships (for example, kinship and marriage patterns), religion, ritual, technology, subsistence, and economic and political systems. Anthropology is also concerned with the biological and evolutionary dimensions of our species, such as genetics, anatomy, skeletal structure, adaptation to disease and other environmental factors, growth, nutrition, and, ultimately, all the evolutionary processes that resulted in the development of modern humans.

In keeping with anthropology's commitment to a broad perspective, aspects of this discipline rest firmly in both science and the humanities: Anthropologists answer many questions by applying the **scientific method**, but they also apply interpretive methods to achieve an understanding of such human qualities as love, individual or group identity, compassion, and ethnicity.

The Biocultural Approach

The concept of **biocultural evolution** underlies the anthropological perspective. Humans are the product of the combined influences of biology and **culture** that have shaped our evolutionary history over the last several million years. It is by tracing the changing interaction between biology and culture and understanding how the process worked in the past and how it continues to work today that we are able to come to grips scientifically with what we are, how and why we came to be the animal that we are today, and the successes and failures we made along the way.

As we'll emphasize in this book, humans have occupied center stage in only one short scene of life's evolutionary play. Our role is fascinating, but many of the cultural factors that we point to as evidence of our extraordinary success as a **species** increas-ingly threaten the existence of many plants and animals, including ourselves. Culture is therefore an extremely important concept, not only as it pertains to modern humans but also in terms of its critical role in human evolution, past as well as future.

Viewed in an evolutionary perspective, human culture can be described as the strategy by which people adapt to the natural and social environments in which they live. Culture includes technologies that range from stone tools to computers; subsistence patterns ranging from hunting and gathering to agri-business; housing types from thatched huts to skyscrapers; and clothing from animal skins to synthetic fibers (**Fig. 1-2**). Because religion, values, social

Figure 1-2

(a) An early stone tool from East Africa. This type of tool was used there about 1.5 million years ago. (b) Hubble space telescope against the earth's horizon. (c) A Samburu woman building a simple, traditional dwelling of stems, plant fibers, and mud. (d) These Hong Kong skyscrapers are typical of cities in industrialized countries today.

(a)

(b)

(c)

(d)

Lynn Kilgore

NASA / Space Telescope Science Institute

Lynn Kilgore

© iStockphoto.com / Justin Horocks

organization, language, kinship, marriage rules, gender roles, and so on, are all aspects of culture, culture shapes people's perceptions of the external environment, or worldview, in particular ways that distinguish each **society** from all others.

One fundamental point to remember is that culture is *learned* and not biologically determined. In other words, we inherit genes that influence our biological characteristics, but those genes have no impact on cultural behavior. Beginning in infancy, each of us begins slowly to learn, through the process called **enculturation**, the language and dialect of our family and community, as well as the shared norms, values, beliefs, and other aspects of culture that we need to be a productive member of the society of which we are a part. Our worldviews are shaped much more by our respective enculturation experiences than by our unique genetic ancestry. We are all products of the culture in which we are socialized, and since most human behavior is learned, it clearly is also culturally patterned.

As biological beings, humans are also subject to the same evolutionary forces that act on all living things On hearing the term *evolution*, many people think of the appearance of new species. Certainly, new species formation is one consequence of evolution; however, biologists see evolution as an ongoing process with a precise genetic meaning. Quite simply, evolution is a change in the genetic makeup of a population from one generation to the next. It's the accumulation of such changes over considerable periods of time that can result in the emergence or extinction of species. In the course of human evolution, biocultural interactions have resulted in such anatomical, biological, and behavioral changes as increased brain size, reorganization of neurological structures, decreased tooth size, and development of language, to list a few. Biocultural interactions are still critically important today; among other things, they are changing patterns of disease worldwide. As one example, changing social and sexual mores in many countries may have influenced the evolutionary rate of HIV, the virus that causes AIDS. Certainly, these cultural factors are influencing the spread of HIV throughout populations in both developed and developing countries.

Biologists study all the biological aspects of humankind, including **adaptation** and evolution, but when such research also considers the role of cultural factors, it falls within the discipline of anthropology. This approach recognizes that the human predisposition to assimilate a culture and to function within it is influenced by biological factors. But in the course of human evolution, as you'll see, the role of culture has increasingly assumed an added importance. In this respect, humans are unlike all other animals.

What Is Anthropology?

Stated ambitiously but simply, anthropology is the study of humankind. The term itself is derived from the Greek words *anthropos*, meaning "human," and *logos*, meaning "word" or "study of." Clearly, anthropologists aren't the only scientists who study humans, and the goals of anthropology are shared by other disciplines within the social, behavioral, and biological sciences. As we noted earlier, the main difference between anthropology and other related fields is anthropology's broad perspective, which integrates the findings of many disciplines, including sociology, economics, history, psychology, and biology.

In the United States, anthropology comprises three main subfields: cultural anthropology, archaeology, and physical anthropology. Additionally, many universities include linguistic anthropology as a fourth subfield. Each of these subdisciplines, in turn, is divided into more specialized areas of interest. The following section briefly describes the main subdisciplines of anthropology.

Cultural Anthropology

Cultural anthropology (also called social anthropology) is the study of all aspects of human behavior. Its beginnings are rooted in the **Enlightenment** of the eighteenth century, which exerted considerable influence on how Europeans viewed

---

society A group of people who share a common culture.

enculturation The process by which individuals, generally as children, learn the values and beliefs of the family, peer groups, and society in which they are raised.

adaptation Functional response of organisms or populations to the environment. Adaptation results from evolutionary change (specifically, as a result of natural selection).

Enlightenment An eighteenth-century philosophical movement in western Europe that assumed a knowable order to the natural world and the interpretive value of reason as the primary means of identifying and explaining this order.

the place of humans in nature, questioned the extent to which there exists a knowable order to the natural world, and introduced fresh concepts of "primitive," or traditional, societies. These changes in political and social philosophy were particularly felt in the spread of European colonial powers between 1500 and 1900.

The interest in traditional societies led many early anthropologists to study and record lifeways that are now mostly extinct. These studies yielded descriptive **ethnographies** that later became the basis for comparisons between societies. Early ethnographies were narratives emphasizing such phenomena as religion, ritual, myth, use of symbols, subsistence and dietary preferences, technology, gender roles, child-rearing practices, taboos, medical practices, and how kinship was reckoned.

The focus of cultural anthropology changed considerably with the global social, political, and economic upheavals of the twentieth century. Researchers using traditional ethnographic methods still spend months or years living in and studying various societies, but the nature of the study groups has shifted. For example, in recent decades, ethnographic techniques have been applied to the study of diverse subcultures and their interactions with one another in contemporary metropolitan areas. The subfield of cultural anthropology that deals with issues of inner cities is appropriately called *urban anthropology*. Among the many issues addressed by urban anthropologists are relationships between various ethnic groups, those aspects of traditional societies that are maintained by immigrant populations, poverty, labor relations, homelessness, access to health care, and problems facing the elderly.

Medical anthropology is the subfield that explores the relationship between various cultural attributes and health and disease. Areas of interest include how different groups view disease processes and how these views affect treatment or the willingness to accept treatment. When medical anthropologists focus on the social dimensions of disease, they may collaborate with physicians and physical anthropologists. Indeed, many medical anthropologists receive much of their training in physical anthropology.

Many subfields of cultural anthropology have practical applications and are pursued by anthropologists working both within and outside the university setting. This approach is aptly termed *applied anthropology*. Although most applied anthropologists regard themselves as cultural anthropologists, the designation is also sometimes used to describe the activities of archaeologists and physical anthropologists. Indeed, the various fields of anthropology, as they are practiced in the United States, overlap to a considerable degree. After all, that was the rationale for combining them under the umbrella of anthropology in the first place.

Physical Anthropology

Physical anthropology (also called biological anthropology) is the study of human biology within the framework of evolution and with an emphasis on the interaction between biology and culture. The origins of physical anthropology are found in two main areas of nineteenth-century research. First, there was increasing curiosity among many scientists (at the time called *natural historians*) regarding the mechanisms by which modern species had come to be. In other words, they were beginning to doubt the literal, biblical interpretation of creation. Although most scientists weren't prepared to believe that humans had evolved from earlier forms, discoveries of several Neandertal fossils (see Chapter 11) in the 1800s raised questions about the origins and antiquity of the human species.

The sparks of interest in biological change over time were fanned into flames by the publication of Charles Darwin's *On the Origin of Species* in 1859. Today, **paleoanthropology**, or the study of human evolution, particularly as revealed in the fossil record, is a major subfield of physical anthropology (**Fig. 1-3**). There are now thousands of specimens of the remains of human ancestors housed in research collections. Taken together, these fossils span at least 4 million years of prehistory; and although incomplete, they provide

ethnographies Detailed descriptive studies of human societies. In cultural anthropology, *ethnography* is traditionally the study of non-Western societies.

paleoanthropology The interdisciplinary approach to the study of earlier hominins—their chronology, physical structure, archaeological remains, habitats, etc.

Figure 1-3

Paleoanthropological research at Omo, Ethiopia.

us with significantly more knowledge than was available just 10 years ago. The ultimate goal of paleoanthropological research is to identify the various early **hominin** species, establish a chronological sequence of relationships among them, and gain insights into their adaptation and behavior. Only then will there emerge a clear picture of how and when humankind came into being.

Observable physical variation was another nineteenth-century interest that had direct relevance to anthropology. Enormous effort was aimed at describing and explaining the biological differences among human populations. Although some endeavors were misguided and even racist, they gave birth to literally thousands of body measurements that could be used to compare people. Physical anthropologists use many of the techniques of **anthropometry** today, not only to study living groups but also to study skeletal remains from archaeological sites (**Fig. 1-4**). Moreover, anthropometric techniques have considerable application in the design of everything from airplane cockpits to office furniture. Today, anthropologists are concerned with human variation because of

Figure 1-4

This anthropology student is measuring the length of a human cranium with spreading calipers.

hominin A member of the tribe Hominini, the evolutionary group that includes modern humans and now-extinct bipedal relatives.

anthropometry Measurement of human body parts. When osteologists measure skeletal elements, the term osteometry is often used.

its *adaptive significance* and because they want to identify the evolutionary factors that have produced variability. In other words, some traits evolved as biological adaptations to local environmental conditions, including infectious disease. Others may simply be the results of geographical isolation or the descent of populations from small founding groups.

Some physical anthropologists examine other aspects of human variation, including how various groups respond physiologically to different kinds of environmentally induced stress (**Fig. 1-5**). Examples of such stresses include high altitude, cold, and heat. Others conduct nutritional studies, investigating the relationships between various dietary components, cultural practices, physiology, and certain aspects of health and disease. Investigations of human fertility, growth, and development are closely related to the topic of nutrition and are fundamental to studies of adaptation in modern human populations.

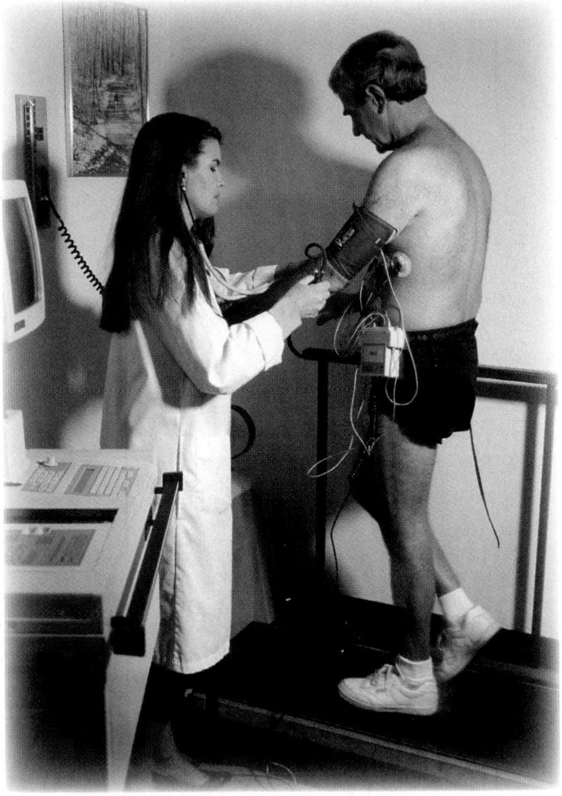

It would be impossible to study evolutionary processes without an understanding of genetic principles. For this reason and others, **genetics** is a crucial field for physical anthropologists. Modern physical anthropology wouldn't exist as an evolutionary science if not for rapidly developing advances in the understanding of genetic mechanisms.

Molecular anthropologists use cutting-edge technologies to investigate evolutionary relationships between human populations as well as between humans and nonhuman **primates**. To do this, they examine similarities and differences in DNA sequences between individuals, populations, and species. In addition, by extracting DNA from certain fossils, they've contributed to our understanding of relationships between extinct and living species. As genetic technologies continue to improve, molecular anthropologists will play a key role in explaining human evolution, adaptation,

Figure 1-5

Researcher using a treadmill test to assess a subject's heart rate, blood pressure, and oxygen consumption.

© Tom McCarthy / Photo Edit

and our biological relationships with other species (**Fig. 1-6**).

Primatology, the study of nonhuman primates, has important implications for many scientific disciplines (**Fig. 1-7**). Because nonhuman primates are our closest living relatives, the identification of underlying factors related to social behavior, communication, infant care, reproductive behavior, and so on, helps us develop a better understanding

© Nelson Ting

Figure 1-6

Molecular anthropologist Nelson Ting collecting red colobus fecal samples for a study of genetic variation in small groups of monkeys isolated from one another by agricultural clearing.

genetics The study of gene structure and action and of the patterns of inheritance of traits from parent to offspring. Genetic mechanisms are the underlying foundation for evolutionary change.

primates Members of the mammalian order Primates (pronounced "pry-may´-tees"), which includes prosimians, monkeys, apes, and humans.

primatology The study of the biology and behavior of nonhuman primates (prosimians, monkeys, and apes).

Figure 1-7

Primatologist Jill Pruetz follows chimpanzees in Senegal.

© Julie Lesnik

the first thing that comes to mind is bones. The emphasis on osteology is due partly to the importance of fossil analysis, which requires a thorough knowledge of the structure and function of the skeleton before one can accurately interpret such basic biological information as the probable habitats and ecological niches of long-ago extinct species.

Bone biology and physiology are also of major importance to many other aspects of physical anthropology. Many osteologists specialize in studies that emphasize various measurements of skeletal elements. This type of research is essential, for example, to the identification of stature and growth patterns in archaeological populations.

One subdiscipline of osteology is the study of disease and trauma in skeletons from archaeological sites. **Paleopathology** is a prominent subfield that investigates the prevalence of trauma, certain infectious diseases (such as syphilis and tuberculosis), nutritional deficiencies, and many other conditions that may leave evidence in bone (**Fig. 1-8**). This research tells us a great deal about the lives of individuals and populations in the past. Paleopathology also provides information pertaining to the history of certain disease processes, making it of interest to scientists in biomedical fields.

Forensic anthropology is directly related to osteology and paleopathology. Technically, this approach is the application of anthropological (usually osteological and sometimes archaeological) techniques to legal issues (**Fig. 1-9**). Forensic anthropologists are routinely called on to help identify skeletal remains in cases of mass disaster or other situations where a human body has been found.

Forensic anthropologists have been involved in numerous cases having important legal, historical, and human consequences. These scientists played a prominent role in identifying the skeletons of most of the Russian imperial family, whose members were executed in 1918. And more recently, many forensic anthropologists participated in the

of the natural forces that have shaped so many aspects of modern human behavior. Another important reason to study nonhuman primates is that most species are threatened or seriously endangered. Only through research will scientists be able to recommend policies that can better ensure their survival in the wild.

Primate paleontology, the study of the primate fossil record, has implications not only for nonhuman primates but also for hominins. Virtually every year, fossil-bearing geological beds in North America, Africa, Asia, and Europe yield important new discoveries. By studying fossil primates and comparing them with anatomically similar living species, primate paleontologists can learn a great deal about such things as diet or locomotion in earlier life-forms. They can also make assumptions about social behavior in some extinct primates and clarify what we know about evolutionary relationships between extinct and living species, including ourselves.

Osteology, the study of the skeleton, is central to physical anthropology. In fact, it's so important that when many people think of physical anthropology,

osteology The study of skeletal material. Human osteology focuses on the interpretation of the skeletal remains of past groups. Some of the same techniques are used in paleoanthropology to study early hominins.

paleopathology The branch of osteology that studies the traces of disease and injury in human skeletal (or, occasionally, mummified) remains.

forensic anthropology An applied anthropological approach dealing with legal matters. Forensic anthropologists work with coroners and law enforcement agencies in the recovery, analysis, and identification of human remains.

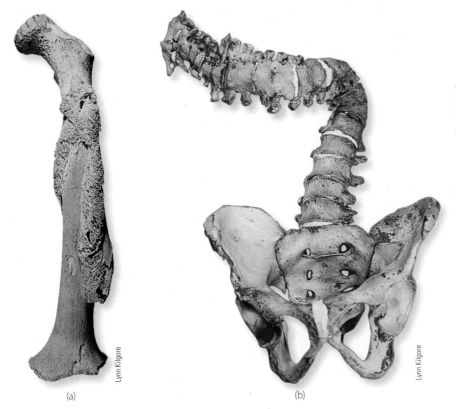

(a)   (b)

Figure 1-8

(a) A partially healed fracture of the femur (thigh bone) from a child's skeleton (estimated age at death is 6 years). Cause of death was probably an infection resulting from this injury. (b) Very severe congenital scoliosis in an adult male from Nubia. The curves are due to several developmental defects that affect individual vertebrae. (This is not the most common form of scoliosis.)

overwhelming task of trying to identify human remains in the aftermath of the September 11, 2001, terrorist attacks in the United States.

Anatomical studies are another area of interest for physical anthropologists. In living organisms, bones and teeth are intimately linked to the muscles and other tissues that surround and act on them. Consequently, a thorough knowledge of soft tissue anatomy is essential to the understanding of biomechanical relationships involved in movement. Knowledge of such relationships is fundamental to the accurate interpretation of the structure and function of limbs and other structures in extinct animals now represented only by fossilized

Figure 1-9

These forensic anthropologists, working in a lab near Baghdad, are examining the skeletal remains of Khurdish victims of genocide. They cataloged the injuries of 114 individuals buried in a mass grave, and some of their evidence was used against Saddam Hussein during his 2006 trial.

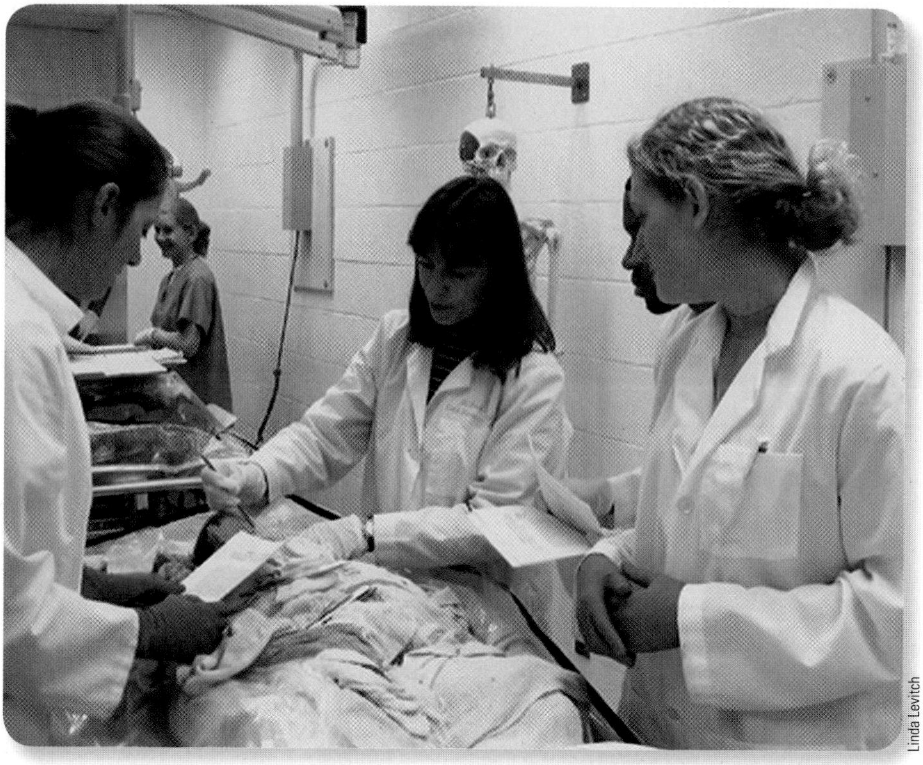

Figure 1-10

Dr. Linda Levitch teaching a human anatomy class at the University of North Carolina School of Medicine.

Linda Levitch

artifacts Objects or materials made or modified for use by hominins. The earliest artifacts tend to be tools made of stone or, occasionally, bone.

material culture The physical manifestations of human activities, such as tools, art, and structures. As the most durable aspects of culture, material remains make up the majority of archaeological evidence of past societies.

paleontologists Scientists whose study of ancient life-forms is based on fossilized remains of extinct animals and plants.

archaeological record The material remains of the human past and the physical contexts of these remains (e.g., stratigraphic relationships, association with other remains).

sites Locations of past human activity, often associated with artifacts and features.

remains. For such reasons, many physical anthropologists specialize in anatomical studies. In fact, several physical anthropologists hold professorships in anatomy departments at universities and medical schools (**Fig. 1-10**).

Archaeology

Stripped to its basics, archaeology is a body of methods designed to understand the human past through the examination and study of its material remains. Its primary data are the **artifacts** and other **material culture**, associations, and contextual information created by past peoples and preserved to the extent that they can be reliably identified and interpreted by modern researchers. From this, it should be clear that archaeologists don't study the fossils of nonprimate species such as dinosaurs or mammoths, a field properly claimed by **paleontologists**.

Given that archaeology is just a body of methods, you won't be surprised to learn that there are lots of different kinds of archaeology. For example, *classical archaeologists* study the Mediterranean world's "classical" civilizations, such as those created by the Romans and Greeks (**Fig. 1-11**). These archaeologists tend

to be found in departments of art history, classics, and architecture rather than anthropology. To these examples we could also add battlefield archaeology, industrial archaeology, underwater archaeology (**Fig. 1-12**), and many more; but you get the picture.

Anthropological archaeology, which is the kind of archaeology dealt with in this book, refers to the application of archaeological methods to the understanding of the origins and diversity of modern humans. As such, its domain covers the entire span of the **archaeological record**—from the earliest identifiable hominin tools, and the **sites** in which these implements were deposited, to the trash cans in our kitchens.

Archaeology exists as a discipline because researchers can justify a key assumption: Many human activities and their by-products tend to enter the archaeological record in patterned, knowable ways that reflect the behaviors, values, and beliefs of the individuals who created them. Given this assumption, archaeologists can study events and processes that are far removed in time from the modern world and interpret developments in the human past that happened at rates rang-

Figure 1-11

Classical archaeologists recording the mosaic floor of a Roman brick and timber building buried deep underneath a modern office structure near St. Paul's Cathedral in London, England. The building dates between A.D. 100 and 200, when London was the Roman settlement of Londinium.

Figure 1-12

An underwater archaeologist places location identification tags on artifacts at the site of an 11th century ship in the Mediterranean Sea off the coast of Turkey. The white lines that crisscross the photo are part of the excavation grid that the archaeologists constructed across the site when they began their fieldwork.

ing from months to millennia. This perspective of the human past is unique to archaeology.

Archaeology is a historical science, much like geology and evolutionary biology. It is scientific because it answers many research questions by applying the scientific method, and it is inherently historical because its primary data cannot be divorced from their context in space and time. The past, as the late paleontologist and evolutionary biologist Stephen Jay Gould (1989) liked to remind us, happened, and it won't happen again. Consequently, archaeology (and paleontology) differs in several fundamental aspects from such fields as physics and chemistry, where primary data are not anchored firmly in time and space (Dunnell, 1982).

As we've mentioned, archaeology is also rooted in the humanities. Archaeology in general—and anthropological archaeology in particular—tries to answer many questions about the past that go beyond the search for expla-

nations of general trends and patterns. Understanding certain cognitive and symbolic aspects of the past requires additional interpretive tools from such humanities disciplines as history, art history, architecture, and comparative literature.

Anthropological archaeologists (from here on, simply called archaeologists) traditionally differ from other anthropologists in their emphasis on the archaeological record as their primary data source. But the boundaries between anthropological subfields are not sharply drawn. Some archaeologists mainly study cultures that existed before the invention of writing (the era commonly known as **prehistory**). Other specialists, sometimes called **historical archaeologists**, examine the archaeological and documentary record of past cultures that left written evidence (**Fig. 1-13**). And **ethnoarchaeologists** blur the past-present dichotomy between archaeology and cultural anthropology by conducting ethnographic research with modern

prehistory The several million years between the emergence of bipedal hominins and the availability of written records.

historical archaeologists Archaeologists who study past societies for which a contemporary written record also exists.

ethnoarchaeologists Archaeologists who use ethnographic methods to study modern peoples so that they can better understand and explain patterning in the archaeological record.

Figure 1-13

Archaeologists expose the foundation of a nineteenth-century farmstead in Illinois.

© Illinois State Archaeological Survey, University of Illinois

peoples in projects designed to achieve archaeological objectives.

Like the other anthropological subfields, modern archaeology largely grew out of the Enlightenment in Europe. Although European awareness of the past can be traced to Roman times, it wasn't until the eighteenth and nineteenth centuries that some scholars began to accept evidence that the existence of living things, including humans, must be considerably older than previously thought. They also began to devise instruments for measuring time as it's reflected in the archaeological and fossil records. Once these factors came together with emerging evolutionary ideas in the mid-nineteenth century, the stage was set for the development of archaeology as the primary means by which the human past can be discovered.

Although the rise of American archaeology was greatly influenced by events in western Europe, it didn't develop along precisely the same lines. In North America, early **antiquarian** interests were fueled by the desire to explain the relationship between contemporary Native Americans and the archaeological record. Although this relationship seems obvious to us in the twenty-first century, it was by no means clear to colonists from the Old World or their descendants, even into the early twentieth century. In the United States, curiosity about the possible solution to this problem motivated what is generally agreed to be the earliest systematically conducted archaeological excavation, conducted in 1782 by Thomas Jefferson (**Fig. 1-14**). He excavated a prehistoric burial mound on his property in Virginia not to find artifacts,

© Everett Collection Inc. / Alamy

Figure 1-14

Long before he became the third president of the United States in 1801, Thomas Jefferson conducted the earliest systematic archaeological excavations in North America and published his results.

antiquarian Relating to an interest in objects and texts of the past.

but to discover how it was constructed. Therefore, he took careful notes on what he found and on the **stratigraphic** relationships. He then published an account of his work and concluded that the mound had been built by the ancestors of modern Native Americans (Jefferson, 1853).

Few of Jefferson's contemporaries on either side of the Atlantic took such care in their excavations, which is hardly surprising: For most early archaeologists, the questions that motivated their excavations were nearly as crude as their methods. By the early twentieth century, this situation had changed; archaeologists began to exploit the patterned nature of the archaeological record as a way to measure the relative sequence of events in the human past and to explain how and why past cultures changed.

Archaeology reached a certain methodological maturity in the second half of the twentieth century. This process was greatly facilitated by the development of new dating techniques, such as radiocarbon dating, and by technological possibilities created by the advent of computers in the 1960s and 1970s. The breadth of questions asked of the archaeological record also expanded greatly throughout the twentieth century in response to theoretical changes in anthropology as a whole. In 1900, many archaeologists were satisfied simply to describe what their excavations revealed and perhaps to arrange these remains in time and space frameworks. By 2000, they also sought to understand how the people who created these sites lived. They asked how or why these groups of people differed culturally from one another, what similarities they shared, and even why they held particular beliefs about themselves, each other, and the cosmos—all this while simultaneously controlling for time and space in the archaeological record.

In addition to the social science perspective of anthropology, archaeology established itself as a scientific discipline in the twentieth century, and it maintains strong ties with the natural and physical sciences. Contemporary archaeological research often involves the specialized expertise of many disciplines. Remote-sensing technology,

including everything from GPS (global positioning system) handhelds to ground-penetrating radar, may be used to locate or define sites. Geologists, soil scientists, and others assist in reconstructing a site's ancient environment. In the subfield of **archaeometry**, archaeologists work with physicists, chemists, engineers, and other scientists to apply the methods and techniques of their respective disciplines to the analysis of ancient materials. Many archaeology students combine their studies with training that prepares them to conduct specialized analyses of ancient plant and animal remains, GIS (geographical information system) spatial data, stable isotopes, ceramics, textiles, and other materials from the archaeological record (**Fig. 1-15**).

Figure 1-15

Bioarchaeologist Kris Hedman processes a bone sample for analysis of strontium levels in prehistoric human skeletons.

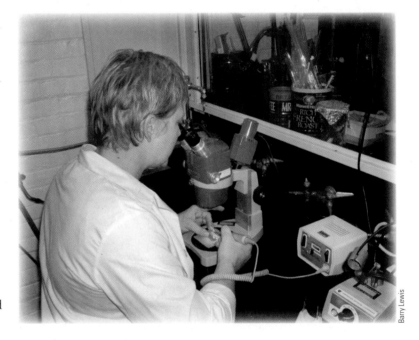

Barry Lewis

In the late twentieth century, **public archaeology** emerged as an important development in American archaeology. This field includes efforts to reach out to communities and involve wider audiences through education and the media. Most public archaeologists are engaged in cultural resource management (CRM) and other heritage management programs. As mandated by government environmental legislation since the 1970s, CRM archaeologists evaluate sites that may be threatened with damage from development and construction on public lands and in connection with

stratigraphic Pertaining to the depositional levels, or strata, of an archaeological site.

archaeometry Application of the methods of the natural and physical sciences to the investigation of archaeological materials.

public archaeology A broad term that covers archaeological research conducted for the public good as part of cultural resource management and heritage management programs; a major growth area of world archaeology.

private land projects that receive federal funds or are licensed or regulated by a federal agency. CRM work utilizes a wide range of archaeological expertise, including that of prehistorians, historical archaeologists, field technicians, archaeological illustrators and writers, and laboratory specialists. Many archaeologists in the CRM field are affiliated with environmental research and engineering firms, and others are employed by state or federal agencies or by educational institutions.

A commitment to the scientific method is also evident in the field of *experimental archaeology*, where researchers attempt to replicate ancient techniques and processes under controlled conditions so that they can better understand the past. Using these approaches, archaeologists have reproduced the entire range of ancient stone tools and employed them in many tasks that replicate the tool wear and breakage patterns on similar tools made and used by prehistoric peoples.

Archaeology's goals also continue to broaden as anthropology changes and as we learn more about the past. Today, anthropological archaeology has several primary goals. The first goal is to reconstruct culture history: This task orders the archaeological record in time and space and creates the archaeological equivalent of the chronologies of history. The second goal is to reconstruct and describe ancient lifeways, and the third is to understand the general processes of culture change and explain how and why past cultures changed in patterned ways. Finally, as an emerging area of research, archaeologists aim to examine and interpret the cognitive and symbolic aspects of past cultures (Demarrais et al., 2005).

As we should expect of any field in which basic goals continue to unfold, archaeologists are engaged in an ongoing negotiation of the discipline's research priorities, the bodies of theory that motivate research, and even the philosophical underpinnings of these theories. No single approach commands a clear consensus in archaeology; but this is a good sign of a healthy, growing, scholarly discipline, not an indication

that something is broken. Every option—from ways of knowing about the past to the inevitable conflict between what C. P. Snow (1965) called the "Two Cultures" of science and humanism—is on the table, and the early twenty-first century is an exciting time to be an archaeologist.

Linguistic Anthropology

Linguistic anthropology is the study of human speech and language, including the origins of language in general as well as specific languages. By examining similarities between contemporary languages, linguists have been able to trace historical ties between languages and groups of languages; in this way, linguistic anthropologists can identify language families and past relationships between human populations.

There is also much interest in the relationship between language and culture: how language reflects the way members of a society perceive phenomena and how the use of language shapes perceptions in different cultures. For example, language dialects can encode many meanings, including geographical origins, identity, and social class. Such encoded meanings influence how a person is treated by those who do or do not speak the same dialects of this or a closely related language. For example, a teacher who speaks with the slow cadence or drawl of Vicksburg, Mississippi, may not be taken seriously by students in Minneapolis or Chicago, where the stereotypical image of the speakers of such dialects is that of hillbillies. However, in Southampton, England, or Adelaide, Australia, the same teacher's voice may simply be viewed as wonderfully exotic, the main difference being cultural—in this case, the social meanings associated with the tones and cadence of speech.

Because the spontaneous acquisition and use of language is a uniquely human characteristic, the topic holds considerable interest for linguistic anthropologists, who, along with specialists in other fields, study the process of language acquisition in infants. This research is also important to physical anthropologists because insights into the process may well have implications for the development of language skills in human evolution.

The Scientific Method

Science is a process of understanding phenomena through observation, generalization, verification, and refutation. By this we mean that there is an objective, **empirical** approach to gaining information through the use of systematic and explicit techniques. Because physical anthropologists and archaeologists are engaged in scientific pursuits, they adhere to the principles of the *scientific method*, whereby a research question is identified and information is subsequently gathered, analyzed, and interpreted to provide an answer.

The gathering of information is referred to as **data** collection, and when researchers use a rigorously controlled approach, they can accurately describe their techniques and results in a manner that facilitates comparisons with the work of others. For example, when scientists collect data on tooth size in hominin fossils, they must specify precisely which teeth are being measured, how they are measured, the validity and reliability of these measures, and what the results of the measurements are (expressed numerically, or **quantitatively**). Subsequently, it's up to the investigators to analyze, interpret, and draw inferences about these measurements. This body of information then becomes the basis of future studies—possibly by other researchers, who can compare their own results with those already obtained. The eventual outcome of this type of inquiry is the acceptance or rejection of proposed answers to the questions that motivated the research.

Once observations have been made, scientists attempt to explain them. First, a **hypothesis**, or provisional explanation of some aspect of the natural world, is developed. To be analytically useful, a hypothesis must be tested by means of data collection and analysis. Indeed, the testing of hypotheses with the possibility of proving them false is the very basis

of the scientific method. Everything that scientists accept as true is always a "working" or "conditional" truth, because subsequent testing may demonstrate it to be false.

In anthropology, the **scientific testing** of hypotheses may take several years or longer and may involve researchers who weren't connected with the original work. In subsequent studies, other investigators may achieve similar results, or their findings may be incompatible with those of the initial study. For example, the archaeologist V. Gordon Childe argued in the 1920s that the earliest prehistoric Near Eastern plant and animal domestication events took place soon after the end of the last Ice Age around the oases, or water holes, of the region (Childe, 1929). Later, Robert Braidwood (1960; Braidwood and Howe, 1960) tested Childe's hypothesis in the field and found that the oldest evidence of Near Eastern plant domestication was actually to be found not around the oases, as Childe's hypothesis predicted, but in village sites scattered among the foothills of the Zagros Mountains in Iraq and Iran. Braidwood's research effectively refuted Childe's hypothesis (just as Braidwood's tentative explanation was itself refuted by subsequent research, which is a story that we'll take up in more detail in Chapter 14). This example illustrates that although it's easier to repeat original studies conducted in laboratory settings, it's no less important to verify research results based on data collected outside of tightly controlled laboratory situations.

After repeated testing, some hypotheses become so well accepted that they're unlikely to be changed by new evidence. At this point, such hypotheses, perhaps combined with others, are accepted as **theories**. In common everyday usage, the word *theory* often means a hunch or guess. But in scientific terms, a theory is a statement or explanation that hasn't been falsified, or shown to be false, by currently available evidence. Of course, theories, or parts of theories, may be altered over time as new technologies and information allow for repeated testing, but in general, they're sustained. For example, it's a fact that when you drop

science A body of knowledge gained through observation and experimentation; from the Latin *scientia*, meaning "knowledge."

empirical Relying on experiment or observation; from the Latin *empiricus*, meaning "experienced."

data (*sing.*, datum) Facts from which conclusions can be drawn; scientific information.

quantitatively Pertaining to measurements of quantity and including such properties as size, number, and capacity.

hypothesis (*pl.*, hypotheses) A provisional explanation of a phenomenon. Hypotheses require repeated testing.

scientific testing The precise repetition of an experiment or expansion of observed data to provide verification; the procedure by which hypotheses and theories are verified, modified, or discarded.

theories Well-substantiated explanations of natural phenomena, supported by hypothesis testing and by evidence gathered over time. Theories also allow scientists to make predictions about as yet unobserved phenomena. Some theories are so well established that no new evidence is likely to alter them substantially.

a stone it falls to the ground. That fact is explained by Isaac Newton's theory of gravity, proposed in 1687. But if you were in earth orbit on board the space shuttle and you dropped a stone, it would seem to float because, even though it would still be influenced by the earth's gravitational field, that field would be weaker on the shuttle than it is on earth. Since 1687, Newton's theory has been enhanced by a greater understanding of the attraction of masses to one another as expressed mathematically. But even after more than 300 years, the theory of gravity remains intact with little modification.

Use of the scientific method permits the development and testing of hypotheses, and it also permits various types of *bias* to be addressed and controlled. It's important to realize that bias occurs in all studies. Sources of bias include the researcher's personal values; how the investigator was trained and by whom; what particular questions interest the researcher; what specific skills and talents he or she possesses; what earlier results (if any) have been established in this realm of study and by whom (for example, the researcher, close colleagues, or those with rival approaches); and what sources of data are available (for example, accessible countries or museums) and thus what samples can be collected.

Bias cannot be entirely eliminated from research, but it's possible to minimize its effects through careful research design, in which the researcher consciously works to identify and control for possible bias effects. Anthropologists, like all researchers, strive to minimize bias in their research outcomes as well as in the articles and books they write.

Science is an approach—indeed, a *tool*—used to minimize bias, enable the replication of relevant tests by other researchers, and maximize the validity and reliability of the results. Application of the scientific method thus requires vigilance by all who practice it. The goal isn't to establish "truth" in any absolute sense, but rather to generate ever more accurate and consistent explanations of how the world around us works.

At its very heart, scientific methodology is an exercise in rational thought and critical thinking. The development of critical thinking skills is an important and lasting benefit of a college education. Such skills enable people to evaluate, compare, analyze, critique, and synthesize information so they won't accept everything they hear at face value. A good example of the need for critical thinking in everyday life is how we evaluate advertising claims. For example, people spend billions of dollars every year on "natural" dietary supplements, basing their purchasing decisions on marketing claims that in fact may not have been tested. So when a salesperson tells you that, for example, extracts made from the roots of echinacea help prevent colds, ask if that statement has been scientifically tested—and if so, how, when, and by whom and how valid and reliable the test results are—before you decide to try this herbal remedy. Similarly, when politicians make claims in 30-second sound bites, check those claims before you accept them as truth. In other words, be skeptical.

The Anthropological Perspective

Perhaps the most important benefit you will derive from this textbook is a wider appreciation of the human experience. To better understand humans, how our species came to be, and why modern humans are the way we are, we need the *anthropological perspective* to broaden our viewpoint across space (comparing individuals, populations, and even species) and through time (considering the past, with special emphasis on evolutionary factors).

From the overview presented in this chapter, we can see that physical anthropologists focus on varied aspects of the biological nature of *Homo sapiens* and that archaeologists discover and interpret the cultural evidence of hominin (including modern human) behavior from sites ranging in age from over 2 million years old up to the present day. Modern humans represent one contemporary component of the vast biological continuum of life on earth. Yes, we're just another animal, but we're also an extraordinary form of life. Like many other organisms, we've been biologically successful when viewed across the depths of evolutionary time. Unlike other organisms, we are conscious of that fact, aware of the responsibilities that our success engenders, and compelled to learn more about how and why it happened.

Answering the question—*How* and *why* did humans become so successful?—provides the main theme of this textbook. Humans are the only species to develop complex culture as a means of buffering the challenges posed by nature, and we're the only species that spontaneously acquires and uses spoken language as a very complex form of communication. Consequently, physical anthropologists are keenly interested in how humans differ from and are similar to other animals, especially nonhuman primates. For example, in Chapters 4 and 16, we will discuss how aspects of human nutrition have been influenced by evolutionary factors. Today, most of the foods people eat are derived from domesticated plants and animals; but these dietary items were unavailable prior to the development of agriculture more than 10,000 years ago. And yet, human physiological mechanisms for chewing and digesting, as well as the types of foods humans are predisposed to eat, are variations of patterns that were well established in nonhuman primate ancestors long before 10,000 years ago. Indeed, these adaptations probably go back millions of years.

In addition to differences in diet prior to the development of agriculture, earlier hominins might well have differed from modern humans in average body size, metabolism, and activity patterns. How, then, does the basic evolutionary "equipment" (that is, physiology) inherited from our hominin and prehominin forebears accommodate our modern diets? Clearly, the way to understand such processes is not simply to look at contemporary human responses, but to place them within the context of evolution and adaptation through time. Indeed, throughout this book, we'll focus on the biocultural interactions that came about after the development of agriculture, an event that was one of the most fundamental revolutions in all of human prehistory. By studying human behavior and anatomy from the broader perspective provided by an evolutionary context, we're better able to understand the factors leading to the development of the human species.

Archaeologists trace the evolution of culture and its ever-expanding role in human affairs over the past 2.5 million years. Information from archaeological research is frequently combined with biological data to explain how cultural and biological factors interacted in the past to produce variations in human adaptive response, disease patterns, and even the genetic diversity that we see today. From such a perspective, we can begin to appreciate the diversity of the human experience and, in so doing, more fully understand human constraints and potentials. Furthermore, by extending the breadth of our knowledge, it's easier to avoid the **ethnocentric** pitfalls inherent in a more limited view of humanity, a view that isolates modern humans from other human groups and places them outside the context of evolution.

We hope that the following pages will help you develop a better understanding of the similarities we share with other organisms as well as the biocultural processes that shaped the traits that make us unique. We live in what may well be the most crucial period for our planet in the last 65 million years. We are members of the one species that, through the very agency of culture, has wrought such changes in ecological systems that we must now alter our technologies or face potentially disastrous consequences. In such a time, it's vital that we attempt to gain the best possible understanding of what it means to be human. We believe that the study of physical anthropology and archaeology is one endeavor that aids in this attempt.

ethnocentric Viewing other cultures from the inherently biased perspective of one's own culture. Ethnocentrism often results in other cultures being seen as inferior to one's own.

Summary of Main Topics

▶ The chapter objective was to introduce the fields of physical anthropology and archaeology and place them within the overall context of anthropology, a social science that also includes cultural anthropology and linguistics as major subfields.

▶ Physical anthropology studies aspects of human biology (emphasizing evolutionary perspectives), nonhuman primates, and the hominin fossil record. Physical anthropologists are interested in how hominins came to possess culture and how this process influenced the direction of human evolution. Especially regarding the study of early hominins, physical anthropologists work in close collaboration with many specialists from archaeology, geology, chemistry, and other disciplines that form the interdisciplinary field of paleoanthropology.

▶ Archaeology provides time depth for our understanding of humans as biocultural organisms. Systematic examination of the archaeological record provides the basis for archaeologists' interpretations of extinct lifeways as well as the construction of cultural chronologies, explanations for observable cultural changes, and interpretations of the cognitive and symbolic patterns that mark our past. Like the larger field of paleoanthropology (which also draws heavily on archaeological methods), archaeological research involves input from many related disciplines. This collaborative examination of the archaeological record yields nearly all we know, if not all we are likely to ever know, about prehistoric human behavior and activities.

Critical Thinking Questions

1. Why does American anthropology describe itself as a three- (often four-) field discipline that includes cultural anthropology, physical anthropology, and archaeology?

2. Is it important to you, personally, to know about human evolution? Why or why not?

3. Why is the biocultural perspective important to understanding human evolution?

4. What fundamental assumption about the relationship between human behavior and the archaeological record makes archaeology's study of the human past possible? Can archaeology exist as a valid and reliable source of understanding the past if this assumption is true only sometimes or only under certain conditions?

5. Do you think that understanding the scientific method and developing critical thinking skills can benefit you personally? Why?

CHAPTER 2

The Development of Evolutionary Theory

LEARNING OBJECTIVES

After you have mastered the material in this chapter, you will be able to:

▶ Describe the key contributions to evolutionary theory made by precursors to Darwin and explain how each influenced the development of evolutionary theory.

▶ Explain how natural selection works.

▶ Contrast the scientific understanding of biological evolution with nonscientific approaches that seek to explain the origins of life and how life has changed on earth.

Has anyone ever asked you, "If humans evolved from monkeys, then why do we still have monkeys?" Or perhaps, "If evolution happens, then why don't we ever see new species?" These are the kinds of questions people sometimes ask if they don't understand evolutionary processes or they don't believe those processes exist. Evolution is one of the most fundamental of biological processes, and yet it's one of the most misunderstood. The explanation for the misunderstanding is simple. Evolution isn't taught in most primary and secondary schools; in fact, it's frequently avoided. In colleges and universities, evolution is covered only in classes that directly relate to it. Indeed, if you're not an anthropology or biology major and you're taking a class in biological anthropology mainly to fill a science requirement, you'll probably never study evolution again.

By the end of this course, you'll know the answers to the questions that opened the previous paragraph. Briefly, no one who studies evolution would ever say that humans evolved from monkeys, because they didn't. They didn't evolve from chimpanzees either. The earliest human ancestors evolved from a species that lived some 5 to 8 million years ago (mya). That ancestral species was the *last common ancestor* we share with chimpanzees. In turn, the lineage that led to the apes and ourselves separated from a monkey-like ancestor some 20 mya, and monkeys are still around because as lineages diverged from a common ancestor, each group went its separate way. Over time, some of these groups became extinct, while others evolved into the species we see today. Therefore, each living species is the current product of processes that go back millions of years. Because evolution takes time, and lots of it, we rarely witness the appearance of new species except in microorganisms. But we do see *microevolutionary* changes in many species.

The subject of evolution is controversial, especially in the United States, because some people think that evolutionary statements run counter to biblical teachings. Indeed, as you're probably aware, there is strong opposition to the teaching of evolution in public schools.

People who deny that evolution happens often say that "evolution is only a theory," implying that evolution is nothing more than supposition. Actually, referring to a concept as "theory" supports it. As we discussed in Chapter 1, theories are hypotheses that have been tested and subjected to verification through accumulated evidence. Evolution *is* a theory, one that has increasingly been supported by a mounting body of genetic evidence. It's a theory that has stood the test of time, and today it stands as the most fundamental unifying force in biological science.

Because physical anthropology is concerned with all aspects of how humans came to be and how we adapt physiologically to the external environment, understanding the details of the evolutionary process is crucial. Therefore, it's beneficial to know how the mechanics of the process came to be discovered. Also, if we want to appreciate the nature of the controversy that still surrounds the issue, we need to see how social and political events influenced the discovery of evolutionary principles.

A Brief History of Evolutionary Thought

The discovery of evolutionary principles first took place in western Europe and was made possible by advances in scientific thinking that date back to the sixteenth century. Having said this, we must recognize that Western science could not have developed without writings from other cultures, especially the Arabs, Indians, and Chinese. In fact, intellectuals in these cultures and in ancient Greece had notions of biological evolution (Teresi, 2002), but they never formulated them into a cohesive theory.

Charles Darwin was the first person to explain the basic mechanics of the evolutionary process. But while he was developing his theory of **natural selection**, a Scottish naturalist named Alfred Russel Wallace independently reached the same conclusion. The fact that natural selection, the single most important force of evolutionary change,

natural selection The most critical mechanism of evolutionary change, first articulated by Charles Darwin; refers to genetic change in the frequencies of certain traits in populations due to differential reproductive success between individuals.

should be proposed at more or less the same time by two British men in the mid-nineteenth century may seem like a strange coincidence. But if Darwin and Wallace hadn't made their simultaneous discoveries, someone else soon would have, and that someone would probably have been British or French. That's because the groundwork had already been laid in Britain and France, and many scientists there were prepared to accept explanations of biological change that would have been unacceptable even 25 years before.

Like other human endeavors, scientific knowledge is usually gained through a series of small steps rather than giant leaps, and just as technological change is based on past achievements, scientific knowledge builds on previously developed theories. For this reason, it's informative to examine the development of ideas that led Darwin and Wallace to independently develop the theory of evolution by natural selection.

Throughout the Middle Ages, one predominant feature of the European worldview was that all aspects of nature, including all forms of life and their relationships to one another, never changed. This view was partly shaped by a feudal society that was itself a hierarchical, rigid class system that hadn't changed much for centuries. It was also influenced by an extremely powerful religious system, and the teachings of Christianity were taken literally. Consequently, it was generally accepted that all life on earth had been created by God exactly as it existed in the present, and the belief that life-forms couldn't change came to be known as **fixity of species**.

The plan of the entire universe was viewed as God's design. In what is called the "argument from design," anatomical structures were engineered to meet the purpose for which they were required. Wings, arms, and eyes fit the functions they performed, and nature was a deliberate plan of the Grand Designer, who was believed to have completed his works fairly recently. In fact, an Irish archbishop named James Ussher (1581–1656) analyzed the "begat" chapter of Genesis and concluded that the earth was created in 4004 B.C.

Archbishop Ussher wasn't the first person to suggest a recent origin of the earth, but he was the first to propose a precise date for it.

The prevailing notion of the earth's brief existence, together with fixity of species, posed a huge obstacle to the development of evolutionary theory because evolution requires time, and the idea of immense geological time, which today we take for granted, simply didn't exist. In fact, until the concepts of fixity and time were fundamentally altered, it was impossible to conceive of evolution by means of natural selection.

The Scientific Revolution

So, what transformed centuries-old beliefs in a rigid, static universe to a view of worlds in continuous motion? How did the earth's brief history become an immense expanse of incomprehensible time? How did the scientific method as we know it today develop? These are important questions, but it would be equally appropriate to ask why it took so long for Europe to break from traditional belief systems when Arab and Indian scholars had developed concepts of planetary motion centuries earlier.

For Europeans, the discovery of the New World and circumnavigation of the globe in the fifteenth century overturned some very basic ideas about the planet. For one thing, the earth could no longer be thought of as flat. Also, as Europeans began to explore the New World, their awareness of biological diversity was greatly expanded as they became aware of plants and animals they hadn't seen before.

There were other attacks on traditional beliefs. In 1514, a Polish mathematician named Copernicus challenged the notion, proposed more than 1,800 years earlier by the Greek philosopher Aristotle, that the earth, circled by the sun, moon, and stars, was the center of the universe (**Fig. 2-1**). In fact, Indian scholars had figured out that the sun was the center of the solar system long before Copernicus did; but Copernicus is generally credited with removing the earth as the center of all things.

Copernicus' theory didn't attract much attention at the time; however,

fixity of species The notion that species, once created, can never change; an idea diametrically opposed to theories of biological evolution.

Figure 2-1

This beautifully illustrated seventeenth-century map shows the earth at the center of the solar system. Around it are seven concentric circles depicting the orbits of the moon, sun, and the five planets that were known at the time. (Note also the signs of the zodiac.)

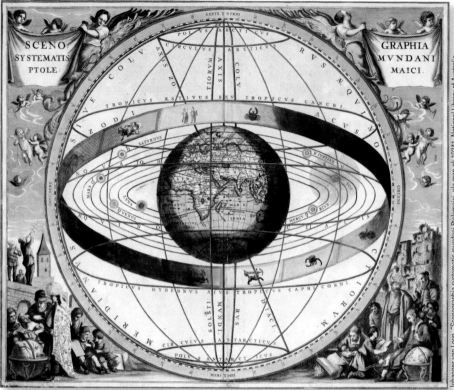

in the early 1600s, it was restated by an Italian mathematician named Galileo Galilei. To his misfortune, Galileo incurred the wrath of the Catholic Church over his publications, and he spent the last nine years of his life under house arrest. Still, in intellectual circles, the universe had changed from earth-centered to sun-centered. Throughout the sixteenth and seventeenth centuries, European scholars developed methods and theories that revolutionized scientific thought. Their technological advances, such as the invention of the telescope, permitted investigations of natural phenomena and opened up entire new worlds for discovery. But even with these advances, the idea that living forms could change over time simply didn't occur to people.

Precursors to the Theory of Evolution

Before early naturalists could begin to understand the many forms of organic life, they had to list and describe them. And as research progressed, scholars were increasingly impressed with the amount of biological diversity they saw.

John Ray   It wasn't until the seventeenth century that John Ray (1627–1705), a minister educated at Cambridge University, developed the concept of species. He was the first person to recognize that groups of plants and animals could be distinguished from other groups by their ability to mate with one another and produce offspring. He placed such groups of reproductively isolated organisms into a single category, which he called the *species* (*pl.*, species). Thus, by the late 1600s, the biological criterion of reproduction was used to define species, much as it is today (Young, 1992). Ray also recognized that species frequently shared similarities with other species, and he grouped these together in a second level of classification he called the *genus* (*pl.*, genera). He was the first to use the labels *genus* and *species* in this way, and they're the terms we still use today.

Carolus Linnaeus   The Swedish naturalist Carolus Linnaeus (1707–1778) is best known for developing a method of classifying plants and animals.

In his famous work *Systema Naturae* (Systems of Nature), first published in 1735, he standardized Ray's use of genus and species terminology and established the system of **binomial nomenclature**. He also added two more categories: class and order. Linnaeus' four-level system became the basis for **taxonomy**, the system of classification we continue to use today.

Another of Linnaeus' innovations was to include humans in his classification of animals, placing them in the genus *Homo* and species *sapiens*. Including humans in this scheme was controversial because it defied contemporary thought that humans, made in God's image, should be considered unique and separate from the animal kingdom.

Linnaeus also believed in fixity of species, although in later years, faced with mounting evidence to the contrary, he came to question it. Indeed, fixity was being challenged on many fronts, especially in France, where voices were being raised in favor of a universe based on change—and, more to the point, in favor of a biological relationship between similar species based on descent from a common ancestor.

Jean-Baptiste Lamarck Linnaeus did not attempt to *explain* the evolutionary process. The first scientist to do this was a French naturalist named Jean-Baptiste Lamarck (1744–1829). Lamarck (**Fig. 2-2**) suggested a dynamic relationship between species and the environment such that if the external environment changed, an animal's activity patterns would also change to accommodate the new circumstances. This would result in the increased or decreased use of certain body parts, and consequently, those body parts would be modified. According to Lamarck, these physical changes would occur in response to bodily "needs," so that if a particular part of the body felt a certain need, "fluids and forces" would be directed to that point and the structure would be modified. Because the alteration would make the animal better suited to its habitat, the new trait would be passed on to its offspring. This theory is known as the *inheritance of acquired characteristics*, or the *use-disuse* theory

One of the most frequently given hypothetical examples of Lamarck's theory is the giraffe, which, having stripped all the leaves from the lower branches of a tree (environmental change), tries to reach leaves on upper branches. As "vital forces" move to tissues of the neck, it becomes slightly longer, and the giraffe can reach higher. The longer neck is then passed on to offspring, with the eventual result that all giraffes have longer necks than their predecessors (**Fig. 2-3**). Thus, according to this theory, *a trait acquired by an animal during its lifetime can be passed on to offspring.* Today we know that this explanation is wrong, because only those traits that are influenced by genetic information contained within sex cells (eggs and sperm) can be inherited (see Chapter 3).

Because Lamarck's explanation of species change isn't genetically correct, it's been made fun of and dismissed. But actually, Lamarck deserves a lot of credit because he emphasized the importance of interactions between organisms and the external environment and tried to explain them. Moreover, he coined the term *biology* to refer to studies of living organisms.

Georges Cuvier Georges Cuvier (1769–1832), the most vehement opponent of Lamarck, was a French vertebrate paleontologist who introduced the concept of extinction to explain the disappearance of animals represented by fossils. Although a brilliant anatomist, Cuvier never grasped the dynamic concept of nature, and he insisted on the fixity of species. So, rather than assume that similarities between certain fossil forms and living species indicated evolutionary relationships, he suggested a variation of a theory known as **catastrophism**.

Catastrophism was the belief that the earth's geological features are the results of sudden, worldwide cataclysmic events like the Noah flood. Cuvier's version of catastrophism suggested that a series of regional disasters had destroyed most or all of the plant and animal life in various places. These areas were then restocked with new, similar forms that migrated

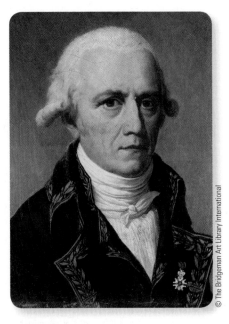

Figure 2-2

Portrait of Jean-Baptiste Lamarck. Lamarck believed that species change was influenced by environmental change. He is best known for his theory of the inheritance of acquired characteristics.

© The Bridgeman Art Library International

binomial nomenclature (*binomial*, meaning "two names") In taxonomy, the convention established by Carolus Linnaeus whereby genus and species names are used to refer to species. For example, *Homo sapiens* refers to human beings.

taxonomy The branch of science concerned with the rules of classifying organisms on the basis of evolutionary relationships.

catastrophism The view that the earth's geological landscape is the result of violent cataclysmic events. This view was promoted by Cuvier, especially in opposition to Lamarck.

Figure 2-3

Contrasting ideas about the mechanism of evolution. **(a)** Lamarck's theory held that acquired characteristics can be passed to offspring. Short-necked giraffes stretched to reach higher into trees for food, and their necks grew longer. According to Lamarck, this acquired trait was passed on to offspring, who were born with longer necks. **(b)** The Darwin-Wallace theory of natural selection states that among giraffes there is variation in neck length. If having a longer neck provides an advantage for feeding (and therefore reproduction), the trait will be passed on to a greater number of offspring, leading to an overall increase in the length of giraffe necks over many generations.

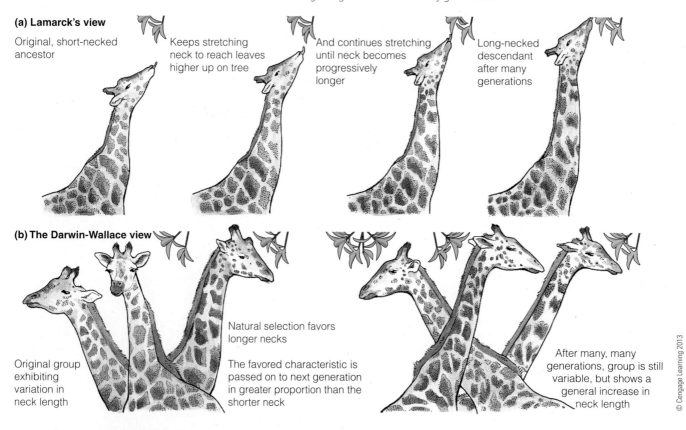

(a) Lamarck's view

Original, short-necked ancestor

Keeps stretching neck to reach leaves higher up on tree

And continues stretching until neck becomes progressively longer

Long-necked descendant after many generations

(b) The Darwin-Wallace view

Original group exhibiting variation in neck length

Natural selection favors longer necks

The favored characteristic is passed on to next generation in greater proportion than the shorter neck

After many, many generations, group is still variable, but shows a general increase in neck length

© Cengage Learning 2013

With permission from the Master of Haileybury

Figure 2-4

Portrait of Thomas Malthus.

in from unaffected regions. But Cuvier needed to account for the emerging fossil evidence that organisms had become more complex over time, so he suggested that after each disaster, the incoming migrants had a more modern appearance because they were the results of more recent creation events. (The last of these events was the one described in Genesis.) So Cuvier's explanation of increased complexity over time avoided any notion of evolution while still being able to account for the evidence for change that was preserved in the fossil record.

Thomas Malthus In 1798, Thomas Malthus (1766–1834), an English clergyman and economist, wrote *An Essay on the Principle of Population*, which inspired both Charles Darwin and

Alfred Wallace in their separate discoveries of natural selection (**Fig. 2-4**). In his essay, Malthus argued for limits to human population growth and pointed out that human populations could double in size every 25 years if they weren't kept in check by limited food supplies. Of course, humans, unlike other species, can increase their food supplies and aren't dependent on natural sources, but Malthus warned that increased numbers of humans would eventually lead to famine.

Darwin and Wallace accepted Malthus' proposition that population size increases exponentially while food supplies remain relatively constant, and they extended it to all organisms. But what impressed them the most was something Malthus hadn't written about. They both recognized the important fact that when population size is limited by the availability of resources, there must be constant competition for food and water. And competition between individuals is the ultimate key to understanding natural selection.

Charles Lyell Charles Lyell (1797–1875), the son of Scottish landowners, is considered the founder of modern geology (**Fig. 2-5**). He was a barrister, a geologist, and for many years Charles Darwin's friend and mentor. Before meeting Darwin in 1836, Lyell had earned acceptance in Europe's most prestigious scientific circles, thanks to his highly praised *Principles of Geology*, first published during the years 1830–1833.

In this immensely important work, Lyell argued that the geological processes observed in the present are the same as those that occurred in the past. This theory, called **uniformitarianism**, didn't originate entirely with Lyell, having been proposed by James Hutton in the late 1700s. Even so, it was Lyell who demonstrated that such forces as wind, water erosion, local flooding, frost, decomposition of vegetation, volcanoes, earthquakes, and glacial movements had all contributed in the past to produce the geological landscape that exists in the present. What's more, the fact that these processes still occurred indicated that geological change was still happening and that the forces driving such change were consistent, or *uniform*, over time. In other words, although various aspects of the earth's surface (for example, climate, plants, animals, and land surfaces) are variable through time, the *underlying processes* that influence them are constant.

The theory of uniformitarianism flew in the face of Cuvier's catastrophism. Additionally, Lyell emphasized the obvious: namely, that for such slow-acting forces to produce momentous change, the earth would have to be far older than anyone had previously suspected. By providing an immense time scale and thereby altering perceptions of earth's history from a few thousand to many millions of years, Lyell changed the framework within which scientists viewed the geological past. Thus, the concept of "deep time" (Gould, 1987) remains one of Lyell's most significant contributions to the discovery of evolutionary principles. The immensity of geological time permitted the necessary time depth for the inherently slow process of evolutionary change (**Fig 2-6**).

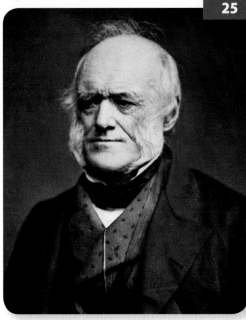

© Hulton-Deutsch Collection / Corbis

Figure 2-5

Portrait of Charles Lyell.

Figure 2-6

(a) These limestone cliffs in southern France were formed around 300 million years ago from shells and the skeletal remains of countless sea creatures. (b) Part of a block of stone cut from the same limestone containing fossilized shells.

Lynn Kilgore

(a)

(b)

Lynn Kilgore

uniformitarianism The theory that the earth's features are the result of long-term processes that continue to operate in the present as they did in the past. Elaborated on by Lyell, this theory opposed catastrophism and contributed strongly to the concept of immense geological time.

The Discovery of Natural Selection

Charles Darwin Charles Darwin (1809–1882) was one of six children of Dr. Robert and Susanna Darwin (**Fig. 2-7**). As a boy, he had a keen interest in nature and spent his days fishing and collecting shells, birds' eggs, rocks, and so forth. However, this interest in natural history didn't dispel the generally held view of family and friends that he was in no way remarkable. In fact, his performance at school was no more than ordinary.

After the death of his mother when he was 8 years old, Darwin was raised by his father and his older sisters. Because he showed little interest in anything except hunting, shooting, and perhaps science, his father sent him to Edinburgh University to study medicine. It was there that Darwin first became acquainted with the evolutionary theories of Lamarck and others.

During that time (the 1820s), notions of evolution were becoming feared in England and elsewhere. Anything identifiable with postrevolutionary France was viewed with suspicion by the established order in England. Lamarck, partly because he was French, was especially vilified by British scientists.

It was also a time of growing political unrest in Britain. The Reform Movement, which sought to undo many of the wrongs of the traditional class system, was under way; and like most social movements, this one had a radical faction. Because many of the radicals were atheists and socialists who also supported Lamarck's ideas, many people came to associate evolution with atheism and political subversion. Such was the growing fear of evolutionary ideas that many believed that if they were generally accepted, "the Church would crash, the moral fabric of society would be torn apart, and civilized man would return to savagery" (Desmond and Moore, 1991, p. 34). It's unfortunate that some of the

most outspoken early proponents of **transmutation** were so vehemently anti-Christian, because their rhetoric helped establish the entrenched suspicion and misunderstanding of evolutionary theory that persist today.

While at Edinburgh, young Darwin studied with professors who were outspoken supporters of Lamarck. Therefore, although he hated medicine and left Edinburgh after two years, his experience there was a formative period in his intellectual development.

Even though Darwin was fairly indifferent to religion, he next went to Christ's College, Cambridge, to study theology. It was during his Cambridge years that he seriously cultivated his interests in natural science, immersing himself in botany and geology. It's no wonder that following his graduation in 1831, he was invited to join a scientific expedition that would circle the globe. And so it was that Darwin set sail aboard HMS *Beagle* on December 17, 1831 (**Fig. 2-8**). The famous voyage of the *Beagle* would take almost five years and would forever change not only the course of Darwin's life but also the history of biological science.

Darwin went aboard the *Beagle* believing in fixity of species. But during the voyage, he privately began to have doubts. For example, he came across fossils of ancient giant animals that, except for size, looked very much like species that still lived in the same vicinity, and he wondered if the fossils represented ancestors of those living forms.

During the famous stopover at the Galápagos Islands (**Fig. 2-9**), Darwin noticed that the vegetation and animals (especially birds) shared many similarities with those on the mainland of South America. But they weren't identical to them. What's more, the birds on one island were somewhat different from those living on another. Darwin collected 13 different varieties of Galápagos finches, and it was clear that they represented a closely affiliated group; but they differed with regard to certain physical traits, particularly the shape and size of their beaks (**Fig. 2-10**). He also collected finches from the mainland, and these appeared to represent only one group, or species.

© Bettmann / Corbis

Figure 2-7
Charles Darwin, photographed five years before the publication of *Origin of Species*.

transmutation The change of one species to another. The term *evolution* did not assume its current meaning until the late nineteenth century.

Figure 2-8

A painting by John Chancellor of HMS *Beagle* sailing through the Galápagos Islands in 1835.

The insight that Darwin gained from the finches is legendary. He recognized that the various Galápagos finches had all descended from a common mainland ancestor and had been modified over time in response to different island habitats and dietary preferences. But actually, it wasn't until *after* he returned to England that he recognized the significance of the variation in beak structure. In fact, during the voyage, he had paid little attention to the finches. It was only later that he considered the factors that could lead to the modification of one species into 13 (Gould, 1985; Desmond and Moore, 1991).

Figure 2-9

The route of HMS *Beagle*.

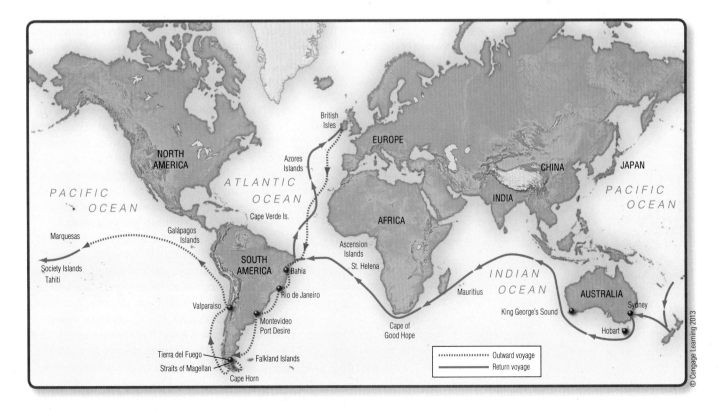

Figure 2-10

Beak variation in Darwin's Galápagos finches.

Ground finch	**Tree finch**	**Tree finch** **(called woodpecker finch)**	**Ground finch** **(known as warbler finch)**
Main Food: seeds	Main food: leaves, buds, blossoms, fruits	Main food: insects	Main food: insects
Beak: heavy	Beak: thick, short	Beak: stout, straight	Beak: slender

Figure 2-11

Down House, as seen from the rear. *On the Origin of Species* and numerous other publications were written here.

Darwin arrived back in England in October 1836 and was immediately accepted into the most prestigious scientific circles. He married his cousin, Emma Wedgwood, and moved to the village of Down, near London, where he spent the rest of his life writing on topics ranging from fossils to orchids (**Fig. 2-11**). But the question of species change was his overriding passion.

At Down, Darwin began to develop his views on what he called *natural selection*. This concept was borrowed from animal breeders, who choose, or "select," as breeding stock those animals that possess certain traits they want to emphasize in offspring. Animals with undesirable traits are "selected against," or prevented from breeding. A dramatic example of the effects of selective breeding can be seen in the various domestic dog breeds shown in **Figure 2-12**. Darwin applied his knowledge of domesticated species to naturally occurring ones, recognizing that in undomesticated organisms, the selective agent is nature, not humans.

By the late 1830s, Darwin had realized that biological variation within a species (that is, differences among individuals) was crucial. Furthermore, he recognized that sexual reproduction increased variation, although he didn't know why. Then, in 1838, he read Malthus' essay, and there he found the answer to the question of how new species came to be. He accepted from Malthus that populations increase at a faster rate than do resources, and he recognized that in nonhuman animals, increase in population size is continuously restricted by limited food supplies. He also accepted that in nature there is a constant "struggle for existence." The idea that in each generation more offspring are born than survive to adulthood, coupled with the notions of competition for resources and biological diversity, was all Darwin needed to develop his theory of natural selection. He wrote: "It at once struck me that under these circumstances favourable variations would tend to be preserved, and unfavourable ones to be destroyed.

The result of this would be the formation of a new species" (F. Darwin, 1950,
pp. 53–54). Basically, this quotation summarizes the entire theory of natural
selection.

By 1844, Darwin had written a short
summary of his views on natural selection, but he didn't think he had enough
data to support his hypothesis, so he
continued his research without publishing. He also had other reasons for
not publishing what he knew would be,
to say the least, a highly controversial
work. He was deeply troubled by the
fact that his wife, Emma, saw his ideas
as running counter to her strong religious convictions (Keynes, 2002). Also,
as a member of the established order, he
knew that many of his friends and associates were concerned with threats to
the status quo, and evolutionary theory
was viewed as a very serious threat. So
he waited.

Alfred Russel Wallace Unlike
Darwin, Alfred Russel Wallace
(1823–1913) was born into a family of
modest means (**Fig. 2-13**). He went to
work at the age of 14, and with little
formal education, he moved from one
job to the next. He became interested
in collecting plants and animals,
and in 1848 he joined an expedition
to the Amazon, where he acquired
firsthand knowledge of many natural
phenomena. Then, in 1854, he sailed
for Southeast Asia and the Malay
Peninsula to collect bird and insect
specimens.

In 1855, Wallace published a paper
suggesting that species were descended from other species and that the
appearance of new species was influenced by environmental factors. The
Wallace paper caused Lyell and others
to urge Darwin to publish, but still he
hesitated.

Figure 2-12

All domestic dog breeds share a common
ancestor, the wolf. The extreme variation exhibited by dog breeds today has been achieved
in a relatively short time through artificial
selection. In this situation, humans allow only
certain dogs to breed to emphasize specific
characteristics. (We should note that not all
traits desired by human breeders are advantageous to the dogs themselves.)

Figure 2-13

Alfred Russel Wallace independently identified natural selection as the key to the evolutionary process.

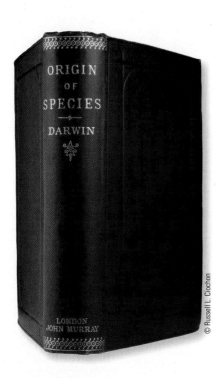

Figure 2-14

Charles Darwin's *Origin of Species*, the book that revolutionized biological science.

reproductive success The number of offspring an individual produces and rears to reproductive age; an individual's genetic contribution to the next generation.

Then, in 1858, Wallace sent Darwin another paper, "On the Tendency of Varieties to Depart Indefinitely from the Original Type." In it, Wallace described evolution as a process driven by competition and natural selection. Once he read it, Darwin feared that Wallace might get credit for a theory (natural selection) that he had already spent decades developing. He quickly wrote a paper presenting his ideas, and both papers were read before the Linnean Society of London. Neither author was present. Wallace was out of the country, and Darwin was mourning the recent death of his young son.

The papers received little notice at the time; but when Darwin completed and published his greatest work, *On the Origin of Species,** in December 1859, the storm broke, and it still hasn't abated (**Fig. 2-14**). Although public opinion was negative, there was much scholarly praise for the book, and scientific opinion gradually came to Darwin's support. The riddle of species was now explained: Species were mutable, not fixed; and they evolved from other species through the mechanism of natural selection.

---

* The full title is *On the Origin of Species by Means of Natural Selection, or the Preservation of Favoured Races in the Struggle for Life.*

Natural Selection

Early in his research, Darwin had realized that natural selection was the key to evolution. With the help of Malthus' ideas, he saw *how* selection in nature could be explained. In the struggle for existence, those *individuals* with favorable variations would survive and reproduce, but those with unfavorable variations wouldn't. For Darwin, the explanation of evolution was simple. The basic processes, as he understood them, are as follows:

1. All species are capable of producing offspring at a faster rate than food supplies increase.
2. There is biological variation within all species.
3. Since in each generation more offspring are produced than can survive, and owing to limited resources, there is competition between individuals. (*Note*: This statement doesn't mean that there is constant fierce fighting.)
4. Individuals who possess favorable variations or traits (for example, speed, resistance to disease, protective coloration) have an advantage over those who don't have them. In other words, favorable traits increase the likelihood of survival and reproduction.
5. The environmental context determines whether or not a trait is beneficial. What is favorable in one setting may be a liability in another. Consequently, the traits that become most advantageous are the result of a natural process.
6. Traits are inherited and passed on to the next generation. Because individuals who possess favorable traits contribute more offspring to the next generation than individuals who don't, over time, such characteristics become more common in the population; less favorable traits aren't passed on as frequently, and they become less common, or are "weeded out." Individuals who produce more offspring in comparison to others are said to have greater **reproductive success**.

7. Over long periods of geological time, successful variations accumulate in a population, so that later generations may be distinct from ancestral ones. Thus, in time, a new species may appear.

8. Geographical isolation also contributes to the formation of new species. As populations of a species become geographically isolated from one another, for whatever reasons, they begin to adapt to different environments. Over time, as populations continue to respond to different **selective pressures** (that is, different ecological circumstances), they may become distinct species. The 13 species of Galápagos finches are presumably all descended from a common ancestor on the South American mainland, and they provide an example of the role of geographical isolation.

Before Darwin, individual members of species weren't considered important, so they weren't studied. But as we've seen, Darwin recognized the uniqueness of individuals and realized that variation among them could explain how selection occurs. Favorable variations are selected, or chosen, for survival by nature; unfavorable ones are eliminated. *Natural selection operates on individuals*, favorably or unfavorably, but *it's the population that evolves*. The unit of natural selection is the individual; the unit of evolution is the population (because individuals don't change genetically, but over time, populations do).

Natural Selection in Action

The most frequently cited example of natural selection concerns changes in the coloration of "peppered" moths around Manchester, England. In recent years, the moth story has come under some criticism; but the basic premise remains valid, so we use it to illustrate how natural selection works.

Before the nineteenth century, the most common variety of the peppered moth was a mottled gray color. During the day, as moths rested on lichen-covered tree trunks, their coloration provided camouflage (**Fig. 2-15**). There

was also a dark gray variety of the same species, but since the dark moths weren't camouflaged, they were eaten by birds more frequently and so they were less common. (In this example, the birds are the *selective agent*, and they apply *selective pressure* on the moths.) Therefore, the dark moths produced fewer offspring than the camouflaged moths. Yet, by the end of the nineteenth century, the common gray form had been almost completely replaced by the darker one.

The cause of this change was the changing environment of industrialized nineteenth-century England. Coal dust from factories and fireplaces settled on trees, turning them dark gray and killing the lichen. The moths continued to rest on the trees, but the light gray ones became more conspicuous as the trees became darker, and they were increasingly targeted by birds. Since fewer of the light gray moths were living long enough to reproduce, they contributed fewer genes to the next generation than

(a)

(b)

Figure 2-15

Variation in the peppered moth. (a) The dark form is more visible on the light, lichen-covered tree. (b) On trees darkened by pollution, the lighter form is more visible.

selective pressures Factors in the environment that influence reproductive success in individuals.

the darker moths did, and the proportion of lighter moths decreased while the dark moths became more common. A similar color shift had also occurred in North America. But when the advent of clean air acts in both Britain and the United States reduced the amount of air pollution (at least from coal), the predominant color of the peppered moth once again became the light mottled gray. This kind of evolutionary shift in response to environmental change is called *adaptation*.

Another example of natural selection is provided by the medium ground finch of the Galápagos Islands. In 1977, drought killed many of the plants that produced the smaller, softer seeds favored by these birds. This forced a population of finches on one of the islands to feed on larger, harder seeds. Even before 1977, some birds had smaller, less robust beaks than others (that is, there was variation); and during the drought, because they were less able to process the larger seeds, more smaller-beaked birds died than larger-beaked birds. Therefore, although overall population size declined, average beak thickness in the survivors and their offspring increased, simply because thicker-beaked individuals were surviving in greater numbers and producing more offspring. In other words, they had greater reproductive success. But during heavy rains in 1982–1983, smaller seeds became more plentiful again and the pattern in beak size reversed itself, demonstrating how reproductive success is related to environmental conditions (Grant, 1986; Ridley, 1993).

The best illustration of natural selection, however, and certainly one with potentially grave consequences for humans, is the recent increase in resistant strains of disease-causing microorganisms. When antibiotics were first introduced in the 1940s, they were hailed as the cure for bacterial disease. But that optimistic view didn't take into account the fact that bacteria, like other organisms, possess genetic variability. Although an antibiotic will kill most bacteria in an infected person, any bacterium with an inherited resistance to that particular therapy will survive. Subsequently, the survivors reproduce and pass their drug resistance

to future generations, so that eventually, the population is mostly made up of bacteria that don't respond to treatment. What's more, because bacteria produce new generations every few hours, antibiotic-resistant strains are continuously being produced. As a result, many types of infection no longer respond to treatment. For example, tuberculosis was once thought to be well controlled, but it has seen a resurgence in recent years because the bacterium that causes it is now resistant to many antibiotics.

These three examples (moths, finches, and bacteria) provide the following insights into the fundamentals of evolutionary change produced by natural selection:

1. *A trait must be inherited if natural selection is to act on it.* A characteristic that isn't hereditary (such as a temporary change in hair color produced by the hairdresser) won't be passed on to succeeding generations. In finches, for example, beak size is a hereditary trait.

2. *Natural selection can't occur without population variation in inherited characteristics.* If, for example, all the peppered moths had initially been gray (you will recall that some dark forms were always present) and the trees had become darker, the survival and reproduction of all moths could have been so low that the population might have become extinct. *Selection can work only with variation that already exists.*

3. **Fitness** *is a relative measure that changes as the environment changes.* Fitness is simply *differential reproductive success.* In the initial stage, the lighter moths were more fit because they produced more offspring. But as the environment changed, the dark gray moths became more fit, and a further change reversed the adaptive pattern. Likewise, the majority of Galápagos finches will have larger or smaller beaks, depending on external conditions. So it should be obvious that statements regarding the "most fit" mean nothing without reference to specific environments.

4. *Natural selection can act only on traits that affect reproduction.* If a character-

fitness Pertaining to natural selection, a measure of the *relative* reproductive success of individuals. Fitness can be measured by an individual's genetic contribution to the next generation compared with that of other individuals. The terms *genetic fitness, reproductive fitness,* and *differential reproductive success* are also used.

istic isn't expressed until later in life, after organisms have reproduced, then natural selection can't influence it. This is because the inherited components of the trait have already been passed on to offspring. Many forms of cancer and cardiovascular disease are influenced by hereditary factors, but because these diseases usually affect people after they've had children, natural selection can't act against them. By the same token, if a condition usually kills or compromises the individual before he or she reproduces, natural selection acts against it because the trait won't be passed on.

So far, our examples have shown how different death rates influence natural selection (for example, moths or finches that die early leave fewer offspring). But mortality isn't the complete picture. Another important aspect of natural selection is fertility, because an animal that gives birth to more young passes its genes on at a faster rate than one that bears fewer offspring. However, fertility isn't the entire story either, because the crucial element is the number of young raised success-fully to the point at which they themselves reproduce. We call this *differential net reproductive success*. The way this mechanism works can be demonstrated through yet another example.

In swifts (small birds that resemble swallows), data show that producing more offspring doesn't necessarily guarantee that more young will be successfully raised. The number of eggs hatched in a breeding season is a measure of fertility. The number of birds that mature and are eventually able to leave the nest is a measure of net reproductive success, or offspring successfully raised. The following table shows the correlation between the number of eggs hatched (fertility) and the number of young that leave the nest (reproductive success), averaged over four breeding seasons (Lack, 1966):

Number of eggs hatched (fertility)	2 eggs	3 eggs	4 eggs
Average number of young raised (reproductive success)	1.92	2.54	1.76
Sample size (number of nests)	72	20	16

At a Glance

The Mechanism of Natural Selection

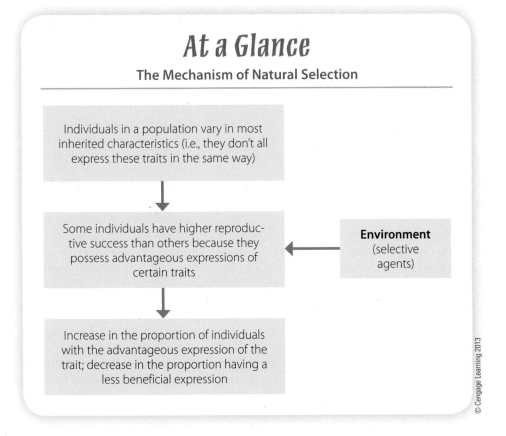

Individuals in a population vary in most inherited characteristics (i.e., they don't all express these traits in the same way)

↓

Some individuals have higher reproductive success than others because they possess advantageous expressions of certain traits

← **Environment** (selective agents)

↓

Increase in the proportion of individuals with the advantageous expression of the trait; decrease in the proportion having a less beneficial expression

As you can see, the most efficient number of eggs is three, because that number yields the highest reproductive success. Raising two offspring is less beneficial to the parents, since the end result isn't as successful as with three eggs. Trying to raise more than three is actually detrimental, since the parents may not be able to provide enough nourishment for any of the offspring. In evolutionary terms, offspring that die before reaching reproductive age are equivalent to never being born. Actually, death of an offspring can be a minus to the parents, because before it dies, it drains parental resources. It may even inhibit their ability to raise other offspring, thereby reducing their reproductive success even further. Selection favors those genetic traits that yield the maximum net reproductive success. If the number of eggs laid is a genetic trait in birds (and it seems to be), natural selection in swifts should act to favor the laying of three eggs as opposed to two or four.

Constraints on Nineteenth-Century Evolutionary Theory

Darwin argued for the concept of evolution in general and the role of natural selection in particular, but he didn't understand the mechanisms of evolutionary change. As we have seen, natural selection acts on variation within species. But neither Darwin nor anyone else in the nineteenth century understood the actual source of variation. Also, no one understood how parents pass traits to offspring. Almost without exception, nineteenth-century scholars believed that inheritance was a *blending* process in which parental characteristics were mixed together to produce intermediate expressions in offspring. Given this notion, we can see why the true nature of genes was unimaginable, and with no alternative explanations, Darwin accepted it. As it turns out, a contemporary of Darwin's had actually worked out the rules of heredity. However, the work of this Augustinian monk named Gregor Mendel (whom you will meet in

Chapter 3) wasn't recognized until the beginning of the twentieth century.

The first three decades of the twentieth century saw the merger of Mendel's discoveries and natural selection. This was a crucial development because until then, scientists thought that these concepts were unrelated. Then, in 1953, the structure of **deoxyribonucleic acid (DNA)** was discovered. This landmark achievement has been followed by even more amazing advances in the field of genetics, including the sequencing of the human **genome**. We may finally be on the threshold of revealing the remaining secrets of the evolutionary process. If only Darwin could know!

Opposition to Evolution

Now, just a little more than 150 years after the publication of *Origin of Species*, the debate over evolution is far from over. For the vast majority of scientists today, evolution is indisputable. The genetic evidence for it is solid and accumulating daily. Anyone who appreciates and understands genetic mechanisms can't avoid the conclusion that populations and species evolve. But surveys consistently show that about half of all Americans don't believe that evolution occurs. There are a number of reasons for this.

The mechanisms of evolution are complex and don't lend themselves to simple explanations. Understanding them requires some familiarity with genetics and biology—a familiarity that people don't have unless they took related courses in school. What's more, people tend to want definitive, clear-cut answers to complex questions. But as you learned in Chapter 1, science doesn't always provide definitive answers to questions, nor does it establish absolute truths. Another thing to consider is that regardless of their culture, most people are raised in belief systems that don't emphasize **biological continuity** between species.

As we said at the beginning of this chapter, much of the opposition to evolutionary concepts is based in cer-

deoxyribonucleic acid (DNA) The double-stranded molecule that contains the genetic code.

genome The entire genetic makeup of an individual or species.

biological continuity Refers to a biological continuum—the idea that organisms are related through common ancestry and that traits present in one species are also seen to varying degrees in others. When expressions of a phenomenon continuously grade into one another so that there are no discrete categories, they exist on a continuum. Color is one such phenomenon, and life-forms are another.

tain religious views. The relationship between science and religion has never been easy (remember Galileo). Even though both systems serve, in their own ways, to explain various phenomena, scientific explanations are based in data analysis, hypothesis testing, and interpretation. Religion, meanwhile, is a system of beliefs based in faith, and it isn't amenable to scientific testing. Religion and science concern different aspects of the human experience, and we should remember that they aren't mutually exclusive approaches. Belief in God doesn't exclude the possibility of biological evolution; and acknowledgment of evolutionary processes doesn't preclude the existence of God. What's more, not all forms of Christianity or other religions are opposed to evolutionary concepts. Some years ago, the Vatican hosted an international conference on human evolution; and in 1996, Pope John Paul II issued a statement that "fresh knowledge leads to recognition of the theory of evolution as more than just a hypothesis." Today, the official position of the Catholic Church is that evolutionary processes occur, but that the human soul is of divine creation and not subject to evolutionary processes. Likewise, mainstream Protestants don't generally see a conflict. But those who believe absolutely in a literal interpretation of the bible (called fundamentalists) accept no compromise.

In 1925, a law banning the teaching of evolution in public schools was passed in Tennessee. To test the validity of the law, the American Civil Liberties Union persuaded a high school teacher named John Scopes to allow himself to be arrested and tried for teaching evolution. The subsequent trial (called the Scopes Monkey Trial) was a 1920s equivalent of current celebrity trials, and in the end, Scopes was convicted and fined $100 (**Fig. 2-16**). In the more than 80 years since that trial, Christian fundamentalists have continued to try to remove evolution from public school curricula. Known as "creationists" because they explain the existence of the universe as the result of a sudden creation event that occurred no more than 10,000 years ago, they are determined either to eliminate the teaching of evolution or to introduce

antievolutionary material into public school classes. In the past 20 years, creationists have insisted that what they used to call "creation science" and now call "intelligent design" (ID) is as valid a scientific explanation of the earth's origins and the life-forms found on our planet. They've argued that, in the interest of fairness, a balanced view should be offered: If evolution is taught as science, then creationism should also be taught as science. Sounds fair, doesn't it? But ID isn't science at all, for the simple reason that creationists insist that their view is absolute and infallible. Therefore, creationism isn't a hypothesis that can be tested, nor is it amenable to falsification. And because hypothesis testing is the basis of all science, creationism, by its very nature, cannot be considered science.

Still, creationists remain active in state legislatures, promoting laws that mandate the teaching of creationism in public schools. In 1981, the Arkansas state legislature passed one such law, but it was overturned in 1982. In his ruling against the state, the judge stated that "a theory that is by its own terms dogmatic, absolutist and never subject to revision is not a scientific theory." And he added: "Since creation is not science, the conclusion is inescapable that the only real effect of [this law] is the advancement

Figure 2-16

Photo taken at the "Scopes Monkey Trial." The well-known defense attorney Clarence Darrow is sitting on the edge of the table. John Scopes, the defendant, is sitting with his arms folded behind Darrow.

of religion." Since that time, numerous similar laws have been passed, only to be overturned because they violate the principle of separation of church and state as provided in the First Amendment to the U.S. Constitution.

It is curious that the biological process that has led to the appearance of millions of plants and animals on our planet should generate such controversy. Our current understanding of evolution is directly traceable to developments in intellectual thought over the past 400 years. Many people contributed to this shift in perspective, and we've named only a few to provide a short historical view. It is quite likely that in the next 20 years, scientists will identify many of the secrets of our evolutionary past through advances in genetic technologies and the continued discovery of fossil material. For evolutionary science, the early twenty-first century is indeed an exciting time.

Summary of Main Topics

▶ Our current understanding of evolutionary processes is directly traceable to developments in intellectual thought in western Europe and the East over the past 400 years. Darwin and Wallace were able to discover the process of natural selection and evolution because of the discoveries of numerous scientists who had laid the groundwork for them. Among others, Galileo, Lyell, Lamarck, Linnaeus, and Malthus all contributed to a dramatic shift in how people viewed the planet and themselves as part of a system governed by natural processes.

▶ Charles Darwin and Alfred Russel Wallace recognized that there was variation among individuals in any population (human or nonhuman). By understanding how animal breeders selected for certain traits in cattle, pigeons, and other species, Darwin formulated the theory of natural selection. Stated in the simplest terms, natural selection is a process whereby individuals who possess favorable traits (characteristics that permit them to survive and reproduce in a specific environment) will produce more offspring than individuals who have less favorable traits. Over time, the beneficial characteristics will become more frequent in the population, and the makeup of the population (or even a species) will have changed.

▶ As populations of a species become reproductively isolated from one another (perhaps due to distance or geographical barriers), they become increasingly different as each population adapts, by means of natural selection, to its own environment. Eventually, the populations may become distinct enough that they can no longer interbreed; at this point, they are considered separate species.

▶ In the United States, and increasingly in some Muslim countries, evolutionary processes are denounced because they are seen as contradictory to religious teaching. In recent years, Christian fundamentalists in the United States have argued in favor of teaching "creation science" or "intelligent design" in public schools. So far, courts have ruled against various attempts to promote "creation science" because of separation of church and state as provided for in the U.S. Constitution.

Critical Thinking Questions

1. After having read this chapter, how would you respond to the question, "If humans evolved from monkeys, why do we still have monkeys?"
2. What are selective agents? Can you think of some examples we didn't discuss? Why did Darwin look at domesticated species as models for natural selection, and what is the selective agent in artificial selection? List some examples of artificial selection that we didn't discuss.
3. Given what you've read about the scientific method in Chapter 1, how would you explain the differences between science and religion as methods of explaining natural phenomena? Do you personally see a conflict between evolutionary and religious explanations of how species come to be?

Heredity and Evolution

© Medi-Mation Ltd / Photo Researchers, Inc.

LEARNING OBJECTIVES

After you have mastered the material in this chapter, you will be able to:

▶ Explain why cells are basic to life and describe the two different types of cells found in animals.

▶ Compare and contrast the two types of cell division.

▶ Describe the basic structure of DNA and explain how it relates to DNA replication.

▶ Describe the basic concepts of heredity that are found in all sexually reproducing organisms, including humans.

You've just gotten home after a rotten day, and you're watching the news on TV. The first story, after about 20 minutes of commercials, is about genetically modified foods, a newly cloned species, synthetic bacteria, or the controversy over stem cell research. What do you do? Change the channel? Press the mute button? Go to sleep? Or do you follow the story? If you watch it, do you understand it, and do you think it's important or relevant to you personally? In fact, it *is* important to you because you live in an age when genetic discoveries and genetically based technologies are advancing daily, and one way or another, they're going to profoundly affect your life.

At some point in your life, you or someone you love will probably need lifesaving medical treatment, perhaps for cancer, and this treatment will almost certainly be based on genetic research. Like it or not, you already eat genetically modified foods, and you may eventually take advantage of developing reproductive technologies. Sadly, you may also see the development of biological weapons based on genetically altered bacteria and viruses. But fortunately, you'll also live to see many of the secrets of evolution revealed through genetic research. So even if you haven't been particularly interested in genetic issues (or maybe you've been intimidated by them), you should be aware that they affect your life every day.

For at least 10,000 years, beginning with the domestication of plants and animals, people have tried to explain how offspring inherit characteristics from their parents. One common belief was that traits of offspring resulted from the blending of parental characteristics. We now know that this isn't true; in fact, thanks to genetic research, mostly in the twentieth century, we actually know a lot about how traits are inherited.

As you already know, this book is about human evolution and adaptation, both of which are intimately linked to life processes that involve cells, the replication and decoding of genetic information, and the transmission of this information between generations. So, to present human evolution and adaptation in the broad sense, we need to examine the fundamental principles of genetics. **Genetics** is the study of how traits are transmitted from one generation to the next, and even though many physical anthropologists don't actually specialize in genetics, it's genetics that ultimately links the various subdisciplines of biological anthropology.

The Cell

To discuss genetic and evolutionary principles, we first need to know how cells function. Cells are the basic units of life in all living things. In some forms, such as bacteria, a single cell constitutes the entire organism. However, more complex *multicellular forms*, such as plants, insects, birds, and mammals, are composed of billions of cells. Indeed, an adult human is made up of perhaps as many as 1,000 billion (1,000,000,000,000) cells, all functioning in complex ways to promote the survival of the individual.

Life on earth can be traced back at least 3.7 billion years to *prokaryotic* cells. Prokaryotes are single-celled organisms, represented today by bacteria and blue-green algae. Structurally more complex cells appeared approximately 1.2 billion years ago, and these are called *eukaryotic* cells. Because eukaryotic cells are found in all multicellular organisms, they're the focus of this discussion. Despite the numerous differences between various life-forms and the cells that constitute them, it's important to understand that the cells of all living organisms share many similarities because they share a common evolutionary history.

In general, a eukaryotic cell is a three-dimensional structure that contains a variety of structures, called organelles, enclosed within a *cell membrane* (**Fig. 3-1**). One of these organelles is the **nucleus** (*pl.,* nuclei), a discrete unit surrounded by a thin nuclear membrane. Within the nucleus are two acids that contain the genetic information that controls the cell's functions: **deoxyribonucleic acid (DNA)** and **ribonucleic acid (RNA)**. The nucleus is surrounded by a gel-like fluid called the **cytoplasm**, which contains several other types of organelles. These organelles are involved in various activities, such as breaking down nutrients

genetics The study of gene structure and action and the pattern of transmission of traits from parent to offspring. Genetic mechanisms are the foundation for evolutionary change.

nucleus A structure (organelle) found in all eukaryotic cells. The nucleus contains chromosomes (nuclear DNA).

deoxyribonucleic acid (DNA) The double-stranded molecule that contains the genetic code. DNA is a main component of chromosomes.

ribonucleic acid (RNA) A molecule similar in structure to DNA. Three different single-stranded forms of RNA are essential to protein synthesis.

cytoplasm The portion of the cell contained within the cell membrane, excluding the nucleus. The cytoplasm consists of a semi-fluid material and contains numerous structures involved in cell function.

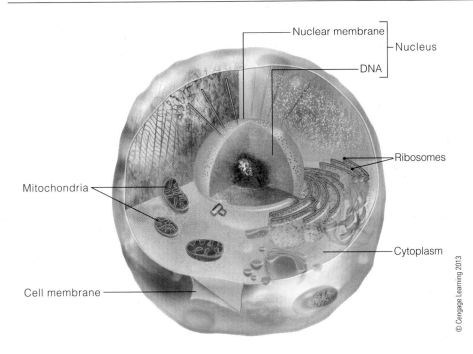

Figure 3-1

Structure of a generalized eukaryotic cell, illustrating the cell's three-dimensional nature. Various organelles are shown, but for simplicity, only those we discuss are labeled.

Labels on figure: Nuclear membrane, Nucleus, DNA, Ribosomes, Cytoplasm, Mitochondria, Cell membrane

© Cengage Learning 2013

and converting them to other substances, storing and releasing energy, eliminating waste, and manufacturing **proteins** (a process called **protein synthesis**).

There are basically two types of cells: **somatic cells** and **gametes**. Somatic cells are the cellular components of body tissues, such as muscle, bone, skin, nerves, heart, and brain. Gametes, or sex cells, are specifically involved in reproduction and are not structural components of the body. There are two types of gametes: egg cells, produced in the ovaries in females; and sperm, which develop in male testes. The sole function of a sex cell is to unite with a gamete from another individual to form a **zygote**, which has the potential to develop into an entire new individual. In this way, gametes transmit genetic information from parent to offspring.

DNA Structure and Function

As already mentioned, cellular functions are directed by DNA. If we want to understand how cells work and how traits are inherited, we must first know something about the structure and function of DNA.

The DNA **molecule** is composed of two chains of even smaller molecules

called **nucleotides**. A nucleotide, in turn, is made up of three components: a sugar molecule (deoxyribose), a phosphate unit, and one of four bases (**Fig. 3-2**). In DNA, nucleotides are stacked on top of one another to form a chain that is bonded along its bases to another nucleotide chain. Together the two twist to form a spiral, or helical, shape. The resulting DNA molecule, then, is two-stranded and is described as forming a *double helix* that resembles a twisted ladder. If we follow the twisted ladder analogy, the sugars and phosphates represent the two sides, while the bases and the bonds that join them form the rungs.

The four bases are the key to how DNA works. These bases are named *adenine, guanine, thymine,* and *cytosine*, but they're usually referred to by their initial letters: A, G, T, and C. In the formation of the double helix, one type of base can pair, or bond, with only one other type: A can pair with T, and G can pair with C (see Fig. 3-2). This specificity is essential to the DNA molecule's ability to replicate, or make an exact copy of itself.

DNA Replication

Cells multiply by dividing to make exact copies of themselves. This, in turn, enables organisms to grow and injured tissues to heal. There are two kinds of

proteins Three-dimensional molecules that serve a wide variety of functions through their ability to bind to other molecules.

protein synthesis The assembly of chains of amino acids into functional protein molecules. The process is directed by DNA.

somatic cells Basically, all the cells in the body except those involved with reproduction.

gametes Reproductive cells (eggs and sperm in animals) developed from precursor cells in ovaries and testes.

zygote A cell formed by the union of an egg and a sperm cell. It contains the full complement of chromosomes (in humans, 46) and has the potential to develop into an entire organism.

molecule A structure made up of two or more atoms. Molecules can combine with other molecules to form more complex structures.

nucleotides Basic units of the DNA molecule, composed of a sugar, a phosphate unit, and one of four DNA bases.

Figure 3-2

Part of a DNA molecule. The illustration shows the two DNA strands with the sugar and phosphate backbone and the bases extending toward the center.

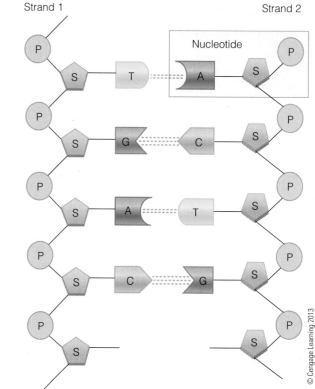

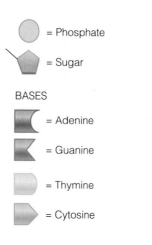

= Phosphate

= Sugar

BASES

= Adenine

= Guanine

= Thymine

= Cytosine

© Cengage Learning 2013

cell division. In the simpler form, cells divide in a way that ensures that each new cell receives a full set of genetic material. This is important, because a cell can't function properly without the appropriate amount of DNA. But before a cell can divide, its DNA must first replicate.

Prior to cell division, **enzymes** break the bonds between bases in the DNA molecule, leaving the two previously joined strands of nucleotides with their bases exposed (**Fig. 3-3**). The exposed bases then attract unattached nucleotides that are constantly being manufactured elsewhere in the cell nucleus. Because one base can be joined to only one other, the attraction between bases occurs in a **complementary** way. Consequently, each of the two previously joined parental nucleotide chains serve as models, or *templates*, for the formation of a new strand of nucleotides. As each new strand is formed, its bases are joined to the bases of an original strand. When the process is completed, there are two double-stranded DNA molecules exactly like the original, and each new molecule consists of one original nucleotide chain joined to a newly formed chain.

Protein Synthesis

One of the most important functions of DNA is to direct the manufacture of proteins (protein synthesis) within the cell. Proteins are complex, three-dimensional molecules that function through their ability to bind to other molecules. For example, the protein **hemoglobin**, found in red blood cells, is able to bind to oxygen, which it transports to cells throughout the body (**Fig. 3-4**)

Proteins function in countless ways. Some are structural components of tissues. Collagen, for example, is the most common protein in the body, and it's a major component of all connective tissues. Enzymes are also proteins, and they regulate chemical reactions. For instance, a digestive enzyme called *lactase* breaks down *lactose*, or milk sugar, into two simpler sugars. Another class of proteins includes many kinds of **hormones**. Specialized cells produce and release hormones into the bloodstream to circulate to other areas of the body, where they produce specific effects in tissues and organs. For example, insulin is a hormone produced by cells in the pancreas, and it causes cells

enzymes Specialized proteins that initiate and direct chemical reactions in the body.

complementary Referring to the fact that DNA bases form base pairs in a precise manner. For example, adenine can bond only to thymine. These two bases are said to be complementary because one requires the other to form a complete DNA base pair.

hemoglobin A protein molecule that occurs in red blood cells and binds to oxygen molecules.

hormones Substances (usually proteins) that are produced by specialized cells and travel to other parts of the body, where they influence chemical reactions and regulate various cellular functions.

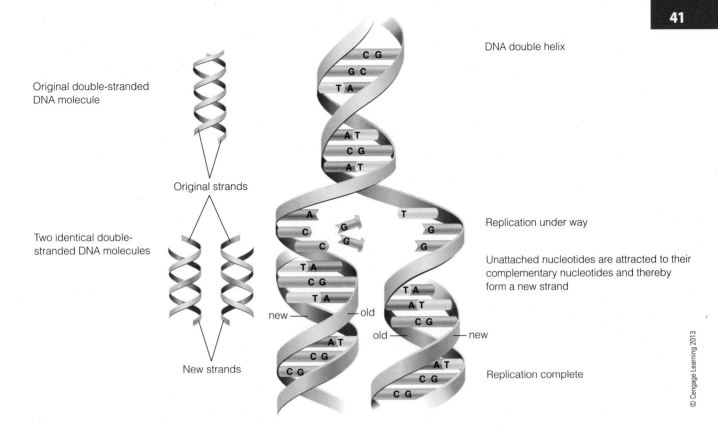

Original double-stranded DNA molecule

Original strands

Two identical double-stranded DNA molecules

New strands

DNA double helix

Replication under way

Unattached nucleotides are attracted to their complementary nucleotides and thereby form a new strand

Replication complete

new — old

old — new

© Cengage Learning 2013

Figure 3-3

DNA replication. During DNA replication, the two strands of the DNA molecule are separated, and each strand serves as a template for the formation of a new strand. When replication is complete, there are two DNA molecules, each molecule consisting of one new strand and one original strand.

in the liver to absorb energy-producing glucose (sugar) from the blood. Lastly, many kinds of proteins can actually enter a cell's nucleus and attach directly to the DNA. These proteins are called regulatory proteins because when they bind to the DNA, they can switch genes on and off, thereby influencing how the genes function. As you can see, proteins make us what we are, so it's critical that protein synthesis occur accurately. If it doesn't, physiological development and activities can be disrupted or even prevented.

Proteins are made up of chains of smaller molecules called **amino acids**. In all, there are 20 amino acids, which are combined in different amounts and sequences to produce potentially millions of proteins. What makes proteins different from one another is the number of amino acids involved and the sequence in which they are arranged. This means that a protein can't function correctly unless its amino acids are arranged in the proper order.

DNA serves as a recipe for making a protein because it's the sequence of DNA bases that ultimately determines the order of amino acids in a protein mole-

cule. In the DNA instructions, a *triplet*, or group of three bases, specifies a particular amino acid. For example, if a triplet consists of the base sequence cytosine, guanine, and adenine (CGA), it specifies the amino acid *alanine*. So, a small portion of the DNA recipe might look like this (except there wouldn't be spaces between the triplets): AGA CGA ACA ACC TAC TTT TTC CTT AAG GTC.

Protein synthesis is a little more complicated than the last paragraph suggests, and it involves an additional molecule similar to DNA called RNA

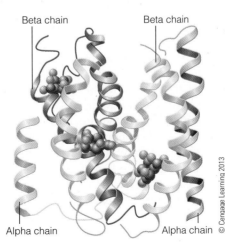

Beta chain   Beta chain

Alpha chain   Alpha chain

© Cengage Learning 2013

Figure 3-4

Diagrammatic representation of a hemoglobin molecule. A hemoglobin molecule is composed of four chains of amino acids (two alpha chains and two beta chains).

amino acids Small molecules that are the components of proteins.

(ribonucleic acid). While DNA provides the instructions for protein synthesis, it's RNA that reads the instructions and actually assembles amino acids to form proteins.

The entire sequence of DNA bases responsible for the synthesis of a protein or, in some cases, part of a protein, is referred to as a **gene**. Or, to put it another way, a gene is a segment of DNA that dictates the sequence of amino acids in a particular protein. A gene may consist of only a few hundred bases, or it may be composed of thousands. If the sequence of DNA bases is changed by a **mutation**, some proteins may not be manufactured, and the cell (or indeed the organism) may not function properly, if at all.

This definition of a gene is technically correct. But it's important to emphasize that gene action is complex and only partly understood. For example, the DNA segments that ultimately are translated into amino acids are called *exons*. But most of the DNA in a gene isn't expressed during protein synthesis, and these unexpressed segments are called *introns* (**Fig. 3-5**). Even though introns aren't involved in protein manufacture, they can and do have other functions, and it's the combination of introns and exons interspersed along a DNA strand that makes up the unit we call a gene.

We usually think of genes as coding for the production of proteins that make up body tissues. But many genes, called **regulatory genes**, make proteins that switch other genes on and off, so they influence how those genes work. Obviously, regulatory genes are critical for individual organisms, and they also play an important role in evolution. For example, many of the anatomical differences between humans and chimpanzees are the results of evolutionary changes in regulatory genes in both lineages.

Homeobox genes, or *Hox* genes, are extremely important regulatory genes.

Hox genes direct early segmentation of embryonic tissues, including those that give rise to the spine and thoracic muscles. They also interact with other genes to determine the identity and characteristics of developing body segments and structures, but not their actual development. For example, homeobox genes determine where limb buds will appear in a developing embryo. They also establish the number and overall pattern of the different types of vertebrae, the bones that make up the spine (**Fig. 3-6**).

Homeobox genes are highly conserved, meaning they've been maintained pretty much throughout evolutionary history. They're present in all invertebrates (such as worms and insects) and vertebrates, and they don't vary greatly from species to species. This type of conservation means not only that these genes are vitally important, but also that they evolved from genes that were present in some of the earliest forms of life. Moreover, changes in the behavior of homeobox genes are responsible for various physical differences between species.

A final point is that the genetic code is universal; at least on earth, DNA is the genetic material in all forms of life. The DNA of all organisms, from bacteria to oak trees to human beings, is composed of the same molecules using the same kinds of instructions. Consequently, the DNA triplet CGA, for example, specifies the amino acid alanine, regardless of species. These similarities imply biological relationships among, and an ultimate common ancestry for, all forms of life. What makes oak trees different from humans isn't differences in their DNA material, but differences in how that material is arranged and regulated.

Cell Division: Mitosis and Meiosis

Throughout much of a cell's life, its DNA exists as an uncoiled, threadlike substance. (Incredibly, the nucleus of every one of your somatic cells contains an estimated 6 feet of DNA!) However, at various times in the life of most types of cells, normal functions are interrupted and the cell divides. Cell division results

Figure 3-5

Diagram of a DNA sequence being transcribed. The introns are deleted from the pre-mRNA before it leaves the cell nucleus. The remaining mature mRNA contains only exons.

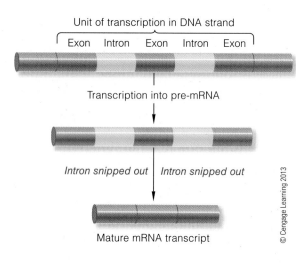

Unit of transcription in DNA strand

Exon Intron Exon Intron Exon

Transcription into pre-mRNA

Intron snipped out | *Intron snipped out*

Mature mRNA transcript

© Cengage Learning 2013

gene A sequence of DNA bases that specifies the order of amino acids in an entire protein, a portion of a protein, or any functional product. A gene may be made up of hundreds or thousands of DNA bases.

mutation A change in DNA. The term can refer to changes in DNA bases as well as changes in chromosome number or structure.

regulatory genes Genes that code for the production of proteins that can influence the action of other genes. Many are active only during certain stages of development.

homeobox (*Hox*) genes An evolutionarily ancient family of regulatory genes. *Hox* genes direct the segmentation and patterning of the overall body plan during embryonic development.

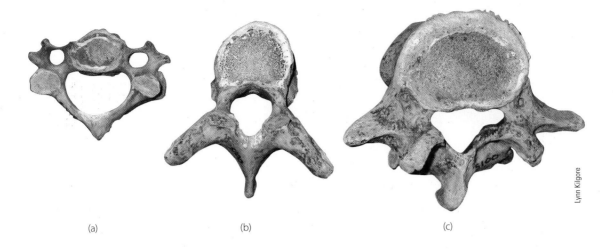

(a)   (b)   (c)

Lynn Kilgore

in the production of new cells, and during this process, the DNA becomes tightly coiled and is visible under a light microscope as a set of discrete structures called **chromosomes** (**Fig. 3-7**).

A chromosome is composed of a DNA molecule and associated proteins (**Fig. 3-8**). If chromosomes were visible during normal cell function, they would appear as single-stranded structures. However, during the early stages of cell division, they are made up of two strands, or two DNA molecules, joined together at a constricted area called the **centromere**. The reason there are two strands is simple: The DNA molecules have *replicated* and one strand is an exact copy of the other.

Every species is characterized by a specific number of chromosomes in somatic cells (**Table 3-1**). In humans there are 46 chromosomes, organized into 23 pairs. Chimpanzees and gorillas have 48 chromosomes, or 24 pairs. This difference in chromosome number doesn't necessarily mean that humans have less DNA; it only indicates that the DNA is packaged differently in the three species.

One member of each chromosomal pair is inherited from the father (paternal), and the other member is inherited from the mother (maternal). Members of chromosomal pairs are alike in size and position of the centromere, but this doesn't mean that partner chromosomes

Figure 3-6

The differences in these three vertebrae, from different regions of the spine, are caused by the action of *Hox* genes during embryonic development. The cervical (neck) vertebrae (a) have characteristics that differentiate them from the thoracic vertebrae (b), which are attached to the ribs, and also from the lumbar vertebrae of the lower back (c). *Hox* genes determine the overall pattern not only of each type of vertebra but also of each individual vertebra.

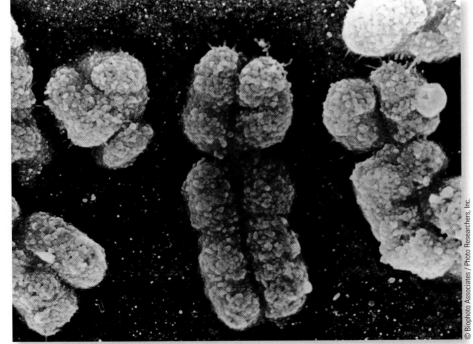

© Biophoto Associates / Photo Researchers, Inc.

Figure 3-7

Colorized scanning electron micrograph of human chromosomes during cell division. Note that these chromosomes are each composed of two DNA molecules.

chromosomes Discrete structures, composed of DNA and protein, found only in the nuclei of cells. Chromosomes are visible only under magnification during certain stages of cell division.

centromere The constricted portion of a chromosome. After replication, the two strands of a double-stranded chromosome are joined at the centromere.

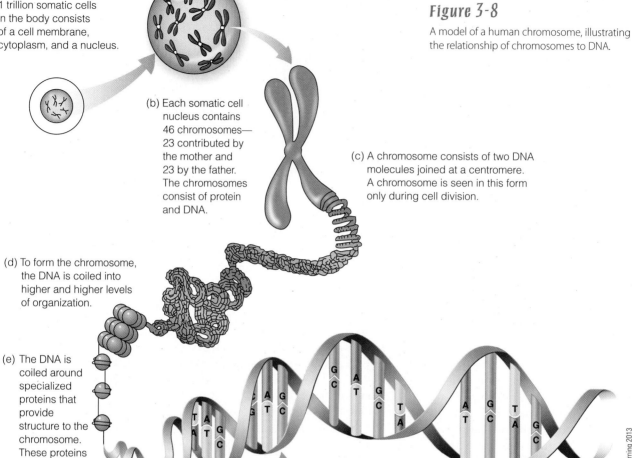

(a) Each of the more than 1 trillion somatic cells in the body consists of a cell membrane, cytoplasm, and a nucleus.

Figure 3-8

A model of a human chromosome, illustrating the relationship of chromosomes to DNA.

(b) Each somatic cell nucleus contains 46 chromosomes— 23 contributed by the mother and 23 by the father. The chromosomes consist of protein and DNA.

(c) A chromosome consists of two DNA molecules joined at a centromere. A chromosome is seen in this form only during cell division.

(d) To form the chromosome, the DNA is coiled into higher and higher levels of organization.

(e) The DNA is coiled around specialized proteins that provide structure to the chromosome. These proteins also interact with the DNA.

(f) A specific sequence of nucleotide base pairs constitutes a gene.

© Cengage Learning 2013

Table 3-1   Standard Chromosomal Complement in Various Organisms

Organism	Chromosome Number in Somatic Cells	Chromosome Number in Gametes
Human (*Homo sapiens*)	46	23
Chimpanzee (*Pan troglodytes*)	48	24
Gorilla (*Gorilla gorilla*)	48	24
Dog (*Canis familiaris*)	78	39
Chicken (*Gallus domesticus*)	78	39
Frog (*Rana pipiens*)	26	13
Housefly (*Musca domestica*)	12	6
Onion (*Allium cepa*)	16	8
Corn (*Zea mays*)	20	10
Tobacco (*Nicotiana tabacum*)	48	24

Source: Cummings, 2000, p. 16.

© Cengage Learning 2013

autosomes All chromosomes except the sex chromosomes.

sex chromosomes The X and Y chromosomes. The Y chromosome determines maleness; in its absence, an embryo develops as a female.

mitosis Simple cell division; the process by which somatic cells divide to produce two identical daughter cells.

are genetically identical because they aren't; but they do influence the same traits.

There are two basic types of chromosomes: **autosomes** and **sex chromosomes**. Autosomes carry genetic information that governs all physical characteristics except primary sex determination. The two sex chromosomes are the X and Y chromosomes, and the Y chromosome is directly involved in determining maleness. Although the X chromosome is called a sex chromosome, it really functions more like an autosome, since it isn't involved in primary sex determination and it carries genes that influence a number of other traits. In mammals, all genetically normal males have one X and one Y chromosome (XY). However, all genetically normal females have two X chromosomes (XX), and they're female simply because they don't have a Y chromosome. Actually, you could say that femaleness is the default setting.

It's extremely important to understand that *all* autosomes occur in pairs. Normal human somatic cells have 22 pairs of autosomes and one pair of sex chromosomes. It's also important to know that abnormal numbers of autosomes, with few exceptions, are fatal to the individual—usually soon after conception. Although abnormal numbers of sex chromosomes aren't usually fatal, they may result in sterility and can also have other consequences. This means that to function normally, a human cell must possess both members of each chromosomal pair, or a total of 46 chromosomes.

Mitosis

Cell division in somatic cells is called **mitosis**. Mitosis is the way somatic cells reproduce, and the reproduction of somatic cells is essential to growth and development. In addition, mitosis is the mechanism by which injured tissues heal and older cells are replaced.

In the early stages of mitosis, a cell contains 46 double-stranded chromosomes, which line up in random order along the center of the cell (**Fig. 3-9**). As the cell wall begins to constrict at the center, the chromosomes split apart

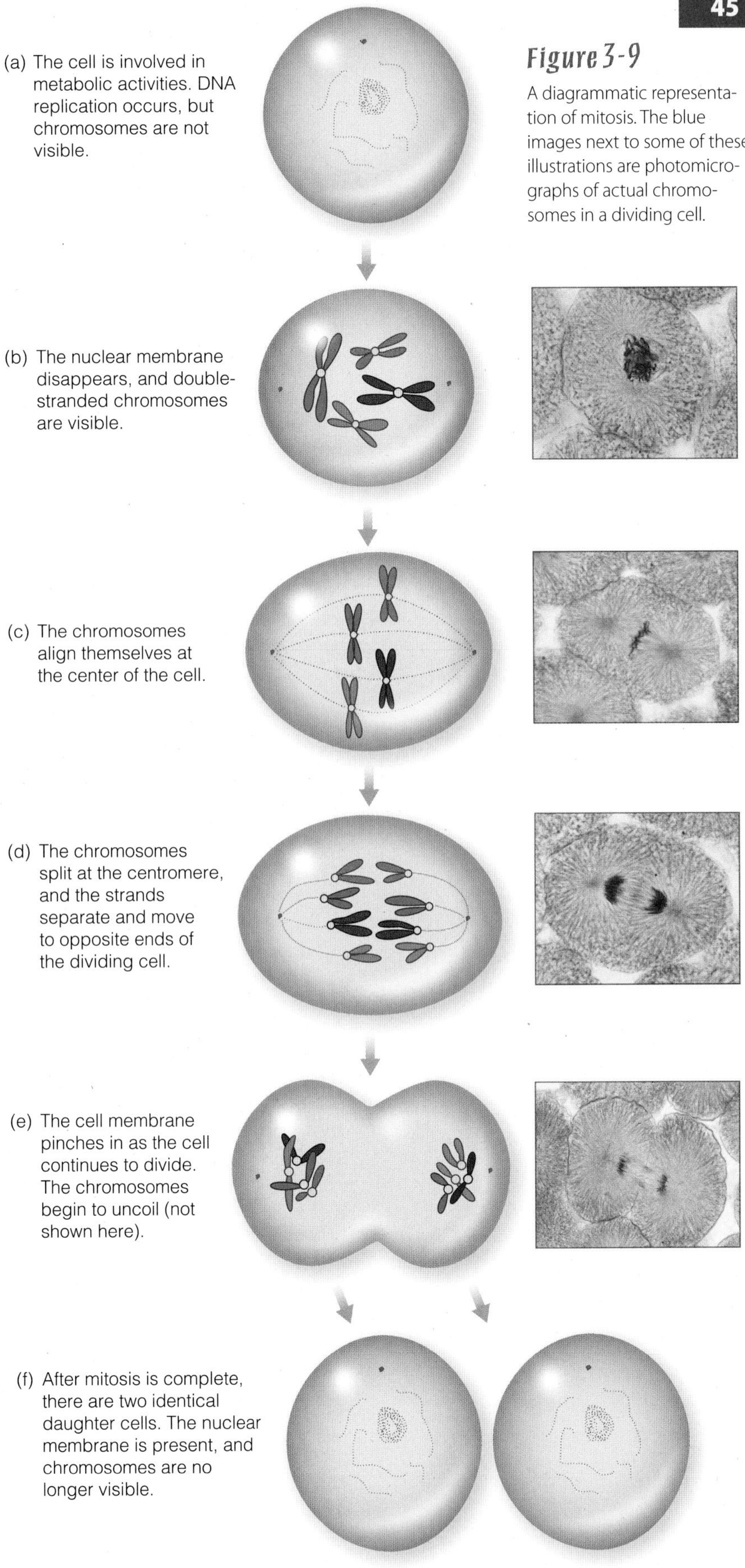

(a) The cell is involved in metabolic activities. DNA replication occurs, but chromosomes are not visible.

(b) The nuclear membrane disappears, and double-stranded chromosomes are visible.

(c) The chromosomes align themselves at the center of the cell.

(d) The chromosomes split at the centromere, and the strands separate and move to opposite ends of the dividing cell.

(e) The cell membrane pinches in as the cell continues to divide. The chromosomes begin to uncoil (not shown here).

(f) After mitosis is complete, there are two identical daughter cells. The nuclear membrane is present, and chromosomes are no longer visible.

Figure 3-9

A diagrammatic representation of mitosis. The blue images next to some of these illustrations are photomicrographs of actual chromosomes in a dividing cell.

at the centromere and the two strands separate, pulling away from each other and moving to opposite ends of the dividing cell. At this point, each strand is now a distinct chromosome, *composed of one DNA molecule.* Following the separation of chromosome strands, the cell wall pinches in and becomes sealed, so that two new cells are formed, each with a full complement of DNA, or 46 chromosomes.

Mitosis is referred to as "simple cell division" because a somatic cell divides one time to produce two daughter cells that are genetically identical to each other and to the original cell. In mitosis, the original cell possesses 46 chromosomes, and each new daughter cell inherits an exact copy of all 46. This precise arrangement is made possible by the ability of the DNA molecule to replicate. Thus, DNA replication ensures that the amount of genetic material remains constant from one generation of cells to the next.

Meiosis

While mitosis produces new cells, **meiosis** can lead to the development of an entire new organism because it produces reproductive cells. Although meiosis is similar to mitosis, it's a more complicated process, because in meiosis there are two divisions instead of one. Also, meiosis produces four daughter cells, not two, and each of these four cells contains only half the original number of chromosomes (**Fig. 3-10**).

During meiosis, specialized cells in male testes and female ovaries divide and eventually develop into sperm and egg cells. Initially, these cells contain the full complement of chromosomes (46 in humans), but after the first division (called *reduction division*), the number of chromosomes in the two daughter cells is 23, or half the original number (see Fig. 3-10). This reduction in chromosome number is crucial because the resulting gamete, with its 23 chromosomes, may eventually unite with another gamete that also has 23 chromosomes. The product of this union is a *zygote,* or fertilized egg, in which the original number of chromosomes (46) has been restored. In other words, a zygote inherits the exact amount of DNA it needs (half from each

parent) to develop and function normally. But if it weren't for reduction division in meiosis, it wouldn't be possible to maintain the correct number of chromosomes from one generation to the next.

During the first division of meiosis, partner chromosomes come together to form *pairs* of double-stranded chromosomes. Then the pairs of chromosomes line up along the cell's equator (see Fig. 3-10). Pairing of partner chromosomes is extremely important, because while they're together, the members of each pair exchange genetic information in a critical process called **recombination** or *crossing over.* Pairing is also important because it facilitates the accurate reduction of chromosome number by ensuring that each new daughter cell receives only one member of each pair.

As a cell begins to divide, the chromosomes themselves remain intact (that is, double-stranded), but *members of pairs* pull apart and move to opposite ends of the cell. After the first division, there are two new daughter cells, but they aren't identical to each other or to the parent cell. They're different because each cell contains only one member of each chromosome pair and therefore only 23 chromosomes. But all the chromosomes still have two strands (see Fig. 3-10).

The second meiotic division happens pretty much the way it does in mitosis. In the two newly formed cells, the 23 double-stranded chromosomes line up at the cell's center, and as in mitosis, the strands of each chromosome separate at the centromere and move apart. Once this second division is completed, there are four daughter cells, each with 23 single-stranded chromosomes. (For a comparison of mitosis and meiosis, see **Fig. 3-11**.)

The Evolutionary Significance of Meiosis Meiosis occurs in all sexually reproducing organisms, and it's an extremely important evolutionary innovation because it increases genetic variation in populations. Members of sexually reproducing species aren't genetically identical **clones** of other individuals because they inherit a combination of genes from two parents. As a result, each individual represents a unique combination

meiosis Cell division in specialized cells in ovaries and testes. Meiosis involves two divisions and results in four daughter cells, each containing only half the original number of chromosomes. These cells can develop into gametes.

recombination The exchange of DNA between paired chromosomes during meiosis; also called *crossing over.*

clones A clone is an organism that is genetically identical to another organism. The term may also be used to refer to genetically identical DNA segments and molecules.

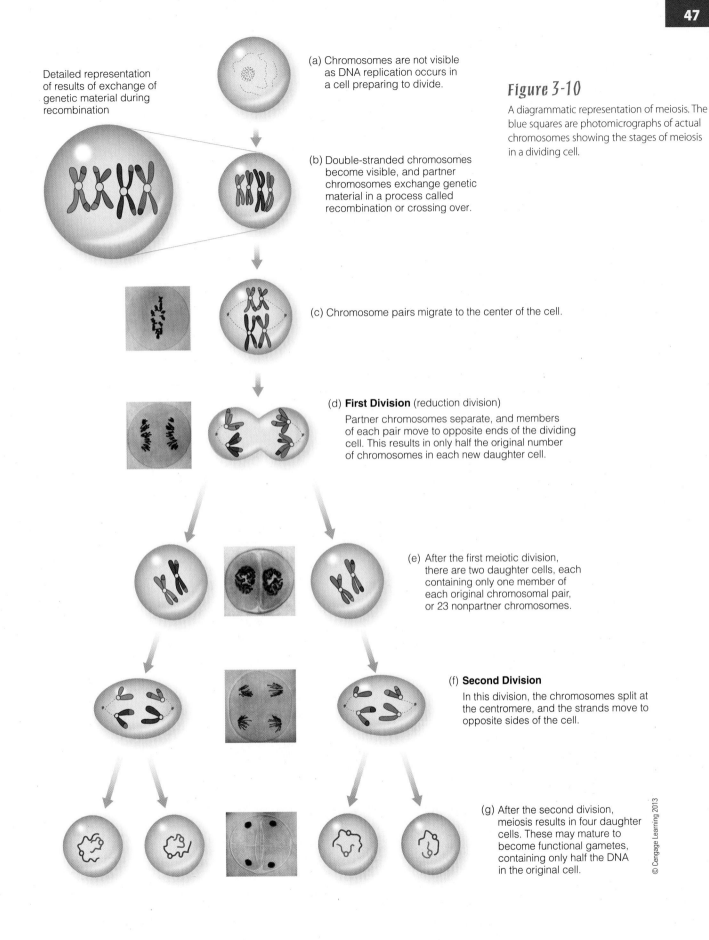

Detailed representation of results of exchange of genetic material during recombination

(a) Chromosomes are not visible as DNA replication occurs in a cell preparing to divide.

(b) Double-stranded chromosomes become visible, and partner chromosomes exchange genetic material in a process called recombination or crossing over.

(c) Chromosome pairs migrate to the center of the cell.

(d) **First Division** (reduction division)

Partner chromosomes separate, and members of each pair move to opposite ends of the dividing cell. This results in only half the original number of chromosomes in each new daughter cell.

(e) After the first meiotic division, there are two daughter cells, each containing only one member of each original chromosomal pair, or 23 nonpartner chromosomes.

(f) **Second Division**

In this division, the chromosomes split at the centromere, and the strands move to opposite sides of the cell.

(g) After the second division, meiosis results in four daughter cells. These may mature to become functional gametes, containing only half the DNA in the original cell.

Figure 3-10

A diagrammatic representation of meiosis. The blue squares are photomicrographs of actual chromosomes showing the stages of meiosis in a dividing cell.

© Cengage Learning 2013

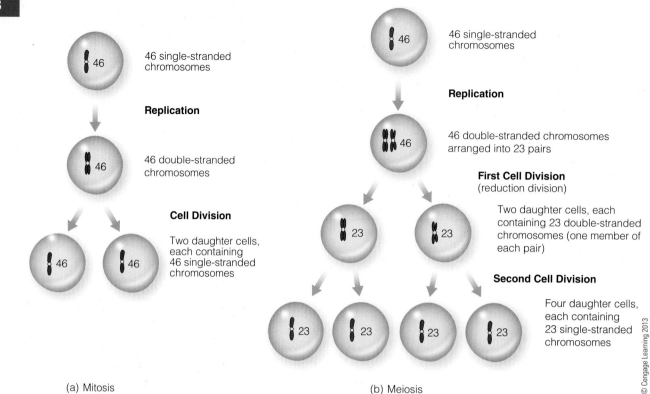

46 single-stranded
chromosomes

Replication

46 double-stranded
chromosomes

Cell Division

Two daughter cells,
each containing
46 single-stranded
chromosomes

46 single-stranded
chromosomes

Replication

46 double-stranded chromosomes
arranged into 23 pairs

First Cell Division
(reduction division)

Two daughter cells, each
containing 23 double-stranded
chromosomes (one member of
each pair)

Second Cell Division

Four daughter cells,
each containing
23 single-stranded
chromosomes

© Cengage Learning 2013

(a) Mitosis

(b) Meiosis

Figure 3-11

Mitosis and meiosis compared. (a) In mitosis, one division produces two daughter cells, each containing 46 chromosomes. (b) In meiosis there are two divisions. After the first division, there are two cells, each containing only 23 chromosomes (one member of each original chromosome pair). Each daughter cell divides again, so that the final result is four cells, each with only half the original number of chromosomes.

of genes that, in all likelihood, has never occurred before and will never occur again. The genetic uniqueness of individuals is further increased by recombination between partner chromosomes during meiosis, because recombination ensures that chromosomes aren't transmitted intact from one generation to the next. Instead, in every generation, parental contributions are reshuffled in an almost infinite number of combinations, altering the genetic composition of chromosomes even before they are passed on.

As we mentioned in Chapter 2, natural selection acts on genetic variation in populations. If all individuals in a population were genetically identical from one generation to the next, natural selection (and evolution) couldn't occur. Although there are other sources of variation (mutation being the only source of *new* variation), sexual reproduction and meiosis are of major evolutionary importance because they enhance the role of natural selection in populations.

The Genetic Principles Discovered by Mendel

It wasn't until Gregor Mendel (1822–1884) addressed the question of heredity that this crucial biological process began to be scientifically resolved (**Fig. 3-12**). Mendel was a monk living in an abbey in what is now the Czech Republic. At the time he began his research, he had already studied botany, physics, and

Figure 3-12

Portrait of Gregor Mendel.

Raychel Ciemma and Precision Graphics

mathematics at the University of Vienna, and he also had performed various experiments in the monastery gardens. These experiments led him to explore the various ways in which physical traits, such as color or height, could be expressed in plant **hybrids**.

Mendel worked with garden peas, concentrating on seven different traits, each of which could be expressed in two different ways (**Fig. 3-13**). We want to emphasize that the principles Mendel discovered apply to all biological organisms, not just peas; so we discuss Mendel's pea experiments only to illustrate the basic rules of inheritance.

Mendel's Principle of Segregation

Mendel began by crossing parent (P) plants that produced only tall plants with others that produced only short ones (**Fig. 3-14**). Blending theories of inheritance would have predicted that the hybrid offspring of the initial crosses (called the F_1 plants) would be intermediate in height, but they weren't. Instead, they were all tall.

Next, he allowed the F_1 plants to self-fertilize and produce a second generation (the F_2 generation). But this time, only about ¾ of the offspring were

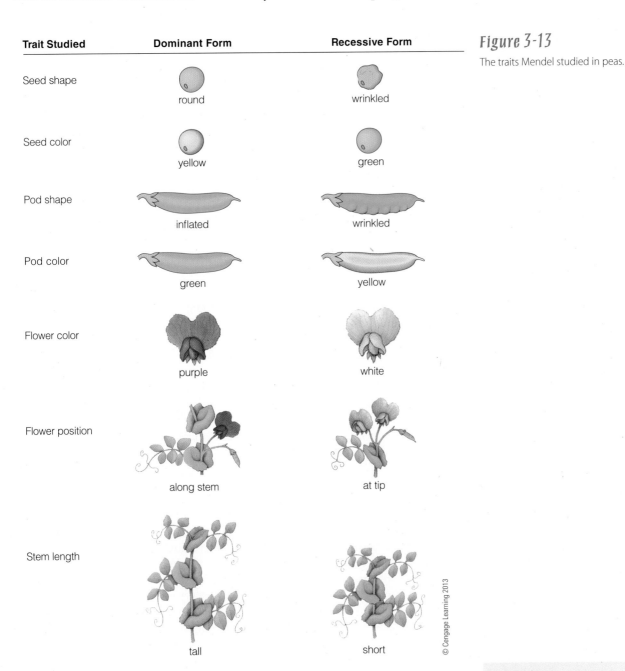

Trait Studied	Dominant Form	Recessive Form
Seed shape	round	wrinkled
Seed color	yellow	green
Pod shape	inflated	wrinkled
Pod color	green	yellow
Flower color	purple	white
Flower position	along stem	at tip
Stem length	tall	short

Figure 3-13

The traits Mendel studied in peas.

© Cengage Learning 2013

hybrids Offspring of mixed ancestry; heterozygotes.

Figure 3-14

Results of crosses when only one trait (height) at a time is considered.

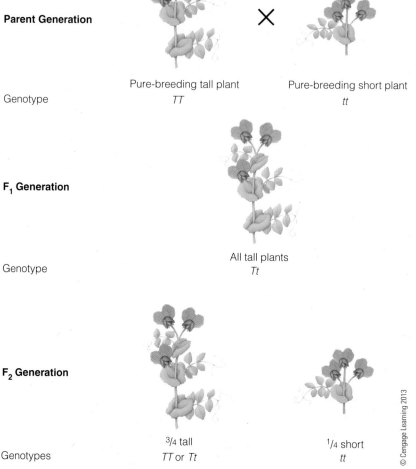

Parent Generation

Genotype

Pure-breeding tall plant
TT

×

Pure-breeding short plant
tt

F₁ Generation

Genotype

All tall plants
Tt

F₂ Generation

Genotypes

¾ tall
TT or *Tt*

¼ short
tt

© Cengage Learning 2013

principle of segregation Genes (alleles) occur in pairs because chromosomes occur in pairs. During gamete production, the members of each gene pair separate, so that each gamete contains one member of each pair. During fertilization, the full number of chromosomes is restored, and members of gene pairs (alleles) are reunited.

recessive Describing a trait that is not expressed in heterozygotes; also refers to the allele that governs the trait. For a recessive allele to be expressed, there must be two copies of the allele (i.e., the individual must be homozygous).

dominant Describing a trait governed by an allele that can be expressed in the presence of another, different allele (i.e., in heterozygotes). Dominant alleles prevent the expression of recessive alleles in heterozygotes. (*Note:* This is the definition of *complete dominance.*)

locus (*pl.*, loci) (lo´-kus, lo-sigh´) The position on a chromosome where a given gene occurs. The term is sometimes used interchangeably with *gene*.

alleles Alternate forms of a gene. Alleles occur at the same locus on paired chromosomes and thus govern the same trait. However, because they are different, their action may result in different expressions of that trait. The term *allele* is often used synonymously with *gene*.

homozygous Having the same allele at the same locus on both members of a chromosome pair.

tall, and the remaining ¼ were short. One expression (shortness) of the trait (height) had completely disappeared in the F₁ plants and reappeared in the F₂ plants. Moreover, the expression that was present in all the F₁ generation was more common in the F₂ generation, occurring in a ratio of approximately 3:1, or three tall plants for every short one.

To Mendel, these results suggested that different expressions of a trait are controlled by discrete *units* or particles, which today we call genes. The units occur in pairs, and offspring inherit one unit from each parent. Mendel also realized that the members of a pair of units separate into different sex cells and are again united with another member during fertilization of the egg. This discovery was the basis of Mendel's *first principle of inheritance*, known as the **principle of segregation**.

Today we know that meiosis explains Mendel's principle of segregation. You will remember that during meiosis, paired chromosomes, and the genes they carry, separate from each other and are distributed to different gametes. However, in the zygote, the full complement of chromosomes is restored, and both members of each chromosome pair are present in the offspring.

Dominance and Recessiveness

Mendel also realized that the expression that was absent in the first generation hadn't actually disappeared at all. It was still there but it was masked somehow and couldn't be expressed. He described the trait that seemed to disappear as **recessive**, and he called the expressed trait **dominant**. With this fact in mind, Mendel developed the important principles of *recessiveness* and *dominance*, and they're still important concepts in the field of genetics.

As you already know, a *gene* is a segment of DNA that directs the production of a specific protein, part of a protein, or any functional element. Each gene has a specific location on a chromosome, and that position is called its **locus** (*pl.*, loci). At numerous genetic loci, however, there may be more than one possible form of the gene, and these variations of genes at specific loci are called **alleles** (**Fig. 3-15**). Simply stated, alleles are different forms of a gene, each of which can direct the cell to make a slightly different version of the same protein and, ultimately, a different expression of a trait.

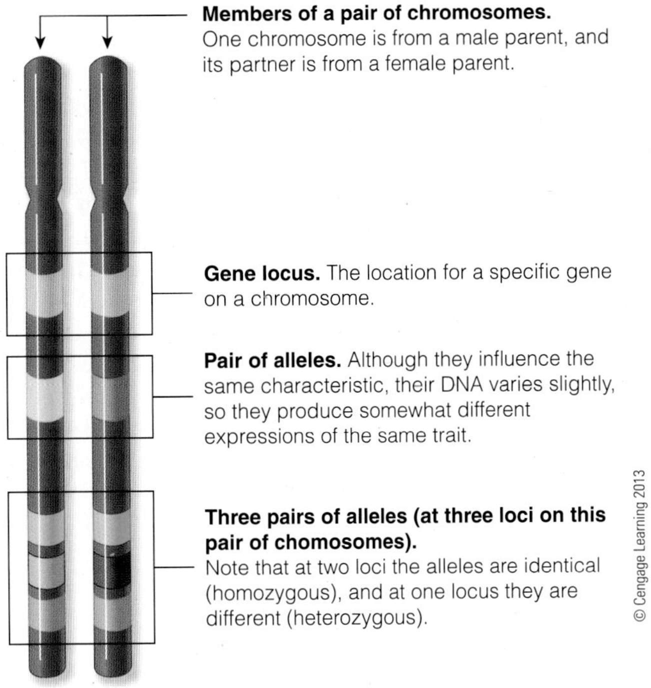

As it turns out, plant height in garden peas is controlled by two different alleles at one genetic locus. The allele that determines that a plant will be tall is dominant to the allele for short. (It's worth mentioning that height isn't governed this way in all plants.) In Mendel's experiments, all the parent (P) plants had two copies of the same allele, either dominant or recessive, depending on whether they were tall or short. When two copies of the same allele are present, the individual is said to be **homozygous**. Thus, all the tall parent plants were homozygous for the dominant allele, and all the short parent plants were homozygous for the recessive allele. (This explains why tall plants crossed with tall plants produced only tall offspring, and short plants crossed with short plants produced only short offspring; they were all homozygous, so they lacked genetic variation at this locus.) However, all the hybrid F_1 plants had inherited one allele from each parent plant, and therefore, they all possessed two different alleles at the locus for height. Individuals that possess two different alleles at a locus are said to be **heterozygous**.

Figure 3-14 illustrates the crosses that Mendel initially performed. Uppercase letters refer to dominant alleles (or dominant traits), and lowercase letters refer to recessive alleles (or recessive traits). Therefore,

T = the allele for tallness
t = the allele for shortness

Members of a pair of chromosomes. One chromosome is from a male parent, and its partner is from a female parent.

Gene locus. The location for a specific gene on a chromosome.

Pair of alleles. Although they influence the same characteristic, their DNA varies slightly, so they produce somewhat different expressions of the same trait.

Three pairs of alleles (at three loci on this pair of chomosomes). Note that at two loci the alleles are identical (homozygous), and at one locus they are different (heterozygous).

© Cengage Learning 2013

Figure 3-15

As this diagram illustrates, alleles are located at the same locus (position) on paired chromosomes, but they aren't always identical.

The same symbols are combined to describe an individual's actual genetic makeup, or **genotype**. The term *genotype* can be used to refer to an organism's entire genetic makeup or to the alleles at a specific genetic locus. Thus, the genotypes of the plants in Mendel's experiments were

TT = homozygous tall plants
Tt = heterozygous tall plants
tt = homozygous short plants

Figure 3-16 is a *Punnett square*. It represents the different ways the alleles can be combined when the F_1 plants are self-fertilized to produce an F_2 generation. In this way, the figure shows the genotypes that are possible in the F_2 generation, and it also demonstrates that approximately ¼ of the F_2 plants are homozygous dominant (TT); ½ are heterozygous (Tt); and the remaining ¼ are homozygous recessive (tt).

The Punnett square also shows the proportions of F_2 **phenotypes**, or the observed physical manifestations of genes, and it illustrates why Mendel saw

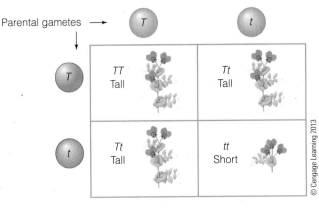

© Cengage Learning 2013

Figure 3-16

Punnett square representing possible genotypes and phenotypes and their proportions in the F_2 generation. The circles across the top and at the left of the Punnett square represent the gametes of the F_1 parents. The four squares illustrate that ¼ of the F_2 plants can be expected to be homozygous tall (TT); another ½ also can be expected to be tall but will be heterozygous (Tt); and the remaining ¼ can be expected to be short (tt). Thus, ¾ can be expected to be tall and ¼ to be short.

heterozygous Having different alleles at a particular locus on the members of a chromosome pair.

genotype The genetic makeup of an individual. Genotype can refer to an organism's entire genetic makeup or to the alleles at a particular locus.

phenotypes The observable or detectable physical characteristics of an organism; the detectable expressions of genotypes.

three tall plants for every short plant in the F$_2$ generation. By examining the Punnett square, you can see that ¼ of the F$_2$ plants will be tall because they have the *TT* genotype. An additional ½ of the plants, which are heterozygous (*Tt*), will also be tall because *T* is dominant to *t* and will therefore be expressed in the phenotype. The remaining ¼ are homozygous recessive (*tt*), and they will be short because no dominant allele is present. It's important to note that the *only* way a recessive allele can be expressed is if it occurs with another recessive allele—that is, if the individual is homozygous recessive at the particular locus in question.

Mendel's Principle of Independent Assortment

Mendel also showed that traits aren't necessarily inherited together by demonstrating that plant height and seed color are independent of each other. In other words, he proposed that any tall plant had a 50-50 chance of producing either yellow or green seeds (peas). This relationship, called the **principle of independent assortment**, says that the units (genes) that code for different traits assort independently of one another during gamete formation. Today we know that this happens because the genes that control plant height and seed color are located on different chromosomes, and during meiosis, the chromosomes travel to newly forming cells independently of one another. But if Mendel had used just *any* two traits, his results would have sometimes been different. For example, if the two traits in question were influenced by genes located on the same chromosome, then they would more likely be inherited together, in which case they wouldn't conform to Mendel's ratios. The ratios came out as he predicted because the loci governing most of the traits he chose were carried on different chromosomes. Even though Mendel didn't know about chromosomes, he was certainly aware that all traits weren't independent of one another in the F$_2$ generation, so he appears to have reported only on those characteristics that did in fact illustrate independent assortment.

In 1866, Mendel's results were published, but their methodology and statistical nature were beyond the thinking of the time, and the significance of his work wasn't appreciated. However, by the end of the nineteenth century, several investigators had made important contributions to the understanding of chromosomes and cell division. These discoveries paved the way for the acceptance of Mendel's work by 1900, when three different groups of scientists came across his paper. Unfortunately, Mendel had died 16 years earlier and never saw his work substantiated.

Mendelian Inheritance in Humans

Mendelian traits (also referred to as *discrete traits* or *traits of simple inheritance*) are controlled by alleles at *one* genetic locus). The most comprehensive listing of Mendelian traits in humans is V. A. McKusick's (1998) *Mendelian Inheritance in Man*. This volume, as well as its continuously updated online version (www.ncbi.nlm.nih.gov/omim/), currently lists almost 18,000 characteristics that are inherited according to Mendelian principles.

Although some Mendelian traits have a visible phenotypic expression, most don't. Most are biochemical in nature, and many genetic disorders (some of which do produce visible phenotypic abnormalities) result from harmful alleles inherited in Mendelian fashion (**Table 3-2**). So if it seems like textbooks overemphasize genetic disease when they discuss Mendelian traits, it's because many of the known Mendelian characteristics are the results of harmful alleles.

Blood groups, like the ABO system, provide some of the best examples of Mendelian traits in humans. The ABO system is governed by three alleles, *A*, *B*, and *O*, that occur at the *ABO* locus on the ninth chromosome.* Although three alleles are present in populations, an individual can possess only two. These alleles determine which ABO blood type

principle of independent assortment The distribution of one pair of alleles into gametes does not influence the distribution of another pair. The genes controlling different traits are inherited independently of one another.

Mendelian traits Characteristics that are influenced by alleles at only one genetic locus. Examples include many blood types, such as ABO. Many genetic disorders, including sickle-cell anemia and Tay-Sachs disease, are also Mendelian traits.

---

* Human chromosomes are numbered in order of size of the autosomes (1 through 22) plus X and Y.

Table 3-2 Some Mendelian Traits in Humans

Dominant Traits Condition	Manifestations	Recessive Traits Condition	Manifestations
Achondroplasia	Dwarfism due to growth defects involving the long bones of the arms and legs; trunk and head size usually normal.	Cystic fibrosis	Among the most common genetic (Mendelian) disorders among European Americans; abnormal secretions of the exocrine glands, with pronounced involvement of the pancreas; most patients develop obstructive lung disease. Until the recent development of new treatments, only about half of all patients survived to early adulthood.
Brachydactyly	Shortened fingers and toes		
Familial hyper-cholesterolemia	Elevated cholesterol levels and cholesterol plaque deposition; a leading cause of heart disease, with death frequently occurring by middle age.		
		Tay-Sachs disease	Most common among Ashkenazi Jews; degeneration of the nervous system beginning at about 6 months of age; lethal by age 2 or 3 years.
Neurofibromatosis	Symptoms range from the appearance of abnormal skin pigmentation to large tumors resulting in severe deformities; can, in extreme cases, lead to paralysis, blindness, and death.	Phenylketonuria (PKU)	Inability to metabolize the amino acid phenylalanine; results in mental impairment if left untreated during childhood; treatment involves strict dietary management and some supplementation.
Marfan syndrome	The eyes and cardiovascular and skeletal systems are affected; symptoms include greater than average height, long arms and legs, eye problems, and enlargement of the aorta; death due to rupture of the aorta is common. Abraham Lincoln may have had Marfan syndrome.	Albinism	Inability to produce normal amounts of the pigment melanin; results in very fair, untannable skin, light blond hair, and light eyes; may also be associated with vision problems. (There is more than one form of albinism.)
Huntington disease	Progressive degeneration of the nervous system accompanied by dementia and seizures; age of onset variable but commonly between 30 and 40 years.	Sickle-cell anemia	Abnormal form of hemoglobin (Hb^S) that results in collapsed red blood cells, blockage of capillaries, reduced blood flow to organs, and, without treatment, death.
Camptodactyly	Malformation of the hands whereby the fingers, usually the little finger, is permanently contracted.	Thalassemia	A group of disorders characterized by reduced or absent alpha or beta chains in the hemoglobin molecule; results in severe anemia and, in some forms, death.
Hypodontia of upper lateral incisors	Upper lateral incisors are absent or only partially formed (peg-shaped). Pegged incisors are a partial expression of the allele.	Absence of permanent dentition	Failure of the permanent dentition to erupt. The primary dentition is not affected.
Cleft chin	Dimple or depression in the middle of the chin; less prominent in females than in males.		
PTC tasting	The ability to taste the bitter substance phenylthiocarbamide (PTC). Tasting thresholds vary, suggesting that alleles at another locus may also exert an influence.		

© Cengage Learning 2013

a person has by coding for the production of special substances, called **antigens**, on the surface of red blood cells. If only antigen A is present, the blood type (phenotype) is A; if only B is present, the blood type is B; if both are present, the blood type is AB; and when neither is present, the blood type is O (**Table 3-3**).

Dominance and recessiveness are clearly illustrated by the ABO system. The *O* allele is recessive to both *A* and *B*; therefore, if a person has type O blood, he or she must be homozygous (*OO*) for the *O* allele. Since both *A* and *B* are dominant to *O*, an individual with blood type A can have one of two genotypes: *AA* or *AO*. The same is true of type B, which results from the genotypes *BB* and *BO*. However, type AB presents a slightly different situation and is an example of **codominance**.

Codominance is seen when two different alleles occur in heterozygotes, but instead of one having the ability to mask the expression of the other, the products of *both* are expressed in the phenotype.

antigens Large molecules found on the surface of cells. Several different loci governing antigens on red and white blood cells are known. (Foreign antigens provoke an immune response in individuals.)

codominance The expression of both alleles in heterozygotes. In this situation, neither allele is dominant or recessive; thus, both influence the phenotype.

So, when both *A* and *B* alleles are present, both A and B antigens can be detected on the surface of red blood cells, and the blood type is AB.

Several genetic disorders are inherited as dominant traits (see Table 3-2). This means that if a person inherits only one copy of a harmful dominant allele, the condition it causes will be present, regardless of the existence of a different, recessive allele on the partner chromosome.

Table 3-3 ABO Genotypes and Associated Phenotypes

Genotypes	Antigens on Red Blood Cells	ABO Blood Type (Phenotype)
AA, AO	A	A
BB, BO	B	B
AB	A and B	AB
OO	None	O

© Cengage Learning 2013

Recessive conditions (see Table 3-2) are commonly associated with the lack of a substance, usually an enzyme. For a person actually to have a recessive disorder, he or she must have *two* copies of the recessive allele that causes it. Heterozygotes who have only one copy of a harmful recessive allele are unaffected (or less affected), and they're frequently called carriers.

Although carriers don't actually have the recessive condition they carry, they can pass the allele that causes it to their children. (Remember, half their gametes will carry the recessive allele.) If the carrier's mate is also a carrier, then it's possible for them to have a child who has two copies of the allele, and that child will be affected. In fact, in a mating between two carriers, the risk of having an affected child is 25 percent (see Fig. 3-16).

Misconceptions Regarding Dominance and Recessiveness

Traditional methods of teaching genetics have led to some misunderstanding of dominance and recessiveness. Thus, most people have the impression that these phenomena are all-or-nothing situations. This misconception especially pertains to recessive alleles, and the general view is that when these alleles occur in carriers, they have absolutely no effect on the phenotype; that is, they are completely inactivated by the other allele. Certainly, this is how it appeared to Gregor Mendel and, until the last two or three decades, to most geneticists.

However, modern biochemical techniques have shown that recessive alleles actually do have some effect on the phenotype, although these effects aren't always apparent through simple observation. It turns out that in heterozygotes, many recessive alleles act to reduce, but not eliminate, the gene products they influence. In fact, it's now clear that our *perception* of recessive alleles greatly depends on whether we examine them at the directly observable phenotypic level or the biochemical level.

Similar misconceptions also relate to dominant alleles. Most people see dominant alleles as somehow "stronger" or "better," and there is always the mistaken notion that dominant alleles are more common in populations. These misconceptions undoubtedly stem from the label "dominant" and some of its connotations. However, in genetic usage, those connotations are misleading. If dominant alleles were always more common, then a majority of people would have such conditions as achondroplasia and Marfan syndrome (see Table 3-2). But, as you know, most people don't.

The relationships between recessive and dominant alleles and their functions are more complicated than they first appeared to be. Previously held views of dominance and recessiveness were guided by available technologies; as genetic technologies continue to change, new theories will emerge, and our perceptions will be further altered. (This is another example of how new techniques and continued hypothesis testing can lead to a revision of hypotheses and theories.) In fact, although dominance and recessiveness will remain important factors in genetics, it's clear that the ways in which these concepts will be taught will be adapted to accommodate new discoveries.

Polygenic Inheritance

Mendelian traits are said to be *discrete*, or *discontinuous*, because their phenotypic expressions don't overlap; instead, they fall into clearly defined categories (**Fig. 3-17a**). For example, Mendel's pea plants were either short or tall, but none was intermediate in height. In the ABO system, the four phenotypes are completely distinct from one another; there is no intermediate form between type A and type B to represent a gradation between the two. In other words, Mendelian traits don't show *continuous* variation.

However, many traits do have a wide range of phenotypic expressions that form a graded series. These are called **polygenic**, or *continuous*, traits (**Fig. 3-17b**). While Mendelian traits are governed by only one genetic locus, polygenic characteristics are governed by two or more loci, with each locus making a contribution to the phenotype. For example, one of the most frequently cited examples of polygenic inheritance in humans is skin color, and the single most important factor influencing skin color is the amount of melanin that is present.

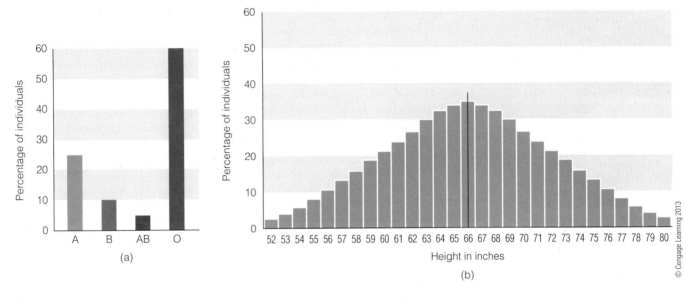

(a)

(b)

© Cengage Learning 2013

Height (feet/inches)

(c)

Ray Carson

Figure 3-17

Comparison of Mendelian and polygenic traits. (a) This bar chart shows the discontinuous distribution of a Mendelian trait (ABO blood type) in a hypothetical population. Expression of the trait is described in terms of frequencies. (b) This histogram represents the continuous expression of a polygenic trait (height) in a large group of people. Notice that the percentage of extremely short or tall individuals is low; most people are closer to the mean, or average, height, represented by the vertical line at the center of the distribution. (c) A group of male students arranged according to height. The most common height is 70 inches (5′10″), which is the mean, or average, for this group.

polygenic Referring to traits that are influenced by genes at two or more loci. Examples of such traits are stature, skin color, and eye color. Many polygenic traits are also influenced by environmental factors.

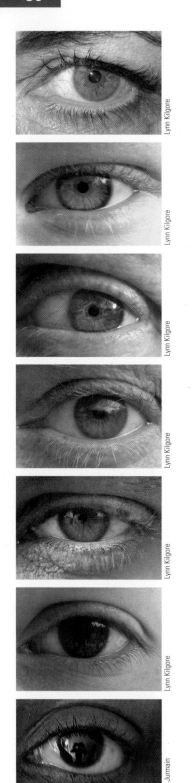

Lynn Kilgore

Lynn Kilgore

Lynn Kilgore

Lynn Kilgore

Lynn Kilgore

Lynn Kilgore

Robert Jurmain

Figure 3-18

Eye color is a polygenic characteristic and is a good example of continuous variation.

Melanin is a pigment that's produced by specialized cells in the skin, and its production is influenced by a number of different loci, some of which have been identified (Lamason et al., 2005). The traditional view has been that each locus has at least two alleles. Given that there are several loci and alleles involved, there are numerous ways in which these alleles can combine to influence skin color. If a person inherits 11 alleles coding for maximum pigmentation and only 1 for reduced melanin production, his or her skin will be very dark. Someone who inherits a higher proportion of reduced pigmentation alleles will have lighter skin. This is because in this system, as in some other polygenic systems, there's an *additive effect*. This means that each allele that codes for melanin production makes a contribution to increased amounts of melanin (although for many characteristics the contributions of the alleles aren't all equal). Likewise, each allele coding for reduced melanin production contributes to lighter skin. The effect of multiple alleles at multiple loci, each making a contribution to a person's skin color, is to produce continuous variation from very dark to very fair skin within the species. (Skin color is also discussed in Chapter 4.)

The additive effects of several alleles at different loci are still believed to play a critical role in human skin color. But a recent study by Lamason and colleagues (2005) showed that one single gene with two alleles makes a significant, and perhaps disproportionate, contribution to the amount of melanin that cells produce. In addition, at least four other pigmentation genes have now been identified. Thus, it appears that many long-standing questions about variation in human skin color may be answered in the foreseeable future.

Polygenic traits actually account for most of the readily observable phenotypic variation seen in humans, and they have traditionally served as a basis for racial classification (see Chapter 4). In addition to skin color, polygenic inheritance in humans is seen in hair color, weight, stature, eye color (**Fig. 3-18**), fingerprint pattern, and shape of the face. Because they exhibit continuous variation, most polygenic traits can be measured on a scale composed of equal increments (see Fig. 3-17b). For example, height (stature) is measured in feet and inches (or meters and centimeters). If we were to measure height in a large number of individuals, the distribution of measurements would continue uninterrupted from the shortest extreme to the tallest. That's what is meant by the term *continuous traits*.

Because polygenic traits can usually be measured in some way, physical anthropologists treat them statistically. (Incidentally, *all* physical traits measured and discussed in fossils are polygenic.) By using simple summary statistics, such as the *mean* (average) or *standard deviation* (a measure of variation within a group), scientists can create basic descriptions of, and make comparisons between, populations. For example, a researcher might be interested in average height in two different populations and whether any differences between the two are significant, and if so, why. However, the types of statistical tests that would be used in such a study can't be used to examine Mendelian traits because Mendelian traits can't be measured in the same way. Mendelian traits are either present or they aren't. Or they're expressed one way or another (for example, blood type A or blood type O). Nevertheless, Mendelian characteristics can be described in terms of frequency within populations, and this permits between-group comparisons regarding prevalence. For example, a majority of people in one population may have blood type A, but in another population, type A may be very rare. Mendelian traits can also be analyzed for mode of inheritance (dominant or recessive). Finally, for many Mendelian traits, the approximate or exact positions of genes have been identified, and this makes it possible to examine the mechanisms and patterns of inheritance at these loci. Because polygenic characters are influenced by several loci, they can't, as yet, be traced to specific loci.

At a Glance

Mendelian vs. Polygenic Traits

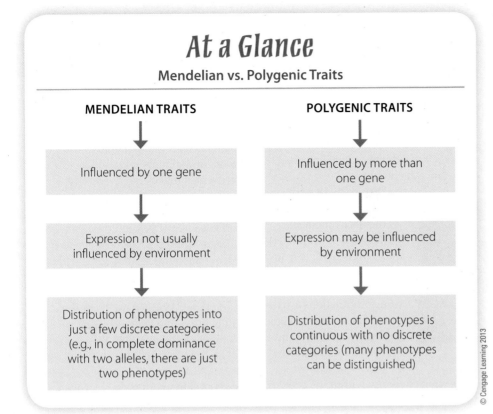

MENDELIAN TRAITS	POLYGENIC TRAITS
Influenced by one gene	Influenced by more than one gene
Expression not usually influenced by environment	Expression may be influenced by environment
Distribution of phenotypes into just a few discrete categories (e.g., in complete dominance with two alleles, there are just two phenotypes)	Distribution of phenotypes is continuous with no discrete categories (many phenotypes can be distinguished)

© Cengage Learning 2013

Genetic and Environmental Factors

By now, you may have the impression that phenotypes are solely the expressions of genotypes, but that's not true. (Here we use the terms *genotype* and *phenotype* in a broader sense to refer to an individual's entire genetic makeup and physical characteristics, respectively.) The genotype sets limits and potentials for development, but it also interacts with the environment, and this genetic-environmental interaction influences many aspects of the phenotype. However, it's usually not possible to identify which specific environmental factors are affecting the phenotype.

Many polygenic traits are influenced by environmental factors. Adult height, for example, is strongly affected by nutrition during growth and development. Other important environmental factors that affect various phenotypes include exposure to altitude, temperature, and, unfortunately, increasing levels of exposure to toxic waste and air-borne pollutants. All these, and many more, contribute in complex ways to the continuous phenotypic variation seen in characteristics governed by several loci.

Mendelian traits are less likely to be influenced by environmental factors. For example, ABO blood type is determined at fertilization and remains fixed throughout an individual's lifetime, regardless of diet, exposure to ultraviolet radiation, temperature, and so forth.

Mendelian and polygenic inheritance produce different kinds of phenotypic variation. In the former, variation occurs in discrete categories, while in the latter, it's continuous. However, it's important to understand that even for polygenic characteristics, Mendelian principles still apply at individual loci. In other words, if a trait is influenced by genes at seven loci, each one of those loci may have two or more alleles, with one perhaps being dominant to the other or with the alleles being codominant. It's the combined action of the alleles at all seven loci, interacting with the environment, that results in observable phenotypic expression.

Mitochondrial Inheritance

Another component of inheritance involves cellular organelles called **mitochondria** (**Fig. 3-19**). All cells contain hundreds of these oval-shaped structures that convert energy (derived from the breakdown of nutrients) to a form that cells can use.

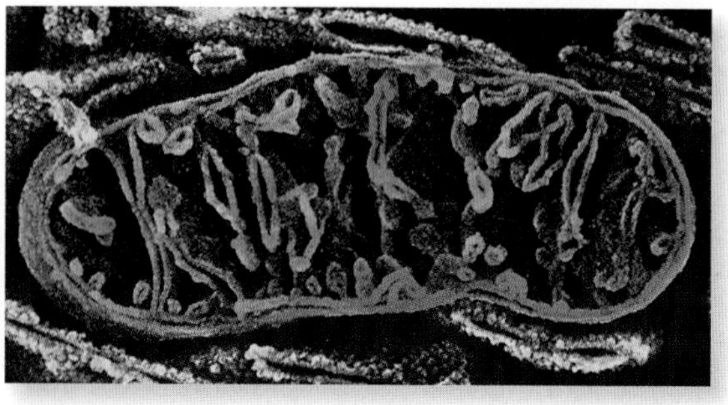

Each mitochondrion contains several copies of a DNA molecule. While **mitochondrial DNA (mtDNA)** is distinct from the DNA found within cell nuclei, its molecular structure and functions are the same. The entire molecule has been sequenced and is known to contain around 40 genes that direct the conversion of energy within the cell.

Mitochondrial DNA is subject to mutations just like nuclear DNA, and some mutations cause certain genetic disorders that result from impaired energy conversion. Importantly, animals of both sexes inherit all their mtDNA, and thus all mitochondrial traits, from their mothers. This is because mitochondria are found only in a cell's cytoplasm, and while egg cells retain their cytoplasm, sperm cells lose theirs just prior to fertilization. Because mtDNA is inherited from only one parent, meiosis and recombination don't occur. This means that all the variation in mtDNA among individuals is caused by mutation, which makes mtDNA extremely useful for studying genetic change over time. So far, geneticists have used mutation rates in mtDNA to investigate evolutionary relationships between species, to trace ancestral relationships within the human lineage, and to study genetic variability among individuals and/or populations. While these techniques are still being refined, it's clear that we have a lot to learn from mtDNA.

New Frontiers

Since the discovery of DNA structure and function in the 1950s, the field of genetics has revolutionized biological science and reshaped our understanding of inheritance, genetic disease, and evolutionary processes. For example, a technique developed in 1986, called **polymerase chain reaction (PCR)**, enables scientists to make thousands of copies of small samples of DNA that can then be analyzed. In the past, DNA samples from crime scenes or fossils were usually too small to be studied. But PCR has made it possible to evaluate tiny amounts of DNA in, for example, Neandertal fossils and Egyptian mummies; and it has limitless potential for many disciplines, including forensic science, medicine, and paleoanthropology.

Another application of PCR allows scientists to identify DNA *fingerprints*, so called because they appear as patterns of repeated DNA sequences that are unique to each individual (**Fig. 3-20**). For example, one person might

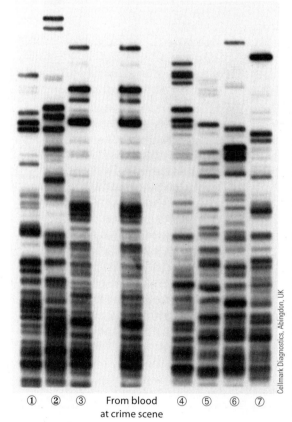

© Professors P. Motta and T. Naguro/SPL / Photo Researchers, Inc.

Figure 3-19

Scanning electron micrograph of a mitochondrion.

Figure 3-20

Eight DNA fingerprints, one of which is from a blood sample left at an actual crime scene. The other seven are from suspects. By comparing the banding patterns, it is easy to identify the guilty person.

① ② ③   From blood at crime scene   ④ ⑤ ⑥ ⑦

Cellmark Diagnostics, Abingdon, UK

mitochondria (*sing.,* mitochondrion) (my´-tow-kond´-dree-uh) Structures contained within the cytoplasm of eukaryotic cells that convert energy, derived from nutrients, to a form that is used by the cell.

mitochondrial DNA (mtDNA) DNA found in mitochondria. mtDNA is inherited only from the mother.

polymerase chain reaction (PCR) A method of producing copies of a DNA segment using the enzyme DNA polymerase.

have a segment of six bases such as ATTCTA repeated 3 times, while another person might have 20 copies of the same sequence. DNA fingerprinting is perhaps the most powerful tool available for human identification. Scientists have used it to identify scores of unidentified remains, including members of the Russian royal family murdered in 1918 and victims of the September 11, 2001, terrorist attacks. Moreover, the technique has been used to exonerate many innocent people wrongly convicted of crimes, in some cases decades after they were imprisoned.

Over the last two decades, scientists have used the techniques of *recombinant DNA technology* to transfer genes from the cells of one species into those of another. One common method has been to insert human genes that direct the production of various proteins into bacterial cells in laboratories. The altered bacteria can then produce human gene products such as insulin. Until the early 1980s, people with diabetes relied on insulin derived from nonhuman animals. However, this insulin wasn't plentiful, and some patients developed allergies to it. But since 1982, abundant supplies of human insulin, produced by bacteria, have been available; and bacteria-derived insulin doesn't cause allergic reactions.

In recent years, genetic manipulation has become increasingly controversial owing to questions related to product safety, environmental concerns, animal welfare, and concern over the experimental use of human embryos. For example, the insertion of bacterial DNA into certain crops has made them toxic to leaf-eating insects, thus reducing the need for pesticides. Cattle and pigs are commonly treated with antibiotics and genetically engineered growth hormone to increase growth rates. (There's no concrete evidence that humans are susceptible to the insect-repelling bacterial DNA or harmed by consuming meat and dairy products from animals treated with growth hormone. But there are concerns over the unknown effects of long-term exposure.)

As exciting as these innovations are, probably the single most important advance in genetics has been the progress made by the **Human Genome Project** (International Human Genome Sequencing Consortium, 2001; Venter et al., 2001). The goal of this international effort, begun in 1990, was to sequence the entire human genome, which consists of some 3 billion bases making up approximately 25,000 protein-coding genes. The initial goals of this extremely important project were completed in 2003.

The potential for anthropological applications is enormous. While scientists were sequencing human genes, the genomes of other organisms were also being studied. As of now, the genomes of hundreds of species have been sequenced, including mice (Waterston et al., 2002), chimpanzees (Chimpanzee Sequencing and Analysis Consortium, 2005), and rhesus macaques (Rhesus Macaque Genome Sequencing and Analysis Consortium, 2007).

In May 2010, researchers finished sequencing the entire Neandertal genome (Green et al., 2010). To date, the most exciting announcement stemming from this research is that modern Europeans and Asians (but not Africans) inherited 1 to 4 percent of their genes from ancient Neandertal ancestors. This finding sheds light on debates concerning whether or not early modern humans interbred with Neandertals. These debates have been ongoing in physical anthropology for more than 50 years, and while this new genetic evidence does not conclusively end the discussion, it strongly supports the argument that interbreeding did indeed take place and that many of us carry a few Neandertal genes (see Chapter 11).

Eventually, comparative genome analysis should provide a thorough assessment of genetic similarities and differences, and thus the evolutionary relationships, between humans and other primates. What's more, we can already look at human variation in an entirely different light than we could even 10 years ago (see Chapter 4). Among other things, genetic comparisons between human groups can inform us about population movements in the past and what selective pressures may have been exerted on different

Human Genome Project An international effort that has mapped the entire human genome.

populations to produce some of the variability we see. We may even be able to speculate on patterns of infectious disease in the past.

Completion of the Neandertal genome sequence wasn't the only groundbreaking achievement in 2010. Using some of the techniques developed in the human genome research, scientists created a functional, synthetic bacterial genome (Gibson et al., 2010). The culmination of 10 years of effort, this synthetic genome is the first life-form ever made by humans, and it has major implications for biotechnology. (Understandably, it has also raised many ethical concerns.) Very basically, some of the geneticists involved in the Human Genome Project sequenced the 1 million bases in a bacterial chromosome. They then produced an artificial chromosome by assembling DNA segments and splicing them together. The new synthetic DNA was then inserted into a bacterial cell of a different species. The original DNA of the recipient cell had been removed, and the cell began to follow the instructions of the new DNA. That is, it produced proteins characteristic of a different bacterial species! Moreover, the recipient cell replicated, and there are now laboratory colonies of the "new" bacterium (**Fig. 3-21**).

It's important to emphasize that this project did not create a completely new synthetic life-form because the genome had been transferred into an already existing cell. Nevertheless, the door has been opened for the development of artificial organisms. While it may never be possible to create new species as complex as birds and mammals, we can almost certainly expect to see the production of artificial single-celled organisms, many of which will have medical applications. Others will perhaps be used to produce food or to

absorb carbon dioxide. But the potential for abuse, especially in the development of biological weapons, will obviously be of grave concern. Still, the human development of a self-replicating bacterium with altered DNA from another species is an extraordinary milestone in biology. It is not an exaggeration to say that this is the most exciting time in the history of evolutionary biology since Darwin published *On the Origin of Species*.

Modern Evolutionary Theory

By the beginning of the twentieth century, the foundations for evolutionary theory had already been developed. Darwin and Wallace had described natural selection 40 years earlier, and the rediscovery of Mendelian genetics in 1900 contributed the other major component, a mechanism for inheritance. We might expect that these two basic contributions would have been combined into a consistent theory of evolution, but they weren't. For the first 30 years of the twentieth century, some scientists argued that mutation was the main factor in evolution, while others emphasized natural selection. What they really needed was a merger of both views (not an either-or situation), but that didn't happen until the mid-1930s.

The Modern Synthesis

In the 1920s and early 1930s, biologists realized that mutation and natural selection weren't opposing processes and that both significantly contributed to biological evolution. The two major foundations of the biological sciences were thus brought together in what a scientist named Julian Huxley called the Modern Synthesis. From such a "modern" (that is, middle of the twentieth century onward) perspective, we define evolution as a two-stage process:

1. The production and redistribution of **variation** (inherited differences among organisms)
2. *Natural selection* acting on this variation, whereby inherited

Figure 3-21

Scanning electron micrograph of a colony of new synthetic bacterial cells.

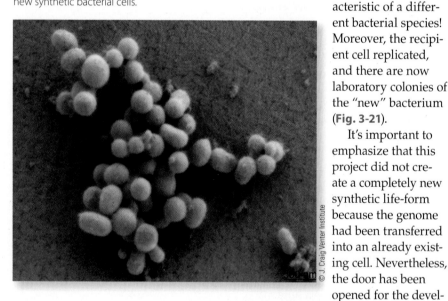

© J. Craig Venter Institute

variation In genetics, inherited differences among individuals; the basis of all evolutionary change.

differences, or variation, among individuals differentially affect their ability to successfully reproduce

A Current Definition of Evolution

As we discussed in Chapter 2, Darwin saw **evolution** as the gradual unfolding of new varieties of life from previous forms over long periods of time. And this is indeed one result of the evolutionary process. But these long-term effects can come about only through the accumulation of many small genetic changes occurring over generations; and today, we can show how evolution works by examining some of these intergenerational genetic changes. From this modern genetic perspective, we define *evolution* as a change in **allele frequency** from one generation to the next.

Allele frequencies are indicators of the genetic makeup of a **population**—an interbreeding group of individuals. To show how allele frequencies change, we'll use a simplified example of an inherited characteristic, again the ABO blood types (see p. 54). (*Note*: In addition to ABO, several other blood type systems are controlled by many other loci.)

Let's assume that the students in your anthropology class represent a population and that we've determined the ABO blood type of each member. (To be considered a population, individuals must choose mates more often from *within* the group than from outside it. Obviously, your class won't meet this requirement, but we'll overlook this point for now.) The proportions of the *A*, *B*, and *O* alleles are the allele frequencies for this trait. Therefore, if 50 percent of all the *ABO* alleles in your class are *A*, 40 percent are *B*, and 10 percent are *O*, then the frequencies of these alleles are $A = .50$, $B = .40$, and $O = .10$.

Since the frequencies for these alleles represent only proportions of a total, it's obvious that allele frequencies can refer only to groups of individuals—that is, populations. Individuals don't have allele frequencies; they have either *A*, *B*, or *O* in any combination of two. Also, from conception onward, a person's genetic composition is fixed. If

you start out with blood type A, you'll always have type A. Therefore, only a population can evolve over time; individuals can't.

Assume that 25 years from now, we calculate the frequencies of the *ABO* alleles for the offspring of our classroom population and find the following: $A = .30$, $B = .40$, and $O = .30$. We can see that the relative proportions have changed: *A* has decreased, *O* has increased, and *B* has remained the same. This wouldn't really be a big deal, but in a biological sense, these kinds of apparently minor changes constitute evolution. Over the short span of just a few generations, such changes in inherited traits may be very small; but if they continue to happen, and particularly if they consistently go in one direction as a result of natural selection, they can produce new adaptations and even new species.

Whether we're talking about the short-term effects (as in our classroom population) from one generation to the next, which is sometimes called **microevolution**, or the long-term effects through time, called speciation or **macroevolution**, the basic evolutionary mechanisms are similar. But how do allele frequencies change? Or, to put it another way, what causes evolution? As we've already seen, evolution is a two-stage process. Genetic variation must first be produced by mutation, and then it can be acted on by natural selection.

Factors That Produce and Redistribute Variation

We've emphasized the importance of genetic variation to the process of evolution and pointed out that mutation is the only source of new variation, because when a gene changes, a new allele is produced. We've also mentioned natural selection several times. But to really understand how evolution works, we need to consider these two factors in greater detail; and we also have to consider a few other mechanisms that contribute to the process.

evolution (modern genetic definition) A change in the frequency of alleles from one generation to the next.

allele frequency In a population, the percentage of all the alleles at a locus accounted for by one specific allele.

population Within a species, a community of individuals where mates are usually found.

microevolution Small changes occurring within species, such as a change in allele frequencies.

macroevolution Changes produced only after many generations, such as the appearance of a new species.

Mutation

You've already learned that a change in DNA is one kind of mutation. Many genes can occur in one of several alternative forms, which we've defined as alleles (*A*, *B*, or *O*, for example). If one allele changes to another—that is, if the gene itself is altered—a mutation has occurred. Even the substitution of one single DNA base for another, called a *point mutation*, can cause an allele to change. But point mutations have to occur in sex cells if they're going to be important to the evolutionary process. This is because evolution is a change in allele frequencies *between* generations, and mutations that occur in somatic cells, but not in gametes, aren't passed on to offspring. If, however, a genetic change occurs in the sperm or egg of one of the students in our classroom (*A* mutates to *B*, for instance), the offspring's blood type will be different from that of the parent, causing a minute shift in the allele frequencies of the next generation.

Actually, it would be rare to see evolution occurring by mutation alone, except in microorganisms. Mutation rates for any given trait are usually low, so we wouldn't really expect to see a mutation at the *ABO* locus in so small a population as your class. In larger populations, mutations might be observed in, say, 1 individual out of 10,000; but by themselves, the mutations wouldn't affect allele frequencies. However, when mutation is combined with natural selection, not only can evolutionary changes occur, but they can occur more rapidly.

It's important to remember that mutation is the basic creative force in evolution, since it's the *only* way to produce *new* genes (that is, variation). Its role in the production of variation is the key to the first stage of the evolutionary process.

Gene Flow

Gene flow is the exchange of genes between populations. The term *migration* is also frequently used; but strictly speaking, migration means movement of people, whereas gene flow refers to the exchange of *genes* between groups, and this can happen only if the migrants interbreed. Also, even if individuals move temporarily and mate in a new population (thus leaving a genetic contribution), they don't necessarily remain in the population. For example, the offspring of U.S. soldiers and Vietnamese women (during the Vietnam War) represent gene flow, even though the fathers returned to their native population.

Population movements (particularly in the last 500 years) have reached unprecedented levels, and few breeding isolates remain. Significant population movements also occurred in the past, although not at current levels. Migration between populations has been a consistent feature of hominin evolution since the first dispersal of our genus, and gene flow between populations (even though sometimes limited) helps explain why, in the last million years, speciation has been rare.

An interesting example of how gene flow influences microevolutionary changes in modern human populations is seen in African Americans. African Americans in the United States are largely of West African descent, but there has also been considerable genetic admixture with European Americans. By measuring allele frequencies for specific genetic loci, we can estimate the amount of migration of European alleles into the African American **gene pool**. Data from northern and western U.S. cities (including New York, Detroit, and Oakland) have shown the migration rate (that is, the proportion of *non*-African genes in the African American gene pool) at 20 to 25 percent (Cummings, 2000). However, more restricted data from the southern United States (Charleston and rural Georgia) have suggested a lower degree of gene flow (4 to 11 percent).

Gene flow doesn't require large-scale movements of entire groups. In fact, significant changes in allele frequencies can come about through long-term patterns of mate selection whereby members of a group obtain mates from one or more other groups. If mate exchange consistently moves in one direction (for example, village A obtains mates from village B, but not vice versa) over a long period of time, allele frequencies in village A will eventually change.

gene flow Exchange of genes between populations.

gene pool The total complement of genes shared by the reproductive members of a population.

Genetic Drift and Founder Effect

Genetic drift is the random factor in evolution, and it's directly related to population size. *Drift occurs because the population is small.* If an allele is rare in a population comprised of, say, a few hundred individuals, then there is a chance that it may not be passed on to offspring. In this type of situation, such an allele can eventually disappear altogether from the population. This may seem like a minor thing, but in effect, genetic variability in this population has been reduced (**Fig. 3-22a**).

One particular kind of genetic drift is called **founder effect**, and we can see its results today in many modern human and nonhuman populations (**Fig. 3-22b**).

Founder effect can occur when a small migrant band of "founders" leaves its parent group and forms a new colony somewhere else. Over time, a new population will be established, and as long as mates are chosen only from within this population, all of its members will be descended from the small group of founders. In effect, all the genes in the expanding group will have come from a few original colonists. In such a case, an allele that was rare in the founders' parent population, but that is carried by even one of the founders, can eventually become common in succeeding generations. This is because a high proportion of members of later generations are all descended from that one founder.

Colonization isn't the only way founder effect can happen. Small

Time

A small population with considerable genetic variability. Note that the dark green and blue alleles are less common than the other alleles.

After just a few generations, the population is approximately the same size but genetic variation has been reduced. Both the dark green and blue alleles have been lost. Also, the red allele is less common and the frequency of the light green allele has increased.

Population size

Original population with considerable genetic variation

A small group leaves to colonize a new area, or a bottleneck occurs, so that population size decreases and genetic variation is reduced.

Population size is restored, but the dark green and purple alleles have been lost. The frequencies of the red and yellow alleles have also changed.

Population size

© Cengage Learning 2013

Figure 3-22

Small populations are subject to genetic drift where rare alleles can be lost because, just by chance, they weren't passed to offspring. Also, although more common alleles may not be lost, their frequencies may change for the same reason. (a) This diagram represents six alleles (different-colored dots) that occur at one genetic locus in a small population. You can see that in a fairly short period of time (three or four generations), rare alleles can be lost and genetic diversity consequently reduced. (b) This diagram illustrates founder effect, a form of genetic drift where diversity is lost because a large population is drastically reduced in size and consequently passes through a genetic "bottleneck." Founder effect also happens when a small group leaves a larger group and "founds" a new population elsewhere. (In this case, the group of founders is represented by the bottleneck.) Those individuals that survive (the founders) and the alleles they carry represent only a sample of the variation that was present in the original population. And future generations, all descended from the survivors (founders), will therefore have less variability.

genetic drift Evolutionary changes—that is, changes in allele frequencies—produced by random factors. Genetic drift is a result of small population size.

founder effect A type of genetic drift in which allele frequencies are altered in small populations that are taken from, or are remnants of, larger populations.

founding groups may consist of a few survivors of a large group that, at some time in the past, was decimated by some type of disaster. The small founder population (the survivors) possesses only a sample of all the alleles that were present in the original group. Just by chance alone, some alleles may be completely removed from the gene pool. Other alleles may become the only allele at a locus that previously had two or more. Whatever the cause, the outcome is reduced genetic diversity, and the allele frequencies of succeeding generations may be substantially different from those of the original large population.

The loss of genetic diversity in this type of situation is called a *genetic bottleneck*, and its effects can be very detrimental to a species (see Fig. 3-22b).

There are many known examples of species or populations that have passed through genetic bottlenecks. Genetically, cheetahs (**Fig. 3-23**) are an extremely uniform species, and biologists believe that at some point in the past, these magnificent cats suffered a catastrophic decline in numbers. For reasons we don't know but that are related to the species-wide loss of numerous alleles, male cheetahs produce a high percentage of defective sperm compared to other cat species. Decreased reproductive potential, greatly reduced genetic diversity, and other factors (including human hunting) have combined to jeopardize the continued existence of this species. Other examples include California elephant seals, sea otters, and condors. Indeed, our own species is genetically uniform, compared to chimpanzees, and it appears that all modern human populations are the descendants of only a few relatively small groups.

Many examples of founder effect in human populations have been documented in small, usually isolated populations (for example, island groups or small agricultural villages in New Guinea or South America). Even larger populations descended from fairly small groups of founders can show the

Figure 3-23

Cheetahs, like many other species, have passed through a genetic bottleneck. Consequently, as a species they have little genetic variation.

effects of genetic drift many generations later. For example, French Canadians in Quebec, who currently number close to 6 million, are all descended from about 8,500 founders who left France during the sixteenth and seventeenth centuries. Because the genes carried by the initial founders represented only a sample of the gene pool from which they were derived, just by chance a number of alleles now occur in different frequencies from those of the current population of France. These differences include an increased presence of several harmful alleles (see Table 3-2), including cystic fibrosis, a variety of Tay-Sachs, thalassemia, and PKU (Scriver, 2001).

In small populations, drift plays a major evolutionary role because fairly sudden fluctuations in allele frequency occur solely because of small population size. Throughout much of human evolution (at least the last 4 to 5 million years), hominins probably lived in small groups, and drift would have had significant impact. But even though genetic drift has caused evolutionary change in certain circumstances, its effects have been irregular. That's because drift isn't directional; that is, it doesn't consistently increase or decrease the frequency of a given allele. But by altering allele frequencies in small populations, drift can provide significantly greater opportunities for natural selection, the only truly directional force in evolution.

As we've seen, both gene flow and genetic drift can produce some evolutionary changes by themselves. However, these changes are usually *microevolutionary* ones; that is, they produce changes within species over the short term. To have the kind of evolutionary changes that ultimately result in entire new groups (for example, the diversification of the first primates or the appearance of the hominins), natural selection would be necessary. But natural selection can't operate independently of the other evolutionary factors—mutation, gene flow, and genetic drift.

Sexual Reproduction and Recombination

As we saw earlier in this chapter, in sexually reproducing species both parents contribute genes to offspring. Also, during meiosis, members of chromosomal pairs exchange segments of DNA. Thus, genetic information is reshuffled every generation. Although these processes won't change allele frequencies (that is, cause evolution), they do produce different combinations of genes that natural selection may be able to act on. In fact, the reshuffling of chromosomes during meiosis can produce literally trillions of gene combinations, making every human being genetically unique.

Natural Selection Acts on Variation

The evolutionary factors just discussed—mutation, gene flow, genetic drift, and sexual reproduction and recombination—interact to produce variation and to distribute genes within and between populations. But there is no long-term *direction* to any of these factors. So how do populations adapt? The answer is natural selection, which causes **directional change** in allele frequencies. This means that natural selection can increase or decrease the frequency of certain alleles over time in ways that are beneficial in specific environmental settings. If you recall the moth example discussed in Chapter 2, the increase in frequency of dark or light moths depended on environmental change. Such a functional shift in allele frequencies is what we mean by *adaptation*. If there are long-term environmental changes in a consistent direction, then allele frequencies should also shift gradually in each generation.

In Chapter 2, we discussed the general principles underlying natural selection and gave some nonhuman examples. The best-documented example of natural selection in humans involves hemoglobin S (Hb^S), an abnormal form of hemoglobin that results from a point mutation in the gene that produces part of the hemoglobin molecule. The allele for hemoglobin S, *Hb^S*, is recessive to the allele for normal hemoglobin, *Hb^A*. Most people are homozygous for the *Hb^A* allele, and they produce normal hemoglobin. But people who inherit the recessive allele from both parents (that is, they

are homozygous with the genotype *Hb^S/ Hb^S*) produce no normal hemoglobin and have a very serious condition called sickle-cell anemia. People who have one copy of each allele (that is, they're heterozygotes with the *Hb^A/Hb^S* genotype) have a condition called *sickle-cell trait*, and although some of their hemoglobin is abnormal, enough of it is normal to enable them to function normally under most circumstances.

Sickle-cell anemia has numerous manifestations, but basically, the abnormal hemoglobin reduces the ability of red blood cells to transport oxygen. When people with sickle-cell anemia increase their body's demand for oxygen (for example, while exercising or traveling to high altitude), their red blood cells collapse and form a shape similar to a sickle (**Fig. 3-24**). These sickled cells can't carry adequate amounts of oxygen; moreover, they clump together and block small capillaries. The result is that vital organs are deprived of oxygen. Even with treatment, life expectancy in the United States today is less than 45 years for patients with sickle-cell anemia. Worldwide, sickle-cell anemia causes an estimated 100,000 deaths each year; in the United States, approximately 40,000 to 50,000 individuals, mostly of African descent, suffer from this disease.

The *Hb^S* mutation occurs at pretty much the same rate in all human populations. In some populations, however, especially in western and central Africa, the *Hb^S* allele is more common than elsewhere, with frequencies as high as 20 percent. It's also fairly common in parts of Greece and India (**Fig. 3-25**). Given the devastating effects of *Hb^S* in homozygotes, you might wonder why it's so common in some populations. It seems like natural selection would act against it, but it doesn't. How do we explain its higher prevalence in some populations? The explanation for this situation can be summed up in one word: malaria.

Malaria is an infectious disease that kills an estimated 1 to 3 million people each year worldwide. It's caused by a single-celled organism that is transmitted to humans by mosquitoes. Very briefly, after an infected mosquito bite, these parasites invade red blood cells, where they get the oxygen they need

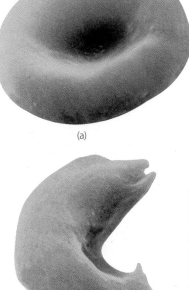

(a)

(b)

© Dr. Stanley Flegler / Visuals Unlimited

Figure 3-24

(a) Scanning electron micrograph of a normal, fully oxygenated red blood cell. (b) Scanning electron micrograph of a collapsed, sickle-shaped red blood cell that contains Hb^S.

directional change In a genetic sense, the nonrandom change in allele frequencies caused by natural selection. The change is directional because the frequencies of alleles consistently increase or decrease (they change in one direction), depending on environmental circumstances and the selective pressures involved.

Figure 3-25

The distribution of the sickle-cell allele in the Old World.

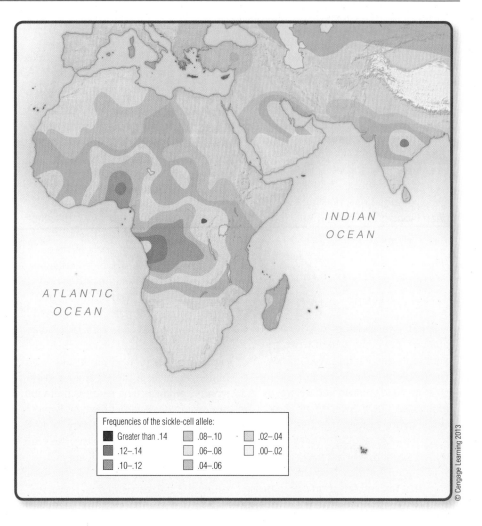

Frequencies of the sickle-cell allele:
- ■ Greater than .14
- ■ .12–.14
- ■ .10–.12
- ■ .08–.10
- ■ .06–.08
- ■ .04–.06
- □ .02–.04
- □ .00–.02

© Cengage Learning 2013

for reproduction. The consequences of this infection to the human host include fever, chills, headache, nausea, vomiting, and frequently death. In parts of western and central Africa, where malaria is always present, children bear the burden of the disease, with as many as 50 to 75 percent of 2- to 9-year-olds being affected.

In the mid-twentieth century, the geographical correlation between malaria and the distribution of the sickle-cell allele (Hb^S) was the only evidence of a biological relationship between the two (**Fig. 3-26**). But now we know that people with sickle-cell trait have greater resistance to malaria than people who have only normal hemoglobin. This is because people with sickle-cell trait have some red blood cells that contain hemoglobin S, and these cells don't provide a suitable environment for the malarial parasite. In other words, having some hemoglobin S is beneficial because it affords some protection from malaria. So, in

malarial areas, malaria acts as a selective agent that favors the heterozygous phenotype, since individuals with sickle-cell trait have higher reproductive success than those with normal hemoglobin, who may die of malaria. But selection for heterozygotes means that the Hb^S allele will be maintained in the population. Thus, there will always be some people with sickle-cell anemia, and they, of course, have the lowest reproductive success, since without treatment, most die before reaching adulthood.

The relationship between malaria and Hb^S provides one of the best examples we have of natural selection in contemporary humans. In this case, natural selection has favored the heterozygous phenotype, thus increasing the frequency of Hb^S, an allele that in homozygotes causes severe disease and early death.

There are many other examples of how disease has been a selective force throughout the course of human evolution and how it has contributed to

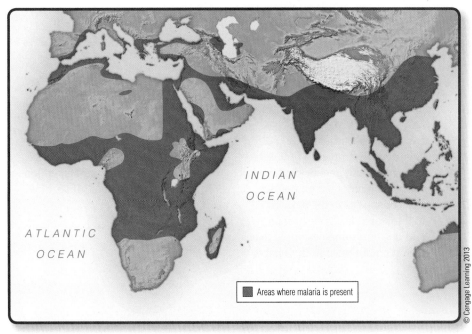

Figure 3-26
The distribution of malaria in the Old World.

INDIAN
OCEAN

ATLANTIC
OCEAN

□ Areas where malaria is present

© Cengage Learning 2013

small, but important, genetic differences between individuals and populations. But the relationship between malaria and the sickle-cell trait is the best single example we have to demonstrate micro-evolution in humans. If you understand this discussion of the complex relationship between environmental factors (mosquitoes), disease, and one slight difference in the gene that governs hemoglobin production, you will comprehend how evolutionary change occurs.

Summary of Main Topics

▶ Cells are the fundamental units of life. They can be either somatic cells, which make up body tissues, or gametes (eggs and sperm), which are reproductive cells that transmit genetic information from parent to offspring.

▶ Genetic information is contained in the DNA molecule, found in a cell's nucleus. The DNA molecule is capable of replication (making copies of itself) during mitosis and meiosis. DNA also controls protein synthesis by directing cells to arrange amino acids in the proper sequence for each particular type of protein.

▶ Gregor Mendel discovered the principles of segregation, independent assortment, and dominance and recessiveness by doing experiments with pea plants. Characteristics influenced by only one genetic locus are called Mendelian traits. In contrast, many characteristics, such as

stature and skin color, are polygenic, meaning that they're influenced by more than one genetic locus and show a continuous range of expression.

▶ Building on fundamental nineteenth-century contributions by Charles Darwin and the rediscovery of Mendel's work in 1900, advances in genetics throughout the twentieth century contributed to contemporary evolutionary thought. In particular, the combination of natural selection with Mendel's principles of inheritance and experimental evidence concerning the nature of mutation have all been synthesized into a modern understanding of evolutionary change, appropriately termed the Modern Synthesis.

▶ In this contemporary theory of evolution, evolutionary change is seen as a two-stage process. The first

stage is the production and redistribution of genetic variation. The second stage is the process whereby natural selection acts on that variation.

▶ Mutation is crucial to all evolutionary change because it's the only source of completely new genetic material (which increases variation).

▶ Natural selection is the crucial factor that influences the long-term direction of evolutionary change. How natural selection works can best be explained as differential net reproductive success—that is, how successful individuals are in producing offspring for succeeding generations. Genetic drift (the random loss of alleles due to small population size) and gene flow (the exchange of genes between populations) are also very important to evolutionary change.

Critical Thinking Questions

1. Before reading this chapter, were you aware that your DNA is structurally the same as that of all other organisms? How do you see this fact as having potential to clarify some of the many questions we still have regarding biological evolution?

2. Has this chapter changed your understanding of genetics and evolution? If so, how?

3. Many people have the misconception that sickle-cell anemia affects only people of African descent. Explain why this isn't true.

4. Give some examples of how selection, gene flow, genetic drift, and mutation have acted on populations or species in the past. Try to think of at least one human and one nonhuman example that weren't mentioned in this chap-ter. Why do you think genetic drift might be important today to endangered species?

5. Did the discussion of misconceptions about dominance and recessiveness change your perceptions of these phenomena? If so, how?

Heredity and Evolution

Modern Human Variation and Adaptation

LEARNING OBJECTIVES

After you have mastered the material in this chapter, you will be able to:

▶ Describe how the history of race studies, particularly in Europe and the United States, has influenced current popular views of human variation.

▶ Explain why anthropologists no longer consider these historical approaches as biologically useful.

▶ Compare and contrast the historical views with a modern biological perspective based on molecular biology and population genetics.

▶ Explain why recent population history of the sickle-cell trait as well as lactase persistence are good examples of biocultural evolution.

Notions about human diversity have played an enormous role in human relations for at least a few thousand years, and they still influence political and social perceptions. While we'd like to believe that informed views have become universal, the gruesome record of genocidal and ethnic cleansing atrocities in recent years tells us that, worldwide, we have a long way to go before tolerance becomes the norm.

In this chapter, we continue to discuss a topic that directly relates to genetics, namely, human biological diversity and how humans adapt physically to environmental challenges. After discussing historical attempts at explaining variations in human phenotypes and racial classification, we examine current methods of interpreting some aspects of variation. In recent years, several techniques have been developed that allow scientists to directly examine the DNA molecule, and this research is revealing differences among people even at the level of single nucleotides. But as discoveries of different levels of diversity emerge, geneticists have also shown that our species is genetically very uniform, particularly when compared with other species.

Historical Views of Human Variation

The first step toward understanding diversity in nature is to organize it into categories that can then be named, discussed, and perhaps studied. Historically, when different groups of people came into contact with one another, they tried to account for the physical differences they saw. Because skin color is so noticeable, it was one of the more frequently explained traits, and most systems of racial classification were based on it.

As early as 1350 B.C., the ancient Egyptians had classified humans based on their skin color: red for Egyptian, yellow for people to the east, white for those to the north, and black for sub-Saharan Africans (Gossett, 1963). In the sixteenth century, after the discovery of the New World, several European countries embarked on a period of intense exploration and colonization in both the New and Old Worlds. One result of this contact was an increased awareness of human diversity.

Throughout the eighteenth and nineteenth centuries, European and American scientists concentrated primarily on describing and classifying the biological variation in humans as well as in nonhuman species. The first scientific attempt to describe variation among human populations was Linnaeus' taxonomic classification (see Chapter 2), which placed humans into four separate categories (Linnaeus, 1758). Linnaeus assigned behavioral and intellectual qualities to each group, with the least complimentary descriptions going to sub-Saharan, dark-skinned Africans. This ranking was typical of the period and reflected the almost universal European ethnocentric view that Europeans were superior to everyone else.

Johann Friedrich Blumenbach (1752–1840), a German anatomist, classified humans into five races, often simply described as white, yellow, red, black, and brown. Although Blumenbach also used criteria other than skin color, he acknowledged that his system had limitations. For example, he emphasized that categories based on skin color were arbitrary and that many traits, including skin color, weren't discrete phenomena because their expression often overlapped between groups. He also pointed out that classifying all humans using such a system would omit everyone who didn't neatly fall into a specific category. (That means ignoring a lot of people!)

Nevertheless, by the mid-nineteenth century, populations were essentially ranked on a scale based on skin color (along with size and shape of the head), again with sub-Saharan Africans at the bottom. The Europeans themselves were also ranked, with northern, light-skinned populations considered superior to their southern, somewhat darker-skinned neighbors in Italy and Greece.

To many Europeans, the fact that non-Europeans weren't Christian suggested that they were "uncivilized" and implied an even more basic inferiority of character and intellect. This view was rooted in a concept called **biological determinism**, which in part holds that there's an association between physical characteristics and such attributes as intelligence, morals, values, abilities, and even social and economic status. In other words, cultural variations were believed to be *inherited* in the same way that biological differences are. It followed, then, that there are inherent behavioral and cognitive differences between groups and that some groups are by nature superior to others.

After 1850, biological determinism was a constant theme underlying common thinking as well as scientific research in Europe and the United States. Most people, including such notables as Thomas Jefferson, Georges Cuvier, Benjamin Franklin, Charles Lyell, Abraham Lincoln, Charles Darwin, and Supreme Court justice Oliver Wendell Holmes, held deterministic (and what today we'd call racist) views. Commenting on this usually de-emphasized characteristic of more respected historical figures, the late evolutionary biologist Stephen J. Gould (1981, p. 32) remarked that "all American culture heroes embraced racial attitudes that would embarrass public-school mythmakers."

Francis Galton (1822–1911), Charles Darwin's cousin, shared an increasingly common fear among nineteenth-century Europeans that "civilized society" was being weakened by the failure of natural selection to eliminate unfit and inferior members (Greene, 1981, p. 107). Galton wrote and lectured on the necessity of "race improvement" and suggested government regulation of marriage and family size, an approach he called **eugenics**. Although eugenics had its share of critics, its popularity flourished throughout the 1930s. Nowhere was it more attractive than in Germany, where the viewpoint took a horrifying turn. The false idea of pure races was increasingly extolled as a means of reestablishing a strong and prosperous state, and eugenics was seen as scientific justification for purging Germany of its "unfit." Many of Germany's scientists supported the policies of racial purity and eugenics during the Nazi period (Proctor, 1988, p. 143), when these ideologies served as

justification for condemning millions of people to death.

But at the same time, many scientists were turning away from racial typologies and classification in favor of a more evolutionary approach. No doubt for some, this shift in direction was motivated by their growing concerns over the goals of the eugenics movement. Probably more important, however, was the synthesis of genetics and Darwin's theories of natural selection during the 1930s. As discussed in Chapter 3, this breakthrough influenced all the biological sciences, and some physical anthropologists soon began applying evolutionary principles to the study of human variation.

The Concept of Race

All contemporary humans are members of the same **polytypic** species, *Homo sapiens*. A polytypic species is composed of local populations that differ in the expression of one or more traits. Still it's crucial to recognize that even *within* local populations, there's a great deal of genotypic and phenotypic variation between individuals.

Nevertheless, in discussions of human variation, most people have traditionally combined various characteristics, such as skin color, face shape, nose shape, hair color, hair form (curly or straight), and eye color. People who have particular combinations of these and other traits have been placed together in categories associated with specific geographical localities. These categories are called *races*.

We all think we know what we mean by the word *race*, but in reality, the term has had various meanings since the 1500s, when it first appeared in the English language. The term *race* has been used synonymously with *species*, as in "the human race." Since the 1600s, race has also referred to various culturally defined groups, and this meaning is still common. For example, you'll hear people say, "the English race" or "the Japanese race," when they actually mean nationality. Another phrase you've probably heard is "the Jewish race," when the

biological determinism The concept that phenomena, including various aspects of behavior (e.g., intelligence, values, morals) are governed by biological (genetic) factors; the inaccurate association of various behavioral attributes with certain biological traits, such as skin color.

eugenics The philosophy of "race improvement" through the forced sterilization of members of some groups and increased reproduction among others; an overly simplified, often racist view that's now discredited.

polytypic Referring to species composed of populations that differ in the expression of one or more traits.

speaker is really talking about an ethnic and religious identity.

So even though *race* is usually a term with biological connotations, it also has enormous social significance. And there's still a widespread perception that certain physical traits (skin color, in particular) are associated with numerous cultural attributes (such as occupational preferences and even morality). As a result, in many cultural contexts, a person's social identity is strongly influenced by the way he or she expresses those physical traits traditionally used to define "racial groups." Characteristics such as skin color are highly visible, and they make it easy to superficially place people into socially defined categories. However, so-called racial traits aren't the only phenotypic expressions that contribute to social identity. Sex and age are also critically important. But aside from these two variables, an individual's biological and/or ethnic background is still inevitably a factor that influences how he or she is initially perceived and judged by others.

References to national origin (for example, African, Asian) as substitutes for racial labels have become more common in recent years, both within and outside anthropology. Within anthropology, the term *ethnicity* was proposed in the early 1950s to avoid the more emotionally charged term *race*. Strictly speaking, ethnicity refers to cultural factors, but the fact that the words *ethnicity* and *race* are used interchangeably reflects the social importance of phenotypic expression and demonstrates once again how phenotype is mistakenly associated with culturally defined variables.

In its most common biological usage, the term *race* refers to geographically patterned phenotypic variation within a species. By the seventeenth century, naturalists were beginning to describe races in plants and nonhuman animals. They had recognized that when populations of a species occupied different regions, they sometimes differed from one another in the expression of one or more traits. But even today, there are no established criteria for assessing races of plants and animals, including humans. As a result,

biologists now almost never refer to "races" of other species, but more typically talk about *populations* or, for major subdivisions, *subspecies*.

Before World War II, most studies of human variation focused on visible phenotypic variation between large, geographically defined populations, and these studies were largely descriptive. But in the last 60 years or so, the emphasis has shifted to examining the differences in allele frequencies (and, more basically, DNA differences) within and between populations, as well as considering the adaptive significance of phenotypic and genotypic variation. This shift in focus occurred partly because of the Modern Synthesis in biology and partly because of further advances in genetics.

In the twentieth century, the application of evolutionary principles to the study of modern human variation replaced the superficial nineteenth-century view of race *based solely on observed phenotype*. Additionally, the genetic emphasis dispelled previously held misconceptions that races are fixed biological entities that don't change over time and that are composed of individuals who all conform to a particular *type*. Clearly, there are phenotypic differences between humans, and some of these differences roughly correspond to particular geographical locations. But we need to ask if there's any adaptive significance attached to these differences. Is genetic drift a factor? What is the degree of underlying genetic variation that influences phenotypic variation? What influence has culture played in the past? These questions place considerations of human variation within a contemporary evolutionary, biocultural framework.

Although physical anthropology is partly rooted in attempts to explain human diversity, no contemporary anthropologist subscribes to pre–Modern Synthesis concepts of races (human or nonhuman) as fixed biological entities. Also, anthropologists recognize that such outdated concepts of race are no longer valid, because the amount of genetic variation accounted for by differences *between* groups is vastly exceeded by the variation that exists *within* groups. Many anthropologists also argue that race is an outdated creation of the human mind that attempts to simplify biological complexity by organizing it into categories. In this view, human races are seen as a product of the human tendency to impose order on complex natural phenomena, and while simplistic classification may have been an acceptable approach 100 years ago, given the current state of genetic and evolutionary science, it's meaningless.

However, even though racial categories based on outwardly expressed variations are invalid, many biological anthropologists continue to study differences in such traits as skin or eye color because these characteristics, and the genes that influence them, can yield information about population adaptation, genetic drift, mutation, and gene flow. Forensic anthropologists, in particular, find the phenotypic criteria associated with ancestry (especially as reflected in the skeleton) to have practical applications. Law enforcement agencies frequently call on these scientists to help identify human remains. Because unidentified human remains are often those of crime victims, identification must be as accurate as possible. The most important variables in such identification are the individual's sex, age, stature, and ancestry ("racial" and ethnic background). Forensic anthropologists use various techniques to determine the ancestry of a person whose remains have been found, and their findings are accurate about 80 percent of the time (Ousley et al., 2009).

Another major limitation of traditional classification schemes derives from their inherently *typological* nature, meaning that categories are distinct and based on stereotypes or ideals that comprise a specific set of traits. So in general, typologies are inherently misleading because any grouping always includes many individuals who don't conform to all aspects of a particular type. In any so-called racial group, there are individuals who fall into the normal range of variation for another group based on one or several characteristics. For example, two people of different ancestry might differ in skin color, but they could share any

number of other traits, including height, shape of head, hair color, eye color, and ABO blood type. In fact, they could easily share more similarities with each other than they do with many members of their own populations (**Fig. 4-1**).

To blur this picture further, the characteristics that have traditionally been used to define races are *polygenic;* that is, they're influenced by more than one gene and therefore exhibit a continuous range of expression. So it's difficult, if not impossible, to draw distinct boundaries between populations with regard to many traits. This limitation becomes clear if you ask yourself, At what point is hair color no longer dark brown but medium brown, or no longer light brown but dark blond? (Look back at Figure 3-18 for an illustration showing variability in eye color.)

The scientific controversy over race will fade as we enhance our understanding of the genetic diversity (and uniformity) of our species. Given the rapid advances in genome studies, dividing the human species into racial categories is not a biologically meaningful way to look at human variation. But among the general public, variations on the theme of race will undoubtedly continue to be the most common view of human variation. Keeping all this in mind, anthropologists must continue exploring the issue so that, to the best of our abilities, accurate information about human variation is available to anyone who seeks informed explanations of complex phenomena.

Contemporary Interpretations of Human Variation

Because the physical characteristics (such as skin color and hair form) that are used to define race are *polygenic*, precisely measuring the genetic influence on them hasn't been possible. But geneticists have now identified some of the genes that influence continuous traits (Gibbons, 2010); thus, the genetic basis of these characteristics is beginning to be revealed.

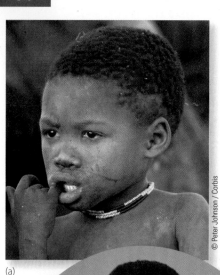

© Peter Johnson / Corbis

(a)

© Charles & Josette Lenars / Corbis

(b)

© Gallo Images / Corbis

(c)

© Otto Lang / Corbis

(d)

Lynn Kilgore

(e)

Figure 4-1

Some examples of phenotypic variation among Africans. (a) San (South African). (b) West African (Bantu). (c) Ethiopian. (d) Ituri (central African). (e) North African (Tunisia).

Beginning in the 1950s, studies of modern human variation focused on various components of blood as well as other aspects of body chemistry. Some phenotypes, such as the ABO blood types, are the direct products of genotypes. (Recall that protein-coding genes direct cells to make proteins, and the antigens on blood cells and many constituents of blood serum are partly composed of proteins; **Fig. 4-2**.) During the twentieth century, studying many Mendelian traits proved very successful, as eventually dozens of loci were identified and the frequencies of many specific alleles were obtained for many human populations. Even so, in all these cases,

it was the phenotype that was observed, and information about the underlying genotype remained largely unobtainable. But beginning in the 1990s, the development of new techniques made genomic studies possible. Thus, it's now possible to directly sequence DNA, and we can actually identify entire genes and even larger DNA segments and make comparisons between individuals and populations. A decade ago, only a small portion of the human genome was accessible to physical anthropologists, but now we have the capacity to obtain DNA profiles for virtually every human population on earth. And we can expect that in the next decade, our understand-

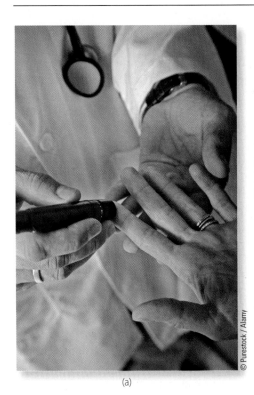

(a)

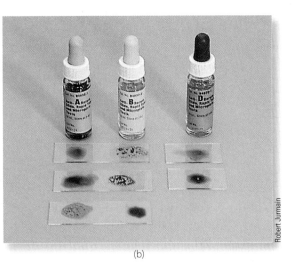

(b)

Figure 4-2

Blood typing. (a) A blood sample is drawn. (b) To determine an individual's blood type, a few drops of blood are treated with specific chemicals. Presence of A and B blood type, as well as Rh, can be detected by using commercially available chemicals. The glass slides below the blue- and yellow-labeled bottles show reactions for the ABO system: The blood on the top slide is type AB; the middle is type B; and the bottom is type A. The two samples to the right depict Rh-negative blood (top) and Rh-positive blood (bottom).

ing and knowledge of human biological variation and adaptation will dramatically increase.

Human Polymorphisms

Traits (or the DNA sequences that code for them) that differ in expression between populations and individuals are called **polymorphisms**, and they're the main focus of human variation studies. A genetic trait is *polymorphic* if the locus that governs it has two or more alleles. A locus can consist of hundreds of nucleotides or just one nucleotide.

Polymorphisms have been essential to the study of evolutionary processes in modern populations. For some time, geneticists have examined polymorphic traits to compare allele frequencies between different populations. These comparisons have then been used to reconstruct the evolutionary events that link human populations with one another.

The ABO system is interesting from an anthropological perspective because the frequencies of the *A*, *B*, and *O* alleles vary tremendously among humans. In most groups, *A* and *B* are rarely found in frequencies greater than 50 percent, and usually their frequencies are

much lower. Still, most human groups are polymorphic for all three alleles, although there are exceptions. For example, the frequency of the *O* allele is virtually 100 percent in indigenous populations of South America. Exceptionally high frequencies of *O* are also found in northern Australia. In these populations, the predominance of the *O* allele is probably due to genetic drift (founder effect), although the influence of natural selection cannot be entirely ruled out.

Examining single traits can be informative regarding potential influences of natural selection or gene flow. This approach, however, is limited when we try to sort out population relationships, since the study of single traits, by themselves, can lead to confusing interpretations of possible relationships between populations. A more meaningful approach is to study several traits simultaneously.

Polymorphisms at the DNA Level

As a result of the Human Genome Project, we've gained remarkable insights into human variation at the DNA level, and molecular biologists have recently discovered many variations in the human genome. For

polymorphisms Loci with more than one allele. Polymorphisms can be expressed in the phenotype as the result of gene action (as in ABO), or they can exist solely at the DNA level within noncoding regions.

example, there are thousands of DNA segments called copy number variants (CNVs) where DNA segments are repeated, in some cases just a few times and in other cases hundreds of times. A type of CNV that is repeated only a few times is called a *microsatellite*, and these segments vary tremendously from person to person. In fact, every person has their own unique arrangement that defines their distinctive "DNA fingerprint."

Researchers are expanding their approach to map patterns of variation for individual nucleotides. As you know, point mutations have been recognized for some time. But what's only been recently appreciated is that single-nucleotide changes also frequently occur in *non-protein-coding* portions of DNA. These point mutations, together with those in coding regions of DNA, are all referred to as *single-nucleotide polymorphisms (SNPs)*. From years of detailed analyses, about 15 million SNPs have been recognized, and they're extraordinarily variable (Durbin et al., 2010). SNPs are only one of several recent genetic discoveries, and indeed, geneticists have gained access to a vast biological "library" that documents the genetic history of our species.

The most recent and most comprehensive population data regarding worldwide patterns of variation come from the analysis of extremely large portions of DNA, called "whole-genome" analysis. Three recent studies have evaluated molecular information for the entire genome in more than 1000 total individuals. The first two studies each identified and traced the patterning of more than 500,000 SNPs in a few dozen populations worldwide (Jakobsson et al., 2008; Li et al., 2008). The most recent study, called the "1000 Genomes Project," is a massive collaboration of more than 400 scientists worldwide, and its preliminary findings reported on close to 15 million SNPs (as well as other DNA variants, such as insertions and deletions); indeed, with more detailed sequencing methods and more sophisticated analyses, the researchers conclude that they have already discovered the molecular basis for 95 percent of all fairly common patterns of human variation (Durbin et al., 2010). They have also identified

between 50 and 100 gene variants associated with disease. This study was also able to reconstruct the *entire* genome for 179 individuals (with an ultimate goal of completing whole-genome sequences for 2,500 people from all around the world). These more complete data, particularly as they are enhanced, will provide the basis for the next generation of human population genetics studies.

The results of these new studies are significant because they confirm earlier findings from more restricted molecular data as well as providing new insights. The higher degree of genetic variation seen in African populations as compared to any other geographical group was once again clearly seen. All human populations outside Africa have much less genetic variation than is seen in Africa. These findings further verify the earlier genetic studies (as well as fossil discoveries) that suggest a fairly recent African origin of all modern humans. Moreover, these new data shed light on the genetic relationships between populations worldwide and the nature of human migrations out of Africa. They also provide evidence of the role of genetic drift (founder effect) in recent human evolution as successively smaller populations split off from larger ones. Finally, preliminary results suggest that the patterning of human variation at the global level may help scientists identify genetic risk factors that influence how susceptible different populations are to various diseases. Specifically, the relative genetic uniformity in non-African populations (for example, European Americans) as compared to those of more recent African descent (such as African Americans) exposes them to a greater risk of developing disease (Lohmueller et al., 2008). How such information might be put to use, however, is controversial.

Human Biocultural Evolution

We've defined culture as the human strategy of adaptation. Humans live in cultural environments that are continually modified by their own activities; thus, evolutionary processes are understandable only within a *cultural* con-

At a Glance

Former and Contemporary Approaches to the Study of Human Variation

TRADITIONAL STUDIES OF HUMAN DIVERSITY— RACIAL STUDIES	CONTEMPORARY STUDIES OF HUMAN DIVERSITY— POPULATION GENETICS STUDIES
Based on superficial phenotypic characteristics (skin color, hair color, head shape, etc.)	Based on specific genetic polymorphisms
All characteristics are polygenic— i.e., many genes influence traits; environment influences phenotype	Mendelian traits ascertained phenotypically (a few dozen known loci that vary between individuals and among groups) / DNA-based traits (millions of ascertained loci showing tremendous variation between individuals)
Emphasis on group differences; only a few large geographical groups ("races") defined	Studies in human populations using population genetics methods
Frequently, behavioral attributes also associated with racial groups (biological determinism)	Hypothesis testing using patterns of human microevolution
Approach scientifically not viewed as accurate or biologically useful— BUT this still is the predominant common view of human diversity	This entire approach generally not recognized or understood by general public

© Cengage Learning 2013

text. You'll recall that natural selection operates within specific environmental settings, and for humans and many of our hominin ancestors, this means an environment dominated by culture. For example, you learned in Chapter 3 that the altered form of hemoglobin called Hb^S confers resistance to malaria. But the sickle-cell allele hasn't always been an important factor in human populations. Before the development of agriculture, humans rarely, if ever, lived close to mosquito-breeding areas for long periods of time. But with the spread in Africa of **slash-and-burn agriculture**, perhaps in just the last 2,000 years, penetration and clearing of tropical forests

occurred. As a result, rainwater was left to stand in open, stagnant pools that provided mosquito-breeding areas close to human settlements. DNA analyses have further confirmed a recent origin and spread of the sickle-cell allele in a population from Senegal, in West Africa. One study estimates that the Hb^S allele appeared (through mutation) in this group sometime between 2,100 and 1,250 ya (Currat et al., 2002). Thus, it appears that at least in some areas, malaria began to have an impact on human populations only recently. But once it did, it became a powerful selective force.

The increase in the frequency of the sickle-cell allele is a biological

slash-and-burn agriculture A traditional land-clearing practice involving the cutting and burning of trees and vegetation. In many areas, fields are abandoned after a few years and clearing occurs elsewhere.

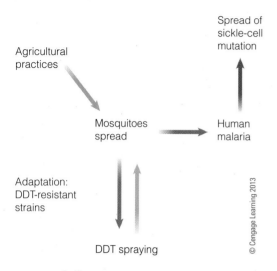

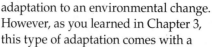

Figure 4-3

Evolutionary interactions affecting the frequency of the sickle-cell allele.

Table 4-1	Frequencies of Lactase Persistence
Population Group	**Percent**
U.S. whites	81–98
Swedes and Danes	>90
Swiss	12
U.S. blacks	70–77
Ibos	99
Bantu	10
Fulani	50
Chinese	1
Thais	1
Asian Americans	<5
Native Australians	85

Source: Lerner and Libby, 1976, Tishkoff et al., 2007. Lerner, I. M., and W. J. Libby, 1976. *Heredity, Evolution, and Society.* San Francisco: W. HJ. Freeman. Tishkoff, S. A., F. A. Reed, et al., 2007. Convergent adaptation of human lactase persistence in Africa and Europe. *Nature Genetics* 39(1): 31-40.

lactase persistence In adults, the continued production of lactase, the enzyme that breaks down lactose (milk sugar). This allows adults in some human populations to digest fresh milk products. The discontinued production of lactase in adults leads to lactose intolerance and the inability to digest fresh milk.

adaptation to an environmental change. However, as you learned in Chapter 3, this type of adaptation comes with a huge cost. Heterozygotes (people with sickle-cell trait) have increased resistance to malaria and presumably higher reproductive success, but prior to modern medical treatment, some of their offspring died from sickle-cell anemia; indeed, this situation still persists in much of the developing world. So there's a counterbalance between selective forces with an advantage for carriers *only* in malarial environments. The genetic patterns of recessive traits such as sickle-cell anemia are discussed in Chapter 3.

Following World War II, the World Health Organization began to spray DDT in mosquito-breeding areas in the tropics. Sixty years of DDT spraying killed millions of mosquitoes; but at the same time, natural selection acted to produce several strains of DDT-resistant mosquitoes (**Fig. 4-3**). Accordingly, especially in the tropics, malaria is again on the rise, with up to 500 million new cases reported annually and more than 1 million people dying each year.

Lactose intolerance, which involves a person's ability to digest milk, is another example of human biocultural evolution. In all human populations, infants and young children are able to digest milk, an obvious necessity for any young mammal. One ingredient of milk is *lactose*, a sugar that's broken down by the enzyme *lactase*. In most mammals, including many humans, the gene that codes for lactase production "switches off" in adolescence. Once this happens, if a person drinks fresh milk, the lactose ferments in the large intestine, leading to diarrhea and severe gastrointestinal upset. So, as you might expect, adults stop drinking milk. Among many African and Asian populations (a majority of humankind today), most adults are lactose-intolerant (**Table 4-1**). But in other populations, including some African and European populations, adults continue to produce lactase and are able to digest fresh milk. This con-

tinued production of lactase is called **lactase persistence**.

Throughout most of hominin evolution, milk was unavailable after weaning. Perhaps, in such circumstances, the continued action of an unnecessary enzyme might inhibit digestion of other foods. Therefore, there may be a selective advantage for the gene coding for lactase production to switch off. So why can some adults (the majority in some populations) tolerate milk? The distribution of lactose-tolerant populations may provide an answer to this question, and it suggests a powerful cultural influence on this trait.

Europeans, who are generally lactose-tolerant, are partly descended from Middle Eastern populations. Often economically dependent on pastoralism, these groups raised cows and/or goats and probably drank considerable quantities of milk. In such a cultural environment, strong selection pressures apparently favored lactose tolerance, a trait that has been retained in modern Europeans. Genetic evidence from north-central Europe recently supports this interpretation.

DNA analysis of both cattle and humans suggests that these species have, to some extent, influenced each other genetically. The interaction between humans and cattle resulted in cattle that produce high-quality milk and humans with the ability to digest it (Beja-Pereira et al., 2003). In other words, more than 5,000 ya, populations of north-central Europe were selectively breeding cattle for higher milk yields. Moreover, as these populations were increasing their dependence on fresh milk, they were inadvertently selecting for the gene that produces lactase persistence in themselves.

Most human populations in Africa are lactose-intolerant, but at some point in the past, certain groups became cattle herders and began to consume fresh milk (**Fig. 4-4**). Interestingly, a pattern of coevolution similar to that seen in Europe has recently been identified in humans and cattle in East Africa (Tishkoff et al., 2007). However, the mutations (SNPs) that allow the continued production of lactase in African adults are different from the European version, suggesting that lactase persis-

Figure 4-4

Fulani cattle herder with his cattle.

© Atlantide Phototravel / Corbis

tence evolved independently in Africa and Europe. Furthermore, the data show that lactase persistence has evolved several times just in East Africa alone. Clearly, the domestication of cattle, partly to provide milk, was a cultural and dietary shift of sufficient importance to cause allele frequencies to change (and lactase persistence to increase) in two distinct areas.

As we've seen, the geographical distribution of lactase persistence is related to a history of cultural dependence on fresh milk products. There are, however, some populations that rely on dairying but don't have high rates of lactase persistence (**Fig. 4-5**). It's been suggested that such populations traditionally have consumed their milk in the form of cheese and yogurt, in which the lactose has been broken down by bacterial action.

The interaction of human cultural environments and changes in lactase persistence in human populations is an excellent example of biocultural evolution. In the last few thousand years, cultural factors have initiated specific evolutionary changes in human groups. Such cultural factors have probably influenced the course of human evolution for at least 3 million years, and today they are still of paramount importance.

© Michael S. Yamashita / Corbis

Population Genetics

Physical anthropologists use the approach of **population genetics** to interpret microevolutionary patterns of human variation. Population genetics is the area of research that, among other things, examines allele frequencies in populations and attempts to identify the various factors that cause allele frequencies to change over time. As we defined it in Chapter 3, a *population* is a group

Figure 4-5

Natives of Mongolia rely heavily on milk products from goats and sheep, but mostly consume these foods in the form of cheese and yogurt.

population genetics The study of the frequency of alleles, genotypes, and phenotypes in populations from a microevolutionary perspective.

of interbreeding individuals that share a common **gene pool**. As a rule, a population is the group within which individuals are most likely to find mates.

In theory, this is a straightforward concept. In every generation, the genes (alleles) in a gene pool are mixed by recombination and then reunited with their counterparts (located on paired chromosomes) through mating. What emerges in the next generation is a direct product of the genes going into the pool, which in turn is a product of who is mating with whom.

Factors that determine mate choice are geographical, ecological, and social. If people are isolated on a remote island in the middle of the Pacific, there isn't much chance they'll find a mate outside the immediate vicinity. Such **breeding isolates** are fairly easily defined and are a favorite subject of microevolutionary studies. Geography plays a dominant role in producing these isolates by strictly determining the range of available mates. But even within these limits, cultural rules can play a deciding role by prescribing who is most appropriate among those who are potentially available.

Most humans today aren't so clearly defined as members of particular populations as they would be if they belonged to breeding isolates. Inhabitants of large cities may appear to be members of a single population, but within the city, socioeconomic, ethnic, and religious boundaries crosscut in complex ways to form smaller population segments. In addition to being members of these smaller local populations, we're also members of overlapping gradations of larger populations: the immediate geographical region (a metropolitan area or perhaps a state), a section of the country, a nation, and ultimately the entire species.

Once specific human populations have been identified, the next step is to ascertain what evolutionary forces, if any, are operating on them. To determine whether evolution is taking place at a given locus, population geneticists measure allele frequencies for specific traits and compare these observed frequencies with a set predicted by a mathematical model called the **Hardy-**

Weinberg equilibrium. Just how this model is used is illustrated in Appendix C. The Hardy-Weinberg formula provides a tool to establish whether allele frequencies in a population are indeed changing. (In Chapter 3, we discussed several factors that act to change allele frequencies, including:

1. New variation (that is, new alleles produced by mutation)
2. Redistributed variation (that is, gene flow or genetic drift)
3. Selection of "advantageous" allele combinations that promote reproductive success (that is, natural selection)

The Adaptive Significance of Human Variation

Today, biological anthropologists view human variation as the result of the evolutionary factors we've already named: mutation; genetic drift (including founder effect), gene flow; and natural selection (the latter is especially seen in adaptations to environmental conditions, both past and present). As we've emphasized, cultural adaptations have also played an important role in the evolution of our species, and although in this discussion we're primarily concerned with biological issues, we must still consider the influence of cultural practices on human adaptive responses.

To survive, all organisms must maintain the normal functions of internal organs, tissues, and cells within the context of an ever-changing environment. Even during the course of a single, seemingly uneventful day, there are numerous fluctuations in temperature, wind, solar radiation, humidity, and so on. Physical activity also places **stress** on physiological mechanisms. The body must accommodate all these changes by compensating in some manner to maintain internal constancy, or **homeostasis**, and all life-forms have evolved physiological mechanisms that, within limits, achieve this goal.

Physiological response to environmental change is influenced by genetic factors. We've already defined adapta-

gene pool The total complement of genes shared by the reproductive members of a population.

breeding isolates Populations that are clearly isolated geographically and/or socially from other breeding groups.

Hardy-Weinberg equilibrium The mathematical relationship expressing—under conditions in which no evolution is occurring—the predicted distribution of alleles in populations; the central theorem of population genetics.

tion as a functional response to environmental conditions in populations and individuals. In a narrower sense, adaptation refers to *long-term* evolutionary (that is, genetic) changes that characterize all individuals within a population or species.

Examples of long-term adaptations in humans include physiological responses to heat (sweating) or excessive levels of ultraviolet (UV) light (deeply pigmented skin in tropical regions). Such characteristics are the results of evolutionary change in species or populations, and they don't vary as a result of short-term environmental change. For example, the ability to sweat isn't lost in people who spend their entire lives in predominantly cool areas. Likewise, people born with dark skin won't become lighter even if they're never exposed to intense sunlight.

Acclimatization is another kind of physiological response to environmental conditions, and it can be short-term, long-term, or even permanent. These responses to environmental factors are partially influenced by genes, but some can also be affected by the duration and severity of the exposure, technological buffers (such as shelter or clothing), and individual behavior, weight, and overall body size.

The simplest type of acclimatization is a temporary and rapid adjustment to an environmental change (Hanna, 1999). Tanning, which can occur in almost everyone, is an example of this kind of acclimatization. Another example (one you've probably experienced but don't know it) is the very rapid increase in hemoglobin production that occurs when people who live at low elevations travel to higher ones. This increase provides the body with more oxygen in an environment where oxygen is less available. In both these examples, the physiological change is temporary. Tans fade once exposure to sunlight is reduced, and hemoglobin production drops to original levels following a return to a lower elevation.

On the other hand, *developmental acclimatization* is irreversible and results from exposure to an environmental challenge during growth and development.

Lifelong residents of high altitude exhibit certain expressions of developmental acclimatization.

In the following discussion, we present some examples of how humans respond to environmental challenges. Some of these examples characterize the entire species. Others illustrate adaptations seen in only some populations. And still others illustrate the more short-term process of acclimatization.

Solar Radiation, Vitamin D, and Skin Color

Skin color is often cited as an example of adaptation through natural selection in humans. In general, prior to European contact, skin color in populations followed a largely predictable geographical distribution, especially in the Old World (**Fig. 4-6**). Populations with the greatest amount of pigmentation are found in the tropics, while lighter skin color is associated with more northern latitudes, particularly the inhabitants of northwestern Europe.

Skin color is mostly influenced by the pigment *melanin*, a granular substance produced by specialized cells (*melanocytes*) in the epidermis (see **Fig. 4-7** on p. 83). All humans have approximately the same number of melanocytes. It's the amount of melanin and the size of the melanin granules that vary. Melanin is important because it acts as a built-in sunscreen by absorbing potentially dangerous UV rays present (although not visible) in sunlight. So melanin protects us from overexposure to UV radiation, which can cause genetic mutations in skin cells. These mutations may lead to skin cancer, which, if left untreated, can eventually spread to other organs and even result in death.

As we previously mentioned, exposure to sunlight triggers a protective mechanism in the form of tanning, the result of temporarily increased melanin production (acclimatization). This response occurs in all humans except albinos, who have a genetic mutation that prevents their melanocytes from producing melanin. But even people who do produce melanin differ in their ability to tan. For instance, many people of northern European descent have very

stress In a physiological context, any factor that acts to disrupt homeostasis; more precisely, the body's response to any factor that threatens its ability to maintain homeostasis.

homeostasis A condition of balance, or stability, within a biological system, maintained by the interaction of physiological mechanisms that compensate for changes (both external and internal).

acclimatization Physiological responses to changes in the environment that occur during an individual's lifetime. Such responses may be temporary or permanent, depending on the duration of the environmental change and when in the individual's life it occurs. The capacity for acclimatization may typify an entire species or population, and because it's under genetic influence, it's subject to evolutionary factors such as natural selection and genetic drift.

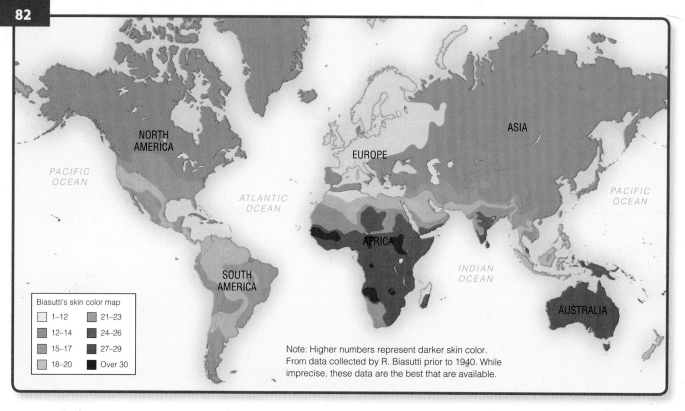

Biasutti's skin color map
- 1–12
- 12–14
- 15–17
- 18–20
- 21–23
- 24–26
- 27–29
- Over 30

Note: Higher numbers represent darker skin color. From data collected by R. Biasutti prior to 1940. While imprecise, these data are the best that are available.

Figure 4-6

Geographical distribution of skin color in indigenous human populations. (After Biasutti, 1959.)

neural tube In early embryonic development, the anatomical structure that develops to form the brain and spinal cord.

spina bifida A condition in which the arch of one or more vertebrae fails to fuse and form a protective barrier around the spinal cord. This can lead to spinal cord damage and paralysis.

fair skin, blue eyes, and light hair. Their melanocytes produce small amounts of melanin, and when exposed to sunlight, they have little ability to increase production. And in all populations, women tend not to tan as deeply as men.

Natural selection has favored dark skin in areas nearest the equator, where the sun's rays are most direct and thus where exposure to UV light is most intense. In considering the cancer-causing effects of UV radiation from an *evolutionary* perspective, three points must be kept in mind:

1. Early hominins lived in the tropics, where solar radiation is more intense than in temperate areas to the north and south.
2. Unlike modern city dwellers, early hominins spent their days outdoors.
3. Early hominins didn't wear clothing that would have protected them from the sun.

Given these conditions, UV radiation was probably a powerful agent selecting for high levels of melanin production in early humans.

Jablonski (1992) and Jablonski and Chaplin (2000) offer an additional explanation for the distribution of skin color, one that focuses on the role of UV radia-

tion in the degradation of folate. Folate is a B vitamin that isn't stored in the body and therefore must be replenished through dietary sources. Folate deficiencies in pregnant women are associated with numerous complications, including maternal death; and in children they can lead to retarded growth and other serious conditions. Folate also plays a crucial role in **neural tube** development very early in embryonic development, and deficiencies can lead to defects, including various expressions of **spina bifida**. The consequences of severe neural tube defects can include pain, infection, paralysis, and even death. It goes without saying that neural tube defects can dramatically reduce the reproductive success of affected individuals.

Some studies have shown that UV radiation rapidly depletes folate serum levels both in laboratory experiments and in fair-skinned individuals. These findings have implications for pregnant women and children and also for the evolution of dark skin in hominins. Jablonski and Chaplin suggest that the earliest hominins may have had light body skin covered with dark hair, as is seen in chimpanzees and gorillas. (Both have darker skin on exposed body parts.) But as loss of body hair in hominins occurred, dark skin evolved rather quickly as a protective response to the damaging effects of UV radiation on folate.

As hominins migrated out of Africa into Europe and Asia, they faced new selective pressures. Not only were they moving away from the tropics, where ultraviolet rays were most direct, but they were also moving into areas where winters were cold and cloudy. Bear in mind, too, that physiological adaptations weren't sufficient to meet the demands of living in colder climates. Therefore, we assume that these populations were wearing animal skins or other types of clothing at least part of the year. Although clothing would have added necessary warmth, it would also have blocked sunlight. Consequently, the advantages provided by deeply pigmented skin in the tropics were no longer important, and selection for darker skin may have been relaxed (Brace and Montagu, 1977).

However, relaxed selection for dark skin isn't sufficient to explain the very depigmented skin seen especially in some northern Europeans. Perhaps another factor, the need for adequate amounts of vitamin D, was also critical. The theory concerning the possible role of vitamin D, known as the *vitamin D hypothesis*, offers the following explanation.

Vitamin D is produced in the body partly as a result of the interaction between UV radiation and a substance similar to cholesterol. It's also available in some foods, including liver, fish oils, egg yolk, butter, and cream. Vitamin D is necessary for normal bone growth and mineralization, and some exposure to ultraviolet radiation is therefore essential. Insufficient amounts of vitamin D during childhood result in *rickets*, a condition that often leads to bowing of the long bones of the legs and deformation of the pelvis (**Fig. 4-8**). Pelvic deformities are of particular concern for women,

Figure 4-7

Ultraviolet rays penetrate the skin and can eventually damage DNA within skin cells. The three major types of cells that can be affected are squamous cells, basal cells, and melanocytes.

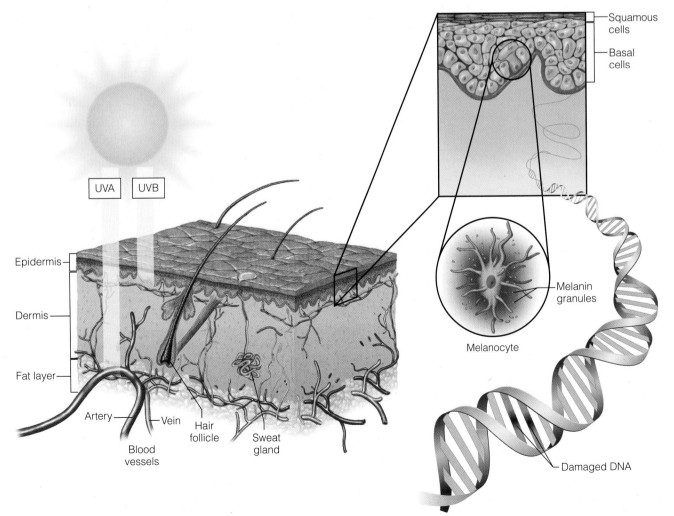

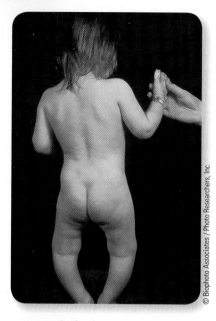

Figure 4-8

A child with rickets. Her leg bones have not been properly mineralized due to lack of vitamin D. Thus, they are bowed because they aren't strong enough to support the weight of her upper body.

© Biophoto Associates / Photo Researchers, Inc.

because they can lead to a narrowing of the birth canal, which, in the absence of surgical intervention, frequently results in the death of both mother and infant during childbirth.

Rickets may have been a significant selective factor that favored lighter skin in regions with less sunlight. Reduced levels of UV light and the increased use of clothing could have been detrimental to dark-skinned individuals in more northern latitudes. In these people, melanin would have blocked absorption of the already reduced amounts of available ultraviolet radiation required for vitamin D synthesis. Therefore, selection pressures would have shifted over time to favor lighter skin. There is substantial evidence, both historically and in contemporary populations, to support this theory.

During the latter decades of the nineteenth century in the United States, African American inhabitants of northern cities suffered a higher incidence of rickets than whites. (The solution to this problem was fairly simple: the supplementation of milk with vitamin D.) Another example is seen in Britain, where darker-skinned East Indians and Pakistanis show a higher incidence of rickets than people with lighter skin (Molnar, 1983).

Jablonski and Chaplin (2000) have also looked at the *potential* for vitamin D synthesis in people with different skin color based on the yearly average UV radiation at various latitudes (**Fig. 4-9**). Their conclusions support the vitamin D hypothesis to the point of stating that the requirement for vitamin D synthesis in northern latitudes was as important to natural selection as the need for protection from UV radiation in tropical regions.

Except for a person's sex, more social importance has been attached to variation in skin color than to any other single human biological trait. But aside from its probable adaptive significance relative to UV radiation, skin color is no more important physiologically than many other characteristics. However, from an evolutionary perspective, it provides a good example of how the forces of natural selection have produced geographically patterned variation as the

consequence of two competing selective forces: the need for protection from overexposure to UV radiation (which can lead to folate depletion and skin cancer) on the one hand, and the necessity for adequate UV exposure to promote vitamin D synthesis on the other.

The Thermal Environment

Mammals and birds have evolved complex mechanisms to maintain a constant internal body temperature. While reptiles rely on exposure to external heat sources to raise body temperature and energy levels, mammals and birds have physiological mechanisms that, within certain limits, increase or reduce the loss of body heat. The optimum internal body temperature for normal cellular functions is species-specific, and for humans it's approximately 98.6°F.

People are found in a wide variety of habitats, with temperatures ranging from over 120°F to less than −60°F. In these extremes, human life wouldn't be possible without cultural innovations. But even accounting for the artificial environments in which we live, such external conditions place the human body under enormous stress.

Response to Heat   All available evidence suggests that the earliest hominins evolved in the warm-to-hot savannas of East Africa. The fact that humans cope better with heat than they do with cold is testimony to the long-term adaptations to heat that evolved in our ancestors.

In humans, as well as certain other species, such as horses, sweat glands are distributed throughout the skin. This wide distribution of sweat glands makes it possible to lose heat at the body surface through evaporative cooling, a mechanism that has evolved to the greatest degree in humans. The ability to dissipate heat by sweating is seen in all humans to an almost equal degree, with the average number of sweat glands per individual (approximately 1.6 million) being fairly constant. However, people who aren't generally exposed to hot conditions do experience a period of acclimatization that initially involves significantly increased perspiration rates (Frisancho, 1993). An additional fac-

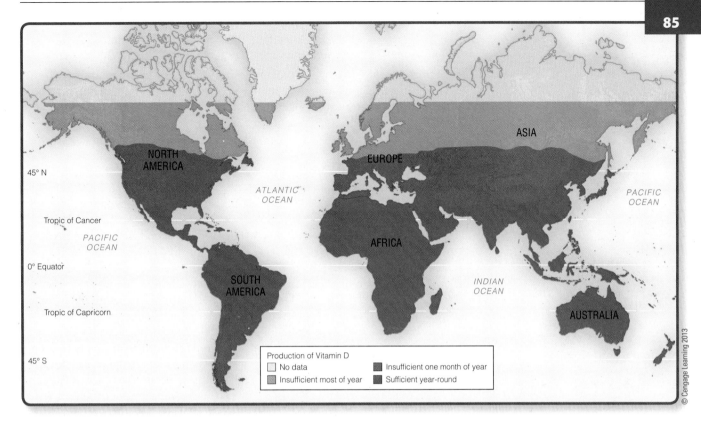

Production of Vitamin D
- No data
- Insufficient most of year
- Insufficient one month of year
- Sufficient year-round

© Cengage Learning 2013

Figure 4-9

Populations indigenous to the tropics (brown band) receive enough UV radiation for vitamin D synthesis year-round. The dark orange band shows areas where people with moderately pigmented skin don't receive enough UV light for vitamin D synthesis for one month of the year. The light orange band shows areas where even light skin doesn't receive enough UV light for vitamin D synthesis during most of the year. (Adapted from Jablonski and Chaplin, 2000, 2002.)

tor that enhances the cooling effects of sweating is increased exposure of the skin because of reduced amounts of body hair. We don't know when in our evolutionary history we began to lose body hair, but it represents a species-wide adaptation.

Although effective, heat reduction through evaporation can be expensive, and indeed dangerous, in terms of water and sodium loss. Up to 3 liters of water can be lost by a human engaged in heavy work in high heat. You can appreciate the importance of this fact if you consider that losing 1 liter of water is approximately equal to losing 1.5 percent of total body weight, and quickly losing 10 percent of body weight can be life threatening. This is why water must be continuously replaced when you exercise on a hot day.

Another mechanism for radiating body heat is **vasodilation**, which occurs when capillaries near the skin's surface widen to permit increased blood flow to the skin. The visible effect of vasodilation is flushing, or increased redness and warming of the skin, particularly of the face. But the physiological effect is to permit heat, carried by the blood from the interior of the body, to be radiated from the skin's surface to the surrounding air. (Some drugs, including alcohol, also produce vasodilation, which accounts for the redder and warmer face some people have after a couple of drinks.)

Body size and proportions are also important in regulating body temperature. Indeed, there seems to be a general relationship between climate and body size and shape in birds and mammals. In general, within a species, body size (weight) increases as distance from the equator increases. In humans, this relationship holds up fairly well, but there are numerous exceptions.

Two rules that pertain to the relationship between body size, body proportions, and climate are *Bergmann's rule* and *Allen's rule.*

1. *Bergmann's rule concerns the relationship of body mass or volume to surface area.* In mammals, body size tends to be greater in populations that live in colder climates. This is because as mass increases, the relative amount of surface area decreases proportionately. Because heat is lost at the surface, it follows that increased mass allows for

vasodilation Expansion of blood vessels, permitting increased blood flow to the skin. Vasodilation permits warming of the skin and facilitates radiation of warmth as a means of cooling. Vasodilation is an involuntary response to warm temperatures, various drugs, and even emotional states (blushing).

greater heat retention and reduced heat loss.

2. *Allen's rule concerns shape of the body, especially appendages.* In colder climates, shorter appendages, with increased mass-to-surface ratios, are adaptive because they're more effective at preventing heat loss. Conversely, longer appendages, with increased surface area relative to mass, are more adaptive in warmer climates because they promote heat loss.

According to these rules, the most suitable body shape in hot climates is linear with long arms and legs. In a cold climate, a more suitable body type is stocky with shorter limbs. Several studies have shown that human populations generally conform to these principles. In colder climates, body mass tends, on average, to be greater and characterized by a larger trunk relative to arms and legs. People living in the Arctic tend to be short and stocky, while many sub-Saharan Africans, especially East African pastoralists, are, on average, tall and linear

(**Fig. 4-10**). But there's a great deal of variability regarding human body proportions, and not all populations conform so readily to Bergmann's and Allen's rules.

Response to Cold   Human physiological responses to cold combine factors that increase heat production with those that enhance heat retention. Of the two, heat retention is more efficient because it requires less energy. This is an important point because energy is derived from food. Unless resources are abundant, and in winter they frequently aren't, any factor that conserves energy can have adaptive value.

Short-term responses to cold include increased metabolic rate and shivering, both of which generate body heat, at least for a short time. **Vasoconstriction**, another short-term response, restricts heat loss and conserves energy. Humans also have a subcutaneous (beneath the skin) fat layer that provides an insulative layer throughout the body. Behavioral modifications include increased activity, wearing warmer clothing, increased food consumption, and even curling up into a ball.

(a)

(b)

Figure 4-10

(a) These Samburu women (and men in the background) have the linear proportions characteristic of many inhabitants of East Africa. The Samburu are cattle-herding people who live in northern Kenya. Here they are shown dancing. (b) By comparison, these Canadian Inuit women are shorter and stockier. Although the people in these two pictures don't typify everyone in their populations, they do serve as good examples of Bergmann's and Allen's rules.

vasoconstriction   Narrowing of blood vessels to reduce blood flow to the skin. Vasoconstriction is an involuntary response to cold and reduces heat loss at the skin's surface.

Increases in metabolic rate (the rate at which cells break up nutrients into their components) release energy in the form of heat. Shivering also generates muscle heat, as does voluntary exercise. But these methods of heat production are expensive because they require an increased intake of nutrients to provide energy. (Perhaps this explains why we tend to have a heartier appetite during the winter and frequently eat more fats and carbohydrates, the very sources of energy our body requires.)

In general, people exposed to chronic cold (meaning much or most of the year) maintain higher metabolic rates than those living in warmer climates. The Inuit (Eskimo) people living in the Arctic maintain metabolic rates between 13 and 45 percent higher than that observed in non-Inuit control subjects (Frisancho, 1993). Moreover, the highest metabolic rates are seen in inland Inuit, who are exposed to even greater cold stress than coastal populations. Traditionally, the Inuit had the highest animal protein and fat diet of any human population in the world. Their diet was dictated by the available resource base (fish and mammals but little to no vegetable material), and it served to maintain the high metabolic rates required by exposure to chronic cold.

Vasoconstriction (the opposite of vasodilation) restricts capillary blood flow to the surface of the skin, thus reducing heat loss at the body surface. Because retaining body heat is more economical than creating it, vasoconstriction is very efficient, provided temperatures don't drop below freezing. If temperatures do fall below freezing, continued vasoconstriction can allow the skin's temperature to decline to the point of frostbite or worse.

Long-term responses to cold vary among human groups. For example, in the past, desert-dwelling native Australian populations were exposed to wide temperature fluctuations from day to night. Since they wore no clothing and didn't build shelters, their only protection from temperatures that hovered only a few degrees above freezing was provided by sleeping fires. They also experienced continuous vasoconstriction throughout the night, and this permitted a degree of skin cooling most people would find extremely uncomfortable. But as there was no threat of frostbite, continued vasoconstriction was an efficient adaptation that helped prevent excessive internal heat loss.

By contrast, the Inuit experience intermittent periods of vasoconstriction and vasodilation. This compromise provides periodic warmth to the skin that helps prevent frostbite in subfreezing temperatures. At the same time, because vasodilation is intermittent, energy loss is restricted, with more heat retained at the body's core.

These examples illustrate two of the ways that adaptations to cold vary among human populations. Obviously, winter conditions exceed our ability to adapt physiologically in many parts of the world. So if they hadn't developed cultural innovations, our ancestors would have remained in the tropics.

High Altitude

Studies of high-altitude residents have greatly contributed to our understanding of physiological adaptation. As you would expect, altitude studies have focused on inhabited mountainous regions, particularly in the Himalayas, Andes, and Rocky Mountains. Of these three areas, permanent human habitation probably has the longest history in the Himalayas (Moore et al., 1998). Today, perhaps as many as 25 million people live at altitudes above 10,000 feet. In Tibet, permanent settlements exist above 15,000 feet, and in the Andes, they can be found as high as 17,000 feet (**Fig. 4-11**).

Because the mechanisms that maintain homeostasis in humans evolved at lower altitudes, we're compromised by conditions at higher elevations. At high altitudes, many factors produce stress on the human body. These include **hypoxia** (reduced available oxygen), more intense solar radiation, cold, low humidity, wind (which increases cold stress), a reduced nutritional base, and rough terrain. Of these, hypoxia exerts the greatest amount of stress on human physiological systems, especially the heart, lungs, and brain.

Hypoxia results from reduced barometric pressure. It's not that there's

hypoxia Lack of oxygen. Hypoxia can refer to reduced amounts of available oxygen in the atmosphere due to lower barometric pressure or to insufficient amounts of oxygen in the body.

less oxygen in the atmosphere at high altitudes; it's just less concentrated. Therefore, to obtain the same amount of oxygen at 9,000 feet as at sea level, people must make certain physiological alterations that increase the body's ability to transport and efficiently use the oxygen that's available.

At high altitudes, reproduction is adversely affected due to increased infant mortality rates, miscarriage, low birth weights, and premature birth. An early study (Moore and Regensteiner, 1983) reported that in Colorado, infant deaths are almost twice as common above 8,200 feet (2,500 m) than at lower elevations. One cause of fetal and mater-

nal death is preeclampsia, a severe elevation of blood pressure in pregnant women after the twentieth gestational week. In another Colorado study, Palmer and colleagues (1999) reported that among pregnant women living at elevations over 10,000 feet, the prevalence of preeclampsia was 16 percent, compared to 3 percent at around 4,000 feet. In general, the problems related to childbearing are attributed to issues that compromise the vascular supply (and thus oxygen transport) to the fetus.

People born at lower altitudes differ from high-altitude natives in how they adapt to hypoxia. In people born at low elevations, acclimatization begins to

(a)

(b)

Figure 4-11

(a) Namche Bazaar, Tibet, is situated at an elevation of over 12,000 feet above sea level. (b) La Paz, Bolivia, at just over 12,000 feet, is home to more than 1 million people.

occur within hours of exposure to high altitude. The responses may be short-term modifications, depending on duration of stay. These changes include an increase in respiration rate, heart rate, and production of red blood cells. (Red blood cells contain hemoglobin, the protein responsible for transporting oxygen to organs and tissues.)

Developmental acclimatization occurs in high-altitude natives during growth and development. This type of acclimatization is present only in people who grow up in high-altitude areas, not in those who move there as adults. Compared with populations at lower elevations, lifelong residents of high altitudes grow somewhat more slowly and mature later. Other differences include greater lung capacity and a relatively larger heart. And people born at high altitudes are more efficient than migrants at diffusing oxygen from blood to body tissues. Developmental acclimatization to high-altitude hypoxia serves as a good example of physiological plasticity by illustrating how, within the limits set by genetic factors, development can be influenced by environment.

We now have firm evidence that natural selection has acted strongly and rapidly to increase the frequency of certain alleles that have produced adaptive responses to altitude in Tibetans living in the Himalayas. Ninety percent of Tibetan highlanders possess a mutation in a gene involved in red blood cell production. In effect, this mutation inhibits the increased red blood cell production normally seen in high-altitude inhabitants so that Tibetan highlanders have red cell counts similar to those of populations living at sea level. Interestingly, in South America, the Quechua and other high-altitude residents of the Andes do not have this mutation and have higher red cell counts than lowland inhabitants. But if increased red blood cell production is advantageous at high altitude, why would selection favor a mutation that acts against it in Tibetans? The answer is that beyond certain levels, elevated numbers of red cells can actually "thicken" the blood and lead to increased risk of stroke, blood clots, and heart attack. In pregnant women, they can also lead to impaired fetal growth

and even fetal death. Thus, although the mechanisms aren't yet understood, Tibetans have acquired a number of genetically influenced adaptations to hypoxic conditions while still producing the same amount of hemoglobin we would expect at sea level. Because the mutation is believed to have appeared only around 4,000 ya, its presence throughout most high-altitude Tibetan populations is the strongest and most rapid example of natural selection documented for humans (Yi et al., 2010).

Infectious Disease

Infection, as opposed to other disease categories, such as degenerative or genetic disease, includes pathological conditions caused by microorganisms (viruses, bacteria, and fungi). Throughout the course of human evolution, infectious disease has exerted enormous selective pressures on populations and consequently has influenced the frequency of certain alleles that affect the immune response. In fact, it would be difficult to overstate the importance of infectious disease as an agent of natural selection in human populations. But as important as infectious disease has been, its role isn't very well documented.

The effects of infectious disease on humans are mediated culturally as well as biologically. Innumerable cultural factors, such as architectural styles, subsistence techniques, exposure to domesticated animals, and even religious practices, all affect how infectious disease develops and persists within and between populations.

Until about 12,000–10,000 ya, all humans lived in small nomadic hunting and gathering groups. These groups rarely remained in one location for long, so they had minimal contact with refuse heaps that house disease **vectors**. But with the domestication of plants and animals, people became more sedentary and began living in small villages. Gradually, villages became towns, and towns, in turn, developed into densely crowded, unsanitary cities.

As long as humans lived in small bands, there was little opportunity for infectious disease to have much impact on large numbers of people. Even if an

vectors Agents that transmit disease from one carrier to another. Mosquitoes are vectors for malaria, just as fleas are vectors for bubonic plague.

entire local group or band were wiped out, the effect on the overall population in a given area would have been negligible. Moreover, for a disease to become **endemic** in a population, sufficient numbers of people must be present. Therefore, small bands of hunter-gatherers weren't faced with continuous exposure to endemic disease.

But with the advent of settled living and close proximity to domesticated animals, opportunities for disease greatly increased. As sedentary life permitted larger group size, it became possible for diseases to become permanently established in some populations. Moreover, exposure to domestic animals, such as cattle and fowl, provided an opportune environment for the spread of several **zoonotic** diseases, such as tuberculosis. Humans had no doubt always contracted diseases occasionally from the animals they hunted; but when they began to live with domesticated animals, they were faced with an entire array of new infectious conditions. Also, the crowded, unsanitary conditions that characterized parts of all cities until the late nineteenth century and that persist in much of the world today further added to the disease burden borne by human inhabitants.

AIDS (acquired immunodeficiency syndrome) provides an excellent example of the influence of human infectious disease as a selective agent. In the United States, the first cases of AIDS were reported in 1981. Since that time, perhaps as many as 1.5 million Americans have been infected by HIV (human immunodeficiency virus), the agent that causes AIDS. However, most of the burden of AIDS is borne by developing countries, where 95 percent of all HIV-infected people live. By the end of 2009, an estimated 33 to 35 million people worldwide were living with HIV infection, and at least 25 million had died.

HIV is transmitted from person to person through the exchange of body fluids, usually blood or semen. It's not spread through casual contact with an infected person. Within six months of infection, most people test positive for anti-HIV antibodies, meaning that their immune system has recognized the presence of foreign antigens and has responded by producing antibodies. However, serious HIV-related symptoms may not appear for years. HIV is a "slow virus" that may persist in a person's body for several years before the onset of severe illness. This asymptomatic state is

endemic Continuously present in a population.

zoonotic (zoh-oh-no´-tic) Pertaining to a zoonosis (*pl.*, zoonoses), a disease that's transmitted to humans through contact with nonhuman animals.

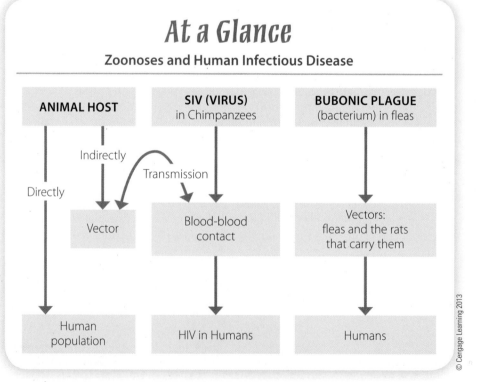

At a Glance
Zoonoses and Human Infectious Disease

| ANIMAL HOST | SIV (VIRUS) in Chimpanzees | BUBONIC PLAGUE (bacterium) in fleas |

Indirectly / Directly — Transmission

| Vector | Blood-blood contact | Vectors: fleas and the rats that carry them |

| Human population | HIV in Humans | Humans |

© Cengage Learning 2013

called a "latency period," and the average latency period in the United States is more than 11 years.

Like all viruses, HIV must invade certain types of cells and alter the functions of those cells to produce more virus particles in a process that eventually leads to cell destruction. HIV can attack various types of cells, but it especially targets so-called T4 helper cells, which are major components of the immune system. As HIV infection spreads and T4 cells are destroyed, the patient's immune system begins to fail. Consequently, he or she develops symptoms caused by various pathogens that are commonly present but usually kept in check by a normal immune response. When an HIV-infected person's T cell count drops to a level indicating that immunity has been suppressed, and when symptoms of "opportunistic" infections appear, the patient is said to have AIDS.

By the early 1990s, scientists were aware of a number of patients who had been HIV positive for 10 to 15 years but continued to show few if any symptoms. Researchers began to suspect that some individuals possess a natural immunity or resistance to HIV infection. This hypothesis was verified in 1996 by two different studies (Dean et al., 1996; Samson et al., 1996) that described a genetic mutation that can provide HIV resistance in some people. Current evidence suggests that people who are homozygous for a particular (mutant) allele may be completely resistant to many types of HIV infection. In heterozygotes, infection may still occur, but the course of HIV disease is slowed.

For unknown reasons, the mutant allele occurs mainly in people of European descent, among whom its frequency is about 10 percent (its frequency is much lower in other populations). Researchers have suggested that this increased allele frequency occurs in Europeans as a result of natural selection favoring an allele that originally occurred as a rare mutation. But we should point out that the original selective agent was *not* HIV. Instead, it was some other, as yet unidentified pathogen that requires the same receptor site as HIV, and some researchers (Lalani et al., 1999) have suggested that it may

have been the virus that causes smallpox. While this conclusion hasn't yet been proved, it offers an exciting avenue of research. It may reveal how a mutation that originally was favored by selection because it provides protection against one type of infection (smallpox) can also increase resistance to another (AIDS).

The best-known epidemic in history was the Black Death (bubonic plague) in the mid-fourteenth century. Bubonic plague is caused by a bacterium and is transmitted from rodents to humans by fleas. In just a few years, this deadly disease had spread (following trade routes and facilitated by rodent-infested ship cargoes) from the Caspian Sea throughout the Mediterranean area to northern Europe. During the initial exposure to this disease, as many as one-third of the inhabitants of Europe died.

A lesser-known but even more devastating example was the influenza pandemic that broke out in 1918 at the end of World War I. This was actually one of a series of influenza outbreaks, but it has remained notable for its still unexplained virulence and the fact that it accounted for the death of an estimated 21 million people worldwide.

While we have no clear-cut evidence of a selective role for bubonic plague or influenza, this doesn't mean that one doesn't exist. The tremendous mortality that these diseases (and others) are capable of causing certainly increases the likelihood that they influenced the development of human adaptive responses in ways we haven't yet discovered.

The Continuing Impact of Infectious Disease

It's important to understand that humans and pathogens exert selective pressures on each other, creating a dynamic relationship between disease organisms and their human (and non-human) hosts. Just as disease exerts selective pressures on host populations to adapt, microorganisms also evolve and adapt to various pressures exerted on them by their hosts.

Evolutionarily speaking, it's to the advantage of any pathogen not to be so deadly that it kills its host too quickly.

pathogens Any agents, especially microorganisms such as viruses, bacteria, or fungi, that infect a host and cause disease.

pandemic An infectious disease epidemic that spreads rapidly through a region, potentially worldwide. A worldwide pandemic becomes much more likely if the disease is "new" to humans (i.e., all populations are vulnerable), spreading quickly owing to rapid means of intercontinental transportation.

virulence A measure of the severity of an infectious disease. Generally, the more virulent a disease, the greater number of deaths of infected people.

If the host dies shortly after becoming infected, the virus or bacterium may not have time to reproduce and infect other hosts. Thus, selection sometimes acts to produce resistance in host populations and/or to reduce the virulence of disease organisms, to the benefit of both. However, members of populations exposed for the first time to a new disease frequently die in huge numbers. This type of exposure was a major factor in the decimation of indigenous New World populations after Europeans introduced smallpox into Native American groups.

Influenza is a contagious respiratory disease caused by various strains of virus. Like HIV, it is a zoonotic disease, and it has probably killed more humans than any other infectious disease. There were two flu pandemics in the twentieth century; the first of these, already mentioned, killed millions of people in 1918. Moreover, "seasonal flu," which comes around every year, killed 36,000 people annually in the United States during the 1990s (Centers for Disease Control, 2009). Worldwide, it accounts for several hundred thousand deaths every year.

The influenza viruses that infect humans are initially acquired through contact with domestic pigs and fowl (**Fig. 4-12**). For this reason, influenza is frequently referred to as swine or avian (bird) flu, depending on which species transmitted it to humans. In 2009, a new swine flu virus called H1N1 caused great fear of another pandemic, partly because it caused more severe illness in younger people than most flu viruses.

Because swine flu epidemics are less frequent than the seasonal avian flu, people have less resistance when confronted with a "new" swine flu virus. Swine flu can also be more deadly, and health professionals are always mindful of, and haunted by, the memory of the catastrophic 1918 pandemic. For all these reasons, health professionals worldwide mobilized an enormous effort in 2009 to prepare for a new swine flu pandemic. Hundreds of millions of doses of vaccine were prepared and distributed, and

in the United States alone, more than 100 million doses were made available.

The H1N1 flu epidemic proved not to be as severe as originally feared. By mid-November 2009, about 50 million Americans had been infected (Reinberg, 2009), but most cases were mild. Still, health officials are always on the alert for the possibility of an influenza pandemic, partly because of the ever-present danger presented by close contact between humans, pigs, and domestic fowl.

Until the twentieth century, infectious disease was the number one cause of death in all human populations. Even today, in many developing countries, as much as half of all mortality is due to infectious disease, compared with only about 10 percent in the United States. For example, there are an estimated 1 million deaths due to malaria every year. That figure computes to one malaria-related death every 30 seconds (Weiss, 2002)! Ninety percent of these deaths occur in sub-Saharan Africa, where 5 percent of children die of malaria before age 5 (Greenwood and Mutabingwa, 2002; Weiss, 2002). In the United States and other industrialized nations, with improved living conditions, better sanitation, and the widespread use of antibiotics since the 1940s, infectious disease has given way to heart disease and cancer as the leading causes of death.

Optimistic predictions held that infectious disease would one day be a thing of the past. You may be surprised to learn that in the United States, mortality due to infectious disease has actually increased in recent years (Pinner et al., 1996). This increase may partly be due to the overuse of antibiotics. It's estimated that half of all antibiotics prescribed in the United States are used to treat viral conditions such as colds and flu. Not only is such misuse of antibiotics useless, it actually has dangerous long-term consequences. There's considerable concern in the biomedical community over the indiscriminate use of antibiotics since the 1950s. Antibiotics have exerted selective pressures on bacterial species that have, over time, evolved antibiotic-resistant strains

Figure 4-12

This woman, selling chickens in a Chinese market, is wearing a scarf over her nose and mouth in an attempt to protect herself from exposure to avian flu.

© Hoang Dinh Nam / AFP / Getty Images

(an excellent example of natural selection). So in the past few years, we've seen the reemergence of many bacterial diseases, including, pneumonia, cholera, and tuberculosis, in forms that are less responsive to treatment.

Tuberculosis is now listed as the world's leading killer of adults by the World Health Organization (Colwell, 1996). In fact, the number of TB cases has risen 28 percent worldwide since the mid-1980s, with an estimated 10 million people infected in the United States alone. Although not all infected people develop active disease, in the 1990s an estimated 30 million persons worldwide are believed to have died from TB. One very troubling aspect of the increase in tuberculosis infection is that new strains of *Mycobacterium tuberculosis* are resistant to many antibiotics and other treatments.

Various treatments for nonbacterial conditions have also become ineffective.

One such example is the appearance of chloroquin-resistant malaria, which has rendered chloroquin (the traditional preventive medication) virtually useless in some parts of Africa. And many insect species have also developed resistance to commonly used pesticides.

Fundamental to all these factors is human population growth. As it continues to soar, it causes more environmental disturbance and, through additional human activity, increased global warming. Moreover, in developing countries, where as much as 50 percent of mortality is due to infectious disease, overcrowding and unsanitary conditions increasingly contribute to increased rates of communicable illness. It's hard to conceive of a better set of circumstances for the appearance and spread of communicable disease, and it remains to be seen if scientific innovation and medical technology will be able to meet the challenge.

Summary of Main Topics

▶ Physically visible traits, traditionally used in attempts to classify humans into clearly defined groups ("races"), have emphasized such features as skin color, hair color, hair form, head shape, and nose shape.

▶ However, all of these physical characteristics are not only influenced by several genetic loci but are also modified by the environment. As a result, these traditional markers of race aren't reliable indicators of genetic relationships, and they're not biologically useful in depicting patterns of human diversity.

▶ Since the 1990s, the development and rapid application of comparative genomics have drastically expanded genetic data. Current population studies are aimed at reconstructing the microevolutionary population history of our species and understanding the varied roles of natural selection, genetic drift, gene flow, and mutation.

▶ For humans, culture also plays a crucial evolutionary role. Interacting with biological influences, these factors define the distinctive biocultural nature of human evolution. Two excellent examples of recent human biocultural evolution relate to resistance to malaria (involving the sickle-cell allele) and lactase persistence.

▶ Another major focus of modern human biological studies concerns adaptation. Skin color variation is one characteristic that is investigated to understand how it has evolved in different populations and the role of natural selection balancing the effects of UV radiation and the requirements for adequate production of vitamin D.

▶ Other well-documented examples of modern human adaptation include adaptations to heat, cold, and high altitude.

▶ Cultural innovations and contact with nonhuman animals have increased the spread of many infectious diseases, including HIV/AIDS, influenza, and malaria.

Critical Thinking Questions

1. Imagine you overhear some friends talking about variation and how many races there are. One person says that there are three, and another thinks that there are five. Would you agree with either one? Why or why not?

2. For the same group of friends in question 1 (none of whom have had a course in biological anthropology), how would you explain how scientific knowledge doesn't support their preconceived notions about human races?

3. In the twentieth century, how did the scientific study of human diversity change from the more traditional approach?

4. Do you think that infectious disease has played an important role in human evolution? Do you think it plays a *current* role in human adaptation? Explain.

5. How have human cultural practices influenced the patterns of infectious disease seen today? Provide as many examples as you can, including some not discussed in this chapter.

Heredity and Evolution

CHAPTER 5

Macroevolution: Processes of Vertebrate and Mammalian Evolution

LEARNING OBJECTIVES

After you have mastered the material in this chapter, you will be able to:

▶ Compare microevolution and macroevolution and explain how they are similar and how they differ.

▶ Describe how animals are classified and explain how humans fit into such classification as vertebrates and as mammals.

▶ Explain why evolutionary relationships are the basis for all scientific biological classifications.

▶ Explain what a fossil is and describe how different kinds of fossils are formed.

▶ Define the major characteristics of mammals, especially placental mammals.

▶ Explain how species are defined by biologists and how they originate from prior species.

Many people think that paleontology is a pretty dreary subject and only interesting to overly serious academics. But have you ever been to a natural history museum—or perhaps to one of the larger, more elaborate toy stores? If so, you may have seen a full-size mockup of *Tyrannosaurus rex*, one that might even have moved its head and arms and screamed threateningly. These displays are usually encircled by enthralled adults and flocks of noisy, excited children. These onlookers, however, show almost no interest in the display cases containing fossils of early marine organisms. And yet, every trace of early life has a fascinating story to tell.

The study of the history of life on earth is full of mystery and adventure. The bits and pieces of fossils are the remains of once living, breathing animals (some of them extremely large and dangerous). Searching for these fossils in remote corners of the globe, from the Gobi Desert in Mongolia, to the rocky outcrops of Madagascar, to the badlands of South Dakota, is not a task for the faint of heart. Piecing together the tiny clues and ultimately reconstructing what *Tyrannosaurus rex* or a small, 50-million-year-old primate looked like and how it might have behaved is really much like detective work. Sure, it can be serious; but it's also a lot of fun.

In this chapter, we'll look back at the very ancient roots of human evolution. We are a primate, which, in turn is one type of mammal; what's more, mammals are one of the major groups of vertebrates. It's important to understand these more general aspects of evolutionary history so that we can place our species in its proper biological context. *Homo sapiens* is only one of millions of species that have evolved. More than that, people have been around for just an instant in the vast expanse of time that life has existed, and we want to know where we fit in this long and complex story of life on earth.

In this chapter, we emphasize concepts relating to large-scale evolutionary processes—that is, *macroevolution* (in contrast to the microevolutionary focus of Chapter 4). The fundamental perspectives reviewed here concern geological history, principles of classification, and the nature of evolutionary change. These perspectives will serve as a basis for topics covered throughout much of the remainder of this book.

How We Connect: Discovering the Human Place in the Organic World

There are millions of species living today; if we were to include microorganisms, the total would likely exceed tens of millions. And if we added in the multitudes of species that are now extinct, the total would be staggering—perhaps *hundreds* of millions! Where do we fit in, and what types of evidence do scientists use to answer this question?

Firstly, biologists need to develop methods to deal scientifically with all this diversity. One way to do this is to develop a system of **classification** that organizes diversity into categories and, at the same time, indicates evolutionary relationships.

Multicellular organisms that move about and ingest food are called animals (**Fig. 5-1**). Within the kingdom Animalia, there are more than 20 major groups called *phyla* (*sing.*, phylum). **Chordata** is one of these phyla, and it includes all animals with a nerve cord, gill slits (at some stage of development), and a supporting cord along the back. In turn, most (but not all) chordates are **vertebrates**—so called because they have a vertebral column. Vertebrates also have a developed brain and paired sensory structures for sight, smell, and balance.

The vertebrates themselves are subdivided into five classes: cartilaginous fishes, bony fishes, amphibians, reptiles/birds, and mammals. We'll discuss mammalian classification later in this chapter.

By putting organisms into increasingly narrow groupings, this arrangement organizes diversity into categories. It also makes statements about evolutionary and genetic relationships

classification In biology, the ordering of organisms into categories, such as orders, families, and genera, to show evolutionary relationships.

Chordata The phylum of the animal kingdom that includes vertebrates.

vertebrates Animals with segmented, bony spinal columns; includes fishes, amphibians, reptiles (including birds), and mammals.

Figure 5-1

In this classification chart, modified from Linnaeus, all animals are placed in certain categories based on structural similarities. Not all members of categories are shown; for example, there are up to 20 orders of placental mammals (8 are depicted). Chapter 6 presents a more comprehensive classification of the primate order.

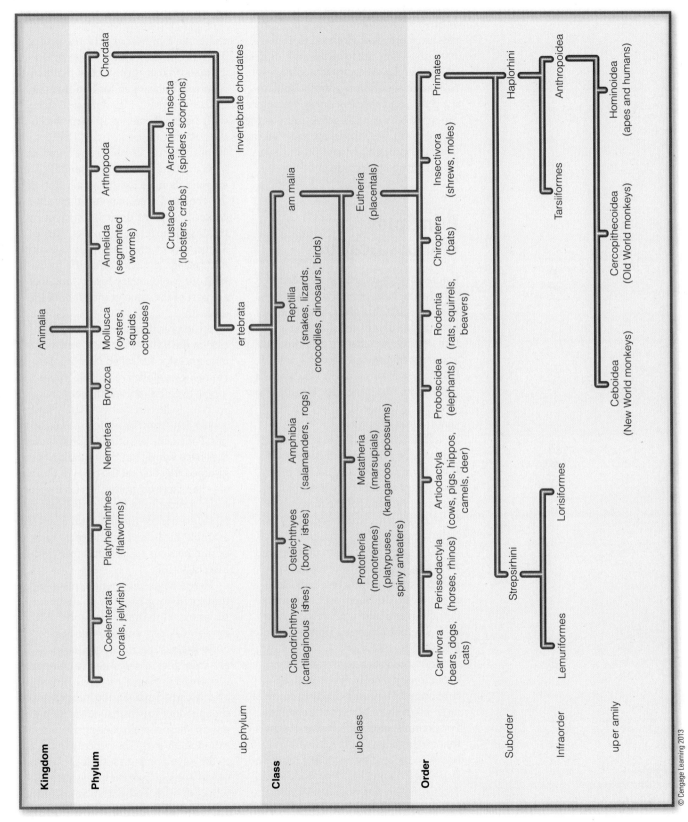

between species and groups of species. Further dividing mammals into orders makes the statement that, for example, all carnivores (Carnivora) are more closely related to each other than they are to any species placed in another order. Consequently, bears, dogs, and cats are more closely related to each other than they are to cattle, pigs, or deer (Artiodactyla). At each succeeding level (suborder, superfamily, family, subfamily, genus, and species), finer distinctions are made between categories until, at the species level, only those animals that can potentially interbreed and produce viable offspring are included.

Principles of Classification

Before we go any further, we need to discuss the basis of animal classification. The field that specializes in establishing the rules of classification is called *taxonomy*. Organisms are classified first, and most traditionally, according to their physical similarities. This was the basis of the first systematic classification devised by Linnaeus in the eighteenth century (see Chapter 2).

Today, basic physical similarities are still considered a good starting point. But for similarities to be useful, they *must* reflect evolutionary descent. For example, the bones of the forelimb of those vertebrates whose ancestors initially adapted to terrestrial (land) environments are so similar in number and form (**Fig. 5-2**) that the obvious explanation for the striking resemblance is that all four kinds of these "four-footed" (tetrapod) animals ultimately derived their forelimb structure from a common ancestor.

How could such seemingly major evolutionary modifications in structure occur? They quite likely began with only relatively minor genetic changes. For example, molecular research shows that forelimb development in all vertebrates is directed by just a few regulatory genes (Shubin et al., 1997; Riddle and Tabin, 1999). A few mutations in certain *Hox* genes in early vertebrates led to the

basic limb plan seen in all subsequent vertebrates, including us. With additional small mutations in these genes or in the genes they regulate, the varied structures that make up the wing of a chicken, the flipper of a porpoise, or the upper limb of a human developed. You should recognize that *basic* genetic regulatory mechanisms are highly conserved in animals; that is, they've been maintained relatively unchanged for hundreds of millions of years. Like a musical score with a basic theme, small variations on the pattern can produce the different "tunes" that differentiate one organism from another. This is the essential genetic foundation for most macroevolutionary change. Large anatomical modifications, therefore, don't always require major genetic rearrangements. This is a crucial point and shows how we connect biologically with other life-forms—how our evolutionary history and theirs are part of the same grand story of life on earth.

Structures that are shared by species on the basis of descent from a common ancestor are called **homologies**. Homologies alone are reliable indicators of evolutionary relationship, but we have to be careful not to draw hasty conclusions from superficial similarities. For example, both birds and butterflies have wings, but they shouldn't be grouped together on the basis of this single characteristic; butterflies (as insects) differ dramatically from birds in several other, even more fundamental ways. (For example, birds have an internal skeleton, central nervous system, and four limbs; insects don't.)

Here's what's happened in evolutionary history: From quite distant ancestors, both butterflies and birds have developed wings *independently*. So their (superficial) similarities are a product of separate evolutionary responses to roughly similar functional demands. Such similarities, based on independent functional adaptation and not on shared evolutionary descent, are called **analogies**. The process that leads to the development of analogies (also called analogous structures) such as wings in birds and butterflies is termed **homoplasy**.

homologies Similarities between organisms based on descent from a common ancestor.

analogies Similarities between organisms based strictly on common function, with no assumed common evolutionary descent.

homoplasy (*homo*, meaning "same," and *plasy*, meaning "growth") The separate evolutionary development of similar characteristics in different groups of organisms..

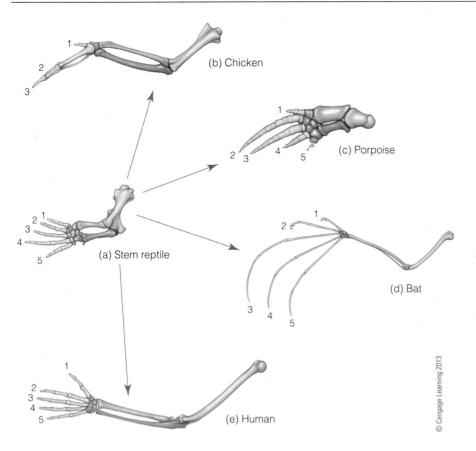

(b) Chicken

(c) Porpoise

(a) Stem reptile

(d) Bat

(e) Human

© Cengage Learning 2013

Figure 5-2

Homologies. Similarities in the forelimb bones of these land vertebrates can be most easily explained by descent from a common ancestor.

Constructing Classifications and Interpreting Evolutionary Relationships

Evolutionary biologists typically use two major approaches, or "schools," when interpreting evolutionary relationships with the goal of producing classifications. The first approach, called **evolutionary systematics**, is the more traditional. The second approach, called **cladistics**, has emerged primarily in the last three decades. While aspects of both approaches are still used by most evolutionary biologists, in recent years cladistic methodologies have predominated among anthropologists. Indeed, one noted primate evolutionist commented that "virtually all current studies of primate phylogeny involve the methods and terminology" of cladistics (Fleagle, 1999, p. 1).

Comparing Evolutionary Systematics with Cladistics

Before we begin drawing distinctions between these two approaches, it's first helpful to note features shared by both evolutionary systematics and cladistics. First, both schools are interested in tracing evolutionary relationships and constructing classifications that reflect these relationships. Second, both schools recognize that organisms must be compared using specific features (called *characters*) and that some of these characters are more informative than others. And third (deriving directly from the previous two points), both approaches focus exclusively on homologies.

But these approaches also have some significant differences—in how characters are chosen, which groups are compared, and how the results are interpreted and eventually incorporated into evolutionary schemes and classifications. The primary difference is that cladistics more explicitly and more rigorously defines the kinds of homologies

evolutionary systematics A traditional approach to classification (and evolutionary interpretation) in which presumed ancestors and descendants are traced in time by analysis of homologous characters.

cladistics An approach to classification that attempts to make rigorous evolutionary interpretations based solely on analysis of certain types of homologous characters (those considered to be derived characters).

that yield the most useful information. For example, at a very basic level, all life (except for some viruses) shares DNA as the molecule underlying all organic processes. However, beyond inferring that all life most likely derives from a single origin, the mere presence of DNA tells us nothing further regarding more specific relationships among different kinds of life-forms. To draw further conclusions, we need to look at particular characters that certain groups share as the result of more recent ancestry.

This perspective emphasizes an important point: Some homologous characters are much more informative than others. We saw earlier that all terrestrial vertebrates share homologies in the number and basic arrangement of bones in the forelimb. Even though these similarities are broadly useful in showing that these large evolutionary groups (amphibians, reptiles, and mammals) are all related through a distant ancestor, they don't provide information we can use to distinguish one group from another (a reptile from a mammal, for example). These kinds of characters (also called traits) that are shared through such remote ancestry are said to be **ancestral**, or primitive. We prefer the term *ancestral* because it doesn't reflect negatively on the evolutionary value of the character in question. In biological anthropology, the term *primitive* or *ancestral* simply means that a character seen in two organisms is inherited in both of them from a distant ancestor.

In most cases, analyzing ancestral characters doesn't supply enough information to make accurate evolutionary interpretations of relationships between different groups. In fact, misinterpretation of ancestral characters can easily lead to inaccurate evolutionary conclusions. Cladistics focuses on traits that distinguish particular evolutionary lineages; such traits are far more informative than ancestral traits. Lineages that share a common ancestor are called a **clade**, giving the name *cladistics* to the field that seeks to identify and interpret these groups.

When we try to identify a clade, the characters of interest are said to be **derived**, or **modified**. Thus, while the general ancestral bony pattern of the

forelimb in land vertebrates doesn't allow us to distinguish among them, the further modification of this pattern in certain groups (as hooves, flippers, or wings, for instance) does.

An Example of Cladistic Analysis: The Evolutionary History of Cars and Trucks

A simplified example might help clarify the basic principles used in cladistic analysis. **Figure 5-3a** shows a hypothetical "lineage" of passenger vehicles. All of the "descendant" vehicles share a common ancestor, the prototype passenger vehicle. The first major division (I) differentiates passenger cars from trucks. The second split (that is, diversification) is between luxury cars and sports cars (you could, of course, imagine many other subcategories). Modified (derived) traits that distinguish trucks from cars might include type of frame, suspension, wheel size, and, in some forms, an open cargo bed. Derived characters that might distinguish sports cars from luxury cars could include engine size and type, wheel base size, and a decorative racing stripe.

Now let's assume that you're presented with an "unknown" vehicle (meaning one not yet classified). How do you decide what kind of vehicle it is? You might note such features as four wheels, a steering wheel, and a seat for the driver, but these are *ancestral* characters (found in the common ancestor) of all passenger vehicles. If, however, you note that the vehicle lacks a cargo bed and raised suspension (so it's not a truck) but has a racing stripe, you might conclude that it's a car, and more than that, a sports car (since it has a derived feature presumably of *only* that group).

All this seems fairly obvious, and you've probably noticed that this simple type of decision making characterizes much of human mental organization. Still, we frequently deal with complications that aren't so obvious. What if you're presented with a sports utility vehicle (SUV) with a racing stripe (**Fig. 5-3b**)? SUVs are basically trucks; the presence of a racing stripe could be seen as a homoplasy with sports cars. The

ancestral Referring to characters inherited by a group of organisms from a remote ancestor and thus not diagnostic of groups (lineages) that diverged after the character first appeared; also called primitive.

clade A group of organisms sharing a common ancestor. The group includes the common ancestor and all descendants.

derived (modified) Referring to characters that are modified from the ancestral condition and thus diagnostic of particular evolutionary lineages.

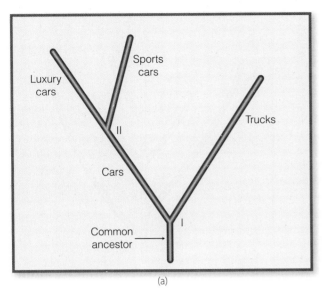

(a)

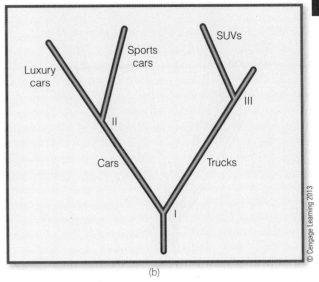

(b)

© Cengage Learning 2013

Figure 5-3

Evolutionary "trees" showing development of passenger vehicles.

lesson here is that we need to be careful, look at several traits, decide which are ancestral and which are derived, and finally try to recognize the complexity (and potential confusion) introduced by homoplasy.

Our example of passenger vehicles is useful up to a point. Because it concerns human inventions, the groupings possess characters that humans can add and delete in almost any combination. Naturally occurring organic systems are more limited in this respect. Any species can possess only those characters that have been inherited from its ancestor or that have been subsequently modified (derived) from those shared with the ancestor. So any modification in *any* species is constrained by that species' evolutionary legacy—that is, what the species starts out with.

Using Cladistics to Interpret Real Organisms

Another example, one drawn from paleontological (fossil) evidence, can help clarify these points. Most people know something about dinosaur evolution, and you may know about the recent controversies surrounding this topic. There are several intriguing issues concerning the evolutionary history of dinosaurs, and recent fossil discoveries have shed considerable light on them. Here we'll consider one of the more fascinating questions: the relationship of dinosaurs to birds.

Traditionally, it was thought that birds were a distinct group from reptiles and not especially closely related to any of them (including extinct forms, such as the dinosaurs; **Fig. 5-4a**). Still, the early origins of birds were clouded in mystery and have been much debated for more than a century. In fact, the first fossil evidence of a very primitive bird (now known to be about 150 million years old) was discovered in 1861, just two years following Darwin's publication of *Origin of Species*. Despite some initial and quite remarkably accurate interpretations linking these early birds to dinosaurs, most experts concluded that there was no close relationship. This view persisted through most of the twentieth century, but discoveries made in the last two decades have supported the hypothesis that birds *are* closely related to some dinosaurs. Two developments in particular have influenced this change of opinion: some remarkable discoveries in the 1990s from China, Madagascar, and elsewhere and the application of cladistic methods to the interpretation of these and other fossils. (Here is another example of how new discoveries as well as new approaches can become the basis for changing hypotheses.)

Recent finds from Madagascar of chicken-sized, primitive birds dated to 70–65 mya* show an elongated second toe (similar, in fact, to that seen in the

_____

* mya = million years ago

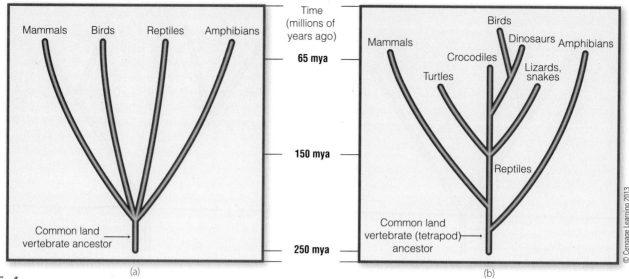

Figure 5-4

Evolutionary relationships of birds and dinosaurs. **(a)** Traditional view, showing no close relationship. **(b)** Revised view, showing common ancestry of birds and dinosaurs.

dinosaur *Velociraptor*, made infamous in the film *Jurassic Park*). Indeed, these primitive birds from Madagascar show many other similarities to *Velociraptor* and its close cousins. Even more extraordinary finds have been unearthed recently in China, where the traces of what were once *feathers* have been found embossed in fossilized sediments! For many researchers, these new finds have finally solved the mystery of bird origins (**Fig. 5-4b**), leading them to conclude that "birds are not only *descended* from dinosaurs, they *are* dinosaurs (and reptiles)—just as humans are mammals, even though people are as different from other mammals as birds are from other reptiles" (Padian and Chiappe, 1998, p. 43).

There are some doubters who remain concerned that the presence of feathers in dinosaurs (145–125 mya) might simply be a homoplasy (that is, dinosaurs may have developed the trait independently from its appearance in birds). Certainly, the possibility of homoplasy must always be considered, as it can add considerably to the complexity of what seems like a straightforward evolutionary interpretation. Indeed, strict cladistic analysis assumes that homoplasy is not a common occurrence; if it were, perhaps no evolutionary interpretation could be very straightforward! When we discuss our own more recent evolutionary lineage (the hominins, beginning in Chapter 9), we'll see that possible homoplasy can really mess up any simple interpretation. Fortunately, in the case of

the proposed relationship between some dinosaurs and birds, the presence of feathers looks like an excellent example of a **shared derived** characteristic, which therefore *does* link the forms. What's more, cladistic analysis emphasizes that several characteristics should be examined, because homoplasy might muddle an interpretation based on just one or two shared traits. In the bird/dinosaur case, several other characteristics further suggest their evolutionary relationship.

One last point needs to be mentioned. Traditional evolutionary systematics illustrates the hypothesized evolutionary relationships using a *phylogeny*, more properly called a **phylogenetic tree**. Strict cladistic analysis, however, shows relationships in a **cladogram** (**Fig. 5-5**). If you examine the charts in Figures 5-4 and 5-5, you'll see some obvious differences. A phylogenetic tree incorporates the dimension of time, as shown in Figure 5-4 (you can find many other examples in this and later chapters). A cladogram doesn't indicate time; all forms (fossil and modern) are shown along one dimension. Phylogenetic trees usually attempt to make hypotheses regarding ancestor-descendant relationships (for example, some dinosaurs are ancestral to modern birds). Cladistic analysis (through cladograms) makes no attempt whatsoever to discern ancestor-descendant relationships. In fact, strict cladists are quite skeptical that the evidence really permits such specific evolutionary hypotheses to be scientifi-

shared derived Relating to specific character traits shared in common between two life-forms and considered the most useful for making evolutionary interpretations.

phylogenetic tree A chart showing evolutionary relationships as determined by evolutionary systematics. It contains a time component and implies ancestor-descendant relationships.

cladogram A chart showing evolutionary relationships as determined by cladistic analysis. It's based solely on interpretation of shared derived characters. It contains no time component and does not imply ancestor-descendant relationships.

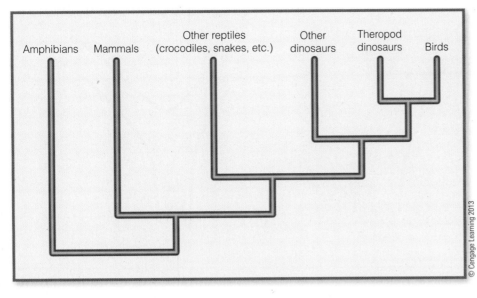

© Cengage Learning 2013

Figure 5-5

This cladogram shows the relationships of birds, dinosaurs, and other terrestrial vertebrates. Notice that there's no time scale, and both living and fossil forms are shown along the same dimension—that is, ancestor-descendant relationships aren't indicated. The chart is slightly simplified, as there are other branches (not shown) within the reptiles (with birds slightly more closely related to crocodiles than to other reptiles, such as snakes and lizards).

cally confirmed (since there are many more extinct species than living ones).

In practice, most physical anthropologists (and other evolutionary biologists) use cladistic analysis to identify and assess the utility of traits and to make testable hypotheses regarding the relationships between groups of organisms. They also frequently extend this basic cladistic methodology to further hypothesize likely ancestor-descendant relationships shown relative to a time scale (that is, in a phylogenetic tree). In this way, aspects of both traditional evolutionary systematics and cladistic analysis are combined to produce a more complete picture of evolutionary history. We'll have lots to say about hominin evolutionary relationships, and we'll use this combined approach to make interpretations.

Definition of Species

Whether biologists are doing a cladistic or more traditional phylogenetic analysis, they're comparing groups of organisms—that is, different species, genera (*sing.,* genus), families, orders, and so forth. Fundamental to all these levels of classification is the most basic, the species. It's appropriate, then, to ask how biologists define species. We addressed this issue briefly in Chapters 1 and 2, where we used the most common definition, one that emphasizes interbreeding and reproductive isolation. While it's not

the only definition of species, this view, called the **biological species concept** (Mayr, 1970), is the one preferred by most biologists.

To understand what species are, you might consider how they come about in the first place—what Darwin called the "origin of species." This most fundamental of macroevolutionary processes is called **speciation**. According to the biological species concept, the way new species are first produced involves some form of isolation. Picture a single species (baboons, for example) composed of several populations distributed over a wide geographical area. Gene exchange between populations (gene flow) will be limited if a geographical barrier, such as an ocean or a large river, effectively separates these populations. This extremely important form of isolating mechanism is called *geographical isolation.*

If one baboon population (A) is separated from another baboon population (B) by a river that has changed course, individual baboons of population A won't mate with individuals from population B (**Fig. 5-6**). As time passes (perhaps hundreds or thousands of generations), genetic differences will accumulate in both populations. If population size is small, we can assume that genetic drift will also cause allele frequencies to change in both populations. And since drift is *random,* we wouldn't expect the effects to be the same. Consequently, the two populations will begin to diverge genetically.

biological species concept A depiction of species as groups of individuals capable of fertile interbreeding but reproductively isolated from other such groups.

speciation The process by which a new species evolves from an earlier species. Speciation is the most basic process in macroevolution.

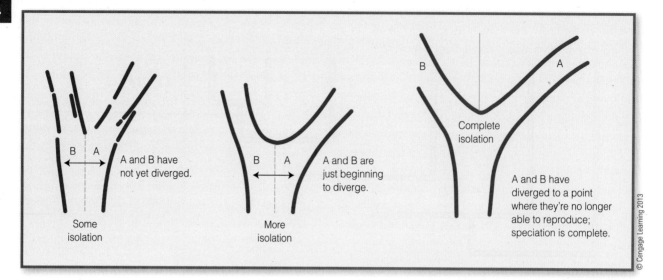

B   A   A and B have
              not yet diverged.

Some
isolation

B   A   A and B are
              just beginning
              to diverge.

More
isolation

B   A

Complete
isolation

A and B have
diverged to a point
where they're no longer
able to reproduce;
speciation is complete.

© Cengage Learning 2013

Figure 5-6

This speciation model illustrates branching evolution, or clado-genesis, which is caused by increasing reproductive isolation.

As long as gene exchange is limited, the populations can only become more genetically different over time. What's more, further difference can be expected if the baboon groups are occupying slightly different habitats. These additional genetic differences would be incorporated through the process of natural selection. Certain individuals in population A would be more reproductively fit in their own environment, but they would show less reproductive success in the environment occupied by population B. So allele frequencies will shift further, resulting in even greater divergence between the two groups.

With the cumulative effects of genetic drift and natural selection acting over many generations, the result will be two populations that—even if they were to come back into contact—could no longer interbreed. More than just geographical isolation might now apply. There may, for instance, be behavioral differences that interfere with courtship—what we call *behavioral isolation*. Using our *biological* definition of species, we would now recognize two distinct species where initially only one existed.

Interpreting Species and Other Groups in the Fossil Record

Throughout much of this text, we'll be using various taxonomic terms to refer to fossil primates (including fos-

sil hominins). You'll be introduced to such names as *Proconsul, Sivapithecus, Australopithecus,* and *Homo.* (Of course, *Homo* is still a living primate.) But it's especially difficult to make these types of designations from remains of animals that are long dead (and only partially preserved as skeletal remains). In these contexts, what do such names mean in evolutionary terms?

Our goal when applying species, genus, or other taxonomic labels to groups of organisms is to make meaningful biological statements about the variation that's represented. When looking at populations of living or long-extinct animals, we certainly are going to see variation; this happens in *any* sexually reproducing organism as a result of recombination (see Chapter 3). Each individual organism is a unique combination of genetic material, and the uniqueness is often reflected to some extent in the phenotype.

Besides such *individual variation,* we see other kinds of systematic variation in all biological populations. *Age changes* alter overall body size, as well as shape, in many mammals. One pertinent example for fossil human and ape studies is the change in number, size, and shape of teeth from deciduous (also known as baby or milk) teeth (only 20 teeth are present) to the permanent dentition (32 are present). It would be an obvious error to distinguish two fossil forms based solely on such age-dependent criteria. If one individual were represented just by milk teeth and another (seemingly very different) individual were represented just by adult teeth, they easily could be different-aged individuals from the *same* population. Researchers dealing with fragmentary remains must be alert to variation of this sort. Otherwise, they might mistakenly assume that fragments from a 2-year-old are from a different species than the mother!

Variation due to sex also plays an important role in the differences observed among individuals in biological populations. Differences in physical characteristics between males and females of the same species, called **sexual dimorphism**, can result in marked variation in body size and proportions in adults of the same species (we'll discuss this important topic in more detail in Chapter 6).

Recognizing Fossil Species

Keeping in mind all the types of variation present within interbreeding groups of organisms, the minimum biological category we'd like to define in fossil primate samples is the *species*. As already defined (according to the biological species concept), a species is a group of interbreeding or potentially interbreeding organisms that is reproductively isolated from other such groups. In modern organisms, this concept is theoretically testable by observations of reproductive behavior. In animals long extinct, such observations are obviously impossible. Our only way, then, to get a handle on the variation we see in fossil groups is to refer to living animals.

When studying a fossil group, we may observe obvious variation, such as some individuals being larger and with bigger teeth than others. The question then becomes: What's the biological significance of this variation? Two possibilities come to mind. Either the variation is accounted for by individual, age, and sex differences seen *within* every biological species (that is, it is **intraspecific**), or the variation represents differences between reproductively isolated groups (that is, it is **interspecific**). How do we decide which answer is correct? To do this, we have to look at contemporary species.

If the amount of variation we observe in fossil samples is comparable to that seen today *within species of closely related forms*, then we shouldn't "split" our sample into more than one species. We must, however, be careful in choosing modern analogues, because rates of evolution vary among different groups of mammals. So, for example, when studying extinct fossil primates, we need to compare them with well-known modern primates. Even so, studies of living groups show that defining exactly where species boundaries begin and end is often difficult. In dealing with extinct species, the uncertainties are even greater. In addition to the overlapping patterns of variation *spatially* (over space), variation also occurs *temporally* (through time). In other words, even more variation will be seen in **paleospecies**, since individuals may be separated by thousands or even millions of years. Applying a strict Linnaean taxonomy to such a situation presents an unavoidable dilemma. Standard Linnaean classification, as used by biologists, is designed to take into account the variation present at any given time; that is, it describes a static situation. But when we deal with paleospecies, the time frame is expanded and the situation can be dynamic (in other words, later forms might be different from earlier forms). In such a dynamic situation, taxonomic decisions (where to draw species boundaries) will unavoidably be somewhat arbitrary.

Because the task of interpreting paleospecies is so difficult, paleoanthropologists have sought various solutions. Most researchers today define species using clusters of derived traits (identified cladistically). But owing to the ambiguity of how many derived characters are required to identify a fully distinct species (as opposed to a subspecies), the frequent mixing of characters into novel combinations, and the always difficult problem of homoplasy, there continues to be disagreement. A good deal of the dispute is driven by philosophical orientation. Exactly how much diversity should we expect among fossil primates, especially among fossil hominins?

Some researchers, called "splitters," claim that speciation occurred frequently during hominin evolution, and they often identify numerous fossil hominin species in a sample being studied. As the

sexual dimorphism Differences in physical characteristics between males and females of the same species. For example, humans are slightly sexually dimorphic for body size, with males being taller, on average, than females of the same population. Sexual dimorphism is very pronounced in many species, such as gorillas.

intraspecific Within species; refers to variation seen within the same species.

interspecific Between species; refers to variation beyond that seen within the same species to include additional aspects seen between two or more different species.

paleospecies Species defined from fossil evidence, often covering a long time span.

nickname suggests, these scientists are inclined to split groups into many species. Others, called "lumpers," assume that speciation was less common and see much variation as being intraspecific. These scientists lump groups together, so that fewer hominin species are identified, named, and eventually plugged into evolutionary schemes. As you'll see in the following chapters, debates of this sort pervade paleoanthropology, perhaps more than in any other branch of evolutionary biology.

Recognizing Fossil Genera

The next and broader level of taxonomic classification, the **genus** (*pl.*, genera), presents another challenge for biologists. To have more than one genus, we obviously must have at least two species (reproductively isolated groups), and the species of one genus must differ in a basic way from the species of another genus. A genus is therefore defined as a group of species composed of members more closely related to each other than they are to species from any other genus.

Grouping species into genera can be quite subjective and is often much debated by biologists. One possible test for contemporary animals is to check for results of hybridization between individuals of different species—rare in nature, but quite common in captivity. If members of two normally separate species interbreed and produce live (though not necessarily fertile) offspring, the two parental species probably are not too different genetically and should therefore be grouped in the same genus. A well-known example of such a cross is horses with donkeys (*Equus caballus* × *Equus asinus*), which normally produces live but sterile offspring (mules).

As previously mentioned, we can't perform breeding experiments with extinct animals, which is why another definition of genus becomes highly relevant. Species that are members of the same genus share the same broad adaptive zone. An adaptive zone represents a general ecological lifestyle more basic than the narrower **ecological niche** characteristic of individual species. This ecological definition of genus can be an immense aid in interpreting

fossil primates. Teeth are the most frequently preserved parts, and they often can provide excellent general ecological inferences. Cladistic analysis also helps scientists to make judgments about evolutionary relationships. That is, members of the same genus should all share derived characters not seen in members of other genera.

As a final comment, we should stress that classification by genus is not always a straightforward decision. For instance, in emphasizing the very close genetic similarities between humans (*Homo sapiens*) and chimpanzees (*Pan troglodytes*), some current researchers (Wildman et al., 2003) place both in the same genus (*Homo sapiens, Homo troglodytes*). This philosophy has caused some to support extending basic human rights to great apes (as proposed by members of the Great Ape Project). Such thinking might startle you. Of course, when it gets this close to home, it's often difficult to remain objective!

What Are Fossils and How Do They Form?

Much of what we know about the history of life comes from studying **fossils**. Fossils are traces of ancient organisms and can be formed in many ways. The oldest fossils found thus far date back to more than 3 billion years ago; because they are the remains of microorganisms, they are extremely small and are called *microfossils*.

These very early traces of life are fragile and very rare. Most of our evidence comes from later in time and usually in the form of pieces of shells, bones, or teeth, all of which, even in a living animal, were already partly made of mineral. After the organism died, these "hard" tissues were further impregnated with other minerals, being eventually transformed into a stone-like composition in a process called **mineralization** (**Fig. 5-7**).

There are, however, many other ways in which life-forms have left traces of their existence. Sometimes insects were trapped in tree sap, which later became hardened and chemically

genus (*pl.*, genera) A group of closely related species.

ecological niche The position of a species within its physical and biological environments. A species' ecological niche is defined by such components as diet, terrain, vegetation, type of predators, relationships with other species, and activity patterns, and each niche is unique to a given species. Together, ecological niches make up an ecosystem.

fossils Traces or remnants of organisms found in geological beds on the earth's surface.

mineralization The process in which parts of animals (or some plants) become transformed into stone-like structures. Mineralization usually occurs very slowly as water carrying minerals, such as silica or iron, seeps into the tiny spaces within a bone. In some cases, the original minerals within the bone or tooth can be completely replaced, molecule by molecule, with other minerals.

(a)

(b)

(c)

(c)

(d)

Figure 5-7

Examples of mineralized fossils.
(a) A mineralized snake caste from geological deposits in Wyoming (dated to about 50 mya).
(b) A fossil dragonfly from Brazil, dated to more than 100 mya. (c) An early primate skull from Egypt, dated to about 30 mya. (d) A fossil fish (a relative of the piranha) from the same deposits as the snake above (also dated to approximately 50 mya). (e) A nautilus, a relative of living snails. (f) A fossilized skull of a hominin from East Africa, dated to 2.5 mya.

(e)

altered. Because there was little or no oxygen inside the hardened amber, the insects have remained remarkably well preserved for millions of years, even with soft tissue and DNA still present (**Fig. 5-8**). This fascinating circumstance led author Michael Crichton to conjure the events depicted in the novel (and motion picture) *Jurassic Park*.

Dinosaur footprints as well as much more recent hominin tracks, leaf imprints in hardened mud or similar impressions of small organisms,

and even the traces of dinosaur feathers—all of these are fossils. Recently, beautifully preserved dinosaur feathers have been discovered in northeastern China (dated to approximately 125 mya). These remains are so superbly preserved that even microscopic cell structures have been identified. These tiny structures directly influenced feather color in ancient dinosaurs; what's more, these same structures influence feather color in modern birds. Researchers are now able to deduce that

Kazuo Unno / Minden Pictures

Figure 5-8

A spider fossilized in amber.

some stripes in the feathers of one dinosaur were chestnut/reddish brown in color (Zhang et al., 2010)!

A spectacular discovery of a 47-million-year-old early primate fossil was widely publicized in 2009. This fossil is remarkable, preserving more than 95 percent of the skeleton as well as outlines of soft tissue and even fossilized remains of digestive tract contents (see Chapter 9) (Franzen et al., 2009). The amazing preservation of this small primate occurred because it died on the edge of a volcanic lake and was quickly covered with sediment. It reminds us that whether a dead animal will become fossilized and how much of it will be preserved depend partly on *how* it dies, but even more on *where* it dies.

Some ancient organisms have left vast amounts of fossil remains. Indeed, limestone deposits can be hundreds of feet thick and are largely made up of fossilized remains of marine shellfish. (see Chapter 2).

Fossils of land animals are not nearly so common. After an animal dies—let's say it's an early hominin from 2 mya—it will probably be eaten and its bones scattered and broken, and eventually they will decompose. After just a few weeks, there will be hardly anything left to fossilize. But suppose, by chance, this recently deceased hominin became quickly covered by sediment, perhaps by sand and mud in a streambed or along a lakeshore or by volcanic ash from a nearby volcano. As a result, the long, slow

process of mineralization may eventually turn at least some parts of the hominin into a fossil.

The study of how bones and other materials come to be buried in the earth and preserved as fossils is called **taphonomy**. Among the topics that taphonomists try to understand are processes of sedimentation, including the action of streams, preservation properties of bone, and carnivore disturbance factors.

Vertebrate Evolutionary History: A Brief Summary

Besides the staggering array of living and extinct life-forms, biologists must also contend with the vast amount of time that life has been evolving on earth. Again, scientists have devised simplified schemes—but in this case to organize *time*, not biological diversity.

Geologists have formulated the **geological time scale** (**Fig. 5-9**), in which immense time spans are organized into eras that include one or more periods. Periods, in turn, can be broken down into epochs. For the time span encompassing vertebrate evolution, there are three eras: the Paleozoic, the Mesozoic, and the Cenozoic. The earliest vertebrate fossils date to early in the Paleozoic at 500 mya, and their origins are probably much older. It's the vertebrate capacity to form bone that accounts for their more complete fossil record *after* 500 mya.

During the Paleozoic, several varieties of fishes (including the ancestors of modern sharks and bony fishes), amphibians, and reptiles appeared. At the end of the Paleozoic, close to 250 mya, several varieties of mammal-like reptiles were also diversifying. It's generally thought that some of these forms gave rise to the mammals.

The evolutionary history of vertebrates and other organisms during the Paleozoic and Mesozoic was profoundly influenced by geographical events. We know that the positions of the earth's continents have dramatically shifted during the last several hundred million years. This process, called **continental drift**, is explained by the geological the-

taphonomy The study of how bones and other materials come to be buried in the earth and preserved as fossils.

geological time scale The organization of earth history into eras, periods, and epochs; commonly used by geologists and paleoanthropologists.

continental drift The movement of continents on sliding plates of the earth's surface. As a result, the positions of large landmasses have shifted drastically during the earth's history.

Figure 5-9

Geological time scale.

	570 mya	500 mya	430 mya	395 mya	345 mya	280 mya	225 mya	190 mya	136 mya	65 mya	0 mya

ERA

PRE-CAMBRIAN	PALEOZOIC	MESOZOIC	CENOZOIC

PERIOD

	Cambrian 570		Silurian 430		Carboniferous 345		Triassic 225		Cretaceous 136	
		Ordovician 500		Devonian 395		Permian 280		Jurassic 190		

EPOCH

Holocene 0.01
Pleistocene 1.8
Pliocene 5
Miocene 23
Oligocene 33
Eocene 56
Paleocene 65

Major extinction event

Major extinction event

© Cengage Learning 2013

ory of *plate tectonics*, which states that the earth's crust is a series of gigantic moving and colliding plates. Such massive geological movements can induce volcanic activity (as, for example, all around the Pacific Rim), mountain building (for example, the Himalayas), and earthquakes. Living on the juncture of the Pacific and North American plates, residents of the Pacific coast of the United States are very much aware of some of these consequences, as illustrated by the explosive volcanic eruption of Mt. St. Helens and the frequent earthquakes in Alaska and California.

While reconstructing the earth's physical history, geologists have determined the earlier positions of major continental landmasses. During the late Paleozoic, the continents came together to form a single colossal landmass called *Pangea*. During the early Mesozoic, the southern continents began to split off from Pangea, forming a large southern landmass called *Gondwanaland* (**Fig. 5-10a**). Similarly, the northern continents were consolidated into a northern landmass called *Laurasia*. During the Mesozoic, Gondwanaland and Laurasia continued to drift apart and

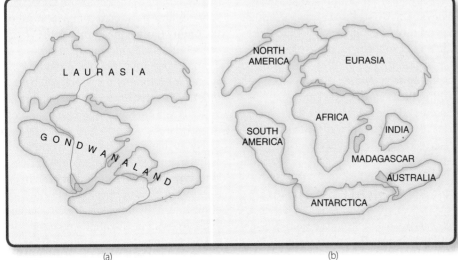

(a)   (b)

Figure 5-10

Continental drift. (a) Positions of the continents during the Mesozoic (ca. 125 mya). Pangea is breaking up into a northern landmass (Laurasia) and a southern landmass (Gondwanaland). (b) Positions of the continents at the beginning of the Cenozoic (ca. 65 mya).

© Cengage Learning 2013

570 mya	500 mya	430 mya	395 mya	345 mya	
ERA					
					PALEOZOIC
PERIOD					
Cambrian	**Ordovician**	**Silurian**	**Devonian**	**Carboniferous**	
Trilobites abundant; also brachiopods, jellyfish, worms, and other invertebrates	First fishes; trilobites still abundant; graptolites and corals become plentiful; possible land plants	Jawed fishes appear; first air-breathing animals; definite land plants	Age of Fishes; first amphibians and first forests appear	First reptiles; radiation of amphibians; modern insects diversify	

Figure 5-11

This time line depicts major events in early vertebrate evolution.

to break up into smaller segments. By the end of the Mesozoic (about 65 mya), the continents were beginning to assume their current positions (**Fig. 5-10b**).

The evolutionary ramifications of this long-term continental drift were profound. Groups of animals became effectively isolated from each other by oceans, significantly influencing the distribution of mammals and other land vertebrates. These continental movements continued in the Cenozoic and indeed are still happening, although without such dramatic results.

During most of the Mesozoic, reptiles were the dominant land vertebrates, and they exhibited a broad expansion into a variety of *ecological niches*, which included aerial and marine habitats. The most famous of these highly successful Mesozoic reptiles were the dinosaurs, which themselves evolved into a wide array of sizes and species and adapted to a variety of lifestyles. (See **Fig. 5-11** for a summary of major events in early vertebrate evolutionary history.)

The Cenozoic is divided into two periods: the Tertiary, about 63 million years in duration, and the Quaternary, from about 1.8 mya up to and including the present (see Fig. 5-9). Paleontologists often refer to the next, more precise level of subdivision within the Cenozoic as the **epochs**. There are seven epochs within the Cenozoic: the Paleocene, Eocene, Oligocene, Miocene, Pliocene, Pleistocene, and Holocene, the last often referred to as the Recent epoch.

Mammalian Evolution

We can learn about mammalian evolution from fossils and from studying the DNA of living species (Bininda-

Emonds et al., 2007). Studies using both of these approaches suggest that all the living groups of mammals (that is, all the orders; see Fig. 5-1) had diverged by 75 mya. Later, only after several million years following the beginning of the Cenozoic, did the various current mammalian subgroups (that is, the particular families) begin to diversify.

Today, there are over 4,000 species of mammals, and we could call the Cenozoic the Age of Mammals. It was during this era that, along with birds, mammals replaced earlier reptiles as the dominant land-living vertebrates.

How do we account for the relatively rapid success of the mammals during the late Mesozoic and early Cenozoic? Several characteristics relating to learning and general flexibility of behavior are of prime importance. Mammals were selected for larger brains than those typically found in reptiles, making them better equipped to process information. In particular, the cerebrum became generally enlarged, especially the outer covering, the neocortex, which controls higher brain functions (**Fig. 5-12**). In some mammals, the cerebrum expanded so much that it came to comprise most of the brain volume; the number of surface convolutions also increased, creating more surface area and thus providing space for even more nerve cells (neurons). As we discuss in Chapter 6, this is a trend even further emphasized among the primates.

For such a large and complex organ as the mammalian brain to develop, a longer, more intense period of growth is required. Slower development can occur internally (*in utero*) as well as after birth. Internal fertilization and internal development aren't unique to mammals, but the latter was a major inno-

epochs Categories of the geological time scale; subdivisions of periods. In the Cenozoic era, epochs include the Paleocene, Eocene, Oligocene, Miocene, and Pliocene (from the Tertiary period) and the Pleistocene and Holocene (from the Quaternary period).

280 mya	225 mya	190 mya	136 mya	65 mya

MESOZOIC

Permian

Reptile radiation; mammal-like reptiles appear

Triassic

Reptiles further radiate; first dinosaurs; egg-laying mammals

Jurassic

Great Age of Dinosaurs; flying and swimming dinosaurs appear; first toothed birds

Cretaceous

Placental and marsupial mammals appear; first modern birds

Major extinction event

Major extinction event

© Cengage Learning 2013

vation among terrestrial vertebrates. Other forms (most fishes and reptiles—including birds) lay eggs, and "prenatal" development occurs externally, outside the mother's body. Mammals, with very few exceptions, give birth to live young. Even among mammals, however, there's considerable variation among the major groups in how mature the young are at birth; and in **placental** mammals, including ourselves, *in utero* development goes farthest.

Another distinctive feature of mammals is the dentition. While many living reptiles (such as lizards and snakes) consistently have similarly shaped teeth (called a *homodont* dentition), mammals have differently shaped teeth (**Fig. 5-13**). This varied pattern, termed a **heterodont** dentition, is reflected in the ancestral (primitive) mammalian arrangement of teeth, which includes 3 incisors, 1 canine, 4 premolars, and 3 molars in each quarter of the mouth. So, with 11 teeth in each quarter of the mouth, the ancestral

mammalian dental complement includes a total of 44 teeth. Such a heterodont arrangement allows mammals to process a wide variety of foods. Incisors are used for cutting, canines for grasping and piercing, and premolars and molars for crushing and grinding.

A final point regarding teeth relates to their disproportionate representation in the fossil record. As the hardest, most durable portion of a vertebrate skeleton, teeth have the greatest likelihood of becoming fossilized (that is, mineralized), since teeth are predominantly composed of mineral to begin with. As a result, the vast majority of available fossil data for most vertebrates, including primates, consists of teeth.

Another major adaptive complex that distinguishes contemporary mammals from reptiles (except birds) is the maintenance of a constant internal body temperature. Known colloquially (and incorrectly) as warm-bloodedness, this crucial physiological adaptation is also seen

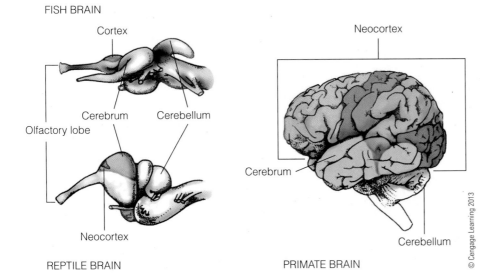

FISH BRAIN

Cortex

Cerebrum   Cerebellum

Olfactory lobe

Neocortex

REPTILE BRAIN

Neocortex

Cerebrum

Cerebellum

PRIMATE BRAIN

© Cengage Learning 2013

Figure 5-12

Lateral view of the brain in fishes, reptiles, and primates. You can see the increased size of the cerebral cortex (neocortex) of the primate brain. The cerebral cortex integrates sensory information and selects responses.

placental A type (subclass) of mammal. During the Cenozoic, placentals became the most widespread and numerous mammals and today are represented by upward of 20 orders, including the primates.

heterodont Having different kinds of teeth; characteristic of mammals, whose teeth consist of incisors, canines, premolars, and molars.

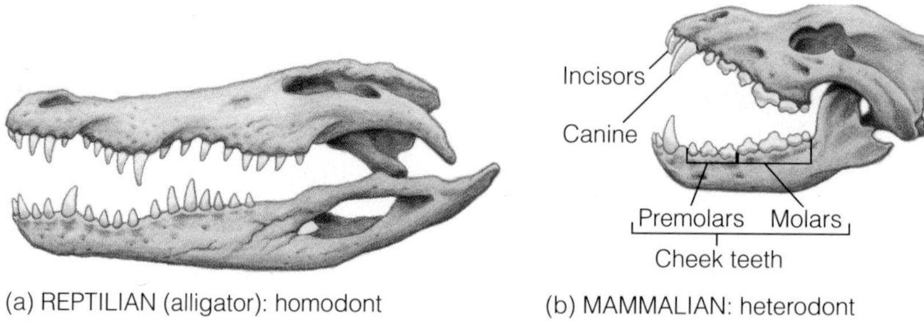

Incisors

Canine

Premolars   Molars

Cheek teeth

© Cengage Learning 2013

(a) REPTILIAN (alligator): homodont

(b) MAMMALIAN: heterodont

Figure 5-13

Reptilian and mammalian teeth.

in contemporary birds and may have characterized many dinosaurs as well. Except for birds, reptiles maintain a constant internal body temperature through exposure to the sun; these reptiles are said to be *ectothermic*. In mammals and birds, however, energy is generated *internally* through metabolic activity (by processing food or by muscle action); for this reason, mammals and birds are said to be **endothermic**.

The Emergence of Major Mammalian Groups

There are three major subgroups of living mammals: the egg-laying mammals, or monotremes; the pouched mammals, or marsupials; and the placental mammals. The monotremes, of which the platypus is one example (**Fig. 5-14**), are

Figure 5-14

A duck-billed platypus (monotreme).

© Tom McHugh / Photo Researchers, Inc.

extremely primitive and are considered more distinct from marsupials or placentals than these two subgroups are from each other. The recent sequencing of the full genome of the platypus (Warren et al., 2008) has confirmed the very ancient orgins of the monotremes and their distinctiveness from other mammals. New fossil evidence from China also shows that the evolutionary split of placental and marsupial mammals had occurred by 160 mya, considerably earlier than previously thought. This discovery of a very well-preserved placental mammal skeleton indicates that it was a small shrewlike animal well adapted to life in the trees (Luo et al., 2011). In this respect it confirms an evolutionary basis for early, primitive primates, which we'll discuss in Chapter 9.

The most notable difference between marsupials and placental mammals concerns fetal development. In marsupials, the young are born extremely immature and must complete development in an external pouch (**Fig. 5-15**). But placental mammals develop over a longer period of time in *utero*, made possible by the evolutionary development of a specialized tissue (the placenta) that provides for fetal nourishment.

With a longer gestation period, the central nervous system develops more completely in the placental fetus. What's more, after birth, the "bond of milk" between mother and young allows more time for complex neural structures to form. We should also emphasize that from a *biosocial* perspective, this dependency period not only allows for adequate physiological development but also provides for a wider range of learning stimuli. That is, a vast amount of information is channeled to the young mammalian brain through observation of the mother's behavior and through play with age-mates. It's not enough to

Figure 5-15

A wallaby with an infant in the pouch (marsupials).

© iStockphoto.com / Michael Sacco

endothermic (*endo*, meaning "within" or "internal") Able to maintain internal body temperature by producing energy through metabolic processes within cells; characteristic of mammals, birds, and perhaps some dinosaurs.

have evolved a brain capable of learning. Collateral evolution of mammalian social systems has ensured that young mammal brains are provided with ample learning opportunities and are thus put to good use.

Processes of Macroevolution

As we noted earlier, evolution operates at both microevolutionary and macroevolutionary levels. We discussed evolution primarily from a microevolutionary perspective in Chapters 3 and 4; in this chapter, our focus is on macroevolution. Macroevolutionary mechanisms operate more on the whole species than on individuals or populations, and they take much longer than microevolutionary processes to have a noticeable impact.

Adaptive Radiation

As we mentioned in Chapter 2, the potential capacity of a group of organisms to multiply is practically unlimited, but its ability to increase its numbers is regulated largely by the availability of resources (food, water, shelter, and space). As population size increases, access to resources decreases, and the environment will ultimately prove inadequate. Depleted resources induce some members of a population to seek an environment in which competition is reduced and the opportunities for survival and reproductive success are increased. This evolutionary tendency to exploit unoccupied habitats may eventually produce an abundance of diverse species.

This story has been played out countless times during the history of life, and some groups have expanded extremely rapidly. This evolutionary process, known as **adaptive radiation**, can also be seen in the divergence of the stem reptiles into the profusion of different forms of the late Paleozoic and especially those of the Mesozoic. It's a process that takes place when a life-form rapidly takes advantage, so to speak, of the many newly available ecological niches.

The principle of evolution illustrated by adaptive radiation is fairly simple, but

important. It may be stated this way: A species, or group of species, will diverge into as many variations as two factors allow. These factors are (1) its adaptive potential and (2) the adaptive opportunities of the available niches.

In the case of reptiles, there was little divergence in the very early stages of evolution, when the ancestral form was little more than one among a variety of amphibian water dwellers. Later, a more efficient egg (one that could incubate out of water) developed in reptiles; this new egg, with a hard, watertight shell, had great adaptive potential, but initially there were few zones to invade. When reptiles became fully terrestrial, however, a wide array of ecological niches became accessible to them. Once freed from their attachment to water, reptiles were able to exploit landmasses with no serious competition from any other animal. They moved into the many different ecological niches on land (and to some extent in the air and sea), and as they adapted to these areas, they diversified into a large number of species. This spectacular radiation burst forth with such evolutionary speed that it may well be termed an adaptive explosion.

Of course, the rapid expansion of placental mammals during the late Mesozoic and throughout the Cenozoic is another excellent example of adaptive radiation. The worldwide major extinction event at the end of the Cenozoic left thousands of econiches vacant as the dinosaurs became extinct. Small-bodied, mostly nocturnal mammals had been around for at least 70 million years, and once they were no longer in competition with the dinosaurs, they were free to move into previously occupied habitats. Thus, over the course of several million years, there was a major adaptive radiation of mammals as they diversified to exploit previously unavailable habitats.

Generalized and Specialized Characteristics

Another aspect of evolution closely related to adaptive radiation involves the transition from *generalized* characteristics to *specialized* characteristics. These two terms refer to the adaptive potential of a

adaptive radiation The relatively rapid expansion and diversification of life-forms into new ecological niches.

Figure 5-16

An aye-aye, a specialized primate native to Madagascar. Note the elongated middle finger, which is used to probe under bark for insects.

particular trait. A trait that's adapted for many functions is said to be generalized, while one that's limited to a narrow set of functions is said to be specialized.

For example, a generalized mammalian limb has five fairly flexible digits, adapted for many possible functions (grasping, weight support, and digging). In this respect, human hands are still quite generalized. On the other hand (or foot), there have been many structural modifications in our feet to make them suited for the specialized function of stable weight support in an upright posture.

The terms *generalized* and *specialized* are also sometimes used when speaking of the adaptive potential of whole organisms. Consider, for example, the aye-aye of Madagascar, an unusual primate spe-

cies. The aye-aye is a highly specialized animal, structurally adapted to a narrow, rodent/woodpecker-like econiche—digging holes with prominent incisors and removing insect larvae with an elongated bony finger (**Fig. 5-16**).

It's important to note that only a generalized ancestor can provide the flexible evolutionary basis for rapid diversification. Only a generalized species with potential for adaptation to varied ecological niches can lead to all the later diversification and specialization of forms into particular ecological niches.

An issue that we've already raised also bears on this discussion: the relationship of ancestral and derived characters. It's not always the case, but ancestral characters *usually* tend to be more generalized. And specialized characteristics are nearly always derived ones as well.

Summary of Main Topics

▶ To understand the large-scale evolutionary history of life on earth, two major organizing perspectives prove indispensable: (1) schemes of formal classification to organize organic diversity and (2) the geological time scale to organize geological time.

▶ There are two differing approaches to classifying and interpreting lifeforms: evolutionary systematics and cladistics.

▶ Because primates are vertebrates and, more specifically, mammals, it's important to understand how these major groups are connected to our own origins.

▶ Theoretical perspectives relating to contemporary understanding of macroevolutionary processes (especially the concepts of species and speciation) are crucial to any interpretation of long-term aspects of

evolutionary history, be it vertebrate, mammalian, or primate.

▶ Because genus and species designation is the common form of reference for both living and extinct organisms (and we use it frequently throughout the text), it's important to understand how these terms are used and their underlying biological significance.

Critical Thinking Questions

1. Remains of a fossil mammal have been found on your campus. If you adopt a cladistic approach, how would you determine (a) that it's a mammal rather than some other kind of vertebrate (discuss specific characters), (b) what kind of mammal it is (again, discuss specific characters), and (c) how it *might* be related to one or more living mammals (again, discuss specific characters)?

2. For the same fossil find (and your interpretation) in question 1, draw an interpretive figure using cladistic analysis (that is, draw a cladogram). Next, using more traditional evolutionary systematics, construct a phylogeny. Lastly, explain the differences between the cladogram and the phylogeny (be sure to emphasize the fundamental ways the two schemes differ).

3. **a.** Humans are fairly generalized mammals. What do we mean by this, and what specific features (characters) would you select to illustrate this statement?
   b. More precisely, humans are *placental* mammals. How do humans, and generally all other placental mammals, differ from the other two major groups of mammals?

CHAPTER **6**

An Overview of the Primates

© iStockphoto.com / Dmitry Rukhlenko

LEARNING OBJECTIVES

After you have mastered the material in this chapter, you will be able to:

▶ Describe the characteristics that set primates apart from other mammals.

▶ Explain how humans are anatomically and behaviorally connected to the other primates.

▶ Explain the differences between the major groupings of nonhuman primates, such as apes and monkeys.

▶ Describe some of the many challenges facing free-ranging nonhuman primates today.

Chimpanzees aren't monkeys, and neither are gorillas or orangutans. They're apes, and even though most people think that monkeys and apes are basically the same, they aren't. Yet, how many times have you seen a greeting card or magazine ad with a picture of a chimpanzee and a caption that says something like, "Don't monkey around" or "No more monkey business"? Or maybe you've seen people at zoos teasing nonhuman **primates**. While these things may seem trivial, they really aren't, because they show just how little most people know about our closest relatives. This is extremely unfortunate, because by getting to know these relatives, we can better know ourselves. Even more important, we can also try to preserve the many nonhuman primate species that are critically endangered today. Indeed, many will go extinct in the next 50 years or so if we don't act now to save them.

One way to understand any organism is to compare its anatomy and behavior with that of other, closely related species. This comparative approach helps explain how and why physiological and behavioral systems evolved as adaptive responses to various selective pressures. This statement applies to humans just as it does to any other species. So if we want to identify the components that have shaped the evolution of our species, a good starting point is to compare ourselves with our closest living relatives, the approximately 230 species of nonhuman primates (lemurs, lorises, tarsiers, monkeys, and apes).

This chapter describes the physical characteristics that define the order Primates, gives a brief overview of the major groups of living primates, and introduces some methods currently used to compare living primates genetically. (For a comparison of human and nonhuman skeletons, see Appendix A.) But before going any further, we again want to call attention to a few common misunderstandings about evolutionary processes.

Evolution is not a goal-directed process. Therefore, the fact that lemurs appeared earlier than **anthropoids** doesn't mean that lemurs "progressed" to become anthropoids. Living primates aren't in any way "superior" to their evolutionary predecessors or to one another. Consequently, when we discuss major groupings of contemporary nonhuman primates, there's no implied superiority or inferiority of any of these groups. Each lineage or species has come to possess unique qualities that make it better suited to a particular habitat and lifestyle. Lastly, you shouldn't make the mistake of thinking that contemporary primates (including humans) necessarily represent the final stage or apex of a lineage, because we all continue to evolve as lineages. Actually, the only species that represent final evolutionary stages of particular lineages are the ones that become extinct.

Primate Characteristics

All primates share many characteristics with other mammals (see Chapter 5). Some of these basic mammalian traits are body hair, a relatively long gestation period followed by live birth, mammary glands (thus the term *mammal*), different types of teeth (incisors, canines, premolars, and molars), the ability to maintain a constant internal body temperature through physiological means, or *endothermy* (see Chapter 5), increased brain size, and a considerable capacity for learning and behavioral flexibility. So, to differentiate primates as a distinct group from other mammals, we need to describe those characteristics that, taken together, set primates apart.

It isn't easy to identify single traits that define the primate order because, compared with most mammals, primates have remained quite *generalized*. This means that primates have retained several ancestral mammalian traits that some other mammals have lost over time. As we discussed in Chapter 5, some mammalian groups have become very specialized, or derived, at least with regard to some traits. For example, through the course of evolution, horses and cattle have undergone a reduction in the number of digits (fingers and toes) from the ancestral pattern of five to one and two, respectively. These species have also developed hard, protective coverings over their feet in the form of hooves

primates Members of the mammalian order Primates (pronounced "pry-may´-tees"), which includes lemurs, lorises, tarsiers, monkeys, apes, and humans.

anthropoids Members of a suborder of Primates, the infraorder Anthropoidea (pronounced "an-throw-poid´-ee-uh"). Traditionally, the suborder includes monkeys, apes, and humans.

(**Fig. 6-1a**). This limb structure is beneficial in prey species because their survival depends on speed and stability, but it restricts them to only one type of locomotion. Moreover, limb function is restricted to support and movement, and the ability to manipulate objects is completely lost.

Primates can't be defined by one or even a few traits they share in common because they *aren't* so specialized. Therefore, primatologists have drawn attention to a group of characteristics that, when taken together, more or less characterize the entire primate order. Still, these are a set of *general* tendencies that aren't all equally expressed in all primates. In addition, while some of these traits are unique to primates, many others are retained ancestral mammalian characteristics shared with other mammals. The following list is meant to give you a general anatomical and behavioral picture of the primates. In their limbs and locomotion, teeth, diet, senses, brain, and behavior, primates reflect a common evolutionary history with adaptations to similar environmental challenges, primarily as highly social, arboreal beings.

A. *Limbs and Locomotion*

1. *A tendency toward an erect posture (especially in the upper body).* All primates show this tendency to some degree, and it's variously associated with sitting, leaping, standing, and, occasionally, bipedal walking.

2. *A flexible, generalized limb structure, which allows most primates to practice various locomotor behaviors.* Primates have retained some bones (such as the clavicle, or collarbone) and certain abilities (like rotation of the forearm) that have been lost in more specialized mammals such as horses. Various aspects of hip and shoulder anatomy also provide primates with a wide range of limb movement and function. Thus, by maintaining a generalized locomotor anatomy, primates aren't restricted to one form of movement, like many other mammals. Primates also

use their limbs for many activities besides locomotion.

3. *Prehensile hands (and sometimes feet).* Many animals can manipulate objects, but not as skillfully as primates (**Fig. 6-1b**). All primates use their hands, and frequently their feet, to grasp and manipulate objects. This ability is

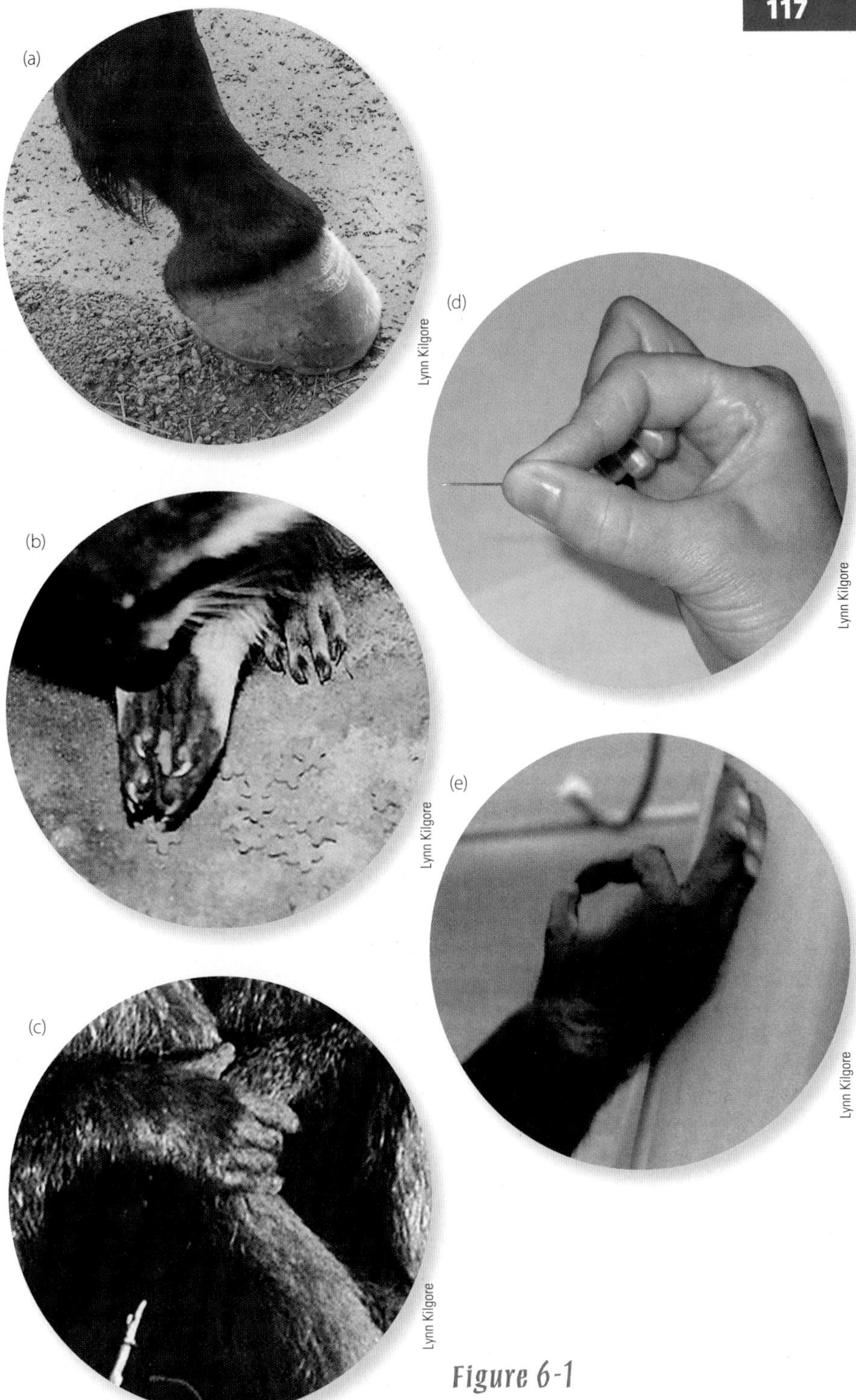

(a)

(b)

(c)

(d)

(e)

Figure 6-1

(a) A horse's front foot, homologous with a human hand, has undergone reduction from five digits to one. (b) While raccoons are capable of considerable manual dexterity and can readily pick up small objects with one hand, they have no opposable thumb. (c) Many monkeys are able to grasp objects with an opposable thumb, while others have very reduced thumbs. (d) Humans are capable of a "precision grip." (e) Chimpanzees, with their reduced thumbs, are capable of a precision grip but frequently use a modified form.

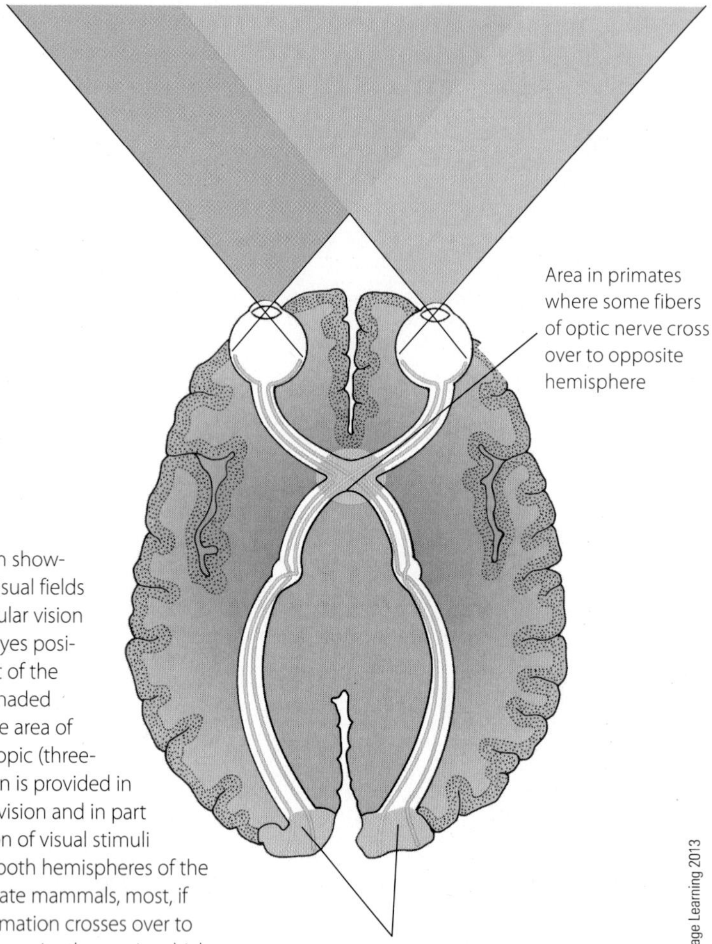

118

Figure 6-2

Simplified diagram showing overlapping visual fields that permit binocular vision in primates with eyes positioned at the front of the face. (The green shaded area represents the area of overlap.) Stereoscopic (three-dimensional) vision is provided in part by binocular vision and in part by the transmission of visual stimuli from each eye to both hemispheres of the brain. (In nonprimate mammals, most, if not all, visual information crosses over to the hemisphere opposite the eye in which it was initially received.)

Area in primates where some fibers of optic nerve cross over to opposite hemisphere

Primary receiving area for visual information

© Cengage Learning 2013

omnivorous Having a diet consisting of many food types, such as plant materials, meat, and insects.

diurnal Active during the day.

nocturnal Active during the night.

stereoscopic vision The condition whereby visual images are, to varying degrees, superimposed. This provides for depth perception, or viewing the external environment in three dimensions. Stereoscopic vision is partly a function of structures in the brain.

binocular vision Vision characterized by overlapping visual fields provided by forward-facing eyes. Binocular vision is essential to depth perception.

hemispheres The two halves of the cerebrum that are connected by a dense mass of fibers. (The cerebrum is the large rounded outer portion of the brain.)

variably expressed and is enhanced by several characteristics, including:

a. *Retention of five digits on the hands and feet.* This trait varies somewhat throughout the order, with some species having reduced thumbs or second digits (first fingers).

b. *An opposable thumb and, in most species, a divergent and partially opposable big toe.* Most primates are capable of moving the thumb so that it comes in contact with the second digit or with the palm of the hand (**Fig. 6-1c–e**).

c. *Nails instead of claws.* This characteristic is seen in all primates except some highly derived New World monkeys (marmosets and tamarins). All lemurs and lorises also have a claw on one digit.

d. *Tactile pads enriched with sensory nerve fibers at the ends of digits.* This characteristic enhances the sense of touch.

B. *Diet and Teeth*

1. *Lack of dietary specialization.* This is typical of most primates, who tend to eat a wide assortment of food items. In general, primates are **omnivorous**.

2. *A generalized dentition.* Primate teeth aren't specialized for processing only one type of food, a trait related to a general lack of dietary specialization.

C. *The senses and the brain.* Primates (**diurnal** ones in particular) rely heavily on vision and less on the sense of smell, especially compared with other mammals. This emphasis is reflected in evolutionary changes in the skull, eyes, and brain.

1. *Color vision.* This is a characteristic of all diurnal primates. **Nocturnal** primates don't have color vision.

2. *Depth perception.* Primates have **stereoscopic vision**, or the ability to perceive objects in three dimensions. This is made possible through a variety of mechanisms, including:

a. *Eyes placed toward the front of the face (not to the sides).* This position provides for overlapping visual fields, or **binocular vision** (**Fig. 6-2**).

b. *Visual information from each eye transmitted to visual centers in both **hemispheres** of the brain.* In nonprimate mammals, most optic nerve fibers cross to the opposite hemisphere through a structure at the base of the brain. In primates, about 40 percent of the fibers remain on the same side, so that both hemispheres receive much of the same information.

c. *Visual information organized into three-dimensional images by specialized structures in the brain itself.* The capacity for stereoscopic vision depends on each hemisphere of the brain

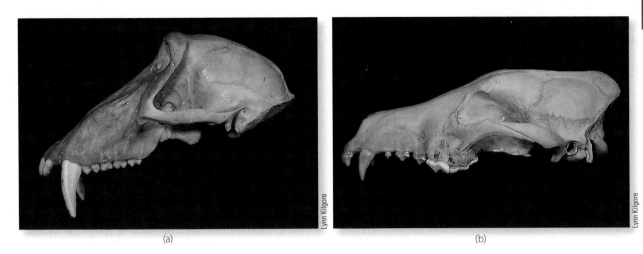

receiving visual information from both eyes and from overlapping visual fields.

3. *Decreased reliance on the sense of smell.* This trend is expressed as an overall reduction in the size of olfactory structures in the brain. Corresponding reduction of the entire olfactory apparatus has also resulted in decreased size of the snout in most species. This is related to an increased dependence on vision. Some species, such as baboons, have large muzzles, but this isn't related to **olfaction**, but rather to the need to accommodate large canine teeth (**Fig. 6-3**).

4. *Expansion and increased complexity of the brain.* This is a general trend among placental mammals,

but it's especially true of primates (**Fig. 6-4**). In primates, this expansion is most evident in the visual and association areas of the **neocortex** (portions of the brain where information from different **sensory modalities** is combined).

D. *Maturation, learning, and behavior*

1. *A more efficient means of fetal nourishment, longer periods of gestation, reduced numbers of offspring (with single births the norm), delayed maturation, and extension of the entire life span.*

2. *A greater dependence on flexible, learned behavior.* This trend is correlated with delayed maturation and longer periods of infant and child dependency on at least one parent. Because of these trends, parental investment in each

Figure 6-3

The skull of a male baboon (a) compared with that of a red wolf (b). Forward-facing eyes are positioned above the snout in baboons; but in wolves, the eyes are positioned more to the side of the face. Also, the baboon's large muzzle doesn't reflect a heavy reliance on the sense of smell as it does in the wolf. Rather, it supports the roots of the large canine teeth, which curve back through the bone for as much as 1½ inches.

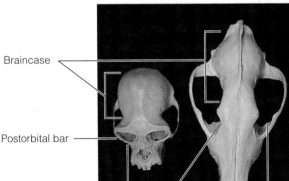

Braincase

Postorbital bar

Eye socket   No postorbital bar

Figure 6-4

The skull of a gibbon (left) compared with that of a red wolf (right). The absolute size of the gibbon braincase is slightly larger than that of the wolf, even though the wolf (at about 80 to 100 pounds) is around six times the size of the gibbon (about 15 pounds).

olfaction The sense of smell.

neocortex The more recently evolved portion of the brain that is involved in higher mental functions and composed of areas that integrate incoming information from different sensory organs.

sensory modalities Different forms of sensation (e.g., touch, pain, pressure, heat, cold, vision, taste, hearing, and smell).

offspring is increased; although fewer offspring are born, they receive more intense rearing.

3. *The tendency to live in social groups and the permanent association of adult males with the group.* Except for some nocturnal species, primates tend to associate with other individuals.

4. *The tendency toward diurnal activity patterns.* This is seen in most primates. Lorises, tarsiers, one monkey species, and some lemurs are nocturnal; all the rest (the other monkeys, apes, and humans) are diurnal.

Primate Adaptations

In this section, we consider how primate anatomical traits evolved as adaptations to environmental circumstances. It's important to remember that when you see the phrase "environmental circumstances," it refers to several interrelated variables, including climate, diet, habitat (woodland, grassland, forest, and so on), and predation.

Evolutionary Factors

Traditionally, the group of characteristics shared by primates has been explained as the result of an adaptation to **arboreal** living. While other mammals were adapting to various ground-dwelling

lifestyles and marine environments, the primates found their **adaptive niche** in the trees. A number of other mammals were also adapting to arboreal living; but while many of them nested in the trees, they continued to forage for food on the ground (**Fig. 6-5**). But throughout the course of evolution, primates increasingly found food (leaves, seeds, fruits, nuts, insects, and small mammals) in the trees themselves. Over time, this dietary shift enhanced a general trend toward *omnivory;* and this trend in turn led to the retention of the generalized dentition that's typical of most primates.

Increased reliance on vision, coupled with grasping hands and feet, are also adaptations to an arboreal lifestyle. In a complex, three-dimensional environment with uncertain footholds, acute color vision with depth perception is, for obvious reasons, extremely beneficial.

An alternative to this traditional *arboreal hypothesis* is based on the fact that animals such as squirrels and raccoons are also arboreal, yet they haven't evolved primate-like adaptations such as prehensile hands or forward-facing eyes. But visual predators, such as cats and owls, do have forward-facing eyes, and this fact may provide insight into an additional factor that could have shaped primate evolution.

Forward-facing eyes (which facilitate binocular vision), grasping hands and feet, and the presence of nails instead of claws may not have come about solely as adaptive advantages in a purely arboreal setting. They may also have been the hallmarks of an arboreal visual predator. So it's possible that early primates may first have adapted to shrubby forest undergrowth and the lowest tiers of the forest canopy, where they hunted insects and other small prey (Cartmill, 1972, 1992). In fact, many smaller primates occupy just such an econiche today.

In a third scenario, Sussman (1991) suggested that the basic primate traits developed along with another major evolutionary occurrence, the appearance and diversification of flowering plants that began around 140 mya. Flowering plants provide numerous resources

Figure 6-5
Gray squirrels are extremely well adapted to life in the trees, where they nest, sleep, play, and frequently eat. Unlike primates, however, they don't have color vision or grasping hands and feet, and they have claws instead of nails.

arboreal Tree-living; adapted to life in the trees.

adaptive niche An organism's entire way of life: where it lives, what it eats, how it gets food, how it avoids predators, and so on.

for primates, including nectar, seeds, and fruits. Sussman argued that because visual predation isn't common among primates, forward-facing eyes, grasping hands and feet, omnivory, and *color vision* may have arisen in response to the demand for fine visual and tactile discrimination, necessary for feeding on small food items such as fruits, berries, and seeds among branches and stems (Dominy and Lucas, 2001).

These hypotheses aren't mutually exclusive. The complex of primate characteristics might well have originated in nonarboreal settings and they certainly could have been stimulated when evolving flowering plants opened up new econiches. But at some point, probably as a result of these and even other factors, primates did take to the trees, and that's where most of them still live today.

Geographical Distribution and Habitats

With just a couple of exceptions, nonhuman primates are found in tropical or semitropical areas of the New and Old Worlds. In the New World, these areas include southern Mexico, Central America, and parts of South America. Old World primates are found in Africa, India, Southeast Asia (including numerous islands), and Japan (**Fig. 6-7** on pages 122–123).

Even though most nonhuman primates are arboreal and live in forest or woodland habitats, some Old World monkeys (for example, baboons) spend much of the day on the ground. The same is true for the African apes (gorillas, chimpanzees, and bonobos). Nevertheless, all nonhuman primates spend some time in the trees, especially when sleeping.

Diet and Teeth

Omnivory is one example of the overall lack of specialization in primates. Although all primates tend to favor some food items over others, most eat a combination of fruits, nuts, seeds, leaves, other plant materials, and insects. Many also get animal protein from birds, amphibians, and small mammals, including

other primates. Others have become more specialized and mostly eat leaves. Such a wide array of choices is highly adaptive, even in fairly predictable environments.

Like nearly all other mammals, almost all primates have four kinds of teeth: incisors and canines for biting and cutting, and premolars and molars for chewing and grinding. Biologists use what's called a **dental formula** to describe the number of each type of tooth that typifies a species. A dental formula indicates the number of each tooth type in each quadrant of the mouth (**Fig. 6-6**). For example, all Old World *anthropoids* have two incisors, one canine, two premolars, and three molars on each side of the midline in both the upper and lower jaws, for a total of 32 teeth. This is represented by the following dental formula:

2.1.2.3 (upper)
2.1.2.3 (lower)

The dental formula for a generalized placental mammal is 3.1.4.3 (three incisors, one canine, four premolars, and three molars). Primates have fewer teeth than this ancestral pattern because of a general evolutionary trend toward fewer teeth in many mammal groups. Consequently, the number of each kind of tooth varies between lineages. For example, humans, apes, and all Old World monkeys share the same dental formula: 2.1.2.3. This formula differs from that of the New World monkeys in that there's one less premolar.

The overall lack of dietary specialization in primates is reflected in the lack of specialization in the size and shape of the teeth, because tooth shape and size are directly related to diet. For example, carnivores typically have premolars and molars with high, pointed **cusps** adapted for tearing meat; but herbivores, such as cattle and horses, have premolars with broad, flat surfaces suited to chewing tough grasses and other plant materials. Most primates have premolars and molars with low, rounded cusps, a pattern that enables them to process most types of foods. So, throughout their evolutionary history, the primates have developed a dentition adapted to a

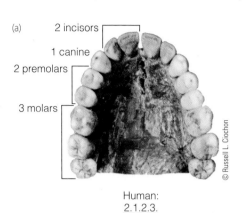

(a) 2 incisors
1 canine
2 premolars
3 molars

Human:
2.1.2.3.
2.1.2.3.

© Russell L. Ciochon

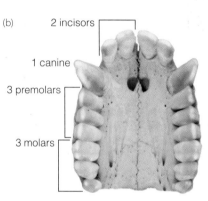

(b) 2 incisors
1 canine
3 premolars
3 molars

New World monkey:
2.1.3.3.
2.1.3.3.

© Russell L. Ciochon

Figure 6-6

(a) The human maxilla illustrates a dental formula characteristic of all Old World monkeys, apes, and humans. (b) The New World monkey (*Cebus*) maxilla shows the dental formula that is typical of most New World monkeys. (Not to scale, the monkey maxilla is actually much smaller than the human maxilla.)

dental formula Numerical device that indicates the number of each type of tooth in each side of the upper and lower jaws.

cusps The bumps on the chewing surface of premolars and molars.

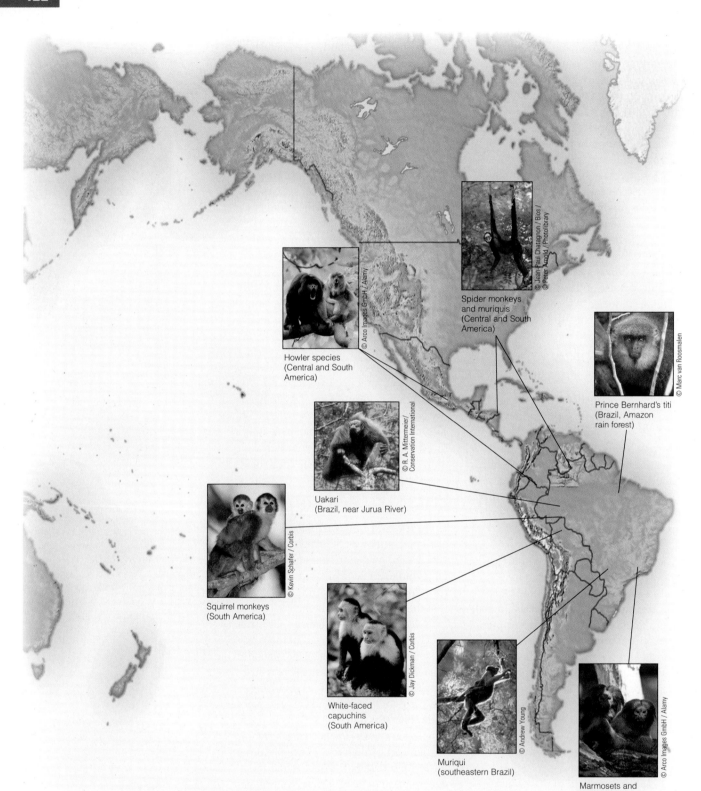

Spider monkeys and muriquis (Central and South America)
© Jean-Paul Chatagnon / Bios / © Peter Arnold / Photolibrary

Howler species (Central and South America)
© Arco Images GmbH / Alamy

Prince Bernhard's titi (Brazil, Amazon rain forest)
© Marc van Roosmalen

Uakari (Brazil, near Jurua River)
© R. A. Mittermeier / Conservation International

Squirrel monkeys (South America)
© Kevin Schafer / Corbis

White-faced capuchins (South America)
© Jay Dickman / Corbis

Muriqui (southeastern Brazil)
© Andrew Young

Marmosets and tamarins (South America)
© Arco Images GmbH / Alamy

Figure 6-7

Geographical distribution of living nonhuman primates. Much original habitat is now very fragmented.

Macaque species
(North Africa, India,
Southeast Asia,
China, and Japan

Jean De Rousseau

Gibbons and siamangs
(Southeast Asia,
islands, and China)

Lynn Kilgore

Baboon species
(throughout sub-Saharan
Africa)

Bonnie Pedersen / Arlene Kruse

Cercopithecus
species (throughout
sub-Saharan Africa)

Robert Jurmain

Tarsier species
(southeast
Asian islands)

© Steve Bloom Images / Alamy

Loris species
(Africa, India, and
Southeast Asia)

© Ian Butler / Alamy

Mountain and lowland
gorillas (western and
central Africa)

Lynn Kilgore

Langur species
(colobines) (India,
southern Asia, and
south China)

© Cyril Ruoso / Bios / Peter Arnold / Photolibrary

Lemurs
(Madagascar)

Fred Jacobs

Orangutans
(Borneo and Sumatra)

© Rolf Nussbaumer Photography / Alamy

Chimpanzees and
bonobos
(across central Africa)

Arlene Kruse / Bonnie Pedersen

Galago species
(throughout sub-Saharan
Africa)

© Federico Veronesi / Gallo Images / Getty Images

Colobus species
(throughout sub-Saharan
Africa)

Robert Jurmain

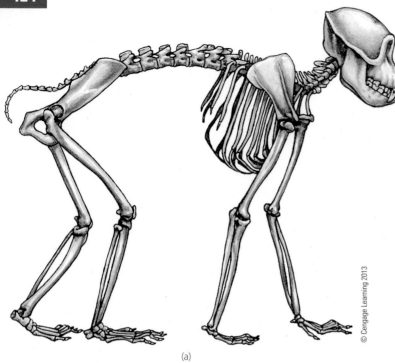

(a)

Figure 6-8

Like most mammals, primate locomotion is primarily quadrupedal, as shown here in (a) a baboon and (b) a chimpanzee with a modified form of quadrupedalism, called knuckle walking (see also Fig. 6-9).

(b)

© Cengage Learning 2013

varied diet, and the capacity to exploit many foods has contributed to their overall success during the last 50 million years.

Locomotion

Almost all primates are, at least to some degree, **quadrupedal.** However, most primates use more than one form of locomotion, and they're able to do this because of their generalized anatomy.

The limbs of terrestrial quadrupeds are approximately the same length (**Fig. 6-8a**). In arboreal quadrupeds, forelimbs are somewhat shorter.

Vertical clinging and leaping, another form of locomotion, is characteristic of some lemurs and tarsiers. As the term implies, vertical clingers and leapers support themselves vertically by grasping onto trunks of trees or other large plants while their knees and ankles are tightly flexed. By forcefully extending their long hind limbs, they can spring

powerfully away either forward or backward.

Brachiation, or arm swinging, is a suspensory form of locomotion, and the body moves by being alternatively suspended by one arm or the other. (You may have brachiated as a child on the "monkey bars" in a playground.) Because of anatomical modifications at the shoulder joint, apes and humans are capable of true brachiation. However, only the small gibbons and siamangs of Southeast Asia use this form of locomotion almost exclusively.

Brachiation is seen in species characterized by arms longer than legs, a short, stable lower back, long curved fingers, and shortened thumbs. As these are traits seen in all the apes, it's believed that although none of the great apes (orangutans, gorillas, bonobos, and chimpanzees) habitually brachiate today, they probably inherited these characteristics from brachiating or climbing ancestors (**Fig. 6-8b**).

quadrupedal Using all four limbs to support the body during locomotion; the basic mammalian (and primate) form of locomotion.

brachiation Arm swinging, a form of locomotion used by some primates. Brachiation involves hanging from a branch and moving by alternately swinging from one arm to the other.

Some New World monkeys, such as spider monkeys, are called *semibrachiators*, since they practice a combination of leaping with some arm swinging. Also, some New World monkeys enhance arm swinging by using a *prehensile tail*, which in effect serves as an extra hand. It's important to mention that no Old World monkeys have prehensile tails.

Lastly, all the apes, to varying degrees, have arms that are longer than legs, and some (gorillas, bonobos, and chimpanzees) practice a special form of quadrupedalism called knuckle walking. Because their arms are so long relative to their legs, they support the weight of their upper body on the back surfaces of their bent fingers (**Fig. 6-9**).

Primate Classification

The living primates are commonly categorized into their respective subgroups, as shown in **Figure 6-10**. This taxonomy is based on the system originally established by Linnaeus (see Chapter 2). The primate order, which includes a diverse array of approximately 230 species, belongs to a larger group, the class Mammalia (see Chapter 5).

As you learned in Chapter 5, in any taxonomic system, animals are organized into increasingly specific categories. For example, the order Primates includes *all* primates. But at the next level down, the *suborder*, primates are divided into two smaller categories: **Strepsirhini** (lemurs and lorises) and **Haplorhini** (tarsiers, monkeys, apes, and humans). Therefore, the suborder distinction is more specific. At the suborder level, the lemurs and lorises are distinct as a group from all the other primates. This classification makes the biological and evolutionary statement that all the lemurs and lorises are more closely related to one another than they are to any of the other primates. Likewise, humans, apes, monkeys, and tarsiers are more closely related to one another than they are to the lorises and lemurs.

The taxonomy shown in Figure 6-10 is a modified version of a similar system that biologists and primatologists have used for decades. The traditional system was based on physical similarities between species and lineages. But that approach isn't foolproof. For instance, some New and Old World monkeys resemble each other anatomically, but evolutionarily they're quite distinct from each other, having diverged from a common ancestor perhaps as long ago as 35 mya. By looking only at physical characteristics, it's possible to overlook the unknown effects of separate evolutionary history (most specifically, the difficulties caused by homoplasy; see Chapter 5). But thanks to the rapidly growing number of species whose genomes have been sequenced, geneticists can now make direct comparisons between the genes, and indeed the entire genetic makeup, of different species. This kind of analysis, called *comparative genomics*, provides a more accurate picture of evolutionary and biological relationships between species than was possible even as recently as the late 1990s. So once again, we see how changing technologies allow scientists to refine older hypotheses and develop new ones.

When a complete draft sequence of the chimpanzee genome was completed in 2005 (Chimpanzee Sequencing and Analysis Consortium, 2005), it was a major milestone in human comparative genomics. Comparisons of the genomes of different species are important because they reveal such differences in DNA as the number of nucleotide substitutions and/or deletions that have occurred since related species last shared a common ancestor. Geneticists estimate the rate at which genes change and then combine this information with the amount of change they observe to estimate when related species last shared a common ancestor.

For example, Wildman and colleagues (2003) compared nearly 100 human genes with their chimpanzee, gorilla, and orangutan counterparts. Their results

Lynn Kilgore

Figure 6-9

Chimpanzee knuckle walking. Note how the weight of the upper body is supported on the knuckles and not on the palm of the hand.

Strepsirhini (strep'-sir-in-ee) The primate suborder that includes lemurs and lorises.

Haplorhini (hap'-lo-rin-ee) The primate suborder that includes tarsiers, monkeys, apes, and humans.

Figure 6-10

Primate taxonomic classification. This abbreviated taxonomy illustrates how primates are categorized from broader groupings (e.g., the order Primates) into increasingly specific ones (species). Only the more general categories are shown, except for the great apes and humans.

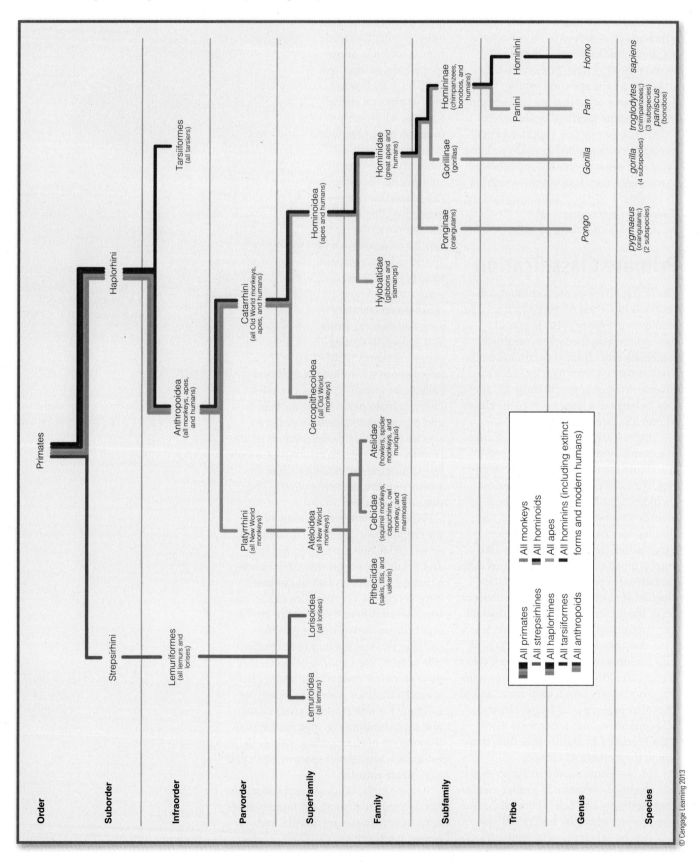

Figure 6-11

As you can see, rhinaria come in different shapes and sizes, but they all enhance an animal's sense of smell.

supported some earlier studies indicating that humans are most closely related to chimpanzees and that the protein-coding DNA sequences of the two species are 98.4 to 99.4 percent identical. This study also revealed that the chimpanzee and human lineages diverged between 7 and 6 mya. These results are consistent with the molecular findings of several other studies (Chen and Li, 2001; Clark et al., 2003; Steiper and Young, 2006). Other research has substantiated these figures but has also revealed more variation in noncoding DNA segments and portions that have been inserted, deleted, or duplicated. So when the *entire* genome is considered, reported DNA differences between chimpanzees and humans range from 2.7 percent (Cheng et al., 2005) to 6.4 percent (Demuth et al., 2006). These aren't substantial differences, but perhaps the most important discovery of all is that humans have much more non-protein-coding DNA than do the other primates that have so far been studied. Now geneticists are beginning to understand some of the functions of non-protein-coding DNA, and they hope to explain why humans have so much of it and how it makes us different from our close relatives.

A Survey of the Living Primates

In this section, we discuss the major primate subgroups. Since it's beyond the scope of this book to cover any species in great detail, we present a brief description of each major grouping, taking a somewhat closer look at the apes.

Lemurs and Lorises

The suborder Strepsirhini includes the lemurs and lorises, the most nonderived, or primitive, living primates. Remember that by "primitive" we mean that lemurs and lorises are more similar anatomically to their earlier mammalian ancestors than are the other primates (tarsiers, monkeys, apes, and humans). For example, they retain certain ancestral characteristics, such as a greater reliance on *olfaction*. Their greater olfactory capabilities (compared with other primates) are reflected in the presence of a relatively long snout and a moist, fleshy pad, or **rhinarium**, at the end of the nose (**Fig. 6-11**).

Many other characteristics distinguish lemurs and lorises from the other primates, including eyes placed more to the side of the face, differences in reproductive physiology, and shorter gestation and maturation periods. Lemurs and lorises also have a unique derived trait called a "dental comb" (**Fig. 6-12**), formed by forward-projecting lower incisors and canines. These modified teeth are used in grooming and feeding.

Lemurs Lemurs are found only on the island of Madagascar and adjacent islands off the east coast of Africa (**Fig. 6-13**). As the only nonhuman primates on Madagascar, lemurs diversified into numerous ecological niches without competition from monkeys and apes. Thus, the approximately 60 surviving species of lemurs on Madagascar today

Figure 6-12

Lemur dental comb, formed by forward-projecting incisors and canines.

rhinarium (rine-air´-ee-um) The moist, hairless pad at the end of the nose seen in most mammalian species. The rhinarium enhances an animal's ability to smell.

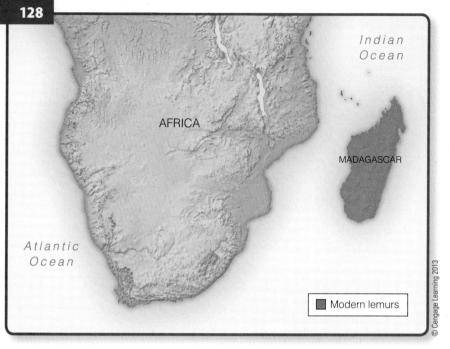

© Cengage Learning 2013

Figure 6-13

Geographical distribution of modern lemurs.

© Cyril Ruoso / JH Editorial / Minden Pictures

Figure 6-14

Ring-tailed lemurs in a typical vertical clinging and leaping posture.

indris) are vertical clingers and leapers (**Fig. 6-15**). Several species (for example, ring-tailed lemurs and sifakas) live in groups of 10 to 25 animals composed of males and females of all ages. However, indris live in "family" units composed of a mated pair and dependent offspring, and several nocturnal species are mostly solitary.

Lorises Lorises (**Fig. 6-16**), which somewhat resemble lemurs, were able to survive in mainland areas by becoming nocturnal. In this way, they were (and are) able to avoid competition with more recently evolved primates (the diurnal monkeys).

There are at least eight loris species, all of which are found in tropical forest and woodland habitats of India, Sri Lanka, Southeast Asia, and Africa. Also included in the same general category are six to nine galago species, also called bush babies (Bearder, 1987; Nowak, 1999), which are widely distributed throughout most of the forested and woodland savanna areas of sub-Saharan Africa (**Fig. 6-17**).

Locomotion in some lorises is a slow, cautious, climbing form of quadrupedalism. All galagos, however, are highly agile vertical clingers and leapers. Some lorises and galagos are almost entirely insectivorous, while others also eat fruits, leaves, and other plant products. Lorises and galagos frequently forage alone, but feeding ranges can overlap, and two or more females may feed and even nest together. Females also leave

represent an evolutionary pattern that vanished elsewhere.

Lemurs range in size from the small mouse lemur, with a body length (head and trunk) of only 5 inches, to the indri, with a body length of 2 to 3 feet (Nowak, 1999). Typically, the larger lemurs are diurnal and eat a wide variety of foods, such as leaves, fruits, buds, bark, and shoots, but the tiny mouse and dwarf lemurs are nocturnal and insectivorous.

There's a great deal of behavioral variation among lemurs. Some are mostly arboreal, but others, such as ring-tailed lemurs (**Fig. 6-14**), are more terrestrial. Some arboreal species are quadrupeds, and others (sifakas and

Figure 6-15

Sifakas.

Fred Jacobs

Figure 6-16

A slow loris in Malaysia. Note the large forward-facing eyes and rhinarium.

Figure 6-17

Galago, or "bush baby."

young infants behind in nests while they search for food, a behavior not seen in most primate species.

Tarsiers

There are five recognized tarsier species (Nowak, 1999), all of which are restricted to islands of Southeast Asia (Malaysia, Borneo, Sumatra, the Philippines), where they inhabit a wide range of habitats, from tropical forest to backyard gardens (**Figs. 6-18** and **6-19**). Tarsiers are nocturnal insectivores that leap from lower branches and shrubs onto small prey. They appear to form stable pair bonds, and the basic tarsier social unit is a mated pair and their young offspring (MacKinnon and MacKinnon, 1980).

Tarsiers are highly specialized (derived) animals that have several unique characteristics. In the past, primatologists thought that tarsiers were more closely related to lemurs and lorises than to other primates because they share several traits with them. However, they actually present a complex blend of characteristics not

seen in any other primate. One of the most obvious is their enormous eyes, which dominate much of the face and are immobile within their sockets. To compensate for the inability to move their eyes, tarsiers, like owls, can rotate their heads 180°.

Figure 6-18

Bornean tarsier. Tarsiers' eyes are almost as large as their brains.

Figure 6-19

Geographical distribution of tarsiers.

ASIA

Pacific Ocean

PHILIPPINES

SUMATRA   BORNEO

■ Tarsiers

Anthropoids: Monkeys, Apes, and Humans

Although there is much variation among anthropoids, they share certain features that, when taken together, distinguish them as a group from lemurs and lorises. Here's a partial list of these traits:

1. Larger average body size
2. Larger brain in absolute terms and relative to body weight
3. Reduced reliance on the sense of smell, as indicated by the absence of a rhinarium and reduction of olfactory-related brain structures
4. Increased reliance on vision, with forward-facing eyes placed more to the front of the face
5. Greater degree of color vision
6. Back of eye socket protected by a bony plate
7. Blood supply to the brain different from that of lemurs and lorises
8. Fusion of the two sides of the mandible at the midline to form one bone (in lemurs and lorises, they're two distinct bones joined by cartilage at the middle of the chin)
9. More generalized dentition, as seen in the absence of a dental comb
10. Differences in female internal reproductive anatomy
11. Longer gestation and maturation periods
12. Increased parental care
13. More mutual grooming

Approximately 85 percent of all primates are monkeys. Primatologists estimate that there are about 195 species, but it's impossible to give precise numbers because the taxonomic status of some monkeys remains in doubt, and previously unknown species are still being discovered. Monkeys are divided into two groups separated by geographical area (New World and Old World) as well as at least 35 million years of separate evolutionary history.

New World Monkeys The approximately 70 New World monkey species can be found in a wide range of environments throughout most forested areas in southern Mexico and Central and South America (**Fig. 6-20**). They exhibit a wide range of variation in size, diet, and ecological adaptations (**Fig. 6-21**). In size, they vary from the tiny marmosets and tamarins that weigh only about 12 ounces (**Fig. 6-22**) to the 20-pound howler monkeys (**Fig. 6-23**). New World monkeys are almost exclusively arboreal, and some never come to the ground. Like the Old World monkeys, all except one species (the owl monkey) are diurnal.

In addition to being the smallest of all monkeys, marmosets and tamarins have several other distinguishing features. They have claws instead of nails, and unlike other primates, they usually give birth to twins instead of one infant. They live in social groups usually composed of a mated pair, or a female and two adult males, and their offspring. This type of mating pattern is rare among mammals, and marmosets and tamarins are among the few primate species in which males are extensively involved in infant care.

Other New World species range in size from squirrel monkeys (weighing

Figure 6-20

Geographical distribution of New World monkeys.

© Cengage Learning 2013

Figure 6-21

Some New World monkeys.

Female muriqui with infant

Squirrel monkeys

Prince Bernhard's titi monkey (discovered in 2002)

White-faced capuchins

Male uakari

Figure 6-22

A pair of golden lion tamarins.

Figure 6-23

Male and female (with infant) howler monkeys. The adults are illustrating why they're called "howlers." The roaring sound they make is among the loudest of mammalian vocalizations.

Figure 6-24

This spider monkey, a New World species, is using its prehensile tail to suspend itself from a tree branch.

Cercopithecidae (serk-oh-pith´-eh-see-dee)

cercopithecines (serk-oh-pith´-eh-seens) Members of the subfamily of Old World monkeys that includes baboons, macaques, and guenons.

colobines (kole´-uh-bines) Members of the subfamily of Old World monkeys that includes the African colobus monkeys and Asian langurs.

ischial callosities Patches of tough, hard skin on the buttocks of Old World monkeys and chimpanzees.

only 1.5 to 2.5 pounds and having a body length of 12 inches) to the larger howlers (as much as 22 pounds in males and around 24 inches long). Diet varies, with most relying on a combination of fruits and leaves supplemented to varying degrees with insects. Most are quadrupedal; but some, such as

spider monkeys (**Fig. 6-24**), are semibrachiators. Howlers, muriquis, and spider monkeys also have prehensile tails that are used not only in locomotion but also for hanging from branches. Socially, most New World monkeys live in groups composed of both sexes and all age categories. Some (such as titis) form monogamous pairs and live with their subadult offspring.

Old World Monkeys Except for humans, Old World monkeys are the most widely distributed of all living primates. They're found throughout sub-Saharan Africa and southern Asia, ranging from tropical jungle habitats to semiarid desert and even to seasonally snow-covered areas in northern Japan (**Fig. 6-25**).

Conveniently, all Old World monkeys are placed in one taxonomic family, **Cercopithecidae**. In turn, this family is divided into two subfamilies: the **cercopithecines** and the **colobines**. Most Old World monkeys are arboreal, but some (such as baboons) spend a lot of time on the ground and return to the trees for the night. They have areas of hardened skin on the buttocks called **ischial callosities** that serve as sitting pads, making it possible to sit and sleep on tree branches for hours at a time.

The cercopithecines are more generalized than the colobines. They're

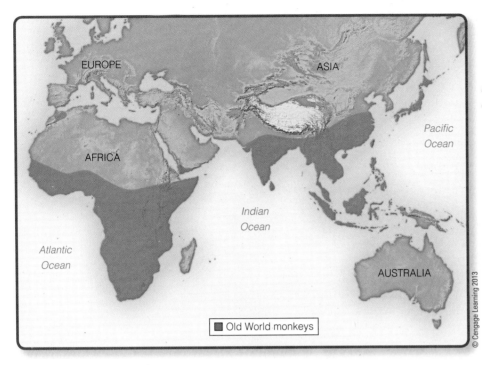

Figure 6-25

Geographical distribution of living Old World monkeys.

© Cengage Learning 2013

more omnivorous, and as a group, they eat almost anything, including fruits, seeds, leaves, grasses, tubers, roots, nuts, insects, birds' eggs, amphibians, small reptiles, and small mammals (the last seen in baboons).

The majority of cercopithecine species, such as the mostly arboreal guenons (**Fig. 6-26**) and the more terrestrial savanna and hamadryas baboons (**Fig. 6-27**), are found in Africa. The many macaque species (including the well-known rhesus monkeys), however,

are widely distributed across southern Asia and India.

Colobine species have a narrower range of food preferences and mainly eat mature leaves, which is why they're also called "leaf-eating monkeys." The colobines are found mainly in Asia, but both red colobus and black-and-white colobus are exclusively African (**Fig. 6-28**).

Locomotion in Old World monkeys includes arboreal quadrupedalism in guenons, macaques, and langurs; terrestrial quadrupedalism in baboons

Figure 6-26

Adult male Sykes monkey, one of many guenon species.

Robert Jurmain

Figure 6-27

Hamadryas baboons are found in Ethiopia. Notice how much larger the male (at right) is than the female. The male also has much longer hair around the head and shoulders, giving him a distinctive mane.

© Thomas Dobner 2006 / Alamy

© Nelson Ting

Figure 6-28

Black-and-white colobus monkeys are mostly arboreal but do come down to the ground occasionally.

sexual dimorphism Differences in physical characteristics between males and females of the same species. For example, humans are slightly sexually dimorphic for body size, with males being taller, on average, than females of the same population.

estrus Period of sexual receptivity in female mammals (except humans), correlated with ovulation. When used as an adjective, the word is spelled "estrous."

hominoids Members of the primate superfamily (Hominoidea) that includes apes and humans.

and macaques; and semibrachiation and acrobatic leaping in colobus monkeys. Marked differences in body size or shape between the sexes, referred to as **sexual dimorphism**, are typical of some terrestrial species and are especially pronounced in baboons. For example, male baboons, which can weigh 80 pounds, can be up to twice the size of females.

Females of several species (especially baboons and some macaques) have pronounced cyclical changes of the external genitalia. These changes, which include swelling and redness, are associated with **estrus**, a hormonally initiated period of sexual receptivity in female nonhuman mammals that is correlated with ovulation. They serve as visual cues to males that females are sexually receptive.

Old World monkeys live in a few different kinds of social groups. Colobines tend to live in small groups, with only one or two adult males. Savanna baboons and most macaque species are found in large social units comprising several adults of both sexes and offspring of all ages. Monogamous pairing isn't common in Old World monkeys, but it's seen in a few langurs and possibly one or two guenon species.

Hominoids: Apes and Humans

Apes and humans are classified together in the same superfamily, the **hominoids**. Apes are found in Asia and Africa. The small-bodied gibbons and siamangs live in Southeast Asia, and the two orangutan subspecies live on the islands of Borneo and Sumatra (**Fig. 6-29**). In Africa, until the mid- to late twentieth century, gorillas, chimpanzees, and bonobos occupied the forested areas of western, central, and eastern Africa, but their habitat is now extremely fragmented, and all are threatened or highly endangered. Apes and humans differ from monkeys in numerous ways:

1. Generally larger body size (except for gibbons and siamangs)
2. No tail
3. Lower back shorter and more stable
4. Arms longer than legs (only in apes)
5. Anatomical differences in the shoulder joint that facilitate suspensory feeding and locomotion
6. Generally more complex behavior
7. More complex brain and enhanced cognitive abilities
8. Increased period of infant development and dependency

Gibbons and Siamangs The eight gibbon species and closely related siamangs are the smallest of the apes, with a long, slender body weighing 13 pounds in gibbons (**Fig. 6-30**) and around 25 pounds in siamangs. Their most distinctive anatomical features are adaptations to feeding while hanging from tree branches, or brachiation. In fact, gibbons and siamangs are more dedicated to brachiation than any other primate, a fact reflected in their extremely long arms, long, permanently curved fingers, short thumbs, and powerful shoulder muscles. (Their arms are so long that when they're on the ground, they have to walk bipedally with their arms raised to the side.) Gibbons and siamangs mostly eat fruits, although they also consume a variety of leaves, flowers, and insects.

The basic social unit of gibbons and siamangs is an adult male and female with dependent offspring. Although they've been described as monogamous, in reality, members of a pair do sometimes mate with other individuals. As in marmosets and tamarins, male gibbons and siamangs are very much involved in rearing their young. Both males and females are highly **territorial** and protect their territories with elaborate whoops and siren-like "songs," lending them the name "the singing apes of Asia."

Orangutans Orangutans (*Pongo pygmaeus*; **Fig. 6-31**) are represented by two subspecies found today only in heavily forested areas on the Indonesian islands of Borneo and Sumatra. The name *orangutan* (which has no final "g" and should *never* be pronounced

© Cengage Learning 2013

Gibbons
Orangutans

Figure 6-29

Geographical distribution of living Asian apes.

© Theo Allofs / Corbis

Figure 6-30

Black-handed gibbon in Indonesia.

territorial Pertaining to the protection of all or a part of the area occupied by an animal or group of animals. Territorial behaviors range from scent marking to outright attacks on intruders.

(a) © Rolf Nussbaumer Photography / Alamy; (b) Thomas Marent / Minden Pictures

Figure 6-31

Bornean orangutans. (a) Female with infant.
(b) Male.

(a)   (b)

"o-rang-utang") means "wise man of the forest" in the language of the local people. But despite this somewhat affectionate-sounding label, orangutans are severely threatened with extinction in the wild due to poaching by humans and continuing habitat loss on both islands.

Orangutans are slow, cautious climbers whose locomotion can best be described as four-handed—referring to their use of all four limbs for grasping and support. Although they're almost completely arboreal, orangutans sometimes travel quadrupedally on the ground. Orangutans exhibit pronounced sexual dimorphism; males are very large and may weigh more than 200 pounds, while females weigh less than 100 pounds. In the wild, orangutans lead largely solitary lives, although adult females are usually accompanied by one or two dependent offspring. They're primarily **frugivorous** but may also eat bark, leaves, insects, and (rarely) meat.

Gorillas The four generally recognized gorilla (*Gorilla gorilla*) subspecies are the largest of all the living primates. Today, they are restricted to forested areas of

western and eastern equatorial Africa (**Fig. 6-32**). Gorillas exhibit marked sexual dimorphism. Males may weigh as much as 400 pounds, while females weigh around 150 to 200 pounds. Adult gorillas, especially males, are primarily terrestrial, and like chimpanzees, they practice a type of quadrupedalism called knuckle walking.

Western lowland gorillas (**Fig. 6-33**) are found in several countries of west-central Africa. In 1998, Doran and McNeilage estimated their population size at perhaps 110,000, but Walsh and colleagues (2003) suggested that their numbers were far lower. Staggeringly, in August 2008, the Wildlife Conservation Society reported the discovery of an estimated 125,000 western lowland gorillas in the northern region of the Democratic Republic of the Congo (DRC—formerly Zaire)! This is extremely encouraging news, but it doesn't mean that gorillas are out of danger. To put this figure into perspective, consider that a large football stadium can hold around 70,000 spectators. So, next time you see a stadium packed with fans, think about the fact that you're looking at a crowd that numbers around half of all the western lowland gorillas on earth.

frugivorous (fru-give´-or-us) Having a diet composed primarily of fruit.

Small populations of Cross River gorillas, another West African subspecies, are found in areas along the border between Nigeria and Cameroon (Sarmiento and Oates, 2000). Primatologists believe that there may be only 250 to 300 of these animals; thus, Cross River gorillas are among the most endangered of all primates. Currently, the International Union for the Conservation of Nature and Natural Resources (IUCN) is developing plans to protect this vulnerable and little-known subspecies (Oates et al., 2007).

Eastern lowland gorillas, which haven't really been studied, live near the eastern border of the DRC. At present, their numbers are unknown but suspected to be around 12,000. Considering that warfare is common in the region, researchers fear that many of these gorillas have been killed, but it's impossible to know how many.

Mountain gorillas (**Fig. 6-34**), the most extensively studied of the four subspecies, are restricted to the mountainous areas of central Africa in Rwanda, the DRC, and Uganda. There have probably never been many mountain gorillas, and today they number only about 700 animals.

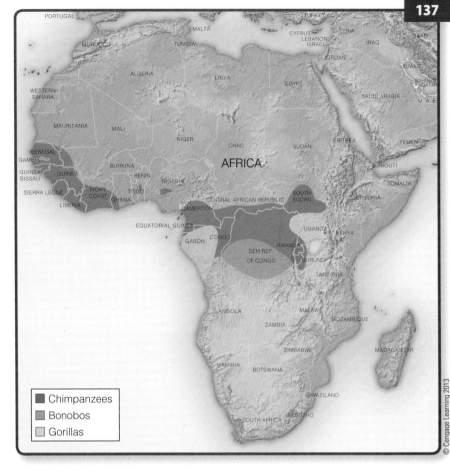

Chimpanzees
Bonobos
Gorillas

© Cengage Learning 2013

Figure 6-32

Geographical distribution of living African apes.

(a)

(b)

(a) © imagebroker / Alamy; (b) © Duncan Usher / Alamy

Figure 6-33

Western lowland gorillas.
(a) Male. (b) Female with infant.

Figure 6-34

Mountain gorillas. (a) A male silverback with his group in the background. (b) Female.

(a)

(b)

Mountain gorillas live in groups consisting of one, or sometimes two, large silverback males, a variable number of adult females, and their subadult offspring. (The term *silverback* refers to the saddle of white hair across the backs of fully adult males that appears around the age of 12 or 13.) A silverback male may tolerate the presence of one or more young adult "blackback" males (probably his sons) in his group. Typically, but not always, both females and males leave their **natal group** as young adults. Females join other groups; and males, who appear to be less likely to emigrate,

may live alone for a while or may join up with other males before eventually forming their own group.

Systematic studies of free-ranging western lowland gorillas weren't begun until the mid-1980s, so even though they're the only gorillas you'll see in zoos, we don't know as much about them as we do about mountain gorillas. The social structure of western lowland gorillas is similar to that of mountain gorillas, but groups are smaller and somewhat less cohesive.

All gorillas are almost exclusively vegetarian. Mountain and western low-

natal group The group in which an animal is born and raised. (*Natal* pertains to birth.)

land gorillas concentrate primarily on leaves, pith, and stalks, but western lowland gorillas eat more fruit. Western lowland gorillas, unlike mountain gorillas (which avoid water), also frequently wade through swamps while foraging on aquatic plants (Doran and McNeilage, 1998).

Perhaps because of their large body size and enormous strength, gorillas have long been considered ferocious; in reality, they're usually shy and gentle. But this doesn't mean they're never aggressive. In fact, among males, competition for females can be extremely violent. As might be expected, males will attack and defend their group from any perceived danger, whether it's another male gorilla or a human hunter. Still, the reputation of gorillas as murderous beasts is the result of uninformed myth making and little else.

Chimpanzees Chimpanzees are probably the best known of all nonhuman primates, even though many people think they're monkeys (**Fig. 6-35**). Often misunderstood because of zoo exhibits, circus acts, and movies, the true nature of chimpanzees didn't become known until years of fieldwork with wild groups provided a more accurate picture. Today, chimpanzees are found in equatorial Africa, in a broad belt from the Atlantic Ocean in the west to Lake Tanganyika in the east (see Fig. 6-32). But within this large geographical area, their range is very patchy, and it's becoming even more so with continuous habitat destruction.

In many ways, chimpanzees are anatomically similar to gorillas. However, the ecological adaptations and behaviors of chimpanzees and gorillas differ, with chimpanzees spending more time in the trees. Chimpanzees are also frequently excitable, active, and noisy, while gorillas tend to be placid and quiet.

Chimpanzees are smaller and less sexually dimorphic than orangutans and gorillas. A male chimpanzee may weigh 150 pounds, but females can weigh at least 100 pounds. In addition to quadrupedal knuckle walking, chimpanzees may brachiate. When on the ground, they frequently walk bipedally for short distances when carrying food or other objects.

Chimpanzees eat a huge variety of foods, including fruits, leaves, insects, birds' eggs, and nuts. Moreover, both males and females occasionally take part in group hunting efforts to kill small mammals such as young bushpigs and antelope. Their prey also includes monkeys, especially red colobus. When hunts are successful, the members of the hunting party share the meat.

Chimpanzees live in large communities ranging in size from 10 to as many as 100 individuals. A group of closely bonded males forms the core of chimpanzee communities in many locations, especially in East Africa (Wrangham and Smuts, 1980; Goodall, 1986; Wrangham et al., 1992). But for some West African groups, females appear to be more central to the community (Boesch, 1996; Boesch and Boesch-Acherman, 2000; Vigilant et al., 2001). Relationships among closely bonded males aren't always peaceful or stable, yet these males cooperatively defend their territory and are highly intolerant of unfamiliar chimpanzees, especially males.

Even though chimpanzees live in communities, it's rare for all members to be together at the same time. Rather,

© Morales / AGE / Photolibrary

Figure 6-35

Male, female, and infant chimpanzees. Chimpanzees do not live in "nuclear families" as this photo might imply, and it's quite possible that the male at left is not the father of the infant.

they tend to come and go, so that the individuals they encounter vary from day to day. Adult females usually forage either alone or with their offspring, a grouping that might include a number of animals, since females with infants sometimes accompany their own mothers and siblings. These associations have especially been reported for the chimpanzees at Gombe National Park, Tanzania, where about 40 percent of females remain in the group they were born in (Williams, 1999). But in most other areas, females leave their natal group to join another community. This behavioral pattern reduces the risk of mating with close male relatives, because males apparently never leave the group in which they were born.

Chimpanzee social behavior is complex, and individuals form lifelong attachments with friends and relatives. If they remain in their natal group, the bond between mothers and infants can remain strong until one of them dies. This may be a long time, because many wild chimpanzees live well into their 40s and occasionally even longer.

Bonobos Bonobos (*Pan paniscus;* **Fig. 6-36**) are found only in an area south of the Zaire River in the DRC (see Fig. 6-32). Not officially recognized by European scientists until the 1920s, they remain among the least studied of the great apes. Although ongoing field stud-

ies have produced much information (Susman, 1984; Kano, 1992), research has been hampered by civil war. There are currently no accurate counts of bonobos, but their numbers are believed to be between 29,000 and 50,000 (IUCN, 2011). The 50,000 estimate is probably optimistic at this point, and bonobos are highly threatened by human hunting, warfare, and habitat loss.

Because bonobos bear a strong resemblance to chimpanzees, but are slightly smaller, they've been inappropriately called "pygmy chimpanzees." Actually, the differences in body size aren't great, although bonobos are less stocky. They also have longer legs relative to arms, a relatively smaller head, and a dark face from birth.

Bonobos are more arboreal than chimpanzees, and they're less excitable and aggressive. While aggression isn't unknown, it appears that physical violence both within and between groups is uncommon. Like chimpanzees, bonobos live in geographically based fluid communities, and they eat many of the same foods, including occasional meat derived from small mammals (Badrian and Malenky, 1984). But bonobo communities aren't centered around a group of males. Instead, male-female bonding is more important than in chimpanzees and most other nonhuman primates (Badrian and Badrian, 1984). This may be related to bonobo sexuality, which differs from that of other nonhuman primates in that copulation is frequent and occurs throughout a female's estrous cycle, so sex isn't linked solely to reproduction. In fact, bonobos are famous for their sexual behavior, copulating frequently and using sex to defuse potentially tense situations. Sexual activity between members of the same sex is also common (Kano, 1992; de Waal and Lanting, 1997).

Humans Humans (*Homo sapiens*) are the only living representatives of the habitually bipedal primates (hominin tribe). Our primate heritage is evident in our overall anatomy, genetic makeup, and many behavioral aspects. Except for reduced canine size, human teeth are typical primate (especially ape) teeth. The human dependence on vision and

Figure 6-36

Group of male, female, and subadult bonobos in the Democratic Republic of the Congo.

© Frans Lanting Studio / Alamy

decreased reliance on olfaction, as well as flexible limbs and grasping hands, are rooted in our primate, arboreal past (**Fig. 6-37**).

Humans in general are omnivorous, although all societies observe certain culturally based dietary restrictions. Even so, as a species with a rather generalized digestive system, we're physiologically adapted to digest an extremely wide assortment of foods. Perhaps to our detriment, we also share with our relatives a fondness for sweets that originates from the importance of high-energy fruits eaten by many nonhuman primates.

But humans are obviously unique among primates and indeed among all animals. No member of any other species has the ability to write or think about issues such as how it differs from other life-forms. This ability is rooted in the fact that during the last 800,000 years of human evolution, brain size has increased dramatically, and there have also been many other neurological changes.

Humans are also completely dependent on culture. Without cultural innovation, it would never have been possible for us to leave the tropics. As it is, humans inhabit every corner of the planet except for Antarctica, and we've established outposts there. And, lest we forget, a fortunate few have even walked on the moon! None of the technologies (indeed, none of the other aspects of culture) that humans have developed over the last several thousand years would have been possible without the highly developed cognitive abilities we alone possess. Nevertheless, the neurological basis for **intelligence** is rooted in our evolutionary past, and it's something that connects us to other primates. Indeed, research has demonstrated that several nonhuman primate species—most notably chimpanzees, bonobos, and gorillas—display a level of problem solving and insight that most people would have considered impossible just 30 years ago.

Humans are uniquely predisposed to use spoken language, and for the last 5,000 years or so, we've also used written language. This ability exists because during the course of human evolution,

certain neurological and anatomical structures have been modified in ways not observed in any other species. But while nonhuman primates aren't anatomically capable of producing speech, research has shown that to varying degrees, the great apes are able to communicate by using symbols, which is a foundation for language that humans and the great apes (to a limited degree) have in common.

Aside from cognitive abilities, the one other trait that sets humans apart from other primates is our unique (among mammals) form of striding, *habitual* bipedal locomotion. This particular trait appeared early in the evolution of our lineage, and over time, we've become more efficient at it because of changes in the musculoskeletal anatomy of our pelvis, leg, and foot. Still, while it's certainly true that human beings are unique intellectually, and in some ways anatomically, we're still primates. As a matter of fact, humans are basically exaggerated African apes.

Endangered Primates

In September 2000, scientists announced that a subspecies of red colobus, named Miss Waldron's red colobus, had officially been declared extinct. This announcement came after a 6-year search for a monkey that hadn't been seen for 20 years (Oates et al., 2000). Sadly, this monkey, indigenous to two West African countries, has the distinction of being the first nonhuman primate to be declared extinct in the twenty-first century. But it won't be the last. In fact, as of this writing, over half of all nonhuman primate species are now in jeopardy, and some face almost certain extinction in the wild.

There are three basic reasons for the worldwide depletion of nonhuman primates: habitat destruction, human hunting, and live capture for export or local trade. Underlying these three causes is one major factor, unprecedented human population growth, particularly in developing countries, where most nonhuman primates live.

The developing nations of Africa, Asia, and Central and South America are

Lynn Kilgore

Figure 6-37

Playground equipment frequently allows children to play in ways that reflect their arboreal heritage.

intelligence Mental capacity; ability to learn, reason, or comprehend and interpret information, facts, relationships, and meanings; the capacity to solve problems, whether through the application of previously acquired knowledge or through insight.

WildlifeDirect.org

Figure 6-38

Congolese villagers carrying the body of the silverback gorilla shot and killed in the July 2007 attack. His body was buried with the other members of his group who were also killed.

home to over 90 percent of all nonhuman primate species. During the 1990s, these countries, aided by Europe, China, and the United States, destroyed an average of 39 million acres of forest per year. The destruction declined between 2000 and 2010 to about 32 million acres a year, largely because of restrictions in Brazil. (Food and Agriculture Organization of the United Nations, 2010). But whether these restrictions will hold remains to be seen.

Tropical forests are cleared for agriculture, pasture, lumber, and large-scale mining operations (with their necessary roads). Moreover, millions of people in many developing countries are critically short of fuel; lacking electricity, they have a critical need for firewood. Lastly, the demand for tropical hardwoods (such as mahogany, teak, and rosewood) in the United States, Europe, and Japan continues unabated, creating an enormously profitable market for rain forest products.

The need for wood has resulted in a conflict with conservationists, especially in central Africa. Mountain gorillas are one of the most endangered nonhuman primate species, and tourism has been the only real hope of salvation for these magnificent animals. For this reason, several gorilla groups have been habituated to humans and are protected by park rangers. Nevertheless, poaching, civil war, and land clearing have contin-

ued to take a toll on these small populations. For example, between January and late July 2007, 10 mountain gorillas were shot in the Virunga Volcanoes Conservation Area (shared by Uganda, Rwanda, and the DRC; **Fig. 6-38**). The gorillas weren't shot for meat or because they were raiding crops. They were shot because the presence and protection of mountain gorillas are obstacles to people who would destroy what remains of the forests. But gorillas are not the only primates to have been shot in the Virungas. In the past few years, more than 120 rangers have been killed while protecting wildlife.

Habitat loss used to be the single greatest threat to nonhuman primates. But in the past few years, human hunting has perhaps become an even more important factor (**Fig. 6-39**). During the 1990s, primatologists and conservationists became aware of a rapidly developing trade in *bushmeat*, meat from wild animals, especially in Africa. The current slaughter, which now accounts for the loss of tens of thousands of nonhuman primates and other animals annually, has been compared to the near extinction of the American bison in the nineteenth century.

Wherever primates live, people have always hunted them for food. But in the past, subsistence hunting wasn't a serious threat to nonhuman primate populations, and certainly not to entire species. But now, hunters armed with automatic rifles can, and do, wipe out an entire group of monkeys or gorillas in minutes. In fact, it's now possible to buy bushmeat in major cities throughout Europe and the United States. Illegal bushmeat is readily available to immigrants who want traditional foods and to nonimmigrants who think that it's trendy to eat meat from exotic, and frequently endangered, animals.

It's impossible to know how many animals are killed each year, but the estimates are staggering. The Society for Conservation Biology estimates that about 6,000 kg (13,228 pounds) of bushmeat are taken through just seven western cities (New York, London, Toronto, Paris, Montreal, Chicago, and Brussels) every month. No one knows how much of this meat is from primates, but this

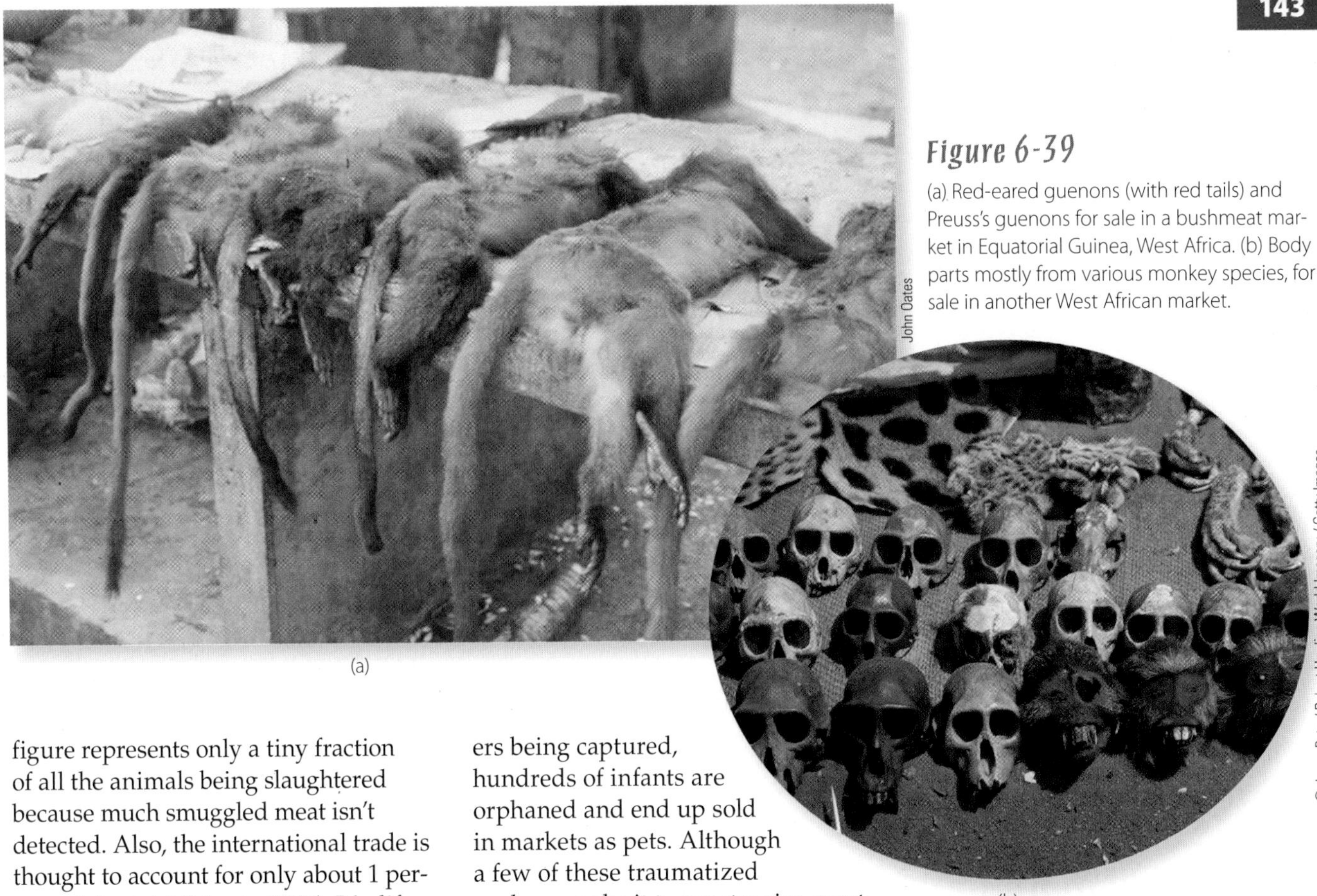

(a)

(b)

John Oates

© Jenny Pate / Robert Harding World Imagery / Getty Images

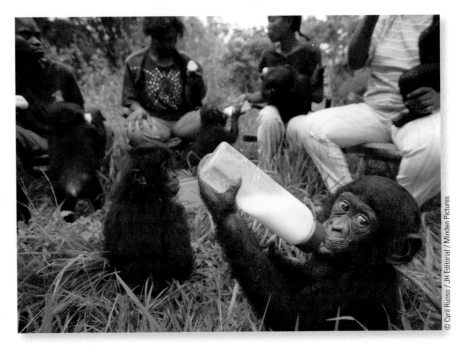

Figure 6-39

(a) Red-eared guenons (with red tails) and Preuss's guenons for sale in a bushmeat market in Equatorial Guinea, West Africa. (b) Body parts mostly from various monkey species, for sale in another West African market.

figure represents only a tiny fraction of all the animals being slaughtered because much smuggled meat isn't detected. Also, the international trade is thought to account for only about 1 percent of the total (Marris, 2006). It's difficult to comprehend, but within a relatively short period of time, hunting wild animals for food, particularly in Africa, has shifted from being a subsistence activity to a commercial enterprise of international scope.

Although the slaughter may be best known in Africa, it's by no means limited to that continent. Hunting and live capture of endangered primates continues unabated in China and Southeast Asia, where nonhuman primates are not only eaten but also funneled into the exotic pet trade. But just as important, primate body parts figure prominently in traditional medicines. With increasing human population size, the enormous demand for these products (and products from other, nonprimate species, such as tigers) has put many species in extreme jeopardy. With some species numbering only a few hundred or a few thousand animals, nonhuman primates cannot survive this onslaught for more than a few years.

Primates are also captured live for zoos, biomedical research, and the exotic pet trade As a result of their mothers being captured, hundreds of infants are orphaned and end up sold in markets as pets. Although a few of these traumatized orphans make it to sanctuaries, most die within days or weeks of capture (**Fig. 6-40**). Live capture has declined since the Convention on International Trade in Endangered Species of Wild Flora and Fauna (CITES) was implemented in 1973. By August 2005, a total

Figure 6-40

Orphaned bonobo infants being cared for at a bonobo sanctuary in the Democratic Republic of the Congo (DRC). It may not be possible to return them to the wild.

© Cyril Ruoso / JH Editorial / Minden Pictures

of 169 countries had signed this treaty, agreeing not to allow trade in species listed by CITES as being endangered (see CITES Handbook, www.cites.org). However, even some CITES members are still occasionally involved in the illegal primate trade (Japan and Belgium, among others).

As a note of optimism, in November 2007, the DRC government and the Bonobo Conservation Initiative (in Washington, D.C.) created a bonobo reserve consisting of 30,500 km². This amounts to about 10 percent of the land in the DRC, and the government has stated that its goal is to set aside an additional 5 percent for wildlife protection (News in Brief, 2007). This is a huge step forward, but it remains to be seen if protection can be enforced.

There are many conservation groups working to protect nonhuman primates. These include, among many others, Conservation International, the World Wildlife Fund, and the Jane Goodall Institute. It goes without saying that these and other organizations must succeed if the great apes are to survive in the wild even until the middle of this century.

If you are in your 20s or 30s, you will certainly live to hear of the extinction of some of our marvelous cousins. Many more will undoubtedly slip away unnoticed. Tragically, this will occur, in most cases, before we've even gotten to know them. Each species on earth is the current result of a unique set of evolutionary events that, over millions of years, has produced a finely adapted component of a diverse, interconnected ecosystem. When it becomes extinct, that adaptation and that part of biodiversity is lost forever. What a tragedy it will be if, through our own mismanagement and greed, we awaken to a world without chimpanzees, mountain gorillas, or the tiny, exquisite lion tamarin. When that day comes, we truly will have lost a part of ourselves, and we will certainly be the poorer for it.

Summary of Main Topics

▶ The mammalian order Primates includes humans and approximately 230 nonhuman species: apes, monkeys, tarsiers, and lemurs. Most nonhuman primates live in tropical and subtropical regions of Africa, India, Asia, Mexico, and South America.

▶ The order Primates is divided into two suborders: Strepsirhini (lemurs and lorises) and Haplorhini (tarsiers, monkeys, apes, and humans).

▶ As a group, the primates are very generalized, meaning they've retained many anatomical characteristics that were present in early ancestral mammalian species. These traits include five digits on the hands and feet, different kinds of teeth, and a skeletal anatomy and limb structure that allow for different forms of locomotion (climbing, brachiation, quadrupedalism, and bipedalism).

▶ In general, primates have relatively larger, more complex brains than other mammals.

▶ Most primates are diurnal and live in social groups.

▶ Because of habitat loss and human hunting, the majority of nonhuman primates are endangered today, and some are on the verge of extinction. Without concerted efforts to preserve primate habitat and control hunting, many species, including mountain gorillas, bonobos, chimpanzees, and many monkeys, could well become extinct by 2050.

Critical Thinking Questions

1. How do you think continued advances in genetic research will influence how we look at our relationship with nonhuman primates?

2. What factors threaten the existence of nonhuman primates in the wild? How much do you care? What can you do to help save nonhuman primates from extinction?

3. How does a classification scheme reflect biological and evolutionary relationships among different primate lineages?

Primates

Primate Behavior

LEARNING OBJECTIVES

After you have mastered the material in this chapter, you will be able to:

▶ Explain how it's possible for natural selection to act on behavior.

▶ Describe the many similarities between human and nonhuman primate behavior.

▶ Explain why primatologists say that many nonhuman primate species have culture.

▶ Describe the ways in which we humans are unique among primates and the ways in which we aren't.

Do you think cats are being cruel when they play with mice? Or if you've ever fallen off a horse when it suddenly jumped aside for no apparent reason, did you think the horse threw you deliberately? If you answered yes to either of these questions, you're not alone. To most people, it does seem cruel for a cat to torment a mouse for no apparent reason; and more than one rider has blamed their horse for intentionally throwing them (it has been known to happen). But these views generally demonstrate how little most people really know about nonhuman animal **behavior**.

In fact, most people think there's a fundamental division between humans and all other animals. In some cultures, this view is fostered by religion; but even when religion isn't a factor, most people see themselves as uniquely set apart from all other species. But at the same time, and in obvious contradiction, they sometimes judge other species from a strictly human perspective and explain certain behaviors in terms of human motivations (for example, cats are cruel to play with mice). Of course, this isn't a valid thing to do for the simple reason that other animals aren't human. Cats sometimes play with mice because that's how, as kittens, they learned to hunt. Cruelty doesn't enter into it because the cat has no concept of cruelty and no idea of what it's like to be the mouse.

Likewise, a horse doesn't deliberately throw you off when it hears leaves rattling in a shrub. It jumps because its behavior has been shaped by thousands of generations of horse ancestors who leaped first and asked questions later. It's important to understand that just as cats evolved as predators, horses evolved as prey animals, and their evolutionary history is littered with unfortunate animals that didn't jump at a sound in a shrub. In many cases, those ancestral horses learned, too late, that the sound wasn't caused by a breeze. This is a mistake that prey animals often don't survive, and those that don't leap first leave few if any descendants.

Obviously, this chapter isn't about cats and horses. It's about what we know and hypothesize about the individual and social behaviors of nonhuman primates. But we begin with the familiar

examples of cats and horses because we want to point out that many basic behaviors have been shaped by the evolutionary history of particular species. So, if we want to discover the underlying principles of behavioral evolution, we first need to identify the interactions between a number of environmental and physiological variables.

The Evolution of Behavior

Scientists study behavior in free-ranging primates from an **ecological** and evolutionary perspective, focusing on the relationship between individual and social behaviors, the natural environment, and various physiological traits of the species in question. This approach is called **behavioral ecology**, and it's based on the underlying assumption that all of the interconnected biological components of ecological systems (animals, plants, and microorganisms) evolved together. Therefore, behaviors are adaptations to environmental circumstances that existed in the past as well as in the present.

Briefly, the cornerstone of this perspective is that *behaviors have evolved through the operation of natural selection* and are therefore subject to natural selection in the same way physical traits are. (Remember that within a specific environmental context, natural selection favors characteristics that provide a reproductive advantage to the individuals who possess them.) Therefore, behavior constitutes a phenotype, and individuals whose behavioral phenotypes increase reproductive fitness will pass on their genes at a faster rate than others. But this doesn't mean that primatologists think that genes code for specific behaviors, such as a gene for aggression, another for cooperation, and so on. Studying complex behaviors from an evolutionary viewpoint doesn't imply a one gene–one behavior relationship, nor does it suggest that behaviors that are influenced by genes can't be modified through learning.

In insects and other invertebrates, behavior is mostly under genetic control. In other words, most behavioral patterns in these species aren't learned; they're

behavior Anything organisms do that involves action in response to internal or external stimuli; the response of an individual, group, or species to its environment. Such responses may or may not be deliberate, and they aren't necessarily the result of conscious decision making.

ecological Pertaining to the relationships between organisms and all aspects of their environment (temperature, predators, nonpredators, vegetation, availability of food and water, types of food, disease organisms, parasites, etc.).

behavioral ecology The study of the evolution of behavior, emphasizing the role of ecological factors as agents of natural selection. Behaviors and behavioral patterns have been favored because they increase the reproductive fitness of individuals (i.e., they are adaptive) in specific environmental contexts.

innate. But in many vertebrates, especially birds and mammals, the proportion of behavior that's due to learning is substantially increased, while the proportion under genetic control is reduced. This is especially true of primates; and in humans, who are so much a product of culture, most behavior is learned. Still, we know that in mammals and birds, some behaviors are at least partly influenced by certain gene products, such as hormones. You may be aware of studies showing that increased levels of the hormone testosterone will increase aggression in many species. You may also know that abnormal levels of certain chemicals produced by brain cells can cause depression, schizophrenia, and bipolar disorder. Because brain cells are directed by the genes within them to produce these chemicals, this is another example of genes influencing behavior.

Because *behavioral genetics*, or the study of how genes affect behavior, is a relatively new field, we don't really know the extent to which genes actually influence behavior in humans or other species. But we do know that behavior must be viewed as the product of *complex interactions between genetic and environmental factors*. The limits and potentials for learning and for behavioral flexibility vary considerably among species. In some species, such as primates, the potentials are extremely broad; but in others, like insects, they aren't. Ultimately, those limits and potentials are set by genetic factors that have been subjected to natural selection throughout the evolutionary history of every species. That history, in turn, has been shaped by the ecological setting not only of living species *but also of their ancestors.*

One of the major goals of primatology is to discover how certain behaviors influence reproductive fitness and how ecological factors have shaped the evolution of those behaviors. While the actual mechanics of behavioral evolution aren't yet fully understood, new technologies and methodologies are helping scientists answer many questions. For example, genetic analysis has recently been used to establish paternity in a few primate groups, and this has helped support hypotheses about some behaviors in males. But in general, an evolutionary approach to the study of behavior doesn't yet provide definitive answers to many research questions. Rather, it offers primatologists a valuable framework within which they can analyze data and generate and test hypotheses concerning behavioral patterns. (Remember, the development and testing of new hypotheses is how scientific research is done.)

Because primates are among the most social of animals, social behavior is one of the major topics in primate research (**Fig. 7-1**). This is a broad subject that includes *all* aspects of behavior occurring in social groupings, even some you may not think of as social behaviors, like

© Barbara Walton / epa / Corbis

Figure 7-1

These proboscis monkeys in Malaysia provide a good example of a small, nonhuman primate social group.

feeding or mating. To understand the function of one behavioral element, it's necessary to determine how it's influenced by numerous interrelated factors. As an example, we'll consider some of the more important variables that influence **social structure**. Bear in mind that social structure itself influences individual behavior, so in many cases, the distinctions between social and individual behaviors are blurred.

Some Factors That Influence Social Structure

Body Size As a rule, larger animals require fewer calories per unit of weight than smaller animals because larger animals have less surface area relative to body mass than smaller animals.

social structure The composition, size, and sex ratio of a group of animals. The social structure of a species is, in part, the result of natural selection in a specific habitat, and it guides individual interactions and social relationships.

Since body heat is lost at the surface, larger animals can retain heat more efficiently, so they need less energy overall. It may seem strange, but two 10-pound monkeys require more food than one 22-pound monkey (Fleagle, 1999).

Basal Metabolic Rate (BMR) The BMR concerns **metabolism**, the rate at which the body uses energy to maintain all bodily functions while in a resting state. It's closely correlated with body size, so in general, smaller animals have a higher BMR than larger ones (**Fig. 7-2**). Consequently, smaller primates, like galagos and marmosets, require an energy-rich diet high in protein (insects), fats (nuts and seeds), and carbohydrates (fruits and seeds). Some larger primates, which tend to have a lower BMR and reduced energy requirements relative to body size, can do well with less energy-rich foods, such as leaves.

Figure 7-2

This small dwarf mouse lemur has a much higher BMR and requires more energy per unit of body weight than a gorilla.

Figure 7-3

This male mountain gorilla has only to reach out to find something to eat.

Diet Since the nutritional requirements of animals are related to the previous two factors, all three have evolved together. Therefore, when primatologists study the relationships between diet and behavior, they consider the

benefits in terms of energy (calories) derived from various food items against the costs (energy expended) of obtaining and digesting them. While small-bodied primates focus on high-energy foods, larger ones don't necessarily need to. For instance, gorillas eat leaves, pith from bamboo stems, and other types of vegetation, and they don't need to use much energy searching for food because they're frequently surrounded by it (**Fig. 7–3**).

Some monkeys, especially colobines (colobus and langur species), are primarily leaf eaters. Compared with many other monkeys, they're fairly large-bodied. They've also evolved elongated intestines and pouched stomachs that enable them, with the assistance of intestinal bacteria, to digest the tough fibers and cellulose in leaves. Moreover, in at least two langur species, there's a duplicated gene that produces an enzyme that further helps with digestion. This gene duplication isn't found in other primates that have been studied, so the duplication event probably occurred after colobines and cercopithecines last shared a common ancestor (Zhang et al., 2002). Since having a second copy of the gene was advantageous to colobine ancestors who were probably already eating some leaves, natural selection favored it to the point that it was established in the lineage. (The discovery of this gene duplication is another example of how new technologies help explain behavior—in this case, dietary differences.)

Distribution of Resources Various kinds of foods are distributed in different ways. Leaves can be abundant and dense and will therefore support large groups of animals. Insects, on the other hand, may be widely scattered, and the animals that rely on them usually feed alone or with only one or two others.

Fruits, nuts, and berries in dispersed trees and shrubs occur in clumps. These are most efficiently exploited by smaller groups of animals, so large groups frequently break up into smaller subunits while feeding. Such subunits may consist of one-male–multifemale groups (some baboons) or **matrilines** (macaques).

metabolism The chemical processes within cells that break down nutrients and release energy for the body to use. (When nutrients are broken down into their component parts, such as amino acids, energy is released and made available for the cell to use.)

matrilines Groups that consist of a female, her daughters, and their offspring. Matrilineal groups are common in macaques.

THE EVOLUTION OF BEHAVIOR

Figure 7-4
Gelada baboons live in one-male groups that combine to form troops that can number more than 300 animals.

Species that feed on abundantly distributed resources may also live in one-male groups, and because food is plentiful, these one-male units are able to join with others to form large, stable communities (for example, howlers and some baboons). To the casual observer, these communities can appear to be multimale-multifemale groups (**Fig. 7-4**).

Some species that depend on foods distributed in small clumps are protective of resources, especially if their feeding area is small enough to be defended. Some live in small groups composed of a mated pair (siamangs) or a female with one or two males (marmosets and tamarins). Naturally, dependent offspring are also included. Lastly, foods such as fruits, nuts, and berries are only seasonally available, and primates that rely on them must eat a wide variety of items. This is another factor that tends to favor smaller feeding groups.

Predation Primates, depending on their size, are vulnerable to many types of predators, including snakes, birds of prey, leopards, wild dogs, and other primates. Their response to predation depends on their body size, social structure, and type of predator. Typically, where predation pressure is high and body size is small, large communities are advantageous. These may be multimale-

multifemale groups or congregations of one-male groups.

Relationships with Other, Nonpredatory Species Many primate species associate with other primate and nonprimate species for various reasons, including predator avoidance. When they do share habitats with other species, they exploit somewhat different resources.

Dispersal Dispersal is another factor that influences social structure and relationships within groups. As is true of most mammals, members of one sex leave the group in which they were born (their *natal group*) about the time they become sexually mature. Male dispersal is the most common pattern (ring-tailed lemurs, vervets, and macaques, to name a few). But female dispersal is seen in some colobus species, hamadryas baboons, chimpanzees, and mountain gorillas. In species where the basic social structure is a mated pair, offspring of both sexes either leave or are driven away by their parents (gibbons and siamangs).

Dispersal may have more than one outcome. When females leave, they join another group. Males may do likewise, but in some species (for example, gorillas), they may live alone for a time, or they may temporarily join an all-male "bachelor" group until they're able to establish a group of their own. But the common theme is that individuals who disperse usually find mates outside their natal group. This has led primatologists to conclude that the most valid explanations for dispersal are related to two major factors: reduced competition between males for mates and, more importantly, the decreased likelihood of close inbreeding.

Life Histories **Life history traits** are characteristics or developmental stages that typify members of a given species and therefore influence potential reproductive rates. Examples of life history traits include length of gestation, length of time between pregnancies (interbirth interval), period of infant dependency and age at weaning, age at sexual maturity, and life expectancy.

© Time Life Pictures / Getty Images

Figure 7-5

When a baboon strays too far from its troop, as this one has done, it's more likely to fall prey to predators. Leopards are the most serious non-human threat to terrestrial primates.

Life history traits have important consequences for many aspects of social life, and they can also be critical to species survival. Species that live only a few years mature rapidly, reproduce within a year or two after birth, and have short interbirth intervals. Thus, shorter life histories are advantageous to species that live in marginal or unpredictable habitats because reproduction can occur at a relatively rapid rate (Strier, 2003). Conversely, longer-lived species, such as gorillas, are better suited to stable envi-

ronmental conditions. The extended life spans of the great apes, characterized by later sexual maturation and long interbirth intervals of three to five years, means that most females will raise only three or four offspring to maturity. Today, this slow rate of reproduction increases the threat of extinction because the great apes are being hunted at a rate that far outpaces their replacement capacities.

Activity Patterns Most primates are diurnal, but galagos, lorises, aye-ayes, tarsiers, and New World owl monkeys are nocturnal. Nocturnal primates tend to forage for food alone or in groups of two or three and many hide to avoid predators.

Human Activities As you saw in Chapter 6, virtually all nonhuman primate populations are now impacted by human hunting and forest clearing. These activities severely disrupt and isolate groups, reduce numbers, reduce resource availability, and eventually can cause extinction.

Why Be Social?

Group living exposes animals to competition with other group members for resources, so why don't primates live alone? After all, competition can lead to injury or even death, and it's costly in terms of energy expenditure. One widely accepted answer to this question is that the costs of competition are offset by the benefits of predator defense. Multimale-multifemale groups are advantageous in areas where predation pressure is high, particularly in mixed woodlands and on open savannas. Leopards are the most significant predator of terrestrial primates (**Fig. 7–5**), but the chances of escaping a leopard attack are greater for animals that live in groups, where there are several pairs of eyes looking about. (There really is safety in numbers.)

Savanna baboons have long been cited as an example of these principles. They live in semiarid grassland and broken woodland habitats throughout sub-Saharan Africa. To avoid nocturnal predators, savanna baboons sleep in trees,

life history traits Characteristics and developmental stages that influence reproductive rates. Examples include longevity, age at sexual maturity, and length of time between births.

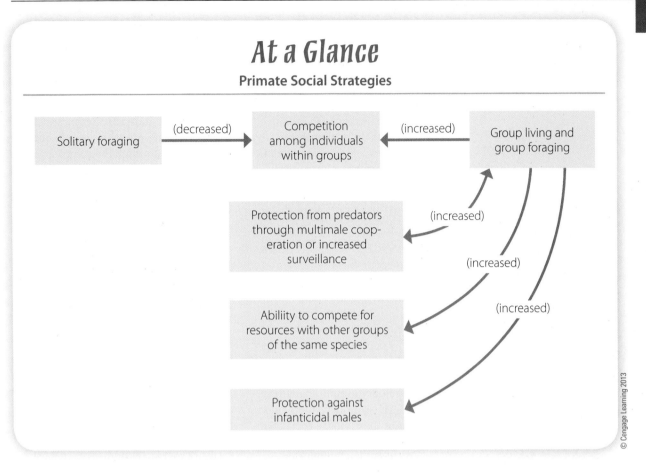

At a Glance
Primate Social Strategies

but they spend much of the day on the ground foraging for food. If a predator appears, baboons flee back into the trees, but if they're some distance from safety, adult males (and sometimes females) may join forces to chase the intruder. The effectiveness of male baboons in this regard should not be underestimated; they've been known to kill domestic dogs and even to attack leopards and lions.

There is probably no single answer to the question of why primates live in groups. More than likely, predator avoidance is a major factor but not the only one. Group living evolved as an adaptive response to a number of ecological variables, and it has served primates well for a very long time.

Primate Social Behavior

Because primates solve their major adaptive problems in a social context, we should expect them to behave in ways that reinforce the integrity of the group. The better known of these behaviors

are described here. Remember, all these behaviors have evolved as adaptive responses during more than 50 million years of primate evolution.

Dominance

Many primate societies are organized into **dominance hierarchies**, which impose a certain degree of order by establishing parameters of individual behavior. Although aggression is frequently used to increase an animal's status, dominance hierarchies usually serve to reduce the amount of actual physical violence. Not only are lower-ranking animals unlikely to attack or even threaten a higher-ranking one, but dominant animals are usually able to exert control simply by making a threatening gesture. Individual rank or status can be measured by access to resources, including food items and mating partners. Dominant animals (alpha males and females) are given priority by others, and they rarely give way in confrontations.

Many primatologists think that the primary benefit of dominance is the

dominance hierarchies Systems of social organization wherein individuals within a group are ranked relative to one another. Higher-ranking animals have greater access to preferred food items and mating partners than lower-ranking individuals.

increased reproductive success of high-ranking animals. This is true in many cases, but there's good evidence that lower-ranking males also successfully mate. High-ranking females also have higher reproductive success; because they have greater access to food than subordinate females, they're able to obtain more energy for the production and care of offspring (Fedigan, 1983).

Pusey and colleagues (1997) demonstrated that the offspring of high-ranking female chimpanzees at Gombe Stream National Park, in Tanzania, had significantly higher rates of infant survival. Moreover, their daughters matured faster, which meant they had shorter interbirth intervals and consequently produced more offspring.

An individual's position in the hierarchy isn't permanent and changes throughout life. It's influenced by many factors, including sex, age, level of aggression, amount of time spent in the group, intelligence, perhaps motivation, and sometimes the mother's social position (particularly true of macaques).

In species organized into groups containing a number of females associated with one or several adult males, the males are generally dominant to females. Within such groups, males and females have separate hierarchies, although very high-ranking females can dominate the lowest-ranking males, particularly young ones. But there are exceptions to this pattern of male dominance. In many lemur species, females are the dominant sex. Moreover, in species that form bonded pairs (for example, indris and gibbons), males and females are codominant.

All primates *learn* their position in the hierarchy. From birth, an infant is carried by its mother, and it observes how she responds to every member of the group. Just as important, it sees how others react to her. Dominance and subordination are indicated by gestures and behaviors, some of which are universal throughout the primate order, including humans, and this gestural repertoire is part of every youngster's learning experience.

Young primates also acquire social rank through play with age peers, and as they spend more time with play

groups, their social interactions widen. Competition and rough-and-tumble play allow them to learn the strengths and weaknesses of peers, and they carry this knowledge with them throughout their lives. Thus, through early contact with their mothers and subsequent exposure to peers, young primates learn to negotiate their way through the complex web of social interactions that make up their daily lives.

Communication

Communication is universal among animals and includes scents and unintentional, **autonomic** responses and behaviors that convey meaning. Such attributes as body posture provide information about an animal's emotional state. For example, a purposeful striding gait implies confidence. Moreover, autonomic responses to threatening or novel stimuli, such as raised body hair (most species) or enhanced body odor (gorillas), indicate excitement.

Many intentional behaviors also serve as communication. In primates, these include a wide variety of gestures, facial expressions, and vocalizations, some of which we humans share. Among many primates, an intense stare indicates a mild threat; and indeed, we humans find prolonged eye contact with strangers very uncomfortable. (For this reason, people should avoid eye contact with captive primates.) Other threat gestures are a quick yawn to expose canine teeth (baboons, macaques; **Fig. 7–6**); bobbing back and forth in a crouched position (patas monkeys); and branch shaking (many monkey species). High-ranking baboons *mount* the hindquarters of subordinates to express dominance (**Fig. 7–7**). Mounting may also serve to defuse potentially tense situations by indicating something like, "It's okay, I accept your apology."

Primates also use a variety of behaviors to indicate submission, reassurance, or amicable intentions. Most primates crouch to show submission, and baboons also present or turn their hindquarters toward an animal they want to appease. Reassurance takes the form of touching, patting, hugging, and holding hands (**Fig. 7–8**). **Grooming** also serves in a

© Martin B Withers / FLPA / Minden Pictures

Figure 7-6

A "yawn" that exposes large canine teeth is a common threat gesture in many primate species. Here, an adult male baboon combines it with an "eyelid flash," closing its eyes to expose light-colored eyelids that enhance the visual effect of the threat.

communication Any act that conveys information, in the form of a message, to another individual. Frequently, the result of communication is a change in the behavior of the recipient. Communication may not be deliberate but may instead be the result of involuntary processes or a secondary consequence of an intentional action.

autonomic Pertaining to physiological responses not under voluntary control. An example in chimpanzees would be the erection of body hair during excitement. Blushing is a human example. Both convey information regarding emotional states, but neither is deliberate, and communication isn't intended.

grooming Picking through fur to remove dirt, parasites, and other materials that may be present. Social grooming is common among primates and reinforces social relationships.

Figure 7-7

One young male savanna baboon mounts another as an expression of dominance.

Figure 7-8

Adolescent savanna baboons holding hands.

number of situations to indicate submission or reassurance.

A wide variety of facial expressions indicating emotional state is seen in chimpanzees and, especially, in bonobos (**Fig. 7-9**). These include the well-known play face (also seen in several other primate and nonprimate species), associated with play behavior, and the fear grin to indicate fear and submission.

Not surprisingly, vocalizations play a major role in primate communication. Some, such as the bark of a baboon that has just spotted a leopard, are unintentional startled reactions. Others, such as the chimpanzee food grunt, are heard only in specific contexts, in this case in the presence of food. These vocalizations, whether deliberate or not, inform others of the possible presence of predators or food.

Primates (and other animals) also communicate through **displays**, which are more complicated, frequently elaborate combinations of behaviors. For example, the exaggerated courtship dances of many male birds, often enhanced by colorful plumage, are displays. Chest slapping and tearing vegetation are common gorilla threat displays.

All nonhuman animals use various body postures, vocalizations, and facial expressions to transmit information. But the array of communicative devices is much richer among nonhuman primates, even though they don't use language the way humans do. Communication is important because it's what makes social living possible. Through submissive gestures, aggression is reduced and physical violence is less likely. Likewise, friendly intentions and relationships are reinforced through physical contact and

displays Sequences of repetitious behaviors that serve to communicate emotional states. Nonhuman primate displays are most frequently associated with reproductive or competitive types of behavior. Examples include chest slapping in gorillas and, in male chimpanzees, dragging and waving branches while charging and threatening other animals.

Figure 7-9

Chimpanzee facial expressions.

| Relaxed | Relaxed with dropped lip | Horizontal pout face (distress) | Fear grin (fear/excitement) | Full play face |

grooming. Indeed, we humans can see ourselves in other primates most clearly in their use of nonverbal communication, particularly because some of their gestures and facial expressions carry the same meaning as ours do.

Aggressive Interactions

Within primate societies, there's an interplay between aggressive behaviors, which can lead to group disruption, and **affiliative behaviors**, which promote group cohesion. Conflict within a group frequently develops out of competition for resources, including mating partners and food. Instead of actual attacks or fighting, most **intragroup** aggression occurs in the form of various signals and displays, frequently within the context of a dominance hierarchy. Therefore, the majority of tense situations are resolved through various submissive and appeasement behaviors.

Figure 7-10

A chimpanzee border patrol.

© Juergen Ritterbach / Alamy

affiliative behaviors Amicable associations between individuals. Affiliative behaviors, such as grooming, reinforce social bonds and promote group cohesion.

intragroup Within the group as opposed to between groups (intergroup).

territories Portions of an individual's or group's home range that are actively defended against intrusion, especially by members of the same species.

core area The portion of a home range containing the highest concentration and most reliable supplies of food and water. The core area is defended.

But conflicts aren't always resolved peacefully; in fact, they can have serious and even fatal consequences. For example, high-ranking female macaques frequently intimidate, harass, and even attack lower-ranking females to keep them away from food. Dominant females consistently chase subordinates away from food and have even been observed taking food from their mouths. Eventually, these actions can cause weight loss and poor nutrition in

low-ranking females and result in lower reproductive success; they're less able to rear offspring to maturity because they simply don't get enough to eat (Silk et al., 2003).

Competition between males for mates frequently results in injury and even death. In species that have a distinct breeding season, such as New World squirrel monkeys, conflict between males is most common during that time. In species not restricted to a mating season, such as baboons and chimpanzees, competition between males can be ongoing.

In recent years, some primatologists have focused on attacks by groups of animals on members of their own species. These conflicts occur when a number of individuals attack and sometimes kill one or two others who may or may not be members of the same group. Lethal aggression is relatively common between groups of chimpanzees, and it's also been reported in several other species, including colobus monkeys, (Starin, 1994), spider monkeys (Aureli et al., 2006; Campbell, 2006), and capuchin monkeys (Gros-Louis et al., 2003).

Between groups, aggression is often used to protect resources or **territories**. Primate groups are associated with a *home range* where they remain permanently. Although individuals may leave their home range and join another community, the group itself remains in a particular area. Within the home range is a portion called the **core area**, which contains the highest concentration of predictable resources, and it's where the group is most frequently found. Although parts of a group's home range may overlap with home ranges of other groups, core areas of adjacent groups don't overlap. The core area can also be said to be a group's territory, and it's the portion of the home range defended against intrusion. However, in some species, other areas of the home range may also be defended (**Fig. 7-10**).

Not all primates are territorial. In general, territoriality is typical of species whose ranges are small enough to be patrolled and protected (gibbons and vervets, for example). But male chimpanzees are highly intolerant of unfa-

© Photoshot Holdings Ltd / Alamy

Figure 7-11

Male chimpanzee display. Note how the hair on his arms and shoulders is raised to make him look larger. Erect hair is also an indication of excitement.

miliar chimpanzees, especially other males, and they fiercely defend their resources. Therefore, chimpanzee intergroup interactions are almost always characterized by aggressive displays, chasing, and sometimes very violent fighting (**Fig. 7-11**).

Beginning in 1974, Jane Goodall and her colleagues witnessed at least five unprovoked and extremely brutal attacks by groups of chimpanzees on other chimpanzees (Goodall, 1986). To explain these attacks, it's necessary to point out that by 1973, the original Gombe community had divided into two distinct groups, one located in the north and the other in the south of what had once been the original group's home range. In effect, the smaller offshoot group had denied the others access to part of their former home range.

By 1977, all seven males and one female of the splinter group were either known or suspected to have been killed. All observed incidents involved several animals, usually adult males, who brutally attacked lone individuals (**Fig. 7-12**). Whether the chimpanzees actually intended to kill their victims is difficult to know, because we don't know to what degree they have a concept of death.

Mitani and colleagues (2010) document a similar situation in a large chimpanzee community at Ngogo, Kibale National Park, Uganda. Between 1999

and 2009, members of this group were observed killing or fatally wounding 18 individuals from other groups, and all but one of the observed attacks were made by coalitions of males on patrol. The entire Ngogo community now regularly uses the area where they frequently conducted border patrols and where 13 of the attacks occurred. Meanwhile, the former residents have not been seen. In effect, these chimpanzees have increased their territory by 2.5 square miles, or 22 percent. Given this fact, the researchers attribute the attacks on a neighboring group to territorial expansion, which increases their resource base and in turn may lead to greater reproductive success.

Figure 7-12

This male chimpanzee cranium exhibits a healed bite wound beneath the nose most likely inflicted by another chimpanzee (arrow). Also, the left margin of the nasal opening shows irregularities that may have been caused by an infection, perhaps related to the injury.

Lynn Kilgore

Even though chimpanzees engage in lethal attacks, the actual number of observed incidents is low. The precise motivation of chimpanzee intergroup aggression may never be fully explained, but it appears that acquiring and protecting resources (including females) are involved (Nishida et al., 1985, 1990; Goodall, 1986; Manson and Wrangham, 1991; Nishida, 1991). Through careful examination of shared aspects of human and chimpanzee social life, we can develop hypotheses regarding how intergroup conflict may have arisen in our own lineage. Early hominins and chimpanzees may have inherited from a common ancestor the predispositions that lead to similar patterns of strife between populations. It's not possible to draw direct comparisons between chimpanzee conflict and modern human warfare owing to later human elaborations of culture: religion, use of symbols (such as flags), and language. But it's important to speculate on the fundamental issues that may have led to the development of similar patterns in both species.

Affiliation and Altruism

Even though conflict can be destructive, a certain amount of aggression helps protect resources and maintain order within groups. Fortunately, to minimize actual violence, promote group cohesion, and defuse potentially dangerous situations, there are many behaviors that reinforce bonds between individuals and enhance group stability. Common affiliative behaviors include reconciliation, consolation, and simple amicable interactions between friends and relatives. Most such behaviors involve various forms of physical contact, such as touching, handholding, hugging, and, among chimpanzees, kissing. In fact, physical contact is one of the most important factors in primate development, and it's crucial in promoting peaceful relationships and reinforcing bonds in many primate social groups.

There are also behaviors that indicate just how important bonds between individuals are; and some of these behaviors can perhaps be said to be examples of caregiving, or compassion. It's somewhat risky to use the term *compassion* because in humans, compassion is motivated by empathy for another person. We don't know for sure whether nonhuman primates can empathize with another's suffering or misfortune, but laboratory research has indicated that some of them probably do. The degree to which chimpanzees and other primates are capable of empathy is debated by primatologists. Some believe that there is substantial evidence for it (deWaal, 1996, 2007), but others remain unconvinced (Silk et al., 2005).

Certainly, there are many examples, mostly from chimpanzee studies, of caregiving actions that resemble compassionate behavior in humans. Examples include protecting victims during attacks, helping younger siblings, and remaining near ill or dying relatives or friends. In a poignant example from Gombe, the young adult female Little Bee brought food to her mother at least twice while the latter lay dying of wounds inflicted by attacking males (Goodall, 1986). When chimpanzees have been observed sitting near a dying relative, they were seen occasionally to shoo flies away or groom the other, as if trying to help in some way.

Grooming is one of the most important affiliative behaviors in many primate species. Although grooming occurs in other animal species, social grooming is mostly a primate activity, and it plays an important role in day-to-day life (**Fig. 7–13**). Because grooming involves using the fingers to pick through the fur of another individual (or one's own) to remove insects, dirt, and other materials, it serves hygienic functions. But it's also an immensely pleasurable activity that members of some species, especially chimpanzees, engage in for long periods of time.

Grooming occurs in a variety of contexts. Mothers groom infants; males groom sexually receptive females; subordinate animals groom dominant ones, sometimes to gain favor; and friends groom friends. In general, grooming is comforting. It restores peaceful relationships after conflict and provides reassurance during tense situations. In

empathy The ability to identify with the feelings and thoughts of another individual.

(a)

(b)

(c)

(d)

short, grooming reinforces social bonds and consequently helps strengthen and maintain a group's structure.

Conflict resolution through reconciliation is another important aspect of primate social behavior. Following a conflict, chimpanzee opponents frequently move, within minutes, to reconcile (de Waal, 1982). Reconciliation takes many forms, including hugging, kissing, and grooming. Even uninvolved individuals may take part, either grooming one or both participants or forming their own grooming parties. In addition, bonobos are unique in their use of sex to promote group cohesion, restore peace after conflicts, and relieve tension within the group (de Waal, 1987, 1989).

Social relationships are crucial to nonhuman primates, and bonds between individuals can last a lifetime. These relationships serve many functions. Individuals of many species form alliances in which members support each other against outsiders. Alliances, or coalitions, as they're also called, can

be used to enhance the status of members. For example, at Gombe, the male chimpanzee Figan achieved alpha status because of support from his brother (Goodall, 1986). In fact, chimpanzees so heavily rely on coalitions and are so skillful politically that an entire book, appropriately titled *Chimpanzee Politics* (de Waal, 1982), is devoted to the topic.

Altruism is behavior that benefits another while involving some risk or sacrifice to the performer. The most fundamental of altruistic behaviors, the protection of dependent offspring, is ubiquitous among mammals and birds, and in the majority of species, altruistic acts are confined to this context. Still, altruism, cooperation, and assistance are fairly common in many primate species, and altruistic acts sometimes contain elements of what might be interpreted as empathy. Chimpanzees routinely come to the aid of relatives and friends; female langurs join forces to protect infants from infanticidal males; and male baboons protect infants and cooperate to

Figure 7-13

Grooming primates. (a) Mandrills. (b) Longtail macaques. (c) Japanese macaques. (d) Chimpanzees.

altruism Behavior that benefits another individual but at some potential risk or cost to oneself.

chase predators. In fact, the primate literature abounds with examples of altruistic acts, whereby individuals place themselves at some risk to protect others from attacks by conspecifics or predators.

Adopting orphans is a form of altruism that has been reported for capuchins, macaques, baboons, gorillas, and especially chimpanzees. When chimpanzee youngsters are orphaned, they are almost always adopted, usually by older siblings, who are attentive and highly protective. Adoption is crucial to the survival of orphans, who certainly wouldn't survive on their own. In fact, it's extremely rare for a chimpanzee orphan less than 3 years of age to survive, even if it is adopted.

There are now hundreds of documented examples of cooperation and altruism in nonhuman primates. Chimpanzees certainly have shown a tendency to perform altruistic acts, and this fact has caused some primatologists to consider the possibility that the common ancestor of humans and chimpanzees had a propensity for cooperation and helping others, at least in certain circumstances (Warneken and Tomasello, 2006).

Evolutionary explanations of altruism are usually based on the premise that individuals are more likely to perform risky or self-sacrificing behaviors that benefit a relative. Therefore, by helping a relative who otherwise might not survive to reproduce, the performer is helping promote the spread of genes they have in common. Another explanation, sometimes called "reciprocal altruism," emphasizes that performers help others to increase the chances that, at a future date, the recipient might return the favor.

Reproduction and Reproductive Behaviors

In most primate species, sexual behavior is tied to the female's reproductive cycle, with females being receptive to males only when they're in estrus. Estrus is characterized by behavioral changes that indicate that a female is receptive. In Old World monkeys and apes that live in multimale groups, estrus is also accompanied by swelling and changes in color of the skin around the genital area. These changes serve as visual cues of a female's readiness to mate (**Fig 7–14**).

Permanent bonding between males and females isn't common among nonhuman primates. However, male and female savanna baboons sometimes form mating *consortships*. These temporary relationships last while the female

Figure 7-14

Estrous swelling in a female Celebes crested macaque.

© Shah, Anup / Animals Animals – Earth Scenes

is in estrus, and the two spend most of their time together, mating frequently. Mating consortships are also sometimes seen in chimpanzees and are common in bonobos. In fact, male and female bonobos may spend several weeks primarily in each other's company. During this time, they mate often, even when the female isn't in estrus. However, these relationships of longer duration aren't typical of chimpanzee (*Pan troglodytes*) males and females.

Such a male-female bond may result in increased reproductive success for both sexes. For the male, there is the increased likelihood that he will be the father of any infant the female conceives. At the same time, the female potentially gains protection from predators or other members of her group; and she may also gain some help in caring for offspring she may already have.

Female and Male Reproductive Strategies

Reproductive strategies, especially how they differ between the sexes, have been a primary focus of primate research. The goal of these strategies is to produce and successfully rear to adulthood as many offspring as possible.

Primates are among the most **K-selected** of mammals. By this we mean that individuals produce only a few young, in whom they invest a tremendous amount of parental care. Contrast this pattern with **r-selected** species, where individuals produce large numbers of offspring but invest little or no energy in parental care. Good examples of r-selected species include insects, most fishes, and, among mammals, mice and rabbits.

Considering the degree of care required by young, dependent primate offspring, it's clear that enormous investment by at least one parent is necessary, and in a majority of species, the mother carries most of the burden certainly before, but also after birth. Primates are totally helpless at birth, and because they develop slowly, they're exposed to expanded learning opportunities within a *social* environment. This trend has been elaborated most dramatically in great apes and humans, especially the

latter. So, what we see in ourselves and our close primate relatives (and presumably in our more recent ancestors as well) is a strategy in which at least one parent, usually the mother, makes an extraordinary investment to produce a few "high-quality," slowly maturing offspring.

Finding food and mates, avoiding predators, and caring for and protecting dependent young are difficult challenges for nonhuman primates. Moreover, in most species, males and females use different strategies to meet these challenges.

Female primates spend almost all their adult lives either pregnant, lactating, and/or caring for offspring, and the resulting metabolic demands are enormous. A pregnant or lactating female, although perhaps only half the size of her male counterpart, may require about the same number of calories per day. Even if these demands are met, her physical resources may be drained. For example, analysis of chimpanzee skeletons from Gombe showed significant loss of bone and bone mineral in older females (Sumner et al., 1989).

Given these physiological costs and the fact that her reproductive potential is limited by lengthy intervals between births, a female's best strategy is to maximize the amount of resources available to her and her offspring. Indeed, as we just discussed, females of many primate species are highly competitive with other females and aggressively protect resources. In other species, females distance themselves from others to avoid competition. Males, however, face a different set of challenges. Having little investment in the rearing of offspring along with the ability to produce sperm continuously, it's to the male's advantage to secure as many mates and produce as many offspring as possible.

Sexual Selection

Sexual selection is an outcome of different mating strategies. First described by Charles Darwin, it is a type of natural selection that operates on only one sex, usually males. The selective agent is male competition for mates and, in some species, mate choice by females. The

reproductive strategies Behaviors or behavioral complexes that have been favored by natural selection to increase individual reproductive success. The behaviors need not be deliberate, and they often vary considerably between males and females.

K-selected Pertaining to K-selection, an adaptive strategy whereby individuals produce relatively few offspring in whom they invest increased parental care. Although only a few infants are born, chances of survival are increased for each one because of parental investments in time and energy. Birds, elephants, and canids (wolves, coyotes, and dogs) are examples of K-selected nonprimate species.

r-selected Pertaining to r-selection, a reproductive strategy that emphasizes relatively large numbers of offspring and reduced parental care compared with K-selected species. *K-selection* and *r-selection* are relative terms; for example, mice are r-selected compared with primates but K-selected compared with fish.

sexual selection A type of natural selection that operates on only one sex within a species. It's the result of competition for mates, and it can lead to sexual dimorphism with regard to one or more traits.

long-term effect of sexual selection is to increase the frequency of those traits in males that lead to greater success in acquiring mates.

In the animal kingdom, numerous male attributes are the results of sexual selection. For example, female birds of many species are attracted to males with more vividly colored plumage. Selection has thus increased the frequency of alleles that influence brighter coloration in males, and in these species (peacocks are a good example), males are more colorful than females.

Sexual selection in primates is most common in species in which mating is **polygynous** and there is considerable male competition for females. In these species, sexual selection produces dimorphism with regard to a number of traits, most noticeably body size (**Fig. 7-15**). As you've seen, the males of many primate species are considerably

Figure 7-15

Mandrills are one of many good examples of sexual dimorphism and sexual selection in primates. Fully adult males are about twice the size of females and are much more colorful.

© Shutterstock / Kfich Bain

larger than females, and they also have larger canine teeth. Conversely, in species that live in pairs (such as gibbons) or where male competition is reduced, sexual dimorphism in body size and canine teeth is either reduced or nonexistent. For this reason, the presence or absence of sexual dimorphism in a species can be a reasonably good indicator of mating structure.

polygynous Pertaining to polygyny, a mating system in which males, and in some cases females, have several mating partners.

Infanticide as a Reproductive Strategy?

One way males may increase their chances of reproducing is to kill infants fathered by other males. This explanation was first offered in an early study of Hanuman langurs in India (Hrdy, 1977). Hanuman langurs (**Fig. 7–16**) typically live in groups composed of one adult male, several females, and their offspring. Other males without mates form "bachelor" groups that frequently forage within sight of one-male–multifemale units. These peripheral males occasionally attack and defeat a reproductive male and drive him from his group. Sometimes, following such a takeover, the new male kills some or all of the group's infants, fathered by the previous male.

At first glance, such behavior would seem to be counterproductive, especially for a species as a whole. However, individuals act to maximize their *own* reproductive success, no matter what effect their actions may have on the group or the species. By killing infants fathered by other animals, male langurs may in fact increase their own chances of fathering offspring, albeit unknowingly. This is because while a female is producing milk and nursing an infant, she doesn't come into estrus and therefore isn't sexually available. But when a female loses an infant, she resumes cycling and becomes sexually receptive. So, by killing nursing infants, a new male avoids waiting two to three years for them to be weaned before he can mate with their mothers. This could be advantageous for him because chances are good that he won't even be in the group for two or three years. He also doesn't expend energy and put himself at risk defending infants who don't carry his genes.

Hanuman langurs aren't the only primates that practice infanticide. Infanticide has been observed or surmised in many species, including gorillas, chimpanzees (Struhsaker and Leyland, 1987), and humans. In the majority of reported nonhuman primate examples, infanticide coincides with the transfer of a new male into a group or, as in chimpanzees, an encounter with an unfamiliar female and infant. (It should

Figure 7-16
Hanuman langurs.

© Cyril Ruoso / Bios / Peter Arnold / Photolibrary

also be noted that infanticide occurs in numerous nonprimate species, including rodents, cats, and horses.)

Numerous objections to this explanation of infanticide have been raised. Alternative explanations have included competition for resources (Rudran, 1973), aberrant behaviors related to human-induced overcrowding (Curtin and Dohlinow, 1978), and inadvertent killing during conflict between animals (Bartlett et al., 1993). Sussman and colleagues (1995), as well as others, have questioned the actual prevalence of infanticide, arguing that although it occurs, it's not particularly common. These authors have also suggested that if indeed male reproductive fitness is increased through the killing of infants, such increases are negligible. Yet others

(Struhsaker and Leyland, 1987; Hrdy et al., 1995) maintain that the incidence and patterning of infanticide by males are not only significant, but also consistent with the assumptions established by theories of behavioral evolution.

More recently, Henzi and Barrett (2003, p. 224) reported that when chacma baboon males migrate into a new group, they "deliberately single out females with young infants and hunt them down" (**Fig. 7-17**). The conclusion is that, at least in chacma baboons, newly arrived males consistently try to kill infants, and their attacks are highly aggressive. However, reports like these don't prove that infanticide increases a male's reproductive fitness. To do this, primatologists must demonstrate two crucial facts:

Figure 7-17
An immigrant male chacma baboon chases a terrified female and her infant (clinging to her back). Resident males interceded to stop the chase.

© Peter Henzi

1. Infanticidal males *don't* kill their own offspring.
2. Once a male has killed an infant, he subsequently fathers another infant with the victim's mother.

These statements are hypotheses that can be tested; and to do this, Borries and colleagues (1999) collected DNA samples from the feces of infanticidal males and their victims' remains in several groups of free-ranging Hanuman langurs. This was done to determine if these males killed their own offspring. The results showed that in all 16 cases where infant and male DNA was available, the males were not related to the infants they either attacked or killed. Moreover, DNA analysis also showed that in four out of five cases where a victim's mother sub-

sequently gave birth, the new infant was fathered by the infanticidal male. The application of DNA technology to a long-unanswered question has provided strong evidence suggesting that infanticide may indeed give males an increased chance of fathering offspring. Moreover, this study provides another example of how hypotheses are further tested as new technologies are developed.

Mothers, Fathers, and Infants

The basic social unit among all primates is a female and her infants (**Fig. 7–18**). Except in those species in which monogamy or **polyandry** occurs or the social group is a bonded pair, males usually don't directly participate in the rearing of offspring. The mother-infant bond begins at birth. Although the exact nature of the bonding process isn't fully understood, there appear to be predisposing innate factors that strongly attract the female to her infant,

Figure 7-18

Primate mothers with young. (a) Mongoose lemurs. (b) Chimpanzees. (c) Sykes monkeys. (d) Japanese macaques. (e) Squirrel monkeys.

(a)

(b)

(c)

(d)

(e)

so long as she herself has had a sufficiently normal experience with her own mother. This doesn't mean that primate mothers have innate knowledge of how to care for an infant. They don't. Monkeys and apes raised in captivity without contact with their own mothers not only don't know how to care for a newborn infant, but may reject or even injure it. Thus, learning is essential to establishing a mother's attraction to her infant.

The role of bonding between primate mothers and infants was clearly demonstrated in a famous series of experiments at the University of Wisconsin. Psychologist Harry Harlow (1959) raised infant rhesus macaques with **surrogate** mothers made of wire or a combination of wire and cloth. Other monkeys were raised with no mother at all. In one experiment, infants retained an attachment to their cloth-covered surrogate mother (**Fig. 7–19**). But those raised with no mother were incapable of forming lasting attachments with other monkeys. None of the motherless males ever successfully copulated, and those females who were (somewhat artificially) impregnated either paid little attention to their infants or were aggressive toward them (Harlow and Harlow, 1961). The point is that monkeys reared in isolation were denied opportunities

Figure 7-19

Infant macaque clinging to cloth surrogate mother.

Harlow Primate Laboratory

to *learn* the rules of social and maternal behavior. Moreover, and just as essential, they were denied the all-important physical contact so necessary for normal primate psychological and emotional development.

The importance of a normal relationship with the mother is demonstrated by field studies as well. From birth, infant primates are able to cling to their mother's fur, and they're in more or less constant physical contact with her for several months. During this critical period, infants develop closeness with their mothers that doesn't always end with weaning. It may even be maintained throughout life. In some species, presumed fathers also participate in infant care (**Fig. 7–20**). Male siamangs are actively involved, and marmoset and tamarin infants are usually carried on the father's back and transferred to their mother only for nursing.

(a)

© Nick Gordon / Minden Pictures

(b)

© Paul Souders / Corbis

Figure 7-20

(a) Male marmoset with youngster on his back. (b) Infant mountain gorilla with silverback male. It's not certain these males are actually the fathers of the infants, but they are exhibiting parental behavior.

polyandry A mating system wherein a female continuously associates with more than one male (usually two or three) with whom she mates. Among nonhuman primates, polyandry is seen only in marmosets and tamarins. It also occurs in a few human societies.

surrogate Substitute. In this case, the infant monkeys were reared with artificial substitute mothers.

Primate Cultural Behavior

Cultural behavior is one important trait that makes primates, and especially chimpanzees and bonobos, attractive as models for behavior in early hominins. Although many cultural anthropologists and others prefer to apply the term *culture* specifically to human activities, most biological anthropologists consider it appropriate to apply the term to many nonhuman primate behaviors too (McGrew, 1992, 1998; de Waal, 1999; Whiten et al., 1999).

Undeniably, most aspects of culture are uniquely human, and we should be cautious when we try to interpret nonhuman animal behavior. But again, since humans are products of the same evolutionary forces that have produced other species, they can be expected to exhibit some of the same *behavioral patterns* seen in other primates. However, because of increased brain size and learning capacities, humans express many characteristics to a greater degree, and culture is one of those characteristics.

Cultural behavior is *learned*. In other words, it's not genetically determined, although the capacity to learn is genetically influenced. Whereas humans deliberately teach their young, free-ranging nonhuman primates (with the exception of a few reports) don't appear to do so. But at the same time, like young nonhuman primates, human children also acquire a tremendous amount of knowledge through observation rather than instruction (**Fig. 7–21**). By watching their mothers and other members of their group, nonhuman primate infants learn about food items, appropriate behaviors, and how to use and modify objects to achieve certain ends. In turn, their own offspring will observe their activities. What emerges is a *cultural tradition* that may eventually come to typify an entire group or even a species.

The earliest reported example of cultural behavior concerned a study group of Japanese macaques on Koshima Island, Japan. In 1952, Japanese researchers began feeding the macaques sweet potatoes. The following year, a young female started washing her potatoes in a freshwater stream before eating them. Within three years, several monkeys were washing their potatoes, though instead of using the stream, they were taking their potatoes to the ocean nearby. Maybe they liked the salt!

Figure 7-21

(a) This little girl is learning basic computer skills by watching her older sister. (b) A young chimpanzee learns the art of termiting through intense observation.

(a)

(b)

Lynn Kilgore

© Manoj Shah / The Image Bank

The researchers pointed out that dietary habits and food preferences are learned and that potato washing is an example of nonhuman culture. Because the practice arose as an innovative solution to a problem (removing dirt) and gradually spread through the troop until it became a tradition, it was seen as containing elements of human culture.

A study of orangutans listed 19 behaviors that showed sufficient regional variation to be classed as "very likely cultural variants" (van Schaik et al., 2003). Four of these were differences in how nests were used or built. Other behaviors that varied included the use of branches to swat insects and pressing leaves or hands to the mouth to amplify sounds.

Reports of tool use by gorillas aren't common, but Breuer and colleagues (2005) reported seeing two female lowland gorillas in the DRC using branches as tools. In one case, a gorilla used a branch to test the depth of a pool of water. Then, as she waded bipedally through the pool, she used the branch again, this time as a walking stick (**Fig. 7-22**).

Chimpanzees exhibit more complex forms of tool use than any other nonhuman primate. This point is very important, because traditionally, tool use (along with language) was said to set humans apart from other animals. Chimpanzees crumple and chew handfuls of leaves, which they dip into tree hollows where water accumulates. Then they suck the water from the newly made "leaf sponges." Leaves are also used to wipe substances from fur, and twigs are used as toothpicks, stones as weapons, and objects such as branches and stones may be dragged or rolled to enhance displays.

"Termite fishing" is a common behavior among many chimpanzee groups. Chimpanzees routinely insert twigs and grass blades into termite mounds. The termites then seize the twig, and unfortunately for them, they become a light snack once the chimpanzee pulls the twig out of the mound. Chimpanzees also modify some of their stems by stripping the leaves or breaking them until they're the right length. In effect, this is making a tool, and chimpanzees have

also been seen making these tools even before the termite mound is in sight.

The modification of natural objects for use as tools has several implications for nonhuman primate intelligence. First, the chimpanzees are involved in an activity that prepares them for a future task at a somewhat distant location, and this implies planning and forethought.

Figure 7-22

A female western lowland gorilla using a wading stick (in her right hand) for support.

Second, attention to the shape and size of the raw material indicates that chimpanzees have a preconceived idea of what the finished product needs to be in order to be useful. To produce a tool, even a simple one, based on a concept is an extremely complex behavior that, as we now know, is not the exclusive domain of humans.

Primatologists have been aware of termite fishing and similar behaviors since the 1960s, but they were surprised by the discovery that chimpanzees also use tools to catch small prey. Pruetz and Bertolani (2007) reported that savanna chimpanzees in Senegal, West Africa, sharpen small branches to use as thrusting spears for capturing galagos. This is the first report of a nonhuman primate hunting with what is basically a manufactured weapon.

On 22 occasions, 10 different animals jabbed sharpened sticks into cavities in branches and trunks to extract galagos from their sleeping nests. In much the same way they modify termiting sticks, these chimpanzees had stripped off side twigs and leaves. But they'd also chewed the ends to sharpen them, in effect producing small thrusting spears.

The spears weren't necessarily used to impale victims so much as to injure or immobilize them because galagos are extremely agile and hard to catch. After several thrusts, the chimpanzee would reach into the opening to see if there was anything to be had. Observers only saw one galago being retrieved and eaten, and although it wasn't moving or vocalizing, it was unclear if it had actually been killed by the "spear" (Pruetz and Bertolani, 2007).

In several West African study groups, chimpanzees use unmodified stones as hammers and **anvils** (**Fig. 7-23**) to crack nuts and hard-shelled fruits (Boesch et al., 1994). Stone hammers and platforms are used only in West African groups and not in East Africa. Likewise, termite fishing is seen in Central and East Africa, but apparently it's not done in West African groups (McGrew, 1992). And using sharpened sticks to capture prey has been seen only in Senegal.

The fact that chimpanzees show regional variation in the types of tools they use is significant because these differences represent cultural variation from one area to another. Chimpanzees also show regional dietary preferences (Nishida et al., 1983; McGrew, 1992, 1998). For example, oil palm fruits and nuts are eaten at many locations, including Gombe. But even though oil palms also grow in the Mahale Mountains (only about 90 miles from Gombe), the chimpanzees there seem to ignore them. Such regional patterns in tool use and food preferences are reminiscent of the cultural differences that are typical of humans. Therefore,

it's likely that this kind of variation probably existed in early hominins, too.

So far, we've focused on tool use and culture in great apes, but they aren't the only nonhuman primates that consistently use tools and exhibit elements of cultural behavior. Primatologists have been studying tool use in capuchin (also called cebus) monkeys for over 30 years. Capuchins are found in South America from Colombia and Venezuela, through Brazil, and as far south as northern Argentina. They have the largest relative brain size of all monkeys, and while forest-dwelling capuchin species are arboreal, other species live in a more savanna-like habitat and spend a fair amount of time on the ground. Many of the tool-using behaviors parallel those we've discussed for chimpanzees. Capuchins use leaves to extract water from cavities in trees (Phillips, 1998), and they use small, modified branches to probe into holes in logs for invertebrates (Westergaard and Fragaszy, 1987). But what they've really become known for is using stones to obtain food. They use stones to smash foods into smaller pieces and crack palm nuts; break open hollow tree branches and logs; and dig for tubers and insects. Capuchins are the only monkeys known to use stones as tools and the only nonhuman primate to dig with stones (Visalberghi, 1990; Moura and Lee, 2004; Ottoni and Izar, 2008).

The importance of palm nuts as a food source is revealed by the enormous effort expended to obtain it. Adult female and male capuchins weigh around 6 and 8 pounds, respectively, yet they walk bipedally carrying stones that weigh as much as 2 pounds, or 25 to 40 percent of their own body weight (Fragaszy et al., 2004; Visalberghi et al., 2007). Because the stones are heavy, it's difficult for capuchins to sit while cracking nuts, so they frequently stand bipedally, raise the hammer stone with both hands, and then pound the nut using their entire body (**Figs. 7-24** and **7-25**).

Even though chimpanzees and capuchins modify sticks to make tools, they haven't been observed modifying the stones they use. However, a male bonobo named Kanzi (see also p. 169) learned to strike two stones together to produce sharp-edged flakes. In a study con-

Figure 7-23

Chimpanzees in Bossou, Guinea, West Africa, use a pair of stones as a hammer and anvil to crack oil palm nuts.

© Tetsuro Matsuzawa

anvils Surfaces on which an object such as a palm nut, root, or seed is placed before being struck with another object such as a stone.

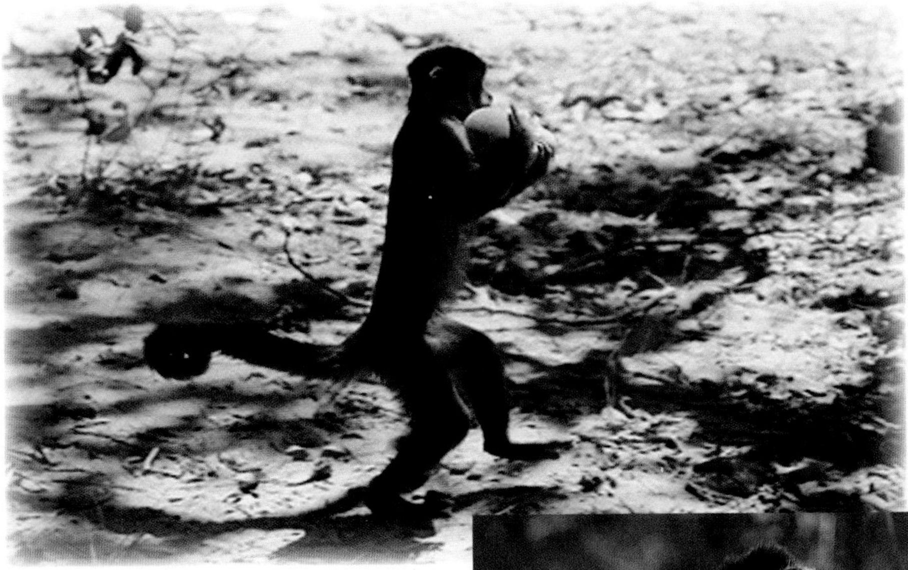

© Barth Wright / Etho*Cebus* Project

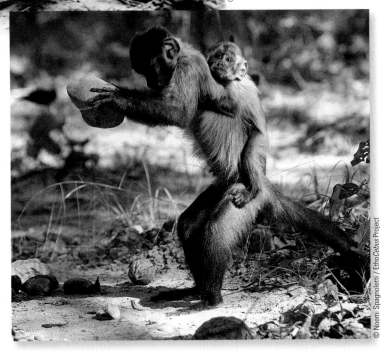

Figure 7-24

A female capuchin is going to considerable effort, walking bipedally and carrying a heavy stone to a palm nut cracking location.

© Noemi Spagnoletti / Etho*Cebus* Project

Figure 7-25

This female capuchin must use most of her strength to smash a pine nut with a heavy stone, especially while carrying an infant on her back. Meanwhile, by watching her, the infant is learning the nut-smashing technique.

ducted by Sue Savage-Rumbaugh and archaeologist Nicholas Toth, Kanzi was allowed to watch as Toth produced stone flakes, which were then used to open a transparent plastic food container (Savage-Rumbaugh and Lewin, 1994).

Bonobos don't commonly use objects as tools in the wild. But Kanzi readily appreciated the usefulness of the flakes to get food. What's more, he was able to master the basic technique of producing flakes without being taught, although at first his progress was slow. But then he realized that if he threw the stone onto a hard floor, it would shatter and he'd have lots of cutting tools. Although his solution wasn't the one that Savage-Rumbaugh and Toth had expected, it was even more significant because it provided an excellent example of bonobo insight and problem-solving ability. Kanzi did eventually learn to produce flakes by striking two stones together, and then he used these flakes to obtain food. These behaviors aren't just examples of tool manufacture and use, albeit in a captive situation; they're also very sophisticated goal-directed activities.

Culture has become the environment in which modern humans live. Quite clearly, the use of sticks in termite fishing and hammer stones to crack nuts is hardly comparable to modern human technology. However, modern human technology had its beginnings in these very types of behaviors. But this doesn't mean that nonhuman primates are "on their way" to becoming human. Remember, evolution isn't goal directed, and even if it were, there's nothing to dictate that modern humans necessarily constitute an evolutionary goal. Such a conclusion is a purely **anthropocentric** view and has no validity in discussions of evolutionary processes.

Language

One of the most significant events in human evolution was the development of **language**. We've already described several behaviors and autonomic responses that convey information in primates. But although we emphasized the importance of communication to nonhuman primate social life, we also

anthropocentric Viewing nonhuman organisms in terms of human experience and capabilities; emphasizing the importance of humans over everything else.

language A standardized system of arbitrary vocal sounds, written symbols, and gestures used in communication.

said that nonhuman primates don't use language the way humans do.

The view traditionally held by most linguists and behavioral psychologists was that nonhuman communication consists of mostly involuntary vocalizations and actions that convey information solely about the emotional state of the animal (anger, fear, and so on). Nonhuman animals haven't been considered capable of communicating about external events, objects, or other animals, either in close proximity or removed in space or time. For example, when a startled baboon barks, other group members know only that it's startled. But they don't know what startled it, and they can only determine this by looking around to find the cause. In general, then, it's been assumed that in nonhuman animals, including primates, vocalizations, facial expressions, body postures, and so on, don't refer to *specific* external phenomena.

But for several years, these views have been challenged (Steklis, 1985; King, 1994, 2004). For example, vervet monkeys (**Fig. 7–26**) use specific vocalizations to refer to particular categories of predators, such as snakes, birds of prey, and leopards (Struhsaker, 1967; Seyfarth, Cheney, and Marler, 1980a, 1980b). When researchers made tape recordings of various vervet alarm calls and played them back within hearing

distance of wild vervets, they saw different responses to various calls. When they heard leopard-alarm calls, the monkeys climbed trees; they looked up when they heard eagle-alarm calls; and they responded to snake-alarm calls by looking around at the ground.

These results show that vervets use distinct vocalizations to refer to specific components of the external environment. These calls aren't involuntary, and they don't refer solely to the emotional state (alarm) of the individual, although this information is conveyed. While these findings dispel certain long-held misconceptions about nonhuman communication (at least for some species), they also indicate certain limitations. Vervet communication is restricted to the present; as far as we know, no vervet can communicate about a predator it saw yesterday or one it might see tomorrow.

Humans use *language*—a set of written or spoken symbols that refer to concepts, other people, objects, and so on. This set of symbols is said to be *arbitrary* because the symbol itself has no inherent relationship with whatever it stands for. For example, the English word *flower*, when written or spoken, doesn't look, sound, smell, or feel like the thing it represents. Humans can recombine their linguistic symbols in an infinite number of ways to create new meanings; and we can use language to refer to events, places, objects, and people far removed in both space and time. For these reasons, language is described as a form of communication based on the human ability to think symbolically.

Language, as distinct from other forms of communication, has always been considered a uniquely human achievement, setting humans apart from the rest of the animal kingdom. But work with captive apes has somewhat revised this view. Although many researchers were skeptical about the capacity of nonhuman primates to use language, reports from psychologists, especially those who work with chimpanzees, leave little doubt that apes can learn to interpret visual signs and use them in communication. Other than humans, no mammal can speak. However, the fact that apes can't speak has less to do with lack

Figure 7-26

A group of vervets.

Lynn Kilgore

of intelligence than to differences in the anatomy of the vocal tract and language-related structures in the brain.

Beginning in the 1960s, after unsuccessful attempts to teach young chimpanzees to speak, researchers designed a study to evaluate language abilities in chimpanzees using American Sign Language for the Deaf (ASL). The research was a success, and in three years a young female named Washoe was using at least 132 signs. Years later, an infant chimpanzee named Loulis was placed in Washoe's care. Psychologist Roger Fouts and colleagues wanted to know if Loulis would acquire signing skills from Washoe and other chimpanzees in the study group. Within just eight days, Loulis began to imitate the signs of others. Moreover, Washoe deliberately *taught* Loulis some signs.

There have been several other chimpanzee language experiments, and work with orangutans, gorillas, and bonobos has shown that all the great apes have the capacity to use signs and symbols to communicate, not only with humans but also with each other. These abilities imply that to some degree, the great apes are capable of symbolic thought.

Questions have been raised about this type of research. Do the apes really understand the signs they learn, or are they merely imitating their trainers? Do they learn that a symbol is a name for an object or simply that using it will produce that object? Partly in an effort to address some of these questions, psychologist Sue Savage-Rumbaugh demonstrated that chimpanzees can use symbols to categorize *classes* of objects. Using a symbol as a label is not the same thing as understanding the *representational value* of the symbol; but if the chimpanzees could classify things into groups, it would indicate that they can use symbols referentially.

Two chimps were taught that familiar food items (for which they used symbols) belonged to a broader category referred to by yet another symbol, "food." Then they were introduced to unfamiliar food items, for which they had no symbols, to see if they would put them in the food category. The fact that they both had excellent scores showed that they could categorize unfamiliar objects. This ability was a strong indication that the chimpanzees understood that the symbols represented objects and groups of objects (Savage-Rumbaugh and Lewin, 1994).

A major assumption throughout the relatively brief history of ape language studies has been that young chimpanzees must be *taught* to use symbols, in contrast to the ability of human children to learn language through exposure, without being taught. Therefore, it was significant when Savage-Rumbaugh and her colleagues reported that the young bonobo Kanzi, before his tool-making days, was *spontaneously* acquiring and using symbols when he was just 2½ years old (Savage-Rumbaugh et al., 1986; **Fig. 7-27**).

© Dr. Duane Rumbaugh, Language Research Center (photo by Elizabeth Pugh)

Figure 7-27

The bonobo Kanzi, as a youngster, using lexigrams to communicate with human observers.

While the great apes that have been involved in the language experiments have shown a remarkable degree of cognitive complexity, it nevertheless remains evident that they don't acquire and use language in the same way humans do. It also appears that not all signing apes understand the relationship between symbol and object, person, or action. Nonetheless, there's now abundant evidence that humans aren't the only species capable of some degree of symbolic thought and complex communication.

At a Glance
Evolution of Human Language

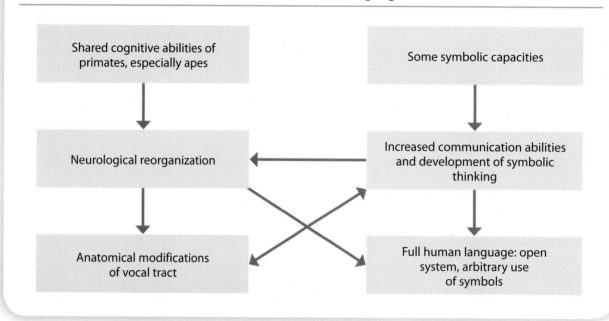

© Cengage Learning 2013

The Primate Continuum

It's an unfortunate fact that humans generally view themselves as separate from the rest of the animal kingdom. This perspective is partly due to a prevailing lack of knowledge about the behavior and abilities of other species. Moreover, these notions are continuously reinforced through exposure to advertising, movies, and television (**Fig. 7–28**).

For decades, behavioral psychology taught that animal behavior represents nothing more than a series of conditioned responses to specific stimuli. (This perspective is very convenient for those who wish to exploit nonhuman animals, for whatever purposes, and remain guilt-free.) Fortunately, this attitude has begun to change in recent years to reflect a growing awareness that humans, although in many ways unquestionably unique, are nevertheless part of a **biological continuum** and behavioral continuum. We are connected not only to our closest relatives, the other primates, but to all life on earth.

Where do humans fit in this continuum? The answer depends on the crite-

ria used. Certainly, we're the most intelligent species if we define intelligence in terms of problem-solving abilities and abstract thought. However, if we look more closely, we recognize that the differences between ourselves and our primate relatives, especially chimpanzees and bonobos, are primarily quantitative, not qualitative.

Although the human brain is absolutely and relatively larger, neurological processes are functionally the same. The necessity of close bonding with at least one parent and the need for physical contact are essentially the same. Developmental stages and dependence on learning are similar. Indeed, even in the capacity for cruelty and aggression combined with compassion, tenderness, and altruism exhibited by chimpanzees, we see a close parallel to the dichotomy between "evil" and "good" so long recognized in ourselves. The main difference between how chimpanzees and humans express these qualities (and therefore the dichotomy) is one of degree. Humans are much more adept at cruelty and compassion, and we can reflect on our behavior in ways that chimpanzees can't. Like the cat that plays with a mouse, chimpanzees

biological continuum Refers to the fact that organisms are related through common ancestry and that behaviors and traits seen in one species are also seen in others to varying degrees. (When expressions of a phenomenon continuously grade into one another so that there are no discrete categories, they are said to exist on a continuum. Color is such a phenomenon.)

Lynn Kilgore

(a)

Allposters.com

(b)

Figure 7-28

(a) Advertising displays such as this reinforce negative and ill-informed stereotypes of non-human primates. (b) This well-intentioned poster is using a common but incorrect and misleading phrase to make a point.

don't seem to understand the suffering they inflict on others. But humans do. Likewise, while an adult chimpanzee may sit next to a dying relative, it doesn't seem to feel the intense grief that a human normally does in the same situation.

To arrive at any understanding of what it is to be human, it's important to recognize that many of our behaviors are elaborate extensions of those of our hominin ancestors and close primate relatives. The fact that so many of us prefer to bask in the warmth of the "sun belt" with literally millions of others reflects our heritage as social animals adapted to life in the tropics. And the sweet tooth that afflicts so many of us is a result of our earlier primate ancestors' predilection for high-energy sugar contained in sweet, ripe fruit. Thus, it's important to recognize our primate heritage as we explore how humans came to be and how we continue to adapt.

Summary of Main Topics

▶ One of the major goals of primatology is to discover how certain behaviors influence reproductive fitness and how ecological factors have shaped the evolution of those behaviors.

▶ Behavioral ecology is the discipline that examines behavior from the perspective of complex ecological relationships and how they influence natural selection as it favors behaviors that increase reproductive fitness.

▶ Primates are among the most social of animals, but within social groups there is competition for resources and conflict. Dominance hierarchies help reduce the amount of physical aggression. Also, there are numerous amicable behaviors, such as grooming, that maintain peaceful relationships between individuals.

▶ Communication makes it possible to live in social groups. It occurs in many forms, including vocalizations and gestures. Some primate species are able to communicate about certain aspects of the external environment, indicating some ability to think symbolically.

▶ Several nonhuman primates exhibit aspects of culture, including tool use and regional variation in dietary preferences. Chimpanzees use stones to crack palm nuts in some populations but not in others;

some savanna chimpanzees use sharpened sticks to hunt for galagos; and capuchins that live in savanna-like habitats use stones to crack nuts and dig for roots.

▶ Long-term language studies with the great apes have shown that these species have the ability to communicate using different kinds of symbols, including sign language.

▶ Biological and behavioral continuity within the primate order reveals how humans are connected to our closest relatives and allows us to explain some aspects of human behavior.

Critical Thinking Questions

1. Speculate on how the behavioral ecology of nonhuman primates may be helpful in explaining some human behaviors.

2. How might infanticide be seen as a reproductive strategy for males? What would you say if you saw a newspaper article that applied this idea (not the act itself) to human males? Do you think some people would object? Why or why not?

3. Do you think that knowing about aggression between groups of chimpanzees is useful in understanding conflicts between human societies? Why or why not?

4. Why are the language capabilities of nonhuman primates important to our understanding of how our own species may have acquired language?

Paleoanthropology/ Fossil Hominins

CHAPTER 8

Understanding the Past: Archaeological and Paleoanthropological Methods

LEARNING OBJECTIVES

After you have mastered the material in this chapter, you will be able to:

▶ Explain, from a biocultural perspective, why scientists need to understand the behavior and anatomy of ancient hominins.

▶ Identify the main objectives of paleoanthropology and archaeology; understand and describe the similarities and differences between these disciplines; and explain why research on human origins requires a multidisciplinary approach.

▶ Compare the similarities and differences between relative and chronometric dating and describe examples of each type.

▶ Explain why archaeologists must assume that the organization and structure of the archaeological record reflects the behavior of humans in the past.

A portion of a pig's tusk, a small sample of volcanic sediment, a battered cobble, a primate's molar tooth: What do these unremarkable remains have in common, and more to the point, why are they of interest to paleoanthropologists and archaeologists? First of all, if they are all discovered at certain sites in Africa or Eurasia, they may be quite ancient—perhaps millions of years old. Further, some of these materials can directly inform scientists of accurate and precise dating of the finds. Last, and most exciting, some of these finds may have been modified, used, and discarded by creatures who looked and behaved in some ways like us, but were, in other respects, very different. And what of that molar tooth? Is it a fossilized remnant of an ancient **hominin**? These are the kinds of questions asked by paleoanthropologists and archaeologists, and to answer them, researchers travel to remote locales throughout the Old World.

How do we distinguish possible hominins from other types of animals, especially when all we may have to study are fragmentary fossil remains from just a small portion of a skeleton? How do humans and our most distant ancestors compare with other animals? In the previous three chapters, we've seen how humans are classified as primates, both structurally and behaviorally, and how our evolutionary history coincides with that of other mammals and, specifically, other primates. But we are a unique kind of primate, and our ancestors have been adapted to a particular lifestyle for several million years. Some primitive hominoid probably began this process close to 7 mya, but with better-preserved fossil discoveries, scientists now have more definitive evidence of hominins shortly after 5 mya. The hominin nature of these remains is revealed by more than the structure of teeth and bones; we know that these animals are hominins also because of the way they behaved—emphasizing once again the biocultural nature of human evolution. Most of what we've learned is the result of paleoanthropological and archaeological research.

Before moving on, let's consider why the paleoanthropologist and the archae-ologist may sometimes be the same person and sometimes be different research specialists. Recall from Chapter 1 that paleoanthropology takes a broad inter-disciplinary perspective on the hom-inin past from more than 5 mya up to the appearance of modern humans. Archaeology, however, focuses only on that part of our past during which hominins have been cultural animals—roughly from 2.6 mya, with the earliest identified early hominin tools and tool-making debris, up to the twenty-first century. In other words, sometimes these anthropology subfields share consid-erable overlap and sometimes they are quite distinct; it all depends on the indi-vidual research question.

In this chapter, we describe the basic concepts of these interrelated lines of investigation so that you can approach the rest of the book with a solid ground-ing in the research methods on which reconstructions of the human past are based. We'll begin with the broader aspects of paleoanthropology. This sets the stage for Chapters 9 through 12, in which we examine the fossil evidence of human ancestors and near relatives.

The present chapter also deals with archaeology and its methods. Archaeological research plays a gradual-ly increasing role in Chapters 9 through 12 and becomes the dominant informa-tion source in Chapters 13 through 15. Toward the end of this chapter, you'll see an example of the integration of paleo-anthropology and archaeology in a short case study of the history of research at Olduvai Gorge, in East Africa, the best-known early hominin site locality in the world.

Biocultural Evolution: The Human Capacity for Culture

One of the most distinctive behavioral features of humans is our extraordi-nary elaboration of and dependence on culture. Certainly other primates, and many other animals, for that matter, modify their environments. As we saw in Chapter 7, chimpanzees especially are

---

hominin   A member of the tribe Hominini, the evolutionary group that includes modern humans and now-extinct bipedal relatives.

known for such behaviors as using ter-mite sticks, and some even carry and use rocks to crush nuts. Because of such observations, it's often hard to draw a sharp line between early hominin tool-making behavior and that exhibited by other animals.

Another point to remember is that human culture, at least as it's defined in contemporary contexts, involves much more than toolmaking capacity. For humans, culture is a fundamental adaptive strategy involving cognitive, political, social, and economic components, as well as technology. Nevertheless, when we examine the archaeological record of early hominins, what is available for study is almost exclusively limited to the material culture they left behind. Researchers are confident that early hominins made and used tools fabricated from perishable materials such as wood long before the earliest stone tools are found in the archaeological record. But a thorough understanding of these first tentative steps toward the development of human culture is elusive because they are so difficult (but fortunately not impossible) to study.

The fundamental basis for human cultural success relates directly to cognitive abilities. Again, we're not dealing with an absolute distinction, but a relative one. As you have already learned, other primates, as documented in chimpanzees and bonobos, have some of the language capabilities exhibited by humans. Even so, modern humans display these abilities in far greater complexity than that seen in any other animal. And only humans are so completely dependent on symbolic communication and its cultural by-products that contemporary *Homo sapiens* could not survive without them.

At this point, you may be wondering just when the unique combination of cognitive, social, and material cultural adaptations became prominent in human evolution. This is hard to pinpoint precisely because we must consider the manifold nature of culture, which cannot be expected to always contain the same elements across species (as when comparing ourselves with nonhuman primates) or through time

(when trying to reconstruct ancient hominin behavior). Richard Potts (1993) has critiqued such overly simplistic perspectives and suggests instead a more dynamic approach, one that incorporates many subcomponents (including aspects of behavior, cognition, and social interaction).

As you'll soon see, by at least 5 mya and perhaps even by 7 mya, hominins had developed one crucial advantage: They were bipedal and could therefore much more easily carry all manner of objects, including rudimentary tools, from place to place. We know that the earliest hominins almost certainly did not regularly manufacture stone tools (at least none that have been found and identified as such). These earliest members of the hominin lineage, which we can call **protohominins**, lived approximately 7–5 mya. They may have carried objects such as naturally sharp stones or stone flakes, parts of carcasses, and pieces of wood around their home ranges. At the very least, we would expect them to have displayed tool-using behavior comparable to that observed among modern chimpanzees and bonobos.

What we know for sure is that over a period of several million years, during the formative stages of hominin emergence, many components interacted, but not all of them developed simultaneously. As cognitive abilities developed, more efficient means of communication and learning resulted. Largely because of consequent neurological reorganization, more elaborate tools and social relationships also emerged. These, in turn, selected for greater intelligence, which in turn selected for further neural elaboration. Quite clearly, then, these mutual dynamic interactions are at the very heart of what we call hominin *biocultural* evolution.

Paleoanthropology

To adequately understand human evolution, we need a broad base of information. It's the paleoanthropologist's task to recover and interpret all the clues left by early hominins. *Paleoanthropology* is defined as the overall study of

protohominins The earliest members of the hominin lineage, as yet only poorly represented in the fossil record; thus, the reconstruction of their structure and behavior is largely hypothetical.

fossil hominins. As such, it's a diverse **multidisciplinary** pursuit seeking to reconstruct every possible bit of information concerning the dating, structure, behavior, and ecology of our hominin ancestors. In the last half century, the study of early humans has drawn on the specialized skills of many different kinds of scientists, including geologists, archaeologists, physical anthropologists, and paleoecologists.

Geologists, usually working with anthropologists, do the initial surveys to locate potential early hominin sites. Many sophisticated techniques aid in this search, including the analysis of aerial and satellite imagery. Paleontologists are usually involved in this early survey work, for they can help find fossil beds containing faunal remains. Where conditions are favorable for the preservation of bone from such species as pigs and elephants, hominin remains may also be preserved. In addition, paleontologists can (through comparison with known faunal sequences) give approximate age estimates of fossil sites without having to wait for the results of more time-consuming analyses.

Fossil beds likely to contain hominin finds are subjected to extensive field surveying. For some sites, generally those postdating 2.6 mya (roughly the age of the oldest identified human artifacts), archaeologists take over in the search for hominin material traces. We don't necessarily have to find the physical remains of early hominins themselves to know that they consistently occupied a particular area. Such material clues as **artifacts** also inform us directly about early hominin activities. Modifying rocks according to a consistent plan or simply carrying them around from one place to another over fairly long distances (assuming the action can't be explained by natural means, such as streams or glaciers) is characteristic of no other animal but a hominin. So, when we see such material evidence at a site, we know that hominins were present.

Because organic materials such as wooden and bone tools aren't usually preserved in the archaeological record of the oldest hominins, we have no solid evidence of the earliest stages of hominin cultural modifications. On the other hand, our ancestors at some point showed a veritable fascination with stones, which were not only easily accessible and transportable (to use as convenient objects for throwing or for holding down other objects, such as skins and windbreaks) but also the most durable and sharpest cutting edges available at that time. Luckily for us, stone is almost indestructible, and some early hominin sites are strewn with thousands of stone artifacts. The earliest artifact sites now documented are from the Gona and Bouri areas in northeastern Ethiopia, dating to close to 2.6 mya (de Heinzelin et al., 1999; Semaw et al., 2003). Other contenders for the "earliest" stone assemblage come from the adjacent Hadar and Middle Awash areas, immediately to the south in Ethiopia, dated 2.5–2 mya.

After an early hominin site is discovered (and money and personnel can be found to study it), much more concentrated research begins. Usually headed by a physical anthropologist or archaeologist, the field crew continues to survey and map the site in great detail (**Fig. 8-1**). In addition, crew members search carefully for bones and artifacts eroding out of the soil, take pollen and soil samples for ecological analysis, and carefully collect rock samples for use in various dating techniques. If, in this early exploration stage, crew members find fossil hominin remains, they will feel very lucky indeed because such remains are very rare. More likely, the crew will accumulate much information on geological setting, ecological data (particularly faunal remains), and, with some luck, artifacts and other archaeological traces.

Although paleoanthropological fieldwork is typically a long hard process, the detailed laboratory analyses of collected

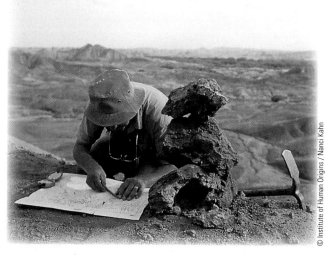

© Institute of Human Origins / Nanci Kahn

Figure 8-1

A paleoanthropologist maps an area in Ethiopia where geological exposures, as well as specific areas containing archaeological, faunal, and other remains are carefully recorded.

multidisciplinary Pertaining to research that involves the cooperation of experts from several scientific fields (i.e., disciplines).

artifacts Objects or materials made or modified for use by hominins. The earliest identified artifacts are made of stone, but hominin tool use is probably older than these artifacts.

samples and other data are even more time-consuming. Archaeologists must clean, sort, label, and identify all artifacts, and paleontologists must do the same for all fossil hominin and faunal remains. Knowing the kinds of animals represented—whether forest browsers, woodland species, or open-country forms—greatly helps in reconstructing the local *paleoecological* settings in which early hominins lived. Analyzing the fossil pollen collected from hominin sites further aids in developing a detailed environmental reconstruction. All these paleoecological analyses can assist in reconstructing the diet of early humans. Also, the **taphonomy** of the site must be worked out in order to understand its depositional history—that is, how the site formed over time.

In the concluding stages of interpretation, the paleoanthropologist draws together the following essential lines of evidence, generated by the many specialists participating in the research: dated samples, paleoecological data, archaeological traces of behavior, and anatomical information from hominin remains.

By analyzing all these data, scientists try to "flesh out" the kind of animal that may have been our direct ancestor, or at least a very close relative. Primatologists may assist here by showing the detailed relationships between the anatomical structure and behavior of humans and that of contemporary nonhuman primates (see Chapters 6 and 7). Cultural anthropologists and ethnoarchaeologists may contribute ethnographic information concerning the varied nature of human behavior, particularly the cultural adaptations of those contemporary hunter-gatherer groups exploiting roughly similar environmental settings as those reconstructed for a hominin site.

The outcome of many such research projects, conducted over decades by scores, if not hundreds, of investigators drawn from many disciplines, is a more complete and accurate understanding of human evolution—how we came to be the way we are. Both biological and cultural aspects of our ancestors contribute to this fundamental understanding of our past, each process developing in relation to the other.

Archaeology

As we noted in Chapter 1, archaeology is best viewed as a body of methods designed to understand the human past through the study of its material remains. Archaeologists use basically the same methods and techniques to research early hominin sites in the Old World as they do to study the prehistory of modern humans. The big differences are, first, that the archaeological record holds much less material evidence of the lifeways of early hominins than of modern humans and, second, that the oldest archaeological data are difficult to interpret accurately because early hominins were physically and culturally quite different from modern humans. As we move closer in time to modern humans, the archaeological record becomes more extensive, more diverse, and more readily interpreted.

Goals of Archaeology

In its study of the human past, anthropological archaeology has four main goals that play a role in every research project. The first goal, a very basic one, is to reconstruct the chronicle of past human events as they were played out across space and through time. This goal is essentially that of providing order to the archaeological record, an order that implicitly answers the fundamental "when" and "where" questions. When did plant domestication arise in the Near East? What sustained contacts existed between the people of western Mexico and northern Peru in 800–400 B.C.? Does the distribution of hand axes (a type of stone tool discussed in Chapter 10) extend into Southeast Asia? Descriptive questions such as these, anchored as they are in time and space, are essential to the successful examination of more challenging questions about the human past.

Archaeology's second main goal is to reconstruct past human lifeways. Using clues from artifacts, archaeological features, sites, and contexts, archaeologists try to understand how people actually created and used those cultural products to interact with each other and their

taphonomy (*taphos*, meaning "grave") The study of how bones and other materials came to be buried in the earth and preserved as fossils. A taphonomist studies the processes of sedimentation, the action of streams, preservation properties of bone, and carnivore disturbance factors.

surroundings. How were these tools made and used? How were people treated in death? What did their huts or shelters look like? Think of this area of research as the archaeological equivalent of the ethnographies that cultural anthropologists create from their studies of contemporary traditional societies.

Third, archaeologists want to *explain* how and why the past happened as it did. Why does the earliest evidence of farming occur after the end of the last Ice Age and not before? Are social inequalities inevitable correlates of the development of the earliest civilizations? Such questions are tough to answer because of their general nature and because the answers can require a lot more information about the past than anyone has yet learned.

Theoretical changes in archaeology over the past two decades also yielded what many researchers now regard as a fourth main goal, which can be loosely described as interpreting the cogni-

tive and symbolic aspects of past societies. This research complements the search for general explanations of past cultural patterns and explores questions that reflect archaeology's roots in the humanities. What can changes in the representational conventions of clothing in medieval Hindu art tell us about the changing nature of kingship and the relations between kings? To what extent is the current scientific understanding of Russian prehistory biased by the values, beliefs, and social history of past generations of archaeologists? Such questions defy *general* explanation but are just as important to our understanding of the human past.

Archaeological Research Projects

Modern archaeology, like paleoanthropology, is a complex undertaking that often draws on the expertise of specialists from many fields. Field projects range in scale from relatively simple tasks that can be completed in a few days (**Fig. 8-2**) to major undertakings that may take decades to complete (**Fig. 8-3**). The justification for allocating resources to such research also varies greatly, from cultural resource management (CRM) projects designed to meet legal guidelines for conserving historical

Figure 8-2

Excavation of this "test pit" at a late prehistoric site in western Kentucky will enable archaeologists to assess the site's depositional history, its approximate age, how well preserved it is, and the diversity and kind of remains preserved there. Researchers will compare this information with the results of similar test pits at other sites in the same region and use it in deciding which sites should be excavated more extensively.

Figure 8-3

Excavation of this large, deeply stratified archaeological site in western Illinois took years of sustained effort by large field crews and support staff to complete. It yielded far greater contextual information than researchers would expect to find in something like a test pit (see Fig. 8–2).

sites and monuments to public or private agency-sponsored projects designed to answer specific questions about the past.

Given an important question or problem to motivate research, archaeological fieldwork assumes a fairly common pattern. First, an appropriate location is chosen for the research, and the archaeological resources of that region are identified and inventoried. Second, sites selected from the region's known sites are carefully examined, often using methods that cause minimal disturbance to the archaeological record . Finally, some sites may be wholly or partially excavated.

Modern archaeologists and other paleoanthropologists can (and do) turn to an extraordinary array of high-tech tools to help them discover the location of sites, including aerial and satellite imagery and remote sensing technologies with such obscure-sounding names as ground-penetrating radar, side-scan sonar, proton magnetometers, and sub-bottom profilers, to name only a few (**Fig. 8-4**). Even so, fieldworkers on foot who look for artifacts and other telltale material evidence on the ground surface probably still discover most sites.

As they identify sites in the field, archaeologists record information about the local terrain, including the kinds of artifacts and other cultural debris that may be present on the surface, the area covered by this scatter of debris, and other basic facts that become part of the permanent record of the site. Later, back in the lab, analyses of these data often yield estimates of the approximate age of each site, what the prehistoric site inhabitants did there, how long they used the site, and sometimes even where they may have come from and the rough age and sex composition of the group (**Fig. 8-5**).

Information from this **site survey**, as it is often called, enables the project directors to make informed decisions about excavating the sites. They'll choose locations that are most likely to yield information necessary to solve the problem that motivated the research or, if it is a CRM project, to comply with relevant heritage management priorities, guidelines, and laws.

The popular stereotype of archaeology and archaeologists is that they spend most of their time digging square

Michael L. Hargrave

Figure 8-4

Dr. Michael L. Hargrave conducts an electrical resistance survey to locate archaeological features at a site in central Missouri. The survey works by measuring the electrical resistance between two electrodes inserted in the earth. By systematically recording these measures across an archaeological site, researchers can plot the data to show soil disturbances such as ditches, walls, roads, and similar features that show no visible traces on the ground surface.

5 Cm

Barry Lewis

Figure 8-5

By analyzing this collection of cultural debris from the surface of a prehistoric site in southeastern Missouri, the archaeologist can estimate the site age and the kinds of activities its inhabitants performed there. Other information about the site—including approximate site area, site preservation conditions, present land use, soil type, ground cover, and visible cultural features—was recorded when this surface collection was made.

site survey The process of discovering the location of archaeological sites; sometimes called site reconnaissance.

holes in the ground. Although this kind of activity will always be archaeology's defining characteristic, the professional attitude toward excavation changed during the twentieth century from a this-is-what-we-do attitude to a deep appreciation of the fact that the archaeological record is a finite resource, much like oil and gas deposits. We can be confident, for example, that all the 2,000-year-old sites that will ever exist were laid down 2,000 years ago. There aren't going to be any more of them, only fewer. And since excavation is obviously destructive, it's not like archaeologists do a site any favor by digging it up! Having come to this realization in the second half of the twentieth century, archaeologists have since tried to take a leadership role in promoting the adoption of national policies that conserve the world's remaining archaeological resources for the maximum public and scientific benefit. So yes, excavation will always be a distinctively archaeological activity. But such excavations should happen only in those situations where the data are needed to answer specific important questions about the human past or to collect basic archaeological information about sites that face imminent threat of destruction. Anything else simply vandalizes our shared heritage of the past.

Piecing Together the Past

Archaeology produces useful information only because we can reasonably assume that the organization and structure of the archaeological record reflects the behavior of humans in the past. Were this assumption to be false, archaeology would cease to exist. It's also undeniably true that it's easier to use archaeological data to examine some aspects of the past than others. Archaeologists, for example, seem to delight in telling us about what ancient people ate. They're typically far less prepared to tell us about such things as regional patterns of Neandertal ethnic identity in southwestern France or the social meaning of tattooed faces among the late prehistoric Native American villagers of the American Southeast.

It's not that no one cares about these things. It's just that it's far easier to talk about the archaeology of food than about the archaeology of identity and body art. After all, the archaeological record really is "other people's garbage" (Peck and Andrade-Watkins, 1988); it only becomes something more than garbage when we attempt to use it to inform ourselves about the past. Only then must we confront the possibility that what we wish to know may not be preserved in the archaeological record or be open to direct examination. If that's the case, then the researcher must explore ways to examine the phenomenon of interest indirectly. And if that doesn't work, the archaeologist smacks up against the state-of-the-art wall, something that exists in every field and beyond which the potentially knowable cannot yet be known until someone develops new technologies or theoretical approaches that make it possible.

Artifacts, Features, and Contexts

Four essential products—artifacts, **features, ecofacts,** and **contexts**—result from archaeological research. The relationships between these categories of remains are most often observed on *archaeological sites,* which are the locations of past human activity, such as the remains of a long-ago abandoned village or the place where an ancient hunter skinned and butchered a buffalo.

Artifacts are tangible objects; in fact, anything that was made or modified by people in the past qualifies as an artifact (**Fig. 8-6**). It might be a stone tool or a sherd (fragment) of broken pottery or even a tin can. Artifacts differ from archaeological features because they can be removed as a single entity from the archaeological record. You can't do that with *features,* such as a medieval Hindu temple, a mud-lined hearth or fireplace, or a human burial, because none of them can be taken from the archaeological record in one piece (**Fig. 8-7**). *Ecofacts* are natural materials that are used mostly to reconstruct the local environment of a site (**Fig. 8-8**). Ecofacts can be found as both artifacts and features.

features Products of human activity that cannot be removed from the archaeological record as a single discrete entity. Examples include hearths, human burials, and the remains of a Paleolithic hut.

ecofacts Natural materials that give environmental information about a site. Examples include plant and animal remains discarded as food waste and also pollen grains preserved in the soil.

contexts The spatial and temporal associations of artifacts and features in an archaeological site. Archaeologists distinguish between *primary context,* which simply means that it has not been disturbed since it was originally deposited, and *secondary context,* which has been disturbed and redeposited.

Figure 8-6

The discovery of these sherds of decorated Native American pottery on the surface of a Mississippi Gulf Coast prehistoric site enables the archaeologist to use them in estimating how old the site is and determining regional ties between the group who lived at this site and groups from other parts of the Gulf Coast.

Context describes the spatial and temporal associations existing in the archaeological record among artifacts and features (**Fig. 8-9**). What was the object's precise location, recorded from several coordinates so as to provide its three-dimensional position within the site? Was it associated somehow with any other artifact or feature? For example, was this projectile point found deep within a trash pit, on the floor of a hunter's shelter, or lodged between the ribs of a large animal? Can we be certain that this apparent association was really contemporaneous and not the result of natural processes of erosion or mixing (a key consideration of taphonomy)? Our point is that the context can be just as important as the artifact itself in understanding the past. With only artifacts,

Figure 8-7

Burials, such as the remains of this cow that were exposed during the excavation of a nineteenth-century Illinois farm, are classic examples of archaeological features. They can be exposed and studied in the archaeological record but cannot be removed without taking them apart.

Figure 8-8

Thousands of land snails like the ones resting on this Lincoln penny were collected from a 4,000-year-old campsite in Illinois. These snails lived on the site location before, during, and after it was used by Native Americans; by analyzing them, archaeologists can reconstruct how the local site environment changed during that time.

Figure 8-9

The large, dark wedge of soil is a partially excavated late prehistoric house in southeast Missouri. Preserved parts of the house wall are dotted along the upper edge of the feature in the upper half of the photo. The remains of this house provide archaeological context for the artifacts, ecofacts, and smaller features found within it.

Figure 8-10

To learn about the pottery-making technology of prehistoric Native Americans in Iowa, archaeologist Colin Betts apprenticed himself to Afro-Caribbean potters who use similar methods on the island of Nevis in the West Indies. Here he stacks freshly made clay vessels so they can be fired, which is the final step that turns them into usable pots.

archaeology would give us a pretty limited understanding of the past, but with artifacts *and* their context, the limitations of what we can potentially know about the past probably rest more with archaeologists than with the archaeological record.

Ethnoarchaeology

In addition to site surveys and excavations, archaeologists sometimes seek to enhance their understanding and interpretations of the past by turning to **ethnoarchaeology**, which examines contemporary societies to gain insights into past human behavior (**Fig. 8-10**).

An ethnoarchaeologist personally conducts in-depth ethnographic research among a living group, such as the !Kung San in southern Africa (Yellen, 1980), Australian aborigines (Gould, 1977; Meehan, 1982), Nunamiut peoples of the Alaskan Arctic (Binford, 1978), or even suburban American households (Rathje and Murphy, 2001). Such studies yield detailed information about hunting or gathering, toolmak-

ing, discard of debris, residence data, and the like. By being "on the scene" as modern people literally create a site, the ethnoarchaeologist can better appreciate the comparable processes that formed the archaeological record (at the same time often becoming painfully aware of how much potential evidence simply decays and disappears between the time a site is created and the time an archaeologist may excavate it thousands or millions of years later).

So, how does ethnoarchaeological information get applied in archaeological research? It gives archaeologists testable ideas about the interpretation of archaeological patterns in much the same way that paleoanthropologists apply observation studies of modern living primates to their understanding of the behavior and biology of hominins known only from the fossil record. The researcher examines the modern information and asks the question, "If early hominins behaved like modern hunter-gatherer X (or supermarket shopper Y or rodeo performer Z), what physical evidence and associations should I expect to find in the archaeological record?" If the predicted evidence and associations are found, then the researcher reasons that the observed modern human behavior can't be excluded as a possible interpretation of comparable patterning in the archaeological record.

ethnoarchaeology Approach used by archaeologists to gain insights into the past by studying contemporary people.

Experimental Archaeology

Yet another way to gain a closer understanding of our ancestors is by learning how they made their tools (**Fig. 8-11**), containers, houses (**Fig. 8-12**), and other artifacts and features and how they used and discarded them. After all, it's the hard evidence of prehistoric tools of stone (and, to a lesser degree, of bone) that constitute our primary information about the earliest identified humanlike behavior. As we mentioned earlier, stone is by far the most common residue of prehistoric cultural behavior, and tons of stone tool debris litter archaeological sites worldwide. For example, if you were taking a casual walk along the bottom of Olduvai Gorge in Tanzania, you'd likely be tripping over prehistoric tools every few seconds!

But what can these artifacts tell us about our ancestors? Quite a lot. Let's say your excavation reveals a bunch of stone axe heads from the remains of an ancient campsite. If you were to make copies of these axe heads using appropriate technology, **haft** them on wooden shafts in ways that replicate the wear patterns found on the ancient axe heads, and use them for a few hours in a set of experiments (say, cutting down a tree with one axe, clearing brush with another, and so on), you'd end up with a much better understanding of how the ancient axes were made and used and, very likely, why they tended to break in patterned ways. You would even be able to compare the wear patterns of modern stone axes used for different tasks with observable wear on the archaeological specimens and identify the tasks for which the ancient tools were used. It's precisely this logic that drives **experimental archaeology**, which, like ethnoarchaeology, uses observations of modern behavior as testable ideas about the interpretation of archaeological patterning.

Figure 8-11
Archaeologist Richard Vanderhoek taught himself how to make and use spear technology like that found in the earliest Alaskan sites so he could better understand and interpret the lifeways of the first inhabitants of the New World.

Richard VanderHoek

Dating Methods

An essential consideration of archaeology and, more generally, paleoanthropology is to establish the age of artifacts, fossils, features, and sites. Only after placing discoveries firmly in time and space can researchers accurately interpret the relationships of archaeological materials and sites to each other and construct a valid and reliable picture of human evolution. Because of the importance of dating in every chapter that follows, in this section we provide a basic introduction to the most widely used dating methods and how they work. **Table 8-1** summarizes the main characteristics of each method.

The question of the age of archaeological and other paleoanthropological materials can be answered in two ways. First, we can say that the hominin that became fossil X lived before or after the hominin that became fossil Y. This is an example of *relative dating*, which establishes the relative order of events but does not scale the amount of time that separates them. Many questions can

William Turnbaugh

Figure 8-12
Drawing upon archaeological research and tribal ingenuity, modern descendants of New England's aboriginal people construct a traditional-style round house, or wigwam, at Plimoth Plantation, Massachusetts. Saplings set into the ground, bent and lashed together, provide a framework for the house, which will be lined and covered with water-deflecting reed matting.

haft To equip a tool or implement with a handle or hilt.

experimental archaeology Research that attempts to replicate ancient technologies and construction procedures to test hypotheses about past activities.

be answered by knowing only relative ages. Second, we can say that a particular village site is X number of years old. This is an example of *chronometric dating*, which establishes the age of events (and obviously their relative order, too) according to some fixed time scale—often, as in this example, in calendar years. Chronometric dating is sometimes called *absolute dating* because the result is a measured quantity of time, not a relative order.

Table 8-1 Summary of Dating Methods Described in This Chapter

Method	Basis	Limitations	Comments
Relative dating methods establish the relative order of events			
Stratigraphy	Principle of superpositioning of strata	Most robust relative dating method	Geological strata and archaeological strata are created by different processes and must be interpreted separately
Biostratigraphy	Estimates of consistent modifications in evolving lineages of animals; presence/absence of species	Requires very well-documented sequences and somewhere must be correlated with chronometric results (e.g., with K/Ar)	Best estimates in East Africa using pigs, monkeys, antelopes, and rodents; has been important dating method in South Africa
Cross-dating	Shared similarities of material remains found in an undated context with remains from a context of known age	Weak when used by itself; best applied in conjunction with other dating methods	Widely applied in archaeological research, the logic of cross-dating is similar to that of biostratigraphy
Seriation	Orders artifacts from different sites or contexts into series based on presence/absence or frequencies of shared attributes	There's no way to know which end of a seriated sequence of artifacts is the oldest unless it is determined by stratigraphic or chronometric methods	Gradually being replaced in archaeological research by a quantitative method called correspondence analysis, which achieves the same end
Chronometric methods give absolute measures of age, often scaled in calendar years			
Potassium-argon (K/Ar)	Regular radioactive decay of potassium isotope	Can be used only on sediments that have been superheated (usually volcanic deposits)	Used to date materials in the 1- to 5-million-year range, especially in East Africa
Argon-argon (^{40}Ar/^{39}Ar)	Works similar to potassium-argon technique	Same as above	Often used to check the validity and reliability of potassium-argon results
Fission-track dating	Regular fission of uranium atoms, leaving microscopic tracks	Usually derived from volcanic deposits; estimates generally less accurate than for K/Ar	Very important corroboratory method in East Africa
Paleomagnetism	Regular shifts in earth's geomagnetic pole; evidence preserved in magnetically charged sediments	Requires precise excavation techniques; both major and minor reversals occur and can easily confuse interpretation	Important corroboratory method in East and South Africa
Radiocarbon dating	Measures the ^{14}C/^{12}C ratio in samples of organic materials	Applications limited to roughly the past 50,000 years	Most widely used chronometric dating method
Thermoluminescence (TL)	Measures the accumulated radiation dose since the last heating or sunlight exposure of an object	Yields the estimated age of the *last* heating event	Widely used for dating ceramics, hearths, and other artifacts and features that were subjected to extremes of heat
Electron spin resonance (ESR)	Measurement (counting) of accumulated trapped electrons	Age estimates can be biased by tooth enamel uptake of uranium; best applied in conjunction with other dating methods	Widely applied in paleoanthropology to date fossil tooth enamel
Uranium series dating	Radioactive decay of short-lived uranium isotopes	Can yield high-precision age estimates; main limitation is the potential range of datable materials	Used to date limestone formations (e.g., stalagmites) and ancient ostrich eggshells
Dendrochronology	Tree-ring dating	Direct archaeological applications limited to temperate regions for which a master chart exists for tree species that were used by humans in the past	Although very important for archaeological dating in some parts of the world (e.g., the American Southwest), its greatest general application is to calibrate radiocarbon age estimates, which greatly enhances their accuracy and precision

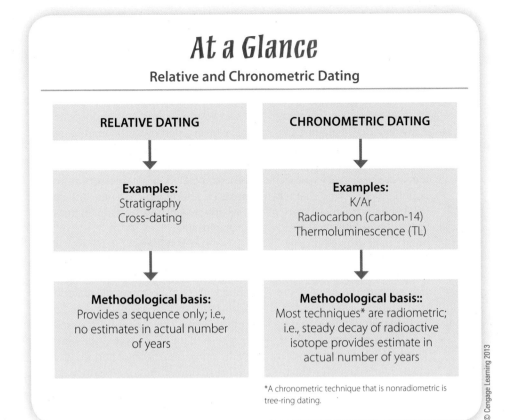

At a Glance
Relative and Chronometric Dating

RELATIVE DATING	CHRONOMETRIC DATING
Examples: Stratigraphy Cross-dating	**Examples:** K/Ar Radiocarbon (carbon-14) Thermoluminescence (TL)
Methodological basis: Provides a sequence only; i.e., no estimates in actual number of years	**Methodological basis::** Most techniques* are radiometric; i.e., steady decay of radioactive isotope provides estimate in actual number of years

*A chronometric technique that is nonradiometric is tree-ring dating.

© Cengage Learning 2013

Both relative and chronometric dating are used daily in archaeological research. Because, like most instruments, every dating method has its strengths and limitations, researchers often employ multiple methods to estimate the age of a given artifact or context. This helps to ensure that their interpretations are based on the most valid and reliable age estimates.

Relative Dating

The oldest relative dating method is **stratigraphy**. A basic understanding of the nature of geological stratigraphy and the **principle of superpositioning** has been critical to the development of the scientific understanding of human evolution for at least the past 150 years. When you stand and look at the rock layers visible in the side of the Grand Canyon, the Rift Valley in East Africa, or even many interstate highway road cuts, there's nothing that cries out to you that the stuff on top must have been put there last and that, therefore, the stuff on the bottom is older than the stuff on the top (**Fig. 8-13**). To make sense of it, you must, like James

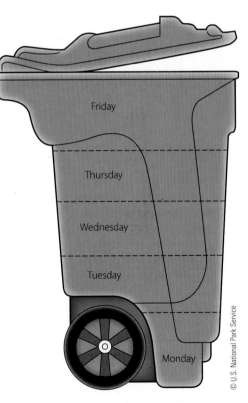

Friday

Thursday

Wednesday

Tuesday

Monday

© U.S. National Park Service

Figure 8-13

A typical garbage bin illustrates the principle of superpositioning. Simply put, this principle asserts that the stuff on the top of a heap was put there last.

Hutton, Charles Lyell, and other nineteenth-century geologists, understand the processes by which sedimentary strata form and how they change. Once you grasp these concepts, then it's obvious that every stratigraphic exposure is

stratigraphy Study of the sequential layering of deposits.

principle of superpositioning In a stratigraphic sequence, the lower layers were deposited before the upper layers. Or, simply put, the stuff on top of a heap was put there last.

Figure 8-14

Archaeological stratigraphy of a prehistoric Native American site in the C & O Canal National Historical Park along the Potomac River. The labels marked on this photo identify major archaeological periods during which Native Americans used this site.

Late woodland

Early woodland

Middle/Late Archaic

Early Archaic

© Chesapeake and Ohio Canal National Historical Park

stratum (*pl.*, strata) A single layer of soil or rock; sometimes called a level.

biostratigraphy A relative dating technique based on regular changes seen in evolving groups of animals as well as the presence or absence of particular species.

index fossils Fossil remains of known age, used to estimate the age of the geological stratum in which they are found. For example, extinct marine arthropods called trilobites can be used as an index fossil of Cambrian and Ordovician geological formations.

cross-dating Relative dating method that estimates the age of artifacts and features based on their similarities with comparable materials from dated contexts.

seriation Relative dating method that orders artifacts into a temporal series based on their similar attributes or the frequency of these attributes.

a time-ordered record that, if systematically studied, can inform you about the past (**Fig. 8-14**).

Conveniently, the layer upon layer of sedimentary rock and other earth strata that compose much of the earth's near-surface geological record also contains most of the fossil evidence of our earliest ancestors and relatives. And even now, when so many chronometric dating methods exist, every researcher in the field knows that when he or she finds a fossil piece of an early hominin skull weathering out of an exposure in a geological **stratum**, then it must be more recent than skull fragments found in context in stratigraphic layers below it and older than fossils found in layers superimposed on it. The principle of superpositioning is therefore both robust, because only one sequence of events is possible, and useful, because this sequence establishes the order, or relative dating, of events.

It's appropriate to note here that geological stratigraphy and archaeological stratigraphy study strata created by quite different processes. As the archaeologist Edward Harris (1989) points out, geological strata are formed only by natural processes, whereas archaeological strata are formed by both cultural and natural processes. Geological strata are also typically sedimentary rocks that formed under water and that cover large areas, but archaeological strata are unconsolidated deposits that cover only small areas. The good news is that the principle of superpositioning applies both to geological and archaeological stratigraphy; the bad news is that these two kinds of stratigraphy differ enough in other ways that the interpretation of many early hominin sites requires stratigraphic interpretations from both perspectives.

Closely connected to geological stratigraphy is the method called **biostratigraphy**, or *faunal correlation*, a dating technique employed in the Early Pleistocene deposits at Olduvai and other African sites. This technique is based on the

regular evolutionary changes in well-known groups of mammals. Animals that have been widely used in biostratigraphic analysis in East and South Africa are fossil pigs, elephants, antelopes, rodents, and carnivores. From areas where evolutionary sequences have been dated by chronometric means (such as potassium-argon dating, discussed shortly), approximate ages can be extrapolated to other lesser-known areas by noting which genera and species are present and treating them as **index fossils**.

In a similar manner, archaeologists use **cross-dating** to estimate the age of artifacts and features based on their similarities with comparable materials from contexts that have been dated by other means. The reasoning is simple. Suppose that you excavated the remains of an ancient burned hut and found several rusted iron hoes of a distinctive design in one corner of the building. If you were to turn to the archaeological literature for that region and research the evidence for similar hoes, you might find that other excavated sites had yielded hoes of the same shape in contexts dated by chronometric techniques to between A.D. 1450 and 1600. By applying the logic of cross-dating, you could tentatively infer that the hoes—and perhaps more important, the hut in which the hoes were found—cannot be older than A.D. 1450. The weakness of such reasoning is its assumption that close material similarities are a reliable measure of contemporaneity of contexts; although it's often true, this assumption is false enough of the time to warrant caution. Consequently, cross-dating is best applied as one of several independent methods of estimating the age of a given context.

Archaeologists also exploit the tendency for many items of material culture to change in patterned ways over time in another relative dating method called **seriation**, which simply orders artifacts into series based on their similar attributes or the frequency of these attributes. The familiar Stone–Bronze–Iron Age sequence long recognized by prehistorians is a good example of seriation: Sites containing metal tools are generally more recent than those where only stone was used, and since bronze technology is known to have developed before iron making, sites containing bronze but no iron occupy an intermediate chronological position.

Likewise, the presence of clay vessels of a specific form in a given site may allow researchers to place that site in a sequence relative to others containing only pots known to be of earlier or later styles. Using this approach, archaeologists working in the southwestern United States determined the correct sequence of ancient Pueblo Indian sites based on the presence or absence of pottery and a comparison of stylistic traits. Later, radiocarbon dating—a chronometric technique—confirmed this sequence. Unless we have some independent means of actually assigning chronometric dates to some or all of the artifacts in the series, we know only that certain types (and, by extension, the sites where they occur) are older or younger than others.

Chronometric Dating

It's impossible to calculate the age in calendar years of a site's archaeological stratum, and the objects in it, by using only relative dating techniques. To estimate absolute measures of age, scientists have developed a variety of chronometric techniques based on the phenomenon of **radiometric decay**. The theory is quite simple: Radioactive isotopes are unstable; over time, these isotopes decay and form an isotopic variation of another element. Since the rate of decay is known, the radioactive material can be used to measure past time in the geological and archaeological records. By measuring the amount of decay in a particular sample, scientists can calculate the number of years it took for the given radioactive isotope to decay to produce the measured level. The result is an age estimate that can be converted to calendar years. As with relative dating methods, chronometric methods have strengths and limitations. Some can be used to date the immense geological age of the earth; others may be limited to artifacts less than 1,000 years old. (For more on these techniques, see Taylor and Aitken 1997; Wagner 2007; Macdougall 2009.)

The most important chronometric technique used to date the earliest hominins involves potassium-40 (^{40}K), which has a **half-life** of 1.25 billion years and produces argon-40 (^{40}Ar). Known as the **potassium-argon (K/Ar) method**, this procedure has been extensively used by paleoanthropologists in dating materials in the 1- to 5-million-year range, especially in East Africa. In addition, a variant of this technique, the **argon-argon (^{40}Ar/^{39}Ar) method**, has recently been used to date a number of hominin localities. The ^{40}Ar/^{39}Ar method allows analysis of smaller samples (even single crystals), reduces experimental error, and is more precise than standard K/Ar dating. Consequently, it can be used to date a wide chronological range—indeed, the entire hominin record, even up to modern times. Recent applications have provided excellent dates for several early hominin sites in East Africa (discussed in Chapter 9) as well as somewhat later sites in Java (discussed in Chapter 10). In fact, the technique was recently used to date the famous Mt. Vesuvius eruption of A.D. 79 (which destroyed the city of Pompeii). Remarkably, the midrange date obtained by the ^{40}Ar/^{39}Ar method was A.D. 73, just six years from the known date (Renne et al., 1997) and a useful cross-check on the accuracy of this dating technique. Organic material, such as bone, cannot be measured by these techniques, but the rock matrix in which the bone is found can be. The K/Ar method was used to provide a minimum date for the deposit containing the *Zinjanthropus* cranium by dating a volcanic layer above the fossil.

Rocks that provide the best samples for K/Ar and ^{40}Ar/^{39}Ar dating are those heated to extremely high temperatures, such as that generated by volcanic activity. When the rock is in a molten state, argon, a gas, is driven off. As the rock cools and solidifies, potassium-40 continues to break down to argon, which is physically trapped in the cooled rock. To obtain the date of the rock, it is reheated and the escaping gas measured.

When dating relatively recent samples (from the perspective of a half-life of 1.25 billion years for K/Ar, *all* paleoanthropological material is relatively recent), the amount of radiogenic argon

radiometric decay A measure of the rate at which certain radioactive isotopes disintegrate.

half-life The time period in which one-half the amount of a radioactive isotope is chemically converted to a daughter product. For example, after 1.25 billion years, half the potassium-40 remains; after 2.5 billion years, one-fourth remains.

potassium-argon (K/Ar) method Dating technique based on accumulation of argon-40 gas as a by-product of the radiometric decay of potassium-40 in volcanic materials; used especially for dating early hominin sites in East Africa.

argon-argon (^{40}Ar/^{39}Ar) method Working on a similar basis as the potassium-argon method, this approach uses the ratio of argon-40 to argon-39 for dating igneous and metamorphic rocks; it offers precision and temporal range advantages for dating some early hominin sites.

Figure 8-15

A geologist carefully takes a sample of sediment containing magnetically charged particles for paleomagnetic dating. He must very precisely record the exact compass orientation so that the sample can be correlated with the known sequence of magnetic orientations.

© Institute of Human Origins, Don Johanson

fission-track dating Dating technique based on the natural radiometric decay (fission) of uranium-238 atoms, which leaves traces in certain geological materials.

paleomagnetism Dating method using known shifts in the earth's magnetic pole to estimate the age of magnetically charged minerals contained in certain kinds of archaeological features.

radiocarbon dating Method for determining the age of organic archaeological materials by measuring the decay of the radioactive isotope of carbon, ^{14}C; also known as carbon-14 dating.

(the argon produced by decay of a potassium isotope) is going to be exceedingly small. Experimental errors in measurement can therefore occur as well as the thorny problem of distinguishing the atmospheric argon normally clinging to the outside of the sample from the radiogenic argon. In addition, the initial sample may have been contaminated, or argon leakage may have occurred while it lay buried. Due to these potential sources of error, K/Ar dating must be cross-checked using other independent methods.

Fission-track dating is one of the most important techniques for cross-checking K/Ar determinations. The key to fission-track dating is that uranium-238 (^{238}U) decays regularly by spontaneous fission. By counting the fraction of uranium atoms that have fissioned (shown as microscopic tracks caused by explosive fission of ^{238}U nuclei), we can determine the age of a mineral or natural glass sample (Fleischer and Hart, 1972). One of the earliest applications of this technique was on volcanic pumice from Olduvai, giving a date of 2.30 ± 0.28 mya—in good accord with K/Ar dates.

Another important means of cross-checking dates is called **paleomagnetism**. This technique is based on the constantly shifting nature of the earth's magnetic pole. Of course, the

earth's magnetic pole is now oriented in a northerly direction, but it hasn't always been. In fact, the orientation and intensity of the geomagnetic field have undergone many changes in the last few million years. The good news is that the major polarity changes are reasonably well documented, providing the temporal framework against which to estimate the age of samples.

Paleomagnetic dating is accomplished by carefully taking samples of sediments that contain magnetically charged particles (**Fig. 8-15**). Since these particles maintain the magnetic orientation they had when they were consolidated into rock (many thousands or millions of years ago), they function as a kind of fossil compass. Then the paleomagnetic sequence can be cross-checked against K/Ar and fission-track age determinations to assess their reliability.

The standard chronometric method for dating later prehistory is carbon-14 (^{14}C) dating, also known as **radiocarbon dating**. This technique has been used to date organic material ranging from less than 1,000 years old up to around 50,000 years old. The radiocarbon dating method is based on the following natural processes (**Fig. 8-16**): Cosmic radiation enters the earth's atmosphere as nuclear particles, some of which react with nitrogen to produce small quantities of an unstable isotope of carbon, ^{14}C. This radioactive ^{14}C diffuses through the atmosphere, mixing with ordinary carbon-12 (^{12}C). Combined with oxygen (O_2) in the form of carbon dioxide (CO_2), carbon is taken up by plants during photosynthesis. Herbivorous animals absorb it by feeding on plants, and carnivores absorb it by feeding on herbivores. So ^{14}C and ^{12}C are found in all living forms at a ratio that reflects the atmospheric proportion. Once an organism dies, it absorbs no more ^{14}C, neither through photosynthesis nor through its diet. Without replacement, the ^{14}C atoms in the tissue continue decaying at a constant rate to nitrogen-14 (^{14}N) and a beta particle, while the ^{12}C remains unchanged. Thus, the ^{14}C/^{12}C ratio in the tissues of a dead plant or animal decreases steadily through time at a rate that can be precisely measured.

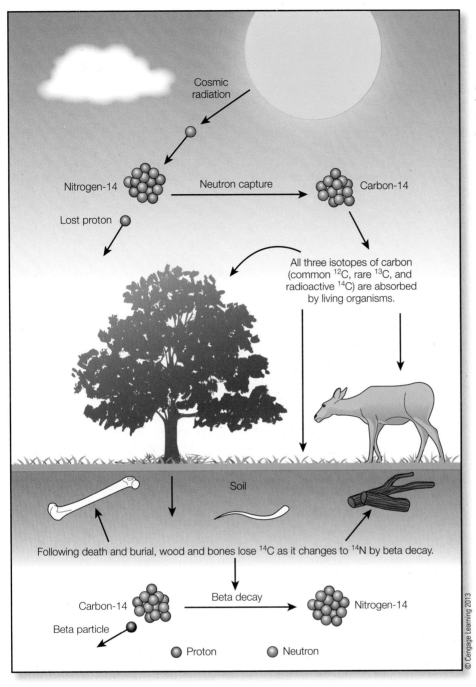

© Cengage Learning 2013

Figure 8-16

The radiocarbon dating method is based on measuring the decay of carbon-14, the radioactive isotope of carbon.

This method is limited primarily to dating organic materials that were once alive and part of the carbon cycle, but the constraint can be a somewhat loose one. For example, South African archaeologist Nikolaas van der Merwe (1969) successfully devised a technique to use radiocarbon dating for archaeological samples of iron alloy, a material that was obviously never alive itself but that does contain carbon from living things due to its manufacturing process. This alone is sufficient for it to be dated by the radiocarbon method.

Carbon-14 has a radiometric half-life of 5,730 years, meaning it takes 5,730 years for half the remaining ^{14}C to decay. Let's say that charred wood, the remains of a campfire, is found at an archaeological site and analyzed for its ^{14}C/^{12}C ratio. First, the sample is carefully collected to avoid contamination. It doesn't have to be a large sample, because even tiny quantities of carbon—just a few milligrams—can be analyzed. In the laboratory, radiation detectors measure the residual ^{14}C. Suppose the findings show that only 25 percent of the original ^{14}C remains, as indicated by the $^{14}C/^{12}C$ ratio. Since we know that it takes 5,730 years for half the original number of ^{14}C atoms to become ^{14}N and another 5,730 years for half the remaining ^{14}C to decay, the sample must be about 11,460 years old. Half of the yet-remaining ^{14}C will disappear over the next 5,730 years (when the charcoal is 17,190 years old), leaving only 12.5 percent of the original amount. This process continues, and, as you can estimate, there would be very little ^{14}C left after 40,000 years, when accurate measurement becomes difficult. Radiocarbon dates (and most other chronometric age determinations) are often reported as a mean age estimate and its associated standard error (1 standard deviation, by convention). So the age estimate of the campfire charcoal, as reported by the dating lab, might be expressed as 11,460 ± 200 radiocarbon years ago. Expressed in words, such an estimate states that the true age of the dated specimen will fall between 11,260 and 11,660 radiocarbon years ago about two times out of three, or roughly 68 percent of the time.

Some inorganic artifacts can be directly dated through the use of **thermoluminescence (TL)**. Used especially for dating ceramics, but also applied to clay cooking hearths and even burned flint tools and hearthstones on later hominin sites, this method, too, relies on the principle of radiometric decay. Clays used in making pottery invariably contain trace amounts of radioactive elements, such as uranium or thorium. As the potter fires the ware (or a campfire burns on a hearth), the rapid heating releases displaced beta particles trapped within the clay. As the particles escape, they emit a dull glow known as thermoluminescence. After that, radioactive decay resumes within the fired clay or stone, again building up electrons at a steady rate. To determine the age of an archaeological sample, the researcher must heat the sample to 500°C and measure its thermoluminescence; from that the date can be calculated. TL is routinely used to authenticate fine ceramic vessels prized by collectors and museums, and the technique has exposed many fake Greek and Maya vases displayed in prominent collections.

Like TL, two other techniques used to date sites from the later phases of hominin evolution (where neither K/Ar nor radiocarbon dating is possible) are uranium series dating and electron spin resonance (ESR) dating. Uranium series dating relies on radioactive decay of short-lived uranium isotopes, and ESR is similar to TL because it's based on measuring trapped electrons. However, while TL is used on heated materials such as clay or stone tools, ESR is used on the dental enamel of animals. All three of these dating methods have been used to provide key dating controls for hominin sites discussed in Chapters 11 and 12.

An archaeologically important chronometric dating technique that does not involve radioactive elements is **dendrochronology**, or dating by tree rings. Its use is limited to contexts in temperate latitudes, where trees show pronounced seasonal growth rings and where ancient wood is commonly preserved. So far, the longest dendrochronological sequences have been developed in the arid American Southwest and the bogs of western Europe, especially Ireland and Germany.

Because tree rings represent seasonal growth layers, the amount of new wood added each year depends directly on rainfall and other factors. People have known for centuries, if not millennia, that the growth rings of an individual tree read like its biography. If we know when the tree was cut and then count from the outer rings inward toward the center, we can readily determine the year the tree began growing. The outstanding contribution of A. E. Douglass, an early twentieth-century astronomer, was to systematically exploit this idea. He reasoned that if we can tell how old a tree is by counting its seasonal growth rings, then we should be able to take a tree of known age and match its growth-ring pattern with the patterns compiled from older and older trees of the same species. The limit on how old this "master chart" of growth rings can extend into the past depends entirely on the extent to which old tree trunks are preserved, because they provide data from which the chart can be built.

thermoluminescence (TL) (ther-mo-loo-min-es´-ence) Technique for dating certain archaeological materials, such as ceramics, that release stored energy of radioactive decay as light upon reheating.

dendrochronology Archaeological dating method based on the study of yearly growth rings in ancient wood.

By cutting or drawing core samples from living trees, recently dead trees, and successively older wood (including archaeological sources such as ancient house posts or beams), archaeologists obtain overlapping life histories of many trees. When compared, these life histories form an extensive record of tree-ring growth through many centuries. Remember, the archaeologist is mostly interested in determining precisely when a tree *stopped* growing and became part of a cultural process such as construction or cooking. As a result, a tree used as a beam in a prehistoric structure in the American Southwest may be dated to the very year in which it was felled (**Fig. 8-17**), since the distinctive pattern of its growth should exactly match some segment of the tree-ring record compiled for the region. Archaeologists studying the ceiling beams in the traditional homes still occupied by the Acoma people in northern New Mexico were able to precisely date construction undertaken in the mid-seventeenth century (Robinson, 1990). Wood from the commonly used pinyon pines and the long-lived Douglas fir trees, sequoia redwoods, and bristlecone pines of the American West, as well as preserved oak logs from western European bogs, afford archaeologists continuous regional tree-ring records extending back thousands of years.

But there is yet another dimension to tree-ring dating. By radiocarbon dating wood taken from individual growth rings of known age, researchers used dendrochronology to fine-tune ^{14}C dating accuracy, factoring in past fluctuations in the atmospheric reservoir of ^{14}C over the past 12,500 years (the period for which usable tree-ring dates are currently available). They then applied these data to recalibrate the raw dates obtained by standard ^{14}C analyses, thereby enabling archaeologists to convert radiocarbon age estimates to calendar year ages, an achievement that greatly enhanced the interpretive utility of radiocarbon dating in archaeology. In a new leap forward a couple of years ago, researchers extended the range of accurate radiocarbon age calibration to 50,000 years ago using fossil corals and other marine data sources (Reimer et al. 2009). Thus, radiocarbon dating has become far

more relevant to the study of the human past than most researchers ever thought possible.

In some regions, including Egypt and Central America, the recorded calendar systems of ancient civilizations have also been cross-referenced to our own, resulting in direct dating of some sites and inferential or cross-dating of others shown to be contemporaneous with them by the presence of distinctive artifacts. For example, firmly dated artifacts originating in the Nile Valley and traded into the Aegean allow us to assign dates to archaeological contexts of Bronze Age Greece. Obviously, this approach is of little use outside those regions having some connection with literate societies.

Since the advent of radiocarbon and other chronometric dating methods in the latter half of the twentieth century, the age of many archaeological and paleoanthropological finds has been precisely and accurately estimated. Although no other dating technique is as widely used as radiocarbon dating, each is an ingenious method with its own special applications. Still, as with any instrument, researchers must consider the strengths and limitations of each chronometric method, both when applying it in the field and when interpreting the lab results.

© Glen Freimuth

Figure 8-17

Roof beams projecting through the wall of a room at Mesa Verde National Park, Colorado. The age of the room can be estimated by dendrochronology, using the tree ring patterns of core samples extracted from each beam.

Paleoanthropology and Archaeology at Olduvai Gorge

We conclude this methodological introduction to paleoanthropology and archaeology with a case study from East Africa—Olduvai Gorge (**Fig. 8-18**), a locality that has yielded the finest quality and greatest abundance of anthropological information concerning the behavior of early hominins and an extraordinarily informative sequence of

Figure 8-18

Olduvai Gorge and the Rift Valley system in East Africa.

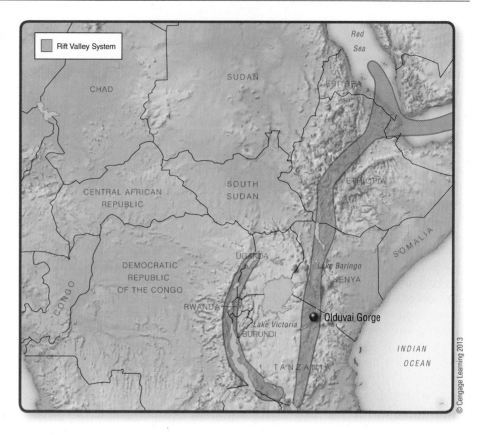

Figure 8-19

Mary Leakey (1913–1996), a major figure in twentieth-century paleoanthropology, devoted most of her life to fieldwork in Olduvai Gorge, where she made many important discoveries, including the *Zinjanthropus* skull (see Fig. 8–21) in 1959.

Lower Paleolithic A unit of archaeological time that begins about 2.6 mya with the earliest identified tools made by hominins and ends around 200,000 years ago.

excavated **Lower Paleolithic** sites. The object of this case study is to illustrate how paleoanthropological methods—especially archaeological approaches—work together to create the modern understanding of early hominin life in this part of East Africa. It also sets the stage for Chapter 9, where we explore in detail the early hominin fossil record and the oldest Lower Paleolithic archaeological evidence.

Beginning in the 1930s, the pioneering team of Louis and Mary Leakey (**Fig. 8-19**) worked at Olduvai. Together, they made Olduvai Gorge one of the most widely known place names in Africa. Located on the Serengeti Plain of northern Tanzania, Olduvai is a steep-sided valley resembling a miniature version of the Grand Canyon (**Fig. 8-20**). A massive ravine some 300 feet deep, Olduvai cuts for more than 25 miles across the grassy plateau of East Africa. The present semiarid climate of the Olduvai region is believed to be similar to what it has been for the last 2 million years. The surrounding countryside is a grassland savanna dotted with scrub bushes and acacia trees. Dry though it may be, this environment presently (as well as

in the past) supports a vast number of mammals (such as zebra, wildebeest, and gazelle), representing an enormous supply of "meat on the hoof."

Geographically, Olduvai is located on the eastern branch of the Great Rift Valley, which stretches for 4,000 miles down the east side of Africa (see Fig. 8-18). The geological processes associated with forming the Rift Valley make Olduvai (and many other East African regions) extremely important because they created an environment that favored the preservation of hominin remains and make it easier for paleoanthropologists and archaeologists to discover these remains. Here are the four most significant results of geological rifting:

1. Faulting, or earth movement, exposes geological strata that are normally hidden deep in the earth.
2. Active volcanic processes cause rapid sedimentation, which often yields excellent preservation of bone and artifacts that normally would be scattered by carnivore activity and erosion forces.
3. Strata formed by rapid sedimentation and, more important, the hom-

Figure 8-20
View of the main gorge at Olduvai. Note the clear sequence of geological beds. The discontinuity in the stratigraphic layers (below the red arrow) is a major fault line.

Robert Jurmain

inin fossils and archaeological sites preserved within them, can be dated by relative methods such as stratigraphy and cross-dating.

4. Volcanic activity provides a wealth of materials datable by chronometric methods.

As a result, Olduvai offers researchers superb preservation of ancient hominins, good evidence of the environments in which these hominins lived, and archaeological sites containing the material remains of their existence in datable contexts, all of which are readily accessible. Such advantages cannot be ignored, and Olduvai continues to be the focus of considerable archaeological and other paleoanthropological research.

Over the decades of paleoanthropological fieldwork, partial remains of more than 40 fossilized hominins have been found at Olduvai. Many of these individuals are quite fragmentary, but a few are excellently preserved. Although the center of hominin discoveries has now shifted to other areas of East Africa, it was the initial discovery by Mary Leakey of the *Zinjanthropus* skull at Olduvai in July 1959 that focused the world's attention on this remarkably rich area (**Fig. 8-21**). "Zinj" is an excellent example of how financial support can result directly from hominin fossil discoveries. Prior to 1959, the Leakeys had worked spo-

radically at Olduvai on a financial shoestring, making marvelous paleontological and archaeological discoveries but never attracting the financial assistance they needed for large-scale excavations. However, following the discovery of Zinj, the National Geographic Society funded the Leakeys' research, and within a year, more than twice as much dirt had been excavated than during the previous 30 years!

Olduvai's greatest contribution to paleoanthropological research in the twentieth century was the establishment of an extremely well-documented and correlated *sequence* of archaeological, geological, paleontological, and hominin remains over the last 2 million years. At the very foundation of all paleoanthropological research is a well-established geological context. At Olduvai, the geological and paleogeographical situation is now known in minute detail. It's been a great help that Olduvai is a geologist's delight, containing sediments in some places 350 feet thick, accumulated from lava flows (basalts), tuffs (windblown

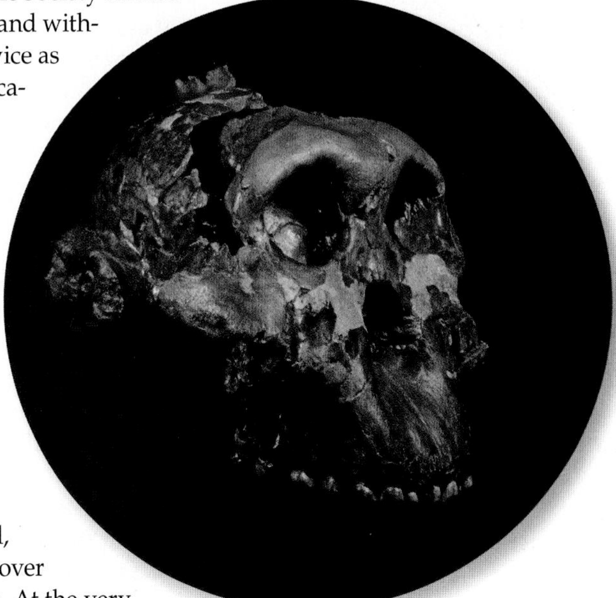

Figure 8-21
Zinjanthropus skull, discovered by Mary Leakey at Olduvai Gorge in 1959. The skull and reconstructed jaw depicted here are casts at the National Museums of Kenya, Nairobi. As we will see in Chapter 9, this fossil is now included as part of the genus *Australopithecus*.

© Javier Trueba / MSF / Photo Researchers, Inc.

or waterborne fine deposits from nearby volcanoes), sandstones, claystones, and limestone conglomerates, all neatly stratified (see Fig. 8-20). A hominin site can therefore be accurately dated relative to other sites in the Olduvai Gorge by cross-correlating known stratigraphic marker beds.

Because the vertical cut of the Olduvai Gorge provides a ready cross section of 2 million years of earth history, sites can be excavated by digging "straight in" rather than first having to remove tons of overlying dirt (**Fig. 8-22**). In fact, sites are usually discovered in Olduvai Gorge by merely walking the stratigraphic exposures and observing what kinds of bones, stones, and so forth, are eroding out, just as archaeologists often do when discovering sites in other parts of the world.

At the most general geological level, the stratigraphic sequence at Olduvai is broken down into four major beds (Beds I–IV), each containing hominin and other animal fossils and sites with artifacts and features created by early hominin cultural behavior. These contexts are reasonably well dated by both relative and chronometric methods. The fossilized remains of more than 150 animal species, including fishes, turtles, crocodiles, pigs, giraffes, horses, and many birds, rodents, and antelopes, have been found throughout these Olduvai beds and provide much of the basis for reconstructing the environmental conditions that existed when the early hominin sites were deposited.

The earliest identified hominin site (circa 1.85 mya) at Olduvai Gorge contains a Lower Paleolithic stone tool assemblage that archaeologists named *Oldowan* (Leakey, 1971). For now, it is enough to know that Oldowan tools are simple and very crude to our eyes and that most were made by knocking small

Robert Jurmain

Figure 8-22

Excavations in progress at Olduvai. This site, more than 1 million years old, was located when a hominin ulna (arm bone) was found eroding out of the side of the gorge.

flakes off bigger rocks and by battering (**Fig. 8-23**). (We'll look at Oldowan tools in more detail in Chapter 9.) Considerable research continues to focus on understanding the nature of these tools, with archaeologists eager to know just why they were made and what they were used for. Many insights about Oldowan tool function and use come from experimental archaeology projects in which researchers try to replicate the wear, breakage, and discard patterns of artifacts found in Lower Paleolithic sites.

For example, in the mid-twentieth century, many archaeologists described Oldowan as primarily a "chopping tool industry" because they concluded that the large, broken cobbles found in these assemblages were used as heavy chopper-like implements (see Fig. 8-23). They also inferred that many of the equally common stone flakes were simply debris from making these so-called "core tools." Over the decades, as archaeologists investigated more Oldowan sites and compared excavated artifacts with similar implements re-created by experimental archaeologists, these initial hypotheses came into question. Many of the choppers or core tools, while they were clearly artifacts, might not have actually been used as tools. In one such study, Richard Potts (1991, 1993), of the Smithsonian Institution, analyzed Olduvai Bed I artifacts and concluded that early hominins were deliberately producing flake tools, not heavy chopper-like core tools, and that the various stone nodule forms (discoids, polyhedrons, choppers, and so on) were simply "incidental stopping points in the process of removing flakes from cores" (Potts, 1993, p. 60).

To many students, the idea that one class of artifacts is not what we once assumed probably seems trivial, but it actually had important implications for how archaeologists view early hominins as cultural animals. If Oldowan tool use emphasized cutting (the flake tools), not chopping (the so-called core tools), then what were they cutting? What kinds of use wear are present on the flake tools, and what kinds of cutting scars are present on the animal bones found in Oldowan sites? And what are the lumps of rock once thought to be core tools? Just broken bits of raw material or something else entirely? Researchers have paid a fair amount of attention to such questions over the past couple of decades, and their results continue to enhance our understanding of how early hominins, as creatures that were still learning to be tool-using animals, exploited the landscapes in which they lived.

The recognition that flake tools were a key part of the Oldowan tool industry forced paleoanthropologists and archaeologists to reassess their ideas about early human tool use. A comparable impact may be felt from recent research on rocks that early humans may not have used at all! The Oldowan industry traditionally includes *manuports*—unmodified rocks of types that are not present in the geology of the immediate vicinity of the Oldowan sites where they are found. In other words, they're just rocks, and the only reasons for not treating them as such are that they are geologically out of place and that they are found in archaeological contexts believed to be the product of hominin behavior.

For decades, archaeologists have believed that the best explanation for the presence of manuports in Oldowan sites was that early hominins picked up the stones where they naturally occurred and carried them to the site where they were much later excavated. If that's true, such an otherwise irrelevant artifact depends for its significance entirely on the assumption that an early human moved it from point A to point B. So long as we believe that the evidence supports only this interpretation, these rocks are artifacts; once we cannot believe this evidence, they're just rocks.

Although they don't seem important, manuports became key elements in some interpretations of the ecological niche of early hominins as tool-using animals on the arid savannas of East Africa. For example, among the several kinds of Oldowan sites excavated in Olduvai Gorge are those originally identified as "multipurpose localities," or campsites, which were interpreted as general-purpose areas where hominins possibly ate, slept, and put the finishing touches on tools. Mary Leakey (1971) and

archaeologist Glynn Isaac (1976) were strong proponents of this interpretation, which carried with it the necessary implication that early hominins were **home-based foragers**. Lewis Binford's (1983) comparisons of bone assemblages from early hominin contexts at Olduvai and similar assemblages drawn from his ethnoarchaeological research in Alaska on modern human and animal behavior led him to a different conclusion. He argued that much of the accumulated bone refuse on Oldowan sites can be explained as the result of nonhominin (that is, predator) activities and that early hominins were little more than passive scavengers of big game kills. This stance opened the door to a continuing debate about whether early hominins were primarily hunters or scavengers (e.g., Domínguez-Rodrigo, 2002; O'Connell et al., 2002; Domínguez-Rodrigo and Pickering, 2003).

One of the alternative interpretations put forth in the hunter versus scavenger debate came from Richard Potts (1988, 1991), who claimed that these sites served as stockpiles, or caches, for raw materials such as manuports in anticipation of future use. Potts' argument was especially important, partly because other researchers picked up the idea and incorporated it into their own models of early hominin behavior and partly because the argument implied a particular set of behaviors as part of the way early hominins used landscapes and interacted with technology. De la Torre and Mora (2005) recently reanalyzed the Olduvai manuport collections and concluded that it's unlikely that they are raw material caches in Potts' sense because (1) they share few characteristics with objects that were modified by early hominins and (2) natural geomorphological processes are sufficient to account for their presence at Olduvai sites. In other words, many, and perhaps most, manuports are just rocks and have

Figure 8-23

Oldowan core tools, such as this "chopper," were made by knocking flakes off a fist-size stone using another rock as a hammer.

home-based foragers Hominins that hunt, scavenge, or collect food and raw materials from the general locality where they habitually live and bring these materials back to some central or home base site to be shared with other members of their coresiding group.

nothing to do with the behavior of early hominins.

Research will undoubtedly continue to focus on Oldowan chopping tools as well as manuports, but their stories make good examples of how we learn about the human past. As in every scientific endeavor, archaeologists and paleoanthropologists will never cease to question everything they may cur-rently think is accurate, knowing full well that tomorrow, or the next day, or 10 years from now, someone will conduct the test, excavate the site, or simply ask a different question that opens the door to a fresh understanding about how and why we made it from the African savannas to exploring other planets. And that's how science is supposed to work!

Summary of Main Topics

▶ To achieve any meaningful understanding of human origins, we must examine both biological and cultural information about the past.

▶ The multidisciplinary approach of paleoanthropology brings together varied scientific specializations to reconstruct the anatomy, behavior, and environments of early hominins.

▶ Archaeology studies the human past primarily through its material remains. Its scope extends roughly from 2.6 mya, with the earliest identified early hominin tools and tool-making debris, up to the twenty-first century. Archaeologists make the key assumption that the organization and structure of the archaeological record reflects the behavior of humans in the past.

▶ One of the main tasks of this chapter has been to describe the varied ways in which researchers estimate past time. For paleoanthropologists and archaeologists alike, *time* rather than space is the important dimension that separates us from those we study.

▶ The Olduvai Gorge example illustrates the application of many of the research and dating methods described in this chapter. It also motivates our examination of early hominin paleoanthropological research, which we take up in the next chapter.

Critical Thinking Questions

1. How are early hominin sites discovered, and what kinds of specialists may be involved in excavating and analyzing such sites?

2. Why are cultural remains so important in interpreting human evolution? What do you think is the most important thing you can learn from cultural remains—say, from a site that is 2 million years old? What is the most important thing you probably *can't* learn?

3. Compare relative dating and chronometric dating. Name one or two examples of each, and briefly explain the principles used in determining the dates for each method that you name.

4. What kinds of cultural information may not be represented by artifacts alone? How do archaeologists attempt to compensate for these shortcomings through approaches such as ethnoarchaeology and experimental archaeology?

Paleoanthropology/ Fossil Hominins

CHAPTER 9

Hominin Origins

LEARNING OBJECTIVES

After you have mastered the material in this chapter, you will be able to:

▶ Explain the general time depth for the earliest primates and explain how they may (or not) be related to living primates.

▶ Define what a "hominin" is and explain what sort of evidence is used to determine whether a fossil form is a hominin.

▶ Describe the time depth and geographical location of early hominins and explain how they relate to later hominins (including us).

Today our species dominates our planet; indeed, we use our brains and cultural inventions to invade every corner of the earth. Yet, 5 million years ago, our ancestors were little more than bipedal apes, confined to a few regions in Africa. What were these creatures like? When and how did they begin their evolutionary journey?

In Chapter 8, we discussed the techniques archaeologists use to locate and excavate sites as well as the multidisciplinary approaches used by paleoanthropologists to interpret discoveries. In this chapter, we turn first to the physical evidence of earlier primates and then to the hominin fossils themselves. The earliest fossils identifiable as hominins are all from Africa, and some of them may date back to more than 6 mya. It's fascinating to think about these early members of our family tree, with different species living side by side for millions of years. Most of these species became extinct. But why? What's more, were some of these apelike animals possibly our direct ancestors?

Hominins, of course, evolved from earlier primates (dating back to almost 50 mya). We'll briefly review this long and abundant prehominin fossil record to provide a better context for understanding the subsequent evolution of the human lineage.

In recent years, paleoanthropologists have made many exciting discoveries from several sites in Africa. However, because many finds have been made so recently, detailed evaluations are still in progress, and conclusions must remain tentative.

One thing is certain, however. The earliest members of the human family were confined to Africa. Only much later did their descendants disperse from the African continent to other areas of the Old World. (This "out of Africa" saga will be the topic of the next chapter.)

Early Primate Evolution

Long before bipedal hominins first evolved in Africa, more primitive primates had diverged from even more distant mammalian ancestors. The roots of the primate order go back to the early stages of the placental mammal radiation at least 65 mya. Thus, the earliest primates evolved from early and still primitive placental mammals.

We have seen (in Chapter 6) that strictly defining living primates using clear-cut derived features is not an easy task. The further back we go in the fossil record, the more primitive and, in many cases, the more generalized the fossil primates become. Such a situation makes classifying them all the more difficult.

The earliest primates date to the Paleocene (65–56 mya) and belong to a large and diverse group of primitive mammals called the plesiadapiforms. These very early primates have been controversial for several decades, with opinions varying as to whether they actually *are* primates or members of a closely related but different group of mammals. Recently discovered quite complete fossils, coming especially from Montana and Wyoming, have now more firmly placed these Paleocene animals as the earliest known primates.

Eocene Primates: Closer Connections to Living Primates

From the succeeding Eocene epoch (56–33 mya), a vast number of fossil primates have been discovered and now total more than 200 recognized species (see Chapter 5 for a geological chart). Unlike the available Paleocene forms, those from the Eocene display more clearly derived primate features. These fossils have been found at many sites in North America and Europe (which for most of the Eocene were still connected). In addition, more recent finds have shown that the radiation of Eocene primates extended to Asia and Africa. It's important to recall that the landmasses that connect continents, as well as the water boundaries that separate them, have an obvious impact on the geographical distribution of all land animals, including primates (see Chapter 5).

The most complete early primate fossil ever found was announced in 2009 and, in honor of the 200th anniversary of Darwin's birth, is called *Darwinius* (**Fig. 9–1**). It comes from the Eocene Messel site in Germany, dates to 47 mya (during the Eocene), and is extraordinarily well preserved (Franzen et al., 2009). At the time of its announcement, it created a public sensation, although the find has a complex and somewhat peculiar history.

Clearly, *Darwinius* was meant to make a big splash, and that it did; yet, virtually no other experts in early primate evolution have had an opportunity to see the original fossil, and thus the wide publicity it received wasn't accompanied by the normal assessments of other researchers. From what has been tentatively concluded by a wide range of scholars, the claims made by the original researchers aren't substantiated and run counter to interpretations of other Eocene primate finds (Gibbons, 2009). There is much to learn about the adaptations of this small Eocene primate, but it seems unlikely that it provides direct evidence of a close connection to us and other anthropoids as claimed. Indeed, it may not be particularly closely related to any living primate.

Looking at this entire array of Eocene fossils, it's certain that they were (1) primates, (2) widely distributed, and (3) mostly extinct by the end of the Eocene. What is less certain is how any of them might be related to the living primates. Some of these forms were probably similar to and are potential ancestors of the lemurs and lorises. Others are probably related to tarsiers. By far, however, most of the Eocene pri-

mates (including *Darwinius* and its close relatives) don't appear to have been ancestral to any later primate, and they became extinct before the end of the Eocene (around 33 mya). Nevertheless, some fossil finds from late in the Eocene have derived features (such as a dental comb) that link them to modern lemurs and lorises.

New evidence of Eocene *anthropoid* origins has recently been discovered at a few sites in North Africa. The earliest of these African fossils go back to 50 mya, but the remains are very fragmentary. More conclusive evidence comes from Egypt and is well dated to 37 mya. At present, it looks likely that the earliest anthropoids first evolved in Africa.

Oligocene Primates: Anthropoid Connections

The Oligocene (33–23 mya) has yielded numerous additional fossil remains of several different early anthropoid species. Most of these are *Old World anthropoids*, all discovered at a single locality in Egypt, the Fayum (**Fig. 9-2**). In

Figure 9-1

Remarkably well-preserved remains of the Eocene primate *Darwinius*, dated to about 47 mya.

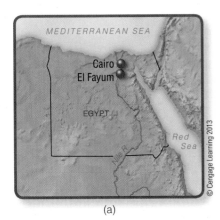

(a)

(b)

Figure 9-2

(a) Fayum site in Egypt (b) Excavations in progress at the Fayum, where dozens of fossil primates have been discovered.

Figure 9-3

Major events in early primate evolution.

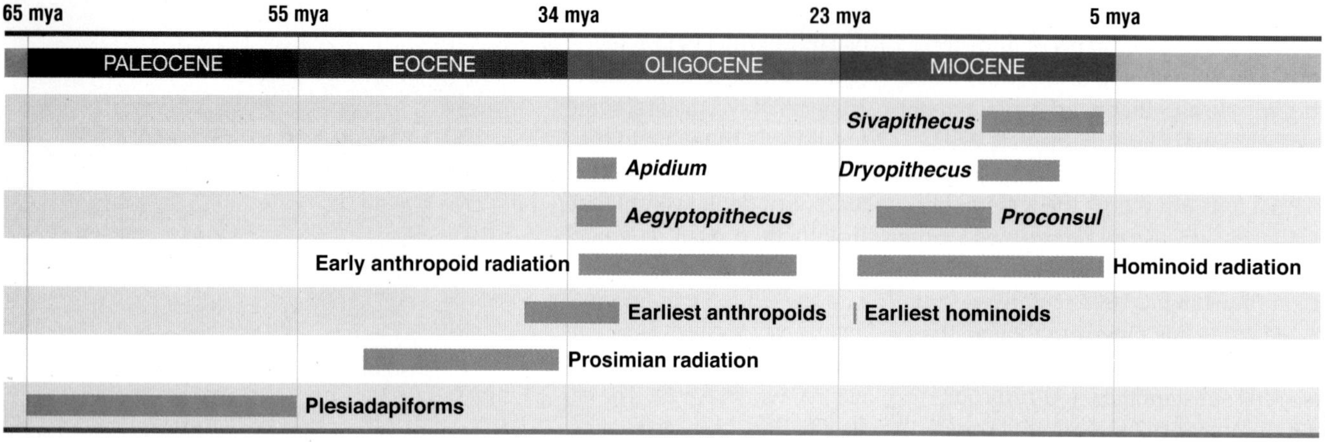

65 mya	55 mya	34 mya	23 mya	5 mya
PALEOCENE	EOCENE	OLIGOCENE	MIOCENE	

Sivapithecus

Apidium   Dryopithecus

Aegyptopithecus   Proconsul

Early anthropoid radiation   Hominoid radiation

Earliest anthropoids   Earliest hominoids

Prosimian radiation

Plesiadapiforms

© Cengage Learning 2013

addition, there are a few known bits from North and South America that relate only to the ancestry of New World monkeys. By the early Oligocene, continental drift had separated the New World (that is, the Americas) from the Old World (Africa and Eurasia). Some of the earliest Fayum species, nevertheless, may potentially be close to the ancestry of both Old and New World anthropoids. It's been suggested that late in the Eocene or very early in the Oligocene, the first anthropoids (primitive "monkeys") arose in Africa and later reached South America by "rafting" over the water separation on drifting chunks of vegetation. What we call "monkey," then, may have a common Old World origin, but the ancestry of New and Old World monkeys was separate after about 35 mya. After this time, the closest evolutionary connections humans have are with other Old World anthropoids—that is, with Old World monkeys and apes.

The possible roots of anthropoid evolution are illustrated by different forms from the Fayum; one is the genus *Apidium*. Well known at the Fayum, *Apidium* is represented by several dozen jaws or partial dentitions as well as many **postcranial** remains. Owing to its primitive dental arrangement, some paleontologists have suggested that *Apidium* may lie near or even before the evolutionary divergence of Old and New World anthro-

poids. Because so much fossil material of teeth and limb bones of *Apidium* has been found, some informed speculation regarding diet and locomotor behavior is possible. It's thought that this small, squirrel-sized primate ate mostly fruits and some seeds and was most likely an arboreal quadruped, adept at leaping and springing.

The other genus of importance from the Fayum is *Aegyptopithecus*. This genus is represented by several well-preserved crania and abundant jaws and teeth. The largest of the Fayum anthropoids, *Aegyptopithecus* is roughly the size of a modern howler monkey (13 to 18 pounds; Fleagle, 1983) and is thought to have been a short-limbed, slow-moving arboreal quadruped. *Aegyptopithecus* is important because, better than any other known form, it bridges the gap between the Eocene fossils and the succeeding Miocene hominoids (**Fig. 9-3**).

Nevertheless, *Aegyptopithecus* is a very primitive Old World anthropoid, with a small brain and long snout and not showing any derived features of either Old World monkeys or hominoids. Thus, it may be close to the ancestry of *both* major groups of living Old World anthropoids. Found in geological beds dating to 35–33 mya, *Aegyptopithecus* further suggests that the crucial evolutionary divergence of hominoids from other Old World anthropoids occurred *after* this time.

postcranial Referring to all or part of the skeleton not including the skull. The term originates from the fact that in quadrupeds, the body is in back of the head; the term literally means "behind the head."

Miocene Fossil Hominoids: Closer Connections to Apes and Humans

During the approximately 18 million years of the Miocene (23–5 mya), a great deal of evolutionary activity took place. In Africa, Asia, and Europe, a diverse and highly successful group of hominoids emerged (**Fig. 9-4**). Indeed, there were many more kinds of hominoids from the Miocene than there are today (now represented by just a few ape species and humans). In fact, the Miocene could be called "the golden age of hominoids." Many thousands of fossils have been found from dozens of sites scattered in eastern Africa, southern Africa, southwest Asia, into western and southern Europe, and extending into southern Asia and China.

During the Miocene, significant transformations relating to climate and repositioning of landmasses took place. By 23 mya, major continental locations approximated those of today (except that North and South America were separate). Nevertheless, the movements of South America and Australia farther away from Antarctica significantly altered ocean currents. Likewise, the continued collision between the South Asian Plate and southern Asia produced the Himalayan Plateau. Both of these geographical changes had significant impacts on the climate, and the early Miocene was considerably warmer than the preceding Oligocene. Moreover, by 19 mya, the Arabian Plate (which had been separate) "docked" with northeastern Africa. As a result, migrations of animals from Africa directly into southwest Asia (and in the other direction as well) became possible. Among the earliest transcontinental migrants (around 16 mya) were African hominoids that colonized both Europe and Asia at this time.

A problem arises in any attempt to simplify the complex evolutionary situation regarding Miocene hominoids. For example, for many years, paleontologists tended to think of these fossil forms as either "apelike" or "humanlike" and used modern examples as models. But as we have just noted, very few hominoids remain. Therefore, we should not hastily generalize from these few living forms to the much more diverse fossil forms; otherwise, we obscure the evolutionary uniqueness of these animals. In addition, we should not expect all fossil forms to be directly or even particularly closely related to living species. Indeed, we should expect the opposite; that is, most lines vanish without descendants.

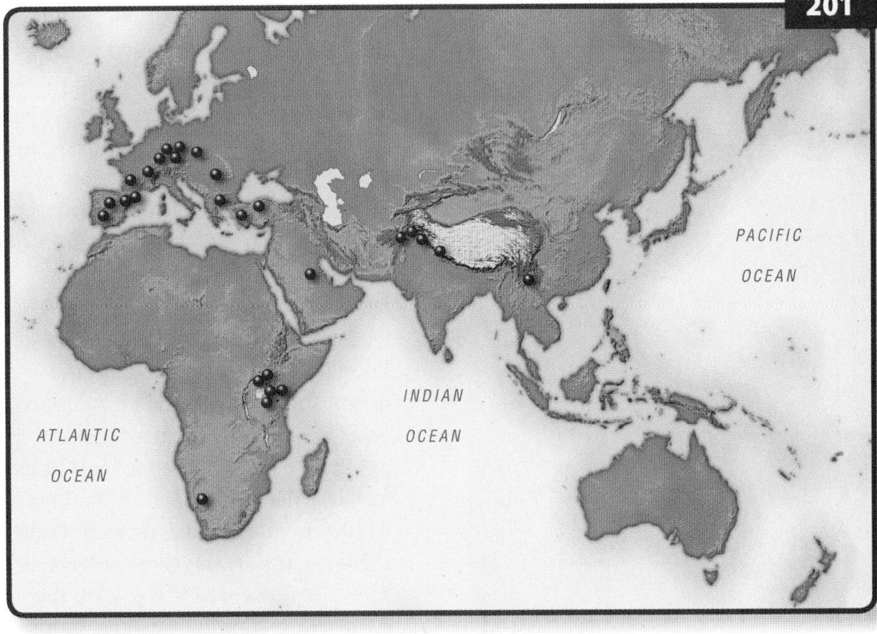

Over the last three decades, the Miocene fossil hominoid assemblage has been interpreted and reinterpreted. As more fossils are found, the evolutionary picture becomes more complicated. What's more, most of the fossils haven't been completely studied, so conclusions remain tenuous. Given this uncertainty, it's probably best, for the present, to group Miocene hominoids geographically:

1. *African forms (23–14 mya)*
   Known especially from western Kenya, these include quite generalized, and in many ways primitive, hominoids. The best-known genus is *Proconsul* (**Fig. 9-5**). In fact, *Proconsul* isn't much like an ape, and postcranially

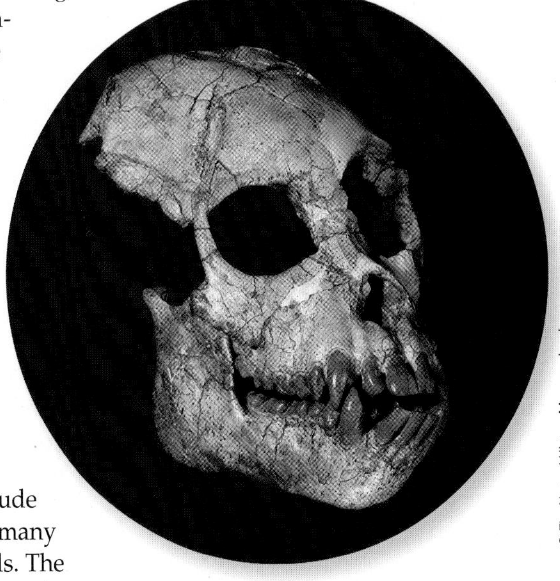

Figure 9-4

Miocene hominoid distribution, from fossils thus far discovered.

Figure 9-5

Proconsul skull, an early Miocene hominoid.

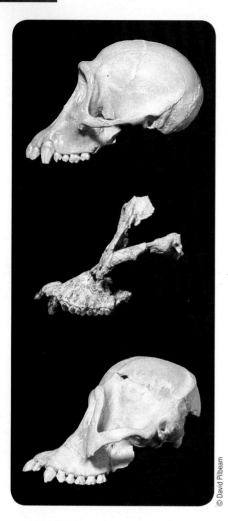

© David Pilbeam

Figure 9-6

Comparison of a modern chimpanzee (top), *Sivapithecus* (middle), and a modern orangutan (bottom). Notice that both *Sivapithecus* and the orangutan exhibit a dished face, broad cheekbones, and projecting upper jaw.

it more closely resembles a monkey. But there are some derived features of the teeth that link *Proconsul* to hominoids.

2. *European forms (16–11 mya)* Known from widely scattered localities in France, Spain, Italy, Greece, Austria, Germany, and Hungary, most of these forms are quite derived. However, this is a varied and not well-understood group. The best known of these are placed in the genus *Dryopithecus*; the Hungarian and Greek fossils are usually assigned to other genera. The Greek fossils, called *Ouranopithecus*, date to 10–9 mya. Evolutionary relationships are uncertain; some researchers have suggested a link with the African ape–hominin group, but most primatologists think that these similarities result from homoplasy (Wood and Harrison, 2011; see Chapter 5).

3. *Asian forms (15–5 mya)* The largest and most varied group of Miocene fossil hominoids was geographically dispersed from Turkey through India/Pakistan and east to Lufeng, in southern China. The best-known genus is *Sivapithecus* (from Turkey and Pakistan), and fossil evidence indicates that most of these hominoids were *highly* derived (**Fig. 9-6**).

Four general points are certain concerning Miocene hominoid fossils: They are widespread geographically; they are numerous; they span essentially the entirety of the Miocene, with *known* remains dated between 23 and 6 mya; and at present, they are poorly understood. However, we can reasonably draw the following conclusions:

1. These are hominoids—more closely related to the ape-human lineage than to Old World monkeys.

2. They are mostly **large-bodied hominoids**, that is, more connected to the lineages of orangutans, gorillas, chimpanzees, and humans than to smaller-bodied apes (gibbons and siamangs).

3. Most of the Miocene species thus far discovered are so derived that they are probably not ancestral to any living form.

4. One lineage that appears well established is *Sivapithecus* from Turkey and Pakistan. *Sivapithecus* shows some highly derived facial features similar to the modern orangutan, suggesting a fairly close evolutionary connection.

5. Evidence of *definite* hominins from the Miocene hasn't yet been indisputably confirmed. However, exciting recent (and not fully studied) finds from Kenya, Ethiopia, and Chad (the latter dating as far back as 7–6 mya) suggest that hominins diverged sometime in the latter Miocene (see pp. 208–213 for further discussion). As we shall see shortly, the most fundamental feature of the early hominins is the adaptation to bipedal locomotion. In addition, recently discovered Miocene remains of the first fossils linked closely to gorillas (Suwa et al., 2007) provide further support for a late Miocene divergence (about 10–7 mya) of our closest ape cousins from the hominin line. The only fossil chimpanzee so far discovered has a much later date of around 500,000 years ago (ya), long after the time that hominins split from African apes (McBrearty and Jablonksi, 2005).

Understanding our Direct Evolutionary Connections: What's a Hominin?

The earliest evidence of hominins dates to the end of the Miocene and mainly includes dental and cranial pieces. But dental remains alone don't describe the special features of hominins, and they certainly aren't distinctive of the later stages of human evolution. Modern humans, as well as our most immediate hominin ancestors, are distinguished from the great apes by more obvious features than tooth and jaw dimensions. For example, various scientists have pointed to such distinctive hominin characteristics as bipedal locomotion, large brain size, and toolmaking behav-

large-bodied hominoids Those hominoids including the great apes (orangutans, chimpanzees, gorillas) and hominins, as well as all ancestral forms back to the time of divergence from small-bodied hominoids (i.e., the gibbon lineage).

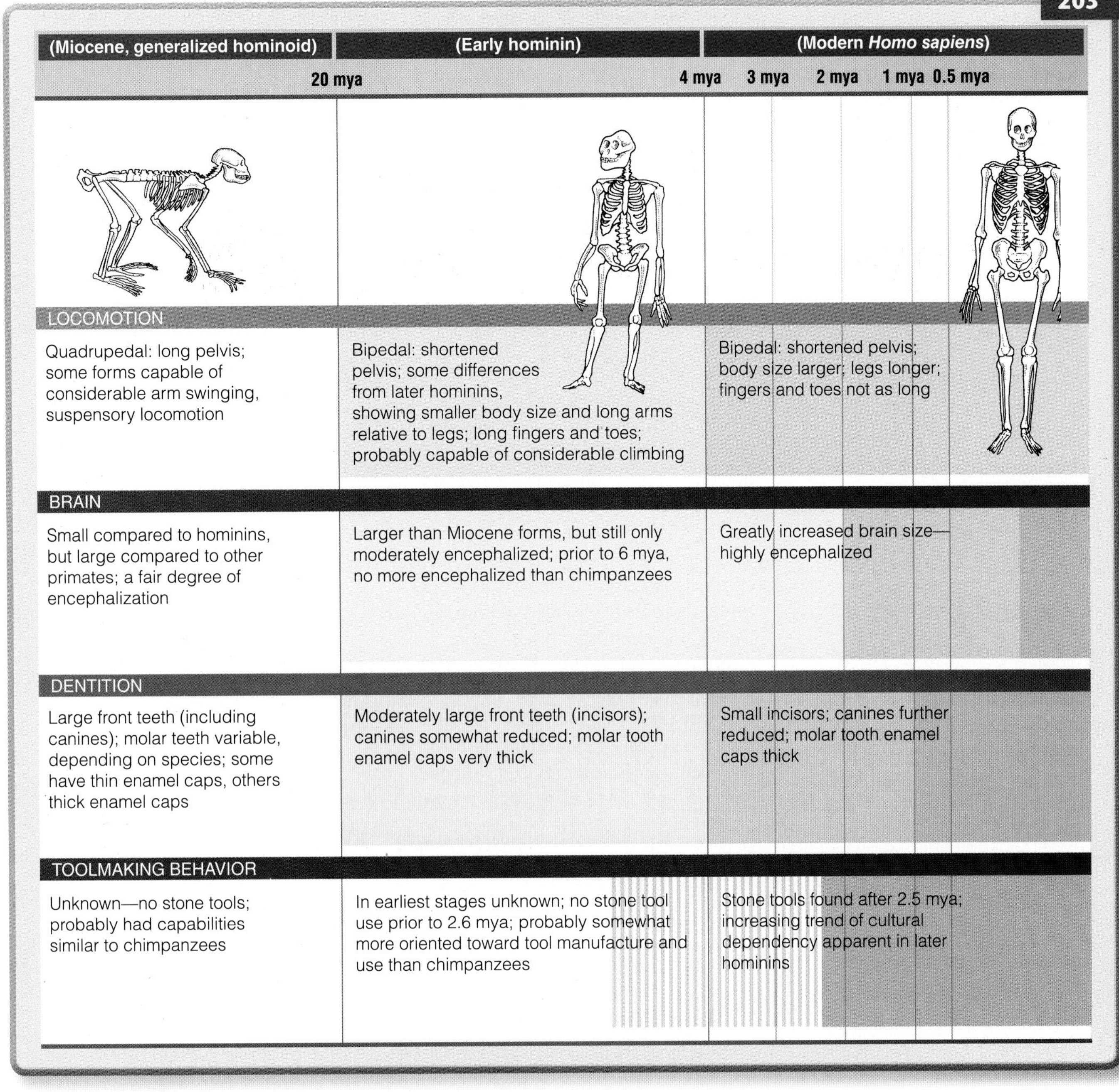

(Miocene, generalized hominoid)	(Early hominin)	(Modern *Homo sapiens*)
20 mya	4 mya 3 mya 2 mya 1 mya 0.5 mya	

LOCOMOTION

| Quadrupedal: long pelvis; some forms capable of considerable arm swinging, suspensory locomotion | Bipedal: shortened pelvis; some differences from later hominins, showing smaller body size and long arms relative to legs; long fingers and toes; probably capable of considerable climbing | Bipedal: shortened pelvis; body size larger; legs longer; fingers and toes not as long |

BRAIN

| Small compared to hominins, but large compared to other primates; a fair degree of encephalization | Larger than Miocene forms, but still only moderately encephalized; prior to 6 mya, no more encephalized than chimpanzees | Greatly increased brain size—highly encephalized |

DENTITION

| Large front teeth (including canines); molar teeth variable, depending on species; some have thin enamel caps, others thick enamel caps | Moderately large front teeth (incisors); canines somewhat reduced; molar tooth enamel caps very thick | Small incisors; canines further reduced; molar tooth enamel caps thick |

TOOLMAKING BEHAVIOR

| Unknown—no stone tools; probably had capabilities similar to chimpanzees | In earliest stages unknown; no stone tool use prior to 2.6 mya; probably somewhat more oriented toward tool manufacture and use than chimpanzees | Stone tools found after 2.5 mya; increasing trend of cultural dependency apparent in later hominins |

© Cengage Learning 2013

ior as being significant (at some stage) in defining what makes a hominin a hominin.

It's important to recognize that not all these characteristics developed simultaneously or at the same pace. In fact, over the last several million years of hominin evolution, quite a different pattern has been evident, in which each of the components (dentition, locomotion, brain size, and toolmaking) have developed at quite different rates. This pattern, in which physiological and behavioral systems evolve at different rates, is called **mosaic evolution**. As we will emphasize in this chapter, the single most important defining characteristic for the entire course of hominin evolution is **bipedal locomotion**. In the earliest stages of hominin emergence, skeletal evidence indicating bipedal locomotion is the only truly reliable indicator that these fossils were indeed hominins. But in later stages of hominin evolution, other features, especially those relating to brain development and behavior, become highly significant (**Fig. 9-7**).

Figure 9-7

Mosaic evolution of hominin characteristics: a postulated time line.

mosaic evolution A pattern of evolution in which the rate of evolution in one functional system varies from that in other systems. For example, in hominin evolution, the dental system, locomotor system, and neurological system (especially the brain) all evolved at markedly different rates.

bipedal locomotion Walking on two feet. Walking on two legs is the single most distinctive feature of the hominins.

What's in a Name?

Throughout this book, we refer to members of the human lineage as hominins (the technical name for members of the tribe Hominini). Most paleoanthropologists now prefer this terminology, since it more accurately reflects evolutionary relationships. As we mentioned briefly in Chapter 6, the more traditional classification of hominoids isn't as accurate and actually misrepresents key evolutionary relationships.

In the last several years, detailed molecular evidence clearly shows that the great apes (traditionally classified as pongids and including orangutans, gorillas, chimpanzees, and bonobos) don't make up a coherent evolutionary group sharing a single common ancestor. Indeed, the molecular/genetic data indicate that the African great apes (gorillas, chimpanzees, and bonobos) are significantly more closely related to humans than is the orangutan. What's more, at an even closer evolutionary level, we now know that chimpanzees and bonobos are yet more closely connected to humans than are gorillas. Hominoid classification has been significantly revised to show

these more complete relationships, and two further taxonomic levels (subfamily and tribe) have been added (**Fig. 9-8**).

We should mention a couple of important ramifications of this new classification. First, it further emphasizes the *very* close evolutionary connection of humans with African apes and most especially with chimpanzees and bonobos. Second, the term *hominid*, which has been used for decades to refer to our specific evolutionary lineage, has a quite different meaning in the revised classification; now it refers to *all* great apes and humans together.

Unfortunately, during the period of transition to the newer classification scheme, confusion is bound to result. For this reason, we won't use the term *hominid* in this book except where absolutely necessary (for example, in a formal classification; see Fig. 6-10). To avoid confusion, we'll simply refer to the grouping of great apes and humans as "large-bodied hominoids." And when you see the term *hominid* in earlier publications (including earlier editions of this text), simply regard it as synonymous with *hominin*, the term we use in this book.

Figure 9-8

(a) Traditional classification of hominoids. (b) Revised classification of hominoids. Note that two additional levels of classification are added (subfamily and tribe) to show more precisely and more accurately the evolutionary relationships among the apes and humans. In this classification, "hominin" is synonymous with the use of "hominid" in part (a).

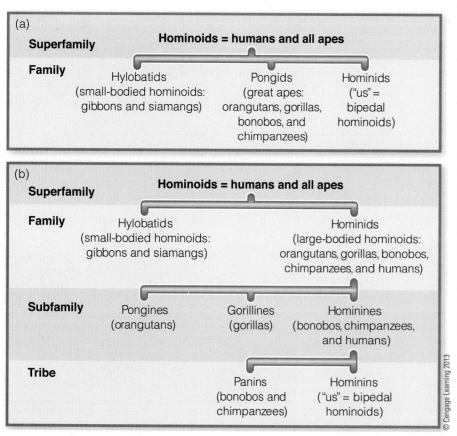

© Cengage Learning 2013

Walking the Walk: The Bipedal Adaptation

As we discussed in Chapter 6, all primates show adaptations for erect body posture, and some species are occasionally bipedal. Of all living primates, however, efficient bipedalism as the primary form of locomotion is seen *only* in hominins. Functionally, the human mode of locomotion is most clearly shown in our striding gait, where weight is alternately placed on a single fully extended hind limb. This specialized form of locomotion has developed to a point where energy levels are used to near peak efficiency. This isn't true of nonhuman primates, who move bipedally with hips and knees bent in a much less efficient manner.

From a survey of our close primate relatives, it's apparent that while still in the trees, our ancestors were adapted to a fair amount of upper-body erectness. Lemurs, lorises, tarsiers, monkeys, and apes all spend considerable time sitting erect while feeding, grooming, or sleeping. Presumably, our early ancestors displayed similar behavior. What caused them to come to the ground and embark on the unique way of life that would eventually lead to humans is still a mystery. Perhaps natural selection favored some Miocene hominoids coming occasionally to the ground to forage for food on the forest floor and forest fringe. In any case, once they were on the ground and away from the immediate safety offered by trees, bipedal locomotion could become a tremendous advantage.

First of all, bipedal locomotion freed the hands for carrying objects and for making and using tools. Hominins were bipedal for at least 2 million years prior to the first archaeological evidence of tool use, and we can reasonably assume that the earliest hominin tool use began considerably before the oldest identifiable evidence. Early cultural developments such as habitual tool use had an even more positive effect on speeding the development of yet more efficient bipedalism—once again emphasizing the dual role of biocultural evolution. In addition, in a bipedal stance, animals have a wider view of the surrounding countryside, and in open (or semi-open) terrain, early spotting of predators (particularly large cats, such as lions, leopards, and saber-tooths) would be of critical importance. We know that modern ground-living primates, including savanna baboons and vervets, occasionally adopt this posture to "look around" when out in open country.

Moreover, bipedal walking is an efficient means of covering long distances, and when large game hunting came into play (several million years after the initial adaptation to ground living), further refinements increasing the

efficiency of bipedalism may have been favored. It's hard to say exactly what initiated the process, but all these factors probably played a role in the adaptation of hominins to their special niche through a special form of locomotion.

The Mechanics of Walking on Two Legs

Our mode of locomotion is indeed extraordinary, involving, as it does, a unique kind of activity in which "the body, step by step, teeters on the edge of catastrophe" (Napier, 1967, p. 56). The problem is to maintain balance on the "stance" leg while the "swing" leg is off the ground. In fact, during normal walking, both feet are simultaneously on the ground only about 25 percent of the time, and as speed of locomotion increases, this percentage becomes even smaller.

Maintaining a stable center of balance calls for many drastic structural/anatomical alterations in the basic primate quadrupedal pattern. The most dramatic changes are seen in the pelvis. The pelvis is composed of three elements: two hip bones, or ossa coxae (*sing.*, os coxae), joined at the back to the sacrum (**Figs. 9-9** and **9-10**). In a quadruped, the ossa coxae are vertically elongated bones positioned along each side of the lower portion of the spine and oriented more or less parallel to it. In hominins, the pelvis is comparatively much shorter and broader and extends around to the side. This configuration helps to stabilize the line of weight transmission in a bipedal posture from the lower back to the hip joint (**Fig. 9-11**).

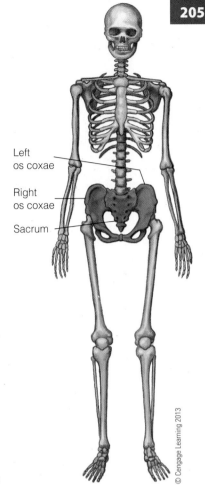

Left os coxae

Right os coxae

Sacrum

© Cengage Learning 2013

Figure 9-9

The human pelvis: various elements shown on a modern skeleton.

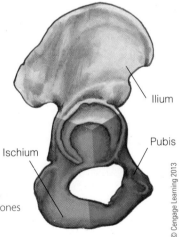

Ilium

Pubis

Ischium

© Cengage Learning 2013

Figure 9-10

The human os coxae, composed of three bones (right side shown).

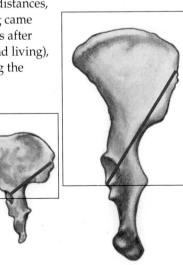

© Cengage Learning 2013

(a)   (b)   (c)

Figure 9-11

Ossa coxae. (a) *Homo sapiens.* (b) Early hominin (australopith) from South Africa. (c) Great ape. Note especially the length and breadth of the iliac blade (boxed) and the line of weight transmission (shown in red).

Major Features of Bipedal Locomotion

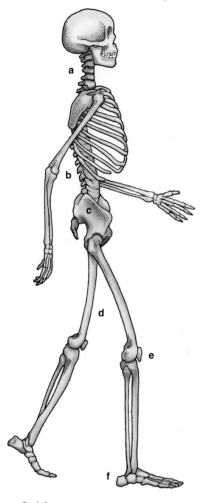

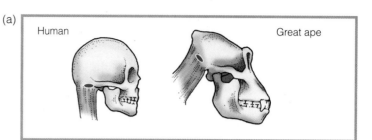

(a)

Human   Great ape

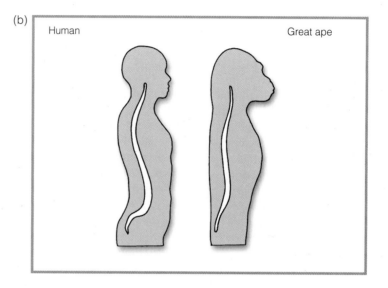

(b)

Human   Great ape

Figure 9-12

During hominin evolution, several major structural features throughout the body have been reorganized (from that seen in other primates), facilitating efficient bipedal locomotion. These are illustrated here, beginning with the head and progressing to the foot: (a) The foramen magnum (shown in blue) is repositioned farther underneath the skull, so that the head is more or less balanced on the spine (and thus requires less robust neck muscles to hold the head upright). (b) The spine has two distinctive curves—a backward (thoracic) one and a forward (lumbar) one—that keep the trunk (and weight) centered above the pelvis. (c) The pelvis is

habitual bipedalism Bipedal locomotion as the form of locomotion shown by hominins most of the time.

obligate bipedalism Bipedalism as the *only* form of hominin terrestrial locomotion. Since major anatomical changes in the spine, pelvis, and lower limb are required for bipedal locomotion, once hominins adapted this mode of locomotion, other forms of locomotion on the ground became impossible.

Moreover, the foot must act as a stable support instead of a grasping limb. When we walk, our foot is used like a prop, landing on the heel and pushing off on the toes, particularly the big toe. In addition, our legs became elongated to increase the length of the stride. An efficient bipedal adaptation required further remodeling of the lower limb to allow full extension of the knee and to keep the legs close together during walking, in this way maintaining the center of support directly under the body (**Fig. 9-12**).

We say that hominin bipedalism is both habitual and obligate. By **habitual bipedalism**, we mean that hominins, unlike any other primate, move bipedally as their standard and most efficient mode of locomotion. By **obligate bipedalism**, we mean that hominins are committed to bipedalism and cannot locomote efficiently in any other way. For example, the loss of grasping ability in the foot makes climbing much more difficult for humans. The central task, then, in trying to understand the earliest members of the hominin lineage is to identify anatomical features that indicate bipedalism and to interpret to what degree these individuals were committed to this form of locomotion (that is, was it habitual and obligate?).

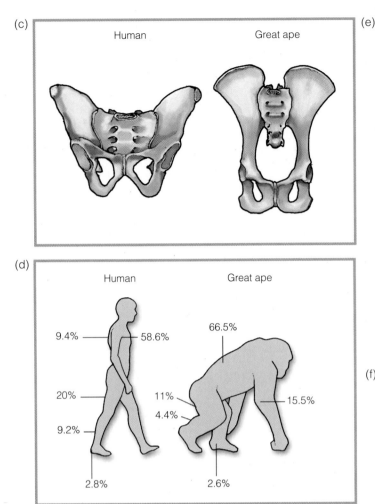

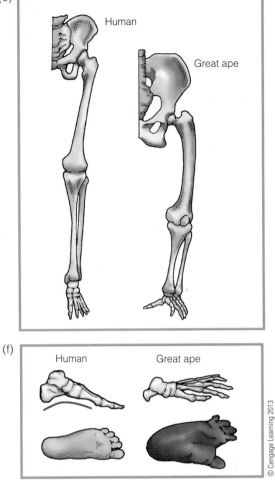

shaped more in the form of a basin to support internal organs; the ossa coxae (specifically, iliac blades) are also shorter and broader, thus stabilizing weight transmission. (d) Lower limbs are elongated, as shown by the proportional lengths of various body segments (for example, in humans the thigh comprises 20 percent of body height, while in gorillas it comprises only 11 percent). (e) The femur is angled inward, keeping the legs more directly under the body; modified knee anatomy also permits full extension of this joint. (f) The big toe is enlarged and brought in line with the other toes; a distinctive longitudinal arch also forms, helping absorb shock and adding propulsive spring.

What structural patterns are observable in early hominins, and what do they imply regarding locomotor function? By 4.4 mya, we have good evidence that hominins had adaptations in their pelvis and feet that allowed for fairly efficient bipedal locomotion while on the ground. They were, however, still surprisingly primitive in many other respects and spent considerable time in the trees (where they could also move about very efficiently).

Only after around 4 mya do we see all the major structural changes required for bipedalism. In particular, the pelvis, as clearly documented by several excellently preserved specimens, was remodeled further to more efficiently support weight in a bipedal stance (see Fig. 9-11b).

Other structural changes shown after 4 mya further confirm the pattern seen in the pelvis. For example, the vertebral column (as known from specimens in East and South Africa) shows the same curves as in modern hominins. The lower limbs are also elongated, and they seem to be proportionately about as long as in modern humans (although the arms are longer in these early hominins). Further, the carrying angle of weight support from the hip to the knee is very similar to that seen in ourselves.

Fossil evidence of early hominin foot structure has come from several sites in South and East Africa. Some of this evidence, especially well-preserved fossils (as well as footprints) from East Africa, show a well-adapted form of bipedalism. However, some earlier (and recently analyzed) finds from East Africa, as well as some from South Africa, indicate that the large toe was divergent like that seen in great apes. Such a configuration is an ancestral trait among hominoids, important in allowing the foot to grasp. In turn, this grasping ability (as in other primates) would have enabled early hominins to more effectively exploit arboreal habitats. Finally, since anatomical remodeling is always constrained by a set of complex functional compromises, a foot highly capable of grasping and climbing is less capable as a stable platform during bipedal locomotion.

From this evidence, some researchers have recently concluded that many forms of early hominins spent considerable time in the trees. What's more, the earliest hominins were likely habitual bipeds when on the ground, but not necessarily obligate bipeds. Only after about 4 mya did further adaptations lead to the fully committed form of bipedalism that we see in all later hominins, including ourselves.

Digging for Connections: Early Hominins from Africa

As you are now aware, a variety of early hominins lived in Africa, and we'll cover their comings and goings over a 5-million-year period, from at least 6 to 1 mya. It's also important to keep in mind that these hominins were geographically widely distributed, with fossil discoveries coming from central, East, and South Africa. Paleoanthropologists generally agree that among these early African fossils, there were at least 6 different genera, which in turn comprised upward of 13 different species. At no time, nor in any other place, were hominins ever as diverse as were these very ancient members of our family tree. As you will soon

see, some of the earliest fossils thought by many researchers to be hominins are primitive in some ways and unusually derived in others. In fact, some paleoanthropologists remain unconvinced that they are really hominins.

As you've already guessed, there are quite a few different fossils from many sites, and you'll find that their formal naming can be difficult to pronounce and not easy to remember. So we'll try to discuss these fossil groups in a way that's easy to understand. Our primary focus will be to organize them by time and by major evolutionary trends. In so doing, we recognize three major groups:

▶ Pre-australopiths—the earliest and most primitive (possible) hominins (6.0+ – 4.4 mya)
▶ Australopiths—diverse forms, some more primitive, others highly derived (4.2 – 1.2 mya)
▶ Early *Homo*—the first members of our genus (2.0+ – 1.4 mya)

Pre-Australopiths (6.0+ – 4.4 mya)

The oldest and most surprising of these earliest hominins is represented by a cranium discovered at a central African site called Toros-Menalla in the modern nation of Chad (Brunet et al., 2002; **Fig. 9-13**). Provisional dating using faunal correlation (biostratigraphy) suggests a date of between 7 and 6 mya (Vignaud et al., 2002). Closer examination of the evidence used in obtaining this biostratigraphic date has led many paleoanthropologists to suggest that the later date (6 mya) is more likely.

The morphology of the fossil is unusual, with a combination of characteristics unlike that found in other early hominins. The braincase is small, estimated at no larger than a modern chimpanzee's (preliminary estimate in the range of 320 to 380 cm³), but it is massively built, with huge browridges in front, a crest on top, and large muscle attachments in the rear. Yet, combined with these apelike features is a smallish vertical face containing front teeth very unlike an ape's. In fact, the lower face, being more tucked in under the

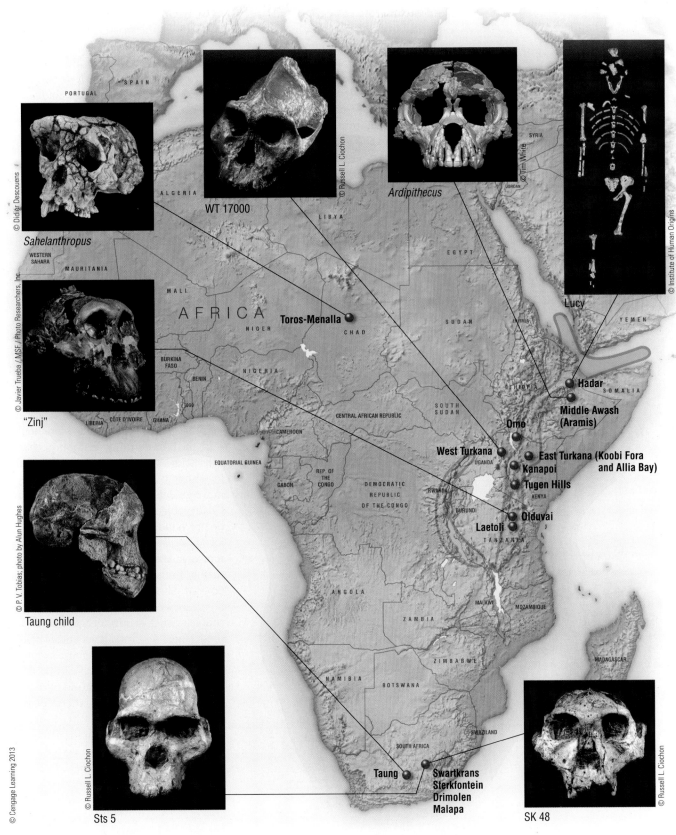

Figure 9-13

Early hominin fossil finds (pre-australopith and australopith localities). The Rift Valley in East Africa is shown in gold.

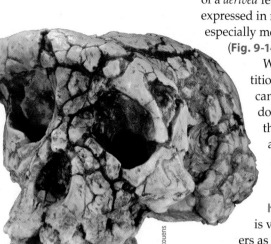

Figure 9-14

A nearly complete cranium of *Sahelanthropus* from Chad, dating to approximately 6 mya or somewhat older.

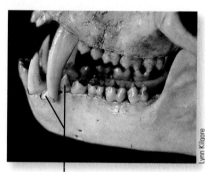

Sectorial lower first premolar

Figure 9-15

Canine/lower first premolar honing complex, typical of most Old World anthropoids but lacking in most hominins, shown here in a male patas monkey. Note how the large upper canine shears against the elongated surface of the lower first premolar.

honing complex The shearing of a large upper canine with the first lower premolar, with the wear leading to honing of the surfaces of both teeth. This anatomical pattern is typical of most Old World anthropoids, but is mostly absent in hominins.

brain vault (and not protruding, as in most other early hominins), is more of a *derived* feature more commonly expressed in much later hominins, especially members of genus *Homo* (**Fig. 9-14**).

What's more, unlike the dentition seen in apes, the upper canine is reduced and is worn down from the tip (rather than shearing along its side against the first lower premolar). The lack of such a shearing canine/premolar arrangement (called a **honing complex; Fig. 9-15**) is viewed by many researchers as an important derived characteristic of early hominins (White et al., 2009). Other experts are not entirely convinced and suggest that it could just as easily have evolved in both hominins

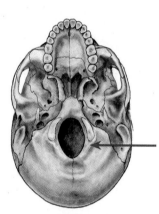

(a)

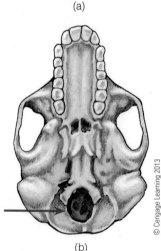

(b)

Figure 9-16

Position of the foramen magnum in (a) a human and (b) a chimpanzee. Note the more forward position in the human cranium.

and other hominoids due to homoplasy (Wood and Harrison, 2011).

In recognition of this unique combination of characteristics, paleoanthropologists have placed the Toros-Menalla remains into a new genus and species of hominin, *Sahelanthropus tchadensis* (Sahel being the region of the southern Sahara in North Africa). These finds from Chad have forced an immediate and significant reassessment of early hominin evolution. Two cautionary comments, however, are in order. First, as we noted, the dating is only approximate, based, as it is, on biostratigraphic correlation with sites in Kenya (1,500 miles to the east). Second, and perhaps more serious, is the hominin status of the Chad fossil. Given the facial structure and dentition, it's difficult to see how *Sahelanthropus* could be anything but a hominin. However, the position of its foramen magnum is intermediate between that of a quadrupedal ape and that of a bipedal hominin (**Fig. 9-16**); for this and other reasons, some researchers (Wolpoff et al., 2002) suggest that at this time, "ape" may be a better classification for *Sahelanthropus*. As we have previously said, the best-defining anatomical characteristics of hominins relate to bipedal locomotion. Unfortunately, no postcranial elements have been recovered from Chad—at least not yet. Consequently, we do not yet know the locomotor behavior of *Sahelanthropus*, and this raises even more fundamental questions: What if further finds show this form not to be bipedal? Should we still consider it a hominin? What, then, are the defining characteristics of our lineage? For all these reasons, several paleoanthropologists have recently grown more skeptical regarding the hominin status of all the pre-australopith finds, and Bernard Wood (2010) prefers to call them "possible hominins."

Probably living at about the same time as *Sahelanthropus*, two other very early (possible) hominin genera have been found at sites in central Kenya in the Tugen Hills and from the Middle Awash area of northeastern Ethiopia. The earlier of these finds (dated by radiometric methods to around 6 mya) comes from the Tugen Hills and includes mostly dental remains, but also some quite complete lower limb bones. The fossils have been placed in a separate early hominin genus called *Orrorin*. The postcranial remains are especially important, since they seem to indicate bipedal locomotion (Pickford and Senut, 2001; Senut et al., 2001; Galik et al., 2004; Richmond and Jungers, 2008). As a result of these further analyses, *Orrorin* is the pre-australopith generally recognized as having the best evidence to establish it as a hominin (compared to less clear evidence for *Sahelanthropus* and *Ardipithecus*).

The last group of possible hominins dating to the late Miocene (that is, earlier than 5 mya) comes from the Middle Awash in the Afar Triangle of Ethiopia. Radiometric dating places the age of these fossils in the very late Miocene, 5.8–5.2 mya. The fossil remains themselves are very fragmentary. Some of the dental remains resemble some later fossils from the Middle Awash (discussed shortly), and Yohannes Haile-Selassie, the researcher who first found and described these earlier materials, has provisionally assigned them to the genus *Ardipithecus* (Haile-Selassie et al., 2004; see "At a Glance: Pre-Australopith Discoveries"). In addition, some postcranial elements have been preserved, most informatively a toe bone, a phalanx from the middle of the foot (see Appendix A, Fig. A-8). From clues in this bone, Haile-Selassie concludes that this primate was a well-adapted biped (once again, the best-supporting evidence of hominin status).

From another million years or so later in the geological record in the Middle Awash region, a very large and significant assemblage of fossil hominins has been discovered at a site called **Aramis**. Radiometric dating firmly places these remains at about 4.4 mya. The site, represented by a 6-foot-thick bed of bones, has yielded more than 6,000 fossils. From this key site, excavations reveal both large and small vertebrates—birds and other reptiles and even very small mammals. Additionally, fossil wood and pollen samples have been recovered. All this information is important for understanding the environments in which these ancient hominins lived.

Hominin fossil remains from Aramis include several individuals, the most

noteworthy being a partial skeleton. At least 36 other hominins are represented by isolated teeth, cranial bones, and a few limb bones. All the bones were extremely fragile and fragmentary and required many years of incredibly painstaking effort to clean and reconstruct. Indeed, it took 15 years before the partial skeleton was in adequate condition to be intensively studied. But the wait was well worth it, and in 2009, Tim White and colleagues published their truly remarkable finds. By far, the most informative fossil is the partial skeleton. Even though it was found crushed and fragmented into hundreds of small pieces, the years of work and computer imaging have now allowed researchers to interpret this 4.4-million-year-old individual. The skeleton, nicknamed "Ardi," has more than 50 percent of the skeleton represented; however, since it was found in such poor condition, any reconstruction must be seen as provisional and open to varying interpretations. Ardi has been sexed as female and contains several key portions, including a skull, a pelvis, and almost complete hands and feet (White et al., 2009; **Fig. 9-17**).

Brain size, estimated between 300 and 350 cm³, is quite small, being no larger than a chimpanzee's. However, it is much like that seen in *Sahelanthropus*, and overall, the skulls of the two hominins also appear to be similar. The fact that remains of the postcranial skeleton are preserved is potentially crucial, because key body elements, such as the pelvis and the foot, are only very rarely discovered. This is the *earliest* hominin for which we have so many different parts of the body represented, and it permits researchers to hypothesize more confidently about body size and proportions and, perhaps most crucially of all, the mode of locomotion.

Height is estimated at close to 4 feet, with a body weight of around 110

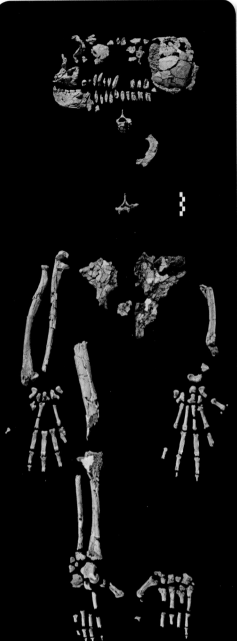

© David L. Brill / Atlanta

Figure 9-17

A mostly complete (but fragmented) skeleton of *Ardipithecus*. Dating to about 4.4 mya, this is the earliest hominin skeleton yet found containing so many different portions of the body.

Aramis (air-ah-miss)

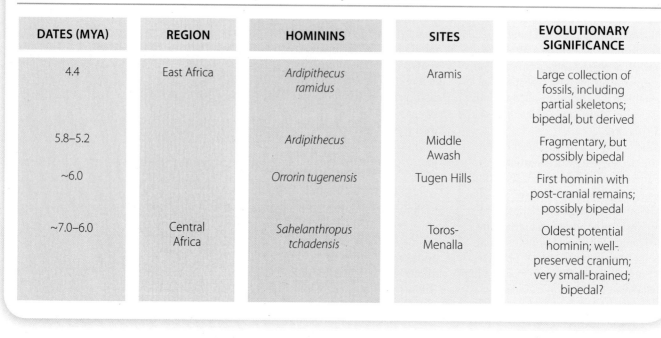

At a Glance

Key Pre-Australopith Discoveries

DATES (MYA)	REGION	HOMININS	SITES	EVOLUTIONARY SIGNIFICANCE
4.4	East Africa	*Ardipithecus ramidus*	Aramis	Large collection of fossils, including partial skeletons; bipedal, but derived
5.8–5.2		*Ardipithecus*	Middle Awash	Fragmentary, but possibly bipedal
~6.0		*Orrorin tugenensis*	Tugen Hills	First hominin with post-cranial remains; possibly bipedal
~7.0–6.0	Central Africa	*Sahelanthropus tchadensis*	Toros-Menalla	Oldest potential hominin; well-preserved cranium; very small-brained; bipedal?

pounds. Compared with other early hominins, such a body size would be similar to that of a male and well above average for a female. The pelvis and foot are preserved well enough to allow good-quality computer reconstructions. According to Tim White and colleagues, both areas of the body show key anatomical changes indicating that *Ardipithecus* was a competent biped. For example, the ilium is short and broad (see Figs. 9-10 and 9-11), and the foot has been modified to act as a prop for propulsion during walking.

However, Ardi also contains some big surprises. While the shape of the ilium seems to show bipedal abilities, other parts of the pelvis show more ancestral ("primitive") hominoid characteristics. In fact, the paleoanthropologists who analyzed the skeleton concluded that Ardi likely walked quite adequately, but might well have had difficulty running (Lovejoy et al., 2009a, 2009b). The foot is also an odd mix of features, showing a big toe that is highly divergent and capable of considerable grasping. Some researchers are not convinced that Ardi was bipedal, and considering all her other primitive characteristics, some have questioned whether *Ardipithecus*

was really a hominin at all (Sarmiento, 2010). The extreme degree of reconstruction that was required (for the skull and pelvis especially) adds further uncertainty to understanding this crucial discovery. One thing that everyone agrees on is that Ardi was an able climber who likely was well adapted to walking on all fours along the tops of branches. It seems clear that she spent a lot of time in the trees.

Accepting for the moment that *Ardipithecus* was a hominin, it was a very primitive one, displaying an array of characteristics quite distinct from all later members of our lineage. The new evidence that Ardi provides has not convinced all paleoanthropologists that *Ardipithecus* or any of the other very early pre-australopiths are hominins; indeed, Ardi's very odd anatomy has caused doubts to increase. One thing is for sure: It would take a considerable adaptive shift in the next 200,000 years to produce the more derived hominins we'll discuss in a moment. All of these considerations have not only intrigued professional anthropologists; they have also captured the imagination of the general public. When did the earliest member of our lineage first appear? The search still goes on, and professional reputations are made and lost in this quest.

Another intriguing aspect of all these late Miocene/early Pliocene locales (that is, Toros-Menalla, Tugen Hills, early Middle Awash sites, and Aramis) relates to the ancient environments associated with these potentially earliest hominins. Rather than the more open grassland savanna habitats so characteristic of most later hominin sites, the environment at all these early locales is more heavily forested. Perhaps we are seeing at Aramis and these other ancient sites the very beginnings of hominin divergence, not long after the division from the African apes.

Australopiths (4.2–1.2 mya)

The best-known, most widely distributed, and most diverse of the early African hominins are colloquially called **australopiths**. In fact, this diverse and very successful group of hominins is made up of two closely related genera, *Australopithecus* and *Paranthropus*. These hominins have an established time range of over 3 million years—stretching back as early as 4.2 mya and not becoming extinct until apparently close to 1 mya—making them the longest-enduring hominins yet documented. In addition, these hominins have been found in all the major geographical areas of Africa that have, to date, produced early hominin finds, namely, South Africa, central Africa (Chad), and East Africa. From all these areas combined, there appears to have been considerable complexity in terms of evolutionary diversity, with numerous species now recognized by most paleoanthropologists.

There are two major subgroups of australopiths, an earlier one that is more anatomically primitive and a later one that is much more derived. These earlier australopiths, dated 4.2–3.0 mya, show several more primitive (ancestral) hominin characteristics than the later australopith group, whose members are more derived, some extremely so. These more derived hominins lived after 2.5 mya and are composed of two different genera, together represented by at least

five different species (see Appendix B for a complete listing and more information about early hominin fossil finds).

Given the 3-million-year time range as well as quite varied ecological niches, there are numerous intriguing adaptive differences between these varied australopith species. We'll discuss the major adaptations of the various species in a moment. But first let's emphasize the major features that all australopiths share:

1. They are all clearly bipedal (although not necessarily identical to *Homo* in this regard).
2. They all have relatively small brains (at least compared to *Homo*).
3. They all have large teeth, particularly the back teeth, with thick to very thick enamel on the molars.

In short, then, all these australopith species are relatively small-brained, big-toothed bipeds.

The earliest australopiths, dating to 4.2–3.0 mya, come from East Africa from a couple of sites in northern Kenya. Among the fossil finds of these earliest australopiths so far discovered, a few postcranial pieces clearly indicate that locomotion was bipedal.

Since these particular fossils have initially been interpreted as more primitive than all the later members of the genus *Australopithecus*, paleoanthropologists have provisionally assigned them to a separate species. This important fossil species is now called *Australopithecus anamensis*, and some researchers suggest that it is a potential ancestor for many later australopiths as well as perhaps early members of the genus *Homo* (White et al., 2006).

Australopithecus afarensis

Slightly later and much more complete remains of *Australopithecus* have come primarily from the sites of Hadar (in Ethiopia) and Laetoli (in Tanzania). Much of this material has been known for three decades, and the fossils have been very well studied; indeed, in certain instances, they are quite famous. For example, the Lucy skeleton was discovered at Hadar in 1974, and the Laetoli footprints were first found in 1978. These

australopiths A colloquial name referring to a diverse group of Plio-Pleistocene African hominins. Australopiths are the most abundant and widely distributed of all early hominins and are also the most completely studied.

Figure 9-18

Hominin footprint from Laetoli, Tanzania. Note the deep impression of the heel and the large toe (arrow) in line (adducted) with the other toes.

© John Reader / Photo Researchers, Inc.

hominins are classified as members of the species *Australopithecus afarensis*.

Literally thousands of footprints have been found at Laetoli, representing more than 20 different kinds of animals (Pliocene elephants, horses, pigs, giraffes, antelopes, hyenas, and an abundance of hares). Several hominin footprints have also been found, including a trail more than 75 feet long made by at least two—and perhaps three—individuals (Leakey and Hay, 1979; **Fig. 9-18**). Such discoveries of well-preserved hominin footprints are extremely important in furthering our understanding of human evolution. For the first time, we can make *definite* statements regarding the locomotor pattern and stature of early hominins.

Studies of these impression patterns clearly show that the mode of locomotion of these hominins was bipedal (Day and Wickens, 1980). Some researchers, however, have concluded that *A. afarensis* was not bipedal in quite the same way that modern humans are. From detailed comparisons with modern humans, estimates of stride length, cadence, and speed of walking have been ascertained, indicating that the Laetoli hominins moved in a slow-moving ("strolling") fashion with a rather short stride.

One extraordinary discovery at Hadar is the Lucy skeleton (**Fig. 9-19**), found eroding out of a hillside by Don Johanson. This fossil is scientifically

designated as Afar Locality (AL) 288-1, but is usually just called Lucy (after the Beatles song "Lucy in the Sky with Diamonds"). Representing almost 40 percent of a skeleton, this is one of the most complete individuals from anywhere in the world for the entire period before about 100,000 ya.

Because the Laetoli area was covered periodically by ashfalls from nearby volcanic eruptions, accurate dating is possible and has provided dates of 3.7–3.5 mya. Dating from the Hadar region hasn't proved as straightforward; however, more complete dating calibration using a variety of techniques has determined a range of 3.9–3.0 mya for the hominin discoveries from this area.

Several hundred *A. afarensis* specimens, representing a minimum of 60 individuals (and perhaps as many as 100), have been removed from Laetoli and Hadar. At present, these materials represent the largest *well-studied* collection of early hominins and as such are among the most significant of the hominins discussed in this chapter.

Without question, *A. afarensis* is more primitive than any of the other later australopith fossils from South or East Africa (discussed shortly). By "primitive" we mean that *A. afarensis* is less evolved in any particular direction than are later-occurring hominin species. That is, *A. afarensis* shares more primitive features with late Miocene apes and with

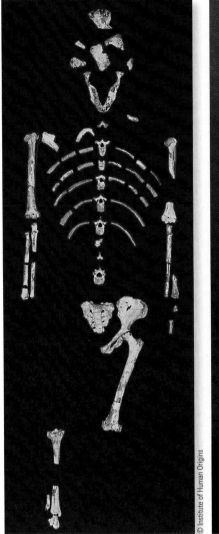

(a)

(b)

Figure 9-19

(a) "Lucy," a partial hominin skeleton, discovered at Hadar in 1974. This individual is assigned to *Australopithecus afarensis*. (b) Artist's reconstruction of Lucy, based upon her skeleton.

living great apes than do later hominins, who display more derived characteristics.

For example, the teeth of *A. afarensis* are quite primitive. The canines are often large, pointed teeth. Moreover, the lower first premolar provides a shearing surface for the upper canine (although it is not a full honing complex as seen in many monkeys and apes). Lastly, the tooth rows are parallel, even converging somewhat toward the back of the mouth (**Fig. 9-20**).

The cranial portions that are preserved also display several primitive hominoid characteristics, including a crest in the back as well as several primitive features of the cranial base. Cranial capacity estimates for *A. afarensis* show a mixed pattern when compared with later hominins. A provisional estimate for the one partially

complete cranium—apparently a large individual—gives a figure of 500 cm³, but another, even more fragmentary cranium is apparently quite a bit smaller and has been estimated at about 375 cm³ (Holloway, 1983). Thus, for some individuals (males?), *A. afarensis* is well within the range of other australopith species, but others (females?) may have a significantly smaller cranial capacity. However, a detailed depiction of cranial size for *A. afarensis* is not possible at this time; this part of the skeleton is unfortunately too poorly represented. One thing is clear: *A. afarensis* had a small brain, probably averaging for the whole species not much over 420 cm³.

On the other hand, a large assortment of postcranial pieces representing almost all portions of the body of *A. afarensis* has been found. Initial impressions

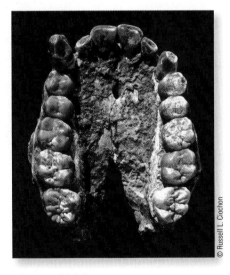

Figure 9-20

Upper jaw of *Australopithecus afarensis* from Hadar, Ethiopia. (Note the parallel tooth rows and large canines.)

suggest that relative to lower limbs, the upper limbs are longer than in modern humans (also a primitive Miocene ape condition). (This statement does not mean that the arms of *A. afarensis* were longer than the legs.) In addition, the wrist, hand, and foot bones show several differences from modern humans (Susman et al., 1985). From such excellent postcranial evidence, stature can be confidently estimated: *A. afarensis* was a short hominin. From her partial skeleton, Lucy is estimated to be only 3 to 4 feet tall. However, Lucy—as demonstrated by her pelvis—was probably a female, and there is evidence of larger individuals as well. The most economical hypothesis explaining this variation is that *A. afarensis* was quite sexually dimorphic: The larger individuals are male, and the smaller ones, such as Lucy, are female. Estimates of male stature can be approximated from the larger footprints at Laetoli, inferring a height of not quite 5 feet. If we accept this interpretation, *A. afarensis* was a very sexually dimorphic form indeed. In fact, for overall body size, this species may have been as dimorphic as *any* living primate (that is, as much as gorillas, orangutans, or baboons).

Significant further discoveries of *A. afarensis* have come from Ethiopia in the last few years, including two further partial skeletons. The first of these is a mostly complete skeleton of an *A. afarensis* infant discovered at the Dikika locale in northeastern Ethiopia, very near the Hadar sites mentioned earlier (**Fig. 9-21**). What's more, the infant comes from the same geological horizon as Hadar, with very similar dating: 3.3–3.2 mya (Alemseged et al., 2006). This find of a 3-year-old infant is remarkable because it's the first example of a very well-preserved immature hominin prior to about 100,000 ya. From the infant's extremely well-preserved teeth, scientists hypothesize that she was female. A comprehensive study of her developmental biology has already begun, and many more revelations are surely in store as the Dikika infant is more completely cleaned and studied.

Figure 9-21

Complete skull with attached vertebral column of the infant skeleton from Dikika, Ethiopia (dated to about 3.3 mya).

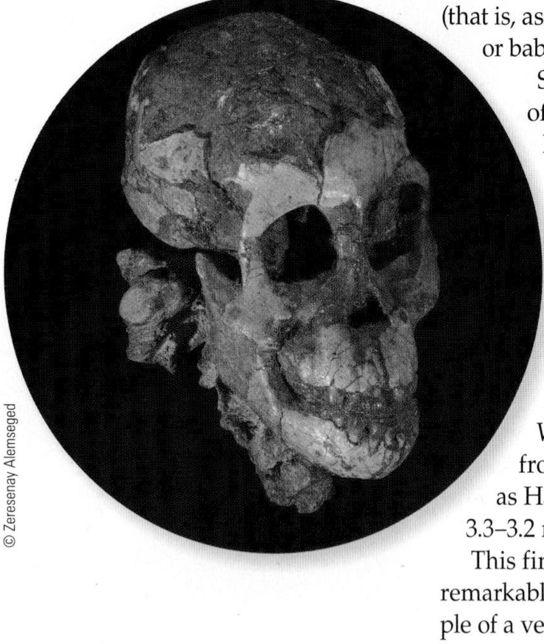

© Zeresenay Alemseged

For now, and accounting for her immature age, the skeletal pattern appears to be quite similar to what we'd expect in an *A. afarensis* adult. What's more, the limb proportions, anatomy of the hands and feet, and shape of the scapula (shoulder blade) reveal a similar "mixed" pattern of locomotion. The foot and lower limb indicate that this infant would have been a terrestrial biped; yet, the shoulder and (curved) fingers suggest that she was also capable of climbing about quite ably in the trees.

The second recently discovered *A. afarensis* partial skeleton comes from the Woranso-Mille research area in the central Afar, only about 30 miles north of Hadar (Haile-Selassie et al., 2010). The dating places the find at close to 3.6 mya (almost 400,000 years earlier than Lucy). Moreover, the individual was considerably larger than Lucy and likely was male. Analysis of bones preserved in this new find reinforces what was previously known about *A. afarensis* as well as adding some further insights. The large degree of sexual dimorphism and well-adapted bipedal locomotion agree with prior evidence. What's more, a portion of a shoulder joint (with a scapula; see Appendix A) confirms that suspensory locomotion was not a mode of arboreal locomotion; nevertheless, arboreal habitats could still have been effectively exploited.

What makes *A. afarensis* a hominin? The answer is revealed by its manner of locomotion. From the abundant limb bones recovered from Hadar and other locales, as well as those beautiful footprints from Laetoli, we know unequivocally that *A. afarensis* walked bipedally when on the ground. (At present, we do not have nearly such good evidence concerning locomotion for *any* of the earlier hominin finds.) Whether Lucy and her contemporaries still spent considerable time in the trees and just how efficiently they walked have become topics of some controversy. Most researchers, however, agree that *A. afarensis* was an efficient habitual biped while on the ground. These hominins were also clearly *obligate* bipeds, which would have hampered their climbing abilities but would not necessarily have precluded arboreal behavior altogether.

Australopithecus afarensis is a crucial hominin group. Since it comes after the earliest, poorly known group of pre-australopith hominins, but prior to all later australopiths as well as *Homo*, it is an evolutionary bridge, connecting together much of what we assume are the major patterns of early hominin evolution. The fact that there are many well-preserved fossils and that they have been so well studied also adds to the paleoanthropological significance of *A. afarensis*. The consensus among most experts over the last several years has been that *A. afarensis* is a potentially strong candidate as the ancestor of all later hominins. Some ongoing analysis has recently challenged this hypothesis (Rak et al., 2007), but at least for the moment, this new interpretation has not been widely accepted. Still, it reminds us that science is an intellectual pursuit that constantly reevaluates older views and seeks to provide more systematic explanations about the world around us. When it comes to understanding human evolution, we should always be aware that things might change. So stay tuned.

Later More Derived Australopiths (3.0–1.2 mya)

Following 3.0 mya, hominins became more diverse in Africa. As they adapted to varied niches, australopiths became considerably more derived. In other words, they show physical changes making them quite distinct from their immediate ancestors.

In fact, there were at least three separate lineages of hominins living (in some cases side by side) between 2.0 and 1.2 mya. One of these is a later form of *Australopithecus*; another is represented by the highly derived three species that belong to the genus *Paranthropus*; and the last consists of early members of the genus *Homo*. Here we'll discuss *Paranthropus* and *Australopithecus*. *Homo* will be discussed in the next section.

The most derived australopiths are the various members of *Paranthropus*. While all australopiths are big-toothed, *Paranthropus* has the biggest teeth of all, especially as seen in its huge premolars and molars. Along with these massive back teeth, these hominins show a vari-ety of other specializations related to powerful chewing (**Fig. 9-22**). For example, they all have large, deep lower jaws and large attachments for muscles associated with chewing. In fact, these chewing muscles are so prominent that major anatomical alterations evolved in the architecture of their face and skull vault. In particular, the *Paranthropus* face is flatter than that of any other australopith; the broad cheekbones (to which the masseter muscle attaches) flare out; and a ridge develops on top of the skull (this is called a **sagittal crest**, and it's where the temporal muscle attaches).

All these morphological features suggest that *Paranthropus* was adapted for a diet emphasizing rough vegetable foods. However, this does not mean that these very big-toothed hominins did not also eat a variety of other foods, perhaps including some meat. In fact, sophisticated recent chemical analyses of *Paranthropus* teeth suggest that their diet may have been quite varied (Sponheimer et al., 2006).

The first member of the *Paranthropus* evolutionary group (clade) comes from a site in northern Kenya on the west side of Lake Turkana. This key find is that of a nearly complete skull, called the "Black Skull" (owing to chemical staining during fossilization), and it dates to approximately 2.5 mya (**Fig. 9-23**). This skull, with a cranial capacity of only 410 cm³, is among the smallest for any hominin known, and it has other primitive traits reminiscent of *A. afarensis*.

But here's what makes the Black Skull so fascinating: Mixed into this array of distinctively primitive traits are a host of derived ones that link it to other, later *Paranthropus* species (including a broad face, a very large palate, and a large area for the back teeth). This mosaic of features seems to place this individual between the earlier *A. afarensis* and the later *Paranthropus* species. Because of its unique position in hominin evolution, the Black Skull (and the population it represents) has been placed in a new species, *Paranthropus aethiopicus*.

Around 2 mya, different varieties of even more derived members of the *Paranthropus* lineage were on the scene in East Africa. As well documented by finds dated after 2 mya from Olduvai

sagittal crest A ridge of bone that runs down the middle of the cranium like a short Mohawk. This serves as the attachment for the large temporal muscles, indicating strong chewing.

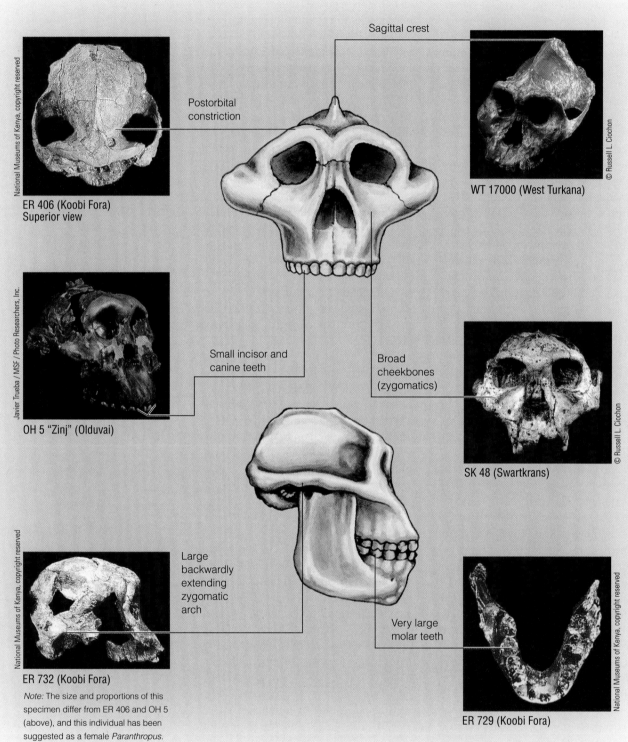

Sagittal crest

Postorbital constriction

ER 406 (Koobi Fora)
Superior view

WT 17000 (West Turkana)

Small incisor and canine teeth

OH 5 "Zinj" (Olduvai)

Broad cheekbones (zygomatics)

SK 48 (Swartkrans)

Large backwardly extending zygomatic arch

Very large molar teeth

ER 732 (Koobi Fora)

Note: The size and proportions of this specimen differ from ER 406 and OH 5 (above), and this individual has been suggested as a female *Paranthropus*.

ER 729 (Koobi Fora)

National Museums of Kenya, copyright reserved

Javier Trueba / MSF / Photo Researchers, Inc.

© Russell L. Ciochon

© Russell L. Ciochon

National Museums of Kenya, copyright reserved

National Museums of Kenya, copyright reserved

© Cengage Learning 2013

Figure 9-22

Morphology and variation in *Paranthropus*. (Note both typical features and range of variation as shown in different specimens.)

and East Turkana, *Paranthropus* continues to have relatively small cranial capacities (ranging from 510 to 530 cm³) and very large, broad faces with massive back teeth and lower jaws. The larger (probably male) individuals also show that characteristic raised ridge (sagittal crest) along the midline of the cranium. Females are not as large or as robust as the males, indicating a fair degree of sexual dimorphism. In any case, the East African *Paranthropus* individuals are all extremely robust in terms of their teeth and jaws—although in overall body size they are much like other australoaths. Since these somewhat later East African *Paranthropus* fossils are so robust, they are usually placed in their own separate species, *Paranthropus boisei*.

Paranthropus fossils have also been found at several sites in South Africa. As we discussed earlier, the geological context in South Africa usually does not allow as precise chronometric dating as is possible in East Africa. Based on less precise dating methods, *Paranthropus* in South Africa existed about 2.0–1.2 mya.

Paranthropus in South Africa is very similar to its close cousin in East Africa, but it's not quite as dentally robust. As a result, paleoanthropologists prefer to regard South African *Paranthropus* as a distinct species—one called *Paranthropus robustus*.

What became of *Paranthropus*? After 1 mya, these hominins seem to vanish without descendants. Nevertheless, we should be careful not to think of them as "failures." After all, they lasted for 1.5 million years, during which time they expanded over a considerable area of sub-Saharan Africa. Moreover, while their extreme dental/chewing adaptations may seem peculiar to us, it was a fascinating "evolutionary experiment" in hominin evolution. And it was an innovation that worked for a long time. Still, these big-toothed cousins of ours did eventually die out. It remains to us, the descendants of another hominin lineage, to find their fossils, study them, and ponder what these creatures were like.

From no site dating after 3 mya in East Africa have fossil finds of the genus *Australopithecus* been found. As you know, their close *Paranthropus* kin were doing quite well during this time.

Whether *Australopithecus* actually did become extinct in East Africa following 3 mya or whether we just haven't yet found their fossils is impossible to say.

South Africa, however, is another story. A very well-known *Australopithecus* species has been found at four sites in southernmost Africa, in a couple of cases in limestone caves very close to where *Paranthropus* fossils have also been found.

In fact, the very first early hominin discovery from Africa (indeed, from *anywhere*) came from the Taung site and was discovered back in 1924. The story of the discovery of the beautifully preserved child's skull from Taung is a fascinating tale (**Fig. 9-24**). When first published in 1925 by a young anatomist named Raymond Dart, most experts were unimpressed. They thought Africa to be an unlikely place for the origins of hominins. These skeptics, who had been long focused on European and Asian hominin finds, were initially unprepared to acknowledge Africa's central place in human evolution. Only years later, following many more African discoveries from other sites, did professional opinion shift. With this admittedly slow scientific awareness came the eventual consensus that Taung (which Dart classified as *Australopithecus africanus*) was indeed an ancient member of the hominin family tree.

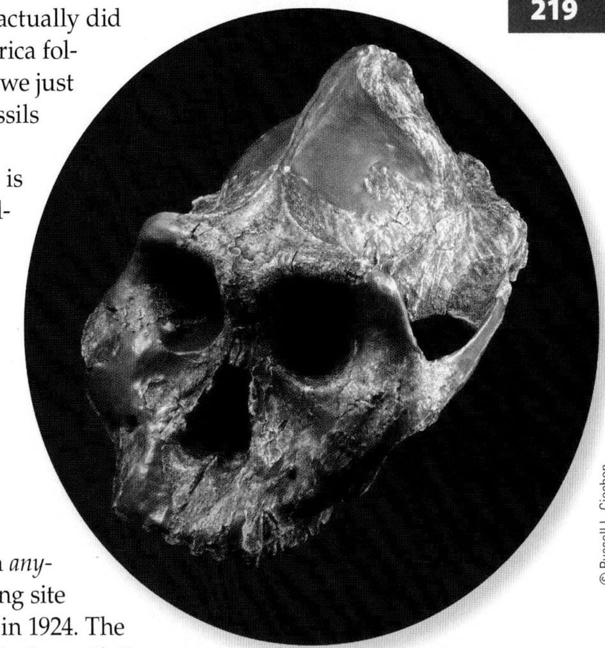

© Russell L. Ciochon

Figure 9-23

The "Black Skull," discovered at West Lake Turkana. This specimen is usually assigned to *Paranthropus aethiopicus*. It's called the Black Skull due to its dark color from the fossilization (mineralization) process.

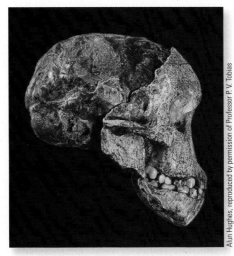

Alun Hughes, reproduced by permission of Professor P. V. Tobias

Figure 9-24

The Taung child's skull, discovered in 1924. There is a fossilized endocast of the brain in back, with the face and lower jaw in front.

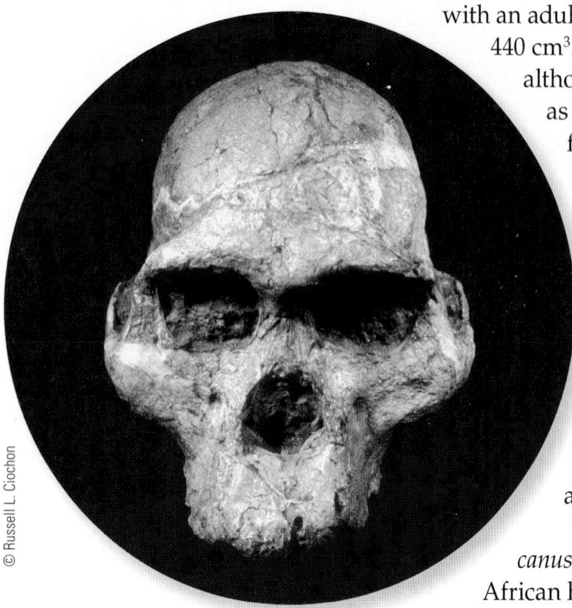

© Russell L. Ciochon

Figure 9-25

Australopithecus africanus adult cranium from Sterkfontein.

Like other australopiths, the "Taung baby" and other *A. africanus* individuals (**Fig. 9-25**) were small-brained, with an adult cranial capacity of about 440 cm³. They were also big-toothed, although not as extremely so as *Paranthropus*. Moreover, from very well-preserved postcranial remains from Sterkfontein, we know that they also were well-adapted bipeds. The ongoing excavation of a remarkably complete skeleton at Sterkfontein should tell us about *A. africanus'* locomotion, body size and proportions, and much more (**Fig. 9-26**).

The precise dating of *A. africanus*, as with most other South African hominins, has been disputed. Over the last several years, it's been assumed that this species existed as far back as 3.3 mya. However, the most recent analysis suggests that *A. africanus* lived approximately between 3 and 2 mya (Walker et al., 2006; Wood, 2010; **Fig. 9-27**).

New Connections: A Transitional Australopith?

As we'll see in the next section, almost all the evidence for the earliest appearance of our genus, *Homo*, has come from East Africa. So it's no surprise that most researchers have assumed that *Homo* probably first evolved in this region of Africa.

However, new and remarkably well-preserved fossil discoveries from South Africa may challenge this view. In 2008, paleoanthropologists discovered two partial skeletons at the Malapa Cave, located just a few miles from Sterkfontein and Swartkrans. Actually, the first find was made by the lead researcher's 9-year-old son, Matthew. His father (Lee Berger, from the University of Witwatersrand) and colleagues have been further investigating inside the cave, where several skeletons may be buried, and they announced and described their finds in 2010 (Berger et al., 2010).

Using paleomagnetic dating as well as more precise radiometric techniques than have been used before in South Africa (Dirks et al., 2010; Pickering et al., 2011), the fossils are dated to just a little less than 2 mya and show a fascinating mix of australopith characteristics along with a few features more suggestive of *Homo*. Because of this unique anatomical combination, these fossils have been assigned to a new species, *Australopithecus sediba* (*sediba* means "wellspring" or "fountain" in the local language). Australopith-like characteristics seen in *A. sediba* include a small brain (estimated at 420 cm³), long arms

Figure 9-26

Paleoanthropologist Ronald Clarke carefully excavates a 2-million-year-old skeleton from the limestone matrix at Sterkfontein Cave. Clearly seen are the cranium (with articulated mandible) and the upper arm bone.

John Hodgkiss

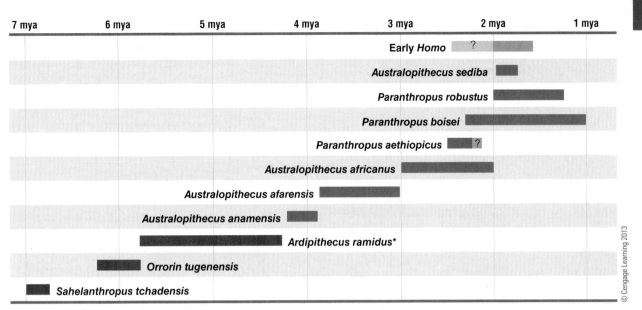

	7 mya	6 mya	5 mya	4 mya	3 mya	2 mya	1 mya

Early *Homo* ?

Australopithecus sediba

Paranthropus robustus

Paranthropus boisei

Paranthropus aethiopicus ?

Australopithecus africanus

Australopithecus afarensis

Australopithecus anamensis

Ardipithecus ramidus*

Orrorin tugenensis

Sahelanthropus tchadensis

© Cengage Learning 2013

*The earlier *Ardipithecus* specimens (5.8–5.2 mya) are placed in a separate species.

Figure 9-27

Time line of early African hominins. Note that most dates are approximations. Question marks indicate those estimates that are most tentative.

with curved fingers, and several primitive traits in the feet. In these respects *A. sediba* most resembles its potential immediate South African predecessor, *A. africanus* (**Figs. 9-28** and **9-29**).

But some other aspects of *A. sediba* more resemble *Homo*. Among these characteristics are short fingers and possible indications of brain reorganization. All this is very new and quite complex. Indeed, initial paleoanthropological interpretations are highly varied (Balter, 2010; Gibbons, 2011). It will take some time for experts to figure it out. Remember, too, that there are more fossils still in the cave. The initial consensus among paleoanthropologists is that *A. sediba* is quite different from other australopiths and shows a surprising and unique mix of primitive and derived characteristics. How it fits in with the origins of *Homo* remains to be determined. Certainly, more detailed studies of the *A. sediba* fossils, including further comparisons with other early hominins, will help further our understanding. For the moment, most paleoanthropologists still think the best evidence for the origins of our genus comes from East Africa.

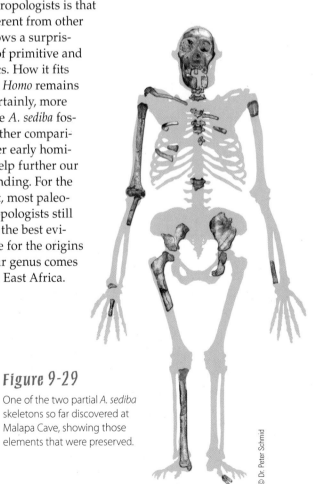

Figure 9-29

One of the two partial *A. sediba* skeletons so far discovered at Malapa Cave, showing those elements that were preserved.

© Dr. Peter Schmid

Figure 9-28

A. sediba skull, found at Malapa Cave, South Africa, precisely dated very close to 2 mya.

© University of the Witwatersrand, Lee Berger. Photo by Brett Eloff.

Closer Connections: Early *Homo* (2.0+ – 1.4 mya)

In addition to the australopith remains, there's another largely contemporaneous hominin that is quite distinctive and thought to be more closely related to us. In fact, as best documented by fossil discoveries from Olduvai and East Turkana, these materials have been assigned to the genus *Homo*—and thus are different from all species assigned to either *Australopithecus* or *Paranthropus*.

The earliest appearance of genus *Homo* in East Africa may date back well before 2 mya (and thus considerably before *A. sediba*). A discovery in the 1990s from the Hadar area of Ethiopia suggested to many paleoanthropologists that early *Homo* was present in East Africa by 2.3 mya; however, we should be cautious, since the find is quite incomplete (including only one upper jaw). Better-preserved evidence of a **Plio-Pleistocene** hominin with a significantly larger brain than seen in australopiths was first suggested by Louis Leakey in the early 1960s on the basis of fragmentary remains found at Olduvai Gorge. Leakey and his colleagues gave a new species designation to these fossil remains, naming them *Homo habilis*. There may, in fact, have been more than one species of *Homo* living in Africa during the Plio-Pleistocene. So, more generally, we'll refer to them all as "early *Homo*." The *Homo habilis* mate-

rial at Olduvai dates to about 1.8 mya, but due to the fragmentary nature of the fossil remains, evolutionary interpretations have been difficult. The most immediately obvious feature distinguishing the *H. habilis* material from the australopiths is cranial size. For all the measurable early *Homo* skulls, the estimated average cranial capacity is 631 cm^3, compared to 520 cm^3 for all measurable *Paranthropus* specimens and 442 cm^3 for *Australopithecus* crania (McHenry, 1988), including *A. sediba*. Early *Homo*, therefore, shows an increase in cranial size of about 20 percent over the larger of the australopiths and an even greater increase over some of the smaller-brained forms. In their initial description of *H. habilis*, Leakey and his associates also pointed to differences from australopiths in cranial shape and in tooth proportions.

The naming of this fossil material as *Homo habilis* ("handy man") was meaningful from two perspectives. First of all, Leakey argued that members of this group were the early Olduvai toolmakers. Second, and most significantly, by calling this group *Homo*, Leakey was arguing for at least *two separate branches* of hominin evolution in the Plio-Pleistocene. Clearly, only one could be on the main branch eventually leading to *Homo sapiens*. By labeling this new group *Homo* rather than *Australopithecus*, Leakey was guessing that he had found our ancestors.

Figure 9-30

A nearly complete early *Homo* cranium from East Lake Turkana (ER 1470), one of the most important single fossil hominin discoveries from East Africa. (a) Lateral view. (b) Frontal view.

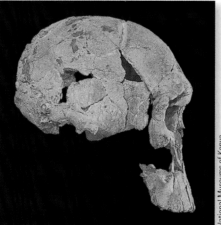

(a)

National Museums of Kenya

(b)

National Museums of Kenya

Plio-Pleistocene Pertaining to the Pliocene and first half of the Pleistocene, a time range of 5–1 mya. For this time period, numerous fossil hominins have been found in Africa.

Much better-preserved fossils from East Turkana have shed further light on early *Homo* in the Plio-Pleistocene.* The most important of this additional material is a nearly complete cranium (**Fig. 9-30**). With a cranial capacity of 775 cm³, this individual is well outside the known range for australopiths and actually overlaps the lower boundary for later species of *Homo* (that is, *H. erectus*, discussed in the next chapter). In addition, the shape of the skull vault is in many respects unlike that of australopiths. However, the face is still quite robust (Walker, 1976), and the fragments of tooth crowns that are preserved indicate that the back teeth in this individual were quite large.† The East Turkana early *Homo* material is generally contemporaneous with the Olduvai remains. The oldest date back to about 1.8 mya, but a recently discovered specimen dates to 1.44 mya, making it by far the latest surviving early *Homo* fossil yet found (Spoor et al., 2007). In fact, this discovery indicates that a species of early *Homo* coexisted in East Africa for several hundred thousand years with *H. erectus*, with both species living in the exact same area on the eastern side of Lake Turkana. This new evidence raises numerous fascinating questions regarding how two closely related species existed for so long in the same region.

As in East Africa, early members of the genus *Homo* have also been found in South Africa, and these fossils are considered more distinctive of *Homo* than is the *transitional* australopith, *A. sediba*. At both Sterkfontein and Swartkrans, fragmentary remains have been recognized as most likely belonging to *Homo* (**Fig. 9-31**).

On the basis of evidence from Olduvai and East Turkana, we can reasonably postulate that at least one species (and possibly two) of early *Homo*

was present in East Africa perhaps a little prior to 2 mya, developing in parallel with an australopith species. These hominin lines lived contemporaneously for a minimum of 1 million years, after which time the australopiths apparently disappeared forever. One lineage of early *Homo* likely evolved into *H. erectus* about 1.8 mya. Any other species of early *Homo* became extinct sometime after 1.4 mya.

The Lower Paleolithic Period: Emergence of Human Culture

As we've seen, the oldest identifiable stone tools date to 2.6 mya, and it is from this evidence that archaeologists determine the beginning of the Lower Paleolithic period. The two major Lower Paleolithic stone tool industries or tool complexes are the Oldowan, which spans roughly 2.6–1.7 mya, and the **Acheulian**, which dates to 1.7–0.2 mya. This section describes the Oldowan tool industry. We'll consider the Acheulian and the end of the Lower Paleolithic in Chapter 10.

The name Oldowan was coined decades ago by Louis and Mary Leakey to describe early stone tools and archaeological sites found at Olduvai Gorge, Tanzania (see Chapter 8). Subsequent research elsewhere in East Africa unearthed Oldowan sites that are more than half a million years older than the oldest Olduvai Gorge locations. These Oldowan assemblages demonstrate that by 2.6 mya, hominins were already inventing and adopting cultural, rather than purely biological, means of dealing with the world around them.

The meager Oldowan archaeological evidence (**Fig 9-32**) may seem unremarkable, especially when you consider that the cultural changes it reflects occurred so slowly that they would have been virtually unnoticeable to the Oldowan tool users themselves. Nevertheless, this seemingly insignificant beginning was profoundly important to the development of humans. As Thomas Plummer (2004, p.118) recently observed: "The appearance of Oldowan sites ca. 2.6

---

* Some early *Homo* fossils from East Turkana are classified by a minority of paleoanthropologists as a different species (*Homo rudolfensis*; see Appendix B). These researchers often identify both *H. habilis* and *H. rudolfensis* at Turkana but only *H. habilis* at Olduvai.

† In fact, some researchers have suggested that all these "early *Homo*" fossils are better classified as *Australopithecus* (Wood and Collard, 1999a).

Acheulian (ash´-oo-lay-en) Pertaining to a stone tool industry from the Early and Middle Pleistocene; characterized by a large proportion of bifacial tools (flaked on both sides). Acheulian tool kits are common in Africa, southwest Asia, and western Europe, but they're thought to be less common elsewhere. Also spelled Acheulean.

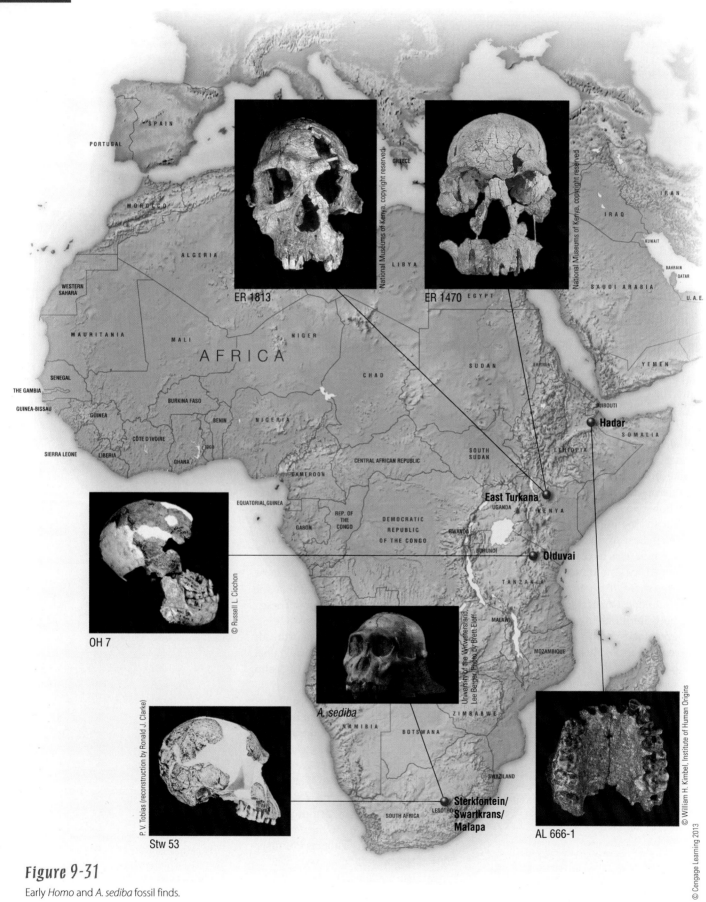

ER 1813

ER 1470

OH 7

Stw 53

A. sediba

AL 666-1

Hadar

East Turkana

Olduvai

Sterkfontein/
Swartkrans/
Malapa

Figure 9-31

Early *Homo* and *A. sediba* fossil finds.

Figure 9-32

The Oldowan assemblage consists of a few simple stone tools, mostly flakes, choppers, cores, and hammerstones.

Barry Lewis

million years ago . . . may reflect one of the most important adaptive shifts in human evolution. Stone artifact manufacture, large mammal butchery, and novel transport and discard behaviors led to the accumulation of the first recognized archaeological debris." These small steps also created a new phenomenon—the archaeological record, the source of the only direct evidence by which researchers can understand the cultural side of our biocultural evolution.

Oldowan tools are extremely rudimentary compared with the simplest known modern human technology. Assemblages mostly consist of stone flakes, which were used for cutting; hammerstones, used as the name implies; core tools such as choppers, which show considerable battering on their edges; and stone cores, which were used only as a source of flakes. These early hominins may have also made bone and wooden tools, but such implements have not survived in the archaeological record.

Most Oldowan stone tools were made by the **"hard hammer" percussion** method (**Fig. 9-33**), which, as the

name implies, means that these toolmakers simply took one rock and smashed it with another rock until they got the sharp flakes or cutting edge they wanted. The resulting tools typically owe most of their shape or form to that of the original pebble or cobble from which they were made. This pattern begins to change during the Acheulian, when we find tools that clearly are the result of the toolmakers sharing a common target design they wished to produce.

Compared with most hunter-gatherer tool kits from, say, 20,000 ya, Oldowan

© Cengage Learning 2013

Figure 9-33

Hard hammer percussion.

"hard hammer" percussion A direct percussion method of making stone tools that uses one rock as a hammer to knock flakes from another rock that serves as a core.

tools were of a generalized nature, where any given tool might serve several tasks. They were also relatively expedient tools, which means that they tended to be made when they were needed, used, and then discarded. Expedient tools are the opposite of curated tools, which are made, used, and kept ("curated") in anticipation of future use. The overall trend, as we shall see in later chapters, is for human tools to become both more specialized and more curated, but it took a long time for this trend to be measurable in the archaeological record. An important exception can be found in areas where suitable stones for tools do not occur naturally. In these cases, the available archaeological evidence suggests that Early Pleistocene hominins carried stones as much as 6 miles from their source areas.

Oldowan tools are properly viewed as the oldest tools that archaeologists can reliably *identify*. Our knowledge of the beginnings of human toolmaking is complicated greatly by the rudimentary nature of the earliest tools and by factors of preservation that removed wooden and other organic tools from the archaeological record. It is reasonable to assume that early hominins were tool users for hundreds of thousands of years before the oldest *identified* Oldowan stone tools were made and used (Harris and Capaldo, 1993).

New discoveries continue to push back the age of the earliest hominin tool use. Recently, for example, researchers found 3.39-million-year-old animal bones at Dikika, Ethiopia, that show stone tool cut marks and battering from the removal of meat and marrow (McPherron et al., 2010). It is important to note that the Dikika evidence is of the *effects* of tool use; no identifiable stone tools were found in association with the cut-marked animal bones. Nevertheless, Dikika is the latest and, thus far, the earliest example of evidence that the beginnings of hominin tool use (and, consequently, of hominin biocultural evolution) have deep roots in our past (de la Torre, 2011; Rogers and Semaw, 2009). The first tool-using hominin was likely one or more species of *Australopithecus*, but which species is far from clear.

So what did Lower Paleolithic hominins use Oldowan tools to do? They are best described as "tool-assisted" gatherers and meat scavengers. We can be reasonably certain that they were not hunters of big game, nor did their technology confer more than a minor competitive advantage over bigger, more aggressive savanna animals. If anything, these hominins were more equipped physically to be prey rather than hunter. Our earliest direct ancestors may have been inching their way up the food chain, but to get there, thousands of generations spent time waiting to pick over what was left after the real predators and scavengers ate their fill.

The Oldowan archaeological record is a controversial area of anthropological research. We are confident that early hominins created the earliest archaeological evidence of human cultural behavior. But which hominins, and why? How did they use the tools they made? Were they hunter, prey, or both? We have answers to these questions, but all too often, they are slippery, chameleon-like ones that can change dramatically with the next fossil find or archaeological excavation. It is a frustrating but fascinating area of science.

Interpretations: What Does It All Mean?

By this time, you may think that anthropologists are obsessed with finding small scraps buried in the ground and then assigning them confusing numbers and taxonomic labels impossible to remember. But it's important to realize that the collection of all the basic fossil data is the foundation of human evolutionary research. Without fossils, our speculations would be largely hollow—and most certainly not scientifically testable. Several large, ongoing paleoanthropological projects are now collecting additional data in an attempt to answer some of the more perplexing questions about our evolutionary history.

The numbering of specimens, which may at times seem somewhat confusing, is an effort to keep the designations neutral and to make reference to each individual fossil as clear as possible. The formal naming of finds as *Australopithecus*, *Paranthropus*, or *Homo habilis* should come much later, since it involves a lengthy series of complex interpretations. Assigning generic and specific names to fossil finds is more than just a convenience; when we attach a particular label, such as *A. afarensis*, to a particular fossil, we should be fully aware of the biological implications of such an interpretation.

From the time that fossil sites are first located until the eventual interpretation of hominin evolutionary patterns, several steps take place. Ideally, they should follow a logical order, for if interpretations are made too hastily, they confuse important issues for many years. Here's a reasonable sequence:

1. Selecting and surveying sites
2. Excavating sites and recovering fossil hominins
3. Designating individual finds with specimen numbers for clear reference
4. Cleaning, preparing, studying, and describing fossils
5. Comparing with other fossil material—in a chronological framework if possible

6. Comparing fossil variation with known ranges of variation in closely related groups of living primates and analyzing ancestral and derived characteristics
7. Assigning taxonomic names to fossil material

But the task of interpretation still isn't complete, for what we really want to know in the long run is what happened to the populations represented by the fossil remains. In looking at the fossil hominin record, we're actually looking for our ancestors. In the process of eventually determining those populations that are our most likely antecedents, we may conclude that some hominins are on evolutionary side branches. If this conclusion is accurate, those hominins necessarily must have become extinct. It's both interesting and relevant to us as hominins to try to find out what influenced some earlier members of our family tree to continue evolving while others died out.

Although a clear evolutionary picture is not yet possible for organizing all the early hominins discussed in this chapter, there are some general patterns that for now make good sense (**Fig. 9-34**). New finds may of course require serious

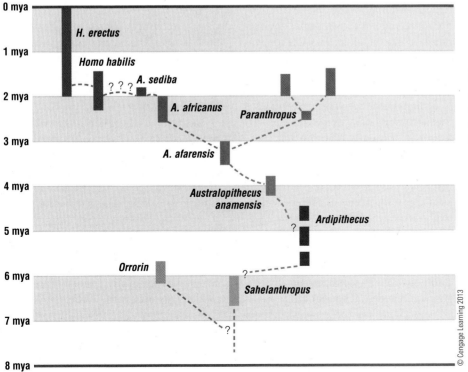

Figure 9-34

A tentative early hominin phylogeny. Note the numerous question marks, indicating continuing uncertainty regarding evolutionary relationships.

© Cengage Learning 2013

alterations to this scheme. Science can be exciting but can also be frustrating to many in the general public looking for simple answers to complex questions. For well-informed students of human evolution, it's most important to grasp the basic principles of paleoanthropology and *how* interpretations are made and *why* they sometimes must be revised. This way you'll be prepared for whatever shows up tomorrow.

Seeing the Big Picture: Adaptive Patterns of Early African Hominins

As you are by now aware, there are several different African hominin genera and certainly lots of species. This, in itself, is interesting. Speciation was occurring quite frequently among the various lineages of early hominins—more frequently, in fact, than among later hominins. What explains this pattern?

Evidence has been accumulating at a furious pace in the last decade, but it's still far from complete. What's clear is that we'll never have anything approaching a complete record of early hominin evolution, so some significant gaps will remain. After all, we're able to discover hominins only in those special environmental contexts where fossilization was likely. All the other potential habitats they might have exploited are now invisible to us.

Still, patterns are emerging from the fascinating data we do have. First, it appears that early hominin species (pre-australopiths, *Australopithecus*, *Paranthropus*, and early *Homo*) all had restricted ranges. It's therefore likely that each hominin species exploited a relatively small area and could easily have become separated from other populations of its own species. So genetic drift (and to some extent natural selection) could have led to rapid genetic divergence and eventual speciation.

Second, most of these species appear to be at least partially tied to arboreal habitats, although there's disagreement

on this point regarding early *Homo* (see Wood and Collard, 1999b; Foley 2002). Also, *Paranthropus* was probably somewhat less arboreal than *Ardipithecus* or *Australopithecus*. These very large-toothed hominins apparently concentrated on a diet of coarse, fibrous plant foods, such as roots. Exploiting such resources may have routinely taken these hominins farther away from the trees than their dentally more gracile—and perhaps more omnivorous—cousins.

Third, except for some early *Homo* individuals, there's very little in the way of an evolutionary trend of increased body size or of markedly greater encephalization. Beginning with *Sahelanthropus*, brain size was no more than that in chimpanzees—although when controlling for body size, this earliest of all known hominins may have had a proportionately larger brain than any living ape. Close to 5 million years later (that is, the time of the last surviving australopith species), relative brain size increased by no more than 10 to 15 percent. Perhaps tied to this relative stasis in brain capacity, there's no absolute association of any of these hominins with patterned stone tool manufacture.

Although conclusions are becoming increasingly controversial, for the moment, early *Homo* appears to be a partial exception. This group shows both increased encephalization and numerous occurrences of potential association with stone tools (though at many of the sites, australopith fossils were *also* found).

Lastly, all of these early African hominins show an accelerated developmental pattern (similar to that seen in African apes), one quite different from the *delayed* developmental pattern characteristic of *Homo sapiens* (and our immediate precursors). This apelike development is also seen in some early *Homo* individuals (Wood and Collard, 1999a). Rates of development can be accurately reconstructed by examining dental growth markers (Bromage and Dean, 1985), and these data may provide a crucial window into understanding this early stage of hominin evolution.

These African hominin predecessors were rather small, able bipeds, but still closely tied to arboreal and/or climbing niches. They had fairly small brains and, compared to later *Homo*, matured rapidly. It would take a major evolutionary jump to push one of their descendants in a more human direction. For the next chapter in this more human saga, read on.

Summary of Main Topics

▶ The earliest very primitive primates evolved in the Paleocene around 65 mya.

▶ Many primate fossil forms more similar to living primates evolved in the Eocene (56–33 mya). Most of these species went extinct, although some show connections to modern lemurs/lorises or to tarsiers.

▶ The first anthropoids probably date to the late Eocene, but are much better documented from the Fayum Oligocene site (about 33 mya).

▶ Large-bodied hominoids are widespread and diverse in the Old World throughout the entire Miocene (23–5 mya).

▶ The first hominins appear 7–6 mya, and for the next 5 million years are all restricted to Africa.

▶ Many species of these early African hominins have been identified and can be summarized within three major subgroups:

• Pre-australopiths (6.0+–4.4 mya)
  – Including three genera of very early, and still primitive (possible) hominins: *Sahelanthropus*, *Orrorin*, and *Ardipithecus*

• Australopiths (4.2–1.2 mya).
  – Early, more primitive australopith species (4.2–3.0 mya), including *Australopithecus anamensis* and *Australopithecus afarensis*
  – Later, more derived australopith species (2.5–1.2 mya), including two genera: *Paranthropus* and a later species of *Australopithecus*

• Early *Homo* (2.4–1.4 mya)
  – The first members of our genus, who around 2 mya likely diverged into more than one species

▶ The earliest known stone tools date to about 2.6 mya, but cut marks on bones and other evidence suggest that hominins were perhaps tool users more than 3.3 mya.

▶ Hominin tool use was such a fundamental change that our subsequent evolution turned in a completely new direction to one that is both biological and cultural. It also marked the beginning of the archaeological record.

What's Important — Key Early Hominin Fossil Discoveries from Africa

Dates (mya)	Hominins	Sites/Regions	The Big Picture
1.8–1.4	Early *Homo*	Olduvai; E. Turkana (E. Africa)	Bigger-brained; possible ancestor of later *Homo*
1.9	*Australopithecus sediba*	Malapa (S. Africa)	Possibly a transitional species between *Australopithecus* and *Homo*
2.5–2.0	Later *Australopithecus* (*A. africanus*)	Taung; Sterkfontein (S. Africa)	Quite derived; likely evolutionary dead end
2.0–1.0 2.4	Later *Paranthropus* *Paranthropus aethiopicus*	Several sites (E. and S. Africa) W. Turkana (E. Africa)	Highly derived; very likely evolutionary dead end Earliest robust australopith; likely ancestor of later *Paranthropus*
3.6–3.0	*Australopithecus afarensis*	Laetoli; Hadar (E. Africa)	Many fossils; very well studied; earliest well-documented biped; possible ancestor of all later hominins
4.4	*Ardipithecus ramidus*	Aramis (E. Africa)	Many fossils; not yet well studied; bipedal, but likely quite derived; any likely ancestral relationship to later hominins not yet possible to say
~6.0	*Sahelanthropus*	Toros-Menalla (central Africa)	The earliest hominin; bipedal?

© Cengage Learning 2013

Critical Thinking Questions

1. In what ways are the remains of *Sahelanthropus* and *Ardipithecus* primitive? Why do many paleoanthropologists classify these forms as hominins? How sure are we?

2. Assume that you are in the laboratory analyzing the Lucy *A. afarensis* skeleton. You also have complete skeletons from a chimpanzee and a modern human. (a) Which parts of the Lucy skeleton are more similar to the chimpanzee? Which are more similar to the human? (b) Which parts of the Lucy skeleton are most informative?

3. The oldest identified hominin tools are roughly 2.6 million years old, but evidence of hominin tool use is much older. Why did hominins become toolmakers?

4. What is a phylogeny? Construct one for early hominins (7.0–1.0 mya). Make sure you can describe what conclusions your scheme makes. Also, try to defend it.

Paleoanthropology/ Fossil Hominins

10

The First Dispersal of the Genus *Homo*: *Homo erectus* and Contemporaries

© David Lordkipanidze

LEARNING OBJECTIVES

After you have mastered the material in this chapter, you will be able to:

▶ Describe the geographical distribution of the earliest *Homo erectus* finds and compare the dating for these discoveries in Africa, Asia, and Europe.

▶ Describe the most important anatomical features found in *Homo erectus* and compare them with early *Homo* and *Homo sapiens*.

▶ Discuss the biocultural evidence (both anatomical and archaeological) that might explain how early hominins dispersed from Africa to other regions of the Old World.

Today it's estimated that more than 1 million people cross national borders every day. Some travel for business, some for pleasure, and others may be seeking refuge from persecution in their own countries. Regardless, it seems that modern humans have wanderlust—a desire to see distant places. Our most distant hominin ancestors were essentially homebodies, staying in fairly restricted areas, exploiting the local resources, and trying to stay out of harm's way. In this respect, they were much like other primate species.

One thing is certain: All these early hominins were restricted to Africa. When did hominins first leave Africa? What were they like, and why did they leave their ancient homeland? Did they differ physically from their australopith and early *Homo* forebears, and did they have new behavioral and cultural capabilities that helped them successfully exploit new environments?

It would be a romantic misconception to think of these first hominin transcontinental emigrants as "brave pioneers, boldly going where no one had gone before." They weren't deliberately striking out to go someplace in particular. It's not as though they had a map! Still, for what they did, deliberate or not, we owe them a lot.

Sometime close to 2 mya, something decisive occurred in human evolution. As the title of this chapter suggests, for the first time, hominins expanded widely out of Africa into other areas of the Old World. Since all the early fossils have been found *only* in Africa, it seems that hominins were restricted to that continent for perhaps as long as 5 million years. The later, more widely dispersed hominins were quite different both anatomically and behaviorally from their African ancestors. They were much larger, were more committed to a completely terrestrial habitat, used more elaborate stone tools, and probably ate meat.

There is some variation among the different geographical groups of these highly successful hominins, and anthropologists still debate how to classify them. In particular, new discoveries from Europe are forcing a major reevaluation of exactly which were the first to leave Africa (**Fig. 10-1**).

Nevertheless, after 2 mya, there's less diversity among these hominins than is apparent in their pre-australopith and australopith predecessors. Consequently, there is universal agreement that the hominins found outside of Africa are all members of genus *Homo*. Thus, taxonomic debates focus solely on how many species are represented. The species for which we have the most evidence is called *Homo erectus*. Furthermore, this is the one group that most paleoanthropologists have recognized for decades and still agree on. Thus, in this chapter we'll focus our discussion on *Homo erectus*. We will, however, also discuss alternative interpretations that "split" the fossil sample into more species.

On the cultural side, the archaeological evidence of the earliest hominins in Europe and Asia is more diverse than that of their African ancestors but generally reflects African roots (Carbonell et al., 2010). While much of the diversity of Lower Paleolithic tool assemblages and sites can be explained as cultural adaptations to the new habitats into which these hominins spread, these early humans were not yet cultural beings in the same sense as modern humans.

Around 1.7–1.6 mya, well after the initial dispersal of hominins, the Lower Paleolithic stone tool industry called Acheulian developed across parts of Africa, western Asia, and eventually Europe. Technologically more advanced than Oldowan (see Chapter 9), the Acheulian tool kit provides us with convincing evidence of increasing tool dependence by hominins.

Throughout this part of the Lower Paleolithic, whether viewed in Africa or beyond, the archaeological record shows that hominins were slowly constructing the basic elements of human culture. And as with the study of the hominin fossils, the archaeology of this dispersal outside of Africa is a quickly changing area of research, about which archaeologists still have much to learn.

A New Kind of Hominin

The discovery of fossils now referred to as *Homo erectus* began in the nineteenth century. Later in this chapter, we'll discuss the historical background of these earliest discoveries in Java and the somewhat later discoveries in China. For these fossils, as well as several from Europe and North Africa, a variety of taxonomic names were suggested.

It's important to realize that such taxonomic *splitting* was quite common in the early years of paleoanthropology. More systematic biological thinking came to the fore only after World War II and with the incorporation of the Modern Synthesis into paleontology. Most of the fossils that were given these varied names are now placed in the species *Homo erectus*—or at least they've all been lumped into one genus (*Homo*).

In the last few decades, discoveries of firmly dated East African fossils have established the clear presence of *Homo erectus* by 1.7 mya. Some researchers see several anatomical differences between these African representatives of an *erectus*-like hominin and their Asian cousins (hominins that almost everybody refers to as *Homo erectus*). Thus, they place the African fossils into a separate species, one they call *Homo ergaster* (Andrews, 1984; Wood, 1991).

While there are some anatomical differences between the African specimens and those from Asia, they are all clearly *closely* related and quite possibly represent geographical varieties of a single species. We'll thus refer to them collectively as *Homo erectus*.

Most analyses show that *H. erectus* represents a type of hominin that is quite different from its more ancient African predecessors. Increase in body size and robustness, changes in limb proportions, and greater encephalization all indicate that these hominins were more like modern humans in their adaptive pattern than their African ancestors were. It's clear from most of the fossils usually classified as *Homo erectus* that a major adaptive shift had taken place—one setting hominin evolution in a distinctly more human direction.

We mentioned that there is considerable variation among different regional populations defined as *Homo erectus*. New discoveries show even more dramatic variation, suggesting that some of these hominins may not fit closely with this general adaptive pattern (more on this presently). For the moment, however, let's review what most of these fossils look like.

The Morphology of *Homo erectus*

Homo erectus populations lived in very different environments over much of the Old World. They all, however, shared several common physical traits.

Body Size

Anthropologists estimate that some *H. erectus* adults weighed well over 100 pounds, with an average adult height of about 5 feet 6 inches (McHenry, 1992; Ruff and Walker, 1993; Walker and Leakey, 1993). Another point to keep in mind is that *H. erectus* was quite sexually dimorphic—at least as indicated by the East African specimens. Some adult males may have weighed considerably more than 100 pounds.

Increased height and weight in *H. erectus* are also associated with a dramatic increase in robusticity. In fact, a heavily built body was to dominate hominin evolution not just during *H. erectus* times, but through the long transitional era of premodern forms as well. Only with the appearance of anatomically modern *H. sapiens* did a more gracile skeletal structure emerge, one that still characterizes most modern populations.

Brain Size

While *Homo erectus* differs in several respects from both early *Homo* and *Homo sapiens*, the most obvious feature is cranial size—which is closely related to brain

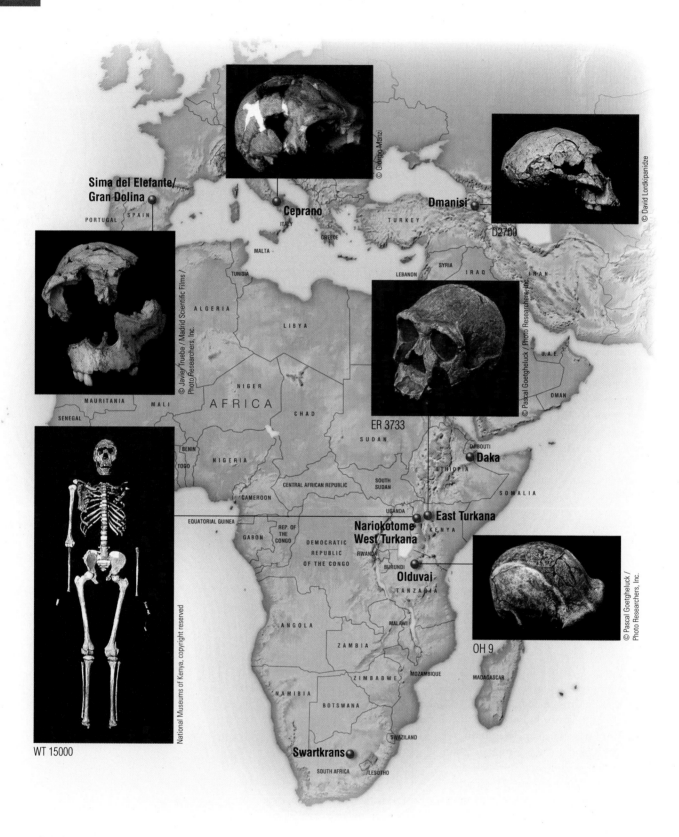

Figure 10-1

Major *Homo erectus* sites and localities of other contemporaneous hominins.

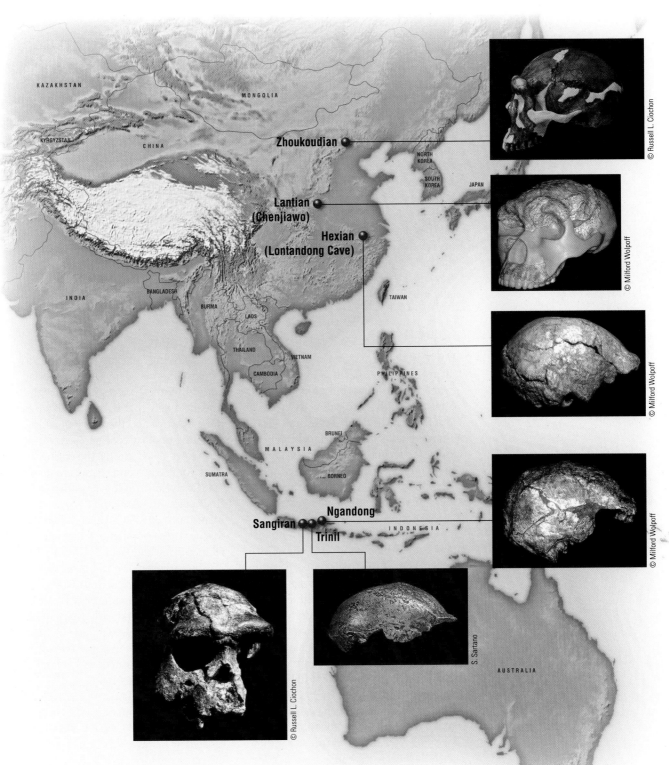

© Russell L. Ciochon

© Milford Wolpoff

© Milford Wolpoff

© Milford Wolpoff

© Russell L. Ciochon

S. Sartano

KAZAKHSTAN

MONGOLIA

KYRGYZSTAN

CHINA

Zhoukoudian

NORTH
KOREA

SOUTH
KOREA

JAPAN

**Lantian
(Chenjiawo)**

INDIA

BANGLADESH

BURMA

LAOS

THAILAND

VIETNAM

CAMBODIA

**Hexian
(Lontandong Cave)**

TAIWAN

PHILIPPINES

MALAYSIA

BRUNEI

SUMATRA

BORNEO

Ngandong

Sangiran

Trinil

INDONESIA

AUSTRALIA

size. Early *Homo* had cranial capacities ranging from as small as 500 cm³ to as large as 800 cm³. *H. erectus*, on the other hand, shows considerable brain enlargement, with a cranial capacity of about 700* to 1,250 cm³ (and a mean of approximately 900 cm³).

As we've discussed, brain size is closely linked to overall body size. So it's important to note that along with an increase in brain size, *H. erectus* was also considerably larger than earlier members of the genus *Homo*. In fact, when we compare *H. erectus* with the larger-bodied early *Homo* individuals, *relative* brain size is about the same (Walker, 1991). What's more, when we compare the relative brain size of *H. erectus* with that of *H. sapiens*, we see that *H. erectus* was considerably less encephalized than later members of the genus *Homo*.

Cranial Shape

Homo erectus crania display a highly distinctive shape, partly because of increased brain size, but probably more correlated with increased body size. The ramifications of this heavily built cranium are reflected in thick cranial bone (in most specimens), large browridges (supraorbital tori) above the eyes, and a projecting **nuchal torus** at the back of the skull (**Fig. 10-2**).

The braincase is long and low, receding from the large browridges with little forehead development. Also, the cranium is wider at the base compared with earlier *and* later species of genus *Homo*. The maximum cranial breadth is below the ear opening, giving the cranium a pentagonal shape (when viewed from behind). In contrast, the skulls of early *Homo* and *H. sapiens* have more vertical sides, and the maximum width is *above* the ear openings.

Most specimens also have a sagittal keel running along the midline of the skull. Very different from a sagittal crest, the keel is a small ridge that runs front to back along the sagittal suture. The sagittal keel, browridges, and nuchal torus don't seem to have served an obvious function, but most likely reflect bone buttressing in a very robust skull.

The First *Homo erectus*: *Homo erectus* from Africa

Where did *Homo erectus* first appear? The answer seems fairly simple: Most likely, this species initially evolved in Africa. Two important pieces of evidence help confirm this hypothesis. First, *all* of the earlier hominins prior to the appearance of *H. erectus* come from Africa. What's more, by 1.7 mya, there are well-dated fossils of this species at East Turkana, in Kenya, and not long after that at other sites in East Africa.

But there's a small wrinkle in this neat view. We now know that at about 1.8 mya, similar populations were already living far away in southeastern Europe, and by 1.6 mya, in Indonesia. So, adding these pieces to our puzzle, it seems likely that *H. erectus* first arose in East Africa and then very quickly migrated to other continents; nevertheless, as we'll see shortly, the dating of sites from Africa and elsewhere does not yet clearly confirm this hypothesis. Let's first review the African *H. erectus* specimens dated at 1.7–1 mya, and then we'll discuss those populations that emigrated to Europe and Asia.

The earliest of the East African *H. erectus* fossils come from East Turkana, from the same area where earlier australopith and early *Homo* fossils have been found (see Chapter 9). Indeed, it seems likely that in East Africa around 2–1.8 mya, some form of early *Homo* evolved into *H. erectus*.

The most significant *H. erectus* fossil from East Turkana is a nearly complete skull (ER 3733; **Fig. 10-3**). Recently redated at 1.7 mya, this fossil is about the same age (or even a little younger) as some other fossils outside of Africa; nevertheless, for now, it certainly is the oldest known member of this species from Africa (Lepre and Kent, 2010). The cranial capacity is estimated at 848 cm³, in the lower range for *H. erectus* (700 to 1,250 cm³), which isn't surprising

---

*Even smaller cranial capacities are seen in recently discovered fossils from the Caucasus region of southeastern Europe at a site called Dmanisi. We'll discuss these fossils in a moment.

nuchal torus (nuke´-ul) (*nucha*, meaning "neck") A projection of bone in the back of the cranium where neck muscles attach. These muscles hold up the head.

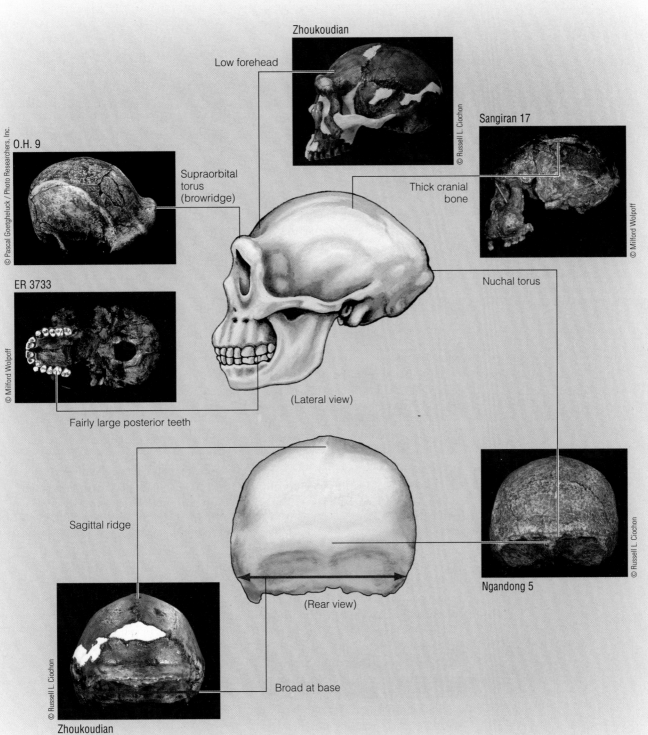

Figure 10-2

Morphology and variation in *Homo erectus*.

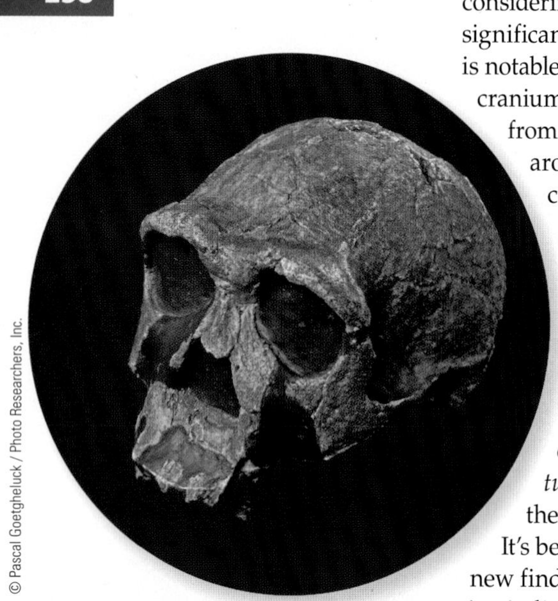

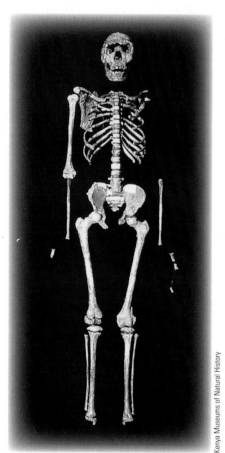

Figure 10-3

Nearly complete skull of *Homo erectus* from East Lake Turkana, Kenya, dated to approximately 1.7 mya.

Figure 10-4

WT 15000 from Nariokotome, Kenya: The "Nariokotome boy" is the most complete *H. erectus* specimen yet found.

Nariokotome (nar´-ee-oh-koh´-tow-may)

considering its early date. A second very significant new find from East Turkana is notable because it has the smallest cranium of any *H. erectus* specimen from anywhere in Africa. Dated to around 1.5 mya, the skull has a cranial capacity of only 691 cm³. As we'll see shortly, there are a couple of crania from southeastern Europe that are even smaller. The small skull from East Turkana also shows more gracile features (such as smaller browridges) than do other East African *H. erectus* individuals, but it preserves the overall *H. erectus* vault shape. It's been proposed that perhaps this new find is a female and that the variation indicates a very high degree of sexual dimorphism in this species (Spoor et al., 2007).

Another remarkable discovery was made in 1984 by Kamoya Kimeu, a member of Richard Leakey's team known widely as an outstanding fossil hunter. Kimeu discovered a small piece of skull on the west side of Lake Turkana at a site known as **Nariokotome**. Excavations produced the most complete *H. erectus* skeleton ever found (**Fig. 10-4**). Known properly as WT 15000, the almost complete skeleton includes facial bones, a pelvis, and most of the limb bones, ribs, and vertebrae and is chronometrically dated to about 1.6 mya.

Such well-preserved postcranial elements make for a very unusual and highly useful discovery, because these elements are scarce at other *H. erectus* sites. The skeleton is that of an adolescent about 8 years of age with an estimated height of about 5 feet 3 inches (Walker and Leakey, 1993; Dean and Smith, 2009). Some estimates have hypothesized that the adult height of this individual could have been about 6 feet. However, this conclusion is contentious, since it assumes that the growth pattern of this species was similar to that of modern humans. More recent and more detailed analyses find the developmental pattern in this and other *H. erectus* individuals to actually be more like that of an ape (Dean and Smith, 2009).

Nevertheless, the postcranial bones look very similar, though not quite identical, to those of modern humans. The

cranial capacity of WT 15000 is estimated at 880 cm³; brain growth was nearly complete, and the adult cranial capacity would have been approximately 909 cm³ (Begun and Walker, 1993).

Other important *H. erectus* finds have come from Olduvai Gorge, in Tanzania, and they include a very robust skull discovered there by Louis Leakey back in 1960. The skull is dated at 1.4 mya and has a well-preserved cranial vault with just a small part of the upper face. Estimated at 1,067 cm³, the cranial capacity is the largest of all the African *H. erectus* specimens. The browridge is huge, the largest known for any hominin, but the walls of the braincase are thin. This latter characteristic is seen in most East African *H. erectus* specimens; in this respect, they differ from Asian *H. erectus*, in which cranial bones are thick.

Three other sites from Ethiopia have yielded *H. erectus* fossils, the most noteworthy coming from the Gona area and the Daka locale, both in the Awash River region of eastern Africa (Gilbert and Asfaw, 2008). As you've seen, numerous remains of earlier hominins have come from this area (see Chapter 9 and Appendix B).

A recently discovered nearly complete female *H. erectus* pelvis comes from the Gona area in Ethiopia and is dated to approximately 1.3 mya (Simpson et al., 2008). This find is particularly interesting because *H. erectus* postcranial remains are so rare, and this is the first *H. erectus* female pelvis yet found. This fossil also reveals some tantalizing glimpses of likely *H. erectus* development. The pelvis has a very wide birth canal, indicating that quite large-brained infants could have developed *in utero* (before birth); in fact, it's possible that a newborn *H. erectus* could have had a brain that was almost as large as what's typical for modern human babies.

This evidence has led Scott Simpson and his colleagues to suggest that *H. erectus* prenatal brain growth was more like that of later humans and quite different from that found in apes *or* in australopiths such as Lucy. However, it's also evident that *H. erectus* brain growth after birth was more rapid than in modern humans. This new pelvis is very different from that of the Nariokotome pelvis and may reflect considerable sexual

At a Glance

Key *Homo erectus* Discoveries from Africa

DATES (MYA)	SITE	EVOLUTIONARY SIGNIFICANCE
1.4	Olduvai	Large individual, very robust (male?) *H. erectus*
1.6	Nariokotome, W. Turkana	Nearly complete skeleton; young male
1.7	E. Turkana	Oldest well-dated *H. erectus* in Africa; great amount of variation seen among individuals, possibly due to sexual dimorphism

© Cengage Learning 2013

dimorphism in skeletal anatomy linked to reproduction as well as body size.

Another recent discovery from the Middle Awash of Ethiopia of a mostly complete cranium from Daka is also important because this individual (dated at approximately 1 mya) is more like Asian *H. erectus* than are most of the earlier East African remains we've discussed (Asfaw et al., 2002). Consequently, the suggestion by several researchers that East African fossils are a different species from (Asian) *H. erectus* isn't supported by the morphology of the Daka cranium.

Who Were the Earliest African Emigrants?

The fossils from East Africa imply that a new adaptive pattern in human evolution appeared in Africa not long after 2 mya. Until recently, *H. erectus* sites outside Africa all have shown dates later than the earliest finds of this species in Africa, leading paleoanthropologists to assume that the hominins who migrated to Asia and Europe descended from earlier African ancestors. Also, these travelers look like *Homo*, with longer limbs and bigger brains. Since *H. erectus* originated in East Africa, they were

close to land links to Eurasia (through the Middle East) and thus were probably the first to leave the continent. We can't be sure why these hominins left— were they following animal migrations, or was it simply population growth and expansion?

What we do know is that we're seeing a greater range of physical variation in the specimens outside of Africa and that the emigration out of Africa happened earlier than we had previously thought. Current evidence shows *H. erectus* in East Africa about 1.7 mya, while similar hominins were living in the Caucasus region of southeastern Europe *even a little earlier*, about 1.8 mya.* Eventually, hominins made it all the way to the island of Java, Indonesia, by 1.6 mya! It took *H. erectus* less than 200,000 years to travel from East Africa to Southeast Asia. Let's look at this fascinating evidence.

The site of **Dmanisi**, in the Republic of Georgia, has produced several individuals and an associated assemblage of Oldowan stone tools, giving us a unique look at these first possible travelers. The age of this crucial site has recently been radiometrically redated to 1.81 mya

---

*Note that these dates are based solely on what has been discovered so far.

Dmanisi (dim´-an-eese´-ee)

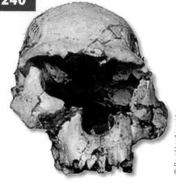
(a)

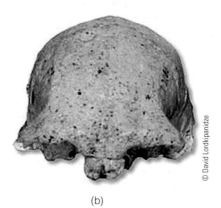
(b)

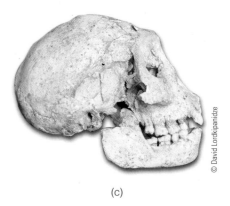
(c)

Figure 10-5

Dmanisi crania discovered in 1999 and 2001 and dated to 1.8–1.7 mya. (a) Specimen 2282. (b) Specimen 2280. (c) Specimen 2700.

Figure 10-6

Most recently discovered cranium from Dmanisi, almost totally lacking in teeth (with both upper and lower jaws showing advanced bone resorption).

(Garcia et al., 2010). The Dmanisi crania are similar to those of *H. erectus* (for example, the long, low braincase, wide base, and sagittal keel; see especially **Fig. 10-5b**, and compare with Fig. 10-2). However, other characteristics of the Dmanisi individuals are different from what is seen in other hominins outside Africa. In particular, the most complete fossil (specimen 2700; **Fig. 10-5c**) has a less robust and thinner brow-ridge, a projecting lower face, and a relatively large upper canine. At least when viewed from the front, this skull is more reminiscent of the smaller early *Homo* specimens from East Africa than it is of *H. erectus*. Also, specimen 2700's cranial capacity is very small—estimated at only 600 cm³, well within the range of early *Homo*. In fact, all four Dmanisi crania so far described have relatively small cranial capacities—the other three estimated at 630 cm³, 650 cm³, and 780 cm³.

Probably the most remarkable find from Dmanisi is the most recently discovered skull. This nearly complete cranium is of an older adult male; and surprisingly for such an ancient find, he died with only one tooth remaining in his jaws (Lordkipanidze et al., 2006). Because his jawbones show advanced bone loss (which occurs after tooth loss), it seems that he lived for several years without being able to efficiently chew his food (**Fig. 10-6**). As a result, it probably would

have been difficult for him to maintain an adequate diet.

The newest evidence from Dmanisi includes several postcranial bones coming from at least four individuals (Lordkipanidze et al., 2007). This new evidence is especially important because it allows us to make comparisons with what is known of *H. erectus* from other areas. The Dmanisi fossils have an unusual combination of traits. They weren't especially tall, having an estimated height ranging from about 4 feet 9 inches to 5 feet 5 inches. Certainly, based on this evidence, they seem smaller than the full *H. erectus* specimens from East Africa or Asia. Yet, although short in stature, they still show body proportions (such as leg length) like that of *H. erectus* (and *H. sapiens*) and quite different from that seen in earlier hominins.

Based on the evidence from Dmanisi, we can assume that *Homo erectus* was the first hominin to leave Africa. While the Dmanisi specimens are small in both stature and cranial capacity, they have specific characteristics that identify them as *H. erectus* (for example, a sagittal keel and low braincase). So, for now, the Dmanisi hominins are thought to be *H. erectus*, although an early and quite different variety from that found almost anywhere else.

While new and thus tentative, the recent evidence raises important and exciting possibilities. The Dmanisi findings suggest that the first hominins to leave Africa were quite possibly a small-bodied very early form of *H. erectus*, possessing smaller brains than later *H. erec-*

tus and carrying with them a typical African Oldowan stone tool culture.

Also, the Dmanisi hominins had none of the adaptations hypothesized to be essential to hominin migration— that is, being tall and having relatively large brains. Another explanation may be that there were *two* migrations out of Africa at this time: one consisting of the small-brained, short-statured Dmanisi hominins and an almost immediate second migration that founded the well-recognized *H. erectus* populations of Java and China. All this evidence is so new, however, that it's too soon even to predict what further revisions may be required.

Homo erectus from Indonesia

After the publication of *On the Origin of Species*, debates about evolution were prevalent throughout Europe. While many theorists simply stayed home and debated the merits of natural selection and the likely course of human evolution, one young Dutch anatomist decided to go find evidence of it. Eugene Dubois (1858–1940) enlisted in the Dutch East Indian Army and was shipped to the island of Sumatra, Indonesia, to look for what he called "the missing link."

In October 1891, after moving his search to the neighboring island of Java, Dubois' field crew unearthed a skullcap along the Solo River near the town of Trinil—a fossil that was to become internationally famous as the first recognized human ancestor (**Fig. 10-7**). The following year, a human femur was recovered about 15 yards upstream in what Dubois claimed was the same level as the skullcap, and he assumed that the skullcap (with a cranial capacity of slightly over 900 cm^3) and the femur belonged to the same individual.

Counting the initial find plus later discoveries, all the *H. erectus* fossil remains have so far come from six sites located in eastern Java. The dating of these fossils has been hampered by the complex nature of Javanese geology, but it's generally accepted that most of the fossils belong to the Early to Middle **Pleistocene** and are between 1.6 and 1 million years old. What's more, there was also a very late surviving *H. erectus* group in Java that apparently managed to survive there until after 100,000 years ago (ya).

These later fossils, from the Ngandong site, are by far the most recent group of *H. erectus* fossils from Java or anywhere else. At Ngandong, an excavation along an ancient river terrace produced 11 mostly complete hominin skulls. Some estimates put the age of the Ngandong *H. erectus* fossils at only 50,000–25,000 ya. These dates have been controversial, but further evidence is establishing a late survival of *H. erectus* in Java (approximately 70,000–40,000 ya; Yokoyama et al., 2008). So these individuals would be contemporary with *H. sapiens*—which, by this time, had expanded widely throughout the Old World and into Australia around 60,000–40,000 ya. Recent work on the old excavation site of Ngandong (first excavated in the early 1930s) has led to a rediscovery of the fossil bed where the *H. erectus* fossils had been found (Ciochon et al., 2009). New dating techniques and fossil identification will be undertaken to better understand site formation and taphonomy. As we'll see in Chapter 12, even later—and very unusual—hominins have been found not far away, apparently evolving while isolated on another Indonesian island.

Homo erectus from China

The story of the first discoveries of Chinese *H. erectus* is another saga filled with excitement, hard work, luck, and misfortune. Europeans had known for a long time that "dragon bones," used by the Chinese as medicine and aphrodisiacs, were actually ancient mammal bones. Scientists eventually located one of the sources of these bones near Beijing at a site called **Zhoukoudian**. Serious excavations were begun there in the 1920s, and in 1929, a fossil skull was

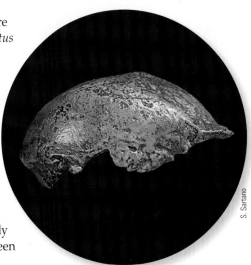

S. Sartano

Figure 10-7

The famous Trinil skullcap discovered by Eugene Dubois near the Solo River in Java. Discovered in 1891, this was the first fossil human found outside of Europe or Africa.

Pleistocene The epoch of the Cenozoic from 1.8 mya until 10,000 ya. Frequently referred to as the Ice Age, this epoch is associated with continental glaciations in northern latitudes.

Zhoukoudian (Zhoh´-koh-dee´-en)

Figure 10-8

Zhoukoudian cave.

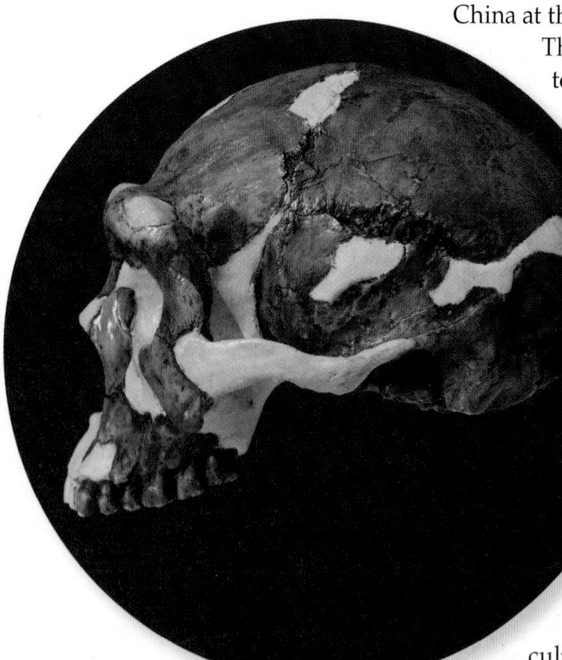

Figure 10-9

Composite cranium of Zhoukoudian *Homo erectus*, reconstructed by Ian Tattersall and Gary Sawyer, of the American Museum of Natural History in New York.

discovered. The skull turned out to be a juvenile's, and although it was thick, low, and relatively small, there was no doubt that it belonged to an early hominin.

Zhoukoudian *Homo erectus*

The fossil remains of *H. erectus* discovered in the 1920s and 1930s, as well as some more recent excavations at Zhoukoudian (**Fig. 10-8**), are by far the largest collection of *H. erectus* material found anywhere. This excellent sample includes 14 skullcaps (**Fig. 10-9**), other cranial pieces, and more than 100 isolated teeth, but only a scattering of postcranial elements (Jia and Huang, 1990). Various interpretations to account for this unusual pattern of preservation have been offered, ranging from ritualistic treatment or cannibalism to the more mundane suggestion that the *H. erectus* remains are simply the leftovers of the meals of giant hyenas. The hominin remains were studied, and casts were made immediately, which proved invaluable, since the original specimens were lost during the American evacuation of China at the start of World War II.

The hominin remains belong to upward of 40 adults and children and together provide a good overall picture of Chinese *H. erectus*. Like the materials from Java, they have typical *H. erectus* features, including a large browridge and nuchal torus. Also, the skull has thick bones, a sagittal keel, and a protruding face and is broadest near the bottom. This site, along with others in China, has been difficult to date accurately. Although Zhoukoudian was previously dated to about 500,000 ya, a new radiometric dating technique that measures isotopes of aluminum and beryllium shows that Zhoukoudian is actually considerably older, with a dating estimate of approximately 780,000 ya (Ciochon and Bettis, 2009; Shen et al., 2009).

Cultural Remains from Zhoukoudian

More than 100,000 artifacts have been recovered from this vast site, which was occupied intermittently for many thousands of years. The earliest tools were generally crude and shapeless, but they became more refined over time. Common tools at the site are choppers and chopping tools, but retouched flakes were fashioned into scrapers, points, burins, and awls (**Fig. 10-10**).

The way of life at Zhoukoudian has traditionally been described as that of **hunter-gatherers** who killed deer, horses, and other animals. Fragments of charred ostrich eggshells and abundant deposits of hackberry seeds unearthed in the cave suggest that these hominins supplemented their diet of meat by gathering herbs, wild fruits, tubers, and eggs. Layers of what has long been thought to be ash in the cave (over 18 feet deep at one point) have been interpreted as indicating the use of fire by *H. erectus*.

More recently, several researchers have challenged this picture of Zhoukoudian life. Lewis Binford and colleagues (Binford and Ho, 1985; Binford and Stone, 1986a, 1986b) reject the description of *H. erectus* as hunters and argue that the evidence clearly points more accurately to scavenging. Using advanced archaeological analyses, Noel Boaz and colleagues have even questioned whether the *H. erectus* remains at Zhoukoudian represent evidence of hominin habitation of the cave. By comparing the types of bones, as well as the damage to the bones, with that seen in contemporary carnivore dens, Boaz and Ciochon (2001) have suggested that much of the material in the cave likely accumulated through the activities of extinct giant hyenas. In fact, they hypothesize that most of the *H. erectus* remains, too, are the leftovers of hyena meals. Boaz and his colleagues do recognize that the tools in the cave, and possibly the cut marks on some of the animal bones, provide evidence of hominin activities at Zhoukoudian.

Probably the most intriguing archaeological aspect of the presumed hominin behavior at Zhoukoudian has been

hunter-gatherers People who make their living by hunting, fishing, and gathering their food and not by producing it.

Graver, or burin

Flint awl

Flint point

Quartzite chopper

Figure 10-10
Chinese tools from Middle Pleistocene sites. (Adapted from Wu and Olsen, 1985.)

the long-held assumption that *H. erectus* deliberately used fire inside the cave. Controlling fire was one of the major cultural breakthroughs of all prehistory. By providing warmth, a means of cooking, light to further modify tools, and protection, controlled fire would have been a giant technological innovation. While some potential early African sites have yielded evidence that to some have suggested hominin control of fire, it's long been assumed that the first *definite* evidence of hominin fire use comes from Zhoukoudian. Now even this assumption has been challenged.

In the course of further excavations at Zhoukoudian during the 1990s, researchers carefully collected and analyzed soil samples for distinctive chemical signatures that would show whether fire had been present in the cave (Weiner et al., 1998). They determined that burnt bone was only rarely found in association with tools. And in most cases, the burning appeared to have taken place *after* fossilization—that is, the bones weren't cooked. In fact, it turns out that the "ash" layers aren't actually ash, but naturally accumulated organic sediment. This last conclusion was derived from chemical testing that showed absolutely no sign of wood having been burnt inside the cave. Finally, the "hearths" that have figured so prominently in archaeological reconstructions of presumed fire control at this site are apparently not hearths at all. They are simply round depressions formed in the past by water.

Another provisional interpretation of the cave's geology suggests that the cave wasn't open to the outside like a habitation site, but was accessed only through a vertical shaft. This theory has led

archaeologist Alison Brooks to remark, "It wouldn't have been a shelter, it would have been a trap" (quoted in Wuethrich, 1998). These serious doubts about control of fire, coupled with the suggestive evidence of bone accumulation by carnivores, have led anthropologists Boaz and Ciochon to conclude that "Zhoukoudian cave was neither hearth nor home" (Boaz and Ciochon, 2001).

Other Chinese Sites

More work has been done at Zhoukoudian than at any other Chinese site. Even so, there are other paleoanthropological sites worth mentioning. Three of the more important regions outside of Zhoukoudian are Lantian County (including two sites, often simply referred to as Lantian), Yunxian County, and several discoveries in Hexian County (usually referred to as the Hexian finds).

Dated to 1.15 mya, Lantian is older than Zhoukoudian (Zhu et al., 2003). From the Lantian sites, the cranial remains of two adult *H. erectus* females have been found in association with fire-treated pebbles and flakes as well as ash (Woo, 1966; **Fig. 10-11a**). One of the specimens, an almost complete mandible containing several teeth, is quite similar to those from Zhoukoudian.

Two badly distorted crania were discovered in Yunxian County, Hubei Province, in 1989 and 1990 (Li and Etler, 1992). A combination of ESR and paleomagnetism dating methods (see Chapter 8) gives us an average dating estimate of 800,000–580,000 ya. If the dates are correct, this would place Yunxian at a similar age to Zhoukoudian in the Chinese

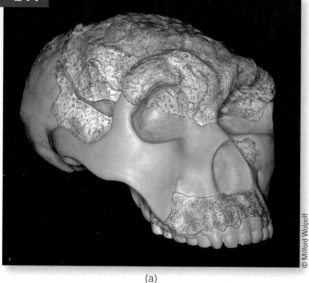

(a)

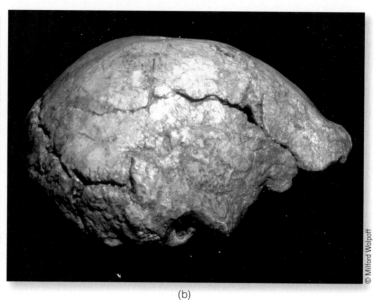

(b)

© Milford Wolpoff

Figure 10-11

(a) Reconstructed cranium of *Homo erectus* from Lantian, China, dated to approximately 1.15 mya. (b) Hexian cranium.

sequence. Due to extensive distortion of the crania from ground pressure, it was very difficult to compare these crania with other *H. erectus* fossils; recently, however, French paleoanthropologist Amélie Vialet has restored the crania using sophisticated imaging techniques (Vialet et al., 2005). And from a recent analysis of the fauna and paleoenvironment at Yunxian, the *H. erectus* inhabitants are thought to have had limited hunting capabilities, since they appear to have been restricted to the most vul-

nerable prey, namely, the young and old animals.

In 1980 and 1981, the remains of several individuals, all bearing some resemblance to similar fossils from Zhoukoudian, were recovered from Hexian County, in southern China (Wu and Poirier, 1995; **Fig. 10-11b**). A close relationship has been postulated between the *H. erectus* specimens from the Hexian finds and those from Zhoukoudian (Wu and Dong, 1985). Dating of the Hexian remains is

At a Glance

Key *Homo erectus* Discoveries from Asia

DATES (YA)	SITE	EVOLUTIONARY SIGNIFICANCE
70,000– 40,000	Ngandong (Java)	Very late survival of *H. erectus* in Java
780,000	Zhoukoudian (China)	Large sample; most famous *H. erectus* site; shows some *H. erectus* populations well adapted to temperate (cold) environments
1.6 mya	Sangiran (Java)	First discovery of *H. erectus* from anywhere; shows dispersal out of Africa into Southeast Asia by 1.6 mya

© Cengage Learning 2013

unclear, but they appear to be later than Zhoukoudian, perhaps by several hundred thousand years.

The Asian crania from Java and China share many similar features, which could be explained by *H. erectus* migration from Java to China perhaps around 1 mya. Asia has a much longer *H. erectus* habitation than Africa (1.8 mya–40,000 or 70,000 ya versus 1.7–1 mya), and it's important to understand the variation seen in this geographically dispersed species.

Asian and African *Homo erectus:* A Comparison

The *Homo erectus* remains from East Africa show several differences from the Javanese and Chinese fossils. Some African cranial specimens—particularly ER 3733, presumably a female, and WT 15000, presumably a male—aren't as strongly buttressed at the browridge and nuchal torus, and their cranial bones aren't as thick. Indeed, some researchers are so impressed by these differences, as well as others in the postcranial skeleton, that they're arguing for a *separate* species status for the African material, to distinguish it from the Asian samples. Bernard Wood, the leading proponent of this view, has suggested that the name *Homo ergaster* be used for the African remains and that *H. erectus* be reserved solely for the Asian material (Wood, 1991). In addition, the very early dates now postulated for the dispersal of *H. erectus* into Asia (Java) would argue that the Asian and African populations were separate (distinct) for more than 1 million years.

With the discovery of the Daka cranium in Ethiopia and continued comparison of these specimens, this species division has not been fully accepted; the current consensus (and the one we prefer) is to continue referring to all these hominins as *Homo erectus* (Kramer, 1993; Conroy, 1997; Rightmire, 1998; Asfaw et al., 2002). So, as with some earlier hominins, our interpretation of *H. erectus* requires us to recognize a considerable degree of variation within this species.

Later *Homo erectus* from Europe

We've talked about *H. erectus* in Africa, the Caucasus region, and Asia, but there are European specimens as well, found in Spain and Italy. While not as old as the Dmanisi material, fossils from the Atapuerca region in northern Spain are significantly extending the antiquity of hominins in western Europe. There are several caves in the Atapuerca region, two of which (Sima del Elefante and Gran Dolina) have yielded hominin fossils contemporaneous with *H. erectus.*

The earliest find from Atapuerca (from Sima del Elefante) has been recently discovered and dates to 1.2 mya, making it clearly the oldest hominin yet found in western Europe (Carbonell et al., 2008). So far, just one specimen has been found here, a partial jaw with a few teeth. Very provisional analysis suggests that it most closely resembles the Dmanisi fossils. There are also tools and animal bones from the site. As at the Dmanisi site, the implements are simple flake tools similar to that of the Oldowan. Some of the animal bones also bear the scars of hominin activity, with cut marks indicating butchering.

Gran Dolina is a later site, and based on specialized techniques discussed in Chapter 8, it's dated to approximately 850,000–780,000 ya (Parés and Pérez-González, 1995; Falguères et al., 1999). Because all the remains so far identified from both these caves at Atapuerca are fragmentary, assigning these fossils to particular species poses something of a problem. Spanish paleoanthropologists who have studied the Atapuerca fossils have decided to place these hominins into another (separate) species, one they call *Homo antecessor* (Bermúdez de Castro et al., 1997; Arsuaga et al., 1999). However, it remains to be seen whether this newly proposed species will prove to be distinct from other species of *Homo.*

Finally, the southern European discovery of a well-preserved cranium from the Ceprano site in central Italy may be the best evidence yet of *H. erectus* in Europe (Ascenzi et al., 1996). Provisional dating of a partial cranium

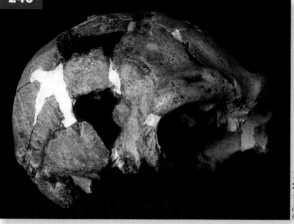

© Giorgio Manzi

Figure 10-12

The Ceprano *Homo erectus* cranium from central Italy, recently dated to 450,000 ya. This is the best evidence for *Homo erectus* in Europe.

Figure 10-13

Time line for *Homo erectus* discoveries and other contemporary hominins. (*Note:* Most dates are only imprecise estimates. However, the dates from East African sites are chronometrically determined and are thus much more secure. The early dates from Java are also radiometric and are gaining wide acceptance.)

from this important site suggested a date between 900,000 and 800,000 ya (**Fig. 10-12**), but more recent paleomagnetic studies have indicated a date of 450,000 ya (Muttoni et al., 2009). Philip Rightmire (1998) has concluded that cranial morphology places this specimen quite close to *H. erectus*. Italian researchers have proposed a different interpretation that classifies the Ceprano hominin as a species separate from *H. erectus*. For the moment, the exact relationship of the Ceprano find to *H. erectus* remains to be fully determined.

After about 400,000 ya, the European fossil hominin record becomes increasingly abundant. More fossils mean more variation, so it's not surprising that interpretations regarding the proper taxonomic assessment of many of these remains have been debated, in some cases for decades. In recent years, several of these somewhat later "premodern" specimens have been regarded either as early representatives of *H. sapiens* or as a separate species, one immediately preceding *H. sapiens*. These enigmatic premodern humans are discussed in Chapter 10. A time line for the *H. erectus* discoveries discussed in this chapter, as well as other finds of more uncertain status, is shown in **Figure 10-13**.

Archaeology of Early Hominin Dispersal

The first hominins to leave Africa were tool-assisted scavenger-gatherers who carried with them the basic concepts and technological capabilities of the Oldowan tool industry (e.g., see Mgeladze et al., 2011). As such, they differed greatly from modern humans. They began their extraordinary journey without the benefit of language, the controlled use of fire, or projectile weapons and other killing tools. Nevertheless, their Lower Paleolithic ancestors' biocultural flexibility to adapt to significant environmental changes (Potts and Teague, 2010) demonstrates that they were equally capable of successfully invading new habitats across the Old World, from the Atlantic to the Pacific.

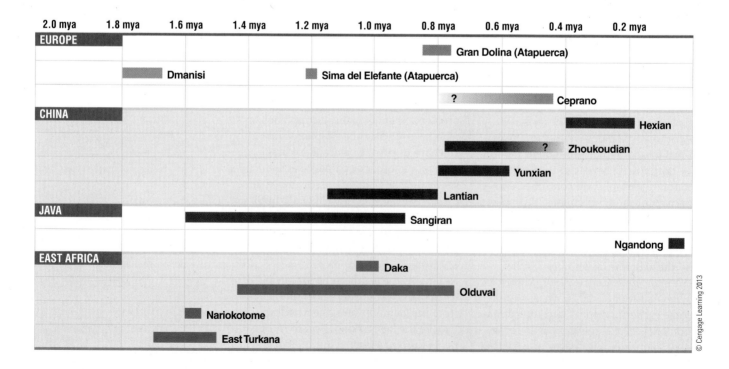

© Cengage Learning 2013

Evidence of butchering is widespread in early *H. erectus* sites, and in the past, such evidence was cited in arguments for consistent hunting. Researchers formerly interpreted any association of bones and tools as evidence of hunting, but many studies now suggest that cut marks on bones from this period often overlay carnivore tooth marks. This means that hominins were gaining access to the carcasses after the carnivores and were therefore scavenging the meat, not hunting the animals. Wild plants, tubers, and fruits were also important foods, but these hominins, who were not fire using, had limited ability to deal with common plant toxins that cooking inactivates.

Just as with the fossil evidence, the stone tools and other artifacts found in the earliest sites are not the same everywhere. The stone tool assemblages of early sites such as Dmanisi in Georgia and Atapuerca in Spain resemble those of Oldowan sites in East Africa, which implies not only a similar grasp of technology but also the technological requirements for its use. By contrast, the assemblages of early East Asian sites in the Nihewan Basin in northern China exhibit patterned differences (for example, smaller artifacts and more artifacts that show evidence of pounding) that may reflect technological requirements and tool kits unlike African Oldowan assemblages (Braun et al., 2010; Potts and Teague, 2010). Equally interesting is the absence of unequivocal Oldowan archaeological evidence in South Asia, where Acheulian sites are known from most of the subcontinent after about 1.5–1.2 mya (Gaillard et al., 2010; Pappu et al., 2011). The problem, of course, is how to explain these important differences. Did stone tool industries other than Oldowan leave Africa with the earliest emigrants? Do differences in these industries mainly reflect noncultural factors, such as local raw material availability or geomorphological conditions that inhibited the preservation of contemporaneous sediments (Chauhan 2010)? Or did new industries develop as early hominins adapted to

new habitats and resources across the Old World? We have the questions, but finding good answers requires more research.

By 1.7–1.6 mya, a new stone tool industry called Acheulian is found in Africa and, soon after, at sites in the Near East, the Indian subcontinent, and parts of East Asia (Semaw et al., 2009). The Acheulian tool kit was both more diverse and more complex than the Oldowan. It represented several new concepts about making stone tools. First, Acheulian toolmakers invented the idea of a *bifacial* stone tool—one that has been worked to create two opposing faces. A notable example of an Acheulian bifacial tool is the hand axe (**Fig. 10-14**), thousands of which have been found at Lower Paleolithic sites from Africa to Europe and eastward to India.

Second, Acheulian toolmakers developed a new way to knock flakes from stone cores, which gave more predictable results than the *"hard hammer"* percussion method used by their Oldowan predecessors. **"Soft hammer" percussion** employs a hammer made of a somewhat flexible material, such as wood, bone, or antler. When struck against a core, the soft hammer absorbs some of the striking force, giving an experienced stone toolmaker greater control over the length, width, and thickness of the

Barry Lewis

Figure 10-14

Hand axe (left) and cleaver (right), both of which were basic tools of the Acheulian tradition.

"soft hammer" percussion A direct percussion method of making stone tools that uses a resilient hammer or billet to gain greater control over the length, width, and thickness of flakes driven from a core.

At a Glance

Key *Homo erectus* and Contemporaneous Discoveries from Europe

DATES (YA)	SITE	EVOLUTIONARY SIGNIFICANCE
900,000–450,000	Ceprano (Italy)	Well-preserved cranium; best evidence of full *H. erectus* morphology from any site in Europe
1.2 mya	Sima del Elefante (Atapuerca, Spain)	Oldest evidence of hominins in western Europe, possibly not *H. erectus*
1.75 mya	Dmanisi (Republic of Georgia)	Oldest well-dated hominins outside of Africa; not like full *H. erectus* morphology, but are small-bodied and small-brained

© Cengage Learning 2013

resulting flakes (**Fig. 10-15**). While this may sound like a small change, it was an era during which such small technological changes could make big differences in how stone tools were made and how they looked when finished.

Finally, some kinds of Acheulian tools tend to reflect shared notions of form, or what they should look like. In other words, not only did Acheulian toolmakers create new stone tools and ways to make them; they were also capable of developing *and communicating to each other* ideas of form and design. For example, pretty much everything was a "Swiss Army knife" to an Oldowan toolmaker; but when an Acheulian toolmaker sat down to make, say, a hand axe, he or she clearly expected to end up with a stone tool that was bifacially worked, often about 6 to 8 inches long, and possessing a pear or teardrop shape with a point at one end and a rounded base at the other (see Fig. 10-14). Conceptualizing tools in this way was something new.

The most distinctive Acheulian artifacts are hand axes, which we just described, and cleavers, which are much like hand axes except that they end in a broad straight edge rather than a point. While we still don't have a clear idea what cleavers were used for, hand axes show wear patterns and other evidence of having been used for many different kinds of tasks, especially cutting and chopping.

The Acheulian tool kit was not just hand axes and cleavers. It also included many kinds of flake tools (**Fig. 10-16**), which were used for cutting, abrading, scraping, piercing, and other tasks, as well as hammerstones, cores, and other artifacts, many of which would also have been familiar to an Oldowan toolmaker.

Seeing the Big Picture: Interpretations of *Homo erectus*

Several aspects of the geographical, physical, and behavioral patterns shown by *Homo erectus* seem clear. But new discoveries and more in-depth analyses are helping us to reevaluate our prior ideas. The fascinating fossil hominins discovered at Dmanisi are perhaps the most challenging piece of this puzzle.

Past theories suggest that *H. erectus* was able to emigrate from Africa owing

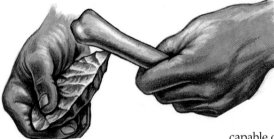

© Cengage Learning 2013

Figure 10-15

Soft hammer percussion. Here the stone tool maker uses a more flexible (bone) hammer, which allows more precise removal of flakes of the desired size and shape.

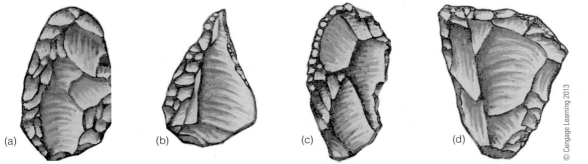

Figure 10-16

Small tools of the Acheulian industry. (a) Side scraper. (b) Point. (c) End scraper. (d) Burin.

to more advanced tools and a more modern anatomy (longer legs, larger brains) compared to earlier African predecessors. Yet, the Dmanisi cranial remains show that these very early Europeans still had small brains; and *H. erectus* in Dmanisi, Java, and Spain was still using Oldowan-style tools.

So it seems that some key parts of earlier hypotheses are not fully accurate. At least some of the earliest emigrants from Africa didn't yet show the entire suite of *H. erectus* physical and behavioral traits. How different the Dmanisi hominins are from the full *H. erectus* pattern remains to be seen, and the discovery of more complete postcranial remains will be most illuminating.

Going a step further, the four crania from Dmanisi are extremely variable; one of them, in fact, does look more like *H. erectus*. It would be tempting to conclude that more than one type of hominin is represented here, but they're all found in the same geological context. The archaeologists who excavated the site conclude that all the fossils are closely associated with each other. The simplest hypothesis is that they're all members of the *same* species. This degree of apparent intraspecific variation is biologically noteworthy, and it's influencing how paleoanthropologists interpret all of these fossil samples.

This growing awareness of the broad intraspecific variation among some hominins brings us to our second consideration: Is *Homo ergaster* in Africa a separate species from *Homo erectus*, as strictly defined in Asia? While this interpretation was popular in the last decade, it's now losing support. The finds from Dmanisi raise fundamental issues of interpretation. Among these four crania from one locality (see Fig. 10-5), we see more variation than between the

African and Asian forms, which many researchers have interpreted as different species. Also, the new discovery from Daka (Ethiopia) of a young African specimen with Asian traits further weakens the separate-species interpretation of *H. ergaster*.

The separate-species status of the early European fossils from Spain (Sima del Elefante and Gran Dolina) is also not yet clearly established. We still don't have much good fossil evidence from these two sites; but dates going back to 1.2 mya for the earlier site are well confirmed. Recall also that no other western European hominin fossils are known until at least 500,000 years later, and it remains to be seen if any of these European hominins dating prior to 500,000 ya are ancestors of any later hominin species. Nevertheless, it's quite apparent that later in the Pleistocene, well-established hominin populations were widely dispersed in both Africa and Europe. These later premodern humans are the topic of the next chapter.

When looking back at the evolution of *H. erectus*, we realize how significant this early human was. *H. erectus* had greater limb length and thus more efficient bipedalism; was the first species with a cranial capacity approaching the range of *H. sapiens*; became a more efficient scavenger and exploited a wider range of nutrients, including meat; and ranged across the Old World, from Spain to Indonesia. In short, it was *H. erectus* that transformed hominin evolution to human evolution. As Richard Foley states, "The appearance and expansion of *H. erectus* represented a major change in adaptive strategy that influenced the subsequent process and pattern of human evolution" (1991, p. 425).

Summary of Main Topics

▶ *Homo erectus* remains have been found in Africa, Europe, and Asia dating from about 1.8 mya to at least 100,000 ya—and probably even later—and thus this species spanned a period of more than 1.5 million years.

▶ *H. erectus* likely first appeared in East Africa and later migrated to other areas. This widespread and highly successful hominin displays a new and more modern pattern of human evolution.

▶ *H. erectus* differs from early *Homo*, with a larger brain, taller stature, robust build, and changes in facial structure and cranial buttressing.

▶ The long period of *H. erectus* existence was marked by a remarkably slow rate of technological change compared to modern human culture. Even so, equipped with more sophisticated tools (as part of the Acheulian industry) and a growing cultural capacity to adapt to new habitats and environments, *H. erectus* populations spread quickly across much of the Old World.

The most important fossil discoveries discussed in this chapter are summarized in "What's Important."

What's Important — Key Fossil Discoveries of *Homo erectus*

Dates (ya)	Region	Site	The Big Picture
1.6 mya–25,000	**Asia** Indonesia	Java (Sangiran and other sites)	Shows *H. erectus* early on (by 1.6 mya) in tropical areas of Southeast Asia; *H. erectus* persisted here for more than 1 million years
780,000–(?)400,000	China	Zhoukoudian	Largest, most famous sample of *H. erectus*; shows adaptation to colder environments; conclusions regarding behavior at this site have been exaggerated and are now questioned
?800,000–450,000	**Europe** (Italy)	Ceprano	Likely best evidence of full-blown *H. erectus* morphology in Europe
1.8–1.7 mya	(Republic of Georgia)	Dmanisi	Very early dispersal to southeastern Europe (by 1.8 mya) of small-bodied, small-brained *H. erectus* population; may represent an earlier dispersal from Africa than one that led to wider occupation of Eurasia
1.6 mya	**Africa** (Kenya)	Nariokotome	Beautifully preserved nearly complete skeleton; best postcranial evidence of *H. erectus* from anywhere
1.7 mya		East Turkana	Earliest *H. erectus* from Africa; some individuals more robust, others smaller and more gracile; such variation has been suggested to represent sexual dimorphism.

© Cengage Learning 2013

Critical Thinking Questions

1. Why is the nearly complete skeleton from Nariokotome so important? What kinds of evidence does it provide?

2. Assume that you're in the laboratory and have the Nariokotome skeleton, as well as a skeleton of a modern human. First, given a choice, what age and sex would you choose for the comparative human skeleton, and why? Second, what similarities and differences do the two skeletons show?

3. What fundamental questions of interpretation do the fossil hominins from Dmanisi raise? Does this evidence completely overturn the earlier views (hypotheses) concerning *H. erectus* dispersal from Africa? Explain why or why not.

4. What are the main differences between Acheulian and Oldowan tool industries? What do these differences tell us about the evolution of human culture? Why did Lower Paleolithic culture change so slowly?

Paleoanthropology/ Fossil Hominins

CHAPTER 11

Premodern Humans

© Robert Franciscus

LEARNING OBJECTIVES

After you have mastered the material in this chapter, you will be able to:

▶ Compare premodern humans with earlier hominins (specifically, *Homo erectus*) both anatomically and in terms of what the archaeological evidence tells us.

▶ Explain why premodern humans are called "humans" and how they relate to modern humans.

▶ Explain how the latest DNA evidence helps resolve the issue of whether the Neandertals are a different species from living people.

What do you think of when you hear the term *Neandertal*? Most people think of imbecilic, hunched-over brutes. Yet, Neandertals were quite advanced; they had brains at least as large as ours, and they showed many sophisticated cultural capabilities. What's more, they definitely weren't hunched over, but were fully erect (as hominins had been for millions of years). In fact, Neandertals and their immediate predecessors could easily be called human.

That brings us to possibly the most basic of all questions: What does it mean to be human? The meaning of this term is highly varied, encompassing religious, philosophical, and biological considerations. Physical anthropologists primarily concentrate on the biological aspects of the human organism, while archaeologists seek to understand how human cultural capacities have developed and changed over time. All living people today are members of one species, sharing a common anatomical pattern and similar behavioral potentials. We call hominins like us "modern *Homo sapiens*," and in the next chapter, we'll discuss the origin of forms that were essentially identical to people living today.

When in our evolutionary past can we say that our predecessors were obviously human? Certainly, the further back we go in time, the less hominins look like modern *Homo sapiens*. This is, of course, exactly what we'd expect in an evolutionary sequence.

We saw in Chapter 10 that *Homo erectus* took crucial steps in the human direction and defined a new adaptive level in human evolution. In this chapter, we'll discuss the hominins who continued this journey. Both physically and behaviorally, they're much like modern *Homo sapiens*, though they still show several significant differences. So while most paleoanthropologists are comfortable referring to these hominins as "human," we need to qualify this recognition a bit to set them apart from fully modern people. Thus, in this text, we'll refer to these fascinating immediate predecessors as "premodern humans."

When, Where, and What

Most of the hominins discussed in this chapter lived during the **Middle Pleistocene**, a period beginning 780,000 ya and ending 125,000 ya. In addition, some of the later premodern humans, especially the Neandertals, lived well into the **Late Pleistocene** (125,000–10,000 ya).

Viewed archaeologically, this chapter addresses significant cultural changes of the late Lower Paleolithic and all of the **Middle Paleolithic**, which began about 200,000 ya and ended around 40,000–30,000 ya. Chapter 12 focuses on the **Upper Paleolithic**, addressing the archaeology of fully modern humans to the end of the Ice Age.

The Pleistocene

The Pleistocene has been called the Ice Age because, as had occurred before in geological history, it was marked by periodic advances and retreats of massive continental **glaciations**. During glacial periods, when temperatures dropped dramatically, ice accumulated as a result of more snow falling each year than melted, causing the advance of massive glaciers measuring nearly a mile thick. As the climate fluctuated, at times it became much warmer. During these **interglacials**, the ice that had built up during the glacial periods melted, and the glaciers retreated back toward the earth's polar regions. The Pleistocene was characterized by numerous advances and retreats of ice, with at least 15 major and 50 minor glacial advances documented in Europe alone (Tattersall et al., 1988).

These glaciations, which enveloped huge swaths of Europe, Asia, and North America as well as Antarctica, were mostly confined to northern latitudes. Hominins living at this time—all still restricted to the Old World—were severely affected as the climate, flora, and animal life shifted during these Pleistocene oscillations. The most dramatic of these effects were in Europe and northern Asia—less so in southern Asia and in Africa.

Still, the climate also fluctuated in the south. In Africa, the main effects were related to changing rainfall patterns. During glacial periods, the climate in Africa became more arid; during interglacials, rainfall increased. The changing availability of food resources certainly affected hominins in Africa; but probably even more importantly, migration routes also swung back and forth. For example, during glacial periods (**Fig. 11-1**), the Sahara Desert expanded, blocking migration in and out of sub-Saharan Africa (Lahr and Foley, 1998).

In Eurasia, glacial advances also greatly affected migration routes. As the ice sheets expanded, sea levels dropped nearly 500 feet (150 m) below modern levels, more northern regions became uninhabitable, and some key passages between areas became blocked by glaciers. For example, during glacial peaks, much of western Europe would have been cut off from the rest of Eurasia (**Fig. 11-2**).

During the warmer—and, in the south, wetter—interglacials, the ice sheets shrank, sea levels rose, and certain migration routes reopened (for example, from central Europe into western Europe). Clearly, to understand Middle Pleistocene hominins, it's crucial to view them within their shifting Pleistocene world.

Dispersal of Middle Pleistocene Hominins

Like their *Homo erectus* predecessors, later hominins were widely distributed

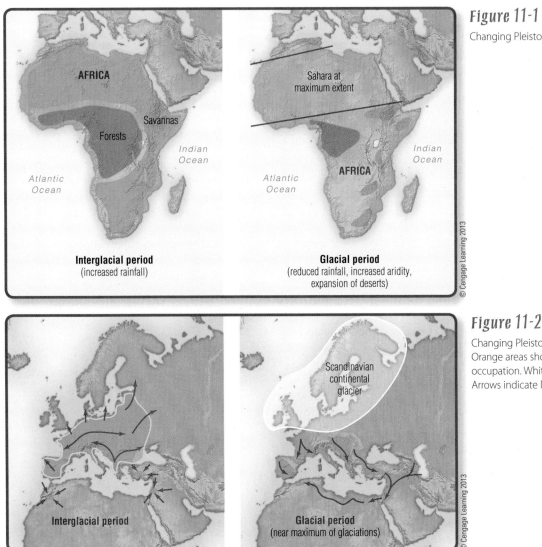

Figure 11-1

Changing Pleistocene environments in Africa.

Figure 11-2

Changing Pleistocene environments in Eurasia. Orange areas show regions of likely hominin occupation. White areas are major glaciers. Arrows indicate likely migration routes.

in the Old World, with discoveries coming from three continents—Africa, Asia, and Europe. For the first time, Europe became more permanently and densely occupied, as Middle Pleistocene hominins have been discovered widely from England, France, Spain, Germany, Italy, Hungary, and Greece. Africa, as well, probably continued as a central area of hominin occupation, and finds have come from North, East, and South Africa. Finally, Asia has yielded several important finds, especially from China. We should point out, though, that these Middle Pleistocene premodern humans didn't vastly extend the geographical range of *Homo erectus*, but rather largely replaced the earlier hominins in previously exploited habitats. One exception appears to be the more successful occupation of Europe, a region where earlier hominins have only sporadically been found.

Middle Pleistocene Hominins: Terminology

The premodern humans of the Middle Pleistocene (that is, after 780,000 ya) generally succeeded *H. erectus*. Still, in some areas—especially in Southeast Asia—there apparently was a long period of coexistence, lasting 300,000 years or longer; you'll recall the very late dates for the Javanese Ngandong *H. erectus* (see Chapter 10).

The earliest premodern humans exhibit several *H. erectus* characteristics: The face is large, the brows are projected, the forehead is low, and in some cases the cranial vault is still thick. Even so, some of their other features show that they were more derived toward the modern condition than were their *H. erectus* predecessors. Compared with *H. erectus*, these premodern humans possessed an increased brain size, a more rounded braincase (that is, maximum breadth is higher up on the sides), a more vertical nose, and a less angled back of the skull (occipital). We should note that the time span encompassed by Middle Pleistocene premodern humans is at least 500,000 years, so it's no surprise that over time we can observe certain trends. Later Middle Pleistocene hominins, for example, show even more

brain expansion and an even less angled occipital than do earlier forms.

We know that premodern humans were a diverse group dispersed over three continents. Deciding how to classify them has been disputed for decades, and anthropologists still have disagreements. However, a growing consensus has recently emerged. Beginning perhaps as early as 850,000 ya and extending to about 200,000 ya, the fossils from Africa and Europe are placed within *Homo heidelbergensis*, named after a fossil found in Germany in 1907. What's more, some Asian specimens possibly represent a regional variant of *H. heidelbergensis*.

Until recently, many researchers regarded these fossils as early, but more primitive, members of *Homo sapiens*. In recognition of this somewhat transitional status, the fossils were called "archaic *Homo sapiens*," with all later humans also belonging to the species *Homo sapiens*. However, most paleoanthropologists now find this terminology unsatisfactory. For example, Phillip Rightmire concludes that "simply lumping diverse ancient groups with living populations obscures their differences" (1998, p. 226). In our own discussion, we recognize *H. heidelbergensis* as a transitional species between *H. erectus* and later hominins (that is, primarily *H. sapiens*). Keep in mind, however, that this species was probably an ancestor of both modern humans and Neandertals. It's debatable whether *H. heidelbergensis* actually represents a fully separate species in the *biological* sense, that is, following the biological species concept (see Chapter 5). Still, it's useful to give this group of premodern humans a separate name to make this important stage of human evolution more easily identifiable. (We'll return to this issue later in the chapter when we discuss the theoretical implications in more detail.)

Premodern Humans of the Middle Pleistocene

Africa

In Africa, premodern fossils have been found at several sites. One of the best known is Kabwe (Broken Hill). At this

© Milford Wolpoff

Figure 11-3

The Kabwe (Broken Hill) *Homo heidelbergensis* skull from Zambia. Note the very robust browridges.

Figure 11-4

Bodo cranium, the earliest evidence of *Homo heidelbergensis* in Africa.

© Robert Franciscus

site in Zambia, fieldworkers discovered a complete cranium (**Fig. 11-3**) together with other cranial and post-cranial elements belonging to several individuals. In this and other African premodern specimens, we can see a mixture of primitive and more derived traits. The skull's massive browridge (one of the largest of any hominin), low vault, and prominent occipital torus recall those of *H. erectus*. On the other hand, the occipital region is less angu-

lated, the cranial vault bones are thinner, and the cranial base is essentially modern. Dating estimates of Kabwe and most of the other premodern fossils from Africa have ranged throughout the Middle and Late Pleistocene, but recent estimates have given dates for most of the sites in the range of 600,000–125,000 ya.

Bodo is another significant African premodern fossil (**Fig. 11-4**). A nearly complete cranium, Bodo has been

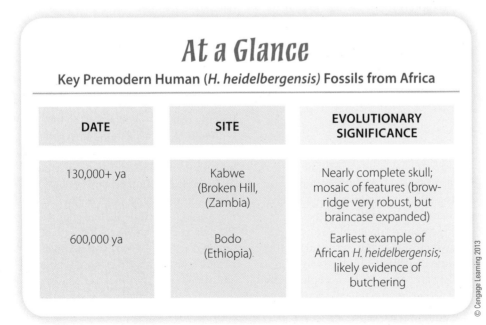

At a Glance

Key Premodern Human (*H. heidelbergensis*) Fossils from Africa

DATE	SITE	EVOLUTIONARY SIGNIFICANCE
130,000+ ya	Kabwe (Broken Hill, (Zambia)	Nearly complete skull; mosaic of features (browridge very robust, but braincase expanded)
600,000 ya	Bodo (Ethiopia)	Earliest example of African *H. heidelbergensis*; likely evidence of butchering

© Cengage Learning 2013

dated to relatively early in the Middle Pleistocene (estimated at 600,000 ya), making it one of the oldest specimens of *H. heidelbergensis* from the African continent. The Bodo cranium is particularly interesting because it shows a distinctive pattern of cut marks, similar to modifications seen on butchered animal bones. Researchers have thus hypothesized that the Bodo individual was defleshed by other hominins, but for what purpose is not clear. The defleshing may have been related to cannibalism, though it also may have been for some other purpose, such as ritual. In any case, this is the earliest evidence of deliberate bone processing of hominins *by* hominins (White, 1986).

A number of other crania from South and East Africa also show a combination of retained ancestral with more derived (modern) characteristics, and they're all mentioned in the literature as being similar to Kabwe. The most important of these African finds come from the sites of Florisbad and Elandsfontein (in South Africa) and Laetoli (in Tanzania).

The general similarities in all these African premodern fossils indicate a close relationship between them, almost certainly representing a single species (most commonly referred to as *H. heidelbergensis*). These African premodern humans also are quite similar to those found in Europe.

Europe

More fossil hominins of Middle Pleistocene age have been found in Europe than in any other region. Maybe it's because more archaeologists have been searching longer in Europe than anywhere else. In any case, during the Middle Pleistocene, Europe was more widely and consistently occupied than it was earlier in human evolution.

The time range of European premodern humans extends the full length of the Middle Pleistocene and beyond. At the earlier end, the Gran Dolina finds from northern Spain (discussed in Chapter 10) are definitely not *Homo erectus*. The Gran Dolina remains may, as proposed by Spanish researchers, be members of a new hominin species. However, Rightmire (1998) has suggested that the Gran Dolina hominins may simply represent the earliest well-dated occurrence of *H. heidelbergensis*, possibly dating as early as 850,000 ya.

More recent and more completely studied *H. heidelbergensis* fossils have been found throughout much of Europe. Examples of these finds come from Steinheim (Germany), Petralona (Greece), Swanscombe (England), Arago (France), and another cave site at Atapuerca (Spain) known as Sima de los Huesos. Like their African counterparts, these European premoderns have retained certain *H. erectus* traits, but they're mixed with more derived ones—for example, increased cranial capacity, less angled occiput, parietal expansion, and reduced tooth size (**Figs. 11-5** and **11-6**).

The hominins from the Atapuerca site of Sima de los Huesos are especially interesting. These finds come from another cave in the same area as the Gran Dolina discoveries, but are slightly younger, likely dating to between 500,000 and 400,000 ya. Using a different dating method, a date as early as 600,000 ya has been proposed (Bischoff et al., 2007), but most researchers prefer the more conservative later dating (Green et al., 2010; Wood, 2010). A total of at least 28 individuals have been recovered from Sima de los Huesos, which literally means "pit of bones." In fact, with more than 4,000 fossil fragments recovered, Sima de los Huesos contains more than 80 percent of all Middle Pleistocene hominin remains in the world (Bermúdez de Castro et al., 2004). Excavations continue at this remarkable site, where bones have somehow accumulated within a deep chamber inside a cave. From initial descriptions, paleoanthropologists interpret the hominin morphology as showing several indica-

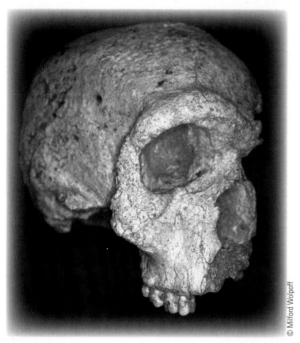

© Milford Wolpoff

Figure 11-5

Steinheim cranium, a representative of *Homo heidelbergensis* from Germany.

At a Glance

Key Premodern Human (*H. heidelbergensis*) Fossils from Europe

DATES (YA)	SITE	EVOLUTIONARY SIGNIFICANCE
300,000?–259,000?	Swanscombe (England)	Partial skull, but shows considerable brain expansion
?600,000–400,000	Sima de los Huesos (Atapuerca, northern Spain)	Large sample; very early evidence of Neandertal ancestry (>400,000 ya); earliest evidence of deliberate body disposal of the dead anywhere

© Cengage Learning 2013

tions of an early Neandertal-like pattern, with arching browridges, projecting midface, and other Neandertal features (Rightmire, 1998).

Asia

Like their contemporaries in Europe and Africa, Asian premodern specimens discovered in China also display both earlier and later characteristics. Chinese paleoanthropologists suggest that the more ancestral traits, such as a sagittal ridge and flattened nasal bones, are shared with *H. erectus* fossils from Zhoukoudian. They also point out that some of these features can be found in modern *H. sapiens* in China today, indicating substantial genetic continuity. That is, some Chinese researchers have argued that anatomically, modern Chinese didn't evolve from *H. sapiens* in either Europe or Africa; instead, they evolved locally in China from a separate *H. erectus* lineage. Whether such regional evolution occurred or whether anatomically modern migrants from Africa displaced local populations has for years been the subject of ongoing debate in paleoanthropology. This important

At a Glance

Key Premodern Human (*H. heidelbergensis*) Fossils from Asia

DATES (YA)	SITE	EVOLUTIONARY SIGNIFICANCE
230,000–180,000	Dali (China)	Nearly complete skull; best evidence of *H. heidelbergensis* in Asia
200,000	Jinniushan (China)	Partial skeleton with cranium showing relatively large brain size; some Chinese scholars suggest it as possible ancestor of early Chinese *H. sapiens*

© Cengage Learning 2013

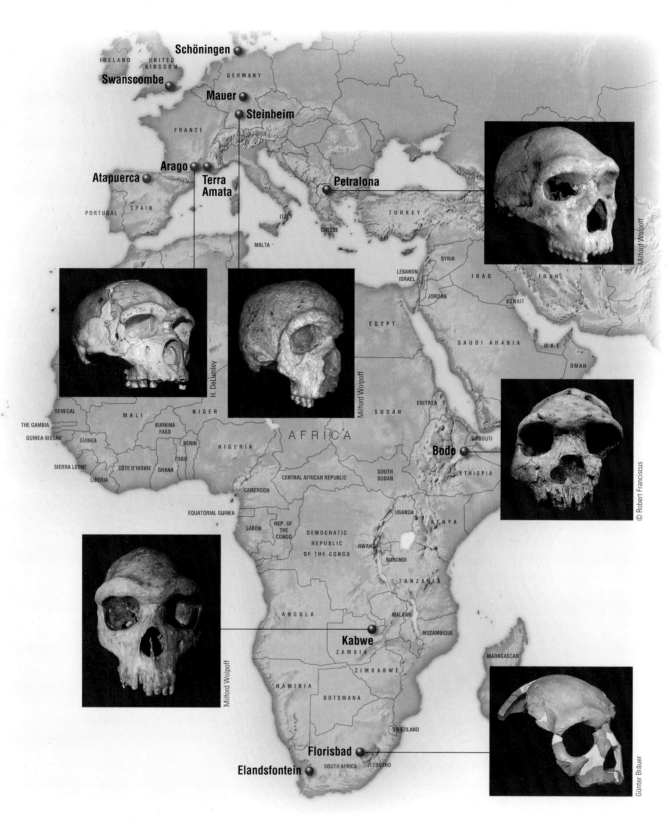

Figure 11-6

Fossil discoveries and archaeological localities of
Middle Pleistocene premodern hominins.

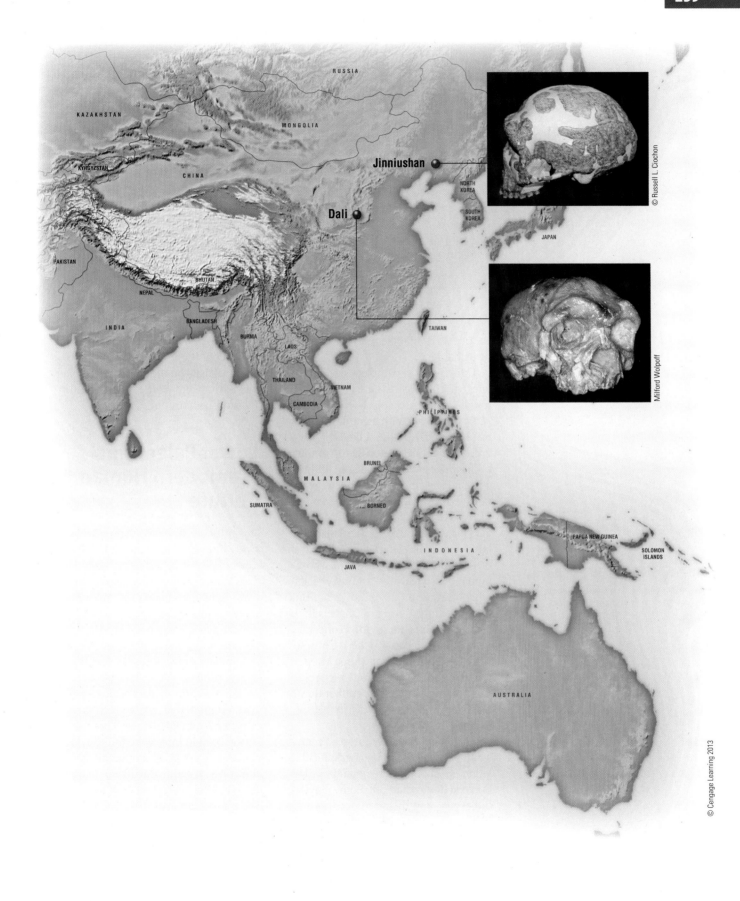

© Russell L. Ciochon

Milford Wolpoff

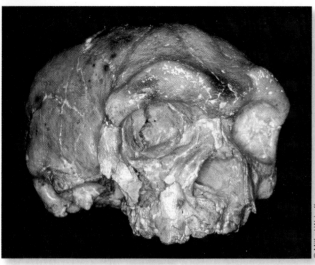

(a)

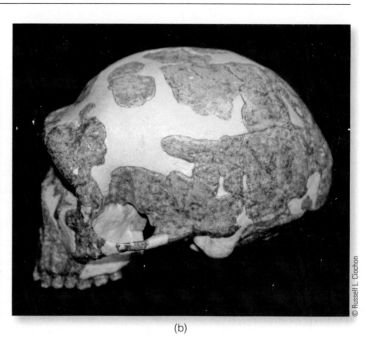

(b)

Figure 11-7

(a) Dali skull and (b) Jinniushan skull, both from China. These two crania are considered by some to be Asian representatives of *Homo heidelbergensis*.

prepared-core method Pertaining to stone cores that a toolmaker shapes into a preplanned form before striking flakes from it; enables predictable flake shape and thickness; can be efficient in the use of raw materials.

controversy will be a central focus of the next chapter.

Dali, the most complete skull of the later Middle or early Late Pleistocene fossils in China, displays *H. erectus* and *H. sapiens* traits, with a cranial capacity of 1,120 cm³ (**Fig. 11-7**). Like Dali, several other Chinese specimens combine both earlier and later traits. In addition, a partial skeleton from Jinniushan, in northeast China, has been given a provisional date of 200,000 ya (Tiemel et al., 1994). The cranial capacity is fairly large (approximately 1,260 cm³), and the walls of the braincase are thin. These are both modern features, and they're somewhat unexpected in an individual this ancient—if the dating estimate is indeed correct. Experts are divided concerning just how to classify these Chinese Middle Pleistocene hominins. More recently, though, a leading paleoanthropologist has concluded that they're regional variants of *H. heidelbergensis* (Rightmire, 2004).

The Pleistocene world forced many small populations into geographical isolation. Most of these regional populations no doubt died out. Some, however, did evolve, and their descendants are likely a major part of the later hominin fossil record. In Africa, *H. heidelbergensis* is hypothesized to have evolved into modern *H. sapiens*. In Europe, *H. heidelbergensis* evolved into Neandertals. Meanwhile, the Chinese premodern

populations may all have met with extinction. Right now, though, there's no consensus on the status or the likely fate of these enigmatic Asian Middle Pleistocene hominins (**Fig. 11-8**).

Lower Paleolithic Premodern Human Culture

Acheulian technology changed relatively little until near the end of the Lower Paleolithic. Flake tools and hand axes, many of which are smaller than early Acheulian hand axes, are commonly found in European assemblages. Amazingly, a few wooden artifacts have also been uncovered in the excavation of several late Acheulian sites. For example, at Schöningen, in the Harz Mountain region of Germany, archaeologists discovered more than six wooden spears between 6 and 8 feet long. These and other wooden tools were found with the remains of horses and other big game, the bones of some bearing cut marks from having been butchered by Lower Paleolithic hunters (Thieme, 2005).

Among their technological accomplishments, about 300,000 ya, later premodern humans in Africa and Europe invented the **prepared-core method** for striking flakes from stone cores (Klein, 1999). Requiring several coordinated

Figure 11-8

Time line of Middle Pleistocene hominins. Note that most dates are approximations. Question marks indicate those estimates that are most tentative.

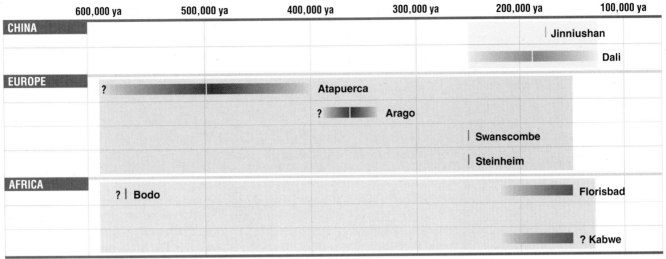

	600,000 ya	500,000 ya	400,000 ya	300,000 ya	200,000 ya	100,000 ya
CHINA						Jinniushan
						Dali
EUROPE	?		Atapuerca			
			?	Arago		
					Swanscombe	
					Steinheim	
AFRICA	? Bodo					Florisbad
						? Kabwe

© Cengage Learning 2013

steps, a prepared-core method called the Levallois technique required a tool-maker to work each stone core into a preplanned shape before beginning to detach flakes from it (**Fig. 11-9**). While this may sound like more trouble than it was worth, the prepared-core method enabled toolmakers to strike off flakes of predictable shape and get more usable flakes from each core.

Hominin populations adapted to the seasonal climatic extremes of life outside the tropics in many ways, eventually including the controlled use of fire and the construction of shelters. Surprisingly, the controlled use of fire does not appear to have been essential to the spread of hominins into northern latitudes. The most convincing archaeological evidence of hominin fire use in Eurasia comes from Gesher Benot Ya'aqov, Israel, where researchers report burned wood, seeds, and flint flakes from contexts

dated stratigraphically to nearly 790,000 ya (Goren-Inbar et al., 2004). Given such evidence, we might reasonably expect to see considerable additional evidence throughout the Pleistocene if it was an important cultural adaptation to life in colder climates. What researchers are actually finding is that the earliest habitual use of fire dates only to about 400,000–300,000 ya in Europe, or some 700,000 years after hominins entered the continent (Roebroeks and Villa, 2011). In other words, the controlled use of fire could not have been an essential cultural component of the initial dispersal of early hominins into Europe or, by implication, other northern-latitude regions.

At roughly the same time that evidence of habitual fire use begins to appear in the archaeological record, researchers also find sites containing patches of artifacts, food waste, stones, and other debris interpreted as the

Figure 11-9

The Levallois technique.

Nodule

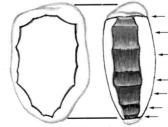

The nodule is chipped on the perimeter.

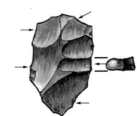

Flakes are radially removed from top surface.

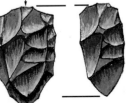

A final blow struck at one end removes a large flake. The flake on the right is the goal of the whole process and is the completed tool.

© Cengage Learning 2013

remains of temporary shelters, as well as burned areas interpreted as the remains of hearths or fireplaces. At Terra Amata, a French site on the Mediterranean coast near Nice, excavators uncovered fascinating evidence relating to short-term, seasonal visits by hominin groups, who built flimsy shelters, gathered plants, ate food from the ocean, and possibly hunted medium- to large-sized mammals (de Lumley and de Lumley, 1973; Villa, 1983).

Archaeologists continue to debate the extent to which later Lower Paleolithic hominins were hunters in the same sense as modern hunter-gatherers. With the notable exception of the Schöningen spears mentioned earlier, late Lower Paleolithic sites include few artifacts that could have been true weapons or killing tools. Meat was apparently an important part of the diet for at least some populations, and plant foods were undoubtedly so, but archaeologists are generally skeptical that these hominins were true hunter-gatherers in the modern sense.

The Middle Paleolithic period began about 200,000 ya in western Europe. Roughly the same period in sub-Saharan Africa is called the Middle Stone Age. As documented by the fossil remains and Middle Paleolithic artifactual evidence, the long period of transitional hominins in Europe continued well into the Late Pleistocene (after 125,000 ya). But with the appearance and expansion of the Neandertals, the evolution of premodern humans took a unique turn.

Neandertals: Premodern Humans of the Late Pleistocene

Since their discovery more than a century ago, the Neandertals have haunted the minds and foiled the best-laid theories of paleoanthropologists. They fit into the general scheme of human evolution, and yet they're misfits. Classified variously either as *H. sapiens* or as belonging to a separate species, they are like us and yet different. It's not easy to put them in their

place. Many anthropologists classify Neandertals within *H. sapiens*, but as a distinctive subspecies, *Homo sapiens neanderthalensis*,[*] with modern *H. sapiens* designated as *Homo sapiens sapiens*. However, not all experts agree with this interpretation. The most recent genetic evidence of interbreeding between Neandertals and early modern humans (Green et al., 2010) suggests that complete speciation was never attained. This argues against a clear designation of Neandertals as a species separate from *H. sapiens*. We'll discuss in a moment this important evidence in more detail.

Neandertal fossil remains have been found at dates approaching 130,000 ya; but in the following discussion of Neandertals, we'll focus on those populations that lived during the last major glaciation, which began about 75,000 ya and ended about 10,000 ya (**Fig. 11-10**). We should also note that the evolutionary roots of Neandertals apparently reach quite far back in western Europe, as evidenced by the 400,000+-year-old remains from Sima de los Huesos, Atapuerca, in northern Spain. The majority of fossils have been found in Europe, where they've been most studied. Our description of Neandertals is based primarily on those specimens, usually called *classic* Neandertals, from western Europe. Not all Neandertals—including others from eastern Europe and western Asia and those from the interglacial period just before the last glacial one—exactly fit our description of the classic morphology. They tend to be less robust, possibly because the climate in which they lived was not as cold as in western Europe during the last glaciation.

One striking feature of Neandertals is brain size, which in these hominins actually was larger than that of *H. sapiens* today. The average for contemporary

---

[*]*Thal*, meaning "valley," is the old spelling; due to rules of taxonomic naming, this spelling is retained in the formal species designation *Homo neanderthalensis* (although the *h* was never pronounced). The modern spelling, *tal*, is used today in Germany; we follow contemporary usage in the text with the spelling of the colloquial *Neandertal*.

Figure 11-10

Correlation of Pleistocene subdivisions with archaeological industries and hominins. Note that the geological divisions are separate and different from the archaeological stages (e.g., Late Pleistocene is not synonymous with Upper Paleolithic).

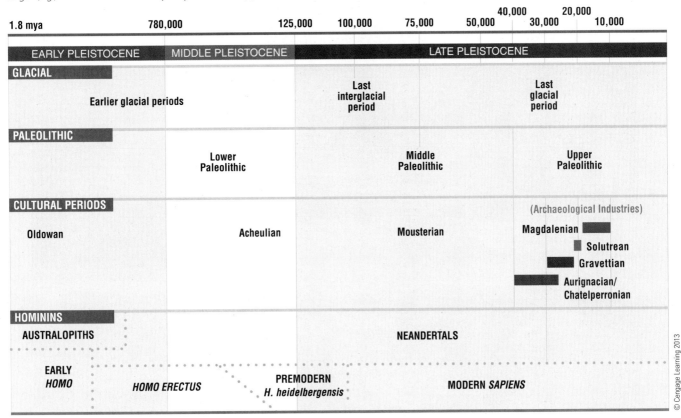

© Cengage Learning 2013

H. sapiens is between 1,300 and 1,400 cm³, while for Neandertals it was 1,520 cm³. The larger size may be associated with the metabolic efficiency of a larger brain in cold weather. The Inuit (Eskimo), also living in very cold areas, have a larger average brain size than most other modern human populations. We should also point out that the larger brain size in both premodern and contemporary human populations adapted to cold climates is partially correlated with larger body size, which has also evolved among these groups (see Chapter 4).

The classic Neandertal cranium is large, long, low, and bulging at the sides. Viewed from the side, the occipital bone is somewhat bun-shaped, but the marked occipital angle typical of many *H. erectus* crania is absent. The forehead rises more vertically than that of *H. erectus*, and the browridges arch over the orbits instead of forming a straight bar (**Fig. 11-11**).

Compared with anatomically modern humans, the Neandertal face stands out. It projects almost as if it were pulled forward. Postcranially, Neandertals were very robust, barrel-chested, and powerfully muscled. This robust skeletal structure, in fact, dominates hominin evolution from *H. erectus* through all premodern forms. Still, the Neandertals appear particularly robust, with shorter limbs than seen in most modern *H. sapiens* populations. Both the facial anatomy and the robust postcranial structure of Neandertals have been interpreted by Erik Trinkaus, of Washington University in St. Louis, as adaptations to rigorous living in a cold climate.

For about 100,000 years, Neandertals lived in Europe and western Asia (**Fig. 11-12**), and their coming and going have raised more questions and controversies than for any other hominin group. As we've noted, Neandertal forebears are transitional forms dating to

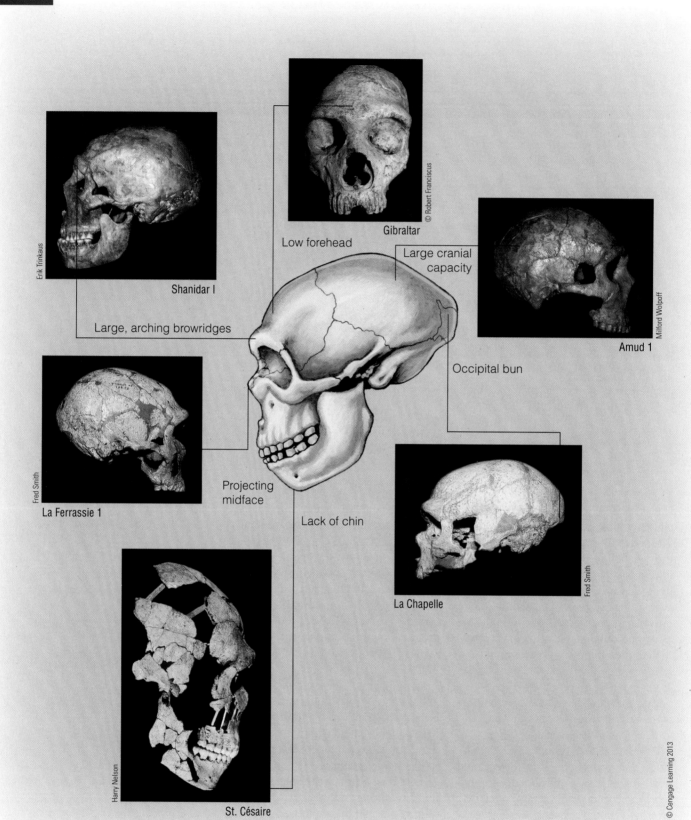

Figure 11-11

Morphology and variation in Neandertal crania.

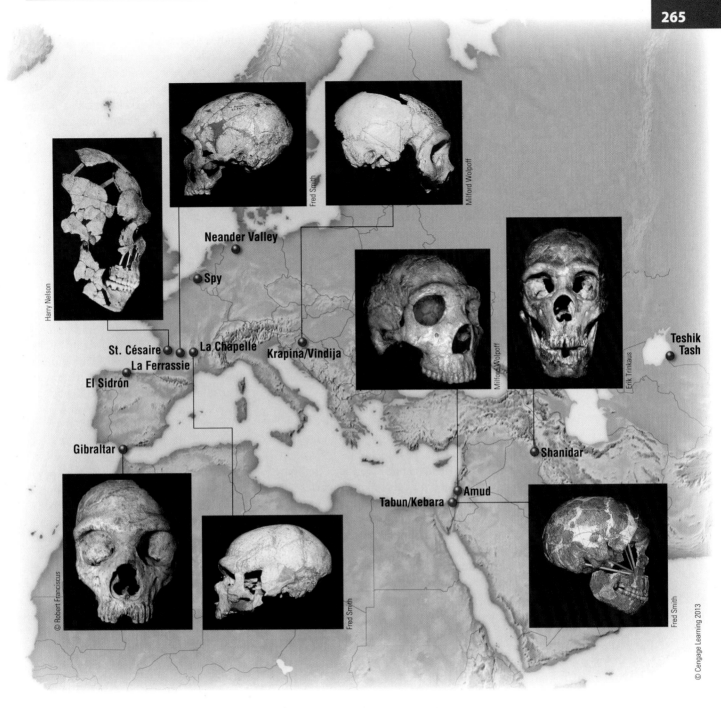

Neander Valley

Spy

St. Césaire

La Ferrassie

El Sidrón

La Chapelle

Krapina/Vindija

Teshik
Tash

Gibraltar

Shanidar

Amud

Tabun/Kebara

Harry Nelson

Fred Smith

Milford Wolpoff

Milford Wolpoff

Erik Trinkaus

© Robert Franciscus

Fred Smith

Fred Smith

© Cengage Learning 2013

the later Middle Pleistocene. However, it's not until the Late Pleistocene that Neandertals become fully recognizable.

Western Europe

One of the most important Neandertal discoveries was made in 1908 at La Chapelle-aux-Saints, in southwestern France. A nearly complete skeleton was found buried in a shallow grave in a **flexed** position (**Fig. 11-13**). Several fragments of nonhuman long bones had

been placed over the head, and over them, a bison leg. Around the body were flint tools and broken animal bones.

The skeleton was turned over for study to a well-known French paleontologist, Marcellin Boule, who depicted the La Chapelle Neandertal as a brutish, bent-kneed, not fully erect biped. Because of this exaggerated interpretation, some scholars, and certainly the general public, concluded that all Neandertals were highly primitive creatures.

Figure 11-12

Fossil discoveries of Neandertals.

flexed The position of the body in a bent orientation, with arms and legs drawn up to the chest.

Figure 11-13

Artist's reconstruction of an adult male Neandertal, based on skeletal remains from La Chapelle-aux-Saints, France.

© 2010 Photo E. Daynes – Reconstruction Atelier Daynes Paris

Why did Boule draw these conclusions from the La Chapelle skeleton? Today, we think he misjudged the Neandertal posture because this adult male skeleton had arthritis of the spine. Also, and probably more important, Boule and his contemporaries found it difficult to fully accept as a human ancestor an individual who appeared in any way to depart from the modern pattern.

The skull of this male, who was possibly at least 40 years of age when he died, is very large, with a cranial capacity of 1,620 cm³. Typical of western European classic forms, the vault is low and long; the browridges are immense, with the

typical Neandertal arched shape; the forehead is low and retreating; and the face is long and projecting. The back of the skull is protuberant and bun-shaped (**Fig. 11-14**; also see Fig. 11-12).

The La Chapelle skeleton isn't a typical Neandertal, but an unusually robust male who "evidently represents an extreme in the Neandertal range of variation" (Brace et al., 1979, p. 117). Unfortunately, this skeleton, which Boule claimed didn't even walk completely erect, was widely accepted as "Mr. Neandertal." But few other Neandertal individuals possess such exaggerated expression of Neandertal traits as the "Old Man of La Chapelle-aux-Saints."

Dramatic new evidence of Neandertal behavior comes from the El Sidrón site in northern Spain. Dated to about 49,000 ya, fragmented remains of 12 individuals show bone changes indicating that they were smashed, butchered, and likely cannibalized—presumably by other Neandertals (Lalueza-Fox et al., 2011).

Because the remains of all 12 individuals were found together in a cave where they had accidentally fallen, they all probably died (were killed) at about the same time. Lying there undisturbed for almost 50,000 years, these individuals reveal several secrets about Neandertals. First, they are hypothesized to all have belonged to the same social group, representing a band of hunter-gatherers. Their ages and sex support this interpretation: three adult males, three adult females, five children/adolescents, and one infant.

What's more, genetic evidence shows that the adult males were all closely related, but the females weren't. It seems that Neandertals practiced a patrilocal form of mating, where related males stay together and mate with females from other groups (**Fig. 11-15**).

Central Europe

There are quite a few other European classic Neandertals, including significant finds from central Europe. At Krapina, Croatia, researchers have recovered an abundance of bones—1,000 fragments representing up to 70 individuals (Trinkaus and Shipman, 1992). Krapina

Figure 11-14

La Chapelle-aux-Saints skull. Note the occipital bun, projecting face, and low vault.

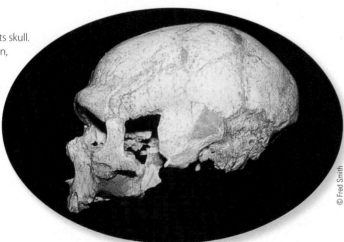

© Fred Smith

is an old site, possibly the earliest showing the full suite of classic Neandertal morphology (**Fig. 11-16**), dating back to the beginning of the Late Pleistocene (estimated at 130,000–110,000 ya).

About 30 miles from Krapina, Neandertal fossils have also been discovered at Vindija. The site is an excellent source of faunal, cultural, and hominin materials stratified in *sequence* throughout much of the Late Pleistocene. Neandertal fossils from Vindija consist of some 35 specimens dated to between 42,000 and 32,000 ya, making them some of the most recent Neandertals ever discovered (Higham et al., 2006).

Anatomically modern humans were living in both western and central Europe by about 35,000 ya or a bit earlier. So it's possible that Neandertals and modern *H. sapiens* were living quite close to each other for several thousand years (**Fig. 11-17**). How did these two groups interact? Based on the evidence from French sites, such as St. Césaire and Grotte du Renne, it has long been argued that Neandertals borrowed technological methods and tools (such as blades) from the anatomically modern populations and thereby modified their own tools, creating a new industry, the **Chatelperronian**, which combines elements of both Middle and Upper Paleolithic technology. However, recent reanalyses of the stratigraphy, dating, and archaeological associations of these sites cast considerable doubt on this interpretation (Bar-Yosef and Bordes, 2010; Higham et al., 2010). It's also possible, of course, that early modern *H. sapiens* borrowed cultural innovations from the Neandertals (who, as we'll soon see, were in many ways quite sophisticated). What's more, we know that the two groups were very likely *interbreeding* with each other!

Figure 11-15

"Clean" excavations at El Sidrón Cave in Spain, where special precautions are used to prevent contamination and allow more controlled DNA analyses. Evidence from mtDNA analyses suggests that these Neandertal males likely practiced a patrilocal mating pattern.

© El Sidrón Research Team

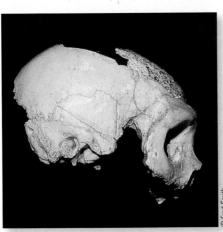
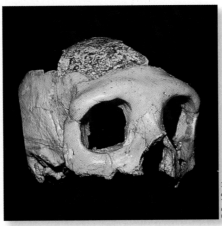

(a)   (b)

© Fred Smith

Figure 11-16

Krapina cranium. (a) Lateral view showing characteristic Neandertal traits. (b) Three-quarters view.

Chatelperronian Pertaining to an Upper Paleolithic industry found in France and Spain.

Figure 11-17

Time line for Neandertal fossil discoveries.

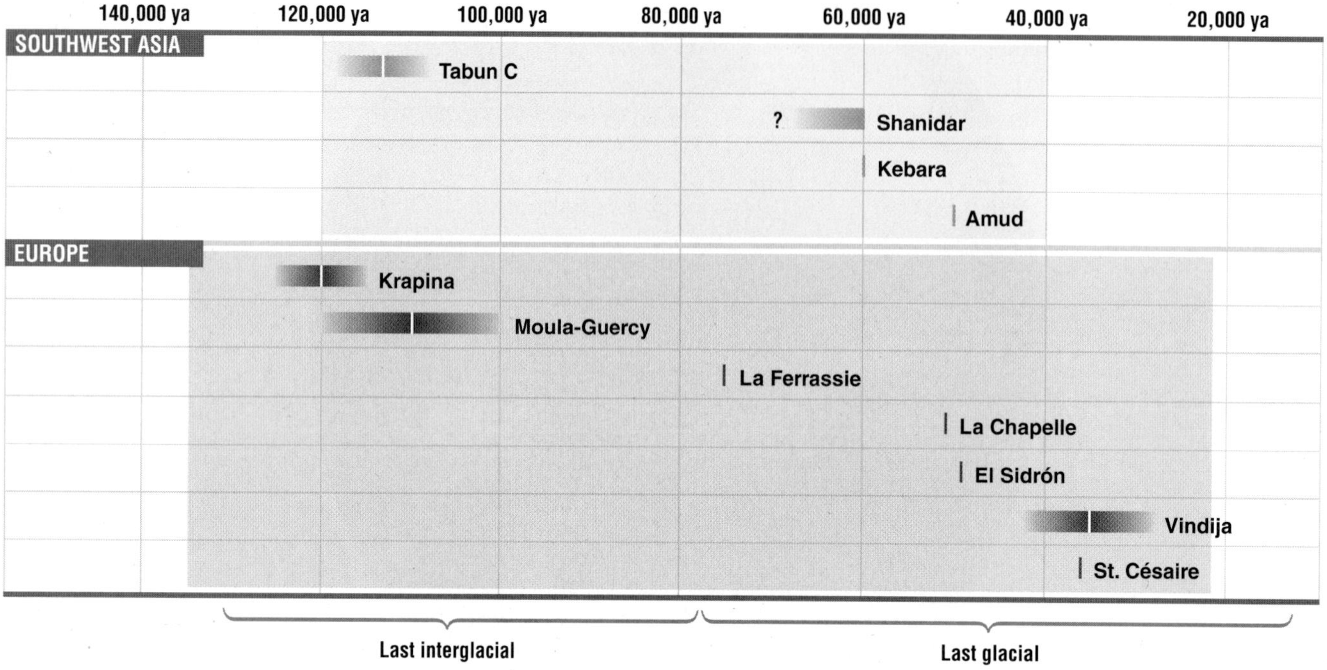

	140,000 ya	120,000 ya	100,000 ya	80,000 ya	60,000 ya	40,000 ya	20,000 ya
SOUTHWEST ASIA							
		Tabun C					
					? Shanidar		
					Kebara		
					Amud		
EUROPE							
		Krapina					
			Moula-Guercy				
				La Ferrassie			
						La Chapelle	
						El Sidrón	
						Vindija	
						St. Césaire	

Last interglacial · Last glacial

© Cengage Learning 2013

Western Asia

Israel In addition to European Neandertals, many important discoveries have been made in southwest Asia. Neandertal specimens from Israel are less robustly built than the classic Neandertals of Europe, though again, the overall pattern is clearly Neandertal. One of the best known of these discoveries is from Tabun (**Fig. 11-18**). Tabun, excavated in the early 1930s, yielded a female skeleton, dated by thermoluminescence (TL) at about 120,000–110,000 ya (TL dating is discussed in Chapter 8). If this dating is accurate, Neandertals

Figure 11-18

Excavation of the Tabun Cave, Mt. Carmel, Israel.

Harry Nelson

at Tabun were generally contemporary with early modern *H. sapiens* found in nearby caves.

A more recent Neandertal burial of a large male comes from Kebara, a neighboring cave at Mt. Carmel. A partial skeleton, dated to 60,000 ya, contains the most complete Neandertal thorax and pelvis yet found. Also recovered at Kebara is a hyoid—a small bone located in the throat and the first ever found from a Neandertal; this bone is especially important because of its usefulness in reconstructing language capabilities.*

Iraq A most remarkable site is Shanidar Cave, in the Zagros Mountains of northeastern Iraq, where fieldworkers found partial skeletons of nine individuals, four of them deliberately buried. One of the more interesting skeletons recovered from Shanidar is that of a male (Shanidar 1) who lived to be approximately 30 to 45 years old, a considerable age for a prehistoric human (**Fig. 11-19**). He is estimated to have stood 5 feet 7 inches tall, with a cranial capacity of 1,600 cm³. The skeletal remains of Shanidar 1 also exhibit several other fascinating features:

> There had been a crushing blow to the left side of the head, fracturing the eye socket, displacing the left eye, and probably causing blindness on that side. He also sustained a massive blow to the right side of the body that so badly damaged the right arm that it became withered and useless; the bones of the shoulder blade, collar bone, and upper arm are much smaller and thinner than those on the left. The right lower arm and hand are missing, probably not because of poor preservation . . . but because they either atrophied and dropped off or because they were amputated. (Trinkaus and Shipman, 1992, p. 340)

Besides these injuries, the man had further trauma to both legs, and he probably limped. It's hard to imagine how he could have performed day-to-day activities without assistance. This is why Erik Trinkaus, who has studied the Shanidar remains, suggests that to survive, Shanidar 1 must have been helped by others: "A one-armed, partially blind, crippled man could have made no pretense of hunting or gathering his own food. That he survived for years after his trauma was a testament to Neandertal compassion and humanity" (Trinkaus and Shipman, 1992, p. 341).

Central Asia

Neandertals extended their range even farther to the east, far into central Asia. A discovery made in the 1930s at the site of Teshik-Tash, in Uzbekistan, of a Neandertal child associated with tools of the Mousterian industry suggested that this species had dispersed a long way into Asia. However, owing to poor archaeological control during excavation and the young age of the individual, the find was not considered by all paleoanthropologists as clearly that of a Neandertal. New finds and molecular evaluation have provided crucial evidence that Neandertals did in fact extend their geographical range far into central Asia and perhaps even farther east.

DNA analysis of the Teshik-Tash remains shows that they are clearly Neandertal. What's more, other fragments from southern Siberia also show a distinctively Neandertal genetic pattern (Krause et al., 2007a). As we'll see shortly, researchers have recently been able to identify and analyze DNA from several Neandertal specimens. It's been shown that Neandertals and modern humans differ in both their mitochondrial DNA (mtDNA) and nuclear DNA, and these results are extremely significant in determining the evolutionary status of the Neandertal lineage. Moreover, in the case of the fragmentary remains from southern Siberia (dating to 44,000–37,000 ya), it was the DNA findings that provided the key evidence in determining whether the hominin is even a Neandertal. In a sense, this is analogous to doing forensic analysis on our ancient hominin predecessors.

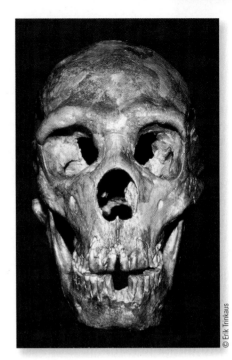

© Erik Trinkaus

Figure 11-19

Shanidar 1. Does he represent Neandertal compassion for the disabled?

---

*The Kebara hyoid is identical to that of modern humans, suggesting that Neandertals did not differ from modern *H. sapiens* in this key element.

At a Glance

Key Neandertal Fossil Discoveries

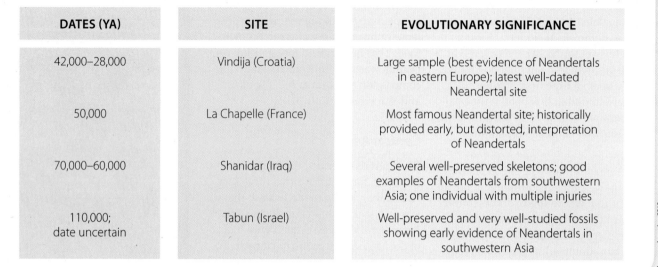

DATES (YA)	SITE	EVOLUTIONARY SIGNIFICANCE
42,000–28,000	Vindija (Croatia)	Large sample (best evidence of Neandertals in eastern Europe); latest well-dated Neandertal site
50,000	La Chapelle (France)	Most famous Neandertal site; historically provided early, but distorted, interpretation of Neandertals
70,000–60,000	Shanidar (Iraq)	Several well-preserved skeletons; good examples of Neandertals from southwestern Asia; one individual with multiple injuries
110,000; date uncertain	Tabun (Israel)	Well-preserved and very well-studied fossils showing early evidence of Neandertals in southwestern Asia

Surprising Connections: Another Contemporary Hominin? In 2000 and 2008, researchers found fragmentary hominin remains in another cave in the Altai Mountains of southern Siberia. Only a finger bone and one tooth were found in Denisova Cave, and they are dated to 50,000–30,000 ya. From such incomplete skeletal remains, accurate anatomical species identification is impossible. In prior years, this seemingly meager find would have been stashed away in a cabinet in a museum or university laboratory and mostly forgotten. But in the twenty-first century, we have new ways to study bits and pieces of ancient hominins. So the finger bone was sent to the Max-Planck Institute for Evolutionary Biology in Germany to see if DNA analysis could determine to which species it belongs.

Mitochondrial DNA analysis was performed on the finger bone and provided a big surprise: The mtDNA did not match that of either modern *H. sapiens* or a Neandertal! What's more, the degree of genetic distance suggested to the researchers that the hominin line of this "new" hominin diverged from the modern *H. sapiens*/Neandertal line almost 1 million years ago (Krause et al., 2010).

These results suggest that the hominins from Denisova Cave were a completely new species, different from modern humans or Neandertals.

Lying in a cool, dry, stable environment inside the cave, the Denisova remains stood a good chance of preserving even more complete ancient DNA. So, the Max Planck team, along with many colleagues from around the world, decided to attempt to sequence the nuclear genome derived from DNA in the finger bone (in which DNA preservation was exceptionally good). Within less than two years, they successfully sequenced the *entire* genome from this one small bone—more than 3 billion base pairs—a truly amazing scientific accomplishment (Reich et al., 2010). These far more complete data confirmed the earlier findings, most notably that the "Denisovans" were a separate branch of hominins living side by side in central Asia with two other lineages of hominins (Neandertals and modern humans). The complete genome also provided another big surprise regarding how these ancient Denisovans are genetically connected to some living human populations (discussed later).

Middle Paleolithic Culture

The best-known Middle Paleolithic tool industry is the Mousterian, which many anthropologists closely associate with the Neandertals. Nevertheless, Mousterian artifacts have occasionally been also found with the remains of early modern *H. sapiens* (although *H. sapiens* remains are more frequently found associated with Upper Paleolithic tool industries). It is because of this archaeological overlap that it wasn't entirely clear until the DNA evidence came in whether the central Asian remains were actually Neandertal. Early in the last glacial episode, Mousterian culture extended across Europe and North Africa into the former Soviet Union, Israel, Iran, and as far east as central Asia and possibly even China. Also, in sub-Saharan Africa, the contemporaneous Middle Stone Age industry is broadly similar to the **Mousterian**.

Technology

One of the most significant Middle Paleolithic technological innovations was the **composite tool** (**Fig. 11-20**), which was developed in Africa as early as the Lower-to-Middle Paleolithic transition, 300,000–200,000 ya. Modern kitchens and garage workshops are stuffed with composite tools—knives, spatulas, hammers, hatchets, pizza cutters, and the like. We take such tools for granted, but somewhere along the line, a long, long time ago, some smart hominin first figured out that you can make many tools more effective if you first attach them to a handle, or shaft. When a Lower Paleolithic hominin used a hand axe, cleaver, or flake tool, it was entirely handheld (now you can see where we get the name "hand axe"); but when a Middle Paleolithic toolmaker picked up a tool, chances are the business end of that implement was embedded in a handle and held in place by glue, leather bindings, or friction.

Some researchers hypothesize that composite tools marked a significant

step forward in other ways, too; their existence clearly implies that hominins had begun to master and communicate complex behavioral sequences. Archaeologist Stanley Ambrose (2001) argues that these complex toolmaking abilities may have coevolved with grammatical language. Both require fine motor skills and the ability to solve problems and plan complex tasks, and both are controlled by adjacent areas of the human brain. Viewed from this perspective, it is no accident that subsequent to the invention of composite tools, the pace of cultural change began to accelerate.

Most Middle Paleolithic stone tools were based on flakes that had been struck from cores and chipped into their final form. Common flake tools include several kinds of scrapers; points for making composite tools such as thrusting spears and knives; and denticulates, which are deeply notched flakes that have a serrated appearance (**Fig. 11-21**). Middle Paleolithic stone toolmakers also developed the **discoid technique**, which enabled a more efficient use of raw material than the Levallois. They trimmed a flint nodule around the edges to form a disk-shaped core. Each time they struck the edge, they drove off a flake toward the center of the core. The flake struck by the discoid technique wasn't preshaped like a Levallois flake, but this technique did make it easier for the toolmaker to get more usable flakes from a given core.

Mousterian A Middle Paleolithic stone tool industry associated with Neandertals and some modern *H. sapiens* groups.

composite tool Minimally, a tool made of several pieces. For example, a prehistoric knife typically included a handle or shaft, a chipped stone blade, and binding materials such as glue or sinew to hold the blade firmly in place.

discoid technique A prepared-core technique in which flakes are struck toward the center of the stone core; greater efficiency of raw material use than Levallois; also called "radial core" technique.

© Randall White

Figure 11-21

Examples of the Mousterian tool kit, including (from left to right) a Levallois point, a perforator, and a side scraper.

While Middle Paleolithic peoples developed many specialized tools for skinning and preparing meat, hunting, woodworking, and hafting, they made little use of bone, antler, and ivory as raw materials. This resource use pattern is in striking contrast to that of the Upper Paleolithic, in which these and other materials were commonly used. Nevertheless, Middle Paleolithic technological advances undoubtedly contributed significantly to the remarkable cultural changes of the Upper Paleolithic, which we'll discuss in the next chapter.

Subsistence

We know, from the abundant remains of animal bones at their sites, that Neandertals and other Middle Paleolithic premodern humans were successful hunters, but many archaeologists characterize them as "generalized" hunter-gatherers, which means that they ate many different kinds of animals and plant foods and didn't specialize on just a few species as staple foods. Researchers question if they were hunter-gatherers in the same sense as some Upper Paleolithic groups, who focused much of their hunting on a few big game species.

These are reasonable questions because it wasn't until the beginning of the Upper Paleolithic that such long-distance weaponry as the spear-thrower, or atlatl, came into use (see Chapter 12),

followed later by the bow and arrow. Middle Paleolithic hunting technology was mostly limited to thrusting spears. Consequently, hunters may have been more prone to serious injury—a hypothesis supported by paleoanthropologists Thomas Berger and Erik Trinkaus. Berger and Trinkaus (1995) analyzed the pattern of trauma, particularly fractures, in Neandertals and compared it with that seen in modern human samples. Interestingly, the Neandertal pattern, which included a relatively high proportion of head and neck injuries, was most similar to that seen in contemporary rodeo performers. Berger and Trinkaus concluded that "the similarity to the rodeo distribution suggests frequent close encounters with large ungulates unkindly disposed to the humans involved" (Berger and Trinkaus, 1995, p. 841).

Speech and Symbolic Behavior

There are a variety of hypotheses concerning the speech capacities of Middle Paleolithic premodern humans, and many of these views are contradictory. Some researchers argue that Neandertals were incapable of human speech. But the prevailing consensus has been that they *were* capable of articulate speech and likely fully competent in producing the full range of sounds used by modern humans.

However, recent genetic evidence may call for a reassessment of just when fully human language first emerged (Enard et al., 2002). In humans today, mutations in a particular gene (locus) are known to produce serious language impairments. From an evolutionary perspective, what's perhaps most significant concerns the greater variability seen in the alleles at this locus in modern humans as compared to other primates. One explanation for this increased variation is intensified selection acting on human populations, and as you'll see shortly, DNA evidence from Neandertal fossils shows that they had already made this transformation. But even if we conclude that Neandertals *could* speak, it doesn't necessarily mean that their abilities were at the level of modern *Homo sapiens*.

Today, paleoanthropologists are quite interested in the apparently sudden expansion of modern *H. sapiens* (discussed in Chapter 12), and they've proposed various explanations for this group's rapid success. Also, as we attempt to explain how and why modern *H. sapiens* expanded its geographical range, we're left with the problem of explaining what happened to the Neandertals. In making these types of interpretations, a growing number of paleoanthropologists suggest that *behavioral* differences are the key.

Researchers have suggested that Upper Paleolithic *H. sapiens* had some significant behavioral advantages over Neandertals and other premodern humans. Was it some kind of new and expanded ability to symbolize, communicate, organize social activities, elaborate technology, obtain a wider range of food resources, or care for the sick or injured—or was it some other factor? Were the Neandertals limited by neurological differences that may have contributed to their demise?

The direct anatomical evidence derived from Neandertal fossils isn't much help in answering these questions. Ralph Holloway (1985) has maintained that Neandertal brains—at least as far as the fossil evidence suggests—aren't significantly different from those of modern *H. sapiens*. What's more, as we've seen, Neandertal vocal tracts (as well as other morphological features), compared with our own, don't appear to have seriously limited them.

Burials

Anthropologists have known for some time that Neandertals deliberately buried their dead. Undeniably, the spectacular discoveries at La Chapelle, Shanidar, and elsewhere were the direct results of ancient burial, which permits preservation that's much more complete. Such deliberate burial treatment goes back at least 90,000 years at Tabun. From a much older site, some form of consistent "disposal" of the dead—not necessarily belowground burial—is evidenced: At Atapuerca, Spain, more than 700 fossilized elements (representing at least 28 different individuals) were found in a cave at the end of a deep vertical shaft. From the nature of the site and the accumulation of hominin remains, Spanish researchers are convinced that the site demonstrates some form of human activity involving deliberate disposal of the dead (Arsuaga et al., 1997).

The recent redating of Atapuerca to more than 400,000 ya suggests that Neandertals—more precisely, their immediate precursors—were, by quite early in the Middle Pleistocene, handling their dead in special ways. Such behavior was previously thought to have emerged only much later, in the Late Pleistocene. As far as current data indicate, this practice is seen in western European contexts well before it appears in Africa or eastern Asia. For example, in the premodern sites at Kabwe and Florisbad (discussed earlier), deliberate disposal of the dead is not documented. Nor is it seen in African early modern sites—for example, the Klasies River Mouth, dated at 120,000–100,000 ya (see Chapter 12).

Lest too much be read into such acts, it's important to remember that humans have lots of reasons to bury their dead. The act of burial and the meaning assigned to it are entirely cultural. Humans invented the concept of burying the dead (along with many other ways of getting rid of bodies), just as they invented all the different ways that we think about the dead. And as Paul Pettitt (2011, p. 5) describes it, "for most of the Palaeolithic what we define as 'burials' were probably very different to what we in the modern world think of as burials." The act of burial, even in the Middle Paleolithic, may have sometimes reflected shared beliefs, symbolic behavior, compassion, or status; at other times, it was just a quick and easy way to dispose of a smelly corpse. Since these two extremes represent very different acts, the problem that nags archaeologists is to identify accurately when it's one thing and not the other

In later contexts (after 35,000 ya), where modern *H. sapiens* remains are found in clear burial contexts, their treatment is considerably more complex than in Neandertal burials. In these later (Upper Paleolithic) sites, grave goods, including bone and stone tools as well as animal bones, are found more consistently and in greater concentrations. Because many Neandertal sites were excavated in the nineteenth or early twentieth century, before more rigorous archaeological methods had been developed, many of these supposed Neandertal burials are now in question. Still, the evidence seems quite clear that deliberate burial was practiced at several localities. In many cases, the body's position was deliberately modified and placed in the grave in a flexed posture (see p. 265).

Finally, as further evidence of Neandertal symbolic behavior, researchers point to the placement of supposed grave goods in burials, including stone tools, animal bones (such as cave bear), and even arrangements of flowers, together with stone slabs on top of the burials. Unfortunately, in many instances, again due to poorly documented excavation, these finds are questionable. Placement of stone tools, for example, is occasionally seen, but it apparently wasn't done consistently. In those 33 Neandertal burials for which we have adequate data, only 14 show definite association of stone tools and/or animal bones with the deceased (Klein, 1989). It's not until the Upper Paleolithic that we see a major behavioral shift, as demonstrated by more elaborate burials and the development of art.

Molecular Connections: The Genetic Evidence

With revolutionary advances in molecular biology (discussed in Chapter 3), fascinating new avenues of research have become possible in the study of earlier hominins. It's becoming fairly commonplace to extract, amplify, and sequence ancient DNA from contexts spanning the last 10,000 years or so. For example, researchers have analyzed DNA from the 5,000-year-old "Iceman" found in the Italian Alps as well the entire nuclear genome from a 4,000-year-old Inuit (Eskimo) from Greenland (Rasmussen et al., 2010).

It's much harder to find usable DNA in even more ancient remains, since the organic components, often including the DNA, have been destroyed during the mineralization process. Still, in the past few years, exciting results have been announced about DNA found in more than a dozen different Neandertal fossils dated between 50,000 and 32,000 ya. These fossils come from sites in France (including La Chapelle), Germany (from the original Neander Valley locality), Belgium, Italy, Spain, Croatia, and Russia (Krings et al., 1997, 2000; Ovchinnikov et al., 2000; Schmitz et al., 2002; Serre et al., 2004; Green et al., 2006). As we previously mentioned, recently ascertained ancient DNA evidence strongly suggests that other fossils from central Asia (Uzbekistan and two caves in southern Siberia) dated at 48,000–30,000 ya are also Neandertals (Krause et al., 2007b) or even an entirely different species (Krause et al., 2010; Reich et al., 2010).

The technique most often used in studying most Neandertal fossils involves extracting mitochondrial DNA (mtDNA), amplifying it through polymerase chain reaction (PCR; see Chapter 3), and sequencing nucleotides in parts of the molecule. Initial results from the Neandertal specimens show that these individuals are genetically more different from contemporary *H. sapiens* populations than modern human populations are from each other—in fact, about three times as much.

Major advances in molecular biology have allowed much more of the Neandertal genetic pattern to be determined with the ability to now sequence the entire mtDNA sequence in several individuals (Briggs et al., 2009) as well as big chunks of the *nuclear* DNA (which, as you may recall, contains more than 99 percent of the human genome). In fact, the most exciting breakthrough yet in ancient DNA studies was achieved in 2010 with the completion of the *entire* nuclear genome of European Neandertals (Green et al., 2010). Just a couple of years ago, this sort of achievement would have seemed like science fiction.

This new information has already allowed for crucial (as well as quite surprising) revisions in our understanding of Neandertal and early modern human evolution. First of all, Neandertal DNA is remarkably similar to modern human DNA, with 99.84 percent of it being identical. However, to detect those few (but possibly informative) genes that do differ, the team sequenced the entire genome of five modern individuals (two from Africa and one each from China, France, and New Guinea). To the surprise of almost everyone, the researchers found that many people today still have Neandertal genes! What's more, these Neandertal genes are found only in non-Africans, strongly suggesting that interbreeding occurred between Neandertals and modern *H. sapiens* after the latter had emigrated out of Africa. In fact, the three modern non-African individuals used for comparison in this study all had the same amount of Neandertal DNA. What makes this finding even more startling is the fact that the three individuals evaluated come from widely scattered regions (western Europe, China, and the far South Pacific). Further evidence, including complete genomes from another seven modern people from even more dispersed populations, have further confirmed these findings (Reich et al., 2010).

The best (and simplest) hypothesis for this genetic pattern is that shortly after modern *H. sapiens* migrants left Africa, a few of them interbred with Neandertals *before* these people and their descendants dispersed to other areas of the world. The best guess is that this intermixing between the two groups occurred in the Middle East, likely sometime between 80,000 and 50,000 ya. DNA data from more individuals, both within and outside of Africa, will help substantiate this hypothesis. For the moment, the degree of interbreeding appears to be small but still significant—about 1 to 4 percent of the total genome for living non-Africans.

Another quite astonishing molecular finding also came in 2010 during the analysis of the Denisovan DNA from Siberia. These ancient hominins from central Asia quite possibly represent a different branch of recent human evolution (Reich et al., 2010). They are also more closely related to just *some* populations of modern humans, sharing about

4 to 5 percent of genes with contemporary people from Melanesia (a region of islands in the south Pacific, including New Guinea, located north and east of Australia). We will focus much more on the ancestral connections of modern humans in the next chapter. As you'll see, all of us derive mostly from fairly recent African ancestors. But when these African migrants came into contact with premodern humans living in Eurasia, some interbreeding occurred with at least two of these premodern groups. And we can tell this by distinctive genetic "signatures" that can still be found in living people.

What's more, we've already had tantalizing clues of how we differ from Neandertals in terms of specific genes. As the data are further analyzed and expanded, we will surely learn more about the evolutionary development of human anatomy *and* human behavior. In so doing, we'll be able to answer far more precisely that age-old question, What does it mean to be human?

Seeing Close Human Connections: Understanding Premodern Humans

As you can see, the Middle Pleistocene hominins are a very diverse group, broadly dispersed through time and space. There is considerable variation among them, and it's not easy to get a clear evolutionary picture. We know that regional populations were small and frequently isolated, and many of them probably died out and left no descendants. So it's a mistake to see an "ancestor" in every fossil find.

Still, as a group, these Middle Pleistocene premoderns do reveal some general trends. In many ways, for example, it seems that they were *transitional* between the hominins that came before them (*H. erectus*) and the ones that followed them (modern *H. sapiens*). It's not a stretch to say that all the Middle Pleistocene premoderns derived from *H. erectus* forebears and that some of them, in turn, were probably ancestors of the earliest fully modern humans.

Paleoanthropologists are certainly concerned with such broad generalities as these, but they also want to focus on meaningful anatomical, environmental, and behavioral details as well as the underlying processes. So they consider the regional variability displayed by particular fossil samples as significant— but just *how* significant is debatable. In addition, increasingly sophisticated theoretical and technological approaches are being used to better understand the processes that shaped the evolution of later *Homo* at both macroevolutionary and microevolutionary levels.

Scientists, like all humans, assign names or labels to phenomena, a point we addressed when discussing classification in Chapter 5. Paleoanthropologists are certainly no exception. Yet, work-

ing from a common evolutionary foundation, paleoanthropologists still come to different conclusions about the most appropriate way to interpret the Middle/Late Pleistocene hominins. Consequently, a variety of species names have been proposed in recent years.

Paleoanthropologists who advocate an extreme lumping approach recognize only one species for all the premodern humans discussed in this chapter. These premoderns are classified as *Homo sapiens* and are thus lumped together with modern humans, although they're partly distinguished by such terminology as "archaic *H. sapiens*." As we've noted, this degree of lumping is no longer supported by most researchers. Alternatively, a second, less extreme view postulates modest species diversity

Figure 11-22

(a) Phylogeny of genus *Homo*. Only very modest species diversity is implied. (b) Phylogeny of genus *Homo* showing considerable species diversity (after Foley, 2002).

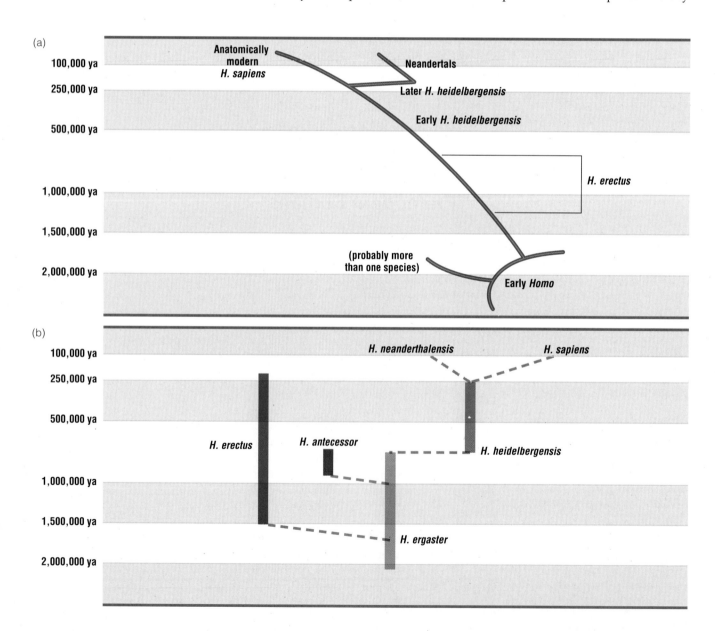

and labels the earlier premoderns as *H. heidelbergensis* (**Fig. 11-22a**).

At the other end of the spectrum, more enthusiastic paleontological splitters have identified at least two (or more) species distinct from *H. sapiens*. The most important of these, *H. heidelbergensis* and *H. neanderthalensis*, have been discussed earlier. This more complex evolutionary interpretation is shown in **Figure 11-22b**.

We addressed similar differences of interpretation in Chapters 8 and 9, and we know that disparities like these can be frustrating to students who are new to paleoanthropology. The proliferation of new names is confusing, and it might seem that experts in the field are endlessly arguing about what to call the fossils.

Fortunately, it's not quite that bad. There's actually more agreement than you might think. No one doubts that all these hominins are closely related to each other as well as to modern humans. And everyone agrees that only some of the fossil samples represent populations that left descendants. Where paleoanthropologists disagree has to do with which hominins are the most likely to be closely related to later hominins. The grouping of hominins into evolutionary clusters (clades) and assigning different names to them is a reflection of different interpretations—and, more fundamentally, of somewhat different philosophies.

But we shouldn't emphasize these naming and classification debates too much. Most paleoanthropologists recognize that a great deal of these disagreements result from simple, practical considerations. Even the most enthusiastic splitters acknowledge that the fossil "species" are not true species as defined by the biological species concept (see Chapter 5). As prominent paleoanthropologist Robert Foley puts it, "It is unlikely they are all biological species. . . . These are probably a mixture of real biological species and evolving lineages of subspecies. In other words, they could potentially have interbred, but owing to allopatry [that is, geographical separation] were unlikely to have had the opportunity" (Foley, 2002, p. 33).

Even so, Foley, along with an increasing number of other professionals, distinguishes these different fossil samples with species names to highlight their distinct position in hominin evolution. That is, these hominin groups are more loosely defined as paleospecies (see Chapter 5) rather than as fully biological species. Giving distinct hominin samples a separate (species) name makes them more easily identifiable to other researchers and makes various cladistic hypotheses more explicit—and equally important, more directly testable.

The hominins that best illustrate these issues are the Neandertals. Fortunately, they're also the best known, represented by dozens of well-preserved individuals and also a complete genome. With all this evidence, researchers can systematically test and evaluate many of the differing hypotheses.

Are Neandertals very closely related to modern *H. sapiens*? Certainly. Are they physically and behaviorally somewhat distinct from both ancient and fully modern humans? Yes. Does this mean that Neandertals are a fully separate biological species from modern humans and therefore theoretically incapable of fertilely interbreeding with modern people? Almost certainly not. Finally, then, should Neandertals really be placed in a separate species from *H. sapiens*? For most purposes, it doesn't matter, since the distinction at some point is arbitrary. Speciation is, after all, a *dynamic* process. Fossil groups like the Neandertals represent just one point in this process (see Chapter 5).

We can view Neandertals as a distinctive side branch of later hominin evolution. It is not unreasonable to say that Neandertals were likely an incipient species. The lesser-known "Denisovans" from Siberia probably represent another partially distinct incipient species, separate from both Neandertals and early modern humans. Given enough time and enough isolation, Neandertals and Denisovans likely would have separated completely from their modern human contemporaries. The new DNA evidence suggests that they were partly on their way, but not yet reaching full speciation from *Homo sapiens*. Their fate, in a sense, was decided for them as more successful competitors expanded into their habitats. These highly successful hominins were fully modern humans, and in the next chapter we'll focus on their story.

Summary of Main Topics

▶ Premodern humans from the Middle Pleistocene show similarities both with their predecessors (*H. erectus*) and with their successors (*H. sapiens*). They've also been found in many areas of the Old World—in Africa, Asia, and Europe.

▶ Most paleoanthropologists call the majority of Middle Pleistocene fossils *H. heidelbergensis*. Similarities between the African and European Middle Pleistocene hominin samples suggest that they all can be reasonably seen as part of this same species, although contemporaneous Asian fossils don't fit as neatly into this model. Further support for this view comes from the Middle Paleolithic archaeological record, which doesn't vary consistently across premodern human species.

▶ Neandertals have been considered quite distinct from modern *H. sapiens*, but recent genetic evidence confirms that some interbreeding took place between these hominins (likely 80,000–50,000 ya).

▶ The composite tool was one of the most significant Middle Paleolithic technological innovations. It enabled the creation of new kinds of tools, made many existing tools more effective, and may have coevolved with grammatical language. The pace of cultural change began to accelerate as the use of composite tools became widespread.

In "What's Important," you'll find a useful summary of the most significant premodern human fossils discussed in this chapter.

What's Important Key Fossil Discoveries of Premodern Humans

Dates (ya)	Region	Site	Hominin	The Big Picture
50,000	Western Europe	**La Chapelle** (France)	Neandertal	Most famous Neandertal discovery; led to false interpretation of primitive, bent-over creature
110,000	Southwestern Asia	**Tabun** (Israel)	Neandertal	Best evidence of early Neandertal morphology in S. W. Asia
130,000	South Africa	**Kabwe** (Broken Hill, Zambia)	*H. heidelbergensis*	Transitional-looking fossil; perhaps a close ancestor of early *H. sapiens* in Africa
?600,000–400,000	Western Europe	**Sima de los Huesos** (Atapuerca, northern Spain)	*H. heidelbergensis* (early Neandertal)	Very early evidence of Neandertal ancestry.
600,000	East Africa	**Bodo** (Ethiopia)	*H. heidelbergensis*	Earliest evidence of *H. heidelbergensis* in Africa—and possibly ancestral to later *H. sapiens*

© Cengage Learning 2013

Critical Thinking Questions

1. Why are the Middle Pleistocene hominins called premodern humans? In what ways are they human?

2. What is the general popular conception of Neandertals? Do you agree with this view? (Cite both anatomical and archaeological evidence to support your conclusion.)

3. What evidence suggests that Neandertals deliberately buried their dead? Do you think the fact that they buried their dead is important? Why? How would you interpret this behavior (remembering that Neandertals were not identical to us)?

4. How are species defined, both for living animals and for extinct ones?

Use the Neandertals to illustrate the problems encountered in distinguishing species among extinct hominins. Contrast specifically the interpretation of Neandertals as a distinct species with the interpretation of Neandertals as a subspecies of *H. sapiens*.

Paleoanthropology/ Fossil Hominins

The Origin and Dispersal of Modern Humans

LEARNING OBJECTIVES

After you have mastered the material in this chapter, you will be able to:

▶ Describe the time frame and geographic locations for the earliest evidence of modern humans in Africa as well as elsewhere in the Old World.

▶ Compare the different models accounting for the origin and dispersal of modern humans and evaluate how fossil and genetic evidence support these models.

▶ Explain from the archaeological evidence how and why modern human behavior in the Upper Paleolithic differed from that of their Middle Paleolithic predecessors.

Today, our species numbers more than 7 billion individuals, spread all over the globe, but there are no other living hominins but us. Our last hominin cousin disappeared several thousand years ago. Perhaps about 80,000 ya, modern peoples in the Middle East encountered beings that walked on two legs, hunted large animals, made fire, lived in caves, and fashioned complex tools. These beings were the Neandertals, and imagine what it would have been like to be among a band of modern people following game into what is now Israel and coming across these other *humans*, so like yourself in some ways, yet so different in others. It's almost certain that such encounters took place, perhaps many times. How strange would it have been to look into the face of a being sharing so much with you, yet a total stranger both culturally and, to some degree, biologically as well? What would you think seeing a Neandertal for the first time? What do you imagine a Neandertal would think seeing you?

Sometime, probably close to 200,000 ya, the first modern *Homo sapiens* populations appeared in Africa. Within 150,000 years or so, their descendants had spread across most of the Old World, even expanding as far as Australia (and somewhat later to the Americas).

Who were they, and why were these early modern people so successful? What was the fate of the other hominins, such as the Neandertals, who were already long established in areas outside Africa? Did they evolve as well, leaving descendants among some living human populations? Or were they completely swept aside and replaced by African emigrants?

In this chapter, we'll discuss the origin and dispersal of modern *H. sapiens*. All contemporary populations are placed within this species (and the same subspecies as well). Most paleoanthropologists agree that several fossil forms, dating back as far as 100,000 ya, should also be included in the same *fully* modern group as us. In addition, some recently discovered fossils from Africa also are clearly *H. sapiens*, but they show some (minor) differences from living people and could thus be described as *near-modern*. Still, we can think of these early African humans as well as their somewhat later relatives as "us."

These first modern humans, who evolved by 195,000 ya, are probably descendants of some of the premodern humans we discussed in Chapter 11. In particular, African populations of *H. heidelbergensis* are the most likely ancestors of the earliest modern *H. sapiens*. The evolutionary events that took place as modern humans made the transition from more ancient premodern forms and then dispersed throughout most of the Old World were relatively rapid, and they raise several basic questions:

1. When (approximately) did modern humans first appear?
2. Where did the transition take place? Did it occur in just one region or in several?
3. What was the pace of evolutionary change? How quickly did the transition occur?
4. How did the dispersal of modern humans to other areas of the Old World (outside their area of origin) take place?
5. What does archaeological evidence tell us about important cultural characteristics of early modern people that allowed them to quickly and successfully disperse throughout the Old World after about 50,000 ya?

These questions concerning the origins and early dispersal of modern *Homo sapiens* continue to fuel much controversy among paleoanthropologists. And it's no wonder, for at least some early *H. sapiens* populations are the direct ancestors of all contemporary humans. They were much like us skeletally, genetically, and (most likely) behaviorally. In fact, it's the various hypotheses regarding the behaviors and abilities of our most immediate predecessors that have most fired the imaginations of scientists and laypeople alike. In every major respect, these are the first hominins that we can confidently refer to as *fully* human.

This chapter also examines archaeological evidence that helps to place Late Pleistocene human biological changes into a cultural context, which in turn gives us a better understanding of the biocultural evolutionary roots of our species. The Upper Paleolithic period begins in western Europe around 40,000 ya and ends roughly 10,000 ya. Unlike the extraordinarily slow rates of cultural change that marked the Lower and Middle Paleolithic periods, the Upper Paleolithic witnessed profound changes in human culture. By 12,000–10,000 ya, the technology of Upper Paleolithic hunter-gatherers was as diverse and effective as that of historically documented hunter-gatherers.

The evolutionary story of *Homo sapiens* is really the biological autobiography of all of us. It's a story that still has many unanswered questions; but some general theories can help us organize the diverse information that's now available.

Approaches to Understanding Modern Human Origins

In attempting to organize and explain modern human origins, paleoanthropologists have proposed a few major theories that can be summarized into two contrasting views: the *regional continuity model* and various versions of *replacement models*. These two views are quite distinct, and in some ways they're completely opposed to each other. Since so much of our contemporary view of modern human origins is influenced by the debates linked to these differing theories, let's start by briefly reviewing them. Then we'll turn to the fossil and archaeological evidence itself to see what it can contribute to answering the five questions we've posed.

The Regional Continuity Model: Multiregional Evolution

The regional continuity model is most closely associated with paleoanthropologist Milford Wolpoff, of the University of Michigan, and his associates (Wolpoff et al., 1994, 2001). They suggest that local populations—not all, of course—in Europe, Asia, and Africa continued their indigenous evolutionary development from premodern Middle Pleistocene forms to anatomically modern humans. But if that's true, then we have to ask how so many different local populations around the globe happened to evolve with such similar morphology. In other words, how could anatomically modern humans arise separately in different continents and end up so much alike, both physically and genetically? The multiregional model answers this question by (1) denying that the earliest modern *H. sapiens* populations originated *exclusively* in Africa and (2) asserting that significant levels of gene flow (migration) between various geographically dispersed premodern populations were extremely likely throughout the Pleistocene.

Through gene flow and natural selection, according to the multiregional hypothesis, local populations would *not* have evolved totally independently from one another, and such mixing would have "prevented speciation between the regional lineages and thus maintained human beings as a *single*, although obviously *polytypic* [see Chapter 4], species throughout the Pleistocene" (Smith et al., 1989). Thus, under a multiregional model, there are no taxonomic distinctions between modern and premodern hominins. That is, all hominins following *H. erectus* are classified as a single species: *H. sapiens*.

In light of emerging evidence over the last few years, almost all advocates of the multiregional model aren't dogmatic about the degree of regional continuity. They recognize that a strong influence of modern humans evolving *first* in Africa has left an imprint on populations throughout the world that is still detectable today. Nevertheless, the most recent data suggest that multiregional models no longer tell us much about the origins of modern humans; nor do they seem to provide much information regarding the dispersal of modern *H. sapiens*.

Replacement Models

Replacement models all emphasize that modern humans first evolved in Africa and only later dispersed to other parts of the world, where they replaced those hominins already living in these other regions. In recent years, two versions of such replacement models have been proposed, the first emphasizing *complete* replacement. The complete replacement model proposes that anatomically modern populations arose in Africa within the last 200,000 years and then migrated from Africa, completely replacing populations in Europe and Asia (Stringer and Andrews, 1988). It's important to note that this model doesn't account for a transition from premodern forms to modern *H. sapiens* anywhere in the world except Africa. A critical deduction of the original Stringer and Andrews theory argued that anatomically modern humans appeared as the result of a biological speciation event. So in this view, migrating African modern *H. sapiens* could not have interbred with local non-African populations, because the African modern humans were a *biologically* different species. Taxonomically, all of the premodern populations outside Africa would, in this view, be classified as belonging to different species of *Homo*. For example, the Neandertals would be classified as *H. neanderthalensis*. This speciation explanation fits nicely with, and in fact helps explain, *complete* replacement; but Stringer has more recently stated that he isn't insistent on this issue. He does suggest that even though there may have been potential for interbreeding, apparently very little actually took place.

Interpretations of the latter phases of human evolution have recently been greatly extended by newly available genetic techniques, and they've recently been applied to the question of modern human origins. Using numerous contemporary human populations as a data source, geneticists have precisely determined and compared a wide variety of DNA sequences. The theoretical basis of this approach assumes that at least some of the genetic patterning seen today can act as a kind of window into the past. In particular, the genetic patterns observed today between geographically widely dispersed humans are thought to partly reflect migrations occurring in the Late Pleistocene. This hypothesis can be fur-

ther tested as contemporary population genetic patterning is better documented.

As these new data accumulate, consistent relationships are emerging, especially in showing that indigenous African populations have far greater diversity than do populations from elsewhere in the world. The consistency of the results is highly significant, because it strongly supports an African origin for modern humans and some mode of replacement elsewhere. What's more, as we discussed in Chapter 4, new, even more complete data on contemporary population patterning for large portions of nuclear DNA further confirm these conclusions.

Certainly, most molecular data come from contemporary species, since DNA is not *usually* preserved in long-dead individuals. Even so, exceptions do occur, and these cases open another genetic window—one that can directly illuminate the past. As discussed in Chapter 11, mtDNA has been recovered from more than a dozen Neandertal fossils.

In addition, researchers have recently sequenced the mtDNA of nine ancient fully modern *H. sapiens* skeletons from sites in Italy, France, the Czech Republic, and Russia (Caramelli et al., 2003, 2006; Kulikov et al., 2004; Serre et al., 2004). MtDNA data, however, are somewhat limited because mtDNA is a fairly small segment of DNA, and it is transmitted between generations as a single unit; genetically it acts like a single gene. Indeed, in just the last few years, comparisons of Neandertal and early modern mtDNA led to some significant misinterpretations. Clearly, data from the vastly larger nuclear genome are far more informative.

As we discussed in Chapter 11, a giant leap forward occurred in 2010 when sequencing of the entire Neandertal nuclear genome was completed. Researchers immediately compared the Neandertal genome with that of people living today and discovered that some populations still retain some Neandertal genes (Green et al., 2010). Without doubt, we can now conclude that some interbreeding took place between Neandertals and modern humans, arguing against *complete* replacement and supporting some form of *partial* replacement.

Partial Replacement Models

For a number of years, several paleoanthropologists, including Günter Bräuer, of the University of Hamburg, suggested that very little interbreeding occurred—a view supported more recently by John Relethford (2001) in what he described as "mostly out of Africa." The new findings from DNA analysis further confirm that the degree of interbreeding was modest, ranging from 1 to 4 percent in modern populations outside Africa; moreover, contemporary Africans have no trace of Neandertal genes, suggesting that any interbreeding occurred *after* modern humans migrated out of Africa. This would seem obvious when you consider that (as far as we know) Neandertals never lived anywhere in Africa. For our African ancestors to even have the opportunity to mate with a Neandertal, they would first have to leave their African homeland. Another fascinating discovery is that among the modern people so far sampled (five individuals), the three non-Africans all have some Neandertal DNA. The tentative conclusion from these preliminary findings suggests that the interbreeding occurred soon after modern humans emigrated out of Africa. The most likely scenario suggests that the intermixing occurred around 80,000–50,000 ya, quite possibly in the Middle East.

These results are very new and are partly based on very limited samples of living people. Technological innovations in DNA sequencing are occurring at an amazing pace, making it faster and cheaper. But it is still a challenge to sequence all the 3 billion+ nucleotides each of us has in our nuclear genome. When we have full genomes from more individuals living in many more geographical areas, the patterns of modern human dispersal should become clearer. Did the modern human-Neandertal interbreeding occur primarily in one area, or did it happen in several regions? And did some modern human populations several thousand years ago inter-

breed with their Neandertal cousins more than others did? Even more interesting, were there still other premodern human groups still around when modern humans emigrated from Africa—and did they interbreed, too?

From his study of fossil remains, Fred Smith, of Illinois State University, has proposed an "assimilation" model that hypothesizes that more interbreeding did take place, at least in some regions (Smith, 2002). To test these hypotheses and answer all the fascinating questions, we will also need more whole-genome DNA from ancient remains, particularly from early modern human skeletons. This, too, won't be an easy task; remember, it took four years of intensive effort to decode and reassemble the Neandertal genome. Then, too, we need to be aware that DNA thousands of years old can be obtained from hominin remains that are found in environments that have been persistently cold (or at least cool). In tropical areas, DNA degrades rapidly; so it seems a long shot that any usable DNA can be obtained from hominins that lived in many extremely large and significant regions (for example, Africa and Southeast Asia).

The Earliest Discoveries of Modern Humans

Africa

In Africa, several early (around 200,000–100,000 ya) fossils have been interpreted as fully anatomically modern forms (**Fig. 12-1**, on p. 284). The earliest of these specimens comes from Omo Kibish, in southernmost Ethiopia. Using radiometric techniques, redating of a fragmentary skull (Omo 1) demonstrates that, coming from 195,000 ya, this is the earliest modern human yet found in Africa—or, for that matter, anywhere else (McDougall et al., 2005). An interesting aspect of fossils from this site concerns the variation shown between the two individuals. Omo 1 (**Fig. 12-2**) is essentially modern in most respects (note the presence of a chin; see **Fig. 12-3**, where a variety

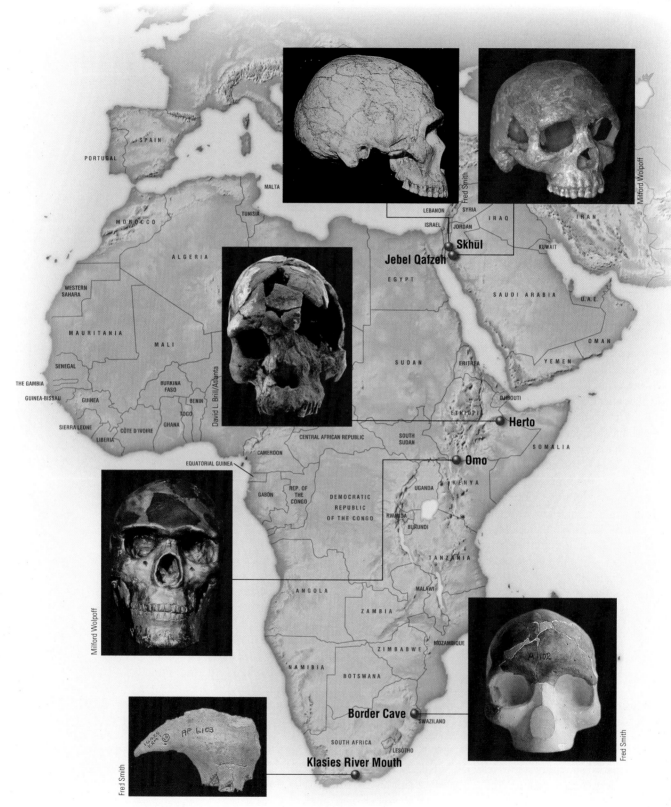

Figure 12-1

Modern humans from Africa and the Near East.

Figure 12-2

Reconstructed skull of Omo 1, an early modern human from Ethiopia, dated to 195,000 ya. Note the clear presence of a chin.

© Milford Wolpoff

of modern human cranial characteristics are shown), but another ostensibly contemporary cranium (Omo 2) is much more robust and less modern in morphology.

Somewhat later modern human fossils come from the Klasies River Mouth on the south coast of Africa and Border Cave, just slightly to the north. Using relatively new techniques, paleoanthropologists have dated both sites to about 120,000–80,000 ya. The original geological context at Border Cave is uncertain, and the fossils may be younger than those at Klasies River Mouth. Although recent reevaluation of the Omo site has provided much more dependable dating, there are still questions remaining about some of the other early modern fossils from Africa. Nevertheless, it now seems very likely that early modern humans appeared in East Africa by shortly after 200,000 ya and had migrated to southern Africa by approximately 100,000 ya. More recently discovered fossils are helping confirm this view.

Herto The announcement in 2003 of well-preserved *and* well-dated *H. sapiens* fossils from Ethiopia has gone a long

way toward filling gaps in the African fossil record. As a result, these fossils are helping to resolve key issues regarding modern human origins. Tim White, of the University of California, Berkeley, and his colleagues have been working for three decades in the Middle Awash area of Ethiopia. They've discovered a remarkable array of early fossil hominins (*Ardipithecus* and *Australopithecus*) as well as somewhat later forms (*H. erectus*). From this same area in the Middle Awash, highly significant new discoveries came to light in 1997. For simplicity, these new hominins are referred to as the Herto remains.

These Herto fossils include a mostly complete adult cranium, an incomplete adult cranium, a fairly complete (but heavily reconstructed) child's cranium, and a few other cranial fragments. Following lengthy reconstruction and detailed comparative studies, White and colleagues were prepared to announce their findings in 2003.

What they said caused quite a sensation among paleoanthropologists, and it was reported in the popular press as well. First, well-controlled radiometric dating ($^{40}Ar/^{39}Ar$) securely places the

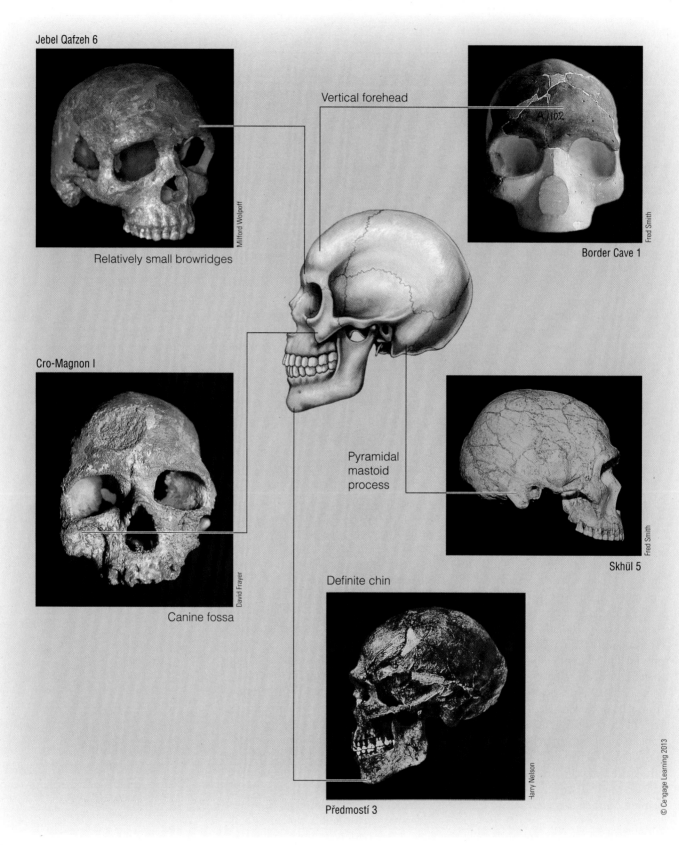

Jebel Qafzeh 6

Relatively small browridges

Vertical forehead

Border Cave 1

Cro-Magnon I

Canine fossa

Pyramidal mastoid process

Skhūl 5

Definite chin

Předmostí 3

Milford Wolpoff

Fred Smith

David Frayer

Fred Smith

Jarry Nelson

© Cengage Learning 2013

Figure 12-3

Morphology and variation in early specimens of modern *Homo sapiens*.

remains at between 160,000 and 154,000 ya, making these the best-dated hominin fossils from this time period from anywhere in the world. Note that this date is clearly *older* than for any other equally modern *H. sapiens* from anywhere else in the world. Moreover, the preservation and morphology of the remains leave little doubt about their relationship to modern humans. The mostly complete adult cranium (**Fig. 12-4**) is very large, with an extremely long cranial vault. The cranial capacity is 1,450 cm³, well within the range of contemporary *H. sapiens* populations. The skull is also in some respects heavily built, with a large, arching browridge in front and a large, projecting occipital protuberance in back. The face does not project, in stark contrast to Eurasian Neandertals.

The overall impression is that this individual is clearly *Homo sapiens*—as are the other fossils from the site. Following comprehensive statistical studies, Tim White and colleagues concluded that, while not identical to modern people, the Herto fossils are near-modern. That is, these fossils "sample a population that is on the verge of ana-

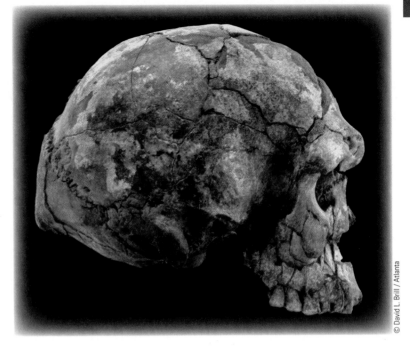

tomical modernity but not yet fully modern." (White et al., 2003, p. 745). To distinguish these individuals from fully modern humans (*H. sapiens sapiens*), the researchers have placed them in a newly defined subspecies: *Homo*

Figure 12-4

Herto cranium from Ethiopia, dated to 160,000–154,000 ya. This is the best-preserved early modern *H. sapiens* cranium yet found.

© David L. Brill / Atlanta

At a Glance

Key Early Modern *Homo sapiens* Discoveries from Africa and the Near East

DATES (YA)	SITE	HOMININ	EVOLUTIONARY SIGNIFICANCE
110,000	Qafzeh (Israel)	*H. sapiens sapiens*	Large sample (at least 20 individuals); definitely modern, but some individuals fairly robust; early date (>100,000 ya)
115,000	Skhūl (Israel)	*H. sapiens sapiens*	Minimum of 10 individuals; like Qafzeh modern morphology, but slightly earlier date (and earliest modern humans known outside of Africa)
160,000–154,000	Herto (Ethiopia)	*H. sapiens idaltu*	Very well-preserved cranium; dated > 150,000 ya, the best-preserved early modern human found anywhere
195,000	Omo (Ethiopia)	*H. sapiens*	Dated to almost 200,000 ya and the oldest modern human found anywhere; two crania found, one more modern looking than the other

© Cengage Learning 2013

Figure 12-5

Mt. Carmel, studded with caves, was home to *H. sapiens sapiens* at Skhūl (and to Neandertals at Tabun and Kebara).

© David Frayer

sapiens idaltu. The word *idaltu*, from the Afar language, means "elder."

What can we conclude? First, we can say that these new finds strongly support an African origin of modern humans. The Herto fossils are the right age, and they come from the right place. Besides that, they look much like what we might have predicted. Considering all these facts, they're the most conclusive fossil evidence yet indicating an African origin of modern humans. What's more, this fossil evidence is compatible with a great deal of strong genetic data indicating some form of replacement model for human origins.

The Near East

In Israel, researchers found early modern *H. sapiens* fossils, including the remains of at least 10 individuals, in the Skhūl Cave at Mt. Carmel (**Figs. 12-5** and **12-6a**). Also from Israel, the Qafzeh Cave has yielded the remains of at least 20 individuals (**Fig. 12-6b**). Although their overall configuration is definitely modern, some specimens show certain premodern features. Skhūl has been dated to between 130,000 and 100,000 ya (Grün et al., 2005), while Qafzeh has been dated to around 120,000–92,000 ya (Grün and Stringer, 1991). The time line for these fossil discoveries is shown in **Figure 12-7**.

Such early dates for modern specimens pose some problems for those advocating the influence of local evolution, as proposed by the multiregional model. How early do the premodern populations—that is, Neandertals—appear in the Near East? A recent chronometric calibration for the Tabun Cave suggests a date as early as 120,000 ya.

Figure 12-6

(a) Skhūl 5. (b) Qafzeh 6. These specimens from Israel are thought to be representatives of early modern *Homo sapiens*. The vault height, forehead, and lack of prognathism are modern traits.

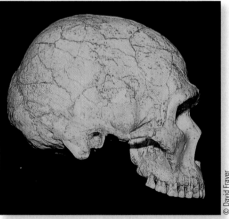

© David Frayer

(a)

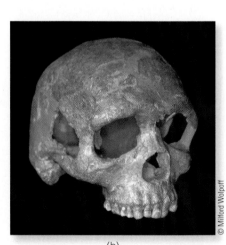

© Milford Wolpoff

(b)

This dating for these sites, all located *very* close to each other, suggests that there's considerable chronological overlap in the occupation of the Near East by Neandertals and modern humans. This chronological overlap in such a small area is the reason anthropologists have suggested this region as a likely place where Neandertals and modern humans might well have interbred.

Asia

There are seven early anatomically modern human localities in China, the most significant of which are Upper Cave at Zhoukoudian, Tianyuan Cave (very near Zhoukoudian), and Ordos, in Mongolia (**Fig. 12-8**). The fossils from these Chinese sites are all fully modern, and all are considered to be from the Late Pleistocene, with dates probably less than 40,000 ya. Upper Cave at Zhoukoudian has been dated to 27,000 ya, and the fossils consist of three skulls found with cultural remains in a cave site that humans clearly regularly inhabited. Considerable antiquity has also been proposed for the Mongolian Ordos skull, but this dating is not very

secure and has therefore been questioned (Trinkaus, 2005).

In addition, some researchers (Tiemel et al., 1994) have suggested that the Jinniushan skeleton discussed in Chapter 10 hints at modern features in China as early as 200,000 ya. If this date—as early as that proposed for direct antecedents of modern *H. sapiens* in Africa—should prove accurate, it would cast doubt on replacement models. This position, however, is a minority view and is not supported by more recent and more detailed analyses.

Just about 4 miles down the road from the famous Zhoukoudian Cave is another cave called Tianyuan, the source of an important find in 2003. Consisting of a fragmentary skull, a few teeth, and several postcranial bones, this fossil is accurately dated by radiocarbon at close to 40,000 ya (Shang et al., 2007). The skeleton shows mostly modern features, but has a few archaic characteristics as well. The Chinese and American team that has analyzed the remains from Tianyuan proposes that they indicate an African origin of modern humans, but there is also evidence of at least some interbreeding in China with resident archaic (that

Figure 12-7

Time line of modern *Homo sapiens* discoveries. Note that most dates are approximations. Question marks indicate those estimates that are most tentative.

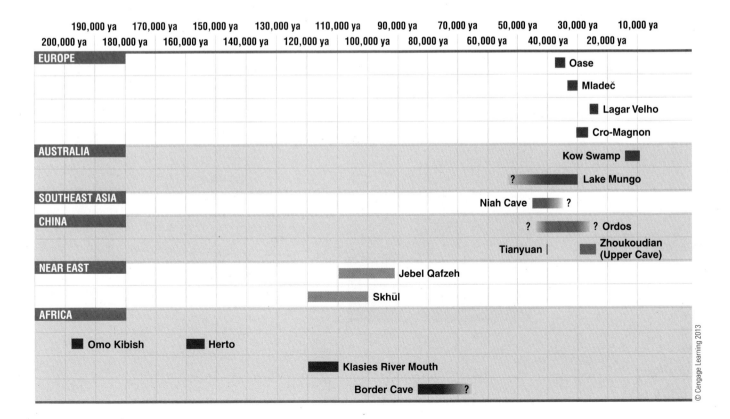

© Cengage Learning 2013

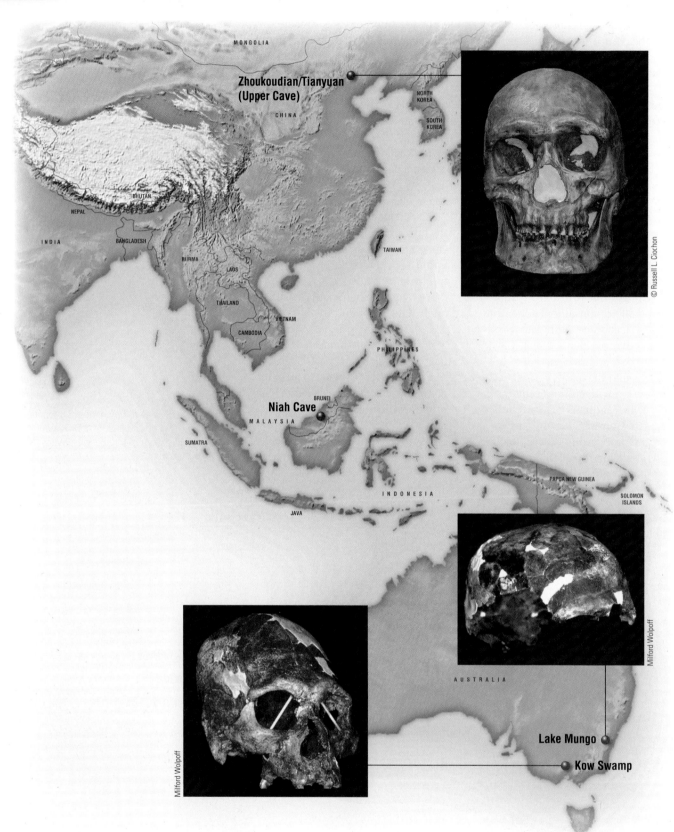

Figure 12-8

Anatomically modern *Homo sapiens* in Asia and Australia.

is, premodern) populations. More complete analysis and (with some luck) further finds at this new site will help provide a better picture of early modern *H. sapiens* in China. For the moment, this is the best-dated early modern *H. sapiens* from China and one of the two earliest from anywhere in Asia.

The other early fossil is a partial skull from Niah Cave, on the north coast of the Indonesian island of Borneo (see Fig. 12-8). This is actually not a new find and was, in fact, first excavated more than 50 years ago. However, until recent more extensive analysis, it had been relegated to the paleoanthropological back shelf due to uncertainties regarding its archaeological context and dating. Now all this has changed with a better understanding of the geology of the site and new dates strongly supporting an age of more than 35,000 ya and most likely as old as 45,000–40,000 ya, making it perhaps older than Tianyuan (Barker et al., 2007). Like its Chinese counterparts, the Niah skull is modern in morphology. It's hypothesized that some population contemporaneous with Niah or somewhat earlier inhabitants of Indonesia were perhaps the first group to colonize Australia.

Australia

During glacial times, the Indonesian islands were joined to the Asian mainland, but Australia wasn't. It's likely that by 50,000 ya, modern humans inhabited Sahul—the area including New Guinea and Australia. Bamboo rafts may have been used to cross the ocean between islands, and this would certainly have been dangerous and difficult. It's not known just where the ancestral Australians came from, but as noted, Indonesia has been suggested.

Human occupation of Australia appears to have occurred quite early, with some archaeological sites dating to 55,000 ya. There's some controversy about the dating of the earliest Australian human remains, which are all modern *H. sapiens*. The earliest finds so far discovered have come from Lake Mungo, in southeastern Australia (see Fig. 12-8). In agreement with archaeological context and radiocarbon dates, the

hominins from this site have been dated at approximately 30,000–25,000 ya.

Fossils from a site called Kow Swamp suggest that the people who lived there between about 14,000 and 9,000 ya were different from the more gracile early Australian forms from Lake Mungo (see Fig. 12-8). The Kow Swamp fossils display certain archaic cranial traits—such as receding foreheads, heavy supraorbital tori, and thick bones—that are difficult to explain, since these features contrast with the postcranial anatomy, which matches that of living indigenous Australians. Regardless of the different morphology of these later Australians, new genetic evidence indicates that all native Australians are descendants of a *single* migration dating back to about 50,000 ya (Hudjashou et al., 2007).

Central Europe

Central Europe has been a source of many fossil finds, including the earliest anatomically modern *H. sapiens* yet discovered anywhere in Europe. Dated to 35,000 ya, these early *H. sapiens* fossils come from recent discoveries at the Oase Cave, in Romania (**Fig. 12-9**). Here, cranial remains of three individuals were recovered, including a complete mandible and a partial skull (**Fig. 12-10**). While quite robust, these individuals are similar to later modern specimens, as seen in the clear presence of both a chin and a canine fossa (see Fig. 12-3; Trinkaus et al., 2003).

Another early modern human site in central Europe is Mladeč, in the Czech Republic. Several individuals have been excavated here and are dated to approximately 31,000 ya. While there's some variation among the

Figure 12-9

Excavators at work within the spectacular cave at Oase, in Romania. The floor is littered with the remains of fossil animals, including the earliest dated cranial remains of *Homo sapiens* in Europe.

© Mircea Gherase

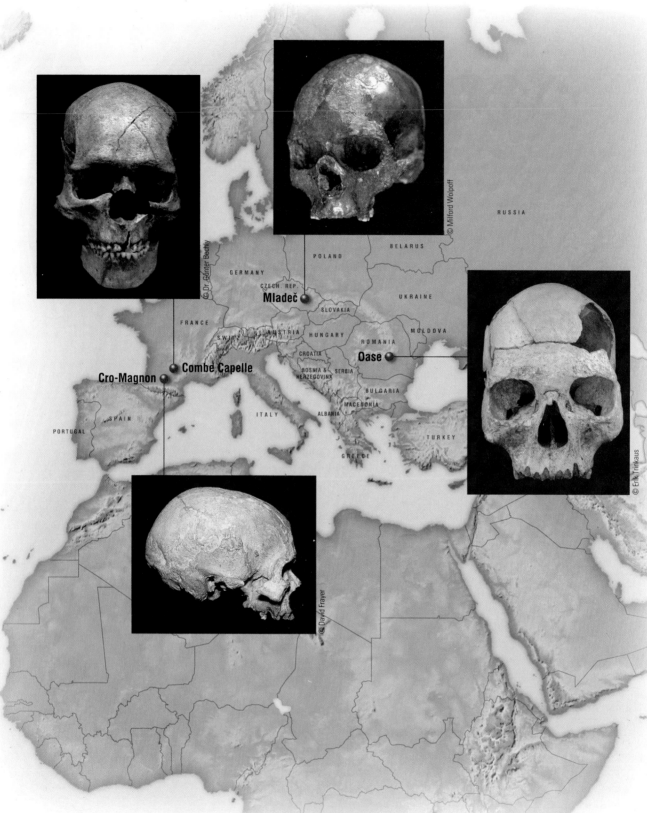

Figure 12-10

Anatomically modern humans in Europe.

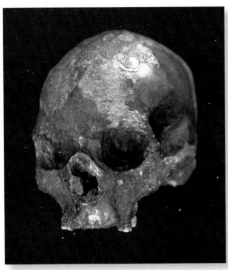

(a) © Milford Wolpoff

(b) © Robert Franciscus

Figure 12-11

The Mladeč (a) and Dolní Věstonice (b) crania, both from the Czech Republic, represent good examples of early modern *Homo sapiens* in central Europe. Along with Oase, in Romania, the evidence for early modern *Homo sapiens* appears first in central Europe before the later finds in western Europe.

crania, including some with big brow-ridges, Fred Smith (1984) is confident that they're all best classified as modern *H. sapiens* (**Fig. 12-11a**). It's clear that by 28,000 ya, modern humans were widely dispersed in central and western Europe (Trinkaus, 2005). Also from the Czech Republic and dated at about 26,000 ya, Dolní Věstonice provides another example of a central European early modern human (see **Fig. 12-11b**).

Western Europe

For several reasons, western Europe and its fossils have received more attention than other regions. Over the last 150 years, many of the scholars doing this research happened to live in western Europe, and the southern region of France also turned out to be a fossil treasure trove.

As a result of this scholarly interest, a great deal of data accumulated beginning back in the nineteenth century, with little reliable comparative information available from elsewhere in the world. Consequently, theories of human evolution were based almost exclusively on the western European material. It's only been in more recent years, with growing evidence from other areas of the world and with the application of new dating techniques, that recent human evolutionary dynamics are being seriously considered from a worldwide perspective.

Western Europe has yielded many anatomically modern human fossils, but by far the best-known sample of western European *H. sapiens* is from the **Cro-Magnon** site, a rock-shelter in southern France. At this site, the remains of eight individuals were discovered in 1868.

The Cro-Magnon materials are associated with an **Aurignacian** tool assemblage, an Upper Paleolithic industry. Dated at about 28,000 ya, these individuals represent the earliest of France's anatomically modern humans. The so-called Old Man (Cro-Magnon 1) became the original model for what was once termed the Cro-Magnon, or Upper Paleolithic, "race" of Europe (**Fig. 12-12**). Actually, of course, there's no such valid biological category, and Cro-Magnon 1 is not typical of Upper Paleolithic western Europeans—and not even all that similar to the other two male skulls found at the site.

Most of the genetic evidence, as well as the newest fossil evidence from Africa, argue against continuous local evolution producing modern groups directly from any Eurasian premodern population (in Europe, these would be Neandertals). Still, for some researchers, the issue isn't completely settled. With all the latest evidence, there's no longer much debate that a *large* genetic contribution from migrating early modern Africans influenced other groups throughout the Old World. What's being debated is just how much admixture

Cro-Magnon (crow-man´-yon)

Aurignacian Pertaining to an Upper Paleolithic stone tool industry in Europe beginning about 40,000 ya.

Figure 12-12

Cro-Magnon 1 (France). In this specimen, modern traits are quite clear. (a) Lateral view. (b) Frontal view.

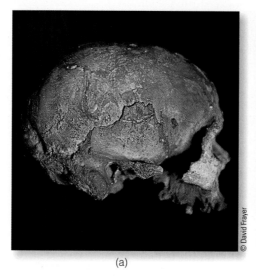

(a)

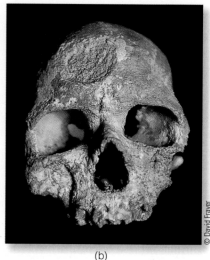

(b)

might have occurred between these migrating Africans and the resident premodern groups. For those paleo-anthropologists (for example, Trinkaus, 2005) who hypothesize that significant admixture (assimilation) occurred in western Europe as well as elsewhere, a recently discovered child's skeleton from Portugal provides some of the best skeletal evidence of possible interbreeding between Neandertals and anatomically modern *H. sapiens*. This important discovery from the Abrigo do Lagar Velho

site was excavated in late 1998 and is dated to 24,500 ya—that's at least 5,000 years more recent than the last clearly identifiable Neandertal fossil (**Fig. 12-13**). Associated with an Upper Paleolithic industry and buried with red ocher and pierced shell is a fairly complete skeleton of a 4-year-old child (Duarte et al., 1999). In studying the remains, Cidália Duarte, Erik Trinkaus, and colleagues found a highly mixed set of anatomical features. From this evidence they concluded that the young child was the result of inter-

At a Glance

Key Early Modern *Homo sapiens* Discoveries from Europe and Asia

DATES (YA)	SITE	HOMININ	EVOLUTIONARY SIGNIFICANCE
24,500	Abrigo do Lagar Velho (Portugal)	*H. sapiens sapiens*	Child's skeleton; some suggestion of possible hybrid between Neandertal and modern human—but is controversial
30,000	Cro-Magnon (France)	*H. sapiens sapiens*	Most famous early modern human find in world; earliest evidence of modern humans in France
40,000	Tianyuan Cave (China)	*H. sapiens sapiens*	Partial skull and a few postcranial bones; oldest modern human find from China
45,000–40,000	Niah Cave (Borneo, Indonesia)	*H. sapiens sapiens*	Partial skull recently redated more accurately; oldest modern human find from Asia

breeding between Neandertals and modern humans, thus supporting a partial replacement model of human origins. It's still debatable from this fossil evidence whether interbreeding with Neandertals took place in Portugal this late in time. Nevertheless, the genetic evidence is unequivocal: Neandertals and modern humans *did* interbreed at some point.

Something New and Different: The "Little People"

As we've seen, by 25,000 ya, modern humans had dispersed to all major areas of the Old World, and they would soon journey to the New World as well. But at about the same time, remnant populations of earlier hominins still survived in a few remote and isolated corners. We mentioned in Chapter 10 that populations of *Homo erectus* in Java managed to survive on this island long after their cousins had disappeared from other areas (for example, China and East Africa). What's more, even though they persisted well into the Late Pleistocene, physically these Javanese

hominins were still similar to other *H. erectus* individuals.

Even more surprising, it seems that other populations possibly branched off from some of these early inhabitants of Indonesia and either intentionally or accidentally found their way to other, smaller islands to the east. There, under even more extreme isolation pressures, they evolved in an astonishing direction. In late 2004, the world awoke to the startling announcement that an extremely small-bodied, small-brained hominin had been discovered in Liang Bua Cave, on the island of Flores, east of Java (see **Fig. 12-14**). Dubbed the "Little Lady of Flores" or simply "Flo," the remains consist of an incomplete skeleton of an adult female (LB1) as well as additional pieces from approximately 13 other individuals, which the press has collectively nicknamed "hobbits." The female skeleton is remarkable in several ways (**Fig. 12-15**), though in some ways similar to the Dmanisi hominins. First, she was barely 3 feet tall—as short as the smallest australopith—and her brain, estimated at a mere 417 cm³ (Falk et al., 2005), was no larger than that of a chimpanzee (Brown et al., 2004). Possibly most startling of all, these extraordinary hominins were still

Figure 12-13

A child's skeleton discovered at Abrigo do Lagar Velho, in Portugal. Some researchers suggest that this child may be a hybrid produced by interbreeding of Neandertals with modern humans.

© Figure 13.1 of Zilhão, J.; Trinkaus, E. (eds.)— *Portrait of the Artist as a Child. The Gravettian Human Skeleton from the Abrigo do Lagar Velho and its Archaeological Context*, Trabalhos de Arqueologia 22, Lisboa, Instituto Português de Arqueologia, 2002, 610 pages). Photo by José Paulo Ruas.

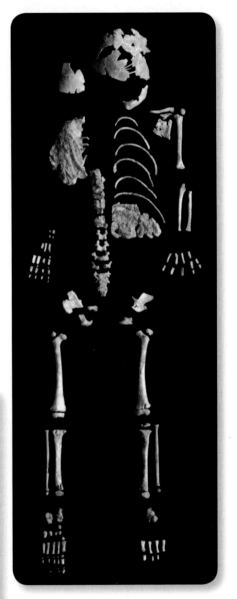

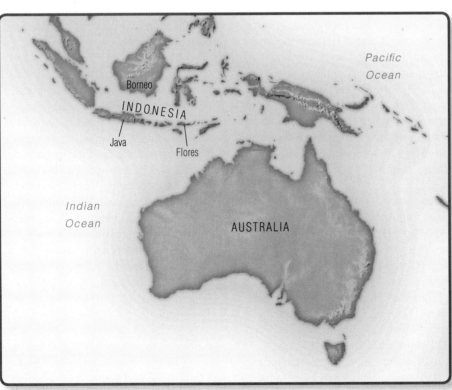

Figure 12-14

Location of the Flores site in Indonesia.

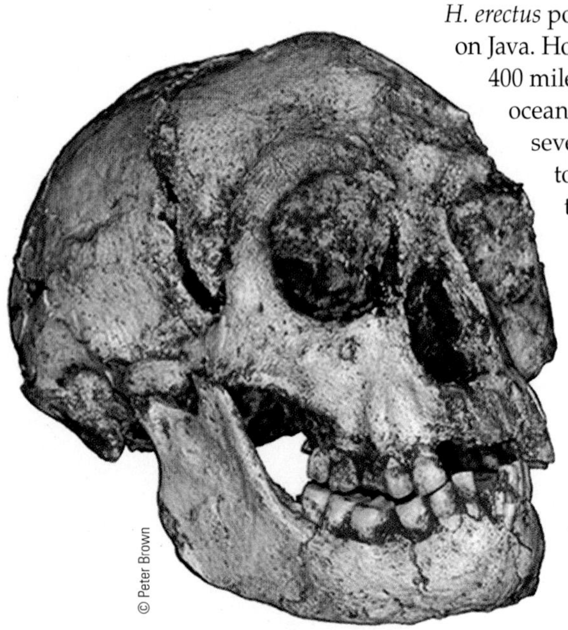

© Peter Brown

Figure 12-15

Cranium of adult female *Homo floresiensis* from Flores, Indonesia, dated to 18,000 ya.

living on Flores just 13,000 ya (Morwood et al., 2004, 2005; Wong, 2009)!

Where did they come from? As we said, their predecessors were perhaps *H. erectus* populations like those found on Java. How they got to Flores—some 400 miles away, partly over open ocean—is a mystery. There are several connecting islands, and to get from one to another these hominins may have drifted across on rafts; but there's no way to be sure of this. What's more, these little hominins were apparently living on Flores for a very long time; recently discovered stone tools have been radiometrically dated to at least 1 mya (Brumm et al., 2010). Such an ancient date, as well as the overall similarities to the Dmanisi hominins, suggest to some researchers that *Homo floresiensis* may derive from an early migration of early *Homo* to Southeast Asia (Jungers et al., 2009; Wong, 2009). In other words, this highly unusual hominin might have evolved from ancestors that left Africa even before *H. erectus* did.

How did they get to be so physically different from all other known hominins? Here we're a little more certain of the answer. Isolated island populations can quite rapidly diverge from their relatives elsewhere. Among such isolated animals, natural selection frequently favors reduced body size. For example, remains of dwarfed elephants have been found on islands in the Mediterranean as well as on some channel islands off the coast of southern California. And perhaps most interesting of all, dwarf elephants *also* evolved on Flores; they were found in the same geological beds with the little hominins. The evolutionary mechanism (called "insular dwarfing") thought to explain such extreme body size reduction in both the elephants and the hominins is an adaptation to reduced resources, with natural selection favoring smaller body size (Schauber and Falk, 2008).

Other than short stature, what did the Flores hominins look like? In their cranial shape, thickness of cranial bone,

and dentition, they most resemble *H. erectus*, and specifically those from Dmanisi. Still, they have some derived features that also set them apart from all other hominins. For that reason, many researchers have placed them in a separate species, *Homo floresiensis*.

Immediately following the first publication of the Flores remains, intense controversy arose regarding their interpretation (Jacob et al., 2006; Martin et al., 2006). Some researchers have argued that the small-brained hominin ("Flo," technically called LB1) is actually a pathological modern *H. sapiens* individual afflicted with a severe disorder (microcephaly has been proposed, among others). The researchers who did most of the initial work reject this conclusion and provide some further details to support their original interpretation (for example, Dean Falk and colleagues' further analysis of microcephalic endocasts; Falk et al., 2009).

The conclusion that among this already small-bodied island population the one individual found with a preserved cranium happened to be afflicted with a severe (and rare) growth defect is highly unlikely. Yet, it must also be recognized that long-term, extreme isolation of hominins on Flores leading to a new species showing dramatic dwarfing and even more dramatic brain size reduction is quite unusual.

So where does this leave us? Because a particular interpretation is unlikely, it's not necessarily incorrect. We do know, for example, that such "insular dwarfing" has occurred in other mammals. For the moment, the most comprehensive analyses indicate that a recently discovered hominin species (*H. floresiensis*) did, in fact, evolve on Flores (Nevell et al., 2007; Tocheri et al., 2007; Falk et al., 2008; Schauber and Falk, 2008; Jungers et al., 2009). The more detailed studies of hand and foot anatomy suggest that in several respects the morphology is like that of *H. erectus* (Nevell et al., 2007; Tocheri et al., 2007) or even early *Homo* (Jungers et al., 2009). In any case, the morphology of the Flores hominins is different in several key respects from that of *H. sapiens*, even those who show pathological conditions. There is some possibility that DNA can be retrieved from the Flores bones and sequenced. Although considered a long shot due to poor bone preservation, analysis of this DNA would certainly help solve the mystery.

Upper Paleolithic Technology and Art

Southwest Asia and Europe

In Eurasia, cultural changes viewed as part of the Upper Paleolithic period spread rapidly, with early sites in southwest Asia (Israel/Lebanon) dated at 47,000 ya. Soon after, Upper Paleolithic culture expanded throughout Europe, and several sites dated to approximately 41,000 ya located from southeastern Russia all the way to southern France and northern Spain have been excavated (**Fig. 12-16**; Mellars, 2006; Anikovich et al., 2007).

The European climate was quite different than it is today. At the beginning of the Upper Paleolithic, glacial ice covered land and sea in northern Europe. Where the glaciers stopped, ice desert and **tundra** began. The tundra gradually merged into vast grasslands that stretched as far south as the northern Mediterranean region. The overall climatic trend was one of gradually cooler average annual temperature, which reached its coldest with the last major glacial advance of the Ice Age between 20,000 and 12,000 ya.

The tundra and grasslands created an enormous pasture for herbivorous animals, large and small, and a rich hunting ground for the predators that ate them. This hunter's paradise stretched from

Spain through Europe and across the Russian steppes. Reindeer herds roamed its vast expanse, along with mammoths, bison, horses, and other animals, many of which were staple foods of Upper Paleolithic hunters. It is also during this period that archaeologists find the earliest evidence of the extensive exploitation of birds and fish as game animals. Bear in mind, however, that our understanding of the human use of marine resources is distorted by how little is known archaeologically of the thousands of square miles of coastal plains, hills, and valleys that were buried by rising sea levels at the end of the Ice Age (Erlandson, 2010).

Upper Paleolithic hunters focused most of their efforts on the immense herds of reindeer, horses, and a few other big game species that seasonally migrated across the European grasslands. Such specialized hunting is viewed by many researchers as a key aspect of the cultural transition from the Middle to the Upper Paleolithic (Mellars, 1989). While the technology of Middle and Upper Paleolithic hunters did indeed differ greatly, recent research shows that the focus of their hunting may have been more similar than once believed possible. Analysis of well-documented faunal remains from the Dordogne region of southern France reveals that the frequency of ungulates (in other words, reindeer, roe deer, and the like) shows little change between late Middle and early Upper Paleolithic strata (Grayson and Delpech, 2003). Farther south, archaeologists also found evidence of similar Middle and Upper Paleolithic land use patterns in three valleys of eastern Spain (Miller and Barton,

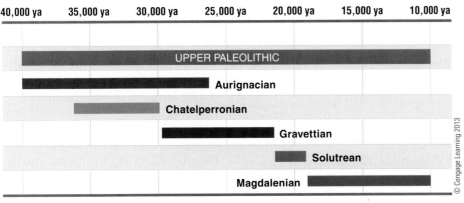

| 40,000 ya | 35,000 ya | 30,000 ya | 25,000 ya | 20,000 ya | 15,000 ya | 10,000 ya |

UPPER PALEOLITHIC

Aurignacian

Chatelperronian

Gravettian

Solutrean

Magdalenian

© Cengage Learning 2013

Figure 12-16

Archaeological industries of the European Upper Paleolithic and their approximate beginning dates.

tundra Treeless plains characterized by permafrost conditions that support the growth of shallow-rooted vegetation such as grasses and mosses.

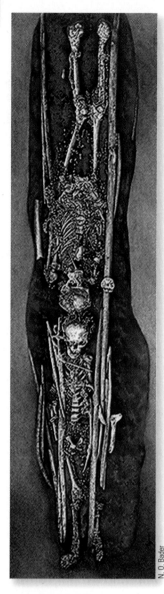

N. O. Bader

Figure 12-17

Skeletons of two teenagers, a male and a female, from Sungir, Russia. Dated to 24,000 ya, this is the richest find of any Upper Paleolithic grave.

Figure 12-18

Spear-thrower (atlatl). Note the carving.

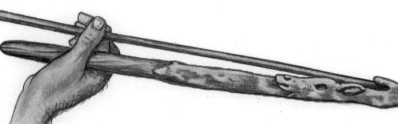

© Cengage Learning 2013

2008). Had the way of life of Upper Paleolithic hunters differed greatly from that of their Middle Paleolithic predecessors, more obvious differences should be seen both in the type and amount of game that was hunted and in overall land use patterns.

Many archaeologists now conclude that "Middle and Upper Palaeolithic hunting and gathering was largely determined by what was available seasonally in the local environment" (Bar-Yosef, 2004, p. 333). While acknowledging the similarities, other researchers remind us that the material culture differences between these two periods are such that cultural continuity cannot simply be assumed (Adler et al., 2006). Our understanding of Upper Paleolithic subsistence also suffers from how little we know about the economic importance of plant foods and other gathered resources.

A potentially important contrast between the Middle and Upper Paleolithic is seen by archaeologists when they examine the remains of Upper Paleolithic sites. They find that these settlements were often larger and used longer than Middle Paleolithic sites in the same regions. These encampments were home to around 25 to 50 people and perhaps even more during the fall and spring, when game herds made their seasonal migrations in search of fresh pasture. Remnants of Upper Paleolithic huts, some of which measure 15 to 20 feet in diameter, have been uncovered at several sites in the grasslands of Ukraine. Similar structures undoubtedly dotted camps across Europe.

Upper Paleolithic human burials provide additional insight into the nature of these communities (Pettitt, 2011). The graves sometimes include ornaments, tools, and other artifacts that were deliberately placed with corpses. Such grave goods may indicate possible status differences among community members, the existence of burial rituals, and possibly even fundamental notions of an afterlife. For example, burials uncovered at the 24,000-year-old Sungir site near Moscow (**Fig. 12-17**) include adults and adolescents dressed in beaded clothing, with grave inclusions of red ocher, thousands of ivory beads, long spears made of straightened mammoth tusks, ivory engravings, and jewelry (Formicola and Buzhilova, 2004). Although child burials are rarely discovered, far to the west at the 27,000-year-old Krems-Wachtberg site in Austria, two newborn infants have been found that were covered in red ocher and buried with scores of ivory beads (Einwögerer et al., 2006).

While Upper Paleolithic groups shared many similarities with their Middle Paleolithic predecessors, there were also many important differences. The Upper Paleolithic was an age of technological innovation that can be compared in its impact on society to the past few hundred years of our own history of amazing technological advances. Modern humans of the Upper Paleolithic not only invented new and specialized tools, but, as we've seen, also turned to new materials, such as bone, ivory, and antler.

Consider, for example, the changes in hunting technology. We noted in Chapter 11 that Neandertals relied on close-encounter weapons, and while these weapons and the tactics that went with them were clearly effective, they placed hunters at great risk of serious injury (see p. 272). Even such seemingly formidable weapons as the Middle Paleolithic wooden spears from Schöningen (see p. 260) may have had an effective range of only 25 feet or less (Shea, 2006). Hunting practices must have changed considerably with the advent of more accurate projectile weaponry such as spear-thrower darts as these weapons spread out of Africa after 50,000 ya (Shea, 2009; Shea and Sisk, 2010). The spear-thrower, or atlatl, was a wooden or bone hooked rod that acted to extend the hunter's arm, thus enhancing the force and distance of a stone projectile-tipped dart or short spear (**Fig. 12-18**; also see Fig. 8-11). Spear-thrower technology and, much later in the period, the bow and arrow undoubtedly had a big impact on hunting, on hunters, and on the game animals they pursued.

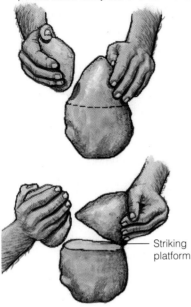

(a) A large core is selected and the top portion removed by use of a hammerstone.

Striking platform

(b) The objective is to create a flat surface called a striking platform.

(c) Next, the core is struck by use of a hammer and punch (made of bone or antler) to remove the long narrow flakes (called blades).

(d) Or the blades can be removed by pressure flaking.

(e) The result is the production of highly consistent sharp blades, which can be used, as is, as knives; or they can be further modified (retouched) to make a variety of other tools (such as burins, scrapers, and awls).

© Cengage Learning 2013

Archaeologists have long recognized five major Upper Paleolithic industries in western Europe: Chatelperronian, Aurignacian, Gravettian, Solutrean, and **Magdalenian**. These industries differ by age, distribution, and the style and type of artifacts. Important among their shared features is the use of **blade technology** for making most stone tools. A chipped stone blade is a flake that is more than twice as long as it is wide. The technology for making ribbonlike blades of predictable length, width, and thickness was invented in Africa more than 100,000 ya, but it wasn't widely adopted until the Upper Paleolithic.

Blades were struck from stone cores using an **indirect percussion** method, the most common of which was the *punch technique*, in which a toolmaker positioned a bone or antler "punch" on a prepared core and then either hit the punch with a billet or applied pressure with a crutch to drive a blade off the core. Given a properly prepared core, blades with razor-like edges could be quickly struck until the core was used up (**Fig. 12-19**).

While blades could be (and were) used without further modification, they were often just the first step in making dart points, knives, scrapers, and other tools. For example, a **burin** could be made by snapping off bits of a blade to create a chisel-like working end (**Fig. 12-20**), which was then mounted in a handle and used to cut bone, antler, ivory, and wood. As anyone who has tried to cut through a big deer bone with a stone flake could tell you, a burin can make the difference between success and failure.

Another technique, called *pressure flaking*, was often used to finish a chipped stone tool. By pressing the tip of a deer antler or similarly shaped piece of bone or wood against the edge of a core, toolmakers found that they could precisely remove small, thin flakes (**Fig. 12-21**). Applied by skilled hands, pressure flaking was used to fashion stone tools, such as **Solutrean** laurel leaf points (**Fig. 12-22**), that reflect an expert command of the technology and are aesthetically pleasing even by modern standards.

© Cengage Learning 2013

Figure 12-19

The punch blade technique.

Figure 12-20

The thick tip of this blade was flaked into a burin (indicated by the red arrow), a chisel-like tool used to cut such dense material as bone and ivory.

Magdalenian A late Upper Paleolithic stone tool industry in Europe that dates to 17,000–11,000 ya.

blade technology Chipped stone toolmaking approach in which blades struck from prepared cores are the main raw material from which tools are made. A blade is a chipped stone flake that is at least twice as long as it is wide.

indirect percussion The method of driving off blades and flakes from a prepared core using a bone or antler punch to press off a thin flake.

burin A small flake tool with a chisel-like end, used to cut bone, antler, and ivory.

Solutrean An Upper Paleolithic stone tool industry in southwestern France and Spain that dates to 21,000–18,000 ya.

© Cengage Learning 2013

Figure 12-21
Pressure flaking.

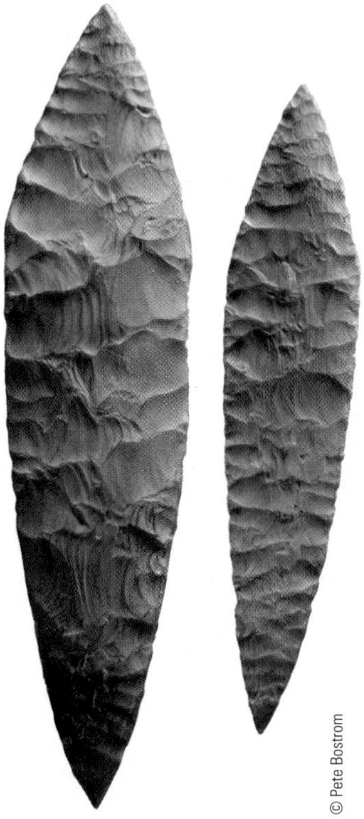

Harry Nelson

© Pete Bostrom

Figure 12-22
Solutrean laurel leaf points, France. Left specimen length 38 cm.

Figure 12-23
Venus of Brassempouy, France. Height 3.6 cm.

Along with the everyday tools of Upper Paleolithic life, archaeologists also find evidence of personal ornaments and clothing , both of which are rarely found in European Middle Paleolithic sites and are unknown from Lower Paleolithic contexts. Personal ornaments included such things as bone necklaces, shell beads, drilled bear canines, and bone and ivory bracelets. Clothing was mostly made from tanned hides and fur, but twined and simply woven fabrics are also known from as early as 27,000 ya (Soffer et al., 2000). Complex fitted clothing probably originated with the basic need for warmth in cooler regions, but it acquired new meanings that went well beyond mere function during the Upper Paleolithic (Gilligan, 2010). Like personal ornaments, clothing also served Upper Paleolithic hunter-gatherers as a medium to express the status of individuals, their roles within society, their gender, and even group identity.

The period between 35,000 and 10,000 ya was an era of "unparalleled creativity and symbolic expression" (Nowell, 2006, p. 240). Best known from sites in Europe, Upper Paleolithic art is now also well documented from Siberia, Africa, and Australia. It found expression in a variety of ways, from painted cave walls to everyday tools that show engraved and carved decorations. New methods of mixing pigments and applying them were important in rendering painted or drawn images. Bone and ivory carving and engraving were made easier with the use of burins (see Fig. 12-20) and other stone tools. Once believed to have originated toward the end of the Upper Paleolithic, recent cave art discoveries demonstrate that it was already well developed by 35,000–32,000 ya (see p. 303).

Upper Paleolithic art divides readily into two broad categories—*portable art*, or that which can be removed from the archaeological record in its entirety, and *cave art*, or that which cannot be so removed. Portable art includes everything from decorated everyday objects to artifacts interpreted as instances of symbolic or artistic expression. For example, many small bone, stone, and ivory sculptures collectively called "Venus figurines" have been excavated at sites from westernmost Europe to western Russia. Some figures were realistically carved, and the faces appear to be modeled after actual women (**Fig. 12-23**). Other female figures are more stylized representations, often with exaggerated sexual characteristics, and they sometimes depict body decoration, clothing, and headgear (**Fig. 12-24**). Although Venus figurines have often been narrowly viewed as objects created for fertility or other ritual purposes, these objects actually represent women in diverse statuses and roles in Upper Paleolithic society (Soffer et al., 2000).

At two sites in the Czech Republic, Dolní Věstonice and Předmostí (both dated at approximately 27,000–26,000 ya), archaeologists have also found small animal figures of fired clay. This is the first documented use of ceramic technology anywhere; in fact, it precedes the earliest documented examples of fired clay pottery by more than 15,000 years.

Upper Paleolithic cave art—material symbolic expressions that can't be removed from the archaeological record without destroying them—comprises what are probably the most widely recognized images of human prehistory in the world. It began during the Aurignacian and continued to the end of the Ice Age. It is beautiful, exotic, rare, old, and only partly understood (Desdemaines-Hugon, 2010).

Most cave art depicts common food animals, such as reindeer, bison, mammoths, and horses, and occasionally even fish, but there are also many pictures of dangerous animals, such as cave bears, rhinos, and lions (**Fig. 12-25**). Many of these animals went extinct at the end of the Ice Age. Other representations include hand stencils (an outline created by blowing pigment over a hand held against a cave wall) and patterns of dots and lines. Images of people are uncommon by comparison with those of other animals.

The importance of cave art ultimately rests in its being far more than just a bunch of pretty pictures executed in strange places. When the first site was discovered in the late 1800s, it caused an immediate sensation because either it was an elaborate hoax, which at first seemed likely, or it truly was old. If the latter, then there was a problem: Its execution defied the then dominant view of cultural "progress" as something that gradually proceeded from a "savage" ancient past to the "civilization" of the present. Since cave art did prove to be quite old, we can reasonably claim that these Upper Paleolithic sites played a role in encouraging a reevaluation of basic notions about the nature of culture change and the course of biocultural evolution.

Cave art is now known from more than 200 sites, many of which are in southwestern France and northern Spain. The most famous of these sites are Altamira, in Spain, and Lascaux and

Figure 12-24
Venus of Willendorf, Austria. Height 11.1 cm.

(a)

Figure 12-25
Cave paintings of the Lascaux Cave in southwestern France. (a) Horse. (b) Cattle.

(b)

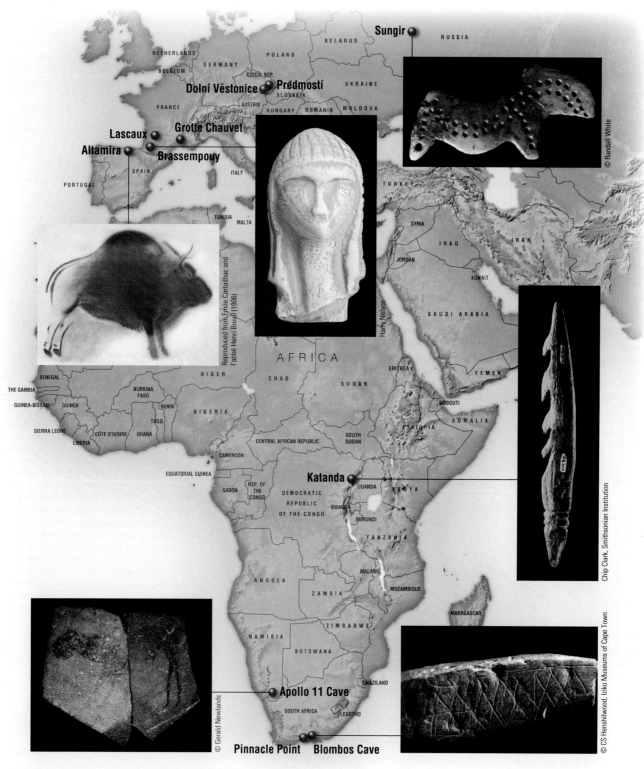

Figure 12-26

Symbolic artifacts from the Middle Stone Age of Africa and the Upper Paleolithic in Europe. It is notable that evidence of symbolism is found in Blombos Cave (77,000 ya) and Katanda (80,000 ya), both in Africa, a full 50,000 years before any comparable evidence is known from Europe. Moreover, the ocher found at Pinnacle Point is yet another 80,000 years older, dating to more than 160,000 ya.

Grotte Chauvet, in France (**Fig. 12-26**). Altamira was discovered by a hunter in 1869. The walls and ceiling of this immense cave are filled with superb portrayals of bison in red and black pigments (Ramos, 1999). The artist even took advantage of bulges in the walls to create the visual illusion of depth in the paintings. Nearly 70 years after the discovery of Altamira, Lascaux Cave came to light and soon attracted worldwide attention for its huge paintings of bulls that dominate the long passage now called the Great Hall of Bulls. Here and elsewhere in the cave, painting after painting of horses, deer, wild bulls, ibex, and other animals were drawn with remarkable skill in black, red, and yellow pigments (Aujoulat, 2005).

Chauvet is one of the most recently discovered art caves, having been found by cave explorers in 1994. It contains more than 200 paintings and engravings of animals, including cave bears, horses, rhinos, lions, and mammoths, as well as stone tools, torches, and fireplaces left by Upper Paleolithic visitors to the cave (Clottes, 2003). Radiocarbon dating of pigments sampled from the paintings shows that they were executed during the Aurignacian, around 35,000–32,000 ya (Balter, 2006; Cuzange et al., 2007), making Chauvet considerably earlier than the Magdalenian sites of Lascaux and Altamira. Pettitt (2008; Pettitt and Pike, 2007) questions current interpretations of Chauvet's age, noting that cave art is hard to date; few examples of Upper Paleolithic cave art have been dated; and Chauvet's art and its execution are most similar to late Upper Paleolithic art, not that of the Aurignacian. Examples of art older than 30,000 ya are also quite rare and, were it not for Chauvet, early Upper Paleolithic art would look much more like the Middle Paleolithic than the late Upper Paleolithic (Pettitt, 2008). Nevertheless, regardless of the age that its paintings ultimately prove to be, Chauvet is extraordinary.

A recent comparative analysis of art cave hand stencils from four French caves has concluded that both men and women participated in cave art (Snow, 2006). And their art was not limited to caves. Evidence discovered during the past 15 years shows that they also painted and engraved images on cliff faces and rocks outside of caves (Bicho et al., 2007), but very little of this art has survived thousands of years of weathering in the open air.

The big question, of course, is why did they paint? There is probably no single reason that explains all Upper Paleolithic art. Certainly, many ideas have been suggested over the decades—for example, that the art represents early religious beliefs, hunting magic (perhaps I can capture the animal if I capture its essence in an image), a visual representation of cosmology or worldview, and group identity or boundaries. It is a question for which archaeologists still have much to learn before they can answer it convincingly.

Africa

As noted in the preceding section, many significant innovations and cultural changes that were traditionally associated with the Upper Paleolithic of Europe actually had their beginnings more than 20,000 years earlier in the Middle Stone Age of Africa (Marean, 2010; Shea and Sisk, 2010). Most research on these important developments in African prehistory dates only to the past couple of decades, and each passing year brings fresh insights that are rapidly changing the scientific understanding of the origins of modern human behavior and its dispersal out of Africa after 50,000 ya (Willoughby, 2009). With these new discoveries, the Middle Stone Age/Middle Paleolithic increasingly looks less like a "transition" to Late Stone Age/Upper Paleolithic modernity and more like "change with considerable continuity" with the past (Straus, in press).

Projectile weaponry such as the spear-thrower and dart and the bow and arrow began in Africa during the Middle Stone age between 100,000 and 50,000 ya, probably in relation to the economic need to broaden the early human diet (Brooks et al., 2006; Shea, 2006; Shea and Sisk, 2010, p. 116). Lombard and Phillipson (2010) argue that the size, shape, and use wear on stone artifacts from Sibudu Cave support the inference that bow and arrow technology was already in use by South African hunter-gatherers as early as 64,000 ya.

Bone projectile points, which are believed to date as early as 90,000–79,000 ya, have been reported from the Katanda site in the Democratic Republic of the Congo (see Fig. 12-26) and at Blombos Cave along the South African coast; in both regions, they may have been part of fishing gear (Brooks et al., 2006).

At Pinnacle Point Cave 13B, not far from Blombos, archaeologists have found a variety of material evidence that "complex cognition" (the basis of modern human behavior) may have occurred in South Africa as long ago as 164,000–75,000 ya (Marean, 2010). The researchers report the discovery of red ocher that was ground to powder and perhaps used for personal adornment (Watts, 2010) as well as clear evidence of systematic exploitation of shellfish and use of very small stone blades (microliths, thumbnail-sized stone flakes hafted to make knives and saws, for example). The Pinnacle Point discoveries are remarkably early: The use of microliths is almost 100,000 years earlier than anywhere else, while the exploitation of marine resources as well as the use of ocher come 40,000 years prior to systematic evidence from any other site.

Early accomplishments in rock art, as early as in Europe, are also seen in southern Africa (Namibia) at the Apollo 11 Rock Shelter site, where painted slabs have been dated to between 28,000 and 26,000 ya (Freundlich et al., 1980; Vogelsang, 1998). At Blombos Cave, engraved ocher fragments (see Fig. 12-26) are dated between 100,000 and 75,000 ya (Henshilwood et al., 2009). At Diepkloof Rock Shelter in South Africa, archaeologists have found 270 fragments of ostrich eggshell containers in contexts dated to about 66,000 ya. As Texier and colleagues (2010, p. 6183) explain, these egghsells "show repetitive patterns, made in accordance with a mental design shared by a group. Such a practice represents the earliest evidence of the existence of a graphic tradition among prehistoric hunter-gatherer populations." What these scattered examples of recent African finds demonstrate is that symbolic behavior and representation did not emerge about 50,000 ya, shortly before the dispersal of "modern" humans out of Africa, but tens of thousands of years before. They also show that we have much to learn about the emergence of modern human behavior in Africa. The only thing on which we can count is that our understanding of fundamental aspects of the beginnings of the Upper Paleolithic is about to change.

Summary of Upper Paleolithic Culture

In looking back at the Upper Paleolithic, we can see it as the culmination of 2 million years of cultural development. Change proceeded incredibly slowly for most of the Pleistocene; but as cultural traditions and materials accumulated, and the brain—and, we assume, intelligence—expanded and reorganized, the rate of change quickened.

Cultural evolution continued with the appearance of early premodern humans and moved a bit faster with later premoderns. Neandertals in Eurasia and their contemporaries elsewhere added deliberate burials, technological innovations, and much more.

Building on existing cultures, Late Pleistocene populations attained sophisticated cultural and material heights in a seemingly short—by previous standards—burst of exciting activity. In Europe as well as in southern and central Africa particularly, there seem to have been dramatic cultural innovations, among them big game hunting with powerful new weapons, such as spear-throwers, harpoons, and the bow and arrow. Other innovations included personal ornaments, needles, "tailored" clothing, and burials with elaborate grave goods—a practice that may indicate some sort of status hierarchy.

The last Ice Age ended about 10,000 ya, and the retreat of glacial ice affected global climate, plants, and animals, including humans. As average annual temperatures slowly increased, coastlines were drowned by rising sea levels, and the vast grasslands of western Europe were replaced by hardwood forests. Many traditional food animals either went extinct or migrated to find better range, and much the same happened to important plant foods. Chapter 13 continues our story of human biocultural evolution by first considering how and when the first humans arrived in the Americas and then exploring how humans everywhere adjusted to the rapidly changing post-Pleistocene world.

Summary of Main Topics

▶ Two main hypotheses have been used to explain the origin and dispersal of modern humans:
- The regional continuity model suggests that different groups of modern people evolved from local populations of premodern humans.
- Various replacement models, especially those emphasizing partial replacement, suggest that modern humans originated in Africa and migrated to other parts of the world. However, when they came into contact with premodern human groups, they did not completely replace them, but interbred with them to some extent.

▶ New DNA evidence from ancient Neandertals as well as from modern people demonstrate that some modest interbreeding did take place, probably between 80,000 and 50,000 ya. These findings clearly support a partial replacement model.

▶ Archaeological finds and some fossil evidence (although the latter is not as well established) also support the view that intermixing occurred between modern *H. sapiens* and Neandertals.

▶ The earliest fossil finds of modern *H. sapiens* come from East Africa (Ethiopia), with the oldest dating to about 200,000 ya. The second find from Herto is very well dated (160,000 ya) and is the best evidence of an early modern human from anywhere at this time.

▶ Modern humans are found in South Africa beginning around 100,000 ya, and the first anatomical modern *H. sapiens* individuals are found in the Middle East dating to perhaps more than 100,000 ya.

▶ The Upper Paleolithic is a cultural period traditionally viewed as showing many innovations in technology, development of more sophisticated (cave) art, and, in many cases, elaborate burials rich in grave goods. Similar cultural developments occurred in Eurasia and Africa.

▶ Many of the cultural innovations that have been long attributed to the Upper Paleolithic appear to have originated tens of thousands of years earlier during the Middle Stone Age of Africa. Recent archaeological research in Africa is rapidly revising our understanding of the beginnings of modern human behavior.

In "What's Important," you'll find a useful summary of the most significant fossil discoveries discussed in this chapter.

What's Important — Key Fossil Discoveries of Early Modern Humans and *Homo floresiensis*

Dates (ya)	Region	Site	Hominin	The Big Picture
95,000–13,000	Southeast Asia	Flores (Indonesia)	*H. floresiensis*	Late survival of very small-bodied and small-brained hominin on island of Flores; designated as different species (*H. floresiensis*) from modern humans
30,000	Europe	Cro-Magnon (France)	*H. sapiens sapiens*	Famous site historically; good example of early modern humans from France
35,000	Europe	Oase Cave (Romania)	*H. sapiens sapiens*	Earliest well-dated modern human from Europe
110,000	Southwest Asia	Qafzeh (Israel)	*H. sapiens sapiens*	Early site; shows considerable variation
115,000	Southwest Asia	Skhūl (Israel)	*H. sapiens sapiens*	Earliest well-dated modern human outside of Africa; perhaps contemporaneous with neighboring Tabun Neandertal site
160,000–154,000	Africa	Herto (Ethiopia)	*H. sapiens idaltu*	Best-preserved and best-dated early modern human from anywhere; placed in separate subspecies from living *H. sapiens*

Critical Thinking Questions

1. What anatomical characteristics define *modern*, as compared with *premodern*, humans? Assume that you're analyzing an incomplete skeleton that may be early modern *H. sapiens*. Which portions of the skeleton would be most informative, and why?

2. What recent evidence supports a partial replacement model for an African origin and later dispersal of modern humans? Do you find this evidence convincing? Why or why not? Can you propose an alternative that has better data to support it?

3. Why are the fossils recently discovered from Herto so important? How does this evidence influence your conclusions in question 2?

4. What archaeological evidence shows that modern human behavior during the Upper Paleolithic was significantly different from that of earlier hominins? Do you think that early modern *H. sapiens* populations were behaviorally superior to the Neandertals? Be careful to define what you mean by "superior."

5. Why do you think some Upper Paleolithic people painted in caves? Why don't we find such evidence of cave painting from a wider geographical area?

CHAPTER 13

Early Holocene Hunters and Gatherers

© Dr. Richard VanderHoek

LEARNING OBJECTIVES

After you have mastered the material in this chapter, you will be able to:

▶ Explain where the first inhabitants of the New World came from and when they arrived.

▶ Identify and contrast the major cultural changes that accompanied the end of the Ice Age in the Americas and the Old World.

▶ Explain why it is unlikely that Paleo-Indian hunters caused widespread extinctions of Pleistocene megafauna at the end of the Ice Age.

During the summer of 1996, two men found a human skull and other bones along the muddy shore of the Columbia River near Kennewick, Washington. They reported the discovery to the police and coroner, who in turn asked James Chatters, a forensic anthropologist and archaeologist, to examine the remains and provide an initial assessment. The results suggested that they were probably dealing with a Caucasian male in his mid-40s, but one who looked thousands of years old. When a CAT scan also showed a large stone spear point embedded in the man's hip, Chatters and others understandably wondered just how old this skeleton was (Chatters, 2001). Bone samples sent for radiocarbon dating returned an early **Holocene** age estimate of roughly 9,300 ya. Instead of explaining this man's past, the analyses just added to the mystery. Who was this guy?

"Kennewick Man," as he was soon called, became the center of an extraordinary controversy, one that was more legal than scientific; it took nine years and more than $8.5 million of taxpayers' money to sort out the case in federal courts (Dalton, 2005). It involved a swarm of attorneys, the U.S. Army Corps of Engineers, the U.S. Department of the Interior, several Native American tribal groups, a handful of internationally known anthropologists, a Polynesian chief, and several federal judges, decisions, and appeals. Several important legal questions were ultimately at issue, not the least of which was the right of the American public to information about the distant past (Bruning, 2006; Malik, 2007). At stake on the scientific side of the picture was what could be learned from the physical remains of a person who lived during the early days of the human presence in North America, when few people were spread over this huge continent. So few human skeletons (currently less than 10 individuals) are known in North America from this period that each new one, like Kennewick Man, is a major discovery that potentially opens a fresh window on the prehistory of the continent.

As we noted in Chapter 12, men, women, and children made the first footprints in New World mud some-time between 30,000 and 13,500 ya. The genetic evidence suggests that this most likely happened after about 16,500 ya (Goebel et al., 2008). With their first steps, they expanded the potential range of our species by more than 16 million square miles, spanning two continents and countless islands, or roughly 30 percent of the earth's land surface. It was a big deal, comparable in scope and significance to the dispersal of the first hominins into Europe and Asia from Africa during the Lower Paleolithic.

In this chapter, we'll consider the story of these first New World inhabitants and also begin to look at the major cultural developments of roughly the past 10,000 years (**Fig. 13-1**), during which world cultural changes increased at a dramatic rate. Following the end of the last Ice Age, the world's modest human population of perhaps a few tens of millions sustained itself by hunting and gathering food, living in small groups, constructing humble shelters, and making use of effective but simple equipment crafted from basic natural materials. Obviously, quite a lot has happened since then! What *is* important to note is that these changes are not primarily the result of human physical evolution, which has played a decreasing role in human changes during the short span since the end of the Pleistocene (see Chapters 4 and 5). Rather, the most radical developments affecting the human condition continue to be the consequences of our uniquely human *biocultural evolution*, mostly stimulated by cultural innovations and the inescapable effects of our ever-growing population.

Let's begin our look at human communities at the end of the Ice Age by examining the archaeological and biological clues relating to the origins of the first Americans and review the evidence indicating not only when they first arrived but also what cultural adjustments they made in their new homeland. We'll then explore how lifeways changed for human groups both in the New and Old Worlds as the glaciers retreated, sea levels rose, plant and animal communities migrated, and even such seemingly permanent entities as rivers and lakes became transformed in a postglacial world.

Holocene The geological epoch during which we now live. The Holocene follows the Pleistocene epoch and began roughly 11,000–10,000 ya.

Entering the New World

Major archaeological problems, such as the entry of the first humans into the New World, inevitably attract a lot of research interest, not to mention a little contentious debate (e.g., Waguespack, 2007). When did the first humans arrive in the Americas? Where did they come from? How did they get here? How did they make a living after they arrived? We want firm answers to these questions, but, as with all research that centers on "first" events, finding the answers is never easy. Consider, for example, the crucial question of *when* the first humans arrived in the New World. Strictly speaking, to answer this question we need to identify the locality —somewhere in the 16 million square miles of two continents—where the oldest material evidence of the presence of humans is preserved in well-dated

archaeological contexts. It's as though we're trying to find a particular sand grain that may or may not be on a beach. Once you understand the difficulty of finding "the" answer, it's easy to see why the question is likely to remain with us for a while.

When people arrived is necessarily tied up with *where* they came from because the two, taken together, tell us where to search in the archaeological record for these first New World immigrants. There's general consensus that the Late Pleistocene marked something of a watershed in human prehistory. For millions of years, continental glaciers waxed and waned while humans evolved from ancestral primates. This activity meant little to our remote ancestors because glaciation primarily affected the higher latitudes, and early hominins lived in the tropics, where relatively few effects of such climatic changes reached them. But by Late Pleistocene times, during the Upper

Figure 13-1

Time line for Chapter 13.

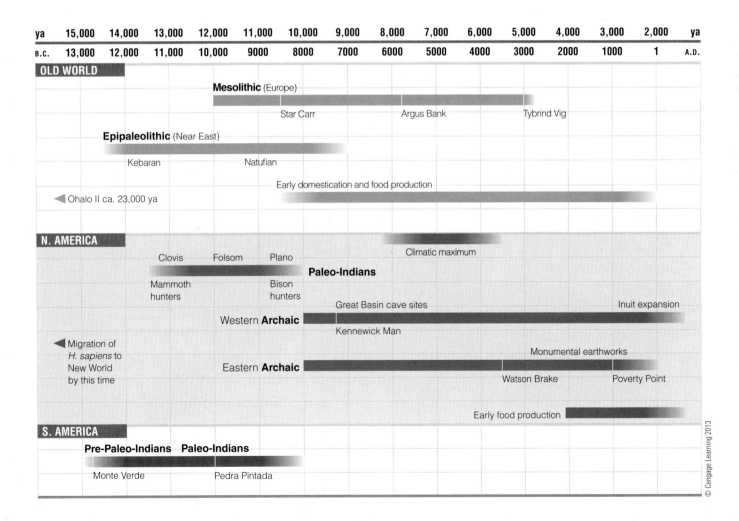

© Cengage Learning 2013

Paleolithic of Europe and the Late Stone Age of Africa, modern humans had long ago pushed well into the temperate latitudes and even into regions just exposed by glacial meltwaters (see Chapter 12). These humans were capable of culturally adapting to changing natural and social environments and could do so at a pace that would have been unthinkable to their Lower Paleolithic ancestors. Members of these human groups became the first New World immigrants.

Archaeologists depend on geographical, biological, archaeological, and linguistic evidence to trace the earliest Americans back to their Old World origins and construct today's answers to the when and where questions. Right now, there are two major hypotheses[*] to explain the route of entry of humans into the New World: first, by way of the Bering land bridge that connected Asia and North America several times during the Late Pleistocene (**Fig. 13-2**), and

---

[*]A third hypothesis, described in previous editions of this textbook, is that the earliest New World inhabitants followed the ice edge across the northern Atlantic Ocean from western Europe to eastern North America (Bradley and Stanford, 2004, 2006). Recent paleoceanographic data show that this route would not have been feasible for Late Pleistocene humans (Wesley and Dix, 2008). Perhaps more significantly, genetic data clearly point to northeastern Asia as the source of the New World inhabitants (Meltzer, 2009; Pitblado, 2011).

second, along the coast of the northern Pacific Rim (**Fig. 13-3**). It's also possible that both routes played important roles in the populating of the New World, but let's keep things simple and consider the evidence for each hypothesis in turn.

Bering Land Bridge

As long ago as the late sixteenth century, José de Acosta, a Jesuit priest with extensive experience in Mexico and Andean South America, examined the geographical and other information available to him and concluded that humans must have entered the New World from Asia (Acosta, 2002). A lot of evidence favors this idea. First, there's the basic geography of the situation. If you cast around for a feasible, low-tech way to get people into the Americas, a quick check of a world map will draw your eyes to the Bering Strait, where northeastern Asia and northwestern North America are separated by only 50 miles of ocean (see Fig 13-2). An equally quick visit to the geology section of your local library will also reveal that there were several long intervals during the Pleistocene when lowered sea levels actually exposed the floor of the shallow Bering Sea, creating a wide "land bridge" (West and West, 1996). The land bridge formed during periods of maximum glaciation, when the volume of water locked up in glacial

Figure 13-2

The earliest inhabitants of North America may have entered the continent during the Late Pleistocene by way of the Bering land bridge, which was exposed during periods of maximum glaciation. These groups may have passed southward into what is now the United States by following the ice-free corridor that periodically emerged between the Cordilleran and Laurentide ice sheets in western Canada.

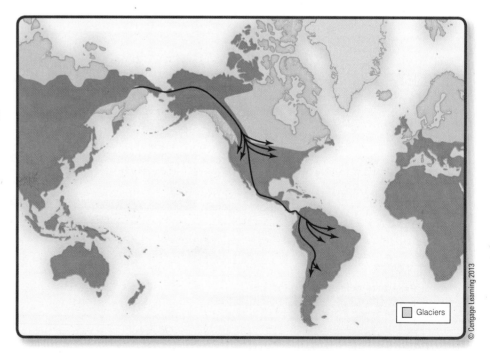

Glaciers

© Cengage Learning 2013

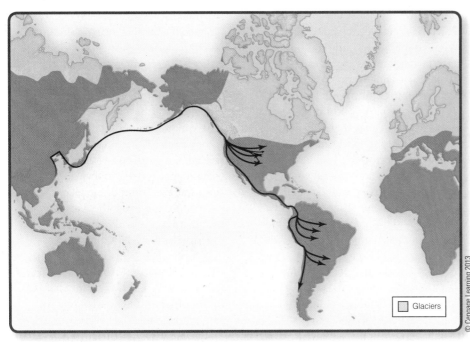

Figure 13-3

The Pacific coastal route hypothesis asserts that the earliest immigrants into the Americas may have traveled by boat along the islands and environmental refugia that dotted the Pacific coast during the Late Pleistocene.

ice sheets reduced worldwide sea levels by 300 to 400 feet.[†] During the Last Glacial Maximum (28,000–15,000 ya), **Beringia**, as it is known, comprised a broad plain up to 1,300 miles wide from north to south (see Fig. 13-2). Ironically, the cold, dry Arctic climate kept Beringia relatively ice-free. Its plant cover included dry grasslands (Zazula et al., 2003), as well as patches, or *refugia*, of boreal trees, shrubs, mosses, and lichens (Brubaker et al., 2005).

Beringia's dry steppes and tundra supported herds of grazing animals and could just as easily have supported human hunters who preyed on them (Pitblado, 2011). The region was, after all, an extension of the familiar landscape of northeastern Asia. Archaeology confirms that humans were well adapted to the cold and dry conditions of the Late Pleistocene in Siberia, including during the harsh conditions of the Last Glacial Maximum (Kuzmin, 2008). Upper Paleolithic hunters pursuing large herbivores with efficient stone- and bone-tipped weapons, and probably with the aid of domesticated dogs, penetrated into the farthest reaches of Eurasia (Soffer and Praslov, 1993). The earliest evidence

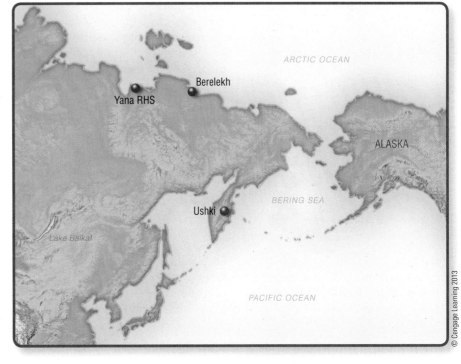

Figure 13-4

Late Pleistocene sites in Siberia and Beringia mentioned in the text.

of their presence in northern Siberia is the recently reported Yana RHS site (**Fig. 13-4**), which lies well within the Arctic Circle. Here archaeologists have found rhinoceros horn and mammoth ivory spear foreshafts as well as stone tools and other artifacts in contexts dated to about 30,000 ya (Pitulko et al., 2004). Yana RHS is at least twice as old as the western Beringia site of Berelekh (see Fig. 13-4), the next oldest candidate for a possible Arctic Circle campsite (Pitulko,

---

[†]To put these glaciers in perspective, visualize a mile-high ice sheet where Chicago is now—not a film of ice on your car's windshield in the winter.

Beringia (bare-in´-jya) The dry-land connection between Asia and America that existed periodically during the Pleistocene epoch.

2011), and it demonstrates that at a very early date, people were successfully adapted to high-latitude conditions similar to what hunters would have encountered in crossing Beringia. Culturally and geographically, these Asian hunters were capable of becoming the first Americans (Goebel et al., 2008).

Geologists have determined that except for short spans, the Bering passage was dry land between about 25,000 and 11,000 ya and for other extended periods even before then (especially between 75,000 and 45,000 ya). If the first humans entered the New World by traveling on foot across Beringia, they probably made their trips during the later episode. As yet, there's no generally accepted evidence of humans in the Americas before that time.

After entering Alaska by way of Beringia, early immigrants would not have had easy access to the rest of the Americas. Major glaciers to the southeast of Beringia blocked the further movement of both game and people throughout most of the Pleistocene epoch. The **Cordilleran** ice mass covered the mountains of western Canada and southern Alaska, and the **Laurentide** glacier, centered on Hudson Bay, spread a vast ice sheet across much of eastern and central Canada and the northeastern United States. Around 20,000 ya, these glaciers coalesced into one massive flow. Toward the close of the Pleistocene, the edges of the Cordilleran and Laurentide glaciers finally separated, allowing animals and, in principle, human hunter-gatherers to gain entry to the south through an "ice-free corridor" along the eastern flank of the Canadian Rockies. Some researchers argue that the ice-free corridor became passable as early as 13,700–13,400 ya (Haynes, 2005). Others point to the geographical pattern of radiocarbon age estimates from western North America that indicate that humans could not have traveled through this ice-free corridor before about 13,400 ya (Arnold, 2006).

For a long time, most archaeologists accepted the ice-free corridor hypothesis because it explained the entry of the earliest humans into the Americas as well as the origins of the **Clovis** complex (13,500–13,000 ya), which, until recently,

was widely believed to be the earliest archaeological evidence of humans in North America. The nagging doubts of critics centered mostly on the lack of any clear antecedents for the sophisticated Clovis stone tool technology in the Upper Paleolithic sites of Siberia. In the long run, it may not matter much who's right because the earliest dates for an ice-free corridor currently fall *after* the earliest archaeological evidence of humans in the Americas south of the glaciers.

To sum things up, the Bering land bridge hypothesis for the entry of people into the New World rests on several key notions. First, the technologically simplest way to get from the Old World to the New World was on foot. Second, lots of other animals arrived by this route during the Pleistocene, so, archaeologists have long reasoned, it was feasible for people to do the same. Third, as we discuss in a later section, the skeletal and genetic evidence clearly favor an Asian origin for Native Americans. On all these points, at least, there's little debate. The main problem with the Bering land bridge explanation is that the age estimates for the earliest humans in North and South America are hard to reconcile with the age estimates for the most favorable intervals during which humans could have crossed Beringia, walked through the ice-free corridor, and populated the Americas. The archaeological evidence currently supports the inference that humans passed the glaciers and established themselves on both continents before, not after, 13,500 ya.

Pacific Coastal Route

The second scenario also envisions the earliest New World inhabitants coming from Asia. But it has them moving along the Pacific coast, where climatic conditions, beginning about 17,000–15,000 ya, were generally not as harsh as those of the interior and where they could simply go around the North American glaciers. Looking again at the northern Pacific Rim between Asia and North America (see Fig. 13-3), we can see that given canoes, rafts, or other forms of water transport, it was geographically possible for humans to enter the New World

Cordilleran (cor-dee-yair´-an) Pleistocene ice sheet originating in mountains of western North America.

Laurentide (lah-ren´-tid) Pleistocene ice sheet centered in the Hudson Bay region and extending across much of eastern Canada and the northern United States.

Clovis North American archaeological complex characterized by distinctive fluted projectile points, dating to roughly 13,500–13,000 ya; once widely believed to be representative of specialized big game hunters, who may have driven many late Pleistocene species into extinction.

At a Glance

Entry of the First Humans into the New World

NORTHEASTERN ASIA

By boat along the northern Pacific Rim → By boat down the west coast of North and South America → Accounts for very ancient pre-Paleo-Indian human presence reported in North and South America

On foot across the Bering land bridge → By land down through the ice-free corridor into the lower 48 United States → Accounts for Paleo-Indian sites, but does not explain evidence of the pre-Paleo-Indian human presence in the Americas

© Cengage Learning 2013

by traveling along the coast. Unlike the Bering land bridge, this route would have been less dependent on the waxing and waning of glaciers. In principle, therefore, humans traveling by this route could have arrived in the New World tens of thousands of years ago (Dixon, 2011; Erlandson, 2002).

But why should we assume that the Late Pleistocene inhabitants of East Asia had water transport capable of making this trip? Here, sound archaeological evidence comes to our rescue. As discussed in Chapter 12, humans colonized Australia roughly 50,000 ya, and it could only be reached by water. So, the rafts or boats necessary to carry humans successfully along the Pacific coast—but not, apparently, across the Pacific Ocean—from Asia to the New World must have existed and been used by at least some Late Pleistocene populations before the first people began to settle in the Americas.

Passage along the Pacific Rim may have been eased by access to the region's diverse marine and terrestrial ecosystems (Erlandson and Braje, 2011). For example, kelp (seaweed) forests provided a rich and diverse coastal ecosystem of fishes, mammals, and birds that were exploited by Native Americans well into the twentieth century. These marine forests, along with rich estuaries, coral reefs, and the like, thrived along the Pacific Rim by 16,000 ya (Erlandson and Braje, 2011; but see Davis, 2011) and would have been important resources for human migrants along the coast.

Many archaeologists find the possibility that people used a coastal route to enter the New World an attractive idea, partly because it avoids the time constraints on the availability of the Bering land bridge and ice-free corridor and partly because migrants traveling by boat along the northern Pacific coast need not have abandoned their boats once they got around the glaciers. They could just as easily have kept going down the west coast of the Americas, following the resource-rich "Pacific Rim Highway" (Erlandson and Braje, 2011). Had they done so, it would help to explain why there are a lot of apparently very early South America sites, but few in the interior of North America (Kelly, 2003).

Still, the coastal route has several possible shortcomings. An often cited problem, one even noted by its proponents, is that the archaeological evidence that could be used to test this hypothesis rests at the bottom of the Pacific Ocean in sites that were covered, if not destroyed, by rising sea levels as the glaciers melted. Fortunately, coastlines react locally, not globally, to such changes. Paleogeographical researchers are beginning to identify specific parts of the modern coasts and offshore islands of Canada that would have been exposed land where human migrants may have traveled (Hetherington et al., 2003). Farther to the south, off the California coast, 13,000-year-old human skeletal remains were recently found in excavations on Santa Rosa Island (Johnson et al., 2007). What makes the Santa Rosa remains particularly relevant is that humans could not have reached this island without some form of water transport. Taken together, these examples show that relevant archaeological evidence is indeed discoverable, even if we cannot (as yet) adequately explore the ocean floor.

Another problem, possibly related to the preceding one, is that we currently have little archaeological evidence of marine-adapted human populations along the coast of northeastern Asia— from which the earliest immigrants into the New World would have been drawn—until *after* the end of the last Ice Age (Erlandson and Braje, 2011). As on the other side of the Pacific, much of the archaeological evidence of marine adaptations may have been buried by rising sea levels at the end of the Pleistocene. Most archaeologists with firsthand experience in the region feel that if immigrants to the New World had arrived by the coastal route, they must have had the necessary technology and Arctic marine experience needed to survive in this harsh, quickly changing environment.

So to sum things up, the Pacific coastal route was feasible in principle. Considering the generally milder climate and rich resources of the coast relative to the interior, the presence of natural refugia, and the apparent technological capabilities of Late Pleistocene populations, the earliest migrants could have pulled it off. Factoring the Bering land bridge and the glaciers out of the equation also removes the temporal bottlenecks on migration that haunt the land bridge hypothesis. These are definitely marks in its favor. The main problem is that if the earliest people came by this route, then much—but hopefully not all—of the most relevant archaeolog-

At a Glance

Important Northeastern Asia Sites and Regions

SITE	DATES (YA)	SIGNIFICANCE
Yana RHS (Russia)	30,000	Earliest evidence of Late Pleistocene hunters beyond the Arctic Circle in northern Siberia; stone tools and horn and ivory spear foreshafts similar to that found much later on North American Paleo-Indian sites
Berelekh (Russia)	ca. 14,000–13,000	Archaeological evidence of Arctic human adaptations
Bering land bridge (Russia & USA)	ca. 75,000–45,000 and 25,000–11,000	Also called "Beringia"; a Pleistocene land bridge that formed between northeastern Asia and northwestern North America during periods of maximum glaciation

ical evidence is buried in the muck on the floor of the Pacific from northeastern Asia to the Americas. Even with this drawback, the coastal route hypothesis is perhaps the most promising explanation of how the first inhabitants arrived in the New World.

The Earliest Americans

We'll now leave behind the question of how the first people arrived in North America and explore some ideas about who they were.

Physical and Genetic Evidence

Biological data bearing directly on the earliest people to reach the New World are frustratingly scarce. Well-documented skeletons are especially

rare. The physical remains of fewer than two dozen North American individuals appear to date much before 9,500 ya, by which time humans had certainly been present in the New World for millennia (**Fig. 13-5**). The tremendous information value of well-preserved and documented early skeletons is the reason archaeologists spent nine years in federal courts contesting what they believed to be the government's well-intentioned but misguided decision to turn over the remains of Kennewick Man to Native American tribal groups for reburial before the remains could be studied.

The rare early finds provide valuable insights on ancient life and death. What little we currently know about Kennewick Man (**Fig. 13-6**), for example, is that he suffered multiple violent trauma and other health problems during his 40 to 50 years of life. His most intriguing injury is an old wound in his pelvis that had healed around a still-embedded

Figure 13-5

Location of some early New World sites. The dates for many of these sites are still disputed as archaeologists grapple with mounting evidence that the earliest evidence of humans in the New World is older than the 13,500–13,000 ya Paleo-Indian Clovis culture of North America.

© Cengage Learning 2013

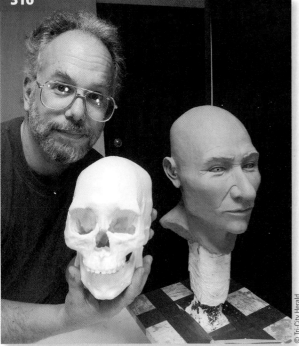

Figure 13-6

Reconstruction of the facial features of Kennewick Man (right), based on a cast of the skull (left) found by two young men in the Columbia River, Washington, in 1996. The reconstruction was the collaborative effort of Tom McClelland (holding the skull) and James Chatters.

stone spear point. To this we can add the largely healed effects of massive blunt trauma to the chest, a depressed skull fracture, and a fracture of the left arm. He also had an infected head injury and a fractured shoulder blade (scapula), neither of which shows the effects of healing, as well as osteoarthritis (Chatters, 2004). What's more, the list is probably incomplete because it was compiled from a preliminary examination of the remains. But by any measure, this man had a pretty hard life. Just how hard it was will become evident in a couple of years, after researchers complete the scientific analysis of his remains.

Anthropologists are also analyzing other cases, all from the American West. The 12,800-year-old partial skeleton of a young woman, discovered in a cave above the Snake River near Buhl, Idaho, reveals signs of interrupted growth in both her long bones and her teeth; this evidence suggests that the woman experienced some metabolic stress in childhood, possibly because of disease or seasonal food shortages (Green et al., 1998). At Spirit Cave, Nevada, researchers discovered the partially desiccated body of a man, wrapped in fine matting, who was in his early 40s when he died some 10,600 years ago; his skeleton exhibits a fractured skull and tooth abscesses as well as signs of back problems (Winslow and Wedding, 1997). Near the Grimes Point rock-shelter, another Nevada site, researchers found a teenager from about the same period who died of his wounds after being stabbed in the chest with an obsidian blade that left slash marks and stone flakes embedded in one of his ribs (Owsley and Jantz, 2000).

Physical anthropologists who made the preliminary studies of Kennewick Man, the Spirit Cave mummy, and other early specimens announced surprising interpretations based on this modest sample. Statistical analyses comparing a series of standard cranial measurements—including those that define overall skull size and proportion, shape of nasal opening, face width, and distance between the eyes—place the earliest-known American remains outside the normal range of variation observed in modern Native American populations (Owsley and Jantz, 2000). The more derived craniofacial morphological traits seen in most modern Asian and Native American populations appear to be absent in this early population. Instead, the archaeological examples display relatively small, narrow faces combined with long skulls. Physical anthropologists note these generalized (nonderived) traits in living populations among the Ainu of Japan and some Pacific Islanders and Australians. Crania that more closely resemble those of modern Native Americans became prevalent only after about 7,000 ya (Owsley and Jantz, 2000; Steele, 2000).

There are, of course, no uniform biological "types" of human beings in the sense once assumed by traditional classifiers of race (see Chapter 4). Generalities regarding human variation must, considering the nature of genetic recombination and the effects of environment and nutrition, be taken simply as that—generalities. Still, the lack of distinctive Native American physical markers on the oldest skeletal specimens has stimulated research on how the early population of the Americas, as represented by these individuals, may be related to contemporary populations.

Neves and colleagues (2004) compared the cranial morphology of nine individuals from central Brazil dated to around 10,200 ya. The researchers concluded that these individuals represent one of possibly several populations that participated in the peopling of the Americas from Asia. The researchers argue that the differences between the cranial morphology of these individuals and that of modern Native American populations are consistent with those seen in morphological comparisons elsewhere in the Americas (e.g., Owsley and Jantz, 2000; Brace et al., 2001). Similar differences also exist between Late Pleistocene and recent populations in Asia, and the modern typical morphological pattern of Asia is likely a recent development that may have followed the adoption of agriculture (Jantz and Owsley, 2001).

Studies like these are a great help in placing recent finds such as Kennewick Man into context. When the facial reconstruction of Kennewick Man (see Fig. 13-6) was completed in 1997, more than a few people wondered why it looked more like the British actor Patrick Stewart of *Star Trek* fame than the popular stereotype of Native Americans (think of the man's profile on the old U.S. buffalo nickel). Quite a lot was read into that reconstruction, but all it really showed was what researchers like Neves, Jantz, Owsley, and others already knew: We don't have much data to work from, but what we do have shows similar morphological variation in Asia and the Americas among Late Pleistocene–early Holocene skeletons. The data support Steele and Powell's (1999) conclusions that there seems to have been more than one prehistoric migration from Asia into the New World. The argument has intuitive appeal. After all, why would the supply of immigrants dry up after the first humans arrived in the New World?

Looking at the entire span of the human presence in the New World, it seems evident that the flow of people to the New World has roughly kept pace with the development of technology to bring them here. In this view, at least, the peopling of the New World can best be viewed as a continuing process, not a one-time event.

The particular physical traits shared by modern Native Americans are almost surely derived from a small founding gene pool and thus a product of founder effect. (For a discussion of founder effect, an example of genetic drift, see Chapter 3.) As in virtually all other areas of biological anthropology, molecular research is shedding new light on where the earliest Americans came from (O'Rourke and Raff, 2010). Recent analyses of mitochondrial DNA among contemporary Native American populations suggest that just four or five genetically related lineages contributed to the early peopling of the Americas and that these groups came from Asia (Tamm et al., 2007). Far

more detailed molecular evidence showing geographical patterns in nuclear DNA support this view (Jacobsson et al., 2008; Li et al., 2008). While these molecular data show very clearly that early Americans share their closest genetic links with East Asian populations, particularly those from Siberia, it remains less certain what route early immigrants took once they reached North America. More detailed analysis using nuclear DNA, which already has provided data on hundreds of thousands of genetic loci, may well provide more complete answers.

Another intriguing source of genetic data that may provide insights has recently come from the Paisley Caves site in Oregon, where 14,000-year-old feces, or **coprolites**, yielded human hair and human DNA (Gilbert et al., 2008). These new data support the coastal route hypothesis for the entry of humans into the continental United States well before the development of the Clovis complex and before the ice-free corridor opened up.

Cultural Traces of the Earliest Americans

Much of the cultural evidence documenting the presence of the earliest Americans is no less controversial than that gained from analyses of the skeletal data. Nearly all archaeologists agree that Native Americans originated in northeastern Asia (yes, Kennewick Man's ancestors, too); yet they have varying opinions about when people first arrived in the New World and the routes by which they traveled (see Meltzer, 2009). Most of the controversy focuses on the span between 30,000 and 13,200 ya. The earlier date represents the time by which modern people first began to appear in those parts of Asia closest to North America—for example, the Yana RHS site in Siberia (see p. 311). And everyone agrees that the **Paleo-Indian** Clovis complex was present in North America by the later date.

Like the biological anthropologists, archaeologists have a tough time reaching consensus on such basic questions as: What are the material remains of the earliest inhabitants of the New World?

coprolites Preserved fecal material, which can be studied for what the contents reveal about diet and health.

Paleo-Indian (*paleo*, meaning "ancient") Referring to early hunter-gatherers who occupied the Americas from about 13,500 to 10,000 ya.

When did they arrive? Where did they come from? That robust answers are not forthcoming isn't for want of research; it is simply the case that the evidence is sparsely scattered over millions of square miles and is not necessarily very distinctive. As biological anthropologists and archaeologists have learned, answering these questions takes decades of hard work—and more than a little luck.

What kind of archaeological evidence can we point to that *has* survived from this early period of American prehistory? The answer depends largely on how one evaluates the "evidence." For example, isolated artifacts, including stone choppers and large flake tools of simple form, are at times recovered from exposed ground surfaces and other undatable contexts in the Americas. They are sometimes proposed as evidence of a period predating the use of bifacial projectile points, which were common in North America by 13,200 ya (see Meltzer, 2009, pp. 97–117). If typologically primitive-looking finds cannot be securely dated, most (but not all) archaeologists regard them with justifiable caution. The appearance of great age or crude condition may be misleading and is all but impossible to verify without corroborating evidence. To be properly evaluated, an artifact must be unquestionably the product of human handiwork and must have been recovered from a geologically sealed and undisturbed context that can be dated reliably.

Sounds pretty straightforward, right? The reality of the situation is not that easy. Take, for example, the projectile points. Alan Bryan and Ruth Gruhn (2003) point out that North American archaeologists' obsession with bifacially flaked stone points may ultimately do more harm than good to research, because we have no basis for believing that such tools were a consistent part of prehistoric assemblages everywhere in the Americas. They note, for example, that bifacially flaked projectile points are far less common in Central and South America than they are in the continental United States and southern Canada. In fact, in some parts of lowland South America, Native American groups never did use bifacially worked stone tool technology (Bryan and Gruhn, 2003, p. 175). The implication is obvious: The criteria that work for identifying the earliest Americans in one part of the two continents may not apply to other parts.

Most difficult to assess are some atypical sites that have been carefully excavated by researchers who sincerely believe that their work offers proof of great human antiquity in the New World. Currently, several South American sites fall into this disputed category (see Fig. 13-5). Pedra Furada is a rock-shelter in northeastern Brazil where excavators found what they claim to be simple stone tools in association with charcoal hearths dating back 40,000 years (Guidon et al., 1996). Others who have examined these materials remain convinced that natural, rather than cultural, factors account for them (Lynch, 1990; Meltzer et al., 1994). The dating of this and other sites in the same general region also continue to be reexamined. Additional radiocarbon age estimates on samples from hearths in the lowest levels of Pedra Furada recently yielded dates in excess of 50,000 ya (Santos et al., 2003). However, fresh radiocarbon dates on Pedra Furada pigments and rock paintings, both of which are thought by their excavators to be nearly 30,000 years old, yielded estimates of only 3,500–2,000 ya (Rowe and Steelman, 2003). So, it could be the oldest site in South America—or it could be so recent as to be irrelevant. Pedra Furada joins several other Central and South American locations that in recent decades have been proposed as extremely early cultural sites (Meltzer, 2009). Archaeologists have been uncertain how to evaluate most of them because the associated cultural materials are so typologically diverse and their contexts are frequently secondary, or mixed, geological deposits.

The United States, too, has its share of potentially early sites that defy easy explanation. The most intriguing recent example is the Debra L. Friedkin site in central Texas, where archaeologists have found a large pre-Clovis assemblage of more than 15,000 artifacts, including bifaces, cores, flake tools, and stone toolmaking debris, stratigraphically beneath the remains of a Clovis assemblage (Pringle, 2011; Waters et al., 2011). The estimated age of the pre-Clovis assemblage, which is based on 18 **optically stimulated luminescence** (Rhodes, 2011) analyses of floodplain clays in which the artifacts were found, is between 15,500 and 13,200 ya, or before the beginning of Clovis. While it is too soon to say how well this site and its dating will bear up under the intense scientific scrutiny to which it will be subjected over the next few years, it is a very promising North American case that may help begin to explain the origins of Clovis and its relationship to the earliest inhabitants of North America.

Far to the east, at the Cactus Hill site along the Nottoway River in southern Virginia and at the Topper site in Allendale County, South Carolina, archaeologists have retrieved unusual assemblages of stone cores, flakes, and tools from strata lying well beneath more typical Paleo-Indian components (Dixon, 1999). The early radiocarbon dates (18,000–15,000 ya) associated with these materials are consistent with their stratigraphic position (e.g., Wagner and McAvoy, 2004), but, as with the Debra L. Friedkin site, the evidence will require cautious review before these sites are generally accepted.

The scientific method is not a democratic process; we can't simply dismiss (or side with) unpopular positions without assessing the evidence as it is presented. The method is, however, a skeptical one; and the burden of proof to substantiate claims of great antiquity falls upon those who make them. Each allegation requires critical evaluation, a process that the general public sometimes perceives as unnecessarily conservative or obstructive. Information regarding dating results, archaeological contexts, and whether or not materials are of cultural origin must all be scrutinized and accepted before intense debate can resolve into consensus.

This evaluation process may take years. Consider, for example, the case of the Meadowcroft Rock Shelter, near Pittsburgh, Pennsylvania. In a meticulous excavation over 25 years ago, archaeologists explored a deeply strati-

fied site containing cultural levels dated at between 19,000 and 14,000 ya by standard radiocarbon methods (Adovasio et al., 1990). Stratum IIa, from which the earliest dates derive, contained several prismatic blades, a retouched flake, a biface, and a knifelike implement (**Fig. 13-7**). None of the tools from this deep stratum are particularly distinctive, and the final detailed excavation report on this important site has yet to be published, so it's hard to assess technological relationships with other assemblages or, indeed, the full significance of Meadowcroft's contribution to the scientific understanding of the early human presence in North America.

Excavations at Monte Verde, in southern Chile, revealed another remarkable site of apparent pre–Paleo-Indian age (Dillehay, 1989, 1997). Here, remnants of the wooden foundations of a dozen rectangular huts were arranged back to back in a parallel row. The structures measured between 10 and 15 feet on a side, and animal hides may have covered their sapling frameworks. Apart from the main cluster, a separate wishbone-shaped building contained stone tools and animal bones (**Fig. 13-8**). The cultural equipment comprised spheroids (possibly sling stones), flaked stone points, perforating tools, a wooden lance, digging sticks, mortars, and fire pits. Mastodon bones represented at least seven individuals, and remains of some 100 species of nuts, fruits, berries, wild tubers, and firewood testify to the major role of plants in subsistence activities at this site. Incredibly, preservation conditions at Monte Verde were such that researchers were able to identify nine species of seaweeds that had been brought from the coast to this inland site for use as food and medicine (Dillehay et al., 2008).

Monte Verde's greatest significance, however, is simply its age, which is about 14,500 years old, with a few features possibly much older. The site's age was hotly contested until 1997, when a "jury" of archaeological specialists reviewed the findings, visited the site, and finally agreed that the excavator's claims for the pre-Clovis age of Monte Verde were substantiated. This was important because it meant that the

Figure 13-7

Knifelike implement from Stratum IIa at the Meadowcroft rock-shelter in Pennsylvania.

optically stimulated luminescence A new (and still developing) dating method that estimates the amount of time that has elapsed since grains of quartz or feldspar were last exposed to daylight. Datable samples can be as small as a single grain.

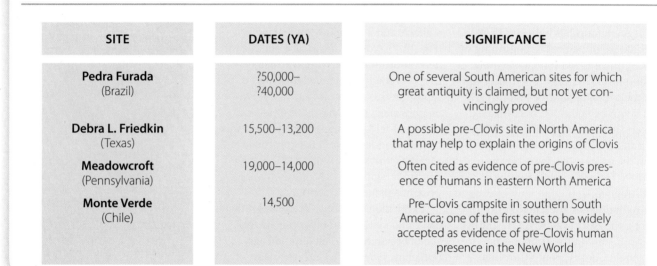

At a Glance

Important Pre-Paleo-Indian Sites in the New World

SITE	DATES (YA)	SIGNIFICANCE
Pedra Furada (Brazil)	?50,000– ?40,000	One of several South American sites for which great antiquity is claimed, but not yet convincingly proved
Debra L. Friedkin (Texas)	15,500–13,200	A possible pre-Clovis site in North America that may help to explain the origins of Clovis
Meadowcroft (Pennsylvania)	19,000–14,000	Often cited as evidence of pre-Clovis presence of humans in eastern North America
Monte Verde (Chile)	14,500	Pre-Clovis campsite in southern South America; one of the first sites to be widely accepted as evidence of pre-Clovis human presence in the New World

© Cengage Learning 2013

Tom Dillehay

Figure 13-8

The semicircular ridge of soil at lower right in the photograph marks the remains of a 14,800-year-old hut at Monte Verde, Chile. Mastodon bones, hide, and flesh were preserved in association with this feature, along with 26 species of medicinal plants.

fluted point A biface or projectile point having had long, thin flakes removed from each face to prepare the base for hafting, or attachment to a shaft.

mainstream of archaeological thought accepted that Monte Verde contained material evidence of a human presence in the New World more than a thousand years before the beginning of the Clovis complex around 13,200 ya in North America. And, more generally, the acceptance of Monte Verde's great antiquity implied that archaeologists had a lot to learn about the colonization of the New World because it had just gotten a lot older (Grayson, 2004; Meltzer, 2004).

Paleo-Indians in the Americas

For much of the twentieth century, most archaeologists held the view that the Clovis complex marked the earliest material evidence for the entry of people into the Americas below the Canadian glaciers about 13,200 ya. These highly mobile Paleo-Indian hunter-gatherers then spread rapidly across the United States (**Fig. 13-9**; Hamilton and Buchanan, 2007).

The distinctive **fluted point** became the Paleo-Indian period's hallmark artifact, at least in North America. Each face of a fluted point typically displays a groove (or "flute") resulting from the removal of a long channel flake, possibly to make it easier to use a special hafting technique for mounting the point on a shaft (**Fig. 13-10**). Other typical Paleo-Indian artifacts include a variety of stone cutting and scraping tools and, less commonly, preserved bone rods and points (Gramly, 1992).

While the general Paleo-Indian tool kit from North America probably would have been familiar to Upper Paleolithic groups in northeastern Asia, no clear technological predecessors of fluted points have yet been identified in Asia.

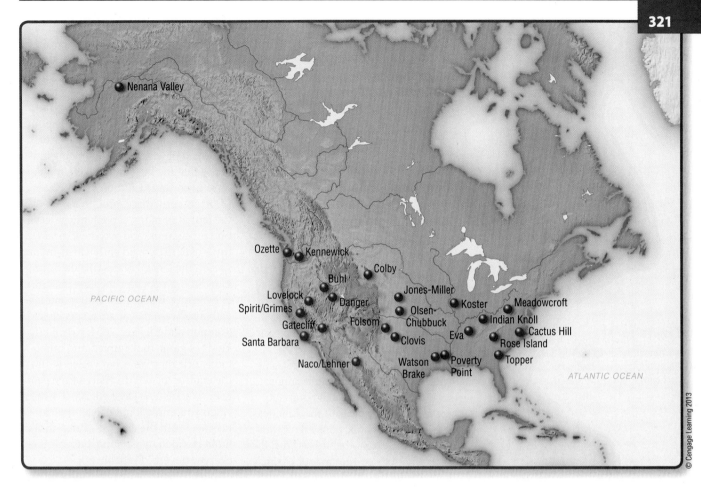

Figure 13-9

North American Paleo-Indian and Archaic sites.

It's possible that fluted point technology is an American invention and there are no ancestral Asian forms to find. Sites such as Yana RHS, in Siberia, demonstrate that Upper Paleolithic hunter-gatherers, like Paleo-Indians, made bifacially worked stone tools and tipped their spears with projectile points—but not *fluted* projectile points. These Siberian hunters set projectile points in bone or ivory foreshafts and were living in the general region of Beringia more than 15,000 years before the earliest evidence of human presence appears in the New World. Bifacial points and knives are also part of the Nenana complex sites of central Alaska and the lower levels of Ushki Lake (see Fig. 13-4) in Siberia's Kamchatka Peninsula. All of these sites are currently believed to date to around 13,400–13,000 ya (Goebel et al., 2003), which is too late for their inhabitants to have been the ancestors of the people who developed Paleo-Indian fluted point technology. Nevertheless, the sites do demonstrate that generally similar tool industries

were moving into the New World at an early date.

Paleo-Indian Lifeways

Current research is chiseling away at the long-standing image of Paleo-Indian uniformity in weaponry and hunting behavior and the rapid spread of Paleo-Indian populations across the Americas about 13,200 ya to reach as far south as Fell's Cave in Patagonia in South America by some 11,000 ya (see Fig. 13-5). It was also long assumed that these rapidly moving Paleo-Indian hunters quickly made cultural adjustments as they dispersed through the varied environments of the New World during the terminal Pleistocene and early Holocene.

The recent acceptance of Monte Verde and other sites as evidence of a human presence in the Americas *before* Clovis is stimulating a major reexamination of these and other interpretations of Paleo-Indian lifeways. One of the main shortcomings of these interpretations is the assumption that the fluted point

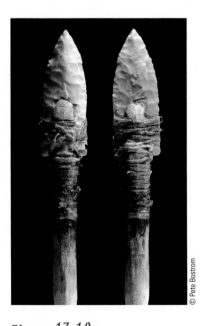

Figure 13-10

Modern copy of a Clovis fluted point mounted in a foreshaft (shows each side).

William Turnbaugh

Figure 13-11

Molar teeth of mastodon (left) and mammoth (right). Mastodons browsed on evergreen branches; mammoths grazed on low vegetation. Paleo-Indian hunters may have contributed to their extinction.

technology was a consistent part of prehistoric assemblages across the Americas and that people everywhere were using the technology to do the same things. As Bryan and Gruhn (2003) point out, there are certainly parts of the Americas in which these assumptions aren't warranted. To the extent that this is true, the uniformity of Paleo-Indian tool kits may often be more the creation of archaeologists than of the archaeology.

The same appears to be true of the long-held view of Paleo-Indians as specialized hunters of Pleistocene **megafauna** —animals over 100 pounds, including the mammoth, mastodon, giant bison, horse, camel, and ground sloth (**Figs. 13-11** and **13-12**). Of the sites associated

with Paleo-Indians, the most impressive are undoubtedly the places where ancient hunters actually killed and butchered such megafauna as mammoth and giant bison (**Fig. 13-13**). At many of these kill sites, knives, scrapers, and finely flaked and fluted projectile points are directly associated with the animal bones, all of which are convincing evidence that the megafauna were human prey. Even so, as Cannon and Meltzer (2004) recently discovered in a review of the faunal remains, taphonomy, excavation procedures, and archaeological features of 62 excavated early Paleo-Indian sites in the United States, the data "provide little support for the idea that all, or even any, Early Paleo-Indian hunter-gatherers were megafaunal specialists" (Cannon and Meltzer, 2004, p. 1955). The kinds of game they hunted and other foodstuffs they collected varied with the environmental diversity of the continent (Walker and Driskell, 2007), which, when you think about it, isn't that surprising. So, in the end, yes, Paleo-Indian hunters killed megafauna, but was it an everyday event? Probably not.

North American archaeologists have identified a sequence of Paleo-Indian cultures in the western Plains and Southwest based on changing tool technology, chronology, and the biggest game species thought to be typical of each period. From about 13,200 to 12,800 ya, hunters employed Clovis-type fluted points (**Fig. 13-14a**; also see

Figure 13-12

The largest American woolly mammoths were over 13 feet high at the shoulder, with long, downward-curving tusks.

© INTERFOTO / Alamy

megafauna Literally, "large animals," those weighing over 100 pounds.

Wyoming State Archaeologist's Office, Department of State Parks and Cultural Resources

Figure 13-13

Partially articulated remains of three mammoths, one of several bone piles that probably represent Paleo-Indian meat caches at the Colby site in Wyoming.

Fig. 13-10). On at least 20 western sites, including Colby, in Wyoming, and Naco and Lehner, in southern Arizona, their spear tips lie embedded in mammoth remains (see Fig. 13-13). Similar points from northern Alaska retain residues that have been biochemically identified as mammoth red blood cells and hemoglobin crystals (Loy and Dixon, 1998). Meat—but not all of it from mammoths—was part of the diet of these early Americans. Isotopic analysis of Buhl Woman's (see p. 316) bone collagen indicates that her diet was largely game and fish, much of it probably preserved by sun-drying or smoking. The heavy wear on her teeth suggests that she regularly ingested grit in her food, probably the residue of grinding stones used to pulverize the dried meat (Green et al., 1998).

Fluted projectile points and evidence of a varied Paleo-Indian diet are also found in eastern North America. While Pleistocene megafauna kill sites are known from the East, these hunter-gatherers also ate caribou, deer, and smaller game (Cannon and Meltzer, 2004). Early Paleo-Indian sites in New Hampshire, Massachusetts, and New York appear to be the remains of caribou-hunting camps (Cannon and Meltzer, 2004, p. 1971). A mixed subsistence of smaller game, fish, and gathered plants supplied Paleo-Indians at a site in eastern Pennsylvania (McNett, 1985). And a Florida site yielded a bison skull that has what looks like part of a Paleo-Indian projectile point embedded in it. The age of this specimen, however, is uncertain (Mihlbachler et al., 2000). Acquiring such resources surely involved the use of a variety of equipment made from perishable materials, such as nets and baskets, but only the stone spear tips survive at most Paleo-Indian sites.

Excavations along the lower Amazon in northern Brazil provide further evidence for other kinds of Paleo-Indian food-getting practices (Roosevelt et al., 1996). Carbonized seeds, nuts, and faunal remains at Pedra Pintada Cave, in the Amazon basin, indicate a broad-based food-collecting, fishing, and small game hunting way of life in the tropical rain forest around 12,000 ya. In other sites along the Pacific slope of the Andes, mastodons, horses, sloths, deer, camelids, and smaller animals were consumed, along with tuberous roots (Lynch, 1983).

During later Paleo-Indian times on the Great Plains of North America, the Clovis fluted spear points gave way to another fluted point style that archaeologists call **Folsom** (Meltzer, 2006; **Fig. 13-14b**). Smaller and thinner than Clovis points, but with a proportionally larger

Folsom Paleo-Indian archaeological complex of the southern Great Plains, around 12,500 ya, characterized by fluted projectile points used for hunting now-extinct bison.

At a Glance

Important Paleo-Indian Sites in the New World

SITE	DATES (YA)	SIGNIFICANCE
Colby (Wyoming) and **Naco/Lehner** (Arizona)	13,500–13,000	Paleo-Indian sites where tools and other artifacts are found associated with the remains of mammoths
Pedra Pintada Cave (Brazil)	ca. 12,000	Early site with evidence of a broad-spectrum hunter-gatherer way of life in the tropical rain forest
Olsen-Chubbuck (Colorado)	9,400	Bison kill site, created when a herd was stampeded across a narrow gully in eastern Colorado
Kennewick (Washington)	9,300	One of the few early North American human skeletons; object of a nine-year court battle to decide if scientists would be permitted to study his remains

© Cengage Learning 2013

central flute, Folsom points are associated exclusively with the bones of the now-extinct giant long-horned bison.

In turn, Folsom points soon gave way to a long sequence of new point forms—a variety of unfluted but slender and finely parallel-flaked projectile points collectively called **Plano** (**Fig. 13-14c**), which came into general use throughout the West even as modern-day *Bison bison* was supplanting its larger Pleistocene relatives. At some Great Plains sites, like Olsen-Chubbuck and Jones-Miller, in Colorado, an effective technique of bison hunting was for hunters to stampede the animals into dry streambeds or over cliffs and then quickly dispatch those that survived the fall (Wheat, 1972; Frison, 1978). Remember, the horse had not yet been reintroduced onto the Plains (the Spanish brought them in the sixteenth century), so these early bison hunters were strictly pedestrians.

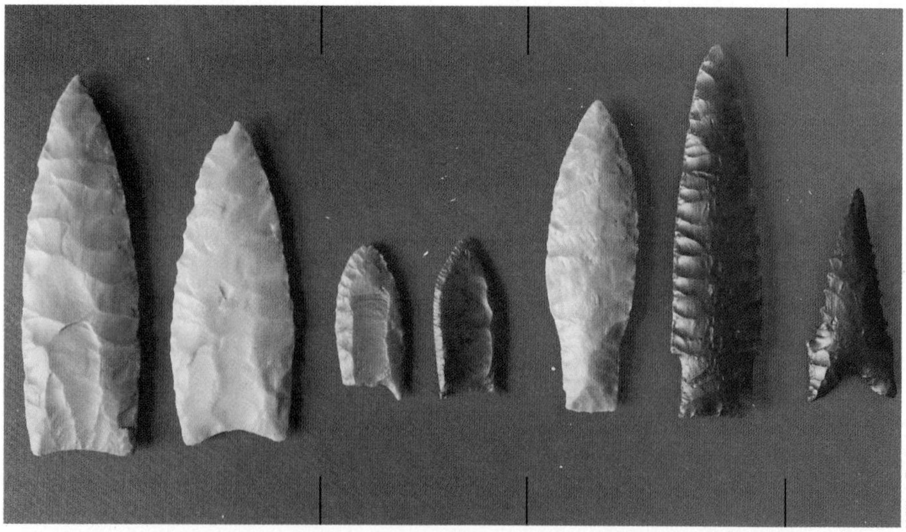

Figure 13-14

North American Paleo-Indian projectile points. (a) Clovis. (b) Folsom. (c) Plano. (d) Dalton (length 2.4 inches).

William Turnbaugh

(a)   (b)   (c)   (d)

Plano Great Plains bison-hunting culture of 11,000–9,000 ya, which employed narrow, unfluted points.

At a Glance

North American Paleo-Indian Cultures

SITE	DATES (YA)	SIGNIFICANCE
Clovis	13,200–12,800	Earliest universally acknowledged Late Pleistocene hunter-gatherers who occupied much of North America below the glacial ice masses of the northern latitudes; used distinctive fluted spear or dart projectile points
Folsom	ca. 12,500	Late Pleistocene hunter-gatherers who hunted now-extinct giant long-horned bison in the American Southwest
Plano	11,000–9,000	Hunter-gatherers of the Great Plains; their unfluted spear or dart points are associated only with modern fauna
Dalton	10,500–10,000	Hunter-gatherers of the American Southeast whose unfluted dart points are associated with modern fauna; distinctive adze woodworking tools

Again, there was regional variation, not only in how different groups of hunter-gatherers made a living in the diverse environments of North America, but also in their technology. The temporal pattern of changing point styles found in the western United States does not hold in the East, where later Paleo-Indians employed other types of projectile points, such as the Dalton variety (**Fig. 13-14d**). Poor bone preservation generally leaves us with little direct information about these groups' hunting techniques or favored prey in this region, though deer probably extended their range at the expense of caribou as oak forests expanded over much of the eastern United States.

Pleistocene Extinctions

Evidence like that found mainly in the American West, where bones of mammoths and other large herbivores have been excavated in undeniable association with the weapons used to kill them, led some researchers to blame Paleo-Indian hunters for the extinction of North American Pleistocene megafauna. Geoscientist Paul S. Martin (1967, 2005), who viewed Clovis sites as evidence of the first people in North America, argued for decades that overhunting by the newly arrived and rapidly expanding human population caused the swift extermination, around 13,000 ya, of these animals throughout the New World. He pointed out that over half of the large mammal species found in the Americas when humans first arrived were gone within just a few centuries, especially those whose habits and habitats would have made them most vulnerable to hunters.

Paleo-Indian hunter-gatherers certainly hunted Pleistocene megafauna. As we noted earlier, archaeologists have excavated several sites where such game was killed and butchered. But evidence that these animals were human prey doesn't also prove that humans hunted them to extinction. The problem is complex for reasons that are still hotly contested (Haynes, 2009). First, it has yet to be proved that Paleo-Indian hunter-gatherers anywhere focused most of their food-getting effort on Pleistocene megafauna (Meltzer, 1993a; Cannon and Meltzer, 2004). What we're finding instead is that Paleo-Indian groups hunted and collected a range of animals and plants, the mix of which varied regionally (Walker and Driskell, 2007).

Second, species extinction is a natural process, and it's no less common than the emergence of new species. It

Dalton Late or transitional Paleo-Indian projectile point type that dates between 10,000 and 8,000 ya in the eastern United States..

happens for various reasons, and at least until modern times, these reasons seldom had anything to do with human agency. Yes, many North American megafaunal species went extinct toward the end of the Pleistocene. But if you look at the North American geological record, you'll find that many species also became extinct in the Pliocene, Miocene, and so on. Our point is that the geological record provides abundant evidence that natural processes are sufficient to account for species extinctions. It has yet to be convincingly demonstrated that Paleo-Indian hunters were a more important factor than natural processes in the extinction of Late Pleistocene megafauna.

One possible exception appears to be the extinction of proboscideans—mammoths, mastodons, elephants, and their relatives. Surovell and colleagues (2005) took a long-term view of the problem and examined the global archaeological record of human exploitation of proboscideans in 41 sites that span roughly the past 1.8 million years. They conclude that local extinctions of proboscideans on five continents correlate well with the global colonization patterns of humans, not climatic changes or other natural factors. This finding suggests that we can't entirely dismiss the possibility that humans played a role in the Late Pleistocene extinctions of some species.

The end of the Pleistocene marked an interval of profound climatic and geographical changes (for example, the creation of the Great Lakes) in North America and elsewhere. Geoarchaeologists also recognize that Late Pleistocene extinctions and the expansion of Paleo-Indian hunters coincided with a time of widespread drought that was immediately followed by rapidly plunging temperatures. The latter climatic event, called the **Younger Dryas** stadial, marked a return to near-glacial conditions and persisted for 1,500 years, from roughly 13,000 to 11,500 ya (Fiedel, 1999). These changing climatic conditions were apparently not necessarily catastrophic for Paleo-Indians in North America (Meltzer and Holliday, 2010). For example, human populations in parts of the Southeast (Anderson et al., 2011) and Great Lakes region (Ellis et al.,

2011) appear to have initially declined but later resurged during the Younger Dryas. As Meltzer and Holliday (2010, p. 32) explain it, "adapting to changing climatic and environmental conditions was nothing new to them [Paleo-Indians]. It was what they did."

And in an extraordinary twist to the North American Younger Dryas story, Firestone and colleagues (2007) recently argued that the explosion of a meteor or other large extraterrestrial object over North America about 12,900 ya contributed directly to the Pleistocene megafaunal extinctions and the onset of the Younger Dryas and, ultimately, to the end of the Paleo-Indian period! Their hypothesis has attracted considerable attention, mostly by the media; the scientific community has expressed considerable skepticism (Kerr, 2008).

The degree of human involvement in these New World extinctions will continue to be controversial. Grayson and Meltzer (2002, 2003, 2004) maintain that no archaeological evidence supports the idea that humans caused the mass extinction of Pleistocene megafauna in North America. They further argue that Paul S. Martin's original hypothesis has been altered into something that is no longer testable and that persists partly because it feeds contemporary political views concerning human effects on the environment. Others take issue with such views, both directly (e.g., Fiedel and Haynes, 2004) and indirectly (Barnosky et al., 2004), and argue for a possible human role.

Early Holocene Hunter-Gatherers

Environmental effects at the end of the last Ice Age extended well beyond the waning glaciers. Much of the Northern Hemisphere experienced radical environmental change during the transition from the Late Pleistocene epoch to the mid-Holocene, which left only the polar regions and Greenland with permanent ice caps. Climatic fluctuations, the redistribution or even extinction of many plant and animal species, and the reshaping of coastlines as sea lev-

Younger Dryas A stadial, or colder stage, between roughly 13,000 and 11,500 ya. The climate became colder and drier but did not return to full glacial conditions in higher latitudes.

els rose hundreds of feet from their Late Pleistocene elevations all affected many of the world's human inhabitants. Their technologies, homes, economic patterns, and lives were transformed as they adapted to the changing world in which they lived.

Environmental Changes

Dramatically higher temperatures after the end of the Younger Dryas—for example, an increase of average July temperature by perhaps 20°F—rapidly melted the glaciers. As they receded to higher latitudes, these great ice sheets left behind thick mantles of silt, mud, rocks, and boulders in **till plains**. Sediment-choked rivers and streams cut fresh channels and deposited new terraces with the ebb and flow of meltwater runoff. Tons upon tons of fine silt were lifted by winds across the newly exposed plains and redeposited as **loess**. In North America, the Great Lakes gradually formed as the glaciers retreated. Eventually, by 5,000 ya, sea levels had risen as much as 400 feet in some parts of the world, drowning the broad Pleistocene coastal plains and flooding into inlets to shape the continental margins we recognize today. By then, overflow from the rising Mediterranean had spilled into a low-lying basin to create the Black Sea, and the North and Baltic seas finally separated the British Isles and Scandinavia from the rest of Europe. To fully appreciate the archaeological significance of these changes, consider the fact that the rise in sea level at the end of the Pleistocene cost Europe as much as 40 percent of its landmass (Bailey and King, 2010). Consequently, much that we have yet to learn about Upper Paleolithic and Archaic/Mesolithic coastal adaptations lies buried under hundreds of feet of seawater off modern coastlines!

As deglaciation proceeded, the major biotic zones expanded northward, so that areas once covered by ice were clothed successively in tundra, grassland, fir and spruce forests, pine, and then mixed deciduous forests (Delcourt and Delcourt, 1991). Like the plants, temperate forest animals displaced their Arctic counterparts. Grazers like the

musk ox and caribou, or reindeer, which had ranged over the Late Pleistocene tundra or grasslands, gave way to browsing species, such as moose and deer, which fed on leaves and the tender twigs of forest plants. Meanwhile, the annual mean summer temperatures continued to climb toward the local **climatic maximum**, attained between 8,000 and 6,000 ya in many areas. By then, July temperatures averaged as much as 5°F higher than at present. Lakes that had formed during the Ice Age as a result of increased precipitation in nonglaciated areas of the American West, southwest Asia (the Near East), and Africa now evaporated under more arid conditions, bringing great ecological changes to those regions, too.

These geoclimatic transformations most directly affected the temperate latitudes, including northern and central Europe and the northern parts of America. They were sufficient to alter conditions of life for plants and animals by creating new niches for some species and pushing others toward extinction. We can't measure precisely how these shifting natural conditions may have affected human populations, although they surely did.

Cultural Adjustments

Environmental readjustments are the natural consequences of climatic change. Although many of the changes that happened at the end of the Pleistocene were slow enough that they passed largely unnoticed by individuals, much depended on the terrain where the changes occurred. For example, on the low-lying coast of Denmark, where sea level rose 1.5 to 2 inches per year during the early Holocene, "during his lifetime many a Stone Age man must have seen his childhood home swallowed up by the sea" (Fischer, 1995, p. 380). The environmental impacts were cumulative, and in time the redistribution of living plant and animal species, plus variations in local topography, drainage, and exposure, created a mosaic of new habitats, some of which invited human exploitation and settlement.

Cultures in both hemispheres kept pace with these changes by adjusting

till plains Accumulations of stones, boulders, mud, sand, and silt deposited by glaciers as they melt; ground moraines.

loess (luss) Fine-grained soil composed of glacially pulverized rock, deposited by the wind.

climatic maximum Episode of higher average annual temperatures that affected much of the globe for several millennia after the end of the last Ice Age; also known as the *altithermal* in the western United States or *hypsithermal* in the East.

Figure 13-15

Mesolithic ground stone axes. Fitted into the socket of a wooden haft or handle, such axes were effective woodworking tools and weapons.

5 Cm

Barry Lewis

their ways of coping with local conditions. Distinctive climatic and cultural circumstances prevailed in different regions. Recognizing this variability (and acknowledging regional differences in the history of archaeological reconstructions of the past), archaeologists have devised specific terms to designate the early and middle Holocene cultures that turned to intensive hunting, fishing, and gathering lifeways in response to post-Pleistocene conditions. In the New World, the **Archaic** period broadly applies to post-Pleistocene hunter-gatherers. In Europe, this period is called the **Mesolithic**. And in the Near East and eastward into parts of Asia, the **Epipaleolithic** period spans much the same interval.

Holocene hunter-gatherers in temperate latitudes extracted their livelihood from a range of local resources by hunting, fishing, and gathering. The relative economic importance of each of these subsistence activities varied from region to region and even from season to season within a given area. In some places, the focus on different food sources, particularly more plants, fish, shellfish, birds, and smaller mammals, corresponded to a lesser emphasis on hunting big game. What accounts for this shift? First, many former prey animals were by then extinct or—like the reindeer—locally unobtainable, having followed their receding habitat north with the waning ice sheets. Additionally, one way to accommodate both the environmental

changes and human population growth was to broaden the definition of *food* by exploiting a wider range of potentially edible species.

New habitats and prey species presented challenges and opportunities. Among the important archaeological reflections of cultural adjustments to the changing natural and social environments of the postglacial world were new tools and ways of making tools that can be found in the sites of these periods. Important raw materials for tools and other implements included stone, bone, antler, and leather, as well as bark and other plant materials (Clark, 1967; Bordaz, 1970). With the spread of temperate forests, ground stone axes, adzes, and other tools became important items in tool kits (**Fig. 13-15**). Wood tended to replace animal bones, tallow, and herbivore dung as the primary fuel and served well for house posts, spear shafts, bowls, and countless smaller items. Wooden dugout canoes and skin-covered boats aided in navigating streams and crossing larger bodies of water. Hunter-gatherers caught large quantities of fish in nets, woven basketry traps, and brushwood or stone fish dams designed to block the mouths of small tidal streams. With the aid of axes and containers, the people extracted the honey of wild bees from hollow trees (**Fig. 13-16**).

© Cengage Learning 2013

Figure 13-16

A Mesolithic forager uses a basket or bag to collect honey from a nest of wild bees in this ancient painting on a rock-shelter wall in southeastern Spain.

Archaic North American archaeological period that follows the end of the Ice Age and traditionally ends with the beginning of the use of ceramics; equivalent to the Mesolithic in the Old World.

Mesolithic (*meso*, meaning "middle," and *lith*, meaning "stone") An early postglacial period of hunter-gatherers, especially in northwestern Europe.

Epipaleolithic (*epi*, meaning "after") Late Pleistocene and early Holocene period of foragers and collectors in the Near East and adjacent parts of Asia.

Hunter-Gatherer Lifeways Under the general category of *hunting and gathering*, researchers recognize a range of subsistence strategies used by early Holocene people as well as their more recent counterparts (Kelly, 1995).

These strategies often vary with the relative mobility of such groups. At one end of the spectrum are **foragers**, who tend to live in small groups that move camp frequently as valued food resources come into season across their home range. Viewed archaeologically, forager campsites often show little investment in substantial shelters, storage facilities, and other features that reflect a long-term commitment to that site. At the other end are **collectors**, who are typically less mobile, staying in some camps for long periods and drawing on a wide range of locally available plant and animal foods that they bring back to camp for consumption. Collector campsites tend to show evidence of long-term occupation, including **middens**, storage facilities, cemeteries, and mounds. As Conneller (2004, p. 920) simply puts it, "foragers can be characterised as people moving to resources, while collectors move resources to people." Most hunter-gatherers lived somewhere between these extremes and emphasized more of one or the other food-getting approaches as the changing natural and social conditions warranted.

Considering the environmental complexity of the temperate regions in the Holocene, including a diverse array of potentially exploitable plants and animals, the food-getting methods that worked well in one region were not always effective in another. Holocene hunter-gatherers invented specialized equipment to help them take advantage of local resources, and we can reasonably assume that they approached cultural solutions to such problems with detailed practical knowledge and understanding of the local environment and its assets.

In foraging, anyone—young or old, male or female—might contribute to the general food supply by taking up whatever resources are at hand. But this isn't the same as saying that foragers eat whatever comes to hand. Human food-getting is selective, whether it's based on what you encounter in the forest that day or find on sale in the local supermarket. Preferred foods are usually those that are most readily available, easily collected and processed, tasty, and nutritious. So, while the San people of the Kalahari Desert in southwestern Africa regard about 80 local plants as edible, they rely mostly on about a dozen of them as primary foods (A. Smith et al., 2000). They use the rest of the foods less often, but know they can eat them when times are tough.

Particularly in regions with only minor seasonal fluctuations in wild food supplies, foraging held prospects for good returns. Jochim (1976, 1998) estimated that foraging activities could maintain a stable population density of about one person per 4 square miles in some regions. More territory might be required to sustain people in less favorable situations or where continuing environmental fluctuations influenced the composition and predictability of animal and plant communities or the stability of estuaries and coastlines.

In areas where dramatic seasonal variations in rainfall or temperature affected resource availability, day-to-day foraging might not always yield a stable diet. Human population density and equilibrium could be maintained only if the group adopted an alternative strategy. Familiarity with their environment enabled people to predict when specific resources should reach peak productivity or desirability. By making well-informed decisions, hunters and gatherers scheduled their movements so they would arrive on the scene at the best season for obtaining a particularly important food. Seasonality and resource scheduling are familiar issues for most, if not all, foragers.

Compared with foragers, food collectors relied much more on a few seasonally abundant resources, and their camps often show evidence of specialized processing and storage technologies that allowed them to balance out fluctuations and remain longer in one place. For example, migratory fish might be split and cured; and nuts or seeds could be parched and stored away in baskets or bags until needed.

foragers Hunter-gatherers who live in small groups that move camp frequently to take advantage of fresh resources as they come into season, with few resources stored in anticipation of future use.

collectors Hunter-gatherers who tend to stay in one place for a long time. A task group may range far afield to hunt and collect food and other resources that are brought back to camp and shared among its inhabitants. Valued food resources are commonly stored in anticipation of future use.

middens Archaeological sites or features within sites formed largely by the accumulation of domestic waste.

Case Studies of Early Holocene Cultures

Now that we've looked at some general hunting and gathering strategies, we can get down to specifics. In this section, we'll consider how the foragers and collectors from various regions found food and adjusted to changes in their environment.

Archaic Hunter-Gatherers of North America

With the retreat of the North American glaciers, the environments, plants, animals, and people of the temperate and boreal latitudes changed significantly. Archaic hunter-gatherers exploited new options in their much-altered environments, which no longer included megafauna (see Fig. 13-9). In eastern North America, dense forests of edible nut-bearing trees spread across the mid-continent and offered rich resources that attracted humans and other animals. Along the coasts, rising sea levels submerged tens of thousands of square miles of low-lying coastlines, creating rich new estuarine and marine environments that Archaic people exploited with a broad array of gear, including fishing equipment, dugout boats, traps, weirs, and nets. The main killing weapon used by these hunter-gatherers was the spear and spear-thrower, or *atlatl* (see p. 298); the bow and arrow came much later, dating to around 1,800–1,500 ya in much of the continental United States.

In many parts of North America, hunter-gatherer lifeways were more the collector than the forager type common among their Paleo-Indian ancestors. These collectors scheduled subsistence activities to coincide with the annual availability of particularly productive resources at specific locations within their territories. They lived in smaller and more circumscribed territories and acquired, through exchange with neighbors or more distant groups, whatever might be lacking locally. Especially in temperate regions, efficient exploitation of edible nuts, deer, fish, shellfish,

and other forest and riverine products was enhanced by new tools, storage techniques, and regional exchange networks. The density of sites and their average size and permanence increased in many localities. Toward the end of the Archaic period, the archaeological remains of some sites exhibit signs of more complex sociopolitical organization, religious ceremonialism, and economic interdependence than had ever existed before.

Archaic Cultures of Western North America Rock-shelters in the **Great Basin**, a harsh arid expanse between the Rocky Mountains and the Sierra Nevadas, preserve material evidence of Desert Archaic lifeways (D'Azevedo, 1986). Hunting weapons, milling stones, twined and coiled basketry, nets, mats, feather robe fragments, fiber sandals and hide moccasins, bone tools, and even gaming pieces are sealed in deeply stratified sites, such as Gatecliff Shelter (Thomas et al., 1983) and Lovelock Cave in Nevada and Danger Cave in Utah, and illuminate nearly 10 millennia of hunting and gathering. Coprolites occasionally found in these deposits contain seeds, insect exoskeletons, and often the tiny scales and bones of fish, rodents, and amphibians, all of which give important information about diet and health (Reinhard and Bryant, 1992). Freshwater and brackish marshes were focal points for many subsistence activities—sources of fish, migratory fowl, plant foods, and raw materials during half the year—but upland resources such as pine nuts and game were important, too. Larger animals might be taken occasionally, though smaller prey, such as jackrabbits and ducks, and the seasonal medley of seed-bearing plants afforded these foragers their most reliable diet. Success in this environment was a direct measure of cultural flexibility (**Fig. 13-17**).

Prehistoric societies throughout California's varied environments likewise sustained themselves without agriculture (McBrinn, 2010). Rich oak forests fed much of the region's human and animal population. Hunter-gatherers routinely ranged across several productive resource zones, from seacoast to interior

Great Basin Rugged, dry plateau between the mountains of California and Utah, comprising Nevada, western Utah, southern Oregon, and Idaho.

William Turnbaugh

Figure 13-17
The arid Great Basin of the American West supported hunter-gatherer cultures for thousands of years.

valleys. Typical California societies, such as the Chumash of the Santa Barbara coast and Channel Islands, obtained substantial harvests of acorns and deer in the fall, supplemented by migratory fish, small game, and plants throughout the year (Glassow, 1996). Collected wild resources sustained permanent villages of up to 1,000 inhabitants. The Chumash were the latest descendants of a long sequence of southern California hunter-gatherers that archaeologists have traced back more than 8,000 years (Moratto, 1984). As environmental fluctuations and population changes necessitated adjustments in coastal and terrestrial resources, Archaic Californians at times ate more fish and shellfish, then more sea mammals or deer, and later more acorns and smaller animal species.

Archaeological and cultural anthropological studies along the northwestern coast of the United States and Canada have identified other impressive non-farming societies whose economies also centered on collecting rich and diverse sea and forest resources. Inhabitants of this region caught, dried, and stored salmon as the fish passed upriver from the sea to spawn each spring or fall. Berries and wild game such as bear and deer were locally plentiful; oily candle-fish, halibut, and whales could be captured with the aid of nets, traps, large seaworthy canoes, and other well-crafted gear. Excavations at Ozette, on Washington's Olympic Peninsula,

revealed a prosperous Nootka whaling community buried in a mud slide 250 years ago (Samuels, 1991).

By historical times along the northwestern coast, clan-based lineages resided in permanent coastal communities of sturdy plank-built cedar houses, guarded by carved cedar **totem** poles proclaiming their owners' genealogical heritage. They vied with one another for social status by staging elaborate public functions (now generally known as the **potlatch**) in which quantities of smoked salmon, fish or whale oil, dried berries, cedar-bark blankets, and other valuables were bestowed upon guests (Jonaitas, 1988). There are archaeological signs that these practices may be quite ancient, with substantial houses, status artifacts, and evidence of warfare dating back some 2,500 years (Ames and Maschner, 1999). While a successful potlatch earned prestige for the hosts and incurred obligations to be repaid in the future, it also served larger purposes. By fostering a network of mutual reciprocity that created both sociopolitical and economic alliances, this ritualized redistribution system ensured a wider availability of the region's dispersed resources. As a result, highly organized **sedentary** communities in the Pacific Northwest prospered without relying on domesticated crops.

Farther to the north, western Arctic Archaic bands pursued coastal sea mammals or combined inland caribou hunting with fishing; however, their diet included

totem An animal or being associated with a kin-group and used for social identification; also, a carved pole representing these beings.

potlatch Ceremonial feasting and gift-giving event among Northwest Coast Indians.

sedentary Residing in a single location for most or all of the year.

virtually no plant foods (McGhee, 1996). Beginning about 2,500 ya, Thule (Inuit/Eskimo) hunters expanded eastward across the Arctic with the aid of a highly specialized tool kit that included effective toggling harpoons for securing sea mammals; blubber lamps for light, cooking, and warmth; and sledges and kayaks (skin boats) for transportation on frozen land or sea.

Archaic Cultures of Eastern North America Locally varied environments across eastern North America supported a range of Archaic cultures after about 10,000 ya. A general warming and drying trend lasting several thousand years promoted deciduous forest growth as far north as the Great Lakes. Archaic societies exploited the temperate oak-hickory forests of the Midwest and the oak-chestnut forests and rivers of the Northeast and Appalachians. Nuts of many kinds were an important staple for these forest groups. Acorn, chestnut, black walnut, butternut, hickory, and beechnut represent plentiful foods that are both nutritious and palatable, rich in fats and oils, and above all easily stored. Some nuts were prepared by parching or roasting, others by crushing and boiling into soups; leaching in hot water neutralized the toxic tannic acids found in acorns. Whitetail deer and black bear provided

meat, hides for clothing, and bone and antler for toolmaking. Other important food items included migratory fowl, wild turkey, fish, turtles, and small mammals such as raccoons, as well as berries and seeds.

In New England, some coastal Archaic groups from Massachusetts to Labrador used canoes to hunt sea mammals and swordfish with bone-bladed harpoons in summer, then relied on caribou and salmon the rest of the year (Snow, 1980). North of the St. Lawrence River, other Archaic bands dispersed widely through the sparse boreal forests, hunting caribou or moose, fishing, and trapping.

In the Midwest around the Great Lakes, seasonally mobile collectors employed an extensive array of equipment to fish, hunt, and gather. The productive valleys of the midcontinent, where several great rivers flow into the Mississippi, supported a riverine focus. Favored sites in this region attained substantial size and were occupied for many generations, some—such as Eva and Rose Island, in Tennessee, and Koster, in southern Illinois—for thousands of years. Trade networks moved valued raw materials and finished goods hundreds, and in some cases thousands, of miles; tools of soft native copper from northern Minnesota and Wisconsin have been found in

At a Glance

Important Archaic Sites in the New World

SITE	DATES (YA)	SIGNIFICANCE
Danger Cave (Utah)	ca. 10,000–historic times	Deeply stratified site that contains rich evidence of Desert Archaic lifeways in the American Southwest
Koster (Illinois)	9,000–4,000	Important stratified sequence of campsites that document the changing lifeways of prehistoric Native Americans in the Midwest during the Archaic period
Poverty Point (Louisiana)	3,500	A large series of earthworks that covers nearly 1 square mile; the most elaborate example of planned communities that were built in the Southeast in late Archaic times

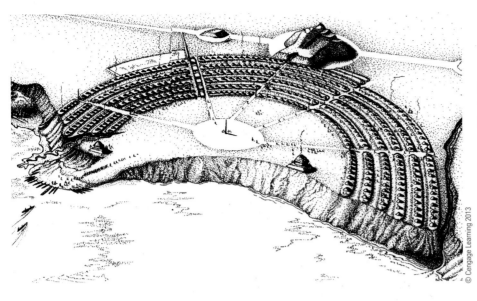

Figure 13-18
The Late Archaic Poverty Point site in north-eastern Louisiana.

© Cengage Learning 2013

Archaic sites as far away as Georgia and Mississippi, and marine shells from the Gulf Coast have been uncovered in western Great Lakes sites.

Eastern Archaic groups at times reinforced their claims to homelands by laying out cemeteries for their dead or by erecting earthwork mounds. These activities imply an emerging social differentiation within some of the preagricultural Archaic societies as well as a degree of sedentism. Archaeologists studying more than 1,000 Archaic burials at Indian Knoll, in Kentucky (Webb, 1974), found possible status indicators reflected in the distribution of grave goods. Though two-thirds of the graves contained no offerings at all, certain females and children had been given disproportionate shares; only a few males were buried with tools and weapons (Rothschild, 1979).

Archaic people in the Lower Mississippi Valley began raising monumental earthworks beginning as early as 5,500 ya. Mound building required communal effort and planning. Near Monroe, Louisiana, Watson Brake is a roughly oval embankment enclosing a space averaging 750 feet across and capped by about a dozen individual mounds up to 24 feet in height (Saunders, 2010). Not far to the east, Poverty Point's elaborate 3,500-year-old complex of six concentric semicircular ridges is flanked by a large platform mound on its west side (**Fig. 13-18**), plus several nearby mounds, and covers a full

square mile (Kidder et al., 2008). That hunter-gatherers chose to invest their energies in creating these planned earthworks with public spaces and dozens of other impressive structures suggests highly developed Archaic social organization and ritualism, though their precise meaning remains unclear.

Mesolithic of Northern Europe

As in North America, people colonized Europe's northern reaches as the glacial ice retreated (Jochim, 1998). Rising waters began to reclaim low-lying coastlines, flooding the North and Baltic seas and burying Paleolithic and Mesolithic sites in the process (Fischer, 1995). On land, temperate plant and animal species succeeded their Ice Age counterparts. Across northwestern Europe, as grasses and then forests invaded the open landscape, red deer, elk, and **aurochs** replaced the reindeer, horse, and bison of Pleistocene times. Human hunters, armed with efficient weapons, accommodated themselves to the relatively low **carrying capacity** of the northern regions (where plant foods, at least, were seasonally scarce) by eating more meat and fish.

Star Carr, near the North Sea coast in east-central England (**Fig. 13-19**), provides clues to the early ecology and foraging economy practiced by northern Mesolithic peoples some 10,500 ya. Periodically over several centuries, this lakeshore site served as a temporary

aurochs European wild oxen, ancestral to domesticated cattle.

carrying capacity In an environment, the maximum population of a specific organism that can be maintained at a steady state.

Figure 13-19

Mesolithic sites of northern Europe mentioned in the text.

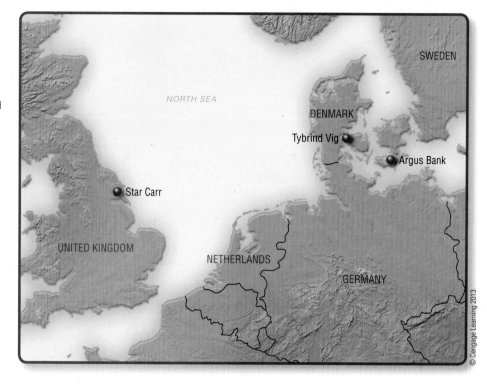

SWEDEN

NORTH SEA

DENMARK

Tybrind Vig

Argus Bank

Star Carr

UNITED KINGDOM

NETHERLANDS

GERMANY

© Cengage Learning 2013

hunting camp, where the people regularly pursued aurochs, deer, elk, and wild pigs (Clark, 1972, 1979; but see Gaffney et al., 2009, pp. 48–50). Because deer grow and shed their antlers annually on a species-specific cycle, the discovery of deer skulls with antlers in different development stages indicates that Mesolithic hunters visited Star Carr throughout the year, though they used it much more in spring and summer (Mellars and Dark, 1999).

Again, as in the New World, Mesolithic hunter-gatherers modified the environment for their own purposes. At Star Carr, people used stone axes and adzes to fell birch trees with which they built platforms and trackways over the marshy ground. In spring, they burned off the reeds along the lake margin to open the view and probably also to induce new growth that would attract game. Hunters employed long wooden or bone arrows, knives, and spear points tipped by *microliths*—small flint blades of geometric shape—set into slots along the shaft and held in place by resin. Another extremely effective weapon, the bow and arrow was used in Europe even before the end of the last Ice Age— that is, considerably earlier than in the New World. Domesticated dogs probably aided in the hunt at Star Carr as well.

Barbed bone and antler spear points, butchering implements, and burins (see p. 299) for working bone and antler were common artifacts.

Coastal resources were economically important to many Mesolithic groups. At an 8,000–7,500-year-old Mesolithic settlement on the Argus Bank, which today lies in 15 to 20 feet of water off the coast of Denmark, preserved food waste and the stable isotopic analysis of human skeletal remains show that fish were the mainstay of the diet, followed by game animals, nuts, and fruits (Fischer et al., 2007). Such favored site locations, sometimes marked by great shell middens, offered a combination of land and sea resources that encouraged year-round residence based on food collecting. The impressive size of some middens—the countless shells of oysters, mussels, periwinkles, and scallops piled along the shore—should not disguise the fact that one red deer carcass may represent the caloric equivalent of 50,000 oysters (Bailey, 1975). Still, for many Mesolithic foragers, shellfish provided a readily available alternative source of protein, probably exploited primarily in the spring when their normal fare of fish, sea mammals, and birds was in shortest supply (Erlandson, 1988). This supplement could have

At a Glance

Important Mesolithic and Epipaleolithic Sites in the Old World

SITE	DATE (YA)	SIGNIFICANCE
Star Carr (England)	10,500	Mesolithic campsite excavated by Grahame Clark; greatly influenced how archaeologists still view the Mesolithic in Europe
Argus Bank and **Tybrind Vig** (Denmark)	ca. 8,000–6,000	Mesolithic villages submerged by rising sea levels off the coast of Denmark; excellent preservation of organic remains including human burials, dugout canoes and paddles, fishing gear, and fabric
Ohalo II (Israel)	23,000	Kebaran or pre-Kebaran campsite; extraordinary preservation of huts, living floors, grass bedding, and plant remains, especially of small-grained grass seeds, which appear to have been a staple food

© Cengage Learning 2013

encouraged people to remain longer in one location.

Since many of these coastal sites were later covered by rising sea level, they can sometimes show extraordinary preservation of organic remains. For example, underwater excavations at Tybrind Vig, a late Mesolithic site that lies in 6 to 9 feet of water about 270 yards off the coast of Denmark, have recovered dugout canoes and paddles, fishing line, fishhooks, and even pieces of fabric, along with plant and animal remains and several human burials (Malm, 1995).

Epipaleolithic of the Near East

Star Carr and other sites of northwestern Europe represent one end of a spectrum of early Holocene lifeways in the Old World. In those regions, plant foods were scarce for much of each year, and hunter-gatherers often relied mostly on hunting or fishing. Farther south, in central and southern Europe and the Near East—regions that were never covered by ice sheets, even during maximum glacial periods—Late Pleistocene and early Holocene environmental and cultural changes proceeded along different lines. People in these regions tended to rely more heavily on wild plant resources, supplemented by animal protein. These distinctions in climate and

culture justify the use of the separate term *Epipaleolithic* to distinguish Late Pleistocene and early Holocene cultural changes of the Near East and adjacent parts of southwest Asia (**Fig. 13-20**) from their contemporaries in northern Europe. For the most part, Epipaleolithic subsistence strategies resulted merely in more efficient hunting and gathering. But in some locations, food-collecting strategies were already taking people quite perceptibly toward an entirely new way of making a living—the development of food production (see Chapter 14).

Figure 13-20

Epipaleolithic sites in the Levant region of the Near East.

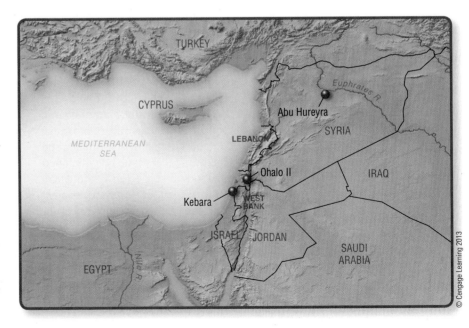

© Cengage Learning 2013

For the moment, let's consider the transition of hunter-gatherers from small-scale, mobile groups to what were essentially permanent communities in the Levant region, in what is today Israel and Lebanon. A Late Pleistocene foraging culture known to archaeologists as the **Kebaran** occupied this region for millennia. Our understanding of Kebaran subsistence has until recently been based mostly on the analysis of faunal remains and tools used in plant food processing, because the direct evidence of plant remains was rarely found in excavations. Ohalo II, a very early Kebaran or pre-Kebaran (23,000 ya) site in the Sea of Galilee, recently demonstrated that archaeologists still have much to learn about Late Pleistocene plant use in the Levant. The Ohalo II excavations revealed a camp comprising several huts, including some with the grass bedding still intact, hearths, tools, and an outstanding collection of more than 90,000 plant remains representing 142 genera and species (Nadel, 2004; Weiss et al., 2004a). Small-grained grass seeds, including brome, foxtail, and alkali grass, were gathered for consumption as staple foods (Weiss et al., 2004b), as were seeds of wild cereals such as barley and wheat. Analysis of starch grains from a grinding slab found in one of the huts revealed that the small-grained grasses and the wild cereal grasses were processed for consumption (Piperno et al., 2004). The Ohalo II remains demonstrate that early Kebaran groups in the Levant were collector-type hunter-gatherers more than 10,000 years farther into the past than we once believed and that the beginnings of agriculture can be traced at least to Epipaleolithic times.

Viewed generally, many Kebaran groups adopted a strategy of **transhumance**, a specific seasonality and scheduling technique by which people divided their activities between resource zones at different elevations. We know from later Kebaran sites that they harvested seeds of wild cereal grasses in the lowlands from fall through springtime (Henry, 1989). In summer, they made extended forays into the sparsely wooded uplands to hunt and to gather nuts. Gazelles (a kind of antelope) and fallow deer were the primary sources of meat, with smaller game becoming more common than deer in site assemblages toward the end of the Epipaleolithic (Bar-Oz, 2004), possibly as deer became scarce.

Between 12,000 and 11,000 ya, a moderating climate associated with the waning Pleistocene took effect in the arid lands bordering the eastern Mediterranean. As both temperatures and precipitation increased, the range of native lowland cereal grasses expanded into the higher forested zones (Henry, 1989). Sites were more permanent than the early Epipaleolithic camps such as Ohalo II, and the newer sites contain house remains, heavy seed-processing equipment and other nonportable items, art objects, and cemeteries; they're also larger, with a five- or tenfold increase in population, accompanied by signs of social ranking (Henry, 1989).

Because the sites of these more sedentary collectors are so dramatically different from earlier camps, archaeologists gave their culture a new label, identifying it as **Natufian** (Belfer-Cohen, 1991). Natufian subsistence depended heavily on diverse resources, including large-seeded legumes, the seeds of wild cereal grasses—but not the small-grained grass seeds that were so common at Ohalo II—and the gazelle (Bar-Yosef, 1987; Savard et al., 2006). Ancient gazelle-hunting practices are revealed through a study of tooth eruption and wear patterns on animal teeth recovered from Natufian sites (Legge and Rowley-Conwy, 1987). After analyzing a nonselective population structure of newborns, yearlings, and adults, these researchers suggested that the dominant hunting method was to surround or ambush an entire herd soon after the females gave birth to their young, probably in late April or early May.

Gazelle-horn sickles with inset flint blades frequently appear on Natufian sites, along with an abundance of grinding stones and mortars (**Fig. 13-21**). Small clusters of semipermanent pit houses with stone foundations, often in close association with cemeteries, such as those excavated at several

Kebaran Late Pleistocene hunter-gatherers of the eastern Mediterranean region and Levant.

transhumance Seasonal migration from one resource zone to another, especially between highlands and lowlands.

Natufian Referring to collector-type hunter-gatherers who established sedentary settlements in parts of the Near East after 12,000 ya.

sites in Israel and Syria (Moore et al., 2000), confirm the Natufians' reliance on local species without moving from place to place. These finds, as well as an increase in human **dental caries** (tooth decay), *hypoplasias* (interrupted enamel formation), periodontal disease, and an overall reduction in tooth size in Natufian skeletons, all testify to the fact that starchy cereal grains figured prominently in this group's diet (P. Smith et al., 1984).

Viewed across the span of the Epipaleolithic, hunter-gatherer groups took a more active role in manipulating the landscape to enhance the productivity or yield of favored species. Whether intentionally or not, they may have created forest clearings or eliminated competing animals or "weed" plants; or,

as their camps expanded into fresh regions, they might have introduced wild food species into new habitats. At times, as among the Natufians in the Near East, these intensive exploitation patterns greatly altered the overall relationship between people and their environment, promoting further changes in their society as well as in the resources on which they depended. So, we see larger populations drawn to certain prime areas, where intergroup competition would be inevitable and where selection pressures on resources could become significant. In some cases, the changes brought about by collector-type hunter-gatherers were actually a prelude to food production, which we'll focus on in the next chapter.

Figure 13-21

Sickles were useful tools for harvesting wild cereal grasses. An embedded row of small flint blades formed the working edge of the sickle, the handle of which could be wood, bone, or horn.

Steve Gorton © Dorling Kindersley

Summary of Main Topics

▶ By the early to middle Holocene, modern humans had expanded into all the inhabitable regions of the globe.

▶ The first humans arrived in the New World from northeastern Asia between 30,000 and 13,500 ya, most likely after 16,500 ya. They entered the New World on foot by way of the Bering land bridge, on foot or by boat along the Pacific coastal route, or by some combination of the two routes.

▶ The earliest New World skeletal evidence shows considerable morphological diversity, but cultural and biological traces clearly link the first Americans with their northeast Asian roots.

▶ There are general similarities of material culture between the earliest sites in the Americas and northeastern Asia.

▶ By about 12,000 ya, after the end of the last Ice Age, significant climatic changes altered the weather, seasonal variations, average temperatures, topography, sea levels, and animal and plant communities across much of the Northern Hemisphere, including North America and Eurasia.

▶ Many species of megafauna became extinct during the Late Pleistocene, particularly in North America; Paleo-Indian hunters may have contributed to the demise of mammoths and a few other species.

▶ Early Holocene foragers in Europe, the Near East, and North America adapted readily to the ongoing environmental changes. Generalized food-getting economies promoted long-term cultural stability for many hunter-gatherers

▶ Long-term, and in some cases permanent, settlements became part of

Holocene hunter-gatherer lifeways in many regions.

▶ Sites like Ohalo II demonstrate that some food-collecting communities experienced economic changes as long ago as the Last Glacial Maximum, which led to the use of a wide range of wild plants and animals as food.

The next two chapters of this text are organized around two primary cultural developments associated with humans in the later Holocene epoch: first, the process of food production, and second, the rise of civilizations. Much of what we associate with modern humanity is linked to these central driving forces.

In "What's Important," you'll find a useful summary of the most important archaeological sites discussed in this chapter.

dental caries Erosions in teeth caused by decay; cavities.

What's Important   The Most Significant Archaeological Sites Discussed in This Chapter

Location	Site	Dates (ya)	The Big Picture
North America	Poverty Point (Louisiana)	3,500	A large series of earthworks that covers nearly 1 square mile; the most elaborate example of planned communities built in the Southeast in late Archaic times
	Koster (Illinois)	9,000–4,000	Important stratified sequence of campsites that document the changing lifeways of prehistoric Native Americans in the Midwest during the Archaic period
	Kennewick (Washington)	9,300	One of the few early North American human skeletons; object of a nine-year court battle to decide if scientists would be permitted to study his remains
	Danger Cave (Utah)	~10,000–historic times	Deeply stratified site that contains rich evidence of Desert Archaic lifeways in the American Southwest
	Debra L. Friedkin (Texas)	15,500–13,200	A possible pre-Clovis site in North America that may help to explain the origins of Clovis
	Meadowcroft (Pennsylvania)	19,000–14,000	Often cited as evidence of pre-Clovis presence of humans in eastern North America
South America	Monte Verde (Chile)	14,500	Pre-Clovis campsite in southern South America; one of the first sites to be widely accepted as evidence of pre-Clovis human presence in the New World
	Pedra Furada (Brazil)	?50,000–?40,000	One of several South American sites for which great antiquity is claimed, but not yet convincingly proved
Old World	Argus Bank and Tybrind Vig (Denmark)	ca. 8,000–6,000	Mesolithic villages submerged by rising sea levels off the coast of Denmark; excellent preservation of organic remains, including human burials, dugout canoes and paddles, fishing gear, and fabric
	Star Carr (England)	10,500	Mesolithic campsite excavated by Grahame Clark; greatly influenced how archaeologists still view the Mesolithic in Europe
	Ohalo II (Israel)	23,000	Kebaran or pre-Kebaran campsite; extraordinary preservation of huts, living floors, grass bedding, and plant remains, especially of small-grained grass seeds, which appear to have been a staple food
	Yana RHS (Russia)	30,000	Earliest evidence of Late Pleistocene hunters beyond the Arctic Circle in northern Siberia; stone tools and horn and ivory spear foreshafts similar to those found much later on North American Paleo-Indian sites

© Cengage Learning 2013

Critical Thinking Questions

1. What are the specific biological and cultural clues that point to an Asian ancestry for the *earliest* American populations? How convincing do you find the evidence?

2. What are some of the significant environmental changes associated with the end of the Pleistocene? Which of these changes would have most affected humans? Do you see parallels with climate changes today?

3. Were Paleo-Indians primarily responsible for the extinction of Pleistocene animals? What archaeological evidence supports your view?

4. Contrast Mesolithic cultural adaptations of northern Europe, as represented at Star Carr and Argus Bank, with those of the Near East, as represented by the Kebarans and Natufians in the Levant. What important factors explain the differences between Mesolithic lifeways in northern Europe and the Levant?

5. In what ways are foragers different from collectors? What are some of the economic and biocultural implications of each of these subsistence strategies?

Archaeology

CHAPTER 14

Food Production

Barry Lewis

LEARNING OBJECTIVES

After you have mastered the material in this chapter, you will be able to:

▶ Explain the important differences between domestication and agriculture.

▶ Compare and contrast environmental and cultural theories that explain the beginnings of farming and herding.

▶ Identify and explain the major kinds of archaeological evidence that researchers use as indicators of early plant and animal domestication.

▶ Explain the major ways in which the development of farming and herding differed in the Old and New Worlds.

By the end of the last Ice Age, humans were living in most of the world's inhabitable places. They achieved a global distribution without becoming multiple species in the process, which isn't the way things usually happen in nature. They were able to do this because they possessed extraordinary adaptive flexibility as biocultural organisms. Without such flexibility, humans might still be restricted to the tropical and subtropical regions of the Old World.

The archaeological record provides abundant evidence that the rate of change in human lifeways accelerated markedly during the past 10,000 years or so. Throughout this long period, human culture accounted for more and more of the changes in how and where our ancestors lived. By making cultural choices and devising new cultural solutions to age-old problems, human groups succeeded in mitigating some of the processes that operate in the natural world (for example, starvation due to seasonal food shortages) and either turned them to their advantage or at least lessened their worst effects. Humans also discovered that the cost of such cultural solutions included consequences for both the natural world and human biology. Chapter 16 will explore these consequences; some were fantastically good; others weren't.

Two of the most profound and far-reaching developments of later prehistory were the shift from hunting and gathering to food production and the emergence of the early civilizations. This chapter deals with plant and animal domestication and the associated spread of farming, both of them integral to the development of the first civilizations, which we will examine in Chapter 15. We'll start by examining competing explanations for the origins of food production. This will give you a sense of the diverse perspectives from which researchers investigate how and why farming developed after the end of the last Ice Age. From there, we'll discuss the archaeological evidence for the origins of food production in several regions around the world (**Fig. 14-1**).

The Neolithic Revolution

The change from hunting and gathering to agriculture is often called the **Neolithic revolution**, a name coined decades ago by archaeologist V. Gordon Childe (1951) to acknowledge the fundamental changes brought about by the beginnings of food production. While hunter-gatherers collected whatever foods nature made available, farmers employed nature to produce only those crops and animals that humans selected for their own exclusive purposes.

Beyond domestication and farming, **Neolithic** activities had other far-reaching consequences, including new settlement patterns, new technologies, and significant biocultural effects. The emergence of food production eventually transformed most human societies either directly or indirectly and, in the process, brought about dramatic changes in the natural realm as well. The world has been a very different place ever since humans began developing agriculture.

Childe argued that maintaining fields and herds demanded a long-term commitment from early farmers. Obliged to stay in one area to oversee their crops, Neolithic people became more or less settled, or sedentary. As storable harvests gradually supported larger and more permanent communities, towns and cities developed in a few areas. Within these larger settlements, fewer people were directly involved in food production, and new **craft specializations** emerged, such as cloth weaving, pottery production, and metallurgy.

While archaeologists still accept his general characterization of the Neolithic revolution, we've learned a lot in the decades since Childe's original study. For example, we now recognize that sedentism actually preceded farming in certain locations where permanent settlements were sustained solely by gathering and hunting or fishing. In Chapter 13, for example, we noted that the Chumash of southern California and the Natufian hunter-gatherers of the Near East, among others, established sizable villages. It's now also widely

Neolithic revolution Childe's term for the far-reaching consequences of food production.

Neolithic (*neo*, meaning "new," and *lith*, meaning "stone") New Stone Age; period of farmers.

craft specializations An economic system in which some individuals do not engage in food production, but devote their labor to the production of other goods and services. Examples include potters, carpenters, smiths, shamen, oracles, and teachers.

Figure 14-1

Time line for Chapter 14.

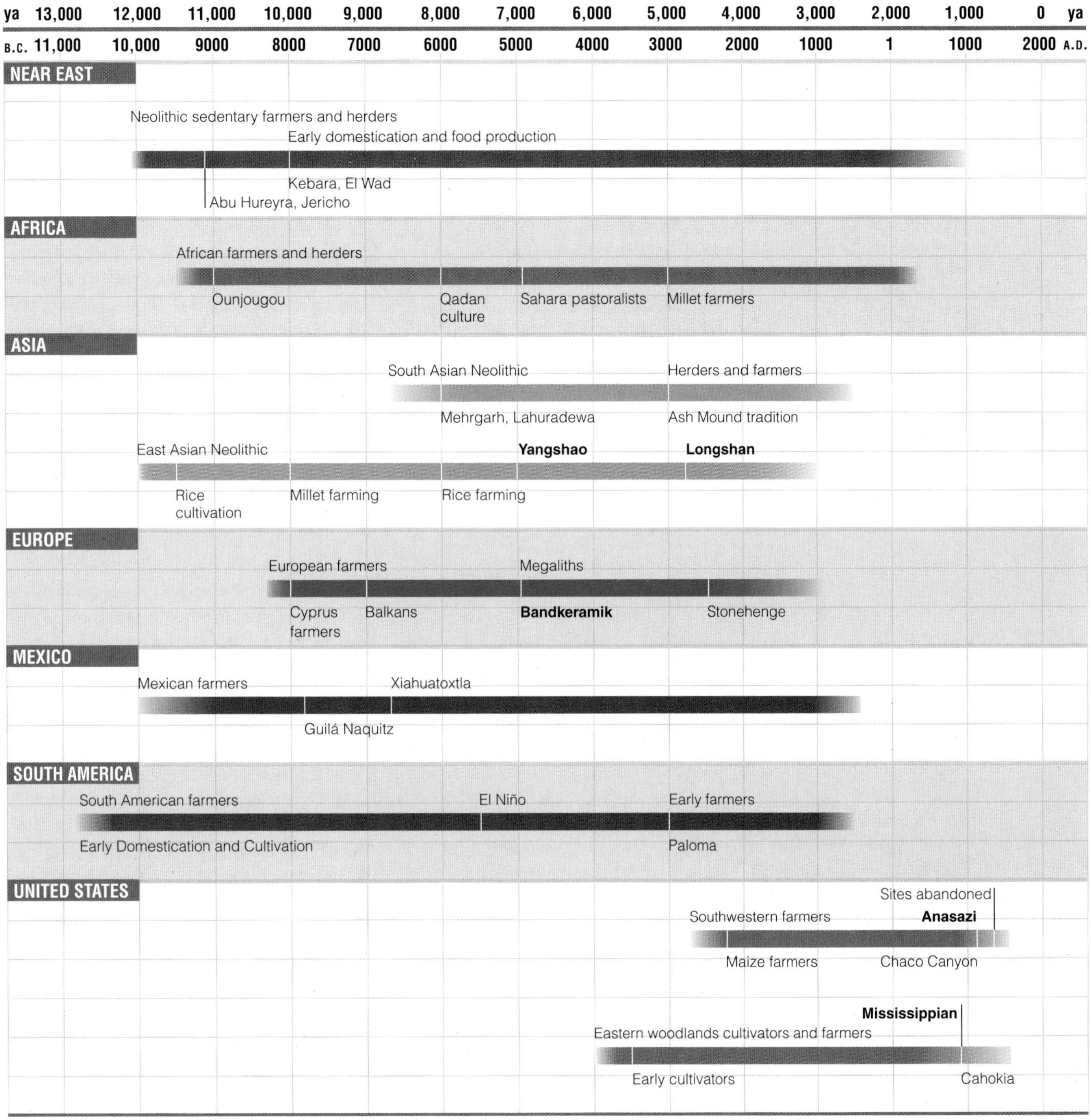

ya	13,000	12,000	11,000	10,000	9,000	8,000	7,000	6,000	5,000	4,000	3,000	2,000	1,000	0	ya
B.C.	11,000	10,000	9000	8000	7000	6000	5000	4000	3000	2000	1000	1	1000	2000	A.D.

NEAR EAST

Neolithic sedentary farmers and herders
Early domestication and food production

Kebara, El Wad
Abu Hureyra, Jericho

AFRICA

African farmers and herders

Ounjougou   Qadan culture   Sahara pastoralists   Millet farmers

ASIA

South Asian Neolithic   Herders and farmers

Mehrgarh, Lahuradewa   Ash Mound tradition

East Asian Neolithic   **Yangshao**   **Longshan**

Rice cultivation   Millet farming   Rice farming

EUROPE

European farmers   Megaliths

Cyprus farmers   Balkans   **Bandkeramik**   Stonehenge

MEXICO

Mexican farmers   Xiahuatoxtla

Guilá Naquitz

SOUTH AMERICA

South American farmers   El Niño   Early farmers

Early Domestication and Cultivation   Paloma

UNITED STATES

Sites abandoned
Southwestern farmers   **Anasazi**

Maize farmers   Chaco Canyon

Mississippian
Eastern woodlands cultivators and farmers

Early cultivators   Cahokia

accepted that sedentism could often stimulate food production, rather than the other way around, and that even Upper Paleolithic hunter-gatherers were perfectly capable of understanding how to manipulate the life histories of plants and animals to their advantage.

Archaeologists also now know that Neolithic lifeways evolved indepen-dently in several places around the world. They are less agreed on how and why it spread from one region to another (e.g., compare Barker, 2006, and Bellwood, 2005). Some researchers see most regional Neolithic developments as the culmination of local cultural sequences. Others argue for migrations and the **diffusion** of agriculture from

diffusion The idea that widely distributed cultural traits originated in a single center and spread from one group to another through contact or exchange.

"heartlands" in which such cultural changes first took place.

Regardless of how it spread, the Neolithic is viewed as revolutionary in its cumulative impact on human lives, not in the amount of time it took for these cultural changes to happen. Measured in human terms, the transition from hunter-gatherer to farmer in any region involved complex, often interrelated biocultural changes that likely played out across as many as 150 generations (Fuller, 2010, p. 11).

In the following discussion, we'll examine the beginnings of domestication and farming by considering evidence drawn from around the world. Although the process everywhere shared many similarities and produced equally dramatic consequences, archaeologists working in the Americas rarely apply the term *Neolithic* to studies of New World farmers. Instead, they use regional terminology, such as *Formative* or *Preclassic* in Mesoamerica and *Mississippian* in eastern North America.

Explaining the Origins of Domestication and Agriculture

Archaeologists have always felt compelled to identify "firsts." When did the earliest humans arrive in Australia? Where are the oldest sites in South America? When did the bow and arrow arrive in the Midwest? Concerns about these firsts also dominate archaeological research on domestication and agriculture and will undoubtedly continue to do so. But we'll never know when or where the first person intentionally planted seeds in the hope of making a crop, and we'll never track down the first person to hitch an animal to a plow or milk a goat. What researchers really hope to achieve by their emphasis on firsts is to understand what made these changes happen.

From research on the origins of agriculture, we know that ancient hunter-gatherers who lived before the earliest identified archaeological evidence of food production were both intelligent and observant enough to figure out what happens to seeds after you put them in the ground. In fact, we have every reason to believe that Mesolithic/Epipaleolithic and Archaic hunter-gatherers had a wealth of practical everyday knowledge and understanding about the natural world around them. So, when we search for the earliest evidence of agriculture in a region, the most important goal is not being able to say, "Ah, here's where we draw the line on our chronology chart of agricultural beginnings" (see, for example, Fig. 14-1). A much more fundamental motivation is simply to understand why these people became farmers. Why then? Why there? What conditions brought about these changes? Why these crops?

From the perspective of the modern world, we may find it hard to accept that earlier peoples didn't generally aspire to be farmers and that many no doubt avoided the opportunity for as long as possible. But the archaeological record and history alike are filled with examples demonstrating that what we now view as the self-evident benefits of food production have seldom been seen in the same light by hunter-gatherers. In recent centuries, many of the remaining hunter-gatherers on every continent resisted, sometimes successfully, the efforts of societies based on food production to convert them to peaceful, taxpaying farmers, voters, and consumers of mass-produced goods. Such attitudes call into question the inevitability of agriculture in biocultural evolution. Did it become the predominant economic basis of human communities because it offered so many obvious advantages? Because it offered the fewest disadvantages? Or because there just weren't a lot of alternatives?

Ironically, although farming didn't get started in a big way until later, it was the hunter-gatherers of the Mesolithic/Epipaleolithic and Archaic periods who actually initiated the critical processes and even developed many of the innovations we usually credit to the Neolithic. Essentially, the lifestyles of some early Holocene hunter-gatherers anticipated many of the developments we associate with agriculture. Neolithic farmers were mostly the *recipients* of domesticated species and agricultural ways from their predecessors.

Defining Agriculture and Domestication

To avoid confusion later on, it's useful to consider the difference between **domestication** and **agriculture**. These terms are often found together in discussions of the beginnings of food production, but they mean different things (Rindos, 1984).

Domestication is an *evolutionary process*. When we say that a certain plant or animal is domesticated, we mean that there's interdependency between this organism and humans, such that part of its life history depends on human intervention. To achieve and maintain this relationship requires the *genetic* transformation of a wild species by selective breeding or other ways of interfering, intentionally or not, with a species' natural life processes.

Agriculture differs from domestication because it's a *cultural activity*, not an evolutionary process. It involves the propagation and exploitation of domesticated plants and animals by humans. Agriculture in its broad sense includes all the activities associated with both farming and animal herding. Although domestication and agriculture are typically examined together in archaeological discussions of Neolithic lifeways, domestication isn't inevitably associated with an economic emphasis on food production. For example, cotton was an early domesticated plant, but it was grown for its fibers, not as human food.

True agriculture would be unthinkable without domesticated plants and animals. Domestication makes agriculture possible, especially when we consider how humans have manipulated the life history strategies of other organisms to maximize particular qualities, such as yield per unit area, growth rate to maturity, ease of processing, seed color, average seed size, and flavor. The cultural activity we call agriculture ensures that the plants and animals with these desirable qualities are predictably available as human food and raw materials. One useful way to view this fundamental change in the relationship between humans and other animals and plants is as **symbiosis**, a mutually beneficial association between members of different species (Rindos, 1984).

Next we'll briefly examine some competing explanations for the beginnings of agriculture. Although most of these approaches address the problem of explaining the development of farming in the Near East, it's important to note that their proponents tend to view them as generally applicable to agricultural origins everywhere. The Near East dominates the discussion mostly because it received the lion's share of research on this problem over the past century, not because it was some sort of primal hearth for the development of agriculture. Also, as you review these competing explanations, bear in mind that the central questions are open areas of research. Right now, no single approach is both sufficient and necessary to explain all known cases.

Loosely following Verhoeven (2004), our overview examines two approaches, those that primarily invoke natural, or environmental, factors to explain the development of agriculture, and those largely based on cultural (including cognitive) factors.

Environmental Approaches

Most approaches to explain the origins of domesticated plants and animals and the beginnings of agriculture identify one or more natural mechanisms, such as climate change or human population growth, that may have promoted the biocultural changes documented in the archaeological record. The reasoning behind such hypotheses is that, when faced with increasing resource needs, a community typically has several options. The least disruption to everyday life can be achieved by reducing the population, extending the territory, or making more intensive use of the environment. Farming, of course, represents a more intensive use of the environment. Through their efforts, farmers attempt to increase the land's carrying capacity by harnessing more of its energy for the production of crops or animals that will feed people (**Fig. 14-2**).

In their most extreme form, environmental approaches call to mind *environmental determinism*, the notion

domestication A state of interdependence between humans and selected plant or animal species. Intense selection activity induces permanent genetic change, enhancing a species' value to humans.

agriculture Cultural activities associated with planting, herding, and processing domesticated species; farming.

symbiosis (*syn*, meaning "together," and *bios*, meaning "life") Mutually advantageous association of two different organisms; also known as *mutualism*.

Figure 14-2

Through a symbiotic relationship with humans, domesticated plants such as lettuce and tomatoes have even spread to Antarctica. There they are grown by hydroponic farming techniques without the benefits of soil or sunlight in New Zealand's Scott Base greenhouse, which consists of two 20-foot shipping containers in which the staff grows vegetables, herbs, and flowers.

that certain cultural outcomes can be predicted from—or are determined by—a combination of purely environmental causes. For example, V. Gordon Childe himself conjectured that climate changes at the end of the Pleistocene increased Europe's rainfall while making southwestern Asia and North Africa much more arid (Childe, 1929, 1934). Humans, animals, and vegetation in the drought areas concentrated into shrinking zones around a few permanent water sources. At these **oases**, Childe hypothesized, the interaction between humans and certain plants and animals resulted in domestication of species such as wheat, barley, sheep, and goats, which people then began to use to their advantage. The eventual result was the spread of sedentary village communities across the Near East.

Hypotheses based on any form of determinism tend to be relatively straightforward, which is both their strength and their weakness. Because they hold so many factors constant, it's easy to see how such approaches should work and why certain important outcomes should arise. The main drawback of such ideas is that their focus is typically too general to explain a given case because they omit the key contextual factors that are unique to a real event. In environmental approaches, such factors are often history and culture. What people are already familiar with and what they and their ancestors did in the past often, if not always, play a big role in their decisions. So, for example, a des-

ert region might simultaneously sustain opportunistic hunter-gatherers, nomadic pastoralists, farmers using special deep-planting procedures, and even lawn-mowing suburbanites willing to pay for piped-in water, not because these groups are unaware of the possibilities posed by alternative ways of living, but because they are living their traditional ways of life and they prefer them.

To return to what has come to be called Childe's oasis theory, its simplicity quickly enabled archaeologist Robert Braidwood to demonstrate that the predicted outcomes didn't exist in the archaeological record (see p. 347 for details). Pollen and sediment profiles now confirm that at least some of the climatic changes hypothesized by Childe did occur in parts of the Near East prior to Neolithic times, and so they may have had a role in fostering new relationships between humans and other species in this marginal environment (Henry, 1989; Wright, 1993). Even so, both the causes and the apparent effects were complex. In places like the Near East, climate change that resulted in diminished or redistributed resources didn't directly push people to become farmers (Munro, 2004), though it may have made farming one of the more reasonable options. Furthermore, the arid conditions familiar to us today in some parts of the Near East may be as much a *result* as a cause of Neolithic activities in the region (see, e.g., Nentwig, 2007). That is, the ecologically disruptive activities of farmers and herd animals during the Neolithic period may have contributed to the destructive process of **desertification**. Their plowed fields exposed soil to wind erosion and evaporation, while the irrigation demands of their crops lowered the water table and increased salinization of the soil. And overgrazing herbivores rapidly reduced the vegetation that holds moisture and binds soil, thus destroying the fragile margin between grassland and desert.

One large group of environmental hypotheses that, unlike Childe's, continues to be examined by researchers looks to increased competition for resources. Whether the competition resulted from natural increases in population density or from climatic changes, such as rising

© D. Rich, Scott Base Greenhouse

oases (*sing.*, oasis) Permanent springs or water holes in an arid region.

desertification Any process resulting in the formation or growth of deserts.

sea levels, increased rainfall, or lower average seasonal temperatures, they're seen as major factors that encouraged the domestication of plants and animals and, ultimately, the beginnings of agriculture (e.g., Boserup, 1965; Binford, 1968; Flannery, 1973; Cohen, 1977). These explanations share the view that agriculture developed in societies where competition for the resources necessary to sustain life favored increasing the diversity of staple foods in the diet. For one reason or another, population control or territorial expansion may not have been feasible or desirable choices in these societies. For example, competition may have arisen from decreased human mortality rates rather than increased fertility or possibly even been driven by the increasing proportion of people living to an old age. The point is that people faced a "prehistoric food crisis" (Cohen, 1977) unlike most modern cases because it was a chronic problem that worsened over decades and showed no sign of ever getting any better. Concentrated in a restricted territory or faced with the dwindling reliability of once-favored resources, such hunter-gatherers might have taken up **horticulture** or herding to enhance the productivity or distribution of one or more particularly useful species. It was this economic commitment that eventually led to the emergence of true farmers.

Binford's (1968) "packing model" develops one such hypothesis involving **demographic** stresses. As modern climatic conditions became established in the early Holocene, people resided in every prime habitat in the temperate regions of Eurasia. Foraging areas became confined as territories filled, leading to increased competition for resources and a more varied diet. Forced to make more intensive use of smaller segments of habitat, hunter-gatherers applied their Mesolithic technology to a broader range of plant and animal species. A few of these resources proved more reliable, easier to catch or process, tastier, or even faster to reproduce than others, so they soon received greater attention. Archaeological evidence of such changes can be found on many Mesolithic/Epipaleolithic sites in the form of sickles, baskets and other containers, grinding slabs, and other processing tools.

As local populations continued to grow and other groups tried to expand their territory, their only choice would be to move into the marginal habitats that lay at the edges of the optimal, resource-rich parts of their territory (Binford, 1968). Because population stress would quickly reach critical levels in these marginal environments, where resources were already sparse, it was here that domesticated plants were first developed. To feed itself, the expanding population might have tried to expand the native ranges of some of the resources they knew from their homeland by sowing seeds of the wild plants. Over time, this activity resulted in domestication of those species and fundamental changes in the relationship between them and the people who by then depended on them.

Aspects of Binford's approach appealed to many archaeologists, who agreed that the wild ancestors of some of the world's most important domesticates originally held a low status in the diet. Many were small, hard seeds that were once seldom used except as secondary or emergency foods. Ethnographic research had also shown that, given their choice, hunter-gatherers everywhere prefer to eat fruit and meat (Yudkin, 1969). Still, grains and roots became increasingly important in the Mesolithic/Epipaleolithic diet—supplemented by available animal or fish protein—and not only when the more desirable foods were in short supply. An interpretation based on increased competition for resources offered a testable explanation for why this happened.

Although he took issue with certain aspects of Binford's approach, Flannery (1973) agreed with the basic thesis because it explained why the earliest archaeological evidence of plant domestication should be found in what would have been marginal environments. Flannery described the increasing breadth of the Epipaleolithic diet as a "broad spectrum revolution" in which hunter-gatherers turned to many kinds of food resources to make up for local shortfalls. Especially in marginal

horticulture Farming method in which only hand tools are used; typical of most early Neolithic societies.

demographic Pertaining to the size or rate of increase of human populations.

At a Glance

Environmental Factors in the Development of Agriculture

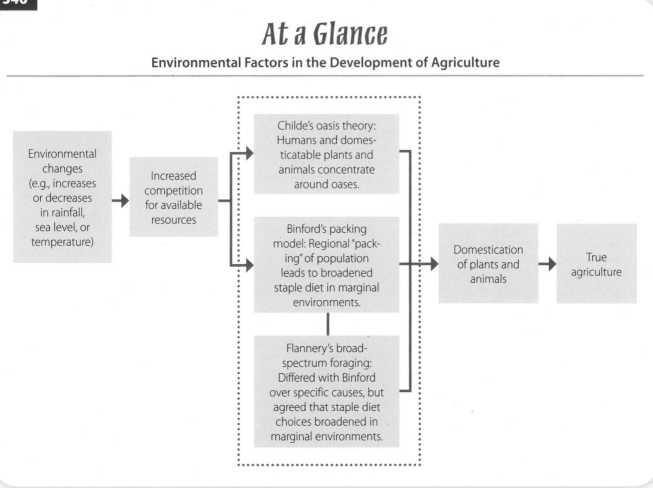

environments, this activity promoted the development of domesticates and, ultimately, the origins of true agriculture.

In short, environmental approaches identify forces external to humans as the active ingredients in the development of agriculture. In these hypotheses, human agency is primarily reactive. Something in the natural environment changes (for example, precipitation patterns, average annual temperature), and it makes life increasingly hard for hunter-gatherers. They react culturally to changed circumstances in various ways, some of which include incorporating a wider range of less preferred foods in their staple diet and colonizing marginal environments. At some point, they take up the alternative of applying cultural means to increase the production of one or more food species. So basically, these approaches envision the development of agriculture more as something that humans backed into from a lack of better

alternatives rather than something they enthusiastically embraced.

Cultural Approaches

Not everyone agrees that the roots of domestication and agriculture are to be explained by the operation of external environmental factors, all of which, by design, place human culture and agency in a passive role. Some archaeologists contend that social and ideological factors, such as competitive feasting to enhance one's status, tribute payments, or offerings to the deities (Price and Bar-Yosef, 2010), may have pushed societies to come up with more food than could be readily obtained on a regular basis from natural sources. The reasoning behind these hypotheses is that human agency and culture alone may be sufficient and necessary to explain many of the fundamental changes documented in the archaeological record.

As you may suspect from your reading of the previous section, these approaches are also not immune to extreme positions. Just as we can identify some environmental approaches as teetering on the brink of determinism, we can find some cultural and cognitive approaches that seek to emphasize the role of human culture to the near exclusion of noncultural factors. In these approaches, such natural phenomena as climatic changes are either irrelevant to the explanation of cultural outcomes or were consciously exploited by people to further cultural objectives, so they weren't merely phenomena to which people reacted.

Robert Braidwood's "nuclear zone" or "hilly flanks" hypothesis (Braidwood and Howe, 1960) is a good mid-twentieth-century example to start with in looking at cultural approaches. Braidwood built on V. Gordon Childe's earlier work (see p. 344) and pointed out that subsequent research didn't find evidence of the environmental changes on which Childe based his oasis theory. What's more, the wild ancestors of common domesticated plants and animals in the Near East were in the foothills of the mountains, not around the oases, which is where they should be if Childe's oasis theory is correct. Without a clear environmental trigger for the origins of domestication and agriculture, Braidwood and Howe (1960) reasoned that domestication and, ultimately, agriculture came about as early Holocene hunter-gatherers gradually became familiar with local plant and animal resources and grew increasingly inclined to the notion of domestication. In other words, domestication and agriculture happened when "culture was ready." But Braidwood never adequately addressed the compelling questions that such an argument stimulates: Why was culture "ready"? Why then and not, say, 30,000 ya? Or 100,000 ya? Or never?

In his examination of the beginnings of agriculture in Europe, Ian Hodder (1990) took a more evenhanded approach than Braidwood. Building on the symbolic meaning assigned to houses and household activities, Hodder developed an argument in which the process of domestication and the activities of agriculture were properly viewed as the human "transformation of nature into culture, with an expansion of cultural control and a domination of nature" (Verhoeven, 2004, p. 210). He identified both social and natural factors as possible pressures in bringing about the transition from foraging to agriculture at the end of the Pleistocene. The strength of Hodder's approach rests in his assignment of considerable weight both to human agency and culture and to the widely accepted effects of environmental factors. Trevor Watkins (2010) makes a broadly similar claim. Watkins argues that the key factor in the "readiness" of human culture was the

At a Glance

Cultural Factors in the Development of Agriculture

Braidwood's hilly flanks or nuclear zone hypothesis	Domestication and agriculture happened when culture was ready to receive it. It developed in the foothills of the mountains of the Near East as hunter-gatherers gradually appreciated the potential value of plant and animal domestication.
Hodder's transformation of nature into culture	Domestication was the product of both the effects of environmental changes and the exercise of human agency to turn "nature into culture."

Hitchcock, Albert S. 1914. *A Text-Book of Grasses with Especial Reference to Economic Species of the United States.* New York: Macmillian, p. 239.

(b)

(a)

Figure 14-3

In seed heads of wild cereal grasses, individual grains are linked together by a flexible jointed stem, or rachis, as they develop. At maturity, the rachis breaks apart and the seeds scatter. In domesticated forms, the rachis remains supple, keeping the seed head intact until harvested. (a) ear of emmer wheat (1:2); (b) grain of emmer wheat (2:1).

emergence of "larger and more cohesive social groups" during the Epipaleolithic, which stimulated human cognitive development and, ultimately, the development of agriculture.

So, to sum things up, cultural approaches to explain the origins of domestication and agriculture assume an active role for human agency and tend to discount, if not deny completely, the importance of natural, or environmental, factors. In these approaches, cultural changes, such as a transformation of the human relationship with the divine or of the conceptualization of self, can be enough in some cases to account for the changes we see in the archaeological record. The main drawback with these hypotheses is that sometimes it's not immediately clear why such transformations would occur.

From Collecting to Cultivating

If today we had to choose an explanation for the origins of domestication and agriculture (and we should at least suggest a preference, since this is an introductory college textbook), we would adopt one of the moderate environmental approaches as the most robust because it explains the most real cases. Most such approaches also consider cultural factors, but they assign the greatest weight to the forces of nature. For us, that's their greatest appeal. They don't require researchers to assume that just because we're biocultural animals, humans are somehow exempt from natural factors that affect all living things. Disasters such as the devastating tsunami of December 2004 that killed more than 180,000 people in a dozen countries are painful reminders that, for all our human posturing to the contrary, nature often has the final word.

Ultimately, we have no reason to believe that the origins of domestication and agriculture can be explained *only* by natural forces or *only* by cultural factors. These are complex problems for which there may be multiple valid explanations. It could easily be the case that approaches such as those recently proposed by Barker (2006) and Verhoeven (2004), which seek explanations in the interaction of both natural and cultural

forces, will prove to be the most productive route to follow.

So, working within our admitted preference for environmental approaches, let's now consider why and how hunter-gatherers became farmers in a real example drawn from the Near East. As Epipaleolithic gatherers in the Levant region harvested natural stands of wild cereal grasses such as wheat or barley, their movements would cause many of the ripened seed heads to shatter spontaneously, with considerable loss of grain. Each time someone used a gazelle-horn sickle to cut through a stalk, some of the seeds would fall to the ground. This normal process of seed dispersal is a function of the **rachis**, a short connector linking each seed to the primary stalk (**Fig. 14-3**). While the embryonic seed develops, the rachis serves as an umbilical that conveys the nutrients to be stored and later used by the germinating seed. Once the seed reaches its full development on the stalk, the rachis normally becomes dry and brittle, enabling the seed to break away easily.

Even without human interference, wild cereal grasses tended to be particularly susceptible to natural genetic modification (much more so than, say, nut-bearing trees), since the plants grew together in dense patches, were highly polytypic, and were quick to reproduce. In fact, a stand of wild grasses was like an enormous genetic laboratory. The normal range of genetic variability among the grasses included some plants with slightly larger seeds and others with tougher or more flexible rachis segments, meaning that their seed heads would be slightly less prone to shattering. As people worked through the stands, seeds from these genetic variants would end up in the gathering baskets slightly more often. Later, as the gatherers carried their baskets to camp, stored or processed the grain, or moved from place to place, a disproportionate number of the seeds they dropped, defecated, or perhaps even scattered purposely in likely growing areas would carry the flexible-rachis allele. (The same thing happened with the larger seeds preferred by the collectors.) As these genetic variants became isolated from the general wild population, each subsequent harvest advanced

rachis The short stem by which an individual seed attaches to the main stalk of a plant as it develops.

the "selection" process in favor of the same desirable traits.

Human manipulation became an evolutionary force in modifying the species, a process Darwin labeled "unconscious selection." People didn't have to be aware of genetic principles to act as effective agents of evolution. And where desirable traits could be readily discerned—larger grain size, plumper seed heads, earlier maturity, and so forth—human choice would even more predictably and consistently favor the preferred characteristics. The result within just a few growing seasons might be a significant shift in allele frequencies—that is, evolution—resulting from Darwinian selection processes, in this case the result of long-term pressure by gatherers, who consistently selected for those traits that improved the plant's productivity and quality (Rindos, 1984).

Of course, the rate of divergent evolution away from the wild ancestral forms of a plant (or animal) species accelerates as people continue to exercise control by selecting for genetically based characteristics they find desirable. With the cereal grasses, such as barley and wheat, the human-influenced varieties typically came to average more grains per seed head than their wild relatives had. The rachis became less brittle in domesticated forms, making it easier for people to harvest the grain with less loss because the seed head no longer shattered to disperse its own seed. At the same time, individual seed coats or husks (glumes) became less tough, making them easier for humans to process or digest. Many of these changes obviously would have been harmful to the plant under natural conditions. Frequently, a consequence of domestication is that the plant species becomes dependent on humans to disperse its seeds. After all, symbiosis is a mutual, two-way relationship.

Whenever favorable plant traits developed, hunter-gatherers could be expected to respond to these improvements by quickly adjusting their collecting behavior to take the greatest advantage, in turn stimulating further genetic changes in the subject plants and eventually producing a **cultigen**, or domesticate, under human control. As continuous selection and isolation from other plants of the

same species favored desirable genetic variants, the steps to full domestication would have been small ones.

Likewise, the distances that separated hunter-gatherers from early farmers were also small ones. It's usually impossible to determine archaeologically when harvesting activities may have expanded to include the deliberate scattering of selected wild seeds in new environments or the elimination of competing plants by "weeding" or even burning over a forest clearing. As they intensified their focus on wheat and barley in the Near East—or on species such as maize or runner beans in Mexico—hunter-gatherers finally abandoned the rhythm of their traditional food-collecting schedules and further committed themselves to increasing the productivity of these plants through cultivation.

Archaeological Evidence for Domestication and Agriculture

Archaeologist Graeme Barker (2006, p. 414) argues that the change from hunting and gathering to agriculture "was the most profound revolution in human history." It also profoundly affected other species and continues to do so. The accumulated archaeological evidence reveals that humans *independently* domesticated local species and developed agriculture in several geographically separate regions relatively soon after the Ice Age ended. From recent applications of genetic research and other methodological advances in archaeology, it's also clear that more independent instances of prehistoric domestication are likely to be identified, some locations currently identified as possible independent centers of domestication may be deleted from the list, and some plants and animals were probably domesticated multiple times in various places (Armelagos and Harper, 2005).

Archaeologists have yet to fully explain how and why agriculture spread and eventually dominated economic life in many parts of the world. Peter Bellwood's (2005) recent "early

cultigen A plant that is wholly dependent on humans; a domesticate.

farming dispersal hypothesis" integrates archaeology, genetics, and historical linguistics in a highly original argument that early farming grew out of the Mesolithic/Epipaleolithic and spread into new lands with the movement or dispersal of farmers from agricultural "homelands." Working within what is essentially an environmental approach that identifies human population growth as the main driving factor of farmer dispersal, or "demic diffusion," this hypothesis offers a controversial explanation for the spread of agriculture, human populations, and languages, as well as major spatial patterns in human genetics (Bellwood, 2005; Bellwood et al., 2007; see Diamond, 1999 for a very similar perspective). Building on much the same archaeological and genetic data, Graeme Barker (2006) reached different conclusions. He essentially questions the existence of such primal hearths or homelands and traces the roots of this revolution back to early Upper Paleolithic hunter-gatherers. It is too soon to tell which of these interpretations offers a more accurate picture of the spread of prehistoric agriculture.

In examining independent centers of domestication around the world, it's important to realize that the domestication of a local species or two would not necessarily trigger the enormous biocultural consequences we usually associate with the Neolithic period in the Near East. In fact, most altered species retained only local significance. For example, in the Eastern Woodlands of the United States, hunter-gatherers domesticated several small-seeded species very early; still, the wild forest products obtained by hunting and gathering retained their primary importance until relatively late prehistoric times, when true farming developed in the East.

In most regions, agriculture didn't develop fully until people were exploiting a mosaic of plants—and sometimes animals, too—from different locations, brought together in various combinations to meet such cultural requirements as nutrition, palatability, hardiness, yield, processing ease, and storage. In the Near East, this threshold was reached around 11,000 ya, when an agricultural complex consisting of wheat, barley, sheep, and goats was widely and rapidly adopted.

Plants

In most areas where agriculture emerged, early farmers relied on local plant species whose wild relatives grew close by. Old World cereal grasses, including barley and some wheat varieties, were native throughout the Near East and perhaps into southeastern Europe (Dennell, 1983). Wild varieties of these plants still flourish today over parts of this range. Therefore, barley or wheat domestication could have occurred anywhere in this region, possibly more than once. The same is true for maize and beans in Mexico. So, as we emphasized earlier, domestication and agriculture were independently invented in different regions around the world.

As we noted earlier, it's best to explain these separate but parallel processes from a combined cultural and ecological perspective. We've already seen that certain kinds of wild plants were more likely than others to become domesticated. Many of these species tend to grow in regions where a very long dry season follows a short wet period (Harlan, 1992). After the last Ice Age, around 10,000 ya, these conditions existed around the Mediterranean basin and the hilly areas of the Near East and in the dry forests and savanna grasslands of portions of sub-Saharan Africa, India, southern California, southern Mexico, and eastern and western South America.

Most scientific understanding of ancient human plant use has come from the **archaeobotanical** study of preserved seeds, fruits, nutshell fragments, and other **plant macrofossils** like those shown in **Figure 14-4**

Barry Lewis

Figure 14-4

Plant remains from a pit feature in an Illinois archaeological site. Clockwise from top are pieces of charred wood, nutshell fragments, and seeds.

archaeobotanical Referring to the analysis and interpretation of the remains of ancient plants recovered from the archaeological record.

plant macrofossils Plant parts such as seeds, nutshells, and stems that have been preserved in the archaeological record and are large enough to be clearly visible to the naked eye.

(Pearsall, 2000). It isn't easy to preserve seeds, tubers, leaves, and other delicate organic materials for thousands of years. Archaeologists recover some macrofossils from depositional environments that are always dry, wet, or frozen, because all of these conditions slow down or halt the process of decomposition. Most, however, are preserved because the way they were harvested, threshed, processed for consumption, or discarded brought them into contact with enough fire to char them, but not enough heat to reduce them to ash. Once charred, macrofossils preserve well in many kinds of archaeological sites and can often be classified to genus, if not to species.

Macrofossils offer direct evidence for important archaeological research, such as reconstructing hunter-gatherer plant use patterns, identifying farming locations, and determining the precise nature of harvested crops. They also provide insights of other kinds. The presence of perennial and biennial weed seeds in an ancient agricultural context may suggest that each year's farming activities only minimally disturbed the soil; the seed planter may have used a digging stick, hoe, or simple scratch plow. If, on the other hand, seeds of annual weeds predominate, the farmer may have used a moldboard plow—one that turns over the soil as it cuts through it.

The major shortcomings of macrofossil-based interpretations of past human plant use are due to potential preservation biases. Most plant macrofossils tend to be preserved because they were charred before entering the archaeological record (see Fig. 14-4 for examples). But not all plant parts char easily, and many don't char at all. For example, it's pretty easy to char a bean, but you'll be disappointed if you try the same thing with a leaf of lettuce. Because the necessary conditions could only be met sometimes in prehistory and by some plants and plant parts, archaeologists are understandably concerned about the validity and reliability of many reconstructions of human plant use that are based only on macrofossils

Fortunately, modern archaeologists can turn to several other important sources in their research on prehistoric human plant use. **Plant microfossils**, such as **pollen**, **phytoliths**, and **starch grains**, often survive even where macrofossils can't—for example, as residues on the cutting edges of ancient stone tools, inside pottery containers, embedded in the pores of grinding stones, and even trapped in the dental calculus that accumulates on human teeth (Bryant, 2003; Henry and Piperno, 2008). Unlike many macrofossils, these remains preserve readily in a wide range of archaeological contexts; they can be classified as to the kind of plant they represent, if not also to the plant part they represent; and they can be archaeologically present even in sites where macrofossils were destroyed or never deposited.

Pollen grains (**Fig. 14-5**) have been a valuable source of environmental and subsistence data for decades (Traverse, 2007). Their strengths are that they're abundant (as any hay fever sufferer can tell you); the grains are taxonomically distinctive and often can be classified to genus, if not to species; the outer shell of each grain is tough; and the wind-borne dispersal of pollen from seed-producing plants continues before, during, and after humans occupy a particular archaeological site. The main shortcoming of pollen grains is that they tend to preserve poorly in many kinds of open sites, depending on soil acidity, moisture, drainage, and weathering.

Phytoliths (**Fig. 14-6**) are microscopic, inorganic structures that form in many seed-producing plants as well as other plants (Piperno, 2006). Like pollen, phytoliths are taxonomically distinctive. They even vary according to where they

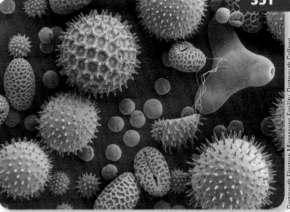

Figure 14-5

Pollen grains from common flowering plants. The spiked ball in the lower left of the photograph is roughly 75 micrometers (μm), or three-thousandths of an inch, in diameter.

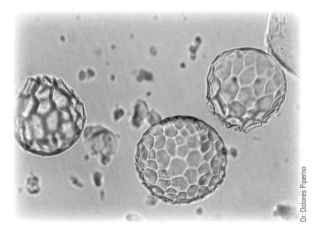

Figure 14-6

Squash (*Cucurbita ficifolia*) phytoliths. The large one in the lower center of the photo measures about 120 μm across.

plant microfossils Small to microscopic plant remains, most falling in a range of 10 to 100 micrometers (μm), or roughly the size of individual grains of wheat flour in the bag from your grocer's shelf.

pollen Microscopic grains containing the male gametes of seed-producing plants.

phytoliths (*phyto*, meaning "plant," and *lith*, meaning "stone") Microscopic silica structures formed in the cells of many plants.

starch grains Subcellular structures that form in all plant parts and can be classified by family or genus; particularly abundant in seeds and tubers.

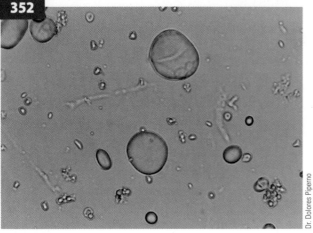

Dr. Dolores Piperno

Figure 14-7

Wild emmer wheat (*Triticum dicoccoides*) starch grains, which show distinctive craterlike surface impressions. The largest starch grain (top center) is about 30 µm in diameter.

form in the plant, so phytoliths from leaves can be distinguished from those that formed in the stems and seeds of the same plant. They are also affected by different preservation biases than macrofossils (Cabanes et al., 2011). Are the plant remains at your site unidentifiable, reduced to a powdery ash, or simply not preserved? Not a problem. Chances are the phytoliths from these plants are not only present in the archaeological deposit but also recoverable and identifiable.

Starch grains (**Fig. 14-7**) are subcellular particles that form in all plant parts. They are particularly abundant in such economically important portions as seeds and tubers (Coil et al., 2003). They are a useful complement to phytoliths as a data source and are a major tool in archaeological investigations of root crops (Piperno, 2008). Like pollen and phytoliths, starch grains can be taxonomically classified, currently mostly to family or genus. A good example of the archaeological application of starch grain analysis is the recent examination of the surface of a grinding stone found on the floor of one of the 23,000-year-old huts at Ohalo II, in Israel. This study, which was based on carefully sampled residues from cracks and pits in the working surface of the grinding stone, enabled archaeobotanists to identify that it was a specialized implement used to grind wild cereal grasses, including barley (Piperno et al., 2004).

As we saw in Chapter 8, some plant species also leave biochemical traces in those who consume them. Because temperate and tropical region plants evolved with slightly different processes for photosynthesis, their chemical compositions vary in the ratio of carbon-13 to carbon-12. This distinctive chemical profile gets passed along the food chain, and the bones of the human skeleton may provide evidence of dietary change. For example, their lower ^{13}C levels reveal that females at Grasshopper Pueblo, in

east-central Arizona, consumed mostly the local plants they gathered, while their male relatives at first enjoyed more maize, a plant higher in ^{13}C. Later, maize became a staple in everyone's diet at Grasshopper, resulting in equivalent carbon isotopes in males and females (Ezzo, 1993).

Other biochemical analyses, using different isotopes, have been devised to assess overall diet—not necessarily just the domesticated portions—from individual skeletons. A higher ratio of nitrogen-15 to nitrogen-14 ($^{15}N/^{14}N$), for instance, corresponds to a greater seafood component to the diet (Schoeninger et al., 1983), while a higher strontium-to-calcium (Sr/Ca) ratio indicates that plant foods were of greater dietary importance than meat (Schoeninger, 1981). Other chemicals taken up by bones may inform us about ancient lifeways. For example, lead (Pb) is a trace element found in unusually high concentration in the bones of Romans who drank wine stored in the lead containers typical of that period. The interplay among culture, diet, and biology is, of course, a prime example of biocultural evolution. But to put it more simply, "You are what you eat," and the odds are increasingly good that archaeologists can measure it.

Microfossil analyses complement and greatly extend the valuable insights that archaeobotanists have achieved through the study of macrofossils. Recent key advances include the growing field of *archaeogenetics*, which applies the methods of molecular genetics to archaeological problems, as well as improvements in radiocarbon dating, which can yield accurate age estimates from samples as small as 100 micrograms (µg)—that's one ten-thousandth of a gram, or roughly one-fifth the weight of a grain of rice (Armelagos and Harper, 2005). As a result, researchers are now able to more completely understand the prehistory of the human use of plants and the beginnings of agriculture.

Animals

The process of animal domestication differed from plant domestication, and it probably varied even from one animal species to another. For example, the dog was one of the first domesticated animals; mtDNA evidence suggests an origin between 40,000 and 15,000 ya (Savolainen, 2002), and dogs may even have accompanied late Ice Age hunter-gatherers (Olsen, 1985). The dog's relationship with humans was different (and still is) from that of most subsequently domesticated animals. Often valued less for its meat or hide, a dog's primary role was most likely as a ferocious hunting weapon under at least a bit of human control and direction. As people domesticated other animals, they changed the dog's behavior even more for service as a herder and later, in the Arctic and among the Native Americans of the Great Plains, as an occasional transporter of possessions. But the burial of a puppy with a Natufian person who died some 12,000 ya in the Near East suggests that dogs may have also earned a role as pets very early (Davis and Valla, 1978).

Most other domesticated animals were maintained solely for their meat at first. Richard J. Harrison's (1985) insightful analysis of faunal collections from Neolithic sites in Spain and Portugal concludes that meat remained the primary product up until about 4,000 ya, when subsequent changes in herd composition (age and sex ratios), slaughter patterns, and popularity of certain breeds all point to new uses for some livestock. Oxen pulled plows, horses carried people and things, cattle and goats contributed milk products, and sheep were raised for wool. Animal waste became fertilizer in agricultural areas. Leather, horn, and bone—and even social status for the animals' owners—were other valued by-products.

Of course, animals are more mobile than plants, and most of them are no less mobile than the early people pursuing them. So it's unlikely that hunters could have promoted useful genetic changes in wild animals just by trying to restrict their movements or by selective hunting alone. Possibly, by simultaneously destroying wild predators and reducing the number of competing herbivores, humans became surrogate protectors of the herds, though this arrangement would not have had the genetic impact of actual domestication.

Since domestication is a process, not an event, it's nearly impossible to say precisely when a plant or animal species has been domesticated. The process involves much more than an indication of "tameness" in the presence of humans. More significant are the changes in allele frequencies that result from selective breeding and isolation from wild relatives. People may have started with young animals spared by hunters or, in the case of large and dangerous species such as the auroch (the wild ancestor of domesticated cattle), with individuals that were exceptionally docile or small (Fagan, 1993). Maintained in captivity, these animals could be selectively bred for desirable traits, such as more meat, fat, wool, or strength. Once early farmers were consistently selecting breeding stock according to certain criteria and succeeding in perpetuating those characteristics through subsequent generations, then domestication—that is, evolution—clearly had begun.

Overall, not many mammal species were ever domesticated. Those most amenable to domestication are animals that form hierarchical herds, are not likely to flee when frightened, and are not strongly territorial (Diamond, 1989). In other words, animals that will tolerate and transfer their allegiance to human surrogates make the best potential domesticates. Several large Eurasian mammals met these specifications, and cultures of Asia, Europe, and Africa came to rely on sheep and goats, pigs, cattle, and horses (listed here in approximately their order of domestication) as well as water buffalo, camels, reindeer, and a few other regionally significant species.

Even fewer New World herd animals were capable of being domesticated. Aside from two South American camelids—the llama and the alpaca—no large American mammal was brought fully under human control (**Fig. 14-8**). Dogs had probably accompanied the first people into the New World. None of these animals were suitable for transporting or pulling heavy loads—llamas balk at carrying more than about 100 pounds, and Plains Indian dogs dragged only small bundles—so the people of the New World continued to carry their own

Figure 14-8

Peoples of highland South America bred the llama primarily as a source of wool and, to a limited extent, to transport loads.

Figure 14-9

A typical collection of faunal remains from an excavation level in an Illinois archaeological site.

burdens, till their fields by hand, and hunt and fight on foot until the introduction of the Old World's livestock in the 1500s.

Archaeological evidence of nonhuman animal domestication is subtle and difficult to assess from the bones themselves (**Fig. 14-9**). Archaeozoologists, who study the skeletal remains of nonhuman fauna from archaeological sites, have also shown that many of the morphological changes long viewed as good proxy measures of domestication (for example, smaller adult size, horn shape) actually follow, by as much as thousands of years, other archaeological measures of domestication in the Near East, such as distinctive demographic patterns typical of managed herds (Zeder, 2008). For example, at Ganj Dareh, in Iran, around 9,900 ya, villagers slaughtered a high proportion of young male goats, but adult females survived long after reaching reproductive maturity. This culling pattern is typical of herded animals (Zeder, 2008). If these villagers were hunting wild goats, the demographic pattern evident in the goat bones would have been different, emphasizing large adults, mostly males.

Among important recent developments, DNA analyses of modern animals and ancient animal bones found in archaeological sites are greatly enhancing our understanding of the domestication of individual animal species as well as the development of farming (Larson, 2011). Although not without their own methodological and interpretive problems, population genetic analyses, coupled with new morphometric analyses and recent advances in small-sample radiocarbon dating, hold considerable promise for answering some of the big questions about the origins of domestication.

Old World Farmers

As we've noted, independent invention accounts best for the diversity of domesticates and the distinctiveness of Neolithic lifeways around the world. What's more, many wild species, such as wheat and sheep, probably occupied more extensive natural ranges in the early Holocene and may in fact have undergone local domestication more than a few times (Armelagos and Harper, 2005).

But as Bellwood (2005) and Diamond (1999) remind us, we can't entirely discount the spread of Neolithic lifeways or people from place to place. As we'll see, in at least some areas—southeastern Europe, for example—colonizing farmers appear to have brought their domesticates and their culture with them as they migrated into new territories in search of suitable farmland. Neolithic practices also spread through secondary contact as people on the margins of established farming societies acquired certain tools, seeds, and ideas and passed them along to cultures still further removed. Seeds and animals must have become commodities in prehistoric exchange networks, just like the Spanish horses obtained by Native Americans did in the sixteenth century. It's important to bear in mind that each archaeological event is unique in its own way. "One-size-fits-all" explanations are rarely adequate, even if the results are the same—in this case, the expansion of Neolithic lifeways. With that in mind, let's consider a sampling of Neolithic societies from around the world to get some idea of the variations on this common theme.

The Near East

As we saw in Chapter 13, Epipaleolithic foraging cultures, such as Kebaran and Natufian, apparently took the first steps, though perhaps inadvertently, toward agriculture in the Near East (**Fig. 14-10**). Many of the archaeologically document-ed changes among Epipaleolithic hunter-gatherers in the Levant offer important support for Flannery's (1973) conception of a broad-spectrum revolution that pre-ceded the development of domestication and agriculture.

For example, the extraordinary pres-ervation of plant remains at Ohalo II, an early Epipaleolithic campsite in northern Israel, shows that small-grained grass and wild cereal seeds were important in hunter-gatherer diets in the Levant by 23,000 ya (see p. 352; Piperno et al., 2004; Weiss et al., 2004a, 2004b). Faunal remains from eight other Epipaleolithic sites in the Levant, all of which date between 18,000 and 12,000 ya, also show a pattern of increased diet breadth as the abundance of big game animals declined and hunters depended more and more on smaller game, such as gazelles (Stutz et al., 2009).

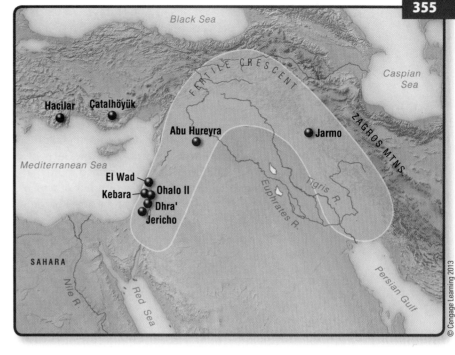

Figure 14-10

Early Neolithic sites of the Fertile Crescent.

At a Glance

Important Near Eastern Sites and Regions

SITE	DATES (YA)	SIGNIFICANCE
Abu Hureyra (Syria)	13,100–12,000	Hunter-gatherer settlement that spans the cold and dry climatic conditions of the Younger Dryas; shows evidence of increasing diet breadth as preferred plant foods became less available across the region
Dhra' (Jordan)	ca. 11,000	Evidence of plant cultivation, food storage, and settled communities after the end of the Younger Dryas
Jericho (West Bank)	<11,000–3,500	One of the early sedentary communities founded in the Levant; Jericho began in Natufian times and was occupied throughout the Neolithic
Kebara and **El Wad** (Israel)	ca. 10,000	Sites where hunter-gatherers supplemented their diet by harvesting the wild ancestral varieties of wheat and barley

The site of Abu Hureyra, in the upper Euphrates valley of Syria, is of particular archaeological interest because its occupation spans the Younger Dryas (roughly 13,000–11,500 ya), a climatic shift to cooler and drier conditions that David Henry (1989) argues was an important environmental factor in the development of agriculture in the Levant. The Abu Hureyra hunter-gatherers consumed more than 250 plant species, only a few of which were staple foods, at the onset of the Younger Dryas (Moore et al., 2000, p. 397). As the climate changed, many of these species vanished from the Abu Hureyra archaeological record, to be replaced by increased frequencies of weed seeds and possible evidence of early domesticated rye, specimens of which date to roughly 11,200–10,600 ya. Moore and colleagues (2010) infer that changing environmental conditions were sufficient to account for these shifts in Abu Hureyra's subsistence economy and that this settlement depended at least partly on the cultivation of domesticated plants (rye, in this case). While the identification of domesticated rye at Abu Hureyra remains a controversial claim (see Colledge and Conolly, 2010, pp. 135–136), the subsistence economy clearly reflects increased diet breadth as higher-ranked foods became less available in the region around Abu Hureyra (Colledge and Conolly, 2010).

Evidence of cultivation, settled communities, and food storage become more common after the end of the Younger Dryas and the return of a slightly more moderate climate. At Dhra', an 11,000-year-old village site near the Dead Sea in Jordan, archaeologists recently uncovered the remains of mud granaries and other food storage features, as well as large quantities of wild barley and oat grains (Kuijt and Finlayson, 2009). The village economy at Dhra' clearly depended on the cultivation and storage of wild plants, and many features traditionally associated with sedentary Neolithic farmers are seen at Dhra'.

Food collectors and the earliest farmers established the first permanent sedentary communities in the Near East.

Drawn by an ever-flowing spring in an otherwise arid region, settlers at the site of Jericho (or Tell es-Sultan), in the West Bank, and at other Natufian sites in Israel built their stone or mud-brick round houses some 11,500 ya. Though they were made of more substantial materials, in form these structures closely resembled the temporary huts of the region's earlier hunters and gatherers. Numerous grinding stones and clay-lined storage pits found in these communities testify to the economic importance of cereal grains (Moore, 1985; Bar-Yosef, 1987).

Finally, around 10,000 ya at Kebara and El Wad, both in Israel, stone-bladed sickles aided the harvest of wild wheat and barley (Henry, 1989). This technology, more efficient than plucking seeds by hand, netted greater yields during a short harvest period. The process of genetic selection that we've considered as the basis for plant domestication must have been well under way by this time. Foraging for the seeds of wild cereals, fruits, nuts, and the meat of wild game long remained an important, but slowly declining, strategy. By 10,000 ya, managed sheep and goat populations were present in the Levant (Munro, 2009). At Abu Hureyra, villagers were cultivating wheat, rye, and lentils by 9,800 ya, but wild plant food staples were still a part of the diet (Moore et al., 2000). By 9,000 ya, sedentary villagers across a broad arc from the Red Sea to western Iran—also known as the *Fertile Crescent* (see Fig. 14-10)—engaged in wheat and barley agriculture and sheep and goat herding. As demonstrated at many sites in this region, Neolithic families lived in adjacent multiroom rectangular houses, in contrast to the compounds of individual small, round shelters commonly built by Epipaleolithic collectors as well as the early Jericho settlers.

Africa

Tracing Africa's Neolithic past is challenging, considering the continent's vast size, its varied climates and vegetation zones, and the extent to which many of its regions are still archaeologically unknown. What's more, because many tropical foods lack woody stems or durable seeds, plant macrofossils often are poorly represented at African archaeological sites. Recent studies based on the analysis of plant microfossils and genetic patterns are helping to construct fresh perspectives on the origins, development, and impacts of plant and animal domestication throughout the African continent.

Northern Africa Archaeologists working in the Nile Valley have found sickles and milling stones relating to early wild grain harvesting (Wendorf and Schild, 1989). Qadan culture sites near present-day Aswan (**Fig. 14-11**) probably typified the Epipaleolithic food collectors who occupied the valley around 8,000 ya (Hoffman, 1991). Qadan people employed spears or nets for taking large Nile perch and catfish. Along the riverbanks they hunted wildfowl and gathered wild produce, processing starchy aquatic tubers on their milling stones. They also stalked the adjacent grasslands for gazelle and other game and may have begun the process of domesticating the local wild cattle (Wendorf and Schild, 1994; but see Gifford-Gonzalez and Hanotte, 2011, p. 6). Considering the wealth of naturally occurring resources along the Nile, this foraging and collecting way of life might have continued indefinitely. So why did farming develop there at all?

Part of the answer rests with shifting rainfall patterns across North Africa since the Late Pleistocene. Long-term cycles brought increased precipitation, which broadened the Nile and its valley and gave the river a predictable seasonal rhythm. Rains falling on its tropical headwaters, thousands of miles to the south, caused the river to overflow its downstream channels by late summer, flooding the low-lying basins of northern Egypt for about three months of the year. Although desiccation followed, the flood-deposited silt grew lush with wild grasses through the following season. Periodically, however, extended drought episodes intervened to narrow the river's life-giving flow.

West of the Nile, the fragile arid environment of the Sahara was particularly susceptible to these fluctuations. It was always marginal for humans, and down

to 11,000 ya, it was uninviting even to hunter-gatherers. Then a period of increased rainfall created shallow lakes and streams that nurtured the Saharan grasslands, attracting game animals and humans. Around 7,000 ya, people in the Sahara devised a strategy of nomadic pastoralism, allowing their herds of sheep, goats, and possibly cattle to act as ecological intermediaries by converting tough grasses to meat and by-products useful to humans (Wendorf and Schild, 1994). Soon after, around 6,000 ya, further deterioration of the region's climate—and possibly overgrazing—forced the herders and their animals to seek greener pastures closer to the Nile and also to the south beyond the Sahara (Williams, 1984; A. Smith, 1992; Kuper and Kröpelin, 2006).

As drought parched the adjacent areas, the Nile Valley attracted more settlers. Wild resources were then insufficient to feed the growing sedentary population, and even the local domesticates that had been casually cultivated on the floodplain gave way to more productive cereals—the domesticated barley and wheat that had been brought under human control elsewhere by people like the Natufians.

Farmers gradually made the river's rhythm their own. Communities of reed-mat or mud-brick houses appeared across the Nile delta and along its banks. Basket-lined storage pits or granaries, milling stones, and sickles indicate a heavy reliance on grain. Pottery vessels of river clay, linen woven from flax fibers, flint tools, and occasional hammered copper items were produced locally. These ordinary Neolithic beginnings laid the foundation for the remarkable Egyptian civilization, which we'll explore in Chapter 15.

Sub-Saharan Africa In West Africa along the southern edge of the Sahara, where little is currently known about the early Holocene human presence, the pattern appears similar to that described for the Sahara. At **Ounjougou**, in the Dogon Plateau region of central Mali, erosional gullies exposed a long sequence of Pleistocene and early Holocene sites (Huysecom et al., 2004). Excavations reveal that hunter-gatherers lived in

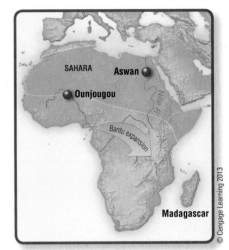

© Cengage Learning 2013

Figure 14-11

Early farming in Africa and Bantu expansion.

Ounjougou (won-joo-goo) A site populated by African hunter-gatherers who made early use of wild cereal grasses on the southern edge of the Sahara between 12,000 and 9,000 ya.

At a Glance

Important African Sites and Regions

SITE	DATES (YA)	SIGNIFICANCE
Qadan culture (Egypt)	ca. 8,000	Epipaleolithic hunter-gatherers who harvested the rich wild plant and animal resources of the Nile region upriver from modern Aswan
Ounjougou (Mali)	12,000–9,000	African hunter-gatherers who made early use of wild cereal grasses on the southern edge of the Sahara

© Cengage Learning 2013

Figure 14-12

A stand of sorghum, which, along with rice and millet, is an important starch grain crop in many parts of Africa and Asia.

millet Small-grained cereal grasses native to Asia and Africa.

sorghum A cereal grass. Some subspecies are grown for food grains, others for their sweet, juicy stalk.

cultivars Wild plants fostered by human efforts to make them more productive.

taro Species of a tropical plant with an edible starchy root.

this region from the earliest Holocene, around 12,000–11,000 ya. By 10,000–9,000 ya, descendants of these groups were harvesting wild cereal grasses and making and using ceramics.

The major Near Eastern cereal crops did not grow well in sub-Saharan Africa or in its tropical regions. Between 5,000 and 3,000 ya, African farmers developed comparable domesticates from local cereal grasses, including varieties of **millet** and **sorghum** (**Fig. 14-12**; Smith, 1999). Pearl millet, an important food grain in parts of Africa and India, was domesticated in Mali around 4,500 ya and was soon found across sub-Saharan Africa. Manning and colleagues (2011) speculate that pearl millet may have spread rapidly because it could grow even where there wasn't much water and it could be easily cultivated by mobile pastoralists. African crops such as pearl millet, finger millet, and sorghum found their way across the Arabian Sea to South Asia more than 3,000 ya (Fuller et al., 2011), where they are still raised today.

Hunters and gatherers in other parts of Africa also experimented with local **cultivars**. For example, mobile foragers and semisedentary fishers of tropical Africa practiced yam horticulture in clearings and along riverbanks by 7,000–6,000 ya (Ehret, 1984; Arnau et al, 2010). With digging sticks, they pried out the starchy tubers and carried them away for cooking. As an added bonus, the people discovered that if they pressed the leafy tops or cuttings of the larg-

est roots into the soil at the edge of the camp clearing, the yams would regenerate into an informal garden. The domestication process for the yam, a tuber that propagates vegetatively (for example, by cuttings rather than by seeds), may have taken far longer, possibly millennia, than for the domestication of cereal grains such as wheat.

More dramatic shifts in sub-Saharan subsistence followed the introduction and spread of several Neolithic domesticated plants and animals from South and Southeast Asia across the Indian Ocean. Among these economically important plants, all of which spread quickly throughout tropical Africa, were bananas (or plantains) and two root crops, **taro** and the greater yam (Fuller et al., 2011, p. 550). The banana, a food crop that is now of global importance, arrived in Africa from Southeast Asia, possibly by 2,500 ya. Based on linguistic evidence, Blench (2009) argues that plantains, taro, and the greater yams were part of the Southeast Asian "crop package," which reached the shores of Africa and quickly spread throughout the interior.

Outside the Nile Valley, cattle herding took priority over farming in much of East Africa, where conditions were generally not suitable for cultivation. Taurine cattle (*Bos taurus*) were first domesticated in the Near East more than 9,000 ya and by 8,000 ya could be found on the savannas that then existed in parts of the Sahara (Gifford-Gonzalez and Hanotte, 2011). Genetic evidence also suggests a possible independent domestication of African taurine cattle (Bradley and Magee, 2006). East African rock paintings show that hump-backed zebu (or indicine) cattle (*Bos indicus*), a South Asian domesticate, reached Africa by 2,500 ya. The resulting African taurine-zebu hybrid played a major role in the success of East African cattle pastoralists (Fuller et al., 2011).

Bantu-speaking peoples, native to west-central Africa, relied on these and other domesticated plants and animals to support their rapid expansion through central and southern Africa (Phillipson, 1984). Driving herds of domestic goats and cattle and acquiring the technology of ironworking as they moved southeastward through central Africa (Van Noten and Raymaekers, 1987), the Bantu easily overwhelmed most hunting and gathering groups. The conventional view is that with iron tools and weapons, they carved out gardens and maintained large semipermanent villages, and today, their numerous descendants live in eastern, southern, and southwestern Africa (see Fig. 14-11). There's at least some evidence that food-producing methods spread into parts of southern Africa before the Bantu. The bones of domesticated sheep found in Late Stone Age sites in South Africa may not be the result of the spread of pastoralists, as once widely believed, but the remains of the camps of Bushmen (also called the San), whom Karim Sadr (2003) describes as "hunters-with-sheep."

Asia

Several centers of domestication in southern and eastern Asia gave rise to separate Neolithic traditions based on the propagation of productive local plant and animal species. The exploitation of these resources spread widely and heralded further economic and social changes associated with the rise of early civilizations in these regions (see Chapter 15).

South Asia Excavations at Mehrgarh, in central Pakistan, have illuminated Neolithic beginnings on the Indian subcontinent (Jarrige and Meadow,

1980; Fuller, 2006). Located at the edge of a high plain west of the broad Indus Valley (**Fig. 14-13**), the site's lower levels, dating between 8,000 and 6,000 ya, reveal the trend toward dietary specialization that accompanied the domestication of local plant and animal species. Early on, the people harvested both wild and domesticated varieties of barley and wheat, among other native plants. Mehrgarh's archaeological deposits also include bones of many local herbivores: water buffalo, gazelle, swamp deer, goats, sheep, pigs, cattle, and even elephants. By 6,000 ya, the cultivated cereals prevailed, along with just three animal species—domestic sheep, goats, and cattle. Researchers believe that this early Neolithic phase at Mehrgarh represents a transition from seminomadic herding to a more sedentary existence that became the basis for later urban development in the Indus Valley. Other planned settlements boasting multiroom mud-brick dwellings and granaries soon appeared in the region, supported by a productive agriculture and bustling trade in copper, turquoise, shells, and cotton.

Rice is the staple crop of much of South and East Asia. The earliest evidence of rice cultivation in India is reported from the Lahuradewa site and adjacent lake deposits in the Ganges Valley, where cultivated rice phytoliths and husks have been found in contexts dated to around 8,360 ya (Saxena et al., 2006). Domesticated rice spread from the Ganges into South India after 3,000 ya, possibly after the emergence of irrigation systems such as paddy-field cultivation (Fuller and Qin, 2009). The relationship between early South Asian domesticated rice and that which was domesticated by Chinese farmers in the lower Yangtze Valley (see next section) is both unclear and an active area of research.

Archaeologists know much less about the origins of agriculture in South India. Recent archaeobotanical analyses of samples taken from southern

Figure 14-13

Early farming in South Asia.

At a Glance

Important South Asian Sites and Regions

SITE	DATES (YA)	SIGNIFICANCE
Lahuradewa (India)	ca. 8,360	Earliest evidence of rice cultivation in India
Mehrgarh (Pakistan)	8,000–6,000	Early Neolithic community in South Asia that depended on domesticated plants and animals; represents a transition from seminomadic herding to sedentary villages and towns
Southern Neolithic, or **Ash Mound** (India)	5,000–4,000	Early evidence of South Indian agriculture based on native crops of lentils and millet, plus introduced domesticates such as wheat and barley

© Cengage Learning 2013

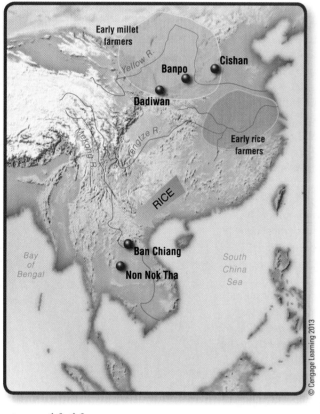

© Cengage Learning 2013

Figure 14-14

Early farming in East and Southeast Asia.

Neolithic, or Ash Mound Tradition, sites in Karnataka and Andhra Pradesh suggest that the earliest agriculture in these regions dates between 5,000 and 4,000 ya and was based on several native domesticated species, principally two lentils (horse-gram and mung bean) and two species of millet (brown-top millet and bristly foxtail grass), along with nonnative crops including wheat and barley (Fuller et al., 2004). The high frequencies of native domesticates in these samples lend support to Vavilov's (1992) identification of India as a possible independent center of domestication.

China By 10,000 ya, hunter-gatherers and East Asia's earliest farmers were already cultivating a crop in the Yellow River basin that became a staple food in the Neolithic villages and towns of northern China. It may surprise you to know that this crop was millet, not rice. The earliest firm evidence of millet cultivation comes from the early Neolithic site of Cishan, in Hebei Province (**Fig. 14-14**), which has yielded caches of common (or broomcorn) millet in storage pits that date between 10,300 and 8,700 ya (Lu et al., 2009). Cishan was part of a regional development of millet farming that began with hunter-gatherer cultivation in several places across northern China. The deep stratigraphic sequence at the Dadiwan site in Gansu Province (Fig. 14-14) shows that the origins of millet farming can be traced to the broad-spectrum resource strategy of Late Pleistocene hunter-gatherers in northern China (Barton et al., 2009; Bettinger et al., 2010).

During the Yangshao period (about 7,000–5,000 ya), millet was a staple of both humans and their domesticated animals, which included pigs, chickens, and dogs, but for a long time foraging continued to provide wild plants, fish, and animals. River terrace deposits of deep loess soil ensured large yields and undoubtedly contributed to the growth of populous settlements. Domesticated rice is found in Yellow River sites by the late Yangshao period, but in minor quantities relative to millet; rice became fairly widespread in this region after 5,000 ya (Fuller et al., 2010)

At the Yangshao site of Banpo, in Henan Province (see Fig. 14-14), more than 100 pit houses were placed around a plaza and its communal house, and a protective ditch surrounded the village. Cemeteries and pottery kilns typically were located near the residential parts of Yangshao villages. The jade carving, painted ceramics of tripod form, silkworm cultivation, and elite burials found in Yangshao sites anticipated some of the hallmarks of the later Neolithic, or Longshan, period beginning 4,700 ya.

Rice may have been cultivated by hunter-gatherers in the lower Yangtze region of southern China by 12,000–10,000 ya (Fuller et al., 2010). Although much is still unknown about the process by which rice was eventually brought into domestication, it was an economically important crop in the lower Yangtze by 8,000 ya (Fuller et al., 2009; Zhao, 2010). The population density of the middle and lower Yangtze basin increased rapidly between 7,000 and 5,500 ya, and substantial permanent villages were present throughout the region (Zhang and Hung, 2008). Some of these villages are considerably larger than their neighbors and show evidence of increased social complexity in their layout and structures.

Farmers introduced rice into Southeast Asia over the next several thousand years, bringing settled village life and domesticated cattle, pigs, and dogs to locations such as Ban Chiang and Non Nok Tha, both in Thailand (see Fig. 14-14). High yields and the varied conditions under which rice could be grown made it the basis for sustained population growth in many parts of this region (Higham and Lu, 1998; Kharakwal et al., 2004).

Europe

Farmers in southeastern Europe already were tilling the Balkan Peninsula by about 9,000 ya at such sites as Argissa and Franchthi Cave, in Greece (**Fig. 14-15**; Perlès, 2001). In the eastern Mediterranean, Neolithic farmers arrived on the island of Cyprus with domesticated plants and animals from the Near East as early as 10,000–9,000 ya (Zeder, 2008, p. 11599). Far to the west, similar farmers reached the east coast of Spain by 7,700 ya.

Researchers continue to debate whether the spread of farming into Europe was caused by the movement of people, ideas, or some combination of the two (Bellwood, 2005; Barker, 2006; Colledge and Conolly, 2007; Rowley-Conwy, 2011). Considerable recent archaeological, genetic, radiocarbon, and other evidence supports the interpretation that the earliest farming cultures in Europe were primarily the result of sporadic migrations by Neolithic farmers, whose pathways stretched ultimately

At a Glance

Important Chinese Sites and Regions

SITE	DATES (YA)	SIGNIFICANCE
Cishan	10,300–8,700	Earliest evidence of millet cultivation in northern China
Dadiwan	8,000–7,200	Deep stratigraphic record that documents the development of millet farming from broad-spectrum exploitation of local plant resources
Banpo	ca. 7,000–6,000	Yangshao period (Neolithic) site near Xi'an, northern China; extensive excavations have exposed about 100 houses that were part of a sedentary community

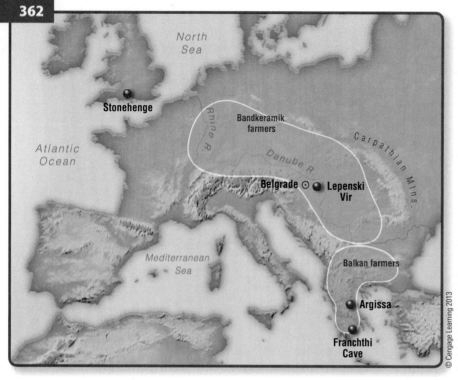

Figure 14-15

Early Neolithic sites of Europe.

Figure 14-16

Bandkeramik vessel from Motzenstein, near Wattendorf, Germany.

Taken from textbook by Timo Seregély (University of Bamberg), to accompany the exhibition "AXT und RAD en miniature, 2005" (Axe and Wheel in Miniature, 2005). Photo by Helmut Voss.

Bandkeramik Literally, "lined pottery"; refers to a Neolithic ceramic ware widely encountered in central Europe and to the culture that produced it.

alluvial Deposited by streams, usually during flood stages.

back to the Fertile Crescent. Rowley-Conwy (2011) and Zeder (2008) argue that in many of the places successfully colonized by these farmers, subsequent interaction with indigenous hunter-gatherers facilitated the spread of farming, as well as domesticated plants and animals, throughout parts of Europe. This interpretation accounts for the seemingly sudden appearance of fully domesticated sheep, goats, wheat, and barley at many sites in Europe and the countries bordering the Mediterranean. Had the Neolithic farming complex diffused throughout Europe primarily through trade and exchange rather than by migrations, farming would have developed gradually in these regions

and the archaeological record would yield evidence of "transitional" local economies between hunting and gathering and farming. No such sites have yet been found.

Neolithic lifeways transformed other parts of Europe somewhat later than southeastern Europe, and the source of these changes has also generated debate. Beginning around 7,000 ya, farming village sites littered with linear-decorated pottery, or **Bandkeramik (Fig. 14-16)**, appeared across central and (still later) northern regions of the continent (Bogucki, 1988). Bandkeramik culture farmers sought deep, well-drained **alluvial** and loess soils located along the Danube, the Rhine, and their tributaries. There they cultivated cereals and legumes, raised cattle and pigs, and collected wild hazelnuts (Whittle, 1985; Howell, 1987). Their settlements consisted of sturdy timber-framed structures averaging 100 feet long, with some up to 150 feet. These longhouses sheltered extended families and possibly served as barns for storing harvested crops or for harboring animals. Wooden fences barred livestock from planted fields during the growing season and then, following the harvest, confined them in the field so that their manure could restore soil nutrients. The fertility of loess soils could be maintained for relatively long periods with simple manuring and crop rotation, and fixed-plot farming on rich alluvium could sustain permanent settlements for up to 500 years (Whittle, 1985; Howell, 1987).

In Britain, Ireland, and southern Scandinavia, the development of Neolithic farming communities was rapid and possibly traumatic (Rowley-Conwy, 2004). In the continuing debate about whether European farming was the product of indigenous development, the cultural influence of farming neighbors, or migration from other regions, a growing body of evidence makes a compelling argument for migration as the main factor. For example, a recent analysis of radiocarbon dates from all regions of Britain concludes that around 6,100–5,400 ya, farmers from northern France settled first in southwestern England and shortly thereafter in central Scotland (Collard et al., 2010). The results of this

At a Glance
Important European Sites and Regions

SITE	DATES (YA)	SIGNIFICANCE
Argissa and **Franchthl Cave** (Greece)	9,000	Early Neolithic farming settlements in Greece
Bandkeramik culture (central Europe)	ca. 7,000	Archaeological culture that contains the earliest Neolithic farming communities in central Europe

© Cengage Learning 2013

study are corroborated by the comparative analysis of pottery, faunal remains, and mortuary practices and by stable isotope data that show a strong Mesolithic/Neolithic diet shift (Richards et al., 2003; Collard et al., 2010). Population density also increased significantly across Britain in the centuries following the arrival of the island's first farmers.

New World Farmers

While Old World Neolithic cultures generally relied on agricultural practices that linked domesticated cereal grasses together with herd animals, the farmers of the Americas focused almost exclusively on plant resources. Most of these plants had very limited ranges, but one important cereal grass—maize, or corn—came to dominate prehistoric Native American agriculture nearly everywhere it could be grown (**Fig. 14-17**).

Cereal grasses suitable for domestication were abundant on several continents, but the people of the Old World brought more of those species under control. Except for maize, whose wild ancestor may at first have been used in a different way, human cultural behavior in the New World did not induce the same genetic transformations in American grasses as it had in the Old World.

New World Domesticates

Considered together, the products of New World farmers make up a remarkable catalog of familiar plants, many of which were domesticated between 10,000 and 7,000 ya (Iriarte, 2009). Besides maize, the list includes important staple foods like white potatoes, sweet potatoes, yams, **manioc**, many bean varieties, peanuts, sunflowers, and **quinoa** (*Chenopodium* sp.). Nearly as important, but not staples, are such domesticated vegetables and fruits as sweet peppers, chili peppers, tomatoes, squashes, and pumpkins, along with pineapples, papayas, avocados, guavas, and passion fruit. Vanilla and chocolate came from American tree beans. Tobacco, coca, and peyote were major stimulants, and a host of other American plant domesticates had medicinal, utilitarian, or ornamental uses long before the arrival of the Europeans. The principal New World domesticates were developed in several locations in Mexico and in South America, but the use of a few of these plants eventually spread far beyond the regions in which they were first domesticated.

One domesticated plant, the bottle gourd (*Lagenaria siceraria*), appears to have had a much different origin than other New World domesticates. It was long suspected that the bottle gourd reached the New World by floating across the Atlantic Ocean from Africa, where it occurs in the wild, but genetic research shows that the closest relatives of the oldest New World specimens were from northeastern Asia. Based on AMS radiocarbon dates of gourd samples and analyses of DNA markers, the

United States Department of Agriculture

Figure 14-17
A sample of modern maize diversity. Maize benefits from a very large gene pool, which was by no means ignored by early Native American farmers.

manioc Cassava, a starchy edible root crop of the tropics.

quinoa (keen-wah´) Seed-bearing member of the genus *Chenopodium*, cultivated by early Peruvians.

domesticated bottle gourd was present in the Americas by 10,000 ya and may have been carried from Asia by Paleo-Indian colonists (Erickson et al., 2005)!

Aside from the dog, which also accompanied the first humans into the New World, domesticated animals had a relatively minor role in the Americas, as we noted earlier (see pp. 353–354). The llama and alpaca, both of which are long-haired relatives of the camel and are found in highland South America, were the only large domesticated species (Stahl, 2008). Other domesticates—the guinea pig (raised for its meat, not as a pet) and Muscovy duck in western South America, turkeys in Mexico—were small in size and not very important beyond their localized distribution areas.

Mexico

Recent archaeological and genetic research is forging a new understanding of the development of Mexican agriculture and of the beginnings of agriculture and settled farming communities in the Americas. Of the more than 100 plant species fully domesticated by Native Americans in Mexico, maize (a grass), beans (legumes), and squashes (cucurbits) ultimately attained the widest prehistoric significance for food purposes (Iriarte, 2009).

Today's many varieties of maize make it one of the world's primary staples (see Fig. 14-17). Maize probably originated somewhere in the valleys of southern and western Mexico and was one of several plants domesticated during the early Holocene. At the Xihuatoxtla site in the Balsas Valley of southwestern Mexico (**Fig. 14-18**), maize starch grains and phytoliths have been recovered from the surfaces of grinding stones and other artifacts dating to about 8,700 ya (Piperno et al., 2009; Ranere et al., 2009). Similar evidence of early agriculture is reported from the Gulf Coast lowlands of Mexico, as well as at sites in Central America and northern South America (Iriarte, 2009).

But early Mexican agriculture was not just all about maize. Other plants were being brought under cultivation in southern Mexico around the same time, including several kinds of beans, squashes, gourds, chili peppers, avocados, and cactus fruit (Flannery, 1986; Smith, 1997). While long believed to have been little more than a dietary supplement for hunter-gatherers for a long time, some of these crops were actually capable of supporting communities. Others played important social and ritual roles in Mesoamerica. The best example of the latter is a tree crop, cacao (the basic ingredient of chocolate). It never became a major prehistoric food crop, but it was ritually important both as a beverage and in solid form. Cacao use began in the Maya lowlands between 3,900 and 3,700 ya (Powis et al., 2007).

Maize, squash, and the common bean make up an important trinity of prehistoric Native North American crops. The common bean appears to have been domesticated in west-central Mexico (and again independently in Peru). Comparative analysis of the genetic diversity of wild and domesticated com-

Figure 14-18

Early farming in the Americas.

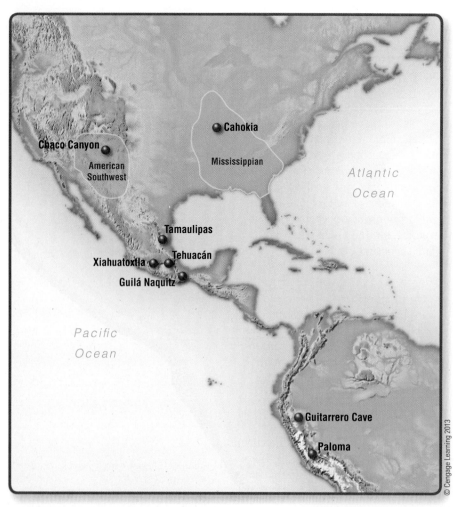

At a Glance

Important Mexican and South American Sites and Regions

SITE	DATES (YA)	SIGNIFICANCE
Xihuatoxtla (Mexico)	ca. 8,700	Early evidence of maize cultivation in the Balsas Valley of southwestern Mexico
Guilá Naquitz (Mexico)	10,200–9,200	Small cave in Oaxaca occupied by 4–6 persons; early dated contexts for pumpkin-like squashes and maize cobs
Guitarrero Cave (Peru)	ca. 8,500	Early evidence of cultivated plants in Andean South America
Paloma (Peru)	ca. 4,500	Small-scale horticulture in nearby river valleys supplemented the predominately seafood diet of these coastal Peruvians

© Cengage Learning 2013

mon beans points to the Lerma and Santiago basin of western Mexico as the region in which the common bean was first domesticated in Mexico (Kwak et al., 2009).

Like the common bean, squashes were probably independently domesticated in several parts of the Americas. In Mexico, domesticated seeds of pumpkin-like squashes from Guilá Naquitz Cave, in Oaxaca, are nearly 10,000 years old. Rinds of domesticated squash have also been recovered from 8,700-year-old contexts at Xihuatoxtla, in northern Guerrero (Ranere et al., 2009). The maize-beans-squash crop trinity eventually came together in the **milpa** intercropping system that was an important part of Mexican agriculture.

South America

Given the analytical value of genetic data and plant microfossils, research into the history of domestication and agriculture in South America is making rapid strides. The current focus is on several major questions. First, what were the relative roles of marine resources and agricultural products throughout prehistory on the continent's west coast? Second, to what extent did Mexican crops, particularly maize, contribute to South American agriculture? Finally, what was the nature of Amazonian agriculture in eastern South America?

Sites in southwestern Ecuador have yielded squash and gourd (cucurbit) phytoliths that date to 12,000–10,000 ya. Their large size suggests they're from domesticated plants; if this is true, it means that the beginnings of food production in lowland South America began about the same time as in Mesoamerica, and maybe even earlier (Piperno and Stothert, 2003).

Sediment cores and other geomorphological evidence indicate that the periodic climatic phenomenon known as **El Niño** became established between 7,000 and 5,000 ya in the Pacific (Sandweiss et al., 1996). El Niño events are triggered when a persistent trough of atmospheric low pressure forces warm equatorial waters southward along South America's west coast, partially displacing the northward flow of deep cold currents. El Niño typically disrupts the maritime food chain and dramatically disturbs precipitation patterns over land, bringing excess rainfall and flooding to some areas, drought to others. El Niño returns every four years or so, on average, and some episodes are more severe or last longer than others.

Early farming in coastal Peru seems somewhat related to the El Niño pattern (Piperno and Pearsall, 1998). At Paloma

milpa Mesoamerican agricultural system of intercropping in which maize, beans, squash and other plants are planted together. Milpas are typically prepared by cutting the forest and bushes to create a small field, farming it through several crop cycles, and then letting it lie fallow for 8 to 10 years.

El Niño Periodic climatic instability, related to temporary warming of Pacific Ocean waters, which may influence storm patterns and precipitation for several years.

(see Fig. 14-18), a short distance south of present-day Lima, summer fishing expeditions had extended into year-round reliance on large and small fish species, shellfish, sea mammals, turtles, and seabirds. Midden contents, analyses of coprolites, and high strontium levels in human skeletons confirm the nearly exclusive role of sea resources at some sites by 5,000 ya (Moseley, 1992). The fishers also began experimenting with nonlocal plant crops, using bottle gourds for carrying water and adding several kinds of squashes and beans to their diet. By about 4,500 ya, they had taken up small-scale horticulture in nearby river valleys, growing cotton for nets and cloth and, significantly, supplementing their predominantly seafood diet with at least 10 more edible plants. While they maintained their basic maritime focus for centuries to come, coastal Peruvians may have decided that a greater variety of foods helped to minimize the periodic shortfalls in sea resources that they could expect with most El Niño events every few years.

The intercontinental dispersal or exchange of American cultigens is a topic of active archaeobotanical research and debate (Smith, 1999; Iriarte, 2009). Maize may have reached coastal South America not long after being domesticated in southern Mexico (see Fig. 14-18). Genetic data, preserved plant macro- and microfossils, maize motifs on pottery, and even the impression of a kernel in the wall of a fired clay vessel, as well as increases in both grinding stones and human dental caries, attest to the early presence of maize in this region. Maize eventually became a significant food source for all the native cultures of western South America. Sixteenth-century Spanish chroniclers noted that many different varieties of maize accommodated Peru's demanding climatic and topographical diversity from sea level to 6,500 feet, with potatoes taking over at higher elevations. Each of these varieties, developed through careful selection and hybridization, probably derived from a common ancestral form of Mexican maize.

Plant cultivation was under way in a few highland areas of South America before 8,500 ya. Nonfood species use-

ful for fiber, containers, tool shafts, bedding, and medicines were tended even more often than edible plants around Guitarrero Cave (see Fig. 14-18), in the Andes Mountains (Lynch, 1980). Native tree fruits, broad lima beans, small-seeded quinoa, and several starchy tubers were among the local food crops grown there (Lynch, 1980). One of these ancient root crops was the white potato, and when eventually adopted into Old World agriculture and cuisine, it became today's familiar baked potato, Dutch *frites met*, and Indian *alu masala*.

Other native South American cultigens were developed in the tropical forests on the eastern slopes of the Andes or in the humid Amazon basin to the east. Roots of manioc shrubs and sweet potatoes became dietary staples in the eastern lowlands, supplying abundant carbohydrate energy but little else. Peanuts added some protein and fats to the starchy diet, but fish and insects remained essential food resources for most of the natives of Amazonia, since their small gardens alone generally couldn't sustain them entirely.

Southwestern United States

Agriculture based on maize and other crops spread into the American Southwest from Mesoamerica. The big questions are currently why, when, and how this northern dispersal of agriculture took place. Researchers are currently examining two possible explanations (Merrill et al., 2009). One view is that maize agriculture was brought to the Southwest by farmers who migrated northward in search of suitable planting areas. Peter Bellwood (1997, 2005, pp. 240–244) and Jane Hill (2001, 2010) argue that these farmers were **Proto-Uto-Aztecan** speakers, who began to spread from their Mesoamerican homeland across the region around 3,500 ya. This hypothesis, if supported by data, would explain the diffusion of agriculture into the American Southwest, as well as the subsequent distribution of the Uto-Aztecan language family.

A competing hypothesis questions the timing and role of the spread of the Proto-Uto-Aztecan language family and argues that maize agriculture entered

Proto-Uto-Aztecan Common ancestor of Uto-Aztecan, a widespread family of Native American languages found from the western United States to south-central Mexico.

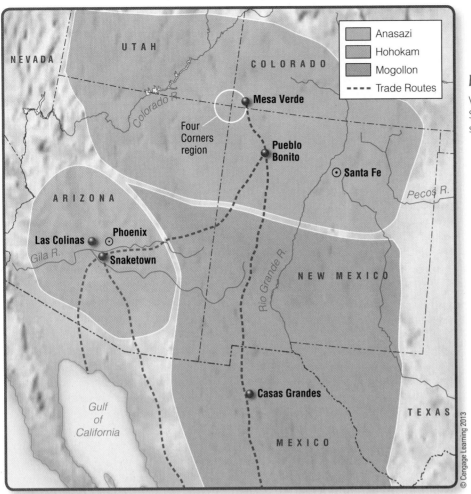

Figure 14-19

Village farming cultures of the American Southwest, showing trade routes (red) and sites mentioned in the text.

the Southwest from Mesoamerica as the result of "group-to-group diffusion," not migration (Merrill et al., 2009, 2010). The proponents of this view argue that Proto-Uto-Aztecan speakers were more likely to have been Great Basin foragers, not Mesoamerican farmers, and that the breakup of the Proto-Uto-Aztecan speech community actually began in the Great Basin nearly 9,000 ya. Merrill and colleagues (2009) further note that mtDNA research does not support a Mesoamerican homeland for the Proto-Uto-Aztecan language family (also see Kemp et al., 2005).

The weight of evidence currently supports the "group-to-group" diffusion hypothesis. The earliest maize is present in the American Southwest around 4,100 ya (Merrill et al., 2009). Notably, other important Mesoamerican cultigens, such as squash, amaranth, beans, and cotton, did not arrive in the region at the same time as part of a coherent agricultural complex, but

reached the Southwest separately over the course of the next two millennia.

Between 2,300 and 1,300 ya, reliance on these domesticated products promoted increased population density and overall cultural elaboration, resulting in the emergence of several distinctive prehistoric cultural traditions in the Southwest (**Fig. 14-19**). Archaeologists distinguish each of these regional traditions based on such features as pottery style, architecture, religious ideas, and sociopolitical organization (Plog, 1997).

The **Hohokam** of southern Arizona were growing both food and cotton by 1,500 ya and possibly much earlier, irrigating their gardens through an extensive system of hand-dug channels that conveyed water from the Gila River or its tributaries. By around 1,000 ya, architecture and artifacts on large Hohokam sites, such as Las Colinas and Snaketown, near Phoenix, reveal links to Mexican centers to the south. They include ball courts and platform

Hohokam (ho-ho-kahm´) Prehistoric farming culture of southern Arizona.

mounds as well as copper bells, parrot feathers, and other Mesoamerican products (Haury, 1976). The Hohokam crafted human figurines and shell and turquoise ornaments in sufficient quantities for trade (Crown, 1991). The Casas Grandes district of northern Chihuahua, Mexico, may have served as a major exchange corridor between Mesoamerica and the Southwest (DiPeso, 1974). But whether the Hohokam maintained direct contact with Mexican civilizations or simply participated in the diffusion of ideas and products passed along trade routes is a matter for debate.

© National Park Service

Figure 14-20

Pueblo Bonito as it would have appeared in the early 12th century A.D. The largest prehistoric structure in Chaco Culture National Historical Park, New Mexico. Its 650 rooms cover nearly two acres.

Mogollon (mo-go-yohn´) Prehistoric village culture of northern Mexico and southern Arizona/New Mexico.

Anasazi (an-ah-saw´-zee) Ancient culture of the southwestern United States, associated with preserved cliff dwellings and masonry pueblo sites.

pueblos Spanish for "town"; multiroom residence structures built by village farmers in the American Southwest; when spelled with an uppercase P, the several cultures that built and lived in such villages.

kivas Underground chambers or rooms used for gatherings and ceremonies by pueblo dwellers.

The **Mogollon**, whose prehistoric culture straddled southern New Mexico and Arizona, lived in pit houses until about A.D. 1000. Around that time, they began constructing aboveground room blocks and—in imitation of their northern neighbors—creating boldly painted black-on-white pottery. Archaeological traces of the Mogollon faded a century or more before Europeans arrived in the mid-1500s, possibly as its people drifted southward into Mexico.

In the Four Corners region to the north, prehistoric farmers known to archaeologists as the **Anasazi** built impressive prehistoric masonry villages and towns, called **pueblos**, beginning around A.D. 900. With their large scale, picturesque settings, and excellent preservation, some Anasazi sites—including

Chaco Canyon (**Fig. 14-20**), in New Mexico, and the so-called cliff dwellings of Mesa Verde (**Fig. 14-21**), in Colorado— are among the most famous archaeological locations in the United States. Anasazi towns consisted of multiroom, multistory residential and storage structures and usually included underground ceremonial chambers, called **kivas**. Their compact sites were situated with good access to the limited agricultural lands and scarce water supply of this high and arid region.

The rise of the Chaco Canyon towns and related villages was probably stimulated by a brief period of increased rainfall and sustained by social factors such as political or religious ideology, trade, and regional strife. A growing body of evidence also points to Chaco-era warfare and terrorism among the Anasazi, extending even to cannibalism (White, 1992; Turner and Turner, 1999). Beginning in the mid-1100s, the Anasazi abandoned Chaco and, eventually, most of the region's other large pueblos. By then, shifting precipitation patterns associated with a general warming period were leaving marginal zones of the Southwest, especially the Colorado Plateau, without adequate rainfall to grow maize (Cordell, 1998). As the drought worsened through the late 1200s, Anasazi townspeople persisted in a few places like Mesa Verde (see Fig. 14-21), where they built their communities into easily defended niches in the steep cliffs and tilled their fields on the canyon rim by day. By A.D. 1300, even Mesa Verde stood empty; the Anasazi of the Four Corners had dispersed toward the south and southeast to become the people known today as Hopi, Zuni, and the Rio Grande Puebloans.

Eastern North America

The earliest domesticated plant in eastern North America was the bottle gourd, a specimen of which has been found with a 7,300-year-old burial at Windover, Florida (Doran et al., 1990). Bottle gourds, which were grown for use as containers, not as food, were probably domesticated in the Old World and entered North America with the earliest human inhabitants.

During the early Holocene, aboriginal peoples developed an independent center of domestication and cultivation in eastern North America (Price, 2009). The first domesticated plant other than the bottle gourd was squash about 5,025 ya, followed soon by sunflower and marsh elder (sumpweed). These plants are associated with ancient campsites and shell heaps along major river valleys, where, about 4,000 ya, people maintained "incidental gardens" of plants that supplemented traditional foraging activities (Smith, 1999; Smith and Yarnell, 2009). Over the next millennium, several more native species, such as knotweed, maygrass, and little barley, were added to the cultivated plants of the region. Stone hoes also began to appear on sites in the Illinois River valley at about the same time (Odell, 1998).

It wasn't easy to harvest and process these weedy, small-seeded species, so they probably weren't much more than supplements to a diet of wild foods. Still, the river valleys of the Southeast and the Midwest, as well as the rich forests covering much of the Northeast, clearly supported large, successful communities even without maize agriculture. For example, the widespread practice of

William Turnbaugh

Figure 14-21

Cliff Palace was the largest of the pueblos built by Anasazi farmers living at Mesa Verde, Colorado, about 800 ya.

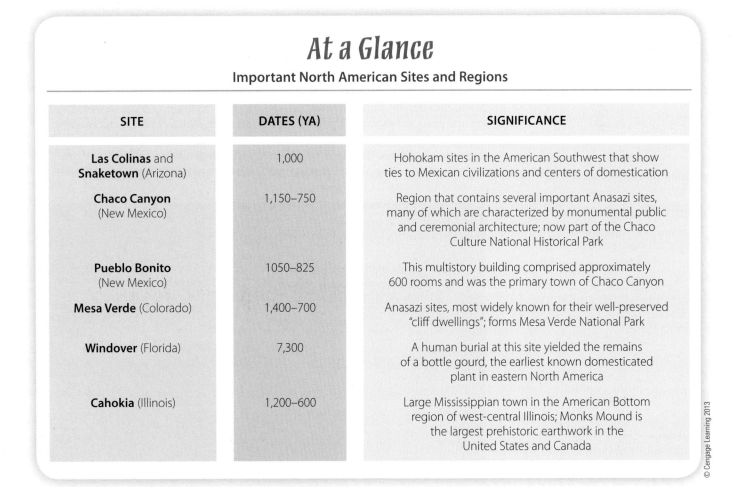

At a Glance

Important North American Sites and Regions

SITE	DATES (YA)	SIGNIFICANCE
Las Colinas and **Snaketown** (Arizona)	1,000	Hohokam sites in the American Southwest that show ties to Mexican civilizations and centers of domestication
Chaco Canyon (New Mexico)	1,150–750	Region that contains several important Anasazi sites, many of which are characterized by monumental public and ceremonial architecture; now part of the Chaco Culture National Historical Park
Pueblo Bonito (New Mexico)	1050–825	This multistory building comprised approximately 600 rooms and was the primary town of Chaco Canyon
Mesa Verde (Colorado)	1,400–700	Anasazi sites, most widely known for their well-preserved "cliff dwellings"; forms Mesa Verde National Park
Windover (Florida)	7,300	A human burial at this site yielded the remains of a bottle gourd, the earliest known domesticated plant in eastern North America
Cahokia (Illinois)	1,200–600	Large Mississippian town in the American Bottom region of west-central Illinois; Monks Mound is the largest prehistoric earthwork in the United States and Canada

Figure 14-22

Flint hoe blade used by Mississippian farmers.

mound building and associated death and burial rituals began long before any significant reliance on maize. As we've seen, Late Archaic hunter-gatherers also constructed major mound groups that, like those at Poverty Point, Louisiana (see Chapter 13), were considerably more than mere stacks of dirt.

Maize was not present in eastern North America until around 2,150 ya, and it appears to have had little economic impact at first. It's not until after 1,200 ya in the Southeast and around 800 ya in the Northeast that we begin to see archaeological evidence of a widespread economic commitment to agriculture, possibly brought about by new varieties of maize and the introduction of domesticated beans (Smith, 1992; Hart and Scarry, 1999). Even then, wild nuts, seeds, fish, and game were staples in the diets of many groups. In the broad river valleys of the Southeast, maize farming was the economic mainstay of **Mississippian** chiefdoms (**Fig. 14-22**).

Mississippian elites relied on elaborate rituals and displays of valued symbols to enhance their privileged positions. Populations and ceremonial centers throughout the region were linked by exchanges of symbolic copper, shell, pottery, and stone items, as well as a common focus on the construction of towns centered on impressive earthen-mound groups that flanked public spaces or plazas (Lewis and Stout, 1998; Emerson and Lewis, 2000). Most buildings that flanked the plazas were erected

on substructure or platform mounds. Some of these buildings were dwellings; others were **charnel houses** and other community structures. The houses and workplaces of the town's rank and file clustered around these mound-and-plaza complexes (**Fig. 14-23**).

The Mississippian site of Cahokia, located below the junction of the Missouri and Mississippi rivers near St. Louis, once boasted some 120 mounds (Milner, 1998; Pauketat and Wright, 2004). The primary earthwork was Monks Mound (**Fig. 14-24**), as long as three football fields and as high as a six-story building—the largest prehistoric structure north of Mexico. Cahokia's homes and garden plots spread over 6 square miles beyond the log stockade that enclosed the central mounds and elite living area. Fields of maize, squash, and pumpkins extending along the river floodplain provided the harvest sheltered in many storage pits and granaries (Iseminger, 1996).

Other New World Regions

Elsewhere in the Americas, farming hadn't gained much importance even by the time Europeans were arriving with their own ways of life and their Old World domesticates (Brown, 1994). In fact, throughout much of western and northern North America and in some South American regions, hunting, fishing, and gathering were still the principal ways of making a living. These

Figure 14-23

Reconstructed Mississippian village huts at Angel Mounds State Historic Site, near Evansville, Indiana.

Mississippian Referring to late prehistoric chiefdoms of the southeastern United States and southern Midwest between roughly 1,100 and 300 ya.

charnel houses Buildings that hold the bones or bodies of the dead.

Figure 14-24

Monks Mound at Cahokia Mounds State Historic Site, near Collinsville, Illinois. Built in late prehistoric times, it is about 1,000 feet long and 100 feet high.

Hannah Lewis

lifeways persisted in part because the more productive American domesticates, especially those native to warm temperate zones, couldn't be introduced and maintained in other geographical settings without sustained effort. Even so, it wasn't always a question of whether farming was possible; it was often a matter of choice. Maize was far from an ideal crop, even where it could be grown most readily. Old World domesticated cereal grasses, including wheat, barley, oat, rye, millet, and rice, grew in dense stands that farmers could harvest readily with a sickle and clean by threshing and winnowing. Maize, the primary New World cereal grass, required more space per plant and more moisture during its

long growing season, and it was much harder to harvest and process by hand.

What's more, these agricultural products could seldom beat the nutritional value of a mixed diet obtained through foraging. Maize itself is deficient in lysine (an amino acid) and niacin and contains a chemical that may promote iron-deficiency anemia. Similarly, in the Amazon basin in South America, the peoples who domesticated manioc, sweet potatoes, and other starchy root crops before 1,500 ya found that these foods supplied bulk and carbohydrates but little protein—a deficiency the people of the Amazon overcame by continuing to rely on hunting, fishing, and gathering.

Summary of Main Topics

▶ The early Holocene rise of plant and animal domestication and the invention of agriculture is called the "Neolithic revolution." Agriculture soon became a major force in human biocultural evolution.

▶ Major theories to explain the development of agriculture fall into two broad groups:

  • Environmental approaches: External or natural forces were the active ingredients in the development of agriculture. Human agency played little role.

  • Cultural approaches: Human agency and culture was sufficient

to push some societies to seek ways to increase locally available food resources. Environmental factors played little role.

▶ The origins of domestication and agriculture are complex problems for which there may be multiple valid explanations.

▶ Plant microfossils (phytoliths, starch grains, pollen) are important new data sources for the reconstruction of the development of plant domestication.

▶ The Old and New World examples show that in those areas where food production was adopted, farming

transformed human subsistence, technology, society, habitation patterns, relationships with other species, and much more.

In a few areas of the world, the emergence of large-scale, complex societies followed quickly on the heels of the Neolithic revolution. In Chapter 15, we'll consider the development and course of early civilizations founded on Neolithic food-producing economies in the Old World and in the Americas.

In "What's Important," you'll find a useful summary of the most important archaeological sites discussed in this chapter.

What's Important The Most Significant Archaeological Sites Discussed in This Chapter

Location	Site	Dates (ya)	The Big Picture
Old World	**Mehrgarh** (Pakistan)	8,000–6,000	Early Neolithic community in South Asia that depended on domesticated plants and animals; represents a transition from seminomadic herding to sedentary villages and towns
	Cishan (China)	10,300–8,700	Earliest evidence of millet cultivation in northern China
	Dhra' (Jordan)	ca. 11,000	Evidence of plant cultivation, food storage, and settled communities after the end of the Younger Dryas
	Abu Hureyra (Syria)	13,100–12,000	Hunter-gatherer settlement that spans the cold and dry climatic conditions of the Younger Dryas; shows evidence of increasing diet breadth as preferred plant foods became less available across the region
New World	**Las Colinas** and **Snaketown** (Arizona)	1,000	Hohokam sites in the American Southwest that show ties to Mexican civilizations and centers of domestication
	Cahokia (Illinois)	1,200–600	Large Mississippian town in the American Bottom region of west-central Illinois; Monks Mound is the largest prehistoric earthwork in the United States and Canada
	Mesa Verde (Colorado)	1,400–700	Anasazi sites, most widely known for their well-preserved "cliff dwellings"; forms Mesa Verde National Park
	Paloma (Peru)	4,500	Coastal preceramic village mostly dependent on marine resources; planting of some crops, such as bottle gourds, squashes, and beans
	Windover (Florida)	7,300	A human burial at this site yielded the remains of a bottle gourd, the earliest known domesticated plant in eastern North America
	Xihuatoxtla (Mexico)	ca. 8,700	Early evidence of maize cultivation in the Balsas Valley of southwestern Mexico
	Guilá Naquitz (Mexico)	10,200–9,200	Small cave in Oaxaca occupied by 4–6 persons; early dated contexts for pumpkin-like squashes and maize cobs
	Guitarrero Cave (Peru)	8,500	Early evidence of cultivated plants in Andean South America

© Cengage Learning 2013

Critical Thinking Questions

1. What are the most important differences between the environmental and cultural approaches explaining why farming began? Your answer should include the basic assumptions, strengths, and weaknesses of each approach.

2. What kinds of evidence from the archaeological record do researchers use as indicators or measures of the extent of plant or animal domestication?

3. In what major ways did the development of agriculture differ between the Old World and the New World? Your answer should consider both plants and animals.

Archaeology

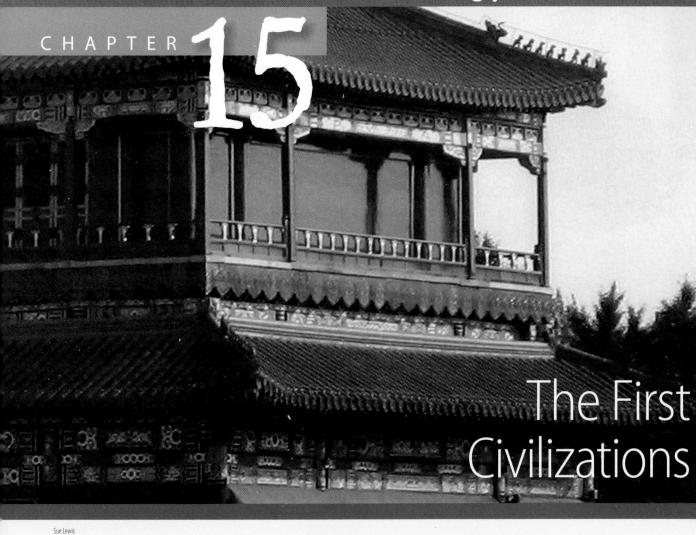

CHAPTER 15

Sue Lewis

The First Civilizations

LEARNING OBJECTIVES

After you have mastered the material in this chapter, you will be able to:

▶ Explain the differences between cities, states, and civilizations.

▶ Compare the fundamental processes that led to the development of the earliest civilizations.

▶ Assess the role that cities played in these developments.

▶ Examine and identify the extent to which the concept of the state, viewed as a political organization, was essential to the emergence of all early civilizations.

The ruins of the city of Vijayanagara lie strewn along the banks of the Tunga-bhadra River in South India (**Fig. 15-1**). As you walk south from the river, you're seldom out of sight of broken granite pillars and the shattered foundations of palaces, temples, and courtyards in fertile valleys surrounded by hills that look like great jumbles of boulders. Founded in the early fourteenth century and destroyed about two centuries later, Vijayanagara had a fairly short life as cities go, but by all accounts, it was an extraordinary place (Fritz and Michell, 2003). With a sixteenth-century population estimated at 500,000 (or about 2½ times the estimated population of London in 1600), the city covered roughly 10 square miles. It was the capital of an empire that included other states, both large and small, across South India. Following the defeat of its armies in A.D. 1565, Vijayanagara was destroyed, its buildings burned, blown apart, or pulled down with the aid of elephants; its citizens were scattered, its riches looted. The remnants of the empire limped along for another century or so, but it never recovered its former strength (Stein, 1994).

The Vijayanagara ruins are now a UNESCO World Heritage site. Where once there were picturesque buildings, crowded markets, busy city streets, royal pageantry, and the fragrance of roses, there are now tour buses, shepherds, security guards, thorn bushes, and the occasional leopard that snatches puppies for late-night snacks. Vijayanagara lives mostly in stories told to small children in villages across South India about such rulers as Krishnadevaraya and their dynasties, their might, and the great events they caused.

Vijayanagara exemplifies three interrelated concepts that are central to this chapter—cities, states, and civilizations, the earliest instances of which can be identified in the archaeological record after the emergence of true agriculture thousands of years ago. Such developments also marked the beginning of history in many parts of the world and laid the foundation for the modern era. By about 5,500 ya, some Old and New Worlds societies were independently transforming themselves into states and civilizations.

Civilizations in Perspective

The term **civilization** is not, as many people think, just another word for culture or society, nor is it the same thing as a city or a state. In this section, we'll clarify our use of the terms *city*, *state*, and *civilization* before discussing theoretical perspectives on their origins and describing some archaeological examples.

Figure 15-1

Ruins of royal buildings in the urban core of the late medieval city of Vijayanagara, Karnataka, India.

civilization The larger social order that includes states related by language, traditions, history, economic ties, and other shared cultural aspects.

Cities

Most of us take **cities** for granted. It just seems natural that they exist, that they're big, and that they're the social, political, and economic centers we often turn to. We even treat some cities, such as London, Paris, and New York, as icons for entire civilizations. But 7,000 ya, the complete absence of cities seemed just as natural to our ancestors. Most settled communities were hamlets, villages, or towns, and that's the way communities had been for thousands of years.

Cities, when they developed in prehistory, were often at the center of ancient states. Commonly, one or more prominent cities dominated smaller dependent towns and villages in a region that also supported farming hamlets. Cities are also characterized by social complexity, formal (nonkin) organization, and diverse craft and administrative specialists (Redman, 1978). The city is the nucleus where production, trade, religion, and administrative activities converge (Cowgill, 2004). These central places usually proclaimed their own importance in prehistory by erecting prominent structures for ceremonial or other civic purposes.

The roots of cities or urbanism are currently best known archaeologically in the Near East, where settled communities existed in some regions before the beginning of the Neolithic and true agriculture (**Fig. 15-2**). In Chapter 14, for example, we saw that Natufians or their contemporaries in the lower Jordan River valley had established a permanent community of dome-shaped dwellings at Jericho centuries before its residents became fully reliant on farming (Kenyon, 1981). Although it never attained the size or status of a true city, early Jericho anticipated some of the characteristics of later urban centers, including evidence of social complexity. Before 10,000 ya, Jericho traders also participated in the regional exchange of

Figure 15-2

Sites associated with early civilizations in Mesopotamia and the Nile Valley.

© Cengage Learning 2013

cities Urban centers that both support and are supported by a hinterland of lesser communities.

such commodities as salt, sulfur, shells, obsidian, and turquoise. Some of these products ended up as offerings in the graves of individuals buried at Jericho. More impressive were Jericho's remarkable construction features, clearly the products of organized communal effort. A massive stone wall 6 feet thick, incorporating a 28-foot stone tower with interior stairs, enclosed the settlement of several hundred modest houses. A deep trench, cut into the bedrock beyond the wall, afforded even greater security, but against whom or what is unknown. Viewed initially as fortifications, Jericho's wall and ditch may have been intended instead to divert mud flows brought on by severe erosion due to deforestation and poor farming practices in the vicinity (Bar-Yosef, 1986). The tower could have functioned either for defense or as a community shrine.

Çatalhöyük, a 32-acre town in south-central Turkey, was both larger and somewhat later than Jericho (Hodder, 1996; Balter, 2005). It served as a trade and religious center some 9,000 ya, during early Neolithic times. Çatalhöyük's timber and mud-brick houses had only rooftop entrances; their painted plaster interiors included living and storage space, sleeping platforms, and hearths. The community's several thousand inhabitants farmed outside the town walls or engaged in craft production within. Some residents exploited nearby sources of obsidian or volcanic glass to make beads, mirrors, and blades to be exported in exchange for raw materials and finished goods. The wealth that this trade generated may have supported religious activities in the elaborately decorated shrines uncovered at this site. Many of these shrines held representations of cattle, then only recently domesticated, as focal points for worshipers.

Trade and religious activities promoted the development of Jericho and Çatalhöyük into relatively large and complex Neolithic communities. Even so, they were not true cities, nor were they part of any larger cultural entity that could be described as a state. The earliest true city yet discovered is Uruk, in southern Iraq. Associated with the Sumerian civilization of the southern Tigris-Euphrates Valley, Uruk boasts remnants of massive mud-brick temples and residential areas that housed tens of thousands of people after 5,500 ya.

States

The **state** is a complex form of political organization characterized by true social classes, the concept of citizenship, administrative bureaucracies, and a monopoly in the use of force (for example, armies), as well as other governing and administrative institutions typical of the societies in which most of us live today.

Other types of political organization also exist, and while researchers disagree about how to define and apply them, they provide the much needed handles by which we can group together politically similar societies and study them. One common view is that of Morton Fried (1967), who describes the simplest, or least complex, societies as *egalitarian*. As the name implies, there's no social differentiation in egalitarian societies; leadership is informal, and "the best idea leads." Examples are most Paleolithic hunter-gatherer bands. *Ranked* societies are more complicated, particularly because some forms of social differentiation are present; a few people are "chiefs," but most are "Indians." These socially differentiated statuses and roles can be inherited, but there are no true social classes. Examples include Neolithic farming villages in the Near East and Mississippian chiefdoms in eastern North America. In *stratified* societies, significant social differentiation is present and true classes exist. An example is the Natchez, a Native American group of west-central Mississippi, whose society was rigidly hierarchical by comparison with other documented Mississippian chiefdoms. Finally, we have the *state*, the complex form of political organization described at the beginning of this section.

The main disadvantage of pigeonholing ancient societies into such categories as egalitarian, ranked, and so on, is that it implies an evolutionary progression of past political institutions—even where there's little or no empirical evidence that such a view

Çatalhöyük (chaetal´-hae-yook´) A large early Neolithic site in southern Turkey. The name is Turkish for "forked mound."

state A governmental entity that persists by politically controlling a territory; examples include most modern nations.

is warranted. In Fried's typology, for example, ranked societies follow egalitarian societies and precede stratified societies, and so on. Through frequent application in research, the built-in sequence of cultural evolutionary stages represented by Fried's scheme and others like it can begin to seem both real and discoverable.

Over the years, researchers have found that it's important to understand both the similarities and the differences between ancient societies as part of the larger task of explaining the development of the earliest states (Trigger, 2003, p. 42). The result is still an evolutionary picture of the development of cities, states, and civilizations, but one that examines cultural changes within a web of possibilities rather than as the outcome of a succession of stages.

For our purposes, the *state* is a governmental entity that persists by politically controlling a territory and "by acting through a generalized structure of authority, making certain decisions in disputes between members of different groups, maintaining the central symbols of society, and undertaking the defense and expansion of the society"(Yoffee, 2005, p. 17). Examples include most modern nations.

With the emergence of the earliest states in antiquity, we also find archaeological evidence of other important changes, among them **social stratification**, typically in the form of true social classes (recalling Fried, 1967). This is so consistent a feature of states that in his recent comparative analysis of early civilizations, archaeologist Bruce Trigger (2003) describes them categorically as "class-based" societies. In ancient states, most people worked the land, while a smaller number performed essential specialized tasks of craft production, military service, trade, and religion. At the top of this social heap were a few elite individuals who closely controlled access to goods and services produced by others, information, the means of force, and symbols of valued status; these individuals also made most essential decisions that affected the working of society—usually with the proclaimed sanction of gods and the assistance of a bureaucracy of lesser officials. Such decisions covered many critical functions, including the capacity to create and enforce laws, levy and collect taxes, store and redistribute food and other basic goods, and defend or expand the state's boundaries.

The development of true social classes implies another important aspect of states: Their main social institutions are commonly organized on the basis of criteria *other than that of kinship*. This doesn't mean that families and kinship cease to be important at every level of society, from the greatest of rulers to the person who hauls out the garbage at the end of the day. What changes is that some of the roles and duties that were once handled by your kin are now decided by the state. For example, states tend to appropriate the right to decide which acts of murder committed by its citizens will be punished as crimes and which will be rewarded with medals and marching bands. They also may take over the authority to pass judgment on local civil disputes, such as village squabbles over property boundaries, contract breaches, and the like. In nonstates, such as the kinds of communities we described in Chapter 14, these decisions were usually decided in kin-centered institutions such as families and lineages.

Civilizations

Civilizations comprise "the larger social order and set of shared values in which states are culturally embedded" (Yoffee, 2005, p. 17). And while cities and states are building blocks of civilizations, the civilizations of which they are a part may show considerable diversity. Unlike what archaeologists believed half a century ago, we can't trace a simple developmental sequence in the archaeological record from villages to cities and then to states. For example, the Vijayanagara empire (roughly A.D. 1300–1650) appears to have been more unified and more urban than Maya civilization during the Classic period (A.D. 250–900). To understand why, we must consider differences of culture, technology, history, external relations, and even terrain, because they all played important roles, as shown in the archaeological records of these regions.

social stratification Class structure or hierarchy, usually based on political, economic, or social standing.

Why Did Civilizations Form?

A half century ago, V. Gordon Childe specified the traits that he believed contributed to the evolution of early civilizations. His list reflects the view that civilization is an outgrowth of increasing productivity, social complexity, and economic advantage (Childe, 1950). The use of writing, mathematics, animal-powered traction, wheeled carts, plows, irrigation, sailing boats, standard units of weight and measure, metallurgy, surplus production, and craft specialization, Childe argued, all had a stimulating effect and were themselves products of changes initiated by earlier Neolithic activities.

It was soon clear that Childe's catalog of inventions and new social institutions was not applicable to all early civilizations. Childe also failed to grasp that a civilization is more than the sum of its parts. His catalog of traits characterized the Near Eastern civilizations with which he was most familiar, but it didn't fit important New World societies such as the Maya and Inca. Nevertheless, these were clearly civilizations, even though they didn't use sailing boats, animal traction, wheeled carts, and so on.

By the later twentieth century, most archaeologists also agreed that descriptive approaches like Childe's were inadequate at best because they couldn't account for why and how the earliest civilizations emerged when and where they did. The search for such answers continues to be one of the most important objectives of archaeological research on complex societies. Let's now consider several competing explanations, with emphasis on Near Eastern civilizations, which offer the advantage of being among the most studied of the world's earliest civilizations. Bear in mind, however, that a good general explanation should apply just as effectively to *all* civilizations, including those in the New World.

Environmental Explanations

At first glance, it may seem unlikely that the rise of civilizations could be the product of purely natural causes, independent of the actions of humans. Nevertheless, researchers have weighed the merits of these and many other possible factors over the past century. Theories that account for the origins of civilization tend to take a position between the extremes of environmental determinism, in which people, culture, and everything else obey the same laws of nature, and cultural determinism, the cultural relativist position that maintains that human behavior can be explained only in cultural and historical terms (Trigger, 2003, pp. 653–655).

Let's look briefly at an example of a strong environmental hypothesis. Arie Issar, a geologist, and his colleague Mattanyah Zohar, an archaeologist, argue that the fluctuating availability of water resources caused by major climatic changes was a key factor in the development of civilization in the Near East (Issar and Zohar, 2004). Based on their chemical analyses of lake sediments and cave stalagmites, these researchers identify several periods between 6,000 and 5,000 ya during which the Near East was drier than present and periods during which it was colder than present. When correlated with major cultural changes documented in the archaeological record of the region, climatic conditions, they argue, are sufficient to account both for production surpluses and for the concentration of the control of these surpluses in the hands of ruling classes. This control gradually became more successful as administrative institutions and such inventions as writing developed in Mesopotamian society. Interregional commerce, the military, administrative bureaucracies, and local ruling dynasties, they argue, emerged because of the changes promoted by optimal climatic conditions. Climatic changes may also account for the catastrophic flood legends that are indigenous to the region (Issar and Zohar, 2004, pp. 112–113).

Elsewhere, however, research has shown that the possible causal relationships between environmental factors and early civilizations are much less likely. In fact, in a recent international conference on the relationship between climatic change and early civilizations, the participants agreed on one main

At a Glance

Environmental Factors in the Development of Early Civilizations

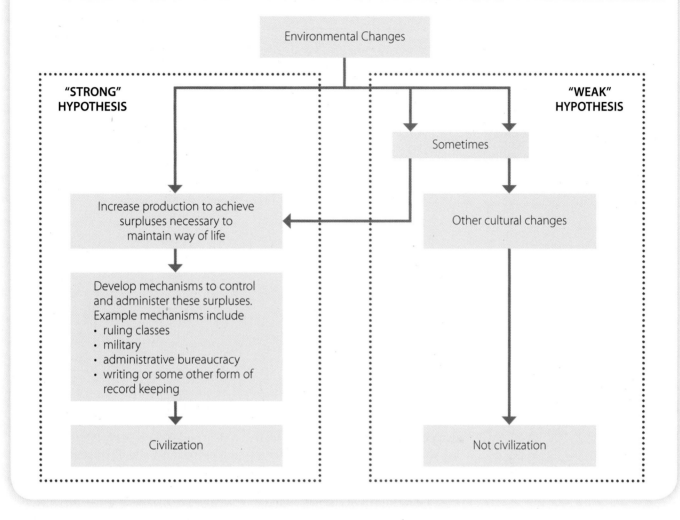

© Cengage Learning 2013

point: "Climatic change for each civilization or community can act as a driving force, or a supporting player, or merely as background noise" (Catto and Catto, 2004). In other words, environmental explanations generally and climatic change in particular can't, by themselves, explain the rise and fall of all early civilizations.

Cultural Explanations

If environmental theories sometimes leave little room for human culture and agency to play important causal roles in the development of civilization, some cultural explanations go to the other extreme and deny the importance of the environment. According to the views of cultural relativists, culture plays the significant role in shaping human behavior, not noncultural factors such as climate, population growth, and the like. From this perspective, culture cannot merely be reduced to the category of human reactions to the whims of nature, but is a force to be reckoned with in explaining major prehistoric changes such as the development of the earliest cities, states, and civilizations.

For example, Kwang-chih Chang argues that the rise of the earliest civilizations in China may have owed more to the differential access by some groups to the means of communication than to the means of production (Chang, 2000). In short, Chang (2000, p. 2) asserts that "the wealth that produced the civilization

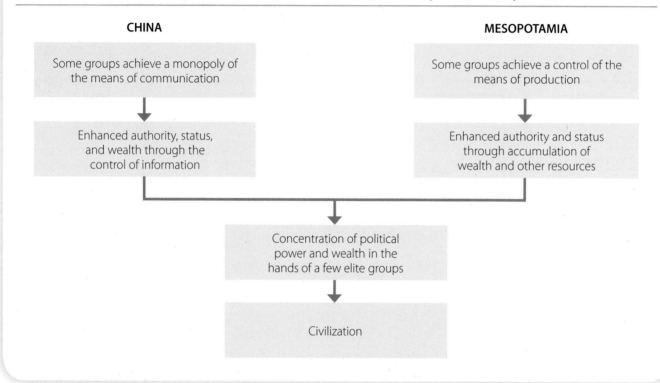

At a Glance

Kwang-chih Chang's View of Cultural Factors in the Development of Early Civilizations

CHINA

Some groups achieve a monopoly of the means of communication

↓

Enhanced authority, status, and wealth through the control of information

MESOPOTAMIA

Some groups achieve a control of the means of production

↓

Enhanced authority and status through accumulation of wealth and other resources

↓

Concentration of political power and wealth in the hands of a few elite groups

↓

Civilization

© Cengage Learning 2013

was itself the product of concentrated political power, and the acquisition of that power was accomplished through the accumulation of wealth. The key to this circular working of the ancient Chinese society was the monopoly of high **shamanism**, which enabled the rulers to gain critical access to divine and ancestral wisdom, the basis of their political authority. Most of the markers of the ancient civilization were in fact related centrally to this shamanism." Chang's hypothesis is particularly interesting because it depends entirely on cultural factors as the active ingredients in developing early Chinese civilization. He pointedly denies the importance of technological advances and increasing control of the means of production, factors that are often mentioned as key aspects in general theories of the development of the early civilizations.

Although it's contested by many specialists on Chinese civilization, Chang's hypothesis has a novel twist in that he also argues that all early civilizations, with the notable exception of

Mesopotamia in the Near East, controlled the means of communication (Chang, 2000, pp. 7–10). It was only in Mesopotamia, Chang reasons, that controlling the means of production was a key factor in developing the region's earliest civilizations. This difference, he conjectures, led to the creation of states that were fundamentally different from those of China and greatly influenced the development of much of Western civilization.

In his recent monumental comparative analysis of early civilizations, Bruce Trigger (2003) identifies several important uniformities that cast doubt on civilization theories that adopt extreme positions, whether they're in the direction of cultural relativism or environmental forces. To take only a few examples, Trigger found no evidence of Chang's control of the means of communication; but in the cases he examined, he did encounter relatively uniform conceptions of kingship, class systems, support of the upper classes through the controlled use of force, and control of

shamanism Traditional practices that mediate between the world of humans and the world of spirits.

the means of production (Trigger, 2003, pp. 272–273, 663). Significantly, Trigger also found that only two types of political organization and two types of general administrative institutions are present in all early civilizations. What's striking about these and the many other cultural similarities he identifies is that it's not the sort of picture we would expect to see if human culture were unconstrained by noncultural forces. If culture were a free agent, so to speak, we would expect considerable diversity in these and other institutions across early civilizations as they respond to local cultural traditions and history. Similarly, these cultural uniformities can't be easily explained by the action of general environmental factors, because the cases Trigger examines are environmentally diverse, ranging from tropical rain forest settings to near-desert conditions.

If culture and natural factors such as climate cannot fully explain the rise of the earliest civilizations, what is the answer? Trigger (2003, pp. 272–274) proposes an essentially functional argument based on information theory. At its root is the observation that the transition from villages to cities and states is fundamentally one of increasing societal complexity, driven by economic or political forces. With the increased complexity of the organization of society, there must also be comparable increases in the institutions that manage this complexity. To put it another way, you can't manage a Fortune 500 multinational corporation from a small storefront in a suburban strip mall. What's missing from that picture is the massive organizational infrastructure necessary to keep a major corporation running on a daily basis, much less to keep it profitable. To Trigger, a state faces the same basic problem. The growth of the earliest cities and states also required the creation of new decision-making institutions and the distribution of power and authority. This is effectively what's seen archaeologically with increased material evidence for the emergence of social classes, ruling elites, administrative bureaucracies, settlement hierarchies, and the like. But Trigger's most important point may be that for all the ways in which early civi-

lizations differed around the world—and there were many—"for societies to grow more complex they may have to evolve specific forms of organization." And as Trigger also observed, humans found only a limited number of ways to do this!

Old World Civilizations

So familiar to most people are the ancient Near Eastern civilizations—Egypt and Mesopotamia—that we instinctively use them as a standard against which to measure all others. Still, it's not appropriate to do so, for as Bruce Trigger (2003) stresses, it's essential to understand both the differences and the similarities between all early civilizations if we are to explain how and why such entities developed. This section is a selective glimpse into the development of the earliest Old World cities, states, and civilizations in several geographical regions: Mesopotamia, Egypt, the Indus Valley in South Asia, and northern China (**Fig. 15-3**). Later, we will take a similar look at the rise of several of the earliest New World civilizations. Each civilization devised ways of grappling with the challenges presented by entirely new social, political, and economic circumstances. Their legacies have survived for millennia, and we can often recognize them within the framework of modern societies.

Mesopotamia

During the centuries after 8,000 ya, pioneering farmers settled **Mesopotamia**, the vast alluvial plains bordering the lower Tigris-Euphrates river system (see Fig. 15-2). These agriculturists shared the heritage of such early Neolithic communities as Jarmo, in the Zagros foothills to the east, and **Çayönü**, at the edge of the Anatolian plateau (Nissen, 1988). In fact, they were probably direct descendants of Samarran farmers, who had practiced small-scale irrigation agriculture along the edges of the central Tigris Valley and obtained painted pottery and obsidian through trade with upland communities. Now expanding onto the southern plains, these **Ubaid** farmers encountered

Mesopotamia (*meso*, meaning "middle," and *potamos*, meaning "river") Land between the Tigris and Euphrates rivers, mostly included in modern-day Iraq.

Çayönü (chayu´-noo)

Ubaid (oo-bide´) Early formative culture of Mesopotamia, 7,500–6,200 ya; predecessor to Sumerian civilization.

Figure 15-3

Time line for Old World civilizations.

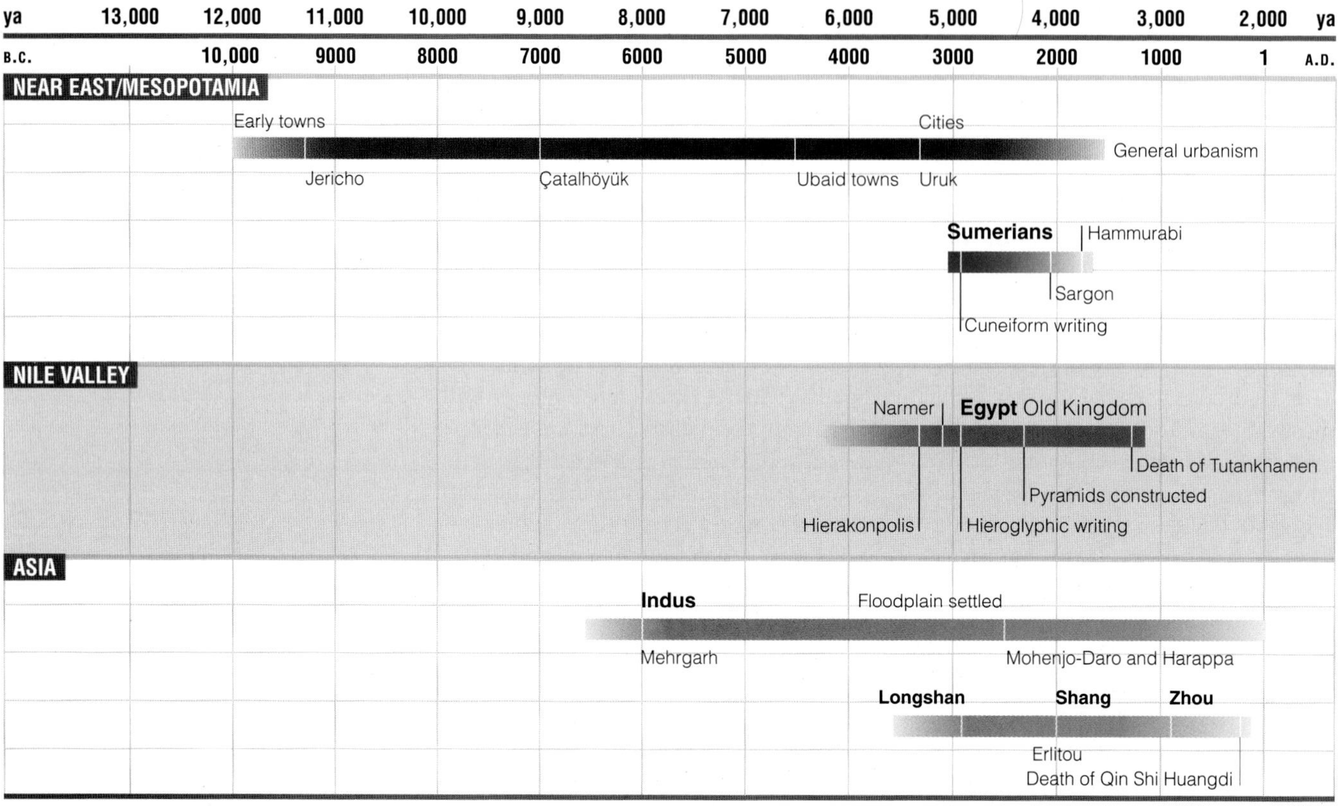

ya	13,000	12,000	11,000	10,000	9,000	8,000	7,000	6,000	5,000	4,000	3,000	2,000	ya
B.C.		10,000	9000	8000	7000	6000	5000	4000	3000	2000	1000	1	A.D.

NEAR EAST/MESOPOTAMIA

Early towns — Cities — General urbanism

Jericho — Çatalhöyük — Ubaid towns — Uruk

Sumerians — Hammurabi — Sargon — Cuneiform writing

NILE VALLEY

Narmer — **Egypt** Old Kingdom — Death of Tutankhamen — Pyramids constructed

Hierakonpolis — Hieroglyphic writing

ASIA

Indus — Floodplain settled — Mehrgarh — Mohenjo-Daro and Harappa

Longshan — **Shang** — **Zhou** — Erlitou — Death of Qin Shi Huangdi

© Cengage Learning 2013

great flood-prone streams bound only by immense mudflats and marshes.

The annual floods in this region began soon after the spring planting season, when young crops were particularly vulnerable. These seasonal overflows deposited rich layers of alluvium, and when the floodwaters receded, a long, dry summer followed. At first, farmers cultivated only the well-drained slopes above the river. Generations later, their descendants began the hard task of redirecting the river's flow, even cutting through its banks to channel floodwater onto low-lying fields. Irrigation unlocked the fertility of the deep, stone-free alluvium that had accumulated on the floodplain for millennia. Barley was the Ubaidians' primary grain, but wheat and millet grew well, too, along with the date palm and vegetable crops. Common domesticated animals included pigs, sheep, donkeys, and oxen. The abundant harvests, supplemented by fish and game, more than kept pace with the rapidly growing floodplain communities.

By around 6,500 ya, Ubaid villagers were beginning to prosper in the southernmost Tigris-Euphrates Valley (Lamberg-Karlovsky and Sabloff, 1995). Each of their more populous towns, such as Nippur, Eridu, and Uruk in the southern valley (see Fig. 15-2), centered on a platform-based temple; even the smaller communities had central shrines. Perhaps to obtain the resources lacking in their new homeland, Ubaidians stayed in touch with distant peoples through trade in decorated pottery, obsidian, ornamental stones, copper, and possibly grain.

Important changes ushered in the late Ubaid period, around 5,500 ya. The population of certain communities rapidly swelled into the thousands as rural villagers migrated to the growing towns. Expanding irrigation systems in the lower Tigris-Euphrates Valley produced more food for the concentrated populace. Altering the riverine environment on this scale by digging drainage and irrigation channels was a challenging enterprise, one that the people could

At a Glance

Important Near Eastern Sites and Regions

SITE	DATES (YA)	SIGNIFICANCE
Uruk (Iraq)	ca. 5,500–1,800	Earliest true city; associated with the Sumerian civilization of the southern Tigris-Euphrates Valley
Ur (Iraq)	ca. 4,600–2,500	City in southern Iraq; its cemetery of >1,800 graves includes 16 "royal" tombs

© Cengage Learning 2013

accomplish only with organized communal effort, including a great deal of cooperation and direction. The activity transformed not only the landscape but also the nature of the agricultural societies themselves.

What might these concentrated populations mean to us? No less than the birth of the Near East's first true cities. But what stimulated their development? It's possible that intensified economic or military rivalries in the region forced populations to come together for protection (Adams, 1981). Alternatively, increased agricultural productivity and efficiency may have fostered cultural changes (social stratification, craft specialization, commerce, and so on) that in turn promoted the development of urban communities. Whatever the reason, these trends happened at settlements along the lower Tigris-Euphrates Valley as people flocked to the developing cities. These cities became the social environments within which the earliest Mesopotamian states emerged (Yoffee, 2005).

Sumerians Over several centuries, Uruk grew to be a city with a population of as many as 20,000 people. Today, the ruins of Uruk's mud-brick buildings cover nearly 1 square mile in southern Mesopotamia, 150 miles southeast of modern Baghdad (Nissen, 2001). The most ancient parts of Uruk reveal some features of the earliest city. Two massive temple complexes, built in stages and dedicated to the sun and to the goddess of love, probably served as focal points of political, religious, economic,

and cultural activities. Inscribed clay tablets associated with these structures record that the temples distributed food to the populace and controlled nearby croplands. Growing social and religious complexity, including the rise of powerful kings and priests, kept pace with the city's physical growth.

The developments associated with Uruk and other urban centers were an immediate prelude and stimulus to a new order in southern Mesopotamia around 5,000 ya. The inscribed tablets, teeming populations, and large-scale religious structures indicate that the essential elements of a Mesopotamian civilization had come together. Uruk marked the beginning of the **Sumerians**, the first complex urban civilization.

The region known as Sumer encompassed about a dozen largely autonomous political units, called **city-states**, in the southernmost Tigris-Euphrates Valley. About the same number of Akkadian city-states hugged the river to the north, near present-day Baghdad. The Sumerians and their neighbors shared the world's first modern society between 4,900 and 4,350 ya. Each Sumerian city-state incorporated a major population center—Ur, Lagash, Umma, Nippur, Eridu, and Uruk are examples—as well as some smaller satellite communities and, of course, a great deal of irrigated cropland. These city-states were controlled by hereditary kings, who often fought for dominance with their counterparts in neighboring cities.

The Sumerians had a technologically accomplished urban culture, economically dependent on large-scale irrigation

Sumerians Earliest civilization of Mesopotamia.

city-states Urban centers that form autonomous sociopolitical units.

agriculture and specialized craft production (Kramer, 1963; Roaf, 1996). The influence of Sumerian cities reached beyond Mesopotamia through exchange and possibly even colonization. Excavations in northern Iraq, Turkey, and the Nile Valley of Egypt have revealed connections with Uruk through trade in prestige goods such as pottery, carved ivory, and lapis (Roaf, 1996). These valued products furnished the tombs of Sumerian elites in a society where social differentiation was becoming more pronounced.

Among the prerogatives of elite members of society was the right to burial in a lavish tomb. Sir Leonard Woolley's excavations of the 4,500-year-old "royal" tombs at Ur in the 1920s revealed that

associated with each city, citizens worshipped many other gods. Chief among them was Enlil, the air god. Like most Mesopotamian gods, Enlil exhibited human characteristics, taking a fatherly concern for mortals and their daily affairs but also meting out punishment and misfortune. Some cities, like Ur, regularly augmented their shrines and eventually created an impressive artificial mountain called a **ziggurat** (**Fig. 15-4**). Rising from an elevated platform roughly the size of a football field, these stepped temples were solidly built of millions of baked mud bricks.

Outside the ceremonial district, narrow unpaved alleyways twisted through crowded residential precincts. Much like city dwellers everywhere, Sumerians endured social problems and pollution in their urban environment. The size and location of individual homes correlated with family wealth and position. The houses of all but the nobility were generally one story, with several rooms opening onto a central courtyard. Wall and floor coverings brightened the interiors, which were furnished with wooden tables, chairs, and beds and an assortment of household equipment for cooking and storage.

From our perspective, their writing system was perhaps the Sumerians' most significant invention, enabling us to discover more about them than their other artifacts and monuments could ever reveal. Literacy was a hard-won accomplishment. By about 5,000 ya, the original pictographic form of Sumerian writing was evolving into a more flexible writing system using hundreds of standardized signs. Highly trained scribes formed the characteristic wedge-shaped, or **cuneiform**, script by pressing a reed stylus onto damp clay tablets, which were then baked to preserve them (**Fig. 15-5**). Ninety percent of early Sumerian writing concerned the kind of economic, legal, and administrative matters that are typical of complex bureaucratic societies. Later scribes recorded more historical and literary works, including several epic accounts featuring the adventures of **Gilgamesh**, an early Uruk king and culture hero reputed to have performed many amazing deeds in the face of overwhelming odds.

© Fotolia / superkiss

Figure 15-4

Reconstructed lower stage of the late Sumerian ziggurat at Ur, Iraq.

King Abargi and Queen Puabi were each accompanied in death by rich offerings—ceremonial vessels, tools, musical instruments, and even chariots complete with their animals and, apparently, also their human attendants—arranged within the burial pits (Woolley, 1929). Woolley interpreted other human remains found in association with these elite individuals as the men and women of their court, who were bedecked with precious jewelry, drugged, and then sealed into the tombs.

Mesopotamian citizens constructed brick walls around their city perimeters for security. The heart of each urban center was its sacred district, dominated by a grand temple and flanked by noble houses. In addition to a patron deity

ziggurat Late Sumerian mud-brick temple-pyramid.

cuneiform (*cuneus*, meaning "wedge") Wedge-shaped writing of ancient Mesopotamia.

Gilgamesh Semilegendary king and culture hero of early Uruk, reputed to have had many marvelous adventures.

The loose conglomeration of Mesopotamian city-states faced hard times after around 4,500 ya. At least part of the problem may have been their long dependence on irrigation agriculture, which was slowly destroying the fertility of their fields because the irrigation water deposited soluble mineral salts in the soil and groundwater (Nentwig, 2007, but see Powell, 1985). Another part of the problem was that this early civilization spent much of its energy in fruitless internal competition. Clustered together in an area about the size of Vermont, the city-states of Sumer and neighboring Akkad, to the north, vied with one another for supremacy in commerce, prestige, and religion.

Finally, around 2334 B.C., a minor Akkadian official assumed the name Sargon of Agade and led armies from the north to victory in the Sumerian lands and united what had been a collection of city-states into a **territorial state**. Military expansion led to economic, political, and linguistic dominance over a broad area. Under Sargon, his sons, and grandsons, the Akkadian state endured only a century before dissolving. But once it began, the unification process continued on and off for many centuries in Mesopotamia—next under the kings of Ur and later (about 3,800 ya) under **Hammurabi** of Babylon, famed for his "eye for an eye" code of law, among other accomplishments.

Egypt

The pyramids of Egypt are unrivaled as the ancient world's most imposing monuments. They have adorned the banks of the Nile for so long that they seem timeless. Even so, as we saw in Chapter 14, Egyptian culture was rooted in the Nile Valley long before the pyramids.

By 6,000 ya, Neolithic villages lined the great river's banks, where early farmers grew wheat and barley, among other crops, and raised pigs, sheep, goats, and cattle (Wenke, 2009). Even then, settlements in the section of the valley known as Upper Egypt—just north of Aswan, the "First Cataract" of ancient times—contrasted somewhat with those in the delta region, called Lower Egypt, close to the river's mouth. Archaeologists recog-

nize a Mesopotamian influence at work among the Upper Egypt villagers, possibly introduced through direct contact or by way of Palestinian traders (Hoffman, 1991). Mineral resources, especially gold, apparently drew outsiders to the region.

Around 5,300 ya, increasing political and social cohesion brought some of these Upper Egypt settlements together as local chiefdoms. Walls protected the towns of Naqada and Hierakonpolis, and well-stocked stone and brick tombs marked the social status enjoyed by important individuals (Wenke, 2009). Pottery making and trading became specialized economic enterprises (**Fig. 15-6**). Continuing contact with Mesopotamian cultures may have stimulated these developments, although researchers do not yet have evidence of comparable Egyptian influence in the other direction.

Over the next few centuries, this part of the Nile Valley developed into a strong territorial state. Historical tradition and written evidence record that one of Upper Egypt's early chiefs took the name Narmer and seized control of both Upper and Lower Egypt (**Fig. 15-7**). Narmer's unification of Nile Valley under one king around 5,000 ya (3000 B.C.) marks the traditional beginning of the First Dynasty of Egyptian civilization.

After the first unification period, a 425-year span known as Old Kingdom times (4,575–4,150 ya) represented the first full flowering of civilization in the Nile Valley. Most of the estimated population of 1 to 3 million people lived in the far south (Trigger, 2003). The ruler, or **pharaoh**, was the supreme power of the society. Under his direction, Egypt became a wonder of the ancient world.

Egyptians soon adopted a complex pictographic script called **hieroglyphics**, a writing system that is Egyptian in form but possibly Mesopotamian in inspiration. The earliest inscriptions are

Figure 15-5

This small Sumerian clay tablet (actual size) is a 4,000-year-old tax receipt with cuneiform impressions on both sides.

Figure 15-6

The design on this pot from Adaima, a Predynastic period center near Hierakonpolis, shows a boat and its passengers. The vessel is about 7 inches tall.

territorial state A form of state political organization with multiple administrative centers and one or more capitals. The cities tended to house the elite and administrative classes, and food producers usually lived and worked in the surrounding hinterland.

Hammurabi (ham-oo-rah´-bee) Early Babylonian king, ca. 1800–1750 B.C.

pharaoh Title of the ruler of ancient Egypt.

hieroglyphics (*hiero*, meaning "sacred," and *glyphein*, meaning "carving") The picture-writing of ancient Egypt.

Figure 15-7

The Narmer Palette, commemorating the unification of Upper and Lower Egypt under Pharoah Narmer. The palette measures about 25 inches high.

© Werner Forman Archive

associated exclusively with the Egyptian royal court, as are other high-status products, such as cylinder seals, certain types of pottery, and specific artistic motifs and architectural techniques that also seem to be derived from beyond the Nile Valley. Advanced methods of copper working came into use as well, including ore refining and alloying, casting, and hammering techniques. Some of these processes likewise were invented elsewhere. An important by-product of copper metallurgy was **faience**, an Egyptian innovation produced by fusing powdered quartz, soda ash, and copper ore in a kiln. The blue-green glassy substance, molded into beads or statuettes, became a popular trade item throughout the region (Friedman, 1998).

Early pharaohs were godlike kings who ruled with divine authority through a bureaucracy of priests and public officials assigned to provinces throughout the kingdom. The pharaoh's power depended to a large degree on his assumed control over the annual Nile flood (Butzer, 1984), and throughout the course of Egypt's long history, pharaonic fortunes tended to fluctuate with the river's flow. Most Old Kingdom pharaohs maintained their royal courts at Memphis, about 15 miles south of present-day Cairo (see Fig. 15-2). In con-

trast to Mesopotamia, few urban centers emerged in the ancient Nile Valley, and even the capital was of modest size. Egypt remained almost entirely an agrarian and rural culture, the vast majority of its citizenry comprising farmers and a few traders engaged in their timeless routines (Aldred, 1998). Only in the immediate vicinity of Memphis and the sacred mortuary complexes along the Nile's west bank was Egypt's grandeur clearly evident.

The familiar Old Kingdom pyramids on the Nile's west bank at Giza evolved out of a tradition of royal tomb building that began at Hierakonpolis. In that early community, brick-lined burial pits were dug with adjoining chambers to stock the offerings for a deceased king's afterlife, and these rooms were then capped with a low, rectangular brick tomb (Lehner, 1997). The scale of these structures increased as successive rulers outdid their predecessors (**Fig. 15-8**). Contrary to popular view, they weren't built by slaves, but by thousands of Egyptian farmers, put to work during the several months each year when the Nile floodwaters covered their fields. The ruins of nearby towns associated with the construction and administration of several of these royal mortuary sites have been found filled with closely packed mud-brick houses aligned along regular street grids (Bard, 2008).

In all, some 25 pyramids honored the Old Kingdom's elite (Lehner, 1997). The first stepped pyramids of stone were built after 2630 B.C. (4,630 ya), and little more than a century later, the imposing tombs of Khufu and Khafra, Fourth Dynasty rulers, were among the last built in true pyramid form. Khufu's Great Pyramid is 765 feet square at its base and 479 feet in height, with 2.3 million massive limestone blocks required in its construction. Although Khafra's tomb is about 20 percent smaller, he compensated by having a nearby rock outcrop carved with the likeness of his face on the body of a lion, today called the Great Sphinx (Hawass and Lehner, 1994). Pyramid building ceased soon after, during a time of political decentralization and greater local control over such practical programs as state irrigation works.

faience (fay-ahnz´) Glassy material, usually of blue-green color, shaped into beads, amulets, and figurines by ancient Egyptians.

Dr. Robert Clouse

Figure 15-8
Egyptian Old Kingdom pyramid and Sphinx at Giza.

The Old Kingdom pyramids represented a remarkable engineering triumph and an enormous cultural achievement that inspired the civilizations that followed. Bear in mind that the stark structures we see along the Nile today were adjoined by extensive complexes of connecting causeways, shrines, altars, and storerooms filled with statuary and furnishings and ornamented with colorful friezes and carved stonework. The mortuary cult of the pharaohs also absorbed a large share of the work and wealth of Egyptian society.

Later kings contented themselves with being buried in smaller but still lavishly furnished tombs in the Valley of the Kings, a cramped desert valley below a natural pyramid-shaped mountain near Thebes. Discovered in the 1920s, the treasure-choked burial chamber of the young pharaoh **Tutankhamen**, who died more than 3,300 ya (about 1323 B.C.) during New Kingdom times, is convincing

Tutankhamen (toot-en-cahm´-en) Egyptian pharaoh of the New Kingdom period, who died at age 19 in 1323 B.C.; informally known today as King Tut.

At a Glance

Important Egyptian Sites and Regions

SITE	DATES (YA)	SIGNIFICANCE
Hierakonpolis	ca. 5,300	Early Nile Valley urban center located about 45 miles to the south of Thebes; associated with the development of the unification of Egypt as one polity; home to the Narmer Palette
Memphis	ca. 5,100–3,300	Old Kingdom capital city located about 10 miles south of Cairo; abandoned after A.D. 641
Giza	ca. 4,500	Old Kingdom pyramid complex and Great Sphinx; located just to the southwest of Cairo
Valley of the Kings	ca. 3,500–3,000	Desert valley near Thebes (modern Luxor), where more than 50 New Kingdom subterranean tombs of pharaohs (including Tutankhamen) and other elites were found

evidence that dead royalty were not neglected even after the era of pyramids had passed (Carter and Mace, 1923).

Much of what we know of ancient Egypt's religion and rulers comes not from the contents of royal tombs, but from the translation of countless hieroglyphic inscriptions (**Fig. 15-9**). In 1799 at Rosetta, a small Nile delta town, French soldiers discovered a 2½-by-2½-foot stone bearing an identical decree engraved in three scripts, including Greek and hieroglyphics. Twenty years later, Jean-François Champollion finally succeeded in deciphering Egyptian hieroglyphic writing by using the Rosetta stone as a guide (Wenke, 2009, pp. 87–90).

Egyptian hieroglyphics are a combination of signs that represent ideas with others indicating sounds. Because hieroglyphics were used primarily in formal contexts by members of the elite classes and bureaucrats (much like Latin in more recent times), their translation tells us much about pharaohs and their concerns, revealing less about the commonplace events and people of the era. In fact, archaeologists can read dis-

appointingly little about daily life in Egypt's Old Kingdom period outside the major administrative and mortuary centers, where tomb scenes occasionally portray peasants at work in their fields or winnowing or grinding grain. Happily, later periods of Egyptian society are more fully documented (Montet, 1981; Casson, 2001).

Although nothing surpassed the original glory of the Old Kingdom period, Egypt proved remarkably resilient through the centuries, surviving foreign invaders such as the Hyksos and Hittites of southwest Asia, as well as frequent episodes of internal misrule and rebellion. Its pharaohs enjoyed periods of resurgence and revival until, in a state of decline and defeated by the Persians (about 2,500 ya), Egypt fell into the Greek sphere under Alexander the Great and eventually came under the rule of Rome.

Indus

As the first great pyramids rose beside the Nile, a collection of urban settlements that dotted a broad floodplain far to the east was forming into the Indus civilization (**Fig. 15-10**). For seven centuries, between about 4,600 and 3,900 ya, the banks of the Indus River and its tributaries in what is now Pakistan and India supported at least five urban centers, each with a population numbering in the tens of thousands (Kenoyer, 1998, 2008; Possehl, 2002). Many hundreds of smaller farming villages were socially and economically, if not politically, linked to these central places.

The people of the Indus were relative newcomers to the Indus Valley. As we saw in Chapter 14, their ancestors cultivated the higher valley margins to the west at sites like Mehrgarh by 8,000 ya. Farming and herding, along with regional trade, sustained village life in these uplands from an early period (Jarrige and Meadow, 1980). Around 5,300 ya, farmers began to populate the Indus floodplain itself, possibly seeking more productive cropland or better access to potential trade routes for valued copper, shell, and colorful stones. Occupying slight natural rises on the flat landscape at places like Kot Diji (see

Figure 15-9

Egyptian hieroglyphic inscriptions on a pillar in the Karnak Temple complex at Thebes (modern Luxor).

Dr. Robert Clouse

Figure 15-10

Location of the Indus civilization in Pakistan and India.

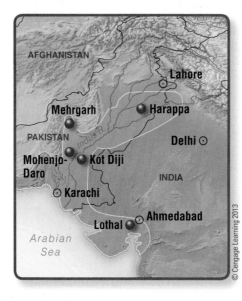

© Cengage Learning 2013

James P. Blair/National Geographic Stock

Figure 15-11
An excavated section of Mohenjo-Daro, Pakistan.

Fig. 15-10), they laid out fields for their vegetables, cereals, and cotton on the deep alluvium. As the new settlements grew, farmers diverted part of the river's flow into canals to irrigate their fields. They also constructed massive retaining walls or elevated platforms to protect their homes from the devastating effects of seasonal floods.

Some of these settlements prospered and grew. By 4,600 ya, several large urban centers hugged the river. Why had people accustomed to living in small farming communities congregated in these cities? Possibly an increased threat of flooding along the river— brought on by extensive deforestation and other poor farming practices—simply forced people to come together in building and maintaining more levees and irrigation canals. An alternative hypothesis proposes that trade was the "integrative force" behind Indus urbanization (Possehl, 1990). A few entrepreneurs may have fostered exchange between the valley settlements and the uplands, promoting resource development, craft specialization, and product distribution to stimulate and reap the economic benefits. As commerce began to pay off, other changes, including urbanism and social stratification, attracted craftspeople, shopkeepers, and foreign traders, all of whom transformed Indus society even more.

Indus Valley cities prospered as busy centers of craft production and trade.

Workshops in different neighborhoods turned out large quantities of wheel-thrown pottery, millions of burnt bricks, cut and polished stone beads and stamp seals, molded figurines, and work in copper, tin, silver, gold, and other metals. Boats plied the Indus River as a commercial highway and also moved goods along the coast as far as Mesopotamia and Oman (Ray 2003). Carts, too, carried the colorfully dyed cotton cloth, pottery, shell, and precious metal goods overland to Mesopotamia. For a while, a distant Harappan trade outpost was even established near Sumerian Ur.

So far, archaeologists have carried out extensive excavations at several of the major cities and a few of the smaller contemporary agricultural and pastoral villages (**Fig. 15-11**). The largest Indus sites excavated so far are **Mohenjo-Daro** and **Harappa**, which flourished between about 4,600 and 3,900 ya in present-day Pakistan. Raised on massive brick terraces above the river's flow, these cities were carefully planned, using grids of approximately 1,300 by 650 feet for the residential blocks. Although these large sites certainly reveal social complexity and a certain degree of central control, the Indus civilization lacks grand picturesque ruins of the type found in Egypt and Sumer. Some large building complexes interpreted as palaces have been excavated at Mohenjo-Daro, but generally speaking, evidence of sumptuous palaces and monumental religious

Mohenjo-Daro (mo-henjo-dar´-o) An early Indus Valley city in south-central Pakistan.

Harappa (ha-rap´-pa) A fortified city in the Indus Valley of northeastern Pakistan.

At a Glance

Important Asian Sites and Regions

SITE	DATES (YA)	SIGNIFICANCE
Mohenjo-Daro, Harappa (Pakistan)	ca. 4,600–3,900	Most extensively excavated large Indus civilization cities in South Asia
Erlitou (China)	ca. 4,000	Elaborate site associated with the earliest phase of civilization in northern China
Erligang, Shixianggou (China)	3,600–3,046	Early Shang cities
Shi Huangdi Tomb (China)	2,200	Tomb of the first emperor of China; his mausoleum at Mount Li, near the modern city of Xian, includes an entire terracotta army

structures is rare (Vidale, 2010). Their absence may suggest a basic feature of Indus society, whose people were less focused on glorifying their individual rulers. Richard H. Meadow, who has been excavating at Harappa since 1987, describes this civilization as "an elaborate middle-class society" (Edwards, 2000, p. 116). Gregory L. Possehl (2002), another archaeologist with decades of Indus civilization research experience, describes it as a socioculturally complex civilization that lacks evidence of the state form of political organization. Possehl (2002, pp. 5–6, 56–57) argues that the criteria by which the state is archaeologically identified—a hierarchy of social classes, kingship, state bureaucracies and the monopolization of power, state religions, and so forth—aren't readily identifiable in the archaeological remains of the Indus civilization. This difference—that of a highly successful, complex society based on a form of political organization other than the state—sets the Indus civilization apart and makes it clear that we still have a lot to learn about this extraordinary development in South Asian prehistory.

Both Mohenjo-Daro and Harappa encompassed a public district and several residential areas. Homes range from modest brick-walled dwellings that bordered unpaved streets and alleys to spacious multistoried houses with interior courtyards. What has been proclaimed as the world's first efficient sewer system carried waste away from these densely packed dwellings, many of them equipped with indoor toilets and baths.

What might this culture have to say for itself? Unfortunately, the writing system, consisting of brief pictographic notations commonly found on seal stones and pottery, remains undeciphered (Parpola, 1994; Possehl, 1996).

After little more than half a millennium, the Indus civilization's major sites declined, but hundreds of smaller towns and villages outlasted them (Lawler, 2008). Without written records or any archaeological evidence of invasion or revolution, we can only guess what caused its demise. Did competing trade routes bypass the Indus? Did the irrigation system fail, or did the river shift in its channel, either flooding the fields or leaving them parched? Could shifts in the Indian summer monsoon toward greater climatic variability and increased aridity have contributed to the Indus civilization's decline, as recently suggested by McDonald (2011)? All we know for sure is that in the end, the river that spawned the principal urban centers gradually reclaimed the surrounding fields and eventually the city sites themselves.

Northern China

As we saw in Chapter 14, the deep roots of China's early civilizations were nurtured in the loess uplands and alluvial plains bordering its great rivers. Specialized production and exchange of valued ritual goods came to characterize the prosperous farming societies along the central and lower Yellow River valley and brought about increased contact and conflict among them. This phase of regional development and interaction continued during the Longshan period (about 4,600–4,000 ya) and culminated in the formation of a distinctive Chinese culture that emphasized social ranking and ritualism accompanied by persistent warfare (Liu, 2009).

During the Longshan period, the circulation of luxury products contributed to the concentration of wealth and the emergence of social hierarchies. Elite consumers supported craft specialties, including fine wheel-thrown pottery, jade carving, and a developing metal industry based on copper and (later) bronze production. Status differences are reflected in the range of burial treatments found in the large Longshan cemeteries—from unusually lavish to mostly austere. Walled towns, some of which were up to 1 mile in circumference, dominated the region's villages and hamlets (Yan, 1999). Town walls were made of stamped earth, compacted to the hardness of cement, more than 20 feet high and 30 feet thick. These enormous constructions obviously required a large supervised labor force. Numerous arrowheads testify to the prevalence of warfare, but no clear explanations for these developments are yet possible.

Perhaps because of the differential access by some individuals and groups to the means of communication within Chinese society (as Chang suggests; see pp. 379–380), their success in organizing and controlling communal agricultural efforts, or more directly through violence and coercion, local leaders who emerged in northern China over the next few centuries commanded the allegiance of ever-larger regions. The rising nobility played an increasingly prominent role in the next era of Chinese civilization.

Many Chinese archaeologists believe that Erlitou (**Fig. 15-12**), in Henan Province, confirms the existence of the legendary **Xia** dynasty, proclaimed in myth as the dawn of Chinese civilization (Chang, 1986). Other researchers question this association and argue that the Xia dynasty has yet to be demonstrated to be more than legend (Liu and Xu, 2007; Lawler, 2009). Regardless of its relationship with the Xia dynasty, this important site, which covered more than 1 square mile, displayed evidence of increased social complexity between 3,900 and 3,600 ya. It's here, for the first time, that walled palaces set onto stamped-earth foundations literally raised members of the royal household above all others. Valuable stone carvings and bronze and ceramic vessels figured in elaborate court ceremonies and rituals. Royal burials contrasted sharply with those of commoners, who were sometimes disposed of in rubbish pits. The economy rested on multicropping of rice, millet, wheat, barley, and possibly soybeans and on extensive trade in utilitarian and ritual goods; salt production and transport may also have figured prominently in the development of this community (Liu, 2009). The earliest evidence of wheeled vehicles in China also comes from Erlitou, where archaeologists have found ruts made by wheeled carts or wagons in a road near the palace complex (Liu and Xu, 2007).

Shang The following **Shang** dynasty, beginning in the eighteenth century B.C., attained a level of sophistication in material culture, architecture, art styles, and writing that only a highly structured society could achieve. Enduring for some six centuries, Shang is generally acknowledged as China's first civilization, but its relationship to older polities, such as that which built Erlitou, is still far from clear. While peasant farmers lived and labored as they always had, an elite and powerful ruling class, supported by slaves, craft specialists, scribes, and other functionaries, topped the rigid Shang social hierarchy. Unlike the Indus civilization, the Shang territorial state included multiple cities and covered roughly 8,900 square miles.

Figure 15-12
Centers of early civilization in Northern China.

Xia (shah) Semilegendary kingdom, or dynasty, of early China.

Shang The first historic civilization in northern China; also called the Yin dynasty.

Figure 15-13

Bronze ritual vessel of the Shang dynasty.

Photo Archive Submitter/National Geographic Stock

Figure 15-14

Section of the Great Wall, erected by Qin Shi Huangdi.

Sue Lewis

divination Foretelling the future.

Qin Shi Huangdi (chin-shee-huangdee) First emperor of a unified China.

Zhou (chew) Chinese dynasty that followed Shang and ruled between 1122 and 221 B.C.

Mesoamerica (*meso*, meaning "middle") Geographical and cultural region from central Mexico to northwestern Costa Rica; formerly called "Middle America" in the archaeological literature.

The power and actions of Shang rulers were sometimes directed through the rite of **divination**, or prophecy. This practice is of immense importance because it also provides the most extensive evidence of early Chinese writing. Divination was performed by first inscribing a question on a specially prepared bone, such as the shoulder blade of an ox or deer or on turtle shells. Applying heat to the thin bones made them crack, and then the answer to the question could be "read" from the patterns formed by the cracks. Divination was a vital activity to the Shang, and thousands of the marked bones survive as a unique historical archive offering insights into early Chinese politics and society (Fitzgerald, 1978). These bones also demonstrate that Chinese writing is older than Shang times. Its roots may lie in the developing social complexity of late Longshan period towns (Demattè, 2010).

Shang cities were significantly larger than older Chinese settlements. By 3,500 ya, the city of Erligang, in Henan Province, covered about 8 square miles (von Falkenhausen, 2008). Its inner enclosure alone, filled with palaces and

temples, was comparable in size to the entire community of Erlitou. The city of Shixianggou, also in Henan Province, was enclosed by an outer ditch and stamped-earth city walls that were 50 to 55 feet thick (von Falkenhausen, 2008). Excavations inside Shixianggou's city walls have exposed elite compounds, some of which were also walled. While most ordinary people appear to have lived outside the city walls, Shixianggou also contained the homes of lesser retainers and servants, as well as workshops and specialized production areas, including several bronze foundries, pottery kilns, and bone workshops.

Shang artisans created remarkable bronze work, particularly elaborate cauldrons cast in sectional molds (**Fig. 15-13**). Decorated with stylized animal motifs and worshipful inscriptions, the massive metal vessels were designed to hold ritual offerings of wine and food dedicated to ancestors and deities. They also served as prominent funerary items in the royal tombs, about a dozen of which were in the vicinity of the later Shang capital at Anyang (Chang, 1986). In addition to bronzes, lavish offerings of carved jade, horse-drawn chariots, and scores of human sacrificial victims accompanied the rulers in death. In much later times, as in the tomb of emperor **Qin Shi Huangdi** (died 2,200 ya) at Xian, life-size clay sculptures of warriors and horses sometimes substituted for their living counterparts.

It seems that the Shang kingdom was only one of several contentious feudal states in northern China. Despite their political competition, all shared a common culture, one that served as a foundation for most future developments in China. After the eclipse of the Shang state, successive **Zhou** rulers (1122–221 B.C.) adopted and extended the social and cultural innovations introduced by their Shang predecessors. Much of China remained apportioned among competitive warlords until the Qin and Han dynasties (221 B.C.–A.D. 220), when this huge region was at last politically unified into a cohesive Chinese empire. Consolidated by Shi Huangdi and protected from the outer world behind his 3,000-mile Great Wall (**Fig. 15-14**),

China in later times maintained many of the cultural traditions linking it to an ancient past.

New World Civilizations

The rise of the earliest civilizations in the Americas was closely intertwined with the development of agriculture. In many regions where early farming prevailed, the combination of maize, beans, and plants such as squash came to substitute for diets rich in animal protein. In time, these primary domesticates supported large populations and established the economic basis for the development of states and civilizations in several New World areas.

Superficially, we can say that early New World cities, states, and civiliza-tions are broadly comparable to those of the Old World. All shared some basic similarities: state economies based on agriculture and long-distance trade; powerful leaders and social stratifica-tion; human labor invested in large-scale constructions; public art styles; state reli-gions; record keeping; and the promi-nent role of warfare. Still, there are sig-nificant points of contrast as well. For example, domesticated animals played only a small part in New World agricul-ture; the technological role of metal was limited; and the wheel had no impor-tant function, nor did watercraft. These differences reflect the unique historical traditions, resources, and geography of the continents on which the earliest civi-lizations developed. This section exam-ines three New World civilizations that developed in very different regions— lowland **Mesoamerica**, highland Mexico, and Peru (**Fig. 15-15**).

Figure 15-15

Time line for New World civilizations.

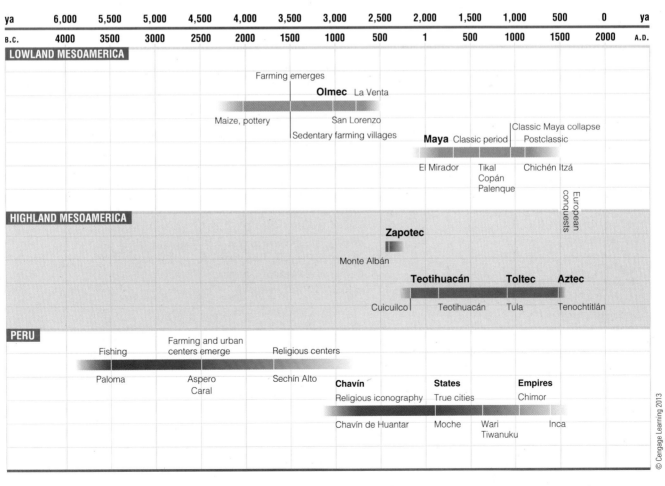

© Cengage Learning 2013

Lowland Mesoamerica

Olmec By roughly 3,500 ya, farming villages dotted the river valleys and lowlands of Mesoamerica. Local chiefdoms arose, and one of these groups, known as the **Olmec**, achieved prominence in the forests and swamps of the southern Gulf Coast of Mexico between about 3,200 and 2,400 ya (**Fig. 15-16**). Richard Diehl (2004) and Michael Coe (Diehl and Coe, 1996) identify Olmec as "America's first civilization" and contend that it exerted considerable influence on later Mesoamerican cultures. Other archaeologists (e.g., Flannery and Marcus, 2000; Spencer and Redmond, 2004) argue that Olmec **polities** were chiefdoms, not states, and that they were simply part of a web of interacting chiefdoms and early states. What's more, Spencer and Redmond (2004) maintain that the most convincing archaeological evidence for the emergence of the earliest Mesoamerican state can be found not in the lowlands, but at the large Zapotec center of Monte Albán in the highlands of Oaxaca around 2,300 ya.

The two best-known Olmec sites are San Lorenzo and La Venta (see Fig. 15-16), which Diehl (2004) identifies as the region's first cities. At both sites, people extensively modified the natural landscape—without the aid of domestic animals or machinery—to convert them to proper settings for impressive constructions and sculptures of ritual significance (Coe, 1994; Diehl, 2004). Earthen-mound alignments enclose the wide courtyards, plazas, and artificial ponds at San Lorenzo. A 100-foot-high cone-shaped earthen pyramid dominates La Venta. Within and near the sites themselves, there are hundreds of smaller earthen platform mounds that once supported homes and workshops.

Figure 15-16

Mesoamerican archaeological sites mentioned in the text.

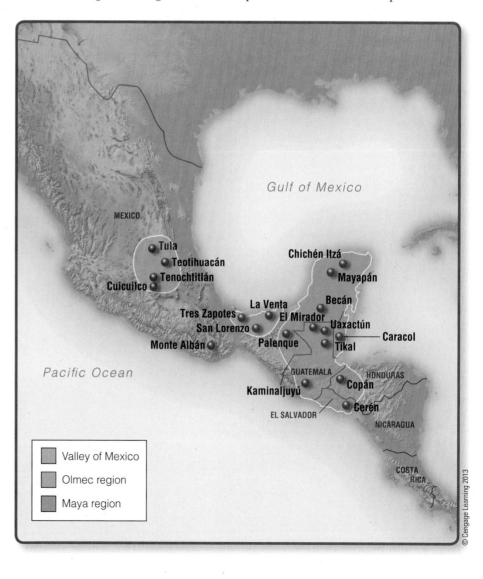

Olmec Prehistoric chiefdom in the Gulf Coast lowlands of Veracruz and Tabasco, Mexico, between 3,200 and 2,400 ya.

polities The political organizations of societies or groups.

anthropomorphic (*anthro*, meaning "man," and *morph*, meaning "shape") Having or being given humanlike characteristics.

glyphs Carved or incised symbolic figures.

In addition to ceremonial architecture, the Olmec produced remarkable monumental sculptures and smaller, well-crafted carvings of jade and other attractive stones (Cyphers and Di Castro, 2009). **Anthropomorphic** forms predominate, including some figurines and bas-reliefs that combine the features of humans with those of felines, probably jaguars. Olmec art and iconography are fascinating but poorly understood. Who or what did these anthropomorphic beings represent? We don't know. Equally intriguing are the colossal Olmec heads, each of which seems to be an individualized portrait of a ruler in helmet-like headgear, carved from massive basalt boulders weighing up to 20 tons (**Fig. 15-17**). Ten of these huge monuments have been found at San Lorenzo itself. Archaeologists estimate that the sustained effort of 1,000 workers was needed to drag and raft these boulders from their distant source, some 60 miles from the site (Lowe, 1989).

Curiously, the Olmec intentionally buried caches of beads, as well as carved figurines and implements made from their highly valued jade. One pit offering at La Venta consisted of 460 green stone blocks, arranged into a giant mosaic design and then buried at a depth of more than 20 feet. Another held an assemblage of small jade figures set into place so that they all seem to be confronting one individual. Then, still in position, the group was buried (**Fig. 15-18**).

The latest Olmec controversy concerns the origins of writing in Mesoamerica. Several artifacts bearing signs reputed to be **glyphs** that could be part of an Olmec writing system have recently been reported from sites in the coastal states of Veracruz and Tabasco (Pohl et al., 2002; del Carmen Rodríguez Martínez et al., 2006). One of these artifacts, a serpentine block that bears 62 signs, or glyphs, could be as old as 900 B.C. Critics argue that these discoveries aren't sufficient evidence of a fully developed system of writing (Stokstad, 2002; see also Bruhns and Kelker, 2007).

To sum things up, the Olmec represent a fascinating early development of complex society in the lowlands of the Mexican Gulf Coast, but one about which archaeologists have more questions than answers. Most evidence supports the view that the Olmec chiefdoms of southern Veracruz and Tabasco were similar in many respects to their neighbors in the highlands to the south

Figure 15-17
Monumental Olmec head excavated at La Venta, Mexico.

At a Glance
Important Lowland Mesoamerican Sites and Regions

SITE	DATES (YA)	SIGNIFICANCE
San Lorenzo (Mexico)	3,150–2,900	Olmec civic-ceremonial center in southern Veracruz
La Venta (Mexico)	ca. 2,800–2,400	Large Olmec civic-ceremonial center in the coastal lowlands of Tabasco
Cerén (El Salvador)	ca. 1,400	Maya village buried by the eruption of a volcano; provides a Pompeii-like snapshot of Classic period Maya life
Tikal (Guatemala)	ca. 2,400–1,200	Important Maya city in northern Guatemala
Copán (Honduras)	ca. 1,600–1,200	Major Maya city in western Honduras with an estimated population of around 27,000 at its peak

Figure 15-18

Buried cache of small Olmec jade figurines found at La Venta, Mexico.

Philip Drucker, Robert Squier, "Excavations at La Venta, Tabasco, 1955." *Smithsonian Institution, Bureau of American Ethnology Bulletin 170, plate 20.* Washington, DC: Government Printing Office, 1959.

and west and to those throughout central Mexico. The archaeological evidence may or may not eventually live up to Diehl's claim that they were America's first civilization (Lawler, 2007).

Classic Maya Some suggest that the roots of Classic **Maya*** rest partly with the Olmec, whose art, architecture, and rituals are reflected in several early Maya sites. However, the development of Maya civilization also clearly owed much to its competitive interaction with contemporary chiefdoms in several Mesoamerican regions, a process that ultimately resulted in some of them becoming true states and civilizations (Flannery and Marcus, 2000; Braswell, 2003).

By roughly 2,100 ya, the elements of Maya civilization were coming together. Crucial materials that were lacking in most of the Maya lowlands, especially suitable stone for making tools and milling slabs, were exchanged for commodities such as salt and the feathers of colorful jungle birds, both of which highland groups desired. Control of trade routes or strategic waterways in northern Guatemala may have promoted

the growth of the Late Preclassic[†] center at El Mirador, where archaeologists have found the earliest evidence of Maya palaces, and, later, at Uaxactún and Tikal (see Fig. 15-16).

At these sites and others, Maya society came to be dominated increasingly by an elite social class. A host of Maya kings, each claiming descent through royal lineages back to the gods themselves, held sway over independent city-states centered on elaborate ceremonial precincts. Under the patronage of these kings, writing, fine arts, and architecture flourished in the Maya lowlands, as did chronic warfare among rival kingdoms (Sharer, 1996; Coe, 1999). Lisa Lucero (2003) argues that successful Maya rulers acquired and maintained their political power by skillfully manipulating domestic rituals, which in turn promoted political cohesion.

The Maya are best known for their impressive Classic period urban centers, with Tikal, Copán (Honduras), and Palenque (Mexico) among them (**Fig. 15-19**). These centers were essentially capitals of regional Maya city-states, despite their somewhat dispersed populace. Including the ruling

---

Maya Mesoamerican culture consisting of regional kingdoms and known for its art and architectural accomplishments; also, Native American ethnic group of southern Mexico, Guatemala, and Belize.

* The word *Classic* refers here to the archaeological period of the same name, which was roughly between A.D. 200 and 900.

† The Late Preclassic is a Mesoamerican archaeological period that dates roughly from 300 B.C. to A.D. 200.

Figure 15-19

The Temple of the Inscriptions at Palenque, Mexico, served as the tomb of the important Maya ruler Pacal, who died in A.D. 683.

elite and their retainers, crafters, other specialists, and farmers, some 27,000 people were attached to the important city of Copán (Webster et al., 2000), although two-thirds of them actually lived in farming compounds scattered through the Copán Valley, within walking distance of the Copán urban center.

Formal, large-scale architecture dominated the largest cities. Tikal, with over 50,000 residents, boasted more than 3,000 structures in its core precinct alone. Most impressive were the stepped, limestone-sided pyramids capped with temples. Facing across the broad stuccoed plazas were multi-room palaces (presumably elite residences), generally a ritual ball court or two (**Fig. 15-20**), and always elaborately carved **stelae** (**Fig. 15-21**). Other features might include graded causeways leading into the complex masonry reservoirs for storing crucial runoff from tropical cloudbursts. The ancient Maya typically painted their structures in bold colors, so the overall effect must have been stunning.

Maya writing was well developed by 300–200 B.C. (Houston, 2006), and scholars are now able to decipher many of the inscriptions found on Maya stelae, temples, and other monuments. Many stelae proclaim the ancestry and noble

Figure 15-20

The ball court at Monte Albán, one of several types built by nearly all the major cultures of Mesoamerica.

Figure 15-21

Maya hieroglyphs on a stela at Copán record the date and purpose of its dedication.

stelae (*sing.*, stela) (stee´-lee) Upright posts or stones, often bearing inscriptions.

Figure 15-22

Detail from a page of the Dresden Codex, one of the few surviving Maya books.

deeds of actual Maya rulers and provide a precise chronology of major events in lowland Mesoamerica (Schele and Miller, 1986). These inscriptions offer direct insights to Classic Maya socio-political organization, including the uneasy and frequently embattled relationships among leading ceremonial centers and their rival aristocracies (Schele and Freidel, 1990; Coe, 1992).

Religion was a key component of Maya society, just as it was in all early civilizations. Architecture and art were dedicated to the veneration of divine kings and the worship of perhaps hundreds of major and minor deities. The nobility included a priestly caste that carefully observed the sun, moon, and planet Venus; predicted the rains; prescribed the rituals; and performed the sacrifices. Most of the priestly lore and learning faithfully recorded in the Maya **codices**, or books (**Fig. 15-22**), was lost when the Spanish burned these ancient texts during the conquest.

Archaeologists historically have devoted much of their attention to the most spectacular Classic Maya sites, but in recent decades they have also begun to learn a lot about the lives of ordinary people. For example, extraordinary discoveries, such as the buried Maya community at Cerén, in El Salvador, give us detailed glimpses of village life (Sheets, 2002, 2006). Cerén—once a hamlet of mud-walled, thatched huts—lay entombed for 1,400 years beneath 18 feet of ash from the eruption of a nearby volcano. The inhabitants fled their homes, which were quickly buried by the volcanic ash. Remarkable traces of Maya peasant life survived, including a plentiful harvest of maize, beans, squash, tomatoes, and chilies stored in baskets and pots, arranged as if they had just been gathered from nearby garden plots.

The rise and fall of Maya city-states continued for centuries, and we now know a great deal about the historical events that figured in the changing fortunes of Maya kings. Things came to a head around A.D. 900, after which artisans no longer turned out their distinctive decorated ceramics, nor did they carve and erect inscribed stelae. The construction of palaces, temples, and other major works ceased altogether, and

nearly all major Classic Maya sites were abandoned.

The remarkable collapse of Classic Maya civilization has intrigued scholars for decades. Archaeologists are not yet sure what happened, let alone why. Proposed explanations, none of which are adequate by themselves to explain every case, include devastation by hurricanes or earthquakes, insect infestations, epidemic diseases, malnutrition, overpopulation, an unbalanced male/female sex ratio, peasant revolts against the elite, and mass migrations. Other researchers argue that Classic Maya city-states collapsed primarily because they failed to integrate into a single unified political system, such as that achieved by the Aztecs in central Mexico and the Inca in highland South America (Cioffi-Revilla and Landman, 1999, pp. 586–588). Recent evidence also points to possible climatic factors, including multiple major droughts and widespread deforestation, as important elements in the demise of many Classic Maya cities (Pringle, 2009).

Highland Mexico

In central Mexico, far to the northwest of the Maya area, the convergence of two mountain ranges forms a great highland of some 3,000 square miles, commonly called the Valley of Mexico (see Fig. 15-16). An elevated plateau rimmed by mountains and volcanic peaks to the west, south, and east, the rich agricultural soils of the Valley of Mexico were watered by several rivers and large lakes. This broad semiarid valley, which is today dominated by Mexico City, was the stage on which several important prehistoric states and civilizations developed. **Teotihuacán**, the earliest city-state to dominate the region, became one of the largest urban centers in the New World up to the nineteenth century (Cowgill, 2000).

Teotihuacán With its fields nourished by a system of irrigation canals, Teotihuacán was a successful, growing community around 2,200 ya. Its closest competitor, Cuicuilco (see Fig. 15-16), had a population of around 20,000 at its peak but vanished from the scene

codices (*sing.*, codex) Illustrated books.

Teotihuacán (tay-oh-tee-wah-cahnˊ) Earliest city-state to dominate the Valley of Mexico. It became one of the largest urban centers in the New World up to the nineteenth century.

around 2,000 ya, when it was buried by a lava flow. This unfortunate event worked to Teotihuacán's advantage, and it soon was the most important polity in the Valley of Mexico. Its influence can be archaeologically recognized in many parts of Mesoamerica, as far away as Guatemala, after 1,700 ya (Spencer and Redmond, 2004).

At its height between 1,700 and 1,400 ya, Teotihuacán had more than 100,000 residents and covered nearly 8 square miles. Somewhat in contrast to the Maya centers, Teotihuacán's layout was more orderly and its population more highly concentrated. Built on a grid pattern with a primary north-south axis, its avenues, plazas, major monuments, and homes alike—and even the San Juan River—were aligned to a master plan.

The city's inhabitants lived in some 2,000 apartment compounds, arranged into formal neighborhoods based on occupation or social class and ranging from merchants to military officers and even foreigners. Civic and religious leaders enjoyed more luxurious facilities in the central district (Millon, 1988). Artisans laboring in hundreds of individual household workshops produced ceramic vessels, obsidian blades, shell and jade carvings, fabrics, leather goods, and other practical or luxury items.

An impressive civic-ceremonial precinct covered nearly 1 square mile in the heart of the city. Imaginative Spanish explorers assigned the name Avenida de los Muertos (literally, "Avenue of the Dead") to the main thoroughfare, which extends northward 2.8 miles to a massive structure, the Pyramid of the Moon. An even greater Pyramid of the Sun, its base equal to that of Khufu's pyramid at Giza in Egypt (though it rises only half as high), occupies a central position along the same avenue. Archaeologists have come to recognize that the Teotihuacán rulers built this immense structure to resemble a sacred mountain, and they raised it directly over a natural cave that symbolized the entry to the underworld. Flanking the south end of the Avenida de los Muertos, the Ciudadela was the administrative complex, and the Great Compound served as Teotihuacán's central marketplace.

Unlike Maya art, that of Teotihuacán doesn't show identifiable rulers or personalized representations. There also are no Teotihuacán counterparts of Maya stelae commemorating the conquests and lineages of a given king. Artistic expression is both impersonal and repetitive, the same elements or motifs appearing again and again; this pattern is particularly evident in Teotihuacán architecture, the repetitive nature of which was relieved mostly by the use of bright colors (**Fig. 15-23**). Although social differentiation clearly existed in Teotihuacán society, it was mostly expressed in art by differences of costume, not by representations of the human body (Cowgill, 2000).

Warfare appears to have been common among Mesoamerican states, but cultural differences determined how war was expressed artistically (Brown and Stanton, 2003). These differences went unappreciated by archaeologists for a long time, and it was believed that Teotihuacán was a relatively peaceful state. Now that researchers better understand Teotihuacán culture, we can see that warfare was an important part of this early state.

Mention of warfare leads us logically to examine the possible influence that Teotihuacán wielded throughout Mexico's central region and beyond. The society's fine orange-slipped ceramics, architectural and artistic styles, and obsidian products are said to be present at distant contemporary centers, such as Monte Albán in Oaxaca; the Maya site of **Kaminaljuyú** in the Guatemalan highlands; and Tikal, Uaxactún, and Becán in the Maya lowlands (Berlo, 1992). Some also argue that Teotihuacán played a large role in the development of Maya states (e.g., Sanders and Michels, 1977; Sanders et al., 1979).

© James Schmeling

Figure 15-23

Feathered Serpent and Tlaloc (god of rain and fertility) figures on a temple facade at Teotihuacán, Mexico.

Kaminaljuyú (cam-en-awl-hoo-yoo´)
Major prehistoric Maya site located at Guatemala City.

At a Glance

Important Highland Mesoamerican Sites and Regions

SITE	DATES (YA)	SIGNIFICANCE
Teotihuacán (Mexico)	ca. 2,200–1,350	Earliest city-state to dominate the Valley of Mexico; one of the largest urban centers in the New World up to the nineteenth century
Cuicuilco (Mexico)	ca. 2,300–2,000	Important early center in the Valley of Mexico; its destruction by a lava flow made it easier for Teotihuacán to take control of the valley
Kaminaljuyú (Guatemala)	ca. 3,000–1,100	Major Maya site located on the outskirts of Guatemala City; similarities of its elaborate tombs and architecture are often cited as evidence of the far-flung influence of Teotihuacán
Tula (Mexico)	ca. 1,200–850	Toltec capital in the Valley of Mexico

© Cengage Learning 2013

As with many—if not most—archaeological generalizations, the more we learn, the more complex the picture gets. And while no one doubts that Teotihuacán interacted with other regions, the precise nature of this interaction is still being explored (Braswell, 2003). Some scholars point to the Escuintla region on the Pacific coast of Guatemala, where evidence was recently found of a Teotihuacán colony that established itself at several sites and soon made itself felt throughout this region as well as in southern Chiapas and western El Salvador (Bove and Busto, 2003). Other scholars, many of them Maya specialists, view the whole notion of Teotihuacán "influence" as greatly exaggerated; in cases where there is indisputable material evidence of contact, they argue that it hasn't yet been proved that Teotihuacán had a significant local impact or that it changed anything (e.g., Iglesias Ponce de Léon, 2003). The truth probably lies somewhere between these opposed views, but precisely where we've yet to discover.

Like the Classic Maya collapse, Teotihuacán's demise remains an archaeological mystery. After prospering for more than 600 years, conditions became unfavorable. Human remains excavated from the site's later features show common skeletal indicators of nutritional stress and disease as well as high infant mortality rates. Still, the city endured and population levels remained stable for another century or so before declining rapidly.

The end came in flames and havoc about 1,350 ya (Cowgill, 2000). The entire ceremonial precinct blazed as temples were thrown down and their icons smashed, though residential areas remained unscathed. In the frenzy, some of the nobility were seized and dismembered, apparently by their own people. As archaeologist George L. Cowgill (2000, p. 290) puts it, "What ended was not just a dynasty, it was the belief system that had supported the state." The city may even have been abandoned, or nearly so, for a brief period, but researchers still have much to learn about this period of the city's past. Regardless, the destruction ended Teotihuacán's political and religious preeminence, and many of its residents scattered to other communities.

Toltecs Teotihuacán's collapse did not leave a political, economic, or religious vacuum in highland Mesoamerica. Of the many groups contending for control over the region during the next few centuries, the **Toltecs** eventually emerged as the most powerful. They established a capital at **Tula**, in the northern Valley of Mexico some 40 miles northwest of Teotihuacán. By 1,200–1,100 ya, the city may have had as many as 50,000 to 60,000 residents. This city-state covered about 5 square miles and included several pyramids and ball courts in two ceremonial precincts (Healan and Stoutamire, 1989).

Although its more modest ceremonial precincts scarcely rivaled those of Classic period times, Tula does show some artistic and architectural continuities with Teotihuacán (Cowgill, 2000). The Toltecs also briefly enjoyed a commercial and military enterprise that expanded through trade and tribute networks, colonization efforts, and probably conquest (Davies, 1983; Healan, 1989). Toltec prestige reached in several directions. We even recognize their influence in the copper bells, ceremonial ball courts, and other exotic products found on Hohokam sites in the American Southwest, from which the Toltecs

acquired their valued blue turquoise stone, probably by making long-distance exchanges (see pp. 367–368).

As Toltec power declined around 850 ya, a prolonged drought was withering many of the farming communities in northern Mexico and the American Southwest, bringing streams of refugees into the Valley of Mexico and throwing the region into chaos once more. One of the groups that appeared on the scene at this point was the **Mexica**, better known historically as the **Aztecs** (Smith, 2003, 2008). They built many city-states, the best known of which is the imperial capital of **Tenochtitlán**, and dominated the Valley of Mexico until 1519, when the Spanish conquered them.

Peru

At first glance, Peru seems an unlikely region for nurturing early civilizations (**Fig. 15-24**). Its narrow coast is a dry fringe of desert broken by deeply entrenched river valleys that slice down from the mountains to the sea.

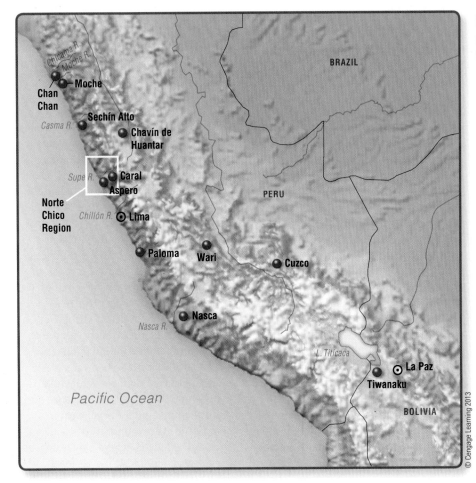

Figure 15-24
Peruvian sites and locations mentioned in the text.

© Cengage Learning 2013

Toltecs Central Mexican highlands people who created a pre-Aztec empire with its capital at Tula in the Valley of Mexico.

Tula (too´-la) Toltec capital in the Valley of Mexico; sometimes known as Tollan.

Mexica (meh-shee´-ka) Original name by which the Aztecs were known before their rise to power.

Aztecs Militaristic people who dominated the Valley of Mexico and surrounding area at the time of the European conquest.

Tenochtitlán (tay-nosh-teet-lahn´) Aztec capital, built on the future site of Mexico City.

Helaine Silverman

Figure 15-25

The arid western flank of the Andes Mountains in Peru. Snow-covered and cloud-wrapped peaks can be seen in the distance.

The Andes Mountains rise abruptly and dramatically behind the coastal plain, forming a rugged, snowcapped continental divide that extends the length of South America (**Fig. 15-25**). These geographical contrasts figured prominently in Peru's prehistory (Bruhns, 1994). In fact, the dynamic tension between coast and highlands—between fishers and farmers—provides a key to understanding the region's cultural past.

Fishing, Farming, and the Rise of Civilization Most of the world's early civilizations were built on the shoulders of farmers. However, in the central Andes region—that is, in Peru and parts of Bolivia and Ecuador—things played out a little differently, and archaeologists continue to explore the relative contributions of both fishing and farming to the development of Peruvian civilization (Moseley, 1975; Wilson, 1981; Bruhns, 1994). Archaeologist Michael Moseley points out that the deep, cold Pacific currents off the Peruvian coast that create the richest fishing waters in the Western Hemisphere are also responsible for the climatic conditions that make the central Andes coastal plain one of the world's driest deserts (Moseley, 1992, p. 102). Marine resources surely supported people in this region from the earliest period of human settlement.

Between 6,000 and 4,500 ya, when farming was already under way in a few highland areas, coastal fishing groups settled as permanent residents at sites such as Paloma (see pp. 365–366). The productive fisheries may have delayed farming in this dry coastal region for some time, until the long-term effects of a stronger, recurring El Niño pattern and other factors promoted the development of a simple form of agriculture. In early farming efforts near the coast, people planted squash, gourds, and beans in the damp beds of seasonal streams flowing down from the Andes.

Social differentiation and the intensification of agriculture spread widely in western South America between 5,500 and 3,800 ya, and evidence can be found at coastal sites in Ecuador and Peru (Pozorski and Pozorski, 2008). For example, the coastal site of Aspero, located in the Norte Chico region to

the north of Lima and dated to 5,000–4,500 ya (see Fig. 15-24), depended on marine resources as well as several domesticated food crops plus cotton. Aspero covers about 37 acres and includes six platform mounds. It provides good evidence that social differentiation and a certain amount of centralized power was present in some coastal centers at a very early date (Haas and Creamer, 2004).

Recent research at inland sites in the Norte Chico region has revealed more than 20 major preceramic sites with monumental architecture and large residential areas between 5,000 and 3,800 ya (Haas et al., 2004). The large urban center of Caral in the Supe Valley covers roughly 270 acres and includes sunken circular plazas, large and small platform mounds, and many residential and other building complexes. Although Caral lies 14 miles inland, the faunal remains found in excavations of this site are all marine animals, principally small fishes such as anchovies and sardines (Haas and Creamer, 2004).

Haas and Creamer (2004) argue that when you consider Norte Chico sites such as Caral and Aspero together, it's evident that a sort of symbiotic economic relationship existed between inland and coastal sites. Coastal sites like Aspero provided the region's main source of animal protein, mostly in the form of anchovies and sardines, and inland sites like Caral provided the main source of plant resources, including cotton for fishnets and gourds for net floats. The inland sites also appear to have had the upper hand in the emergence of leadership and political power in the region. At the inland sites, we find archaeologically identifiable status differences, larger monumental architecture, motifs and features such as sunken circular plazas that appear to be precursors of pan-Andean patterns, control over agricultural resources, and evidence of agricultural intensification (Haas and Creamer, 2004, pp. 46–47).

Peru's coastal regions were wholeheartedly committed to subsistence agriculture after about 3,800 ya. Farming communities are found in river valleys such as the Moche, where irrigation was feasible (see Fig. 15-24). There, local communities dug canals to irrigate crops of maize, peanuts, and potatoes, plants originally domesticated in Mexico and the Andean highlands. Such staple crops made farming a worthwhile endeavor, especially considering the periodic unreliability of coastal resources due to El Niño. The success of these lowland communities may be measured by the imposing size of ceremonial complexes found in more than two dozen coastal valleys and several upland sites in central and northern Peru.

Sechín Alto, on the Casma River, is an early example of the "corporate construction" projects that became common in Peru at this time. At Sechín Alto and other sites, huge U-shaped arrangements of temples, platforms, and courtyards—as well as irrigation networks in many instances—represent the efforts of large labor forces. Sites of this kind became important ceremonial and possibly market centers for several neighboring valleys (Pozorski and Pozorski, 1988).

What inspired the collective efforts that produced the early Peruvian civic architecture and art styles? Most archaeologists interpret these developments as evidence of greater social complexity and greater authority invested in civil or religious leaders. Under their direction, public energies were applied to large-scale construction projects. But what motivated individuals to participate in these collective enterprises? And what guided their leaders? What was the source of their persuasive or coercive powers? In Peru, as elsewhere, archaeologists have considered such factors as militarism, religion, and control of resources to explain the rise of civilizations (e.g., Haas et al., 1987).

Chavín Around 3,200–2,850 ya, the peoples of the northern Peruvian highlands and coast came together in a religious fervor that brought a degree of cultural unity to this broad region. Underlying their unity was some form

At a Glance
Important Peruvian Sites and Regions

SITE	DATES (YA)	SIGNIFICANCE
Caral	ca. 5,200–4,500	Large preceramic urban center in the Supe Valley
Aspero (Peru)	ca. 5,000–4,500	Important early center on the Peruvian coast that shows evidence of social differentiation and a certain amount of centralized power
Sechin Alto (Peru)	ca. 3,800–2,900	Proto-urban settlement on the northwest coast of Peru
Chavín de Huantar	ca. 2,900–2,500	Civic-ceremonial center in the northern highlands
Moche	ca. 1,900–1,300	Early state on Peru's north coast; its capital city (also called Moche) was possibly the earliest true city in the Andes
Wari	ca. 1,460–1,100	Early state in the central highlands
Tiwanaku	ca. 2,400–1,000	Early state in the southern highlands near Lake Titicaca
Chan Chan	ca. 1,000–600	Capital city of the Chimor (Chimú) state

of centralized authority (Kembel and Rick, 2004), with a shared ideology that the people expressed especially through their ritual art. **Chavín de Huantar**, an intriguing civic-ceremonial center set in a high Andean valley, is the best-known archaeological example of this iconography (Burger, 1992, 2008). There, raised stone tiers flank sunken courtyards where ceremonies took place near a temple riddled by underground chambers and passageways. Anthropomorphic stone sculptures and other art at the site combine human characteristics with the features of jaguars, snakes, birds of prey, and mythological beings. Although Chavín may have been an agent of widespread cultural change in the region, at least on a stylistic and ideological level, its influence had faded considerably by about 2,500 ya.

Early States Several Peruvian kingdoms, or states, including the **Moche** culture of Peru's north coast, formed between 1,900 and 1,300 ya (Stanish, 2001). The Moche rulers consolidated their hold over neighboring valleys initially through warfare and then by greatly expanding irrigated agricultural lands in the conquered areas. The archaeologist Charles Stanish (2001, p. 53) suggests that the Moche capital (of the same name) may have been "the first true city in the Andes." Among this city's monumental works, the **Huaca del Sol**, or Pyramid of the Sun, incorporated some 100 million hand-formed bricks and was one of the largest prehistoric structures in the Americas.

Artistic specialists created remarkable objects that served the elite as status symbols in life and in death. Unique **polychrome** ceramic vessels modeled to represent portraits, buildings, everyday scenes, or imaginative fantasies were a Moche specialty (**Fig. 15-26**). Metalsmiths also hammered, alloyed, and cast beautiful ornaments, ceremonial weapons, and religious paraphernalia from precious gold, silver, and copper. Unlike Old World societies, those in the Americas seldom employed metal for technological purposes, generally reserving it for ornamental use as a badge of social standing.

The contents of excavated tombs of Moche warrior-priests rival those of the rulers of Egypt or Mesopotamia (Alva and Donnan, 1993). These high officials, both male and female, officiated over the human sacrifice ceremony that was an important component of Moche state religion. Upon their own deaths, these officials were dressed in the elaborate and distinctive regalia of their elevated position. Protected by dead attendants, llamas, and dogs, their tombs have yielded ceremonial headdresses, earrings, necklaces, and goblets.

As Moche influences faded around 1,400 ya, the **Wari** and **Tiwanaku** states emerged in the central and southern highlands (Isbell, 2008). The name Wari (also spelled Huari) derives from the capital city of Wari, the urban core of which covered roughly 2 square miles in an architectural plan that was repeated in other Wari centers (Stanish, 2001).

Like Wari, Tiwanaku, which was situated near Lake Titicaca, in Bolivia (**Fig. 15-27**; also see Fig. 15-24), used trade, control of food and labor resources, religion, and military conquest to extend its interests from the Andes to the coast (Isbell and Vranich, 2004). Wari and Tiwanaku shared similar expressions of religious art, including the prominent Staff God deity (**Fig. 15-28**), the origins of which can be traced back before Chavín to early representations known from the Norte Chico region around 3,250 ya (Haas and Creamer, 2004, pp. 48–49). Beneath these similarities, however, their architecture, lifeways, and cultural landscapes appear to have been fundamentally different (Isbell and Vranich, 2004).

The rise and fall of highland states was not limited to Moche, Wari, and Tiwanaku. Peru's north coast, for example, became the center of yet another episode of expansion beginning around 1,100–1,000 ya. The **Chimor** (archaeologically called Chimú) kingdom of the north was centered in the Moche Valley (Moore and Mackey, 2008). The eroded mud-brick architecture of its capital, Chan Chan (**Fig. 15-29**), still blankets several square miles of coastal desert there. Among its ruins are nearly a dozen walled compounds, each of which served as a grand palace, storehouse, and tomb for the successive monarchs of ruling lineages. By contrast, the insubstantial quarters of tens

Figure 15-26
Moche portrait jar from northern Peru.

Chavín de Huantar Chavín civic-ceremonial center in the northern highlands of Peru.

Moche (moh´-chay) Regional state, city, and valley of the same name in northern Peru.

Huaca del Sol (wah´-ka dell sole) Massive adobe pyramid built at Moche, in northern Peru.

polychrome Many-colored.

Wari (wah´-ree) Regional state and city of the same name in southern Peru.

Tiwanaku (tee-wahn-ah´-koo) Regional state, city, and valley of the same name near Lake Titicaca, in Bolivia.

Chimor A powerful culture that dominated the northern Peruvian coast between about 1,000 and 500 ya.

Figure 15-27
Ruins of the Kalasasaya Temple at Tiwanaku, in Bolivia.

Figure 15-28
Staff God, Tiwanaku, Bolivia.

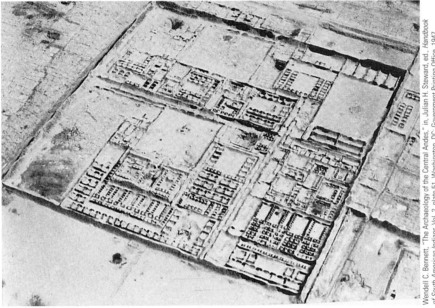

Wendell C. Bennett, "The Archaeology of the Central Andes," in, Julian H. Steward, ed., *Handbook of South American Indians*, Vol. 2, plate 51. Washington, DC: Government Printing Office, 1947.

Figure 15-29
Aerial view of one of the royal enclosures at Chan Chan, the Chimor capital, Peru.

of thousands of urban peasants once crammed the spaces below the massive compound walls (Moseley and Day, 1982).

The pattern of conquest and control set by Chimor was seen again in their successors—the **Inca**, the last native empire builders of ancient Peru. From its beginnings in the **Cuzco** area around 1,000 ya, this highland society used bold military initiatives and strategic alli-ances to dominate the southern highlands by 550 ya. The aging Chimor kingdom itself was conquered by the Inca about A.D. 1470. The Inca soon controlled all of modern Peru and the neighboring region, briefly becoming the largest empire in the pre-Hispanic Americas (Covey, 2003, 2008), only to succumb in the 1500s, like Tenochtitlán in the Valley of Mexico, to the invasion of the New World by the Old.

Inca People whose sophisticated culture dominated Peru at the time of the European arrival; also, the term for that people's highest ruler; also spelled Inka.

Cuzco (coos'-koh)

Summary of Main Topics

▶ The earliest civilizations developed independently in several world regions directly after people achieved sustainable food production.

▶ Environmental and cultural factors are insufficient by themselves to explain the rise of the earliest civilizations.

▶ The earliest civilizations found only a limited number of ways to create new decision-making institutions

and the distribution of power and authority.

▶ Broad similarities exist between the earliest Old and New World civilizations, but there are also important differences.

▶ New World civilizations emerged in more ecologically diverse locations than those of the Old World.

▶ New World civilizations also relied less than their Old World coun-

terparts on domesticated animals, wheels, or metal for technological purposes.

In "What's Important," you'll find a useful summary of the most important archaeological sites discussed in this chapter. And in the final chapter of the book, we'll consider some of the important points to be derived from the story of human biocultural evolution.

What's Important The Most Significant Archaeological Sites Discussed in This Chapter

Site	Dates (ya)	Comments
Uruk (Iraq)	ca. 5,500–1,800	Earliest true city; associated with the Sumerian civilization of the southern Tigris-Euphrates Valley
Ur (Iraq)	ca. 4,600–2,500	City in southern Iraq; its cemetery of >1,800 graves includes 16 "royal" tombs
Giza (Egypt)	ca. 4,500	Old Kingdom pyramid complex and Great Sphinx; located just to the southwest of Cairo
Mohenjo-Daro and **Harappa** (Pakistan)	ca. 4,600–3,900	Most extensively excavated large Indus civilization cities in South Asia
Erlitou (China)	ca. 4,000	Elaborate site associated with the earliest phase of civilization in northern China
Erligang, Shixianggou (China)	3,600–3,046	Early Shang cities
San Lorenzo (Mexico)	3,150–2,900	Olmec civic-ceremonial center in southern Veracruz
Tikal (Guatemala)	ca. 2,400–1,200	Important Maya city in northern Guatemala
Tiwanaku (Peru)	ca. 2,400–1,000	Early state in the southern highlands near Lake Titicaca
Teotihuacán (Mexico)	ca. 2,200–1,350	Earliest city-state to dominate the Valley of Mexico; one of the largest urban centers in the New World up to the nineteenth century
Tula (Mexico)	ca. 1,200–850	Toltec capital in the Valley of Mexico
Chavín de Huantar (Peru)	ca. 2,900–2,500	Chavín civic-ceremonial center in the northern highlands of Peru

Critical Thinking Questions

1. List some of the basic differences between the lifeways of ancient village farmers and the residents of early cities. What are the social, economic, and political implications of city life?

2. Why were major river valleys the primary setting for so many early civilizations?

3. In what ways did Old World and New World civilizations develop along similar lines? In what ways were they fundamentally different? Most importantly, how can we explain these similarities and differences?

Archaeology

Biocultural Evolution and the Anthropocene

LEARNING OBJECTIVES

After you have mastered the material in this chapter, you will be able to:

▶ Identify and evaluate the global impact of human biocultural evolution.

▶ Express the obligation everyone shares to be stewards of the earth and its plants, animals, and resources for the benefit of future generations.

Australia's Great Barrier Reef is a UNESCO World Heritage Area, an honor that places it on a par with other sites of "outstanding universal appeal," such as the Statue of Liberty and the Grand Canyon in the United States. Its status as a world landmark aside, the Great Barrier Reef is hurting. A recent Australian government study (Reef Water Quality Protection Plan Secretariat, 2011) estimates that the reef annually receives 34,000 tons of dissolved nitrogen from agricultural fertilizer runoff, about 62,000 pounds of pesticides, and nearly 19,000,000 tons of sediments (of which roughly 15,500,000 tons are the product of human activity). Given these data, it is painfully obvious that humans are killing the Great Barrier Reef, not maliciously, not from indifference, but slowly and surely nevertheless. The Australian government recognizes the severity of the environmental effects and is working to reduce human-generated pollution of the reef. It will not be an easy task.

The Great Barrier Reef illustrates an important point about humans: We've become rather dangerous to ourselves, other living things, and the earth itself. This textbook has given you the background needed to understand how and why this happened. In Chapter 1, we observed that modern humans are cultural and biological beings whose present and future reflect their past. But where did we come from? And how did we create the present? Answers to such questions can help us understand some of our strengths and limitations as a species and, if used wisely, inform decisions that will affect our future.

Our story of the human past, which we traced over 15 chapters, closes with a look at some of the consequences of biocultural evolution, perhaps the most chilling of which is our new-found ability to trash the planet. We touch only on a few key issues because the topic is another textbook in itself. Our goal is to impress upon you how unique our species has become and what this can mean in practical terms for the quality of your life, your children's lives, and the well-being of the communities in which we all live.

Human Success and the Anthropocene

Humans are the most successful species ever to inhabit the earth. Sounds like a wild claim, right? After all, there are vastly more bacteria than humans, and bacteria are literally everywhere, including inside of us! But it's true. The earth has never witnessed the rise of a species quite like humans. The most telling measure of our success is that we humans grew to be a major force of nature over the last 10,000 years, and our global impact accelerated greatly during the past couple of centuries. Geologists and other scientists are beginning to hammer out a new concept, the **Anthropocene**, the geological epoch during which human behavior became one of the earth's major geomorphological and geological processes (e.g., see Crutzen, 2002; *The Economist*, 2011). The Anthropocene concept implies that millions of years from now, long after humans have vanished from the scene, the record of our brief existence will be a distinct geological formation, formed by a unique set of processes that we largely created and left indelibly stamped on the earth. Now that's success, perhaps in a blunt instrument sort of way, we admit, but no other species can lay claim to the global effects *that we have already achieved*, whether it be our impact on the Great Barrier Reef, the air we breath, or our next drink of water!

Consequences of Biocultural Evolution

We owe our success to biocultural evolution and our primate ancestry. Without them, all this would have never happened. To explain why, let's examine how our past informs our present and future.

Hominins to the End of the Ice Age

Glimmers of our future success are not easily found in the fossil record of our australopith ancestors (see Chapter 9). For millions of years, these homi-

Anthropocene The geological epoch during which human behavior became one of the earth's major geomorphological and geological processes.

nins were just another primate on the African savanna. If we had to point to one thing that made them stand out from their primate cousins, it was that they walked erect on their two hind limbs; they were bipedal. This peculiarity aside, the australopiths were successful in the same biological sense as any other animal—they survived and successfully reproduced.

The game changer for our ancestors, whether they were australopiths or early *Homo*, was our first rudimentary attempts at technological solutions to problems between roughly 3 and 2.5 mya. This, along with the behavioral changes that accompanied tool use, launched an adaptive process that eventually became a distinctive part of the life history strategy of early hominins.

The core components of hominin biocultural evolution took a long time to develop. For hundreds of thousands of years, we were tool-assisted hominins living in small groups that were spread thinly across the landscape. The rate of biocultural change was so slow that a thousand generations could pass, and yet the tool kits of each succeeding generation looked basically the same. Even after our ancestors began spreading out of Africa into parts of Europe and Asia around 2 mya (see Chapter 10), our impact on animals, plants, and the earth itself was negligible. There were too few hominins on the ground, and they could scarcely manage their own lives, much less have a measurable environmental impact on the regions in which they lived. If any part of the human success story can be said to be miraculous, it is simply that hominins did not go extinct during this, our training-wheel period as a biocultural bipedal primate.

The archaeological record shows that our Paleolithic ancestors were capable of expanding into new habitats, largely by adapting culturally. Nevertheless, the rate of cultural evolution continued its slow pace throughout the Lower Paleolithic and much of the Middle Paleolithic, while hominin population density remained low everywhere (see Chapter 11).

Things began to get a bit more complicated after about 200,000 ya with the earliest appearance of anatomically and behaviorally modern *Homo sapiens* in southern Africa (see Chapter 12). Modern humans began spreading into Asia and Europe after about 150,000 ya. The rate of cultural changes also increased at a faster pace; an Upper Paleolithic hunter-gatherer might have tools, huts, clothing, and even foods that would have been unfamiliar to his or her great-grandparents. Toward the end of the Ice Age, around 12,000–10,000 ya, Upper Paleolithic hunter-gatherers differed little in technology and behavior from hunter-gatherer groups that survived into the twentieth century.

Throughout the past couple of million years, the lives of hunter-gatherers and their predecessors weren't easy or disease-free. Our hominin ancestors suffered periodic food shortages that sometimes ended in starvation, and they certainly weren't strangers to traumatic injury and infectious disease. However, hominin populations up to the beginning of early farming probably did not suffer from epidemic diseases or from such "crowd" infections as the common cold. Because hunter-gatherer populations generally were small and mobile, the reservoir of human hosts for harmful viruses and bacteria wasn't sufficient to sustain itself in such groups.

For most of hominin history, our ancestors' reproductive capacity also wasn't much different from that of our ape cousins. A woman who gave birth every three or four years was probably typical of hominins up to just a few thousand years ago. Infant mortality rates were high, as they continued to be after the Ice Age for early farmers (and, regrettably, still are for some communities).

Looking back, hominins had a pretty good environmental record up to the end of the Ice Age. According to the archaeological record, it wasn't because our ancestors were natural conservationists who lived "in harmony with nature." If anything, it was simply because there weren't very many of us. What mattered was that we had extraordinary potential as a species: Biocultural evolutionary factors greatly enhanced our chances of biological success and gave us exceptional flexibility in different habitats.

By the end of the Ice Age, there may have been 5 million humans (**Fig. 16-1**), or less than one person for every 10 square miles of land surface. It sounds like very little, but it was sufficient for some human groups to drive local populations of food animals to extinction or nearly so. It also gives us a handy baseline against which to measure some of the events that happened next.

Earliest Farmers and Cities

As we saw in Chapters 13 and 14, the end of the last Ice Age marked a watershed moment in which we can find the roots of the so-called Neolithic revolution. Domestication and agriculture were the driving forces of this revolution, but the impact of Neolithic lifeways went far beyond subsistence, and opinions differ as to the effects. The physiologist and popular writer Jared Diamond (1987) bluntly refers to the invention of agriculture as "the worst mistake in the history of the human race." At the other extreme, Paul Colinvaux (1979), an eminent ecologist, expresses the same glowing perspective as archaeologist Graeme Barker (see p. 349), calling agriculture the "most momentous event in the history of life."

Some researchers argue that human population growth initiated the agricultural response; others see it happening the other way around. But there's no question that population size and density both tended to increase as farming produced larger and more predictable yields. World population doubled in the 5,000 years after the end of the Ice Age (see Fig. 16-1). In many places, permanent villages and towns sprang up surrounded by fields and pastures. Sedentary living (which in many cases began *before* agriculture) permitted closer birth spacing, since mothers no longer had to carry infants from camp to camp, and the availability of soft cereal grains for infant food allowed for earlier weaning. Potentially, therefore, a woman might bear more children. And they did. Even very early Neolithic settlements, such as Jericho in the Jordan River valley and Çatalhöyük in Turkey (see Chapter 15), quickly reached considerable size. By A.D. 1, world population had grown to 200,000,000, or roughly 3.5 persons per square mile.

As agricultural techniques and resulting harvests improved, surplus production served as a kind of capital, or wealth, that stimulated new kinds of socioeconomic interactions. Some members of society also came to fill specialized roles as priests, merchants, crafters, administrators, and

Figure 16-1

World population growth.

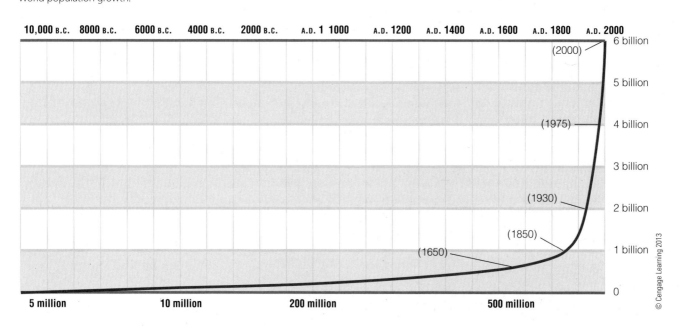

the like. A social and economic hierarchy of productive peasants, nonfarming specialists of many kinds, and a small but dominant elite emerged in a few Neolithic state societies, or civilizations (see Chapter 15).

Unlike hunter-gatherers, who extracted their livelihood from available natural resources, Neolithic farmers altered the environment by substituting their own domesticated plants and animals for native species. Neolithic plowing, terracing, cutting of forests, draining of wetlands, and animal grazing contributed to severe soil erosion and the decline of many plant and animal species. Moreover, many of these practices encouraged the growth of weeds and created fresh habitats for crop-damaging insects, malaria-bearing mosquitoes, and other pests. Intensive agriculture also depletes soil nutrients, especially potassium. In the lower Tigris-Euphrates Valley, high levels of soluble salts carried by irrigation waters slowly poisoned the fields once farmed by Ubaidians and Sumerians. In North Africa, Neolithic herders allowed their animals to overgraze the fragile Sahara grasslands, furthering the development of the world's largest desert. These early farming practices left many areas so damaged that they remained unproductive for thousands of years, until they could begin to be reclaimed with the aid of modern technology.

As with other biocultural aspects relating to the development of food production, the effects on human health were a mixed bag of benefits and costs. As farming villages and towns grew larger, infectious disease became prevalent (see Chapter 4). As you know, infectious diseases can cause epidemics, some small, some catastrophic—for example, the Black Death of the Middle Ages or the worldwide influenza epidemic of 1918. They can potentially kill thousands or even millions of people. Hunter-gatherer populations generally were little affected by infectious disease because they lived in small mobile groups. Farmers weren't so lucky.

One major contributor to heightened disease exposure came from close proximity of humans to domestic animals.

Many pathogens—including viruses, bacteria, and intestinal parasites—can be transferred from nonhuman animals to humans. For example, influenza and tuberculosis can be transmitted to humans by contact with some common domesticated animals.

Several other significant human diseases are associated with sedentism and increasing population size and density. Measles, for example, has been shown to require a very large population pool—in the thousands—to sustain itself long-term (Cohen, 1989). So, measles became prevalent only with the emergence of larger urban centers, making it a "disease of civilization." Likewise, cholera is most commonly found in urban contexts, especially where large numbers of people share a common (and contaminated) water source.

As if this list of diseases and potential human suffering isn't enough, bio-archaeological studies have also shown that overall health quality declined with the development of agriculture (Cohen and Armelagos, 1984; Steckel and Rose, 2002). Essentially, our ancestors had traded the uncertain possibility of starvation as a hunter-gatherer for probable malnutrition as a farmer. If it seems paradoxical that average health was declining among food producers at the same time that populations were expanding, that's because it is. As one researcher commented, "Although humans became physically worse-off in marked respects, they also became more numerous. The agricultural age made possible far denser populations, but less healthy ones than ever before. Historians, anthropologists, and others concerned with this apparent paradox are still exploring its implications in detail" (Curtin, 2002, p. 606).

Nevertheless, even with greater exposure to disease pathogens and other health risks associated with living in denser populations, the health picture for early farmers wasn't all that bleak. After all, it's ultimately our success as a species (that is, more people) that helped infectious pathogens to be more successful. The advent of farming and the emergence of the earliest civilizations were important components of humankind's success.

Industrial Revolution to the Present

Chapter 15 finished this textbook's story of biocultural evolution with a recounting of the earliest civilizations and the beginning of written history. But by ending the story there, we left a particularly important (and environmentally devastating) part of the human story untold. A graph of world population growth makes the point best (see Fig. 16-1). During the past couple of centuries, we humans began to be far more successful as a species than is good for us and the planet. By the year 1800, the Industrial Revolution was well under way, and

Figure 16-2

Plastic bags and containers are cheap, functional, and nearly indestructible. As waste, they kill tens of thousands of marine and other animals each year, clog sewers, pollute the oceans, rivers and creeks, and generally degrade the environment.

world population approached 1 billion, or about 18 persons per square mile. Two centuries later, by the year. 2000, we achieved a staggering 105 persons per square mile of every bit of dry land on earth. The current birth rate is such that we now add roughly 10,000 new mouths to feed every hour, 24 hours a day, 7 days a week.

Although we chose the Industrial Revolution as our point of departure in this section, no single factor explains the dangerously accelerating growth of world population over the past few hundred years. The growth rate also is not equally distributed among nations. The most recent United Nations report on world population notes that 95 percent

of population growth happens in developing countries. Likewise, resources are not distributed equally among all nations. Only a small percentage of the world's population, located in a few industrialized nations, control and consume most of the world's resources. A 2009 study estimated that 48 percent of the world's population exist on less than $2 per day (Population Reference Bureau, 2009).

As biologists can tell you, a natural population growth function similar to the one plotted in Figure 16-1 is unsustainable, regardless of whether we're talking about *E. coli* bacteria or humans. It is pointless to hope that humans will somehow be the lucky exception to the rule. Dying coral reefs, algal blooms in our lakes, pesticides in our drinking water, air pollution levels that kill the elderly and weak in our cities, rapid melting of the polar ice—all these things are nature's way of telling us to slow down, control our growth rate, and actively work toward a brighter and more sustainable future for our children (**Fig. 16-2**). If we can't or won't change, then nature can make the point more bluntly (for example, a global pandemic of a deadly disease like Ebola), and common sense tells us that we don't want to go there.

Today, the earth's human population still relies for food primarily on the seeds of just a half dozen grasses (wheat, barley, oats, rice, millet, maize), several root crops (potatoes, yams, manioc), and a few domesticated fowl and mammals (in addition to fish). Because of their relative genetic similarity, these domesticated species are susceptible to disease, drought, and pests. Agricultural scientists are trying to prevent potential disaster by reestablishing some genetic diversity in these plants and animals through the controlled introduction of heterogeneous (usually "wild") strains. A few farmers have also rediscovered the benefits of multicropping—interspersing different kinds of crops in a single agricultural plot. Combining grains, root crops, fruit trees, herbs, and plants used for fiber or tools mimics the natural species diversity and reduces soil depletion and insect infestation. The challenge farmers face is to make environmentally friendly approaches like multicropping scalable, such that they are technologically and economically feasible to meet world food demands.

Global Climate Change

At the global level, the biggest environmental problem we currently face concerns climate change, sometimes also called "global warming." This phenomenon has been researched for more than three decades by thousands of scientists. So, there's a lot of information out there. Unfortunately, there's also a good deal of misinformation.

Throughout this book, we have emphasized that science is an approach based on data collection, hypothesis testing, generalization, and verification. We have shown that scientific investigation typically can be a long process and one that frequently involves debate regarding alternative approaches and conclusions. It's important to recognize that science advances as these debates occur in the pages of scientific journals and at organized scientific meetings. Little is gained by uninformed, ideology-driven claims coming from television commentators or from politicians in the heat of partisan disputes.

Given all the accumulated scientific data and decades of analysis within the scientific community, there are no major disagreements on two major points:

1. Rapid global climate change has been occurring and continues to occur, including marked warming of the earth's atmosphere and acidification of the world's oceans (threatening habitats like the coral reefs that we mentioned earlier).
2. Human activity in the last two centuries is the most significant cause of this climate change.

As many of you know, humans have caused these changes as a result of the burning of fossil fuels—that is, coal and petroleum products. This burning leads to about 10 billion tons of carbon dioxide emissions into the atmosphere every year. Along with other "greenhouse gases," such as methane, these products trap heat in the atmosphere. In turn, the increased heat leads to melting of polar ice, raising of sea levels, and major impacts on weather, including intensification and greater unpredictability regarding droughts, flooding, and hurricanes.

What's more, the vast majority of countries and their leaders recognize that global climate change is a very serious and urgent problem. The United Nations has organized two extraordinary international conferences specifically to take global action. The first of these took place in 1997 in Kyoto, Japan, and as of 2011, its agreements were ratified by 194 countries; the only major country that failed to sign on was the United States.

The second conference was held in December 2009 and was attended by representatives of 192 countries, including 60 world leaders. Much anticipation and hopes for building on and strengthening the earlier Kyoto agreements preceded the conference. Unfortunately, and to the collective disappointment of most of the world, even less resulted from this meeting. Another such attempt won't take place until 2014, at the earliest. Meanwhile, humans pour increasing amounts of greenhouse gases into the atmosphere.

Learning from the Past and Facing an Uncertain Future

Throughout this textbook, we've tried to draw your attention to some of the costs and benefits of biocultural evolution, especially those relating to overall human health. As the evidence shows, the rate of cultural changes increased in a manner like that of the world population (see Fig. 16-1), and the effects of increasing cultural changes and population growth are inseparably intertwined. Biologically, however, most humans are still well adapted to being hunter-gatherers, not suburban, pizza-eating couch potatoes. And in some ways, our bodies haven't even adjusted to the fact that thousands of years ago, many of our ancestors became farmers. These problems are easier to understand if you view them in the context of biocultural evolution.

Some people, even some scientists, claim that the costs of these changes outweigh the benefits. Others feel just as strongly that the opposite is true. Regardless of the perspective you take about the effects of biocultural evolution, whether you see our future as rosy or depressing, there's no going back. The world we live in is the cumulative product of remarkable contributions made over millions of years by our ancestors who became the first tool users, crossed over into the next valley to see what was there, mastered the use of fire, invented the first composite tools and projectile weapons, domesticated the dog, learned to navigate by the stars, raised the first crop, invented the first printing press, and, yes, even invented the cell phone. Without the benefit of their hard work, sacrifices, and brilliant insights, most of us wouldn't be here at all. There would be no cities, no art, no educational institutions, no writing, no books—meaning, of course, no text-books and exams either. And for all the extremely serious damage that can be traced back to our increasing population density over the past few millennia (and particularly over the past couple of centuries), the effects of biocultural evolution, at least in the developed world, also doubled the average modern human life span and brought us affordable mass transportation, high-tech communication and entertainment, and a diverse and easily obtainable assortment of foods, clothing, and shelters. Our challenge, and one that we will bequeath to subsequent generations, is to identify and repair the damage that we've caused along the way and to learn how to make things better for all living things and the earth itself.

Summary of Main Topics

▶ By virtue of their biological success, humans have become a major threat to other living things, the earth itself, and even their descendants' future.

▶ Due to their low population density, slow population growth rate, and limited technology, humans exerted very little environmental impact until the end of the Ice Age.

▶ The world population growth rate and the rate of cultural change both increased slightly with the beginnings of agriculture and the earliest cities and civilizations; measurable environmental impacts resulted, but their effects tended to be only locally felt.

▶ Population growth and cultural changes accelerated greatly since the late 1700s and the beginning of the Industrial Revolution; measurable environmental impacts are now global.

▶ The fossil and archaeological record of the rise of humans shows that our current course is unsustainable. We can change or nature can force the issue. You choose.

Critical Thinking Questions

1. Based on your reading of this chapter as well as other materials outside of class, identify the most important consequences, both good and bad, of biocultural evolution for the future of our species. For each consequence you name, write a sentence that explains why it is important. Compare your list with that of your classmates and discuss the differences.

2. Assess the impacts of human population growth on humans, other living things, and the earth over the past 10,000 years. Write a paragraph describing the obligations each of us shares to change these impacts. Compare your paragraph with that of your classmates and discuss the differences.

Appendix A
Atlas of Primate Skeletal Anatomy

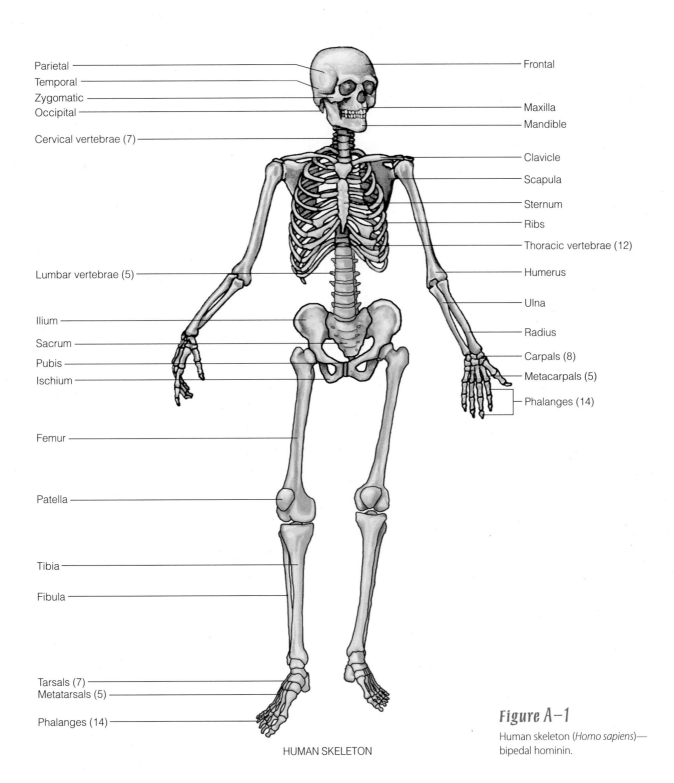

Parietal

Temporal

Zygomatic

Occipital

Cervical vertebrae (7)

Lumbar vertebrae (5)

Ilium

Sacrum

Pubis

Ischium

Femur

Patella

Tibia

Fibula

Tarsals (7)

Metatarsals (5)

Phalanges (14)

Frontal

Maxilla

Mandible

Clavicle

Scapula

Sternum

Ribs

Thoracic vertebrae (12)

Humerus

Ulna

Radius

Carpals (8)

Metacarpals (5)

Phalanges (14)

HUMAN SKELETON

Figure A–1

Human skeleton (*Homo sapiens*)—bipedal hominin.

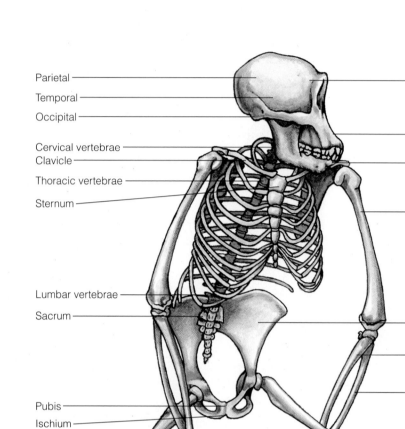

Parietal

Temporal

Occipital

Cervical vertebrae

Clavicle

Thoracic vertebrae

Sternum

Lumbar vertebrae

Sacrum

Pubis

Ischium

Femur

Patella

Tibia

Fibula

Tarsals

Metatarsals

Phalanges

Frontal

Maxilla

Mandible

Humerus

Ilium

Radius

Ulna

Carpals

Metacarpals

Phalanges

CHIMPANZEE SKELETON

Figure A-2

Chimpanzee skeleton (*Pan troglodytes*)—
knuckle-walking ape.

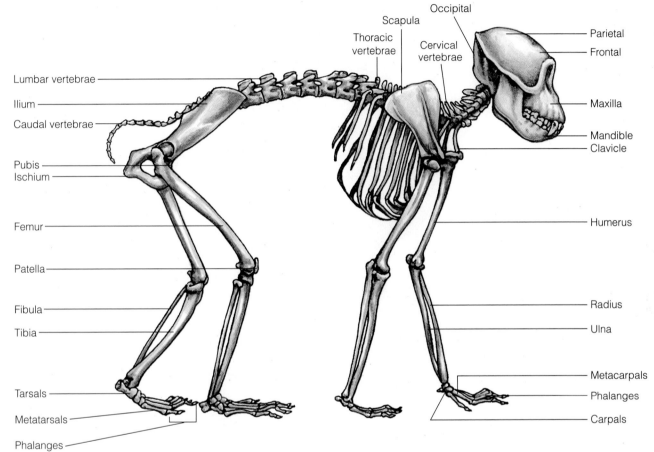

Occipital
Scapula
Thoracic vertebrae
Cervical vertebrae
Parietal
Frontal

Lumbar vertebrae
Maxilla
Ilium
Caudal vertebrae
Mandible
Clavicle

Pubis
Ischium

Femur
Humerus

Patella

Fibula
Radius
Tibia
Ulna

Metacarpals
Phalanges
Tarsals
Carpals
Metatarsals

Phalanges

MONKEY SKELETON

Figure A-3

Monkey skeleton (rhesus macaque; *Macaca mulatta*)—a typical quadrupedal primate.

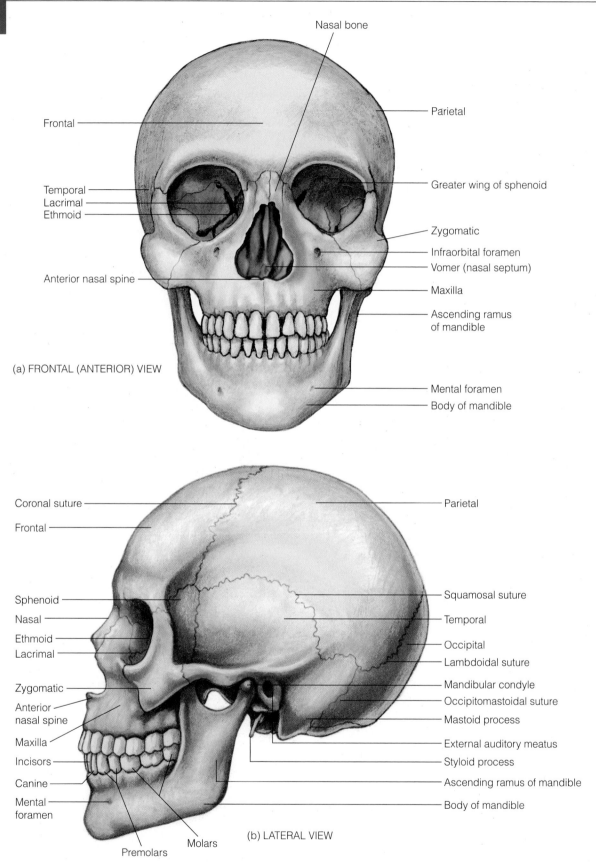

Nasal bone

Frontal

Parietal

Temporal
Lacrimal
Ethmoid

Greater wing of sphenoid

Zygomatic

Infraorbital foramen

Vomer (nasal septum)

Anterior nasal spine

Maxilla

Ascending ramus
of mandible

(a) FRONTAL (ANTERIOR) VIEW

Mental foramen

Body of mandible

Coronal suture

Parietal

Frontal

Sphenoid

Squamosal suture

Nasal

Temporal

Ethmoid

Occipital

Lacrimal

Lambdoidal suture

Zygomatic

Mandibular condyle

Anterior
nasal spine

Occipitomastoidal suture

Mastoid process

Maxilla

External auditory meatus

Incisors

Styloid process

Canine

Ascending ramus of mandible

Mental
foramen

Body of mandible

Premolars

Molars

(b) LATERAL VIEW

Figure A-4

Human cranium.
(continued on next page)

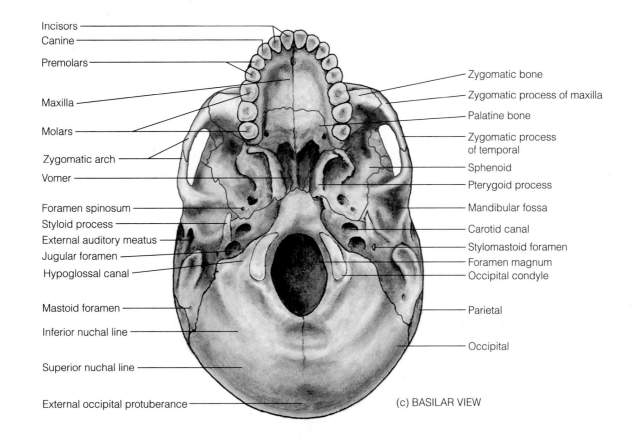

Incisors
Canine
Premolars
Maxilla
Molars
Zygomatic arch
Vomer
Foramen spinosum
Styloid process
External auditory meatus
Jugular foramen
Hypoglossal canal
Mastoid foramen
Inferior nuchal line
Superior nuchal line
External occipital protuberance

Zygomatic bone
Zygomatic process of maxilla
Palatine bone
Zygomatic process of temporal
Sphenoid
Pterygoid process
Mandibular fossa
Carotid canal
Stylomastoid foramen
Foramen magnum
Occipital condyle
Parietal
Occipital

(c) BASILAR VIEW

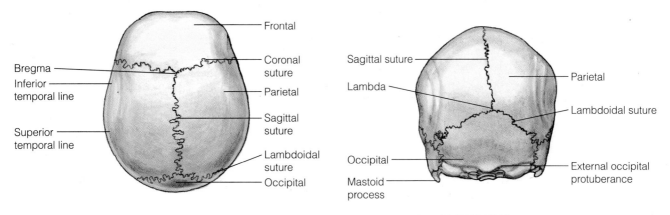

Bregma
Inferior temporal line
Superior temporal line

Frontal
Coronal suture
Parietal
Sagittal suture
Lambdoidal suture
Occipital

(d) SUPERIOR VIEW

Sagittal suture
Lambda
Occipital
Mastoid process

Parietal
Lambdoidal suture
External occipital protuberance

(e) REAR VIEW

Figure A-4

Human cranium.
(continued)

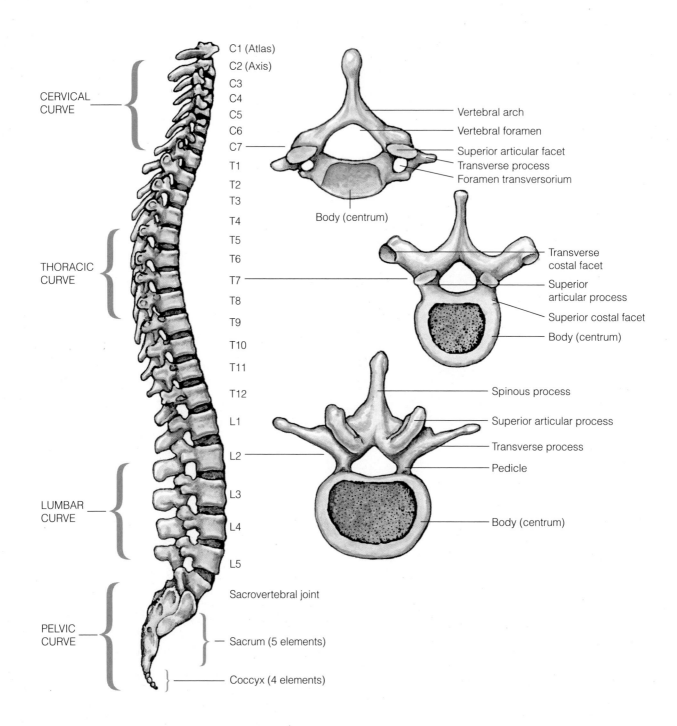

CERVICAL CURVE

C1 (Atlas)
C2 (Axis)
C3
C4
C5
C6
C7

Vertebral arch
Vertebral foramen
Superior articular facet
Transverse process
Foramen transversorium

Body (centrum)

T1
T2
T3
T4
T5

THORACIC CURVE

T6
T7
T8
T9
T10
T11
T12

Transverse costal facet
Superior articular process
Superior costal facet
Body (centrum)

Spinous process
Superior articular process
Transverse process
Pedicle

Body (centrum)

L1
L2

LUMBAR CURVE

L3
L4
L5

Sacrovertebral joint

PELVIC CURVE

Sacrum (5 elements)

Coccyx (4 elements)

Figure A-5

Human vertebral column (lateral view) and representative cervical, thoracic, and lumbar vertebrae (superior views).

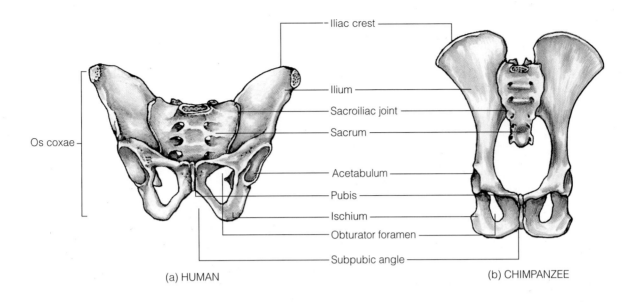

(a) HUMAN   (b) CHIMPANZEE

Figure A-6

Pelvic girdles.

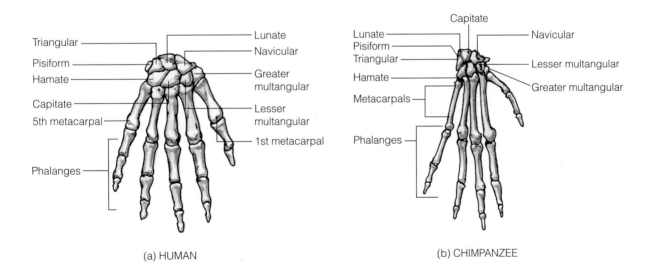

(a) HUMAN   (b) CHIMPANZEE

Figure A-7

Hand anatomy.

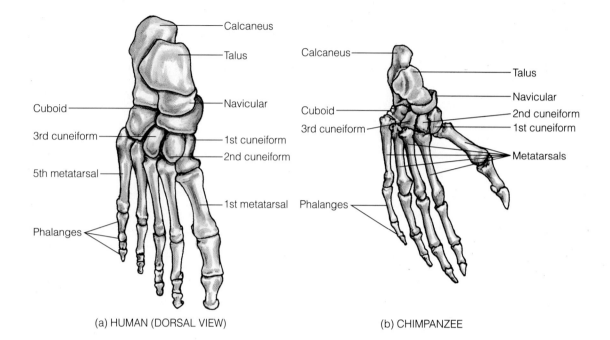

(a) HUMAN (DORSAL VIEW)

(b) CHIMPANZEE

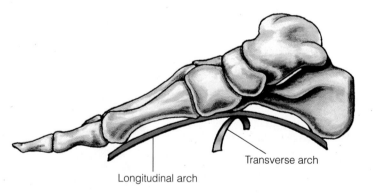

(c) HUMAN (MEDIAL VIEW)

Figure A-8

Foot (pedal) anatomy.

Appendix B
Summary of Early Hominin Fossil Finds from Africa

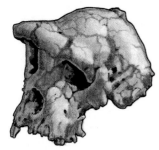

Sahelanthropus

Taxonomic designation:
Sahelanthropus tchadensis

Year of first discovery: 2001

Dating: ~7–6 mya

Fossil material: Nearly complete cranium, 2 jaw fragments, 3 isolated teeth

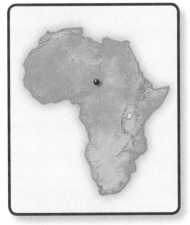

Location of finds: Toros-Menalla, Chad, central Africa

Orrorin

Taxonomic designation:
Orrorin tugenensis

Year of first discovery: 2000

Dating: ~6 mya

Fossil material: 2 jaw fragments, 6 isolated teeth, postcranial remains (femoral pieces, partial humerus, hand phalanx). No reasonably complete cranial remains yet discovered.

Location of finds: Lukeino Formation, Tugen Hills, Baringo District, Kenya, East Africa

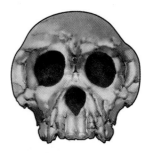

Ardipithecus

Taxonomic designation:
Ardipithecus ramidus; earlier species designated as *Ardipithecus kadabba*

Year of first discovery: 1992

Dating: Earlier sites, 5.8–5.6 mya; Aramis, 4.4 mya

Fossil material: Earlier materials: Jaw fragment, isolated teeth, 5 postcranial remains. Later sample (Aramis): partial skeleton, 110 other specimens representing at least 36 individuals

Location of finds: Middle Awash region, including Aramis (as well as earlier localities), Ethiopia, East Africa

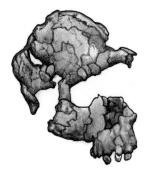

Australopithecus anamensis

Taxonomic designation:
Australopithecus anamensis

Year of first discovery: 1965 (but not recognized as separate species at that time); more remains found in 1994 and 1995

Dating: 4.2–3.9 mya

Fossil material: Total of 22 specimens, including cranial fragments, jaw fragments, and postcranial pieces (humerus, tibia, radius). No reasonably complete cranial remains yet discovered.

Australopithecus afarensis

Taxonomic designation:
Australopithecus afarensis

Year of first discovery: 1973

Dating: 3.6–3.0 mya

Fossil material: Large sample, with up to 65 individuals represented: 1 partial cranium, numerous cranial pieces and jaws, many teeth, numerous postcranial remains, including partial skeleton. Fossil finds from Laetoli also include dozens of fossilized footprints.

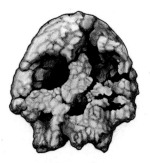

Kenyanthropus

Taxonomic designation:
Kenyanthropus platyops

Year of first discovery: 1999

Dating: 3.5 mya

Fossil material: Partial cranium, temporal fragment, partial maxilla, 2 partial mandibles

Location of finds: Kanapoi, Allia Bay, Kenya, East Africa

Location of finds: Laetoli (Tanzania), Hadar/Dikika (Ethiopia), also likely found at East Turkana (Kenya) and Omo (Ethiopia), East Africa

Location of finds: Lomekwi, West Lake Turkana, Kenya, East Africa

Australopithecus garhi

Taxonomic designation:
Australopithecus garhi
Year of first discovery: 1997
Dating: 2.5 mya
Fossil material: Partial cranium, numerous limb bones

Paranthropus aethiopicus

Taxonomic designation:
Paranthropus aethiopicus (also called *Australopithecus aethiopicus*)
Year of first discovery: 1985
Dating: 2.4 mya
Fossil material: Nearly complete cranium

Paranthropus boisei

Taxonomic designation:
Paranthropus boisei (also called *Australopithecus boisei*)
Year of first discovery: 1959
Dating: 2.2–1.0 mya
Fossil material: 2 nearly complete crania, several partial crania, many jaw fragments, dozens of teeth. Postcrania less represented, but parts of several long bones recovered.

Location of finds: Bouri, Middle Awash, Ethiopia, East Africa

Location of finds: West Lake Turkana, Kenya

Location of finds: Olduvai Gorge and Peninj (Tanzania), East Lake Turkana (Koobi Fora), Chesowanja (Kenya), Omo (Ethiopia)

Paranthropus robustus

Taxonomic designation:
Paranthropus robustus
(also called *Australopithecus robustus*)

Year of first discovery: 1938

Dating: ~2–1 mya

Fossil material: 1 complete cranium, several partial crania, many jaw fragments, hundreds of teeth, numerous postcranial elements

Australopithecus africanus

Taxonomic designation:
Australopithecus africanus

Year of first discovery: 1924

Dating: ~3.0?–2.0 mya

Fossil material: 1 mostly complete cranium, several partial crania, dozens of jaws/partial jaws, hundreds of teeth, 4 partial skeletons representing significant parts of the postcranium

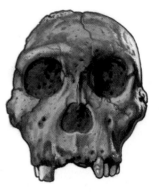

Australopithecus sediba

Taxonomic designation:
Australopithecus sediba
(also called *Homo sediba*)

Year of first discovery: 2008

Dating: 1.95-1.78 mya

Fossil material: 2 partial skeletons (Note: further fossils remains still in cave but not yet published)

Location of finds: Kromdraai, Swartkrans, Drimolen, Cooper's Cave, possibly Gondolin (all from South Africa)

Location of finds: Taung, Sterkfontein, Makapansgat, Gladysvale (all from South Africa)

Location of finds: Malapa Cave (South Africa)

Early *Homo*

Taxonomic designation:
Homo habilis

Year of first discovery: 1959/1960

Dating: ?2.4–1.8 mya

Fossil material: 2 partial crania, other cranial pieces, jaw fragments, several limb bones, partial hand, partial foot, partial skeleton

Location of finds: Olduvai Gorge (Tanzania), Lake Baringo (Kenya), Omo (Ethiopia), Sterkfontein (?) (South Africa)

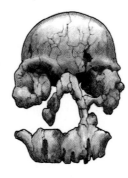

Early *Homo*

Taxonomic designation:
Homo rudolfensis

Year of first discovery: 1972

Dating: 1.8–1.4 mya

Fossil material: 4 partial crania, 1 mostly complete mandible, other jaw pieces, numerous teeth, a few postcranial elements (none directly associated with crania)

Location of finds: East Lake Turkana (Koobi Fora), Kenya, East Africa

Abbreviations Used for Fossil Hominin Specimens

For those hominin sites where a number of specimens have been recovered, standard abbreviations are used to designate the site as well as the specimen number (and occasionally museum accession information as well).

Abbreviation	Explanation	Example
AL	Afar locality	AL-288-1
LH	Laetoli hominin	LH 4
OH	Olduvai hominin	OH 5
KNM-ER (or simply ER)	Kenya National Museums, East Rudolf*	ER 1470
KNM-WT (or simply WT)	Kenya National Museums, West Turkana	WT 17000
Sts	Sterkfontein, main site	Sts 5
Stw	Sterkfontein, west extension	Stw 53
SK	Swartkrans	SK 48

* East Rudolf is the former name for Lake Turkana; the abbreviation was first used before the lake's name was changed. All these fossils (as well as others from sites throughout Kenya) are housed in Nairobi at the National Museums of Kenya.

Appendix C

Population Genetics

As noted in Chapter 4, the basic approach in population genetics makes use of a mathematical model called the Hardy-Weinberg equilibrium equation. The Hardy-Weinberg theory of genetic equilibrium postulates a set of conditions in a population where *no* evolution occurs. In other words, none of the forces of evolution are acting, and all genes have an equal chance of recombining in each generation (that is, there is random mating of individuals). More precisely, the hypothetical conditions that such a population would be *assumed* to meet are as follows:

1. The population is infinitely large. This condition eliminates the possibility of random genetic drift or changes in allele frequencies due to chance.
2. There is no mutation. Thus, no new alleles are being added by molecular changes in gametes.
3. There is no gene flow. There is no exchange of genes with other populations that can alter allele frequencies.
4. Natural selection is not operating. Specific alleles confer no advantage over others that might influence reproductive success.
5. Mating is random. There are no factors that influence who mates with whom. Thus, any female is assumed to have an equal chance of mating with any male.

If all these conditions are satisfied, allele frequencies will not change from one generation to the next (that is, no evolution will take place), and a permanent equilibrium will be maintained as long as these conditions prevail. An evolutionary "barometer" is thus provided that may be used as a standard against which actual circumstances are compared. Similar to the way a typical barometer is standardized under known temperature and altitude conditions, the Hardy-Weinberg equilibrium is standardized under known evolutionary conditions.

Note that the idealized conditions that define the Hardy-Weinberg equilibrium are just that: an idealized, *hypothetical* state. In the real world, no actual population would fully meet any of these conditions. But do not be confused by this distinction. By explicitly defining the genetic distribution that would be *expected* if *no* evolutionary change were occurring (that is, in equilibrium), we can compare the *observed* genetic distribution obtained from actual human populations. The evolutionary barometer is thus evaluated through comparison of these observed allele and genotype frequencies with those expected in the predefined equilibrium situation.

If the observed frequencies differ from those of the expected model, then we can say that evolution is taking place at the locus in question. The alternative, of course, is that the observed and expected frequencies do not differ sufficiently to state unambiguously that evolution is occurring at a locus in a population. Indeed, frequently this is the result that is obtained, and in such cases, population geneticists are unable to delineate evolutionary changes at the particular locus under study. Put another way, geneticists are unable to reject what statisticians call the *null hypothesis* (where "null" means nothing, a statistical condition of randomness).

The simplest situation applicable to a microevolutionary study is a genetic trait that follows a simple Mendelian pattern and has only two alleles (*A, a*). As you recall from earlier discussions, there are then only three possible genotypes: *AA, Aa, aa*. Proportions of these genotypes (*AA:Aa:aa*) are a function of the *allele frequencies* themselves (percentage of *A* and percentage of *a*). To provide uniformity for all genetic loci, a standard notation is employed to refer to these frequencies:

Frequency of dominant allele (*A*) = p
Frequency of recessive allele (*a*) = q

Since in this case there are only two alleles, their combined total frequency must represent all possibilities. In other words, the sum of their separate frequencies must be 1:

$$p \quad + \quad q \quad = \quad 1$$

| (frequency of A alleles) | (frequency of a alleles) | (100% of alleles at that locus) |

To ascertain the expected proportions of genotypes, we compute the chances of the alleles combining with one another into all possible combinations. Remember, they all have an equal chance of combining, and no new alleles are being added.

These probabilities are a direct function of the frequency of the two alleles. The chances of all possible combinations occurring randomly can be simply shown as

$$
\begin{array}{r}
p \;+\; q \\
\times \quad p \;+\; q \\
\hline
pq \;+\; q^2 \\
p^2 \;+\; pq \;+\; q^2 \\
\hline
p^2 \;+\; 2pq \;+\; q^2
\end{array}
$$

Mathematically, this is known as a binomial expansion and can also be shown as

$$(p + q)(p + q) = p^2 + 2pq + q^2$$

What we have just calculated is simply:

Allele Combination	Genotype Produced	Expected Proportion in Population
Chances of A combining with A	AA	$p \times p = p^2$
Chances of A combining with a;	Aa	$p \times q$
a combining with A	aA	$p \times q$ $\Big\} = 2pq$
Chances of a combining with a	aa	$q \times q = q^2$

Thus, p^2 is the frequency of the AA genotype, $2pq$ is the frequency of the Aa genotype, and q^2 is the frequency of the aa genotype, where p is the frequency of the dominant allele and q is the frequency of the recessive allele in a population.

Calculating Allele Frequencies: An Example

How geneticists use the Hardy-Weinberg formula is best demonstrated through an example. Let us assume that a population contains 200 individuals, and we will use the MN blood group locus as the gene to be measured. This gene produces a blood group antigen—similar to ABO—located on red blood cells. Because the M and N alleles are codominant, we can ascertain everyone's phenotype by taking blood samples and observing reactions with specially prepared antisera. From the phenotypes, we can then directly calculate the *observed* allele frequencies. So let us proceed.

All 200 individuals are tested, and the results are shown in Table C-1. Although the match between observed and expected frequencies is not perfect, it is close enough statistically to satisfy equilibrium conditions. Since our population is not a large one, sampling may easily account for the small observed deviations. Our population is therefore probably in equilibrium (that is, at this locus, it is not evolving). At the minimum, what we can say scientifically is that we cannot reject the *null hypothesis*.

Table C-1 Calculating Allele Frequencies in a Hypothetical Population

Observed Data

Genotype	Number of Individuals	Percentage	Number of Alles					
			M	N				
MM	80	40%	160	0				
MN	80	40%	80	80				
NN	40	20%	0	80				
Totals	200	100%	240	+	160	=	400	
		Proportion:	.6	+	.4	=	1	

*Each individual has two alleles. Thus, a person who is *MM* contributes two *M* alleles to the total gene pool. A person who is *MN* contributes one *M* and one *N*. Two hundred individuals, then, have 400 alleles for the *MN* locus.

Observed Allele Frequencies

$M = .6(p)$	
$N = .4(q)$	($p + q$ should equal 1, and they do)

Expected Frequencies

What are the predicted genotypic proportions if genetic equilibrium (no evolution) applies to our population? We simply apply the Hardy-Weinberg formula: $p^2 + 2pq + q^2$.

p^2	=	$(.6)(.6)$	=	.36
$2pq$	=	$2(.6)(.4) = 2(.24)$	=	.48
q^2	=	$(.4)(.4)$	=	.16
Total				1.00

There are only three possible genotypes (*MM:MN:NN*), so the total of the relative proportions should equal 1; as you can see, they do.

Comparing Frequencies

How do the expected frequencies compare with the observed frequencies in our population?

	Expected Frequency	Expected Number of Individuals	Observed Frequency	Actual Number of Individuals with Each Genotype
MM	.36	72	.40	80
MN	.48	96	.40	80
NN	.16	32	.20	40

Glossary

acclimatization Physiological responses to changes in the environment that occur during an individual's lifetime. Such responses may be temporary or permanent, depending on the duration of the environmental change and when in the individual's life it occurs. The capacity for acclimatization may typify an entire species or population, and because it's under genetic influence, it's subject to evolutionary factors such as natural selection and genetic drift.

Acheulian (ash´-oo-lay-en) Pertaining to a stone tool industry from the Early and Middle Pleistocene; characterized by a large proportion of bifacial tools (flaked on both sides). Acheulian tool kits are common in Africa, southwest Asia, and western Europe, but they're thought to be less common elsewhere. Also spelled Acheulean.

adaptation Functional response of organisms or populations to the environment. Adaptation results from evolutionary change (specifically, as a result of natural selection).

adaptive niche An organism's entire way of life: where it lives, what it eats, how it gets food, how it avoids predators, and so on.

adaptive radiation The relatively rapid expansion and diversification of life-forms into new ecological niches.

affiliative behaviors Amicable associations between individuals. Affiliative behaviors, such as grooming, reinforce social bonds and promote group cohesion.

agriculture Cultural activities associated with planting, herding, and processing domesticated species; farming.

allele frequency In a population, the percentage of all the alleles at a locus accounted for by one specific allele.

alleles Alternate forms of a gene. Alleles occur at the same locus on paired chromosomes and thus govern the same trait. However, because they are different, their action may result in different expressions of that trait. The term *allele* is often used synonymously with *gene*.

alluvial Deposited by streams, usually during flood stages.

altruism Behavior that benefits another individual but at some potential risk or cost to oneself.

amino acids Small molecules that are the components of proteins.

analogies Similarities between organisms based strictly on common function, with no assumed common evolutionary descent.

Anasazi (an-ah-saw´-zee) Ancient culture of the southwestern United States, associated with preserved cliff dwellings and masonry pueblo sites.

ancestral Referring to characters inherited by a group of organisms from a remote ancestor and thus not diagnostic of groups (lineages) that diverged after the character first appeared; also called primitive.

Anthropocene The geological epoch during which human behavior became one of the earth's major geomorphological and geological processes.

anthropocentric Viewing nonhuman organisms in terms of human experience and capabilities; emphasizing the importance of humans over everything else.

anthropoids Members of a suborder of Primates, the infraorder Anthropoidea (pronounced "an-throw-poid´-ee-uh"). Traditionally, the suborder includes monkeys, apes, and humans.

anthropology The field of inquiry that studies human culture and evolutionary aspects of human biology; includes cultural anthropology, archaeology, linguistics, and physical anthropology.

anthropometry Measurement of human body parts. When osteologists measure skeletal elements, the term osteometry is often used.

anthropomorphic (*anthro*, meaning "man," and *morph*, meaning "shape") Having or being given humanlike characteristics.

antigens Large molecules found on the surface of cells. Several different loci governing antigens on red and white blood cells are known. (Foreign antigens provoke an immune response in individuals.)

antiquarian Relating to an interest in objects and texts of the past.

anvils Surfaces on which an object such as a palm nut, root, or seed is placed before being struck with another object such as a stone.

arboreal Tree-living; adapted to life in the trees.

archaeobotanical Referring to the analysis and interpretation of the remains of ancient plants recovered from the archaeological record.

archaeological record The material remains of the human past and the physical contexts of these remains (e.g., stratigraphic relationships, association with other remains).

archaeometry Application of the methods of the natural and physical sciences to the investigation of archaeological materials.

Archaic North American archaeological period that follows the end of the Ice Age and traditionally ends with the beginning of the use of ceramics; equivalent to the Mesolithic in the Old World.

argon-argon ($^{40}Ar/^{39}Ar$) method Working on a similar basis as the potassium-argon method, this approach uses the ratio of argon-40 to argon-39 for dating igneous and metamorphic rocks; it offers precision and temporal range advantages for dating some early hominin sites.

artifacts Objects or materials made or modified for use by hominins. The earliest artifacts tend to be tools made of stone or, occasionally, bone.

Aurignacian Pertaining to an Upper Paleolithic stone tool industry in Europe beginning about 40,000 ya.

aurochs European wild oxen, ancestral to domesticated cattle.

australopiths A colloquial name referring to a diverse group of Plio-Pleistocene African hominins. Australopiths are the most abundant and widely distributed of all early hominins and are also the most completely studied.

autonomic Pertaining to physiological responses not under voluntary control. An example in chimpanzees would be the erection of body hair during excitement. Blushing is a human example. Both convey information regarding emotional states, but neither is deliberate, and communication isn't intended.

autosomes All chromosomes except the sex chromosomes.

Aztecs Militaristic people who dominated the Valley of Mexico and surrounding area at the time of the European conquest.

Bandkeramik Literally, "lined pottery"; refers to a Neolithic ceramic ware widely encountered in central Europe and to the culture that produced it.

behavior Anything organisms do that involves action in response to internal or external stimuli; the response of an individual, group, or species to its environment. Such responses may or may not be deliberate, and they aren't necessarily the result of conscious decision making.

behavioral ecology The study of the evolution of behavior, emphasizing the role of ecological factors as agents of natural selection. Behaviors and behavioral patterns have been favored because they increase the reproductive fitness of individuals (i.e., they are adaptive) in specific environmental contexts.

Beringia (bare-in´-jya) The dry-land connection between Asia and America that existed periodically during the Pleistocene epoch.

binocular vision Vision characterized by overlapping visual fields provided by forward-facing eyes. Binocular vision is essential to depth perception.

binomial nomenclature (*binomial*, meaning "two names") In taxonomy, the convention established by Carolus Linnaeus whereby genus and species names are used to refer to species. For example, *Homo sapiens* refers to human beings.

biocultural evolution The mutual, interactive evolution of human biology and culture; the concept that biology makes culture possible and that developing culture further influences the direction of biological evolution; a basic concept in understanding the unique components of human evolution.

biological continuity Refers to a biological continuum—the idea that organisms are related through common ancestry and that traits present in one species are also seen to varying degrees in others. When expressions of a phenomenon continuously grade into one another so that there are no discrete categories, they exist on a continuum. Color is one such phenomenon, and life-forms are another.

biological continuum Refers to the fact that organisms are related through common ancestry and that behaviors and traits seen in one species are also seen in others to varying degrees. (When expressions of a phenomeon continuously grade into one another so that there are no discrete categories, they are said to exist on a continuum. Color is such a phenomenon.)

biological determinism The concept that phenomena, including various aspects of behavior (e.g., intelligence, values, morals) are governed by biological (genetic) factors; the inaccurate association of various behavioral attributes with certain biological traits, such as skin color.

biological species concept A depiction of species as groups of individuals capable of fertile interbreeding but reproductively isolated from other such groups.

biostratigraphy A relative dating technique based on regular changes seen in evolving groups of animals as well as the presence or absence of particular species.

bipedal locomotion Walking on two feet. Walking on two legs is the single most distinctive feature of the hominins.

blade technology Chipped stone toolmaking approach in which blades struck from prepared cores are the main raw material from which tools are made. A blade is a chipped stone flake that is at least twice as long as it is wide.

brachiation Arm swinging, a form of locomotion used by some primates. Brachiation involves hanging from a branch and moving by alternately swinging from one arm to the other.

breeding isolates Populations that are clearly isolated geographically and/or socially from other breeding groups.

burin A small flake tool with a chisel-like end, used to cut bone, antler, and ivory.

carrying capacity In an environment, the maximum population of a specific organism that can be maintained at a steady state.

Çatalhöyük (chaetal´-hae-yook´) A large early Neolithic site in southern Turkey. The name is Turkish for "forked mound."

catastrophism The view that the earth's geological landscape is the result of violent cataclysmic events. This view was promoted by Cuvier, especially in opposition to Lamarck.

centromere The constricted portion of a chromosome. After replication, the two strands of a double-stranded chromosome are joined at the centromere.

cercopithecines (serk-oh-pith´-eh-seens) Members of the subfamily of Old World monkeys that includes baboons, macaques, and guenons.

charnel houses Buildings that hold the bones or bodies of the dead.

Chatelperronian Pertaining to an Upper Paleolithic industry found in France and Spain.

Chavín de Huantar Chavín civic-ceremonial center in the northern highlands of Peru.

Chimor A powerful culture that dominated the northern Peruvian coast between about 1,000 and 500 ya.

Chordata The phylum of the animal kingdom that includes vertebrates.

chromosomes Discrete structures, composed of DNA and protein, found only in the nuclei of cells. Chromosomes are visible only under magnification during certain stages of cell division.

city-states Urban centers that form autonomous sociopolitical units.

civilization The larger social order that includes states related by language, traditions, history, economic ties, and other shared cultural aspects.

clade A group of organisms sharing a common ancestor. The group includes the common ancestor and all descendants.

cladistics An approach to classification that attempts to make rigorous evolutionary interpretations based solely on analysis of certain types of homologous characters (those considered to be derived characters).

cladogram A chart showing evolutionary relationships as determined by cladistic analysis. It's based solely on interpretation of shared derived characters. It contains no time component and does not imply ancestor-descendant relationships.

classification In biology, the ordering of organisms into categories, such as orders, families, and genera, to show evolutionary relationships.

climatic maximum Episode of higher average annual temperatures that affected much of the globe for several millennia after the end of the last Ice Age; also known as the

altithermal in the western United States or *hypsithermal* in the East.

clones A clone is an organism that is genetically identical to another organism. The term may also be used to refer to genetically identical DNA segments and molecules.

Clovis North American archaeological complex characterized by distinctive fluted projectile points, dating to roughly 13,500–13,000 ya; once widely believed to be representative of specialized big game hunters, who may have driven many late Pleistocene species into extinction.

codominance The expression of both alleles in heterozygotes. In this situation, neither allele is dominant or recessive; thus, both influence the phenotype.

collectors Hunter-gatherers who tend to stay in one place for a long time. A task group may range far afield to hunt and collect food and other resources that are brought back to camp and shared among its inhabitants. Valued food resources are commonly stored in anticipation of future use.

colobines (kole´-uh-bines) Members of the subfamily of Old World monkeys that includes the African colobus monkeys and Asian langurs.

communication Any act that conveys information, in the form of a message, to another individual. Frequently, the result of communication is a change in the behavior of the recipient. Communication may not be deliberate but may instead be the result of involuntary processes or a secondary consequence of an intentional action.

complementary Referring to the fact that DNA bases form base pairs in a precise manner. For example, adenine can bond only to thymine. These two bases are said to be complementary because one requires the other to form a complete DNA base pair.

composite tool Minimally, a tool made of several pieces. For example, a prehistoric knife typically included a handle or shaft, a chipped stone blade, and binding materials such as glue or sinew to hold the blade firmly in place.

contexts The spatial and temporal associations of artifacts and features in an archaeological site. Archaeologists distinguish between *primary context*, which simply means that it has not been disturbed since it was originally deposited, and *secondary context*, which has been disturbed and redeposited.

continental drift The movement of continents on sliding plates of the earth's surface. As a result, the positions of large landmasses have shifted drastically during the earth's history.

coprolites Preserved fecal material, which can be studied for what the contents reveal about diet and health.

Cordilleran (cor-dee-yair´-an) Pleistocene ice sheet originating in mountains of western North America.

core area The portion of a home range containing the highest concentration and most reliable supplies of food and water. The core area is defended.

craft specializations An economic system in which some individuals do not engage in food production, but devote their labor to the production of other goods and services. Examples include potters, carpenters, smiths, shamen, oracles, and teachers.

cross-dating Relative dating method that estimates the age of artifacts and features based on their similarities with comparable materials from dated contexts.

cultigen A plant that is wholly dependent on humans; a domesticate.

cultivars Wild plants fostered by human efforts to make them more productive.

culture All aspects of human adaptation, including technology, traditions, language, religion, and social roles. Culture is a set of learned behaviors; it is transmitted from one generation to the next through learning and not by biological or genetic means.

cuneiform (*cuneus*, meaning "wedge") Wedge-shaped writing of ancient Mesopotamia.

cusps The bumps on the chewing surface of premolars and molars.

cytoplasm The portion of the cell contained within the cell membrane, excluding the nucleus. The cytoplasm consists of a semi-fluid material and contains numerous structures involved in cell function.

Dalton Late or transitional Paleo-Indian projectile point type that dates between 10,000 and 8,000 ya in the eastern United States..

data (*sing.,* datum) Facts from which conclusions can be drawn; scientific information.

demographic Pertaining to the size or rate of increase of human populations.

dendrochronology Archaeological dating method based on the study of yearly growth rings in ancient wood.

dental caries Erosions in teeth caused by decay; cavities.

dental formula Numerical device that indicates the number of each type of tooth in each side of the upper and lower jaws.

deoxyribonucleic acid (DNA) The double-stranded molecule that contains the genetic code. DNA is a main component of chromosomes.

derived (modified) Referring to characters that are modified from the ancestral condition and thus diagnostic of particular evolutionary lineages.

desertification Any process resulting in the formation or growth of deserts.

diffusion The idea that widely distributed cultural traits originated in a single center and spread from one group to another through contact or exchange.

directional change In a genetic sense, the nonrandom change in allele frequencies caused by natural selection. The change is directional because the frequencies of alleles consistently increase or decrease (they change in one direction), depending on environmental circumstances and the selective pressures involved.

discoid technique A prepared-core technique in which flakes are struck toward the center of the stone core; greater efficiency of raw material use than Levallois; also called "radial core" technique.

displays Sequences of repetitious behaviors that serve to communicate emotional states. Nonhuman primate displays are most frequently associated with reproductive or competitive types of behavior. Examples include chest slapping in gorillas and, in male chimpanzees, dragging and waving branches while charging and threatening other animals.

diurnal Active during the day.

divination Foretelling the future.

domestication A state of interdependence between humans and selected plant or animal species. Intense selection activity induces permanent genetic change, enhancing a species' value to humans.

dominance hierarchies Systems of social organization wherein individuals within a group are ranked relative to one another. Higher-ranking animals have greater access to preferred food items and mating partners than lower-ranking individuals.

dominant Describing a trait governed by an allele that can be expressed in the presence of another, different allele (i.e., in heterozygotes). Dominant alleles prevent the expression of recessive alleles in heterozygotes. (*Note:* This is the definition of *complete* dominance.)

ecofacts Natural materials that give environmental information about a site. Examples include plant and animal remains discarded as food waste and also pollen grains preserved in the soil.

ecological niche The position of a species within its physical and biological environments. A species' ecological niche is defined by such components as diet, terrain, vegetation, type of predators, relationships with other species, and activity patterns, and each niche is unique to a given species. Together, ecological niches make up an ecosystem.

ecological Pertaining to the relationships between organisms and all aspects of their environment (temperature, predators, non-predators, vegetation, availability of food and water, types of food, disease organisms, parasites, etc.).

El Niño Periodic climatic instability, related to temporary warming of Pacific Ocean waters, which may influence storm patterns and precipitation for several years.

empathy The ability to identify with the feelings and thoughts of another individual.

empirical Relying on experiment or observation; from the Latin *empiricus*, meaning "experienced."

enculturation The process by which individuals, generally as children, learn the values and beliefs of the family, peer groups, and society in which they are raised.

endemic Continuously present in a population.

endothermic (*endo,* meaning "within" or "internal") Able to maintain internal body temperature by producing energy through metabolic processes within cells; characteristic of mammals, birds, and perhaps some dinosaurs.

Enlightenment An eighteenth-century philosophical movement in western Europe that assumed a knowable order to the natural world and the interpretive value of reason as the primary means of identifying and explaining this order.

enzymes Specialized proteins that initiate and direct chemical reactions in the body.

Epipaleolithic (*epi,* meaning "after") Late Pleistocene and early Holocene period of foragers and collectors in the Near East and adjacent parts of Asia.

epochs Categories of the geological time scale; subdivisions of periods. In the Cenozoic era, epochs include the Paleocene, Eocene, Oligocene, Miocene, and Pliocene (from the Tertiary period) and the Pleistocene and Holocene (from the Quaternary period).

estrus Period of sexual receptivity in female mammals (except humans), correlated with ovulation. When used as an adjective, the word is spelled "estrous."

ethnoarchaeologists Archaeologists who use ethnographic methods to study modern peoples so that they can better understand and explain patterning in the archaeological record.

ethnoarchaeology Approach used by archaeologists to gain insights into the past by studying contemporary people.

ethnocentric Viewing other cultures from the inherently biased perspective of one's own culture. Ethnocentrism often results in other cultures being seen as inferior to one's own.

ethnographies Detailed descriptive studies of human societies. In cultural anthropology, *ethnography* is traditionally the study of non-Western societies.

eugenics The philosophy of "race improvement" through the forced sterilization of members of some groups and increased reproduction among others; an overly simplified, often racist view that's now discredited.

evolution A change in the genetic structure of a population from one generation to the next. The term is also frequently used to refer to the appearance of a new species.

evolutionary systematics A traditional approach to classification (and evolutionary interpretation) in which presumed ancestors and descendants are traced in time by analysis of homologous characters.

experimental archaeology Research that attempts to replicate ancient technologies and construction procedures to test hypotheses about past activities.

faience (fay-ahnz´) Glassy material, usually of blue-green color, shaped into beads, amulets, and figurines by ancient Egyptians.

features Products of human activity that cannot be removed from the archaeological record as a single discrete entity. Examples include hearths, human burials, and the remains of a Paleolithic hut.

fission-track dating Dating technique based on the natural radiometric decay (fission) of uranium-238 atoms, which leaves traces in certain geological materials.

fitness Pertaining to natural selection, a measure of the *relative* reproductive success of individuals. Fitness can be measured by an individual's genetic contribution to the next generation compared with that of other individuals. The terms *genetic fitness*, *reproductive fitness*, and *differential reproductive success* are also used.

fixity of species The notion that species, once created, can never change; an idea diametrically opposed to theories of biological evolution.

flexed The position of the body in a bent orientation, with arms and legs drawn up to the chest.

fluted point A biface or projectile point having had long, thin flakes removed from each face to prepare the base for hafting, or attachment to a shaft.

Folsom Paleo-Indian archaeological complex of the southern Great Plains, around 12,500 ya, characterized by fluted projectile points used for hunting now-extinct bison.

foragers Hunter-gatherers who live in small groups that move camp frequently to take advantage of fresh resources as they come into season, with few resources stored in anticipation of future use.

forensic anthropology An applied anthropological approach dealing with legal matters. Forensic anthropologists work with coroners and law enforcement agencies in the recovery, analysis, and identification of human remains.

fossils Traces or remnants of organisms found in geological beds on the earth's surface.

founder effect A type of genetic drift in which allele frequencies are altered in small populations that are taken from, or are remnants of, larger populations.

frugivorous (fru-give´-or-us) Having a diet composed primarily of fruit.

gametes Reproductive cells (eggs and sperm in animals) developed from precursor cells in ovaries and testes.

gene A sequence of DNA bases that specifies the order of amino acids in an entire protein, a portion of a protein, or any functional product. A gene may be made up of hundreds or thousands of DNA bases.

gene flow Exchange of genes between populations.

gene pool The total complement of genes shared by the reproductive members of a population.

genetic drift Evolutionary changes—that is, changes in allele frequencies—produced by random factors. Genetic drift is a result of small population size.

genetics The study of gene structure and action and of the patterns of inheritance of traits from parent to offspring. Genetic mechanisms are the underlying foundation for evolutionary change.

genome The entire genetic makeup of an individual or species.

genotype The genetic makeup of an individual. Genotype can refer to an organism's entire genetic makeup or to the alleles at a particular locus.

genus (*pl.*, genera) A group of closely related species.

geological time scale The organization of earth history into eras, periods, and epochs; commonly used by geologists and paleoanthropologists.

Gilgamesh Semilegendary king and culture hero of early Uruk, reputed to have had many marvelous adventures.

glaciations Climatic intervals when continental ice sheets cover much of the northern continents. Glaciations are associated with colder temperatures in northern latitudes and more arid conditions in southern latitudes, most notably in Africa.

glyphs Carved or incised symbolic figures.

Great Basin Rugged, dry plateau between the mountains of California and Utah, comprising Nevada, western Utah, southern Oregon, and Idaho.

grooming Picking through fur to remove dirt, parasites, and other materials that may be present. Social grooming is common among primates and reinforces social relationships.

habitual bipedalism Bipedal locomotion as the form of locomotion shown by hominins most of the time.

haft To equip a tool or implement with a handle or hilt.

half-life The time period in which one-half the amount of a radioactive isotope is chemically converted to a daughter product. For example, after 1.25 billion years, half the potassium-40 remains; after 2.5 billion years, one-fourth remains.

Hammurabi (ham-oo-rah´-bee) Early Babylonian king, ca. 1800–1750 B.C.

Haplorhini (hap'-lo-rin-ee) The primate suborder that includes tarsiers, monkeys, apes, and humans.

Harappa (ha-rap´-pa) A fortified city in the Indus Valley of northeastern Pakistan.

"hard hammer" percussion A direct percussion method of making stone tools that uses one rock as a hammer to knock flakes from another rock that serves as a core.

Hardy-Weinberg equilibrium The mathematical relationship expressing—under conditions in which no evolution is occurring—the predicted distribution of alleles in populations; the central theorem of population genetics.

hemispheres The two halves of the cerebrum that are connected by a dense mass of fibers. (The cerebrum is the large rounded outer portion of the brain.)

hemoglobin A protein molecule that occurs in red blood cells and binds to oxygen molecules.

heterodont Having different kinds of teeth; characteristic of mammals, whose teeth consist of incisors, canines, premolars, and molars.

heterozygous Having different alleles at a particular locus on the members of a chromosome pair.

hieroglyphics (*hiero*, meaning "sacred," and *glyphein*, meaning "carving") The picture-writing of ancient Egypt.

historical archaeologists Archaeologists who study past societies for which a contemporary written record also exists.

Hohokam (ho-ho-kahm´) Prehistoric farming culture of southern Arizona.

Holocene The geological epoch during which we now live. The Holocene follows the Pleistocene epoch and began roughly 11,000–10,000 ya.

home-based foragers Hominins that hunt, scavenge, or collect food and raw materials from the general locality where they habitually live and bring these materials back to some central or home base site to be shared with other members of their coresiding group.

homeobox (Hox) genes An evolutionarily ancient family of regulatory genes. *Hox* genes direct the segmentation and patterning of the overall body plan during embryonic development.

homeostasis A condition of balance, or stability, within a biological system, maintained by the interaction of physiological mechanisms that compensate for changes (both external and internal).

hominin A member of the Tribe Hominini, the evolutionary group that includes modern humans and now-extinct bipedal relatives.

hominoids Members of the primate superfamily (Hominoidea) that includes apes and humans.

homologies Similarities between organisms based on descent from a common ancestor

homoplasy (*homo*, meaning "same," and *plasy*, meaning "growth") The separate evolutionary development of similar characteristics in different groups of organisms..

homozygous Having the same allele at the same locus on both members of a chromosome pair.

honing complex The shearing of a large upper canine with the first lower premolar, with the wear leading to honing of the surfaces of both teeth. This anatomical pattern is typical of most Old World anthropoids, but is mostly absent in hominins.

hormones Substances (usually proteins) that are produced by specialized cells and travel to other parts of the body, where they influence chemical reactions and regulate various cellular functions.

horticulture Farming method in which only hand tools are used; typical of most early Neolithic societies.

Huaca del Sol (wah´-ka dell sole) Massive adobe pyramid built at Moche, in northern Peru.

Human Genome Project An international effort that has mapped the entire human genome.

hunter-gatherers People who make their living by hunting, fishing, and gathering their food and not by producing it.

hybrids Offspring of mixed ancestry; heterozygotes.

hypothesis (*pl.,* hypotheses) A provisional explanation of a phenomenon. Hypotheses require repeated testing.

hypoxia Lack of oxygen. Hypoxia can refer to reduced amounts of available oxygen in the atmosphere due to lower barometric pressure or to insufficient amounts of oxygen in the body.

Inca People whose sophisticated culture dominated Peru at the time of the European arrival; also, the term for that people's highest ruler; also spelled Inka.

index fossils Fossil remains of known age, used to estimate the age of the geological stratum in which they are found. For example, extinct marine arthropods called trilobites can be used as an index fossil of Cambrian and Ordovician geological formations.

indirect percussion The method of driving off blades and flakes from a prepared core using a bone or antler punch to press off a thin flake.

intelligence Mental capacity; ability to learn, reason, or comprehend and interpret information, facts, relationships, and meanings; the capacity to solve problems, whether through the application of previously acquired knowledge or through insight.

interglacials Climatic intervals when continental ice sheets are retreating, eventually becoming much reduced in size. Interglacials in northern latitudes are associated with warmer temperatures, while in southern latitudes the climate becomes wetter.

interspecific Between species; refers to variation beyond that seen within the same species to include additional aspects seen between two or more different species.

intragroup Within the group as opposed to between groups (intergroup).

intraspecific Within species; refers to variation seen within the same species.

ischial callosities Patches of tough, hard skin on the buttocks of Old World monkeys and chimpanzees.

K-selected Pertaining to K-selection, an adaptive strategy whereby individuals produce relatively few offspring in whom they invest increased parental care. Although only a few infants are born, chances of survival are increased for each one because of parental investments in time and energy. Birds, elephants, and canids (wolves, coyotes, and dogs) are examples of K-selected nonprimate species.

Kaminaljuyú (cam-en-awl-hoo-yoo´) Major prehistoric Maya site located at Guatemala City.

Kebaran Late Pleistocene hunter-gatherers of the eastern Mediterranean region and Levant.

kivas Underground chambers or rooms used for gatherings and ceremonies by pueblo dwellers.

lactase persistence In adults, the continued production of lactase, the enzyme that breaks down lactose (milk sugar). This allows adults in some human populations to digest fresh milk products. The discontinued production of lactase in adults leads to lactose intolerance and the inability to digest fresh milk.

language A standardized system of arbitrary vocal sounds, written symbols, and gestures used in communication.

large-bodied hominoids Those hominoids including the great apes (orangutans, chimpanzees, gorillas) and hominins, as well as all ancestral forms back to the time of divergence from small-bodied hominoids (i.e., the gibbon lineage).

Late Pleistocene The portion of the Pleistocene epoch beginning 125,000 ya and ending approximately 10,000 ya.

Laurentide (lah-ren´-tid) Pleistocene ice sheet centered in the Hudson Bay region and extending across much of eastern Canada and the northern United States.

life history traits Characteristics and developmental stages that influence reproductive rates. Examples include longevity, age at sexual maturity, and length of time between births.

locus (*pl.*, loci) (lo´-kus, lo-sigh´) The position on a chromosome where a given gene occurs. The term is sometimes used interchangeably with *gene*.

loess (luss) Fine-grained soil composed of glacially pulverized rock, deposited by the wind.

Lower Paleolithic A unit of archaeological time that begins about 2.6 mya with the earliest identified tools made by hominins and ends around 200,000 years ago.

macroevolution Changes produced only after many generations, such as the appearance of a new species.

Magdalenian A late Upper Paleolithic stone tool industry in Europe that dates to 17,000–11,000 ya.

manioc Cassava, a starchy edible root crop of the tropics.

material culture The physical manifestations of human activities, such as tools, art, and structures. As the most durable aspects of culture, material remains make up the majority of archaeological evidence of past societies.

matrilines Groups that consist of a female, her daughters, and their offspring. Matrilineal groups are common in macaques.

Maya Mesoamerican culture consisting of regional kingdoms and known for its art and architectural accomplishments; also, Native American ethnic group of southern Mexico, Guatemala, and Belize.

megafauna Literally, "large animals," those weighing over 100 pounds.

meiosis Cell division in specialized cells in ovaries and testes. Meiosis involves two divisions and results in four daughter cells, each containing only half the original number of chromosomes. These cells can develop into gametes.

Mendelian traits Characteristics that are influenced by alleles at only one genetic locus. Examples include many blood types, such as ABO. Many genetic disorders, including sickle-cell anemia and Tay-Sachs disease, are also Mendelian traits.

Mesoamerica (*meso*, meaning "middle") Geographical and cultural region from central Mexico to northwestern Costa Rica; formerly called "Middle America" in the archaeological literature.

Mesolithic (*meso*, meaning "middle," and *lith*, meaning "stone") An early postglacial period of hunter-gatherers, especially in northwestern Europe.

Mesopotamia (*meso*, meaning "middle," and *potamos*, meaning "river") Land between the Tigris and Euphrates rivers, mostly included in modern-day Iraq.

metabolism The chemical processes within cells that break down nutrients and release energy for the body to use. (When nutrients are broken down into their component parts, such as amino acids, energy is released and made available for the cell to use.)

Mexica (meh-shee´-ka) Original name by which the Aztecs were known before their rise to power.

microevolution Small changes occurring within species, such as a change in allele frequencies.

middens Archaeological sites or features within sites formed largely by the accumulation of domestic waste.

Middle Paleolithic Cultural period that began about 200,000 ya and ended around 40,000–30,000 ya. Roughly the same period in sub-Saharan Africa is called the Middle Stone Age.

Middle Pleistocene The portion of the Pleistocene epoch beginning 780,000 ya and ending 125,000 ya.

millet Small-grained cereal grasses native to Asia and Africa.

milpa Mesoamerican agricultural system of intercropping in which maize, beans, squash and other plants are planted together. Milpas are typically prepared by cutting the forest and bushes to create a small field, farming it through several crop cycles, and then letting it lie fallow for 8 to 10 years.

mineralization The process in which parts of animals (or some plants) become transformed into stone-like structures. Mineralization usually occurs very slowly as water carrying minerals, such as silica or iron, seeps into the tiny spaces within a

bone. In some cases, the original minerals within the bone or tooth can be completely replaced, molecule by molecule, with other minerals.

Mississippian Referring to late prehistoric chiefdoms of the southeastern United States and southern Midwest between roughly 1,100 and 300 ya.

mitochondria (*sing.,* mitochondrion) (my´-tow-kond´-dree-uh) Structures contained within the cytoplasm of eukaryotic cells that convert energy, derived from nutrients, to a form that is used by the cell.

mitochondrial DNA (mtDNA) DNA found in mitochondria. mtDNA is inherited only from the mother.

mitosis Simple cell division; the process by which somatic cells divide to produce two identical daughter cells.

Moche (moh´-chay) Regional state, city, and valley of the same name in northern Peru.

Mogollon (mo-go-yohn´) Prehistoric village culture of northern Mexico and southern Arizona/New Mexico.

Mohenjo-Daro (mo-henjo-dar´-o) An early Indus Valley city in south-central Pakistan.

molecule A structure made up of two or more atoms. Molecules can combine with other molecules to form more complex structures.

mosaic evolution A pattern of evolution in which the rate of evolution in one functional system varies from that in other systems. For example, in hominin evolution, the dental system, locomotor system, and neurological system (especially the brain) all evolved at markedly different rates.

Mousterian A Middle Paleolithic stone tool industry associated with Neandertals and some modern *H. sapiens* groups.

multidisciplinary Pertaining to research that involves the cooperation of experts from several scientific fields (i.e., disciplines).

mutation A change in DNA. The term can refer to changes in DNA bases as well

as changes in chromosome number or structure.

natal group The group in which an animal is born and raised. (*Natal* pertains to birth.)

Natufian Referring to collector-type hunter-gatherers who established sedentary settlements in parts of the Near East after 12,000 ya.

natural selection The most critical mechanism of evolutionary change, first articulated by Charles Darwin; refers to genetic change in the frequencies of certain traits in populations due to differential reproductive success between individuals.

neocortex The more recently evolved portion of the brain that is involved in higher mental functions and composed of areas that integrate incoming information from different sensory organs.

Neolithic (*neo*, meaning "new," and *lith*, meaning "stone") New Stone Age; period of farmers.

Neolithic revolution Childe's term for the far-reaching consequences of food production.

neural tube In early embryonic development, the anatomical structure that develops to form the brain and spinal cord.

nocturnal Active during the night.

nuchal torus (nuke´-ul) (*nucha*, meaning "neck") A projection of bone in the back of the cranium where neck muscles attach. These muscles hold up the head.

nucleotides Basic units of the DNA molecule, composed of a sugar, a phosphate unit, and one of four DNA bases.

nucleus A structure (organelle) found in all eukaryotic cells. The nucleus contains chromosomes (nuclear DNA).

oases (*sing.,* oasis) Permanent springs or water holes in an arid region.

obligate bipedalism Bipedalism as the *only* form of hominin terrestrial locomotion. Since major anatomical changes in the spine, pelvis, and lower limb are required for bipedal locomotion, once hominins adapted this mode of locomotion, other forms of locomotion on the ground became impossible.

olfaction The sense of smell.

Olmec Prehistoric chiefdom in the Gulf Coast lowlands of Veracruz and Tabasco, Mexico, between 3,200 and 2,400 ya.

omnivorous Having a diet consisting of many food types, such as plant materials, meat, and insects.

optically stimulated luminescence A new (and still developing) dating method that estimates the amount of time that has elapsed since grains of quartz or feldspar were last exposed to daylight. Datable samples can be as small as a single grain.

osteology The study of skeletal material. Human osteology focuses on the interpretation of the skeletal remains of past groups. Some of the same techniques are used in paleoanthropology to study early hominins.

Ounjougou (won-joo-goo) A site populated by African hunter-gatherers who made early use of wild cereal grasses on the southern edge of the Sahara between 12,000 and 9,000 ya.

Paleo-Indian (*paleo*, meaning "ancient") Referring to early hunter-gatherers who occupied the Americas from about 13,500 to 10,000 ya.

paleoanthropology The interdisciplinary approach to the study of earlier hominins—their chronology, physical structure, archaeological remains, habitats, etc.

paleomagnetism Dating method using known shifts in the earth's magnetic pole to estimate the age of magnetically charged minerals contained in certain kinds of archaeological features.

paleontologists Scientists whose study of ancient life-forms is based on fossilized remains of extinct animals and plants.

paleopathology The branch of osteology that studies the traces of disease and injury in human skeletal (or, occasionally, mummified) remains.

paleospecies Species defined from fossil evidence, often covering a long time span.

pandemic An infectious disease epidemic that spreads rapidly through a region, potentially worldwide. A worldwide pandemic becomes much more likely if the disease is "new" to humans (i.e., all populations are vulnerable), spreading quickly owing to rapid means of intercontinental transportation.

pathogens Any agents, especially microorganisms such as viruses, bacteria, or fungi, that infect a host and cause disease.

pharaoh Title of the ruler of ancient Egypt.

phenotypes The observable or detectable physical characteristics of an organism; the detectable expressions of genotypes.

phylogenetic tree A chart showing evolutionary relationships as determined by evolutionary systematics. It contains a time component and implies ancestor-descendant relationships.

phytoliths (*phyto*, meaning "plant," and *lith*, meaning "stone") Microscopic silica structures formed in the cells of many plants.

placental A type (subclass) of mammal. During the Cenozoic, placentals became the most widespread and numerous mammals and today are represented by upward of 20 orders, including the primates.

Plano Great Plains bison-hunting culture of 11,000–9,000 ya, which employed narrow, unfluted points.

plant macrofossils Plant parts such as seeds, nutshells, and stems that have been preserved in the archaeological record and are large enough to be clearly visible to the naked eye.

plant microfossils Small to microscopic plant remains, most falling in a range of 10 to 100 micrometers (μm), or roughly the size of individual grains of wheat flour in the bag from your grocer's shelf.

Pleistocene The epoch of the Cenozoic from 1.8 mya until 10,000 ya. Frequently referred to as the Ice Age, this epoch is associated with continental glaciations in northern latitudes.

Plio-Pleistocene Pertaining to the Pliocene and first half of the Pleistocene, a time range of 5–1 mya. For this time period, numerous fossil hominins have been found in Africa.

polities The political organizations of societies or groups.

pollen Microscopic grains containing the male gametes of seed-producing plants.

polyandry A mating system wherein a female continuously associates with more than one male (usually two or three) with whom she mates. Among nonhuman primates, polyandry is seen only in marmosets and tamarins. It also occurs in a few human societies.

polychrome Many-colored.

polygenic Referring to traits that are influenced by genes at two or more loci. Examples of such traits are stature, skin color, and eye color. Many polygenic traits are also influenced by environmental factors.

polygynous Pertaining to polygyny, a mating system in which males, and in some cases females, have several mating partners.

polymerase chain reaction (PCR) A method of producing copies of a DNA segment using the enzyme DNA polymerase.

polymorphisms Loci with more than one allele. Polymorphisms can be expressed in the phenotype as the result of gene action (as in ABO), or they can exist solely at the DNA level within noncoding regions.

polytypic Referring to species composed of populations that differ in the expression of one or more traits.

population Within a species, a community of individuals where mates are usually found.

population genetics The study of the frequency of alleles, genotypes, and pheno-types in populations from a microevolution-ary perspective.

postcranial Referring to all or part of the skeleton not including the skull. The term originates from the fact that in quadrupeds, the body is in back of the head; the term literally means "behind the head."

potassium-argon (K/Ar) method Dating technique based on accumulation of argon-40 gas as a by-product of the radiometric decay of potassium-40 in volcanic materials; used especially for dating early hominin sites in East Africa.

potlatch Ceremonial feasting and gift-giving event among Northwest Coast Indians.

prehistory The several million years between the emergence of bipedal homi-nins and the availability of written records.

prepared-core method Pertaining to stone cores that a toolmaker shapes into a preplanned form before striking flakes from it; enables predictable flake shape and thickness; can be efficient in the use of raw materials.

primates Members of the mammalian order Primates (pronounced "pry-may´-tees"), which includes lemurs, lorises, tarsiers, monkeys, apes, and humans.

primatology The study of the biology and behavior of nonhuman primates (prosimians, monkeys, and apes).

principle of independent assortment The distribution of one pair of alleles into gam-etes does not influence the distribution of another pair. The genes controlling different traits are inherited independently of one another.

principle of segregation Genes (alleles) occur in pairs because chromosomes occur in pairs. During gamete production, the members of each gene pair separate, so that each gamete contains one member of each pair. During fertilization, the full number of chromosomes is restored, and members of gene pairs (alleles) are reunited.

principle of superpositioning In a strati-graphic sequence, the lower layers were deposited before the upper layers. Or, sim-ply put, the stuff on top of a heap was put there last.

protein synthesis The assembly of chains of amino acids into functional protein molecules. The process is directed by DNA.

proteins Three-dimensional molecules that serve a wide variety of functions through their ability to bind to other molecules.

Proto-Uto-Aztecan Common ancestor of Uto-Aztecan, a widespread family of Native American languages found from the west-ern United States to south-central Mexico.

protohominins The earliest members of the hominin lineage, as yet only poorly repre-sented in the fossil record; thus, the recon-struction of their structure and behavior is largely hypothetical.

public archaeology A broad term that cov-ers archaeological research conducted for the public good as part of cultural resource management and heritage management programs; a major growth area of world archaeology.

pueblos Spanish for "town"; multiroom resi-dence structures built by village farmers in the American Southwest; when spelled with an uppercase P, the several cultures that built and lived in such villages.

Qin Shi Huangdi (chin-shee-huangdee) First emperor of a unified China.

quadrupedal Using all four limbs to sup-port the body during locomotion; the basic mammalian (and primate) form of locomotion.

quantitatively Pertaining to measurements of quantity and including such properties as size, number, and capacity.

quinoa (keen-wah´) Seed-bearing member of the genus *Chenopodium*, cultivated by early Peruvians.

r-selected Pertaining to r-selection, a repro-ductive strategy that emphasizes relatively large numbers of offspring and reduced

parental care compared with K-selected species. *K-selection* and *r-selection* are rela-tive terms; for example, mice are r-selected compared with primates but K-selected compared with fish.

rachis The short stem by which an indi-vidual seed attaches to the main stalk of a plant as it develops.

radiocarbon dating Method for deter-mining the age of organic archaeological materials by measuring the decay of the radioactive isotope of carbon, ^{14}C; also known as carbon-14 dating.

radiometric decay A measure of the rate at which certain radioactive isotopes disintegrate.

recessive Describing a trait that is not expressed in heterozygotes; also refers to the allele that governs the trait. For a recessive allele to be expressed, there must be two copies of the allele (i.e., the individual must be homozygous).

recombination The exchange of DNA between paired chromosomes during meiosis; also called *crossing over*.

regulatory genes Genes that code for the production of proteins that can influence the action of other genes. Many are active only during certain stages of development.

reproductive strategies Behaviors or behavioral complexes that have been favored by natural selection to increase indi-vidual reproductive success. The behaviors need not be deliberate, and they often vary considerably between males and females.

reproductive success The number of off-spring an individual produces and rears to reproductive age; an individual's genetic contribution to the next generation.

rhinarium (rine-air´-ee-um) The moist, hairless pad at the end of the nose seen in most mammalian species. The rhinarium enhances an animal's ability to smell.

ribonucleic acid (RNA) A molecule similar in structure to DNA. Three different single-stranded forms of RNA are essential to protein synthesis.

sagittal crest A ridge of bone that runs down the middle of the cranium like a short Mohawk. This serves as the attachment for the large temporal muscles, indicating strong chewing.

science A body of knowledge gained through observation and experimentation; from the Latin *scientia*, meaning "knowledge."

scientific method An approach to research whereby a problem is identified, a hypothesis (or hypothetical explanation) is stated, and that hypothesis is tested through the collection and analysis of data.

scientific testing The precise repetition of an experiment or expansion of observed data to provide verification; the procedure by which hypotheses and theories are verified, modified, or discarded.

sedentary Residing in a single location for most or all of the year.

selective pressures Factors in the environment that influence reproductive success in individuals.

sensory modalities Different forms of sensation (e.g., touch, pain, pressure, heat, cold, vision, taste, hearing, and smell).

seriation Relative dating method that orders artifacts into a temporal series based on their similar attributes or the frequency of these attributes.

sex chromosomes The X and Y chromosomes. The Y chromosome determines maleness; in its absence, an embryo develops as a female.

sexual dimorphism Differences in physical characteristics between males and females of the same species. For example, humans are slightly sexually dimorphic for body size, with males being taller, on average, than females of the same population. Sexual dimorphism is very pronounced in many species, such as gorillas.

sexual selection A type of natural selection that operates on only one sex within a species. It's the result of competition for mates, and it can lead to sexual dimorphism with regard to one or more traits.

shamanism Traditional practices that mediate between the world of humans and the world of spirits.

Shang The first historic civilization in northern China; also called the Yin dynasty.

shared derived Relating to specific character traits shared in common between two life-forms and considered the most useful for making evolutionary interpretations.

site survey The process of discovering the location of archaeological sites; sometimes called site reconnaissance.

sites Locations of past human activity, often associated with artifacts and features.

slash-and-burn agriculture A traditional land-clearing practice involving the cutting and burning of trees and vegetation. In many areas, fields are abandoned after a few years and clearing occurs elsewhere.

social stratification Class structure or hierarchy, usually based on political, economic, or social standing.

social structure The composition, size, and sex ratio of a group of animals. The social structure of a species is, in part, the result of natural selection in a specific habitat, and it guides individual interactions and social relationships.

society A group of people who share a common culture.

"soft hammer" percussion A direct percussion method of making stone tools that uses a resilient hammer or billet to gain greater control over the length, width, and thickness of flakes driven from a core.

Solutrean An Upper Paleolithic stone tool industry in southwestern France and Spain that dates to 21,000–18,000 ya.

somatic cells Basically, all the cells in the body except those involved with reproduction.

sorghum A cereal grass. Some subspecies are grown for food grains, others for their sweet, juicy stalk.

speciation The process by which a new species evolves from an earlier species. Speciation is the most basic process in macroevolution.

species A group of organisms that can interbreed to produce fertile offspring. Members of one species are reproductively isolated from members of all other species (i.e., they can't mate with them to produce fertile offspring).

spina bifida A condition in which the arch of one or more vertebrae fails to fuse and form a protective barrier around the spinal cord. This can lead to spinal cord damage and paralysis.

starch grains Subcellular structures that form in all plant parts and can be classified by family or genus; particularly abundant in seeds and tubers.

state A governmental entity that persists by politically controlling a territory; examples include most modern nations.

stelae (*sing.*, stela) (stee´-lee) Upright posts or stones, often bearing inscriptions. codices (*sing.*, codex) Illustrated books.

stereoscopic vision The condition whereby visual images are, to varying degrees, superimposed. This provides for depth perception, or viewing the external environment in three dimensions. Stereoscopic vision is partly a function of structures in the brain.

stratigraphic Pertaining to the depositional levels, or strata, of an archaeological site.

stratigraphy Study of the sequential layering of deposits.

stratum (*pl.*, strata) A single layer of soil or rock; sometimes called a level.

Strepsirhini (strep'-sir-in-ee) The primate suborder that includes lemurs and lorises.

stress In a physiological context, any factor that acts to disrupt homeostasis; more precisely, the body's response to any factor that threatens its ability to maintain homeostasis.

Sumerians Earliest civilization of Mesopotamia.

surrogate Substitute. In this case, the infant monkeys were reared with artificial substitute mothers.

symbiosis (*syn,* meaning "together," and *bios,* meaning "life") Mutually advantageous association of two different organisms; also known as *mutualism.*

taphonomy (*taphos,* meaning "grave") The study of how bones and other materials came to be buried in the earth and preserved as fossils. A taphonomist studies the processes of sedimentation, the action of streams, preservation properties of bone, and carnivore disturbance factors.

taro Species of a tropical plant with an edible starchy root.

taxonomy The branch of science concerned with the rules of classifying organisms on the basis of evolutionary relationships.

Tenochtitlán (tay-nosh-teet-lahn´) Aztec capital, built on the future site of Mexico City.

Teotihuacán (tay-oh-tee-wah-cahn´) Earliest city-state to dominate the Valley of Mexico. It became one of the largest urban centers in the New World up to the nineteenth century.

territorial Pertaining to the protection of all or a part of the area occupied by an animal or group of animals. Territorial behaviors range from scent marking to outright attacks on intruders.

territorial state A form of state political organization with multiple administrative centers and one or more capitals. The cities tended to house the elite and administrative classes, and food producers usually lived and worked in the surrounding hinterland.

territories Portions of an individual's or group's home range that are actively defended against intrusion, especially by members of the same species.

theories Well-substantiated explanations of natural phenomena, supported by hypothesis testing and by evidence gathered over time. Theories also allow scientists to make predictions about as yet unobserved phenomena. Some theories are so well established that no new evidence is likely to alter them substantially.

thermoluminescence (TL) (ther-mo-loo-min-es´-ence) Technique for dating certain archaeological materials, such as ceramics, that release stored energy of radioactive decay as light upon reheating.

till plains Accumulations of stones, boulders, mud, sand, and silt deposited by glaciers as they melt; ground moraines.

Tiwanaku (tee-wahn-ah´-koo) Regional state, city, and valley of the same name near Lake Titicaca, in Bolivia.

Toltecs Central Mexican highlands people who created a pre-Aztec empire with its capital at Tula in the Valley of Mexico.

totem An animal or being associated with a kin-group and used for social identification; also, a carved pole representing these beings.

transhumance Seasonal migration from one resource zone to another, especially between highlands and lowlands.

transmutation The change of one species to another. The term *evolution* did not assume its current meaning until the late nineteenth century.

Tula (too´-la) Toltec capital in the Valley of Mexico; sometimes known as Tollan.

tundra Treeless plains characterized by permafrost conditions that support the growth of shallow-rooted vegetation such as grasses and mosses.

Tutankhamen (toot-en-cahm´-en) Egyptian pharaoh of the New Kingdom period, who died at age 19 in 1323 B.C.; informally known today as King Tut.

Ubaid (oo-bide´) Early formative culture of Mesopotamia, 7,500–6,200 ya; predecessor to Sumerian civilization.

uniformitarianism The theory that the earth's features are the result of long-term processes that continue to operate in the present as they did in the past. Elaborated on by Lyell, this theory opposed catastrophism and contributed strongly to the concept of immense geological time.

Upper Paleolithic Cultural period beginning roughly 40,000–30,000 ya and ending about 10,000 ya and distinguished by major technological innovations, the creation of the earliest human art widely recognized as such, and many other accomplishments. Best known from western Europe; similar industries are also known from central and eastern Europe and Africa.

variation In genetics, inherited differences among individuals; the basis of all evolutionary change.

vasoconstriction Narrowing of blood vessels to reduce blood flow to the skin. Vasoconstriction is an involuntary response to cold and reduces heat loss at the skin's surface.

vasodilation Expansion of blood vessels, permitting increased blood flow to the skin. Vasodilation permits warming of the skin and facilitates radiation of warmth as a means of cooling. Vasodilation is an involuntary response to warm temperatures, various drugs, and even emotional states (blushing).

vectors Agents that transmit disease from one carrier to another. Mosquitoes are vectors for malaria, just as fleas are vectors for bubonic plague.

vertebrates Animals with segmented, bony spinal columns; includes fishes, amphibians, reptiles (including birds), and mammals.

virulence A measure of the severity of an infectious disease. Generally, the more virulent a disease, the greater number of deaths of infected people.

Wari (wah´-ree) Regional state and city of the same name in southern Peru.

Xia (shah) Semilegendary kingdom, or dynasty, of early China.

Younger Dryas A stadial, or colder stage, between roughly 13,000 and 11,500 ya. The climate became colder and drier but did not return to full glacial conditions in higher latitudes.

Zhou (chew) Chinese dynasty that followed Shang and ruled between 1122 and 221 B.C.

ziggurat Late Sumerian mud-brick temple-pyramid.

zoonotic (zoh-oh-no´-tic) Pertaining to a zoonosis (*pl.*, zoonoses), a disease that's transmitted to humans through contact with nonhuman animals.

zygote A cell formed by the union of an egg and a sperm cell. It contains the full complement of chromosomes (in humans, 46) and has the potential to develop into an entire organism.

Bibliography

Acosta, J. de
2002　*Natural and Moral History of the Indies*, J. E. Mangan (ed.). Durham, NC: Duke University Press.

Adams, R. McC.
1981　*Heartland of Cities*. Chicago: University of Chicago Press.

Adler, D. S., G. Bar-Oz, A. Belfer-Cohen, et al.
2006　Ahead of the game: Middle and Upper Palaeolithic hunting behaviors in the southern Caucasus. *Current Anthropology* 47:89–118.

Adovasio, J. M., J. Donahue, and R. Stuckenrath
1990　The Meadowcroft Rockshelter radiocarbon chronology 1975–1990. *American Antiquity* 55(2): 348–354.

Aldred, C.
1998　*The Egyptians*. (Rev. Ed.). New York: Thames & Hudson.

Alemseged, Z., F. Spoor, W. H. Kimbel, et al.
2006　A juvenile early hominin skeleton from Dikika, Ethiopia. *Nature* 443:296–301.

Alva, W., and C. Donnan
1993　*Royal Tombs of Sipan*. Los Angeles: Fowler Museum of Cultural History, University of California.

Ambrose, S. H.
2001　Paleolithic technology and human evolution. *Science* 291:1748–1753.

Ames, K. M., and H. D. Maschner
1999　*Peoples of the Northwest Coast: Their Archaeology and Prehistory*. New York: Thames & Hudson.

Anderson, D. G., A. C. Goodyear, J. Kennett, and A. West
2011　Multiple lines of evidence for possible human population decline/settlement reorganization during the early Younger Dryas. *Quaternary International* 242:570–583.

Andrews, P.
1984　An alternative interpretation of the characters used to define *Homo erectus*. *Courier Forschungsinstitut Senckenberg* 69:167–175.

Anikovich, M.V., A. A. Sinitsy, John F. Hoffecker, et al.
2007　Early Upper Paleolithic in eastern Europe and implications for the dispersal of modern humans. *Science* 315:223–229.

Armelagos, G. J., and K. N. Harper
2005　Genomics at the origins of agriculture. Part One. *Evolutionary Anthropology* 14:68–77.

Arnau, G., K. Abraham, M. N. Sheela, et al.
2010　Yams. In: *Root and Tuber Crops*, J. E. Bradshaw (ed.), pp. 127–148. New York: Springer.

Arnold, T. G.
2006　*The Ice-Free Corridor: Biogeographical Highway or Environmental Cul-de-sac*. Unpublished Ph.D. dissertation. Department of Archaeology, Simon Fraser University, Burnaby, British Columbia.

Arsuaga, J.-L., C. Lorenzo, A. Gracia, et al.
1999　The human cranial remains from Gran Dolina Lower Pleistocene site (Sierra de Atapuerca, Spain). *Journal of Human Evolution* 37:431–457.

Arsuaga, J.-L., I. Martinez, A. Gracia, et al.
1997　Sima de los Huesos (Sierra de Atapuerca, Spain): The site. *Journal of Human Evolution* 33:109–127.

Ascenzi, A., I. Biddittu, et al.
1996　A calvarium of late *Homo erectus* from Ceprano, Italy. *Journal of Human Evolution* 31:409–423.

Asfaw, B., W. H. Gilbert, Y. Beyene, et al.
2002　Remains of *Homo erectus* from Bouri, Middle Awash, Ethiopia. *Nature* 416:317–320.

Aujoulat, N.
2005　*Lascaux: Movement, Space and Time*. New York: Abrams.

Aureli, F., C. M. Schaffner, et al.
2006　Raiding parties of male spider monkeys: Insights into human warfare? *American Journal of Physical Anthropology* 131:486–497.

Badrian, A., and N. Badrian
1984　Social organization of *Pan paniscus* in the Lomako Forest, Zaire. In: *The Pygmy Chimpanzee*, R. L. Susman (ed.), pp. 325–346. New York: Plenum Press.

Badrian, N., and R. K. Malenky
1984　Feeding ecology of *Pan paniscus* in the Lomako Forest, Zaire. In: *The Pygmy Chimpanzee*, R. L. Susman (ed.), pp. 275–299. New York: Plenum Press.

Bailey, G.
1975　The role of molluscs in coastal economies. *Journal of Archaeological Science* 2:45–62.

Bailey, G. N., and G. C. P. King
2010　Living with sea level change and dynamic landscapes: An archaeological perspective. In: *Macroengineering Seawater in Unique Environments*, V. Badescu and R. B. Cathcart (eds.), pp. 1–26. Berlin: Springer.

Balter, M.
2005　*The Goddess and the Bull*. New York: Free Press.

———
2006　Radiocarbon dating's final frontier. *Science* 313:1560–1563.

———
2010　Candidate human ancestor from South Africa sparks praise and debate. *Science* 328:154–155.

Bar-Oz, G.
2004   *Epipaleolithic Subsistence Strategies in the Levant: A Zooarchaeological Perspective.* Boston: Brill Academic Publishers.

Bar-Yosef, O.
1986   The walls of Jericho: An alternative explanation. *Current Anthropology* 27(2):157–162.

_____
1987   Late Pleistocene adaptations in the Levant. In: *The Pleistocene in the Old World: Regional Perspectives,* O. Soffer (ed.), pp. 219–236. New York: Plenum.

_____
2004   Eat what is there: Hunting and gathering in the world of Neanderthals and their neighbours. *International Journal of Osteoarchaeology* 14:333–342.

Bar-Yosef, O., and J.-G. Bordes
2010   Who were the makers of the Chatelperronian culture? *Journal of Human Evolution* 59(5): 586–593.

Bard, K.
2008   Royal cities and cult centers, administrative towns, and workmen's settlements in ancient Egypt. In: *The Ancient City: New Perspectives on Urbanism in the Old and New World,* J. Marcus and J. A. Sabloff (eds.), pp.165–182. Santa Fe: School for Advanced Research Press.

Barker, G.
2006   *The Agricultural Revolution in Prehistory: Why Did Foragers Become Farmers?* Oxford: Oxford University Press.

Barker, G., H. Barton, M. Bird, et al.
2007   The human revolution in lowland tropical Southeast Asia: The antiquity and behavior of anatomically modern humans at Niah Cave (Sarawak, Borneo). *Journal of Human Evolution* 52:243–261.

Barnosky, A., P. L. Koch, R. S. Feranec, et al.
2004   Assessing the causes of Late Pleistocene extinctions on the continents. *Science* 306:70–75.

Bartlett, T. Q., R. W. Sussman, and J. M. Cheverud
1993   Infant killing in primates: A review of observed cases with specific references to the sexual selection hypothesis. *American Anthropologist* 95:958–990.

Barton, L., S. D. Newsome, F. H. Chen, et al.
2009   Agricultural origins and the isotopic identity of domestication in northern China. *Proceedings of the National Academy of Sciences,* 106(14): 5523–5528.

Bearder, S. K.
1987   Lorises, bush babies & tarsiers: Diverse societies in solitary foragers. In: *Primate Societies,* B. B. Smuts, D. L. Cheney, and R. M. Seyfath (eds.), pp. 11–24. Chicago: University of Chicago Press.

Begun, D,. and A. Walker
1993   The Endocast. In: *The Nariokotome* Homo erectus *Skeleton,* A. Walker and R. E. Leakey (eds.), pp. 326–358. Cambridge, MA: Harvard University Press.

Beja-Pereira, A., G. Luikart, P. R. England, et al.
2003   Gene-culture coevolution between cattle milk protein genes and human lactase genes. *Nature Genetics* 35:311–313.

Belfer-Cohen, A.
1991   The Natufians in the Levant. *Annual Review of Anthropology* 20:167–186.

Bellisari, A.
2008   Evolutionary origins of obesity. *Obesity Reviews* 9(2): 165–180.

Bellwood, P.
1997   Prehistoric cultural explanations for widespread linguistic families. In: *Archaeology and Linguistics: Aboriginal Australia in Global Perspective,* P. McConvell and N. Evans (eds.), pp. 123–134. Melbourne: Oxford University Press.

Bellwood, P. S.
2005   *The First Farmers: The Origins of Agricultural Societies.* Malden, MA: Blackwell.

Bellwood, P. S., C. Gamble, S. A. Le Blanc, et al.
2007   Review feature: *First Farmers: The Origins of Agricultural Societies,* by Peter Bellwood. *Cambridge Archaeological Journal* 17(1): 87–109.

Berger, L. R., D. J. de Ruiter, S. E. Churchill, et al.
2010   *Australopithecus sediba:* A new species of *Homo*-like australopith from South Africa. *Science* 328:195–204.

Berger, T. D., and E. Trinkaus
1995   Patterns of trauma among the Neandertals. *Journal of Archaeological Science* 22(6): 841–852.

Berlo, J. (ed.)
1992   *Art, Ideology, and the City of Teotihuacán.* Washington, DC: Dumbarton Oaks.

Bermúdez de Castro, J. M., J. Arsuaga, E. Carbonell, et al.
1997   A hominid from the Lower Pleistocene of Atapuerca, Spain. Possible ancestor to Neandertals and modern humans. *Science* 276:1392–1395.

Bermúdez de Castro, J. M., M. Martinon-Torres, E. Carbonell, et al.
2004   The Atapuerca sites and their contribution to the knowledge of human evolution in Europe. *Evolutionary Anthropology* 13:25–41.

Bettinger, R. L, L. Barton, and C. Morgan
2010   The origins of food production in North China: A different kind of agricultural revolution. *Evolutionary Anthropology: Issues, News, and Reviews* 19:9–21.

Biasutti, R.
1959   La Razze e i Popoli della Terra (3rd Ed.). 4 vols. *Turin: Unione Tipografico-Editrice Torinese.*

Bicho, N., A. F. Carvalho, C. González-Sainz, et al.
2007   The Upper Paleolithic rock art of Iberia. *Journal of Archaeological Method and Theory* 14(1): 81–151.

Binford, L. R.
1968   Post-Pleistocene adaptations. In: *New Perspectives in Archaeology*, S. Binford and L. R. Binford (eds.), pp. 313–341. Chicago: Aldine.

_____
1978   *Nunamiut Ethnoarchaeology*. New York: Academic Press.

_____
1983   *In Pursuit of the Past*. New York: Thames & Hudson.

Binford, L. R., and C. K. Ho
1985   Taphonomy at a distance: Zhoukoudian, "the cave home of Beijing Man." *Current Anthropology* 26:413–442.

Binford, L. R., and N. M. Stone
1986a   The Chinese Paleolithic: An outsider's view. *AnthroQuest* 1:14–20.

_____
1986b   Zhoukoudian: A closer look. *Current Anthropology* 27:453–475.

Bininda-Emonds, R. P. Olaf, M. Cordillo, et al.
2007   The delayed rise of present-day mammals. *Nature* 446:507–512.

Bischoff, J. L., R. W. Williams, R. J. Rosebauer, et al.
2007   High-resolution U-series dates from the Sima de los Huesos hominids yields 600+/−66 kyrs: Implications for the evolution of the early Neanderthal lineage. *Journal of Archaeological Science* 34:763–770.

Blench, R.
2009   Bananas and plantains in Africa: Re-interpreting the linguistic evidence. *Ethnobotany Research & Applications* 7:363–380.

Boaz, N. T., and R. L. Ciochon
2001   The scavenging of *Homo erectus pekinensis*. *Natural History* 110(2): 46–51.

Boesch, C.
1996   Social grouping Tai chimpanzees. In: *Great Ape Societies*, W. C. McGrew, L. Marchant, and T. Nishida (eds.), pp. 101–113. Cambridge, UK: Cambridge University Press.

Boesch, C., and H. Boesch-Achermann
2000   *The Chimpanzees of the Tai Forest*. New York: Oxford University Press.

Boesch, C., P. Marchesi, et al.
1994   Is nut cracking in wild chimpanzees a cultural behaviour? *Journal of Human Evolution* 26:325–338.

Bogucki, P.
1988   *Forest Farmers and Stockherders: Early Agriculture and Its Consequences in North Central Europe*. Cambridge, UK: Cambridge University Press.

Bordaz, J.
1970   *Tools of the Old and New Stone Age*. Garden City, NY: Natural History Press.

Borries, C., K. Launhardt, C. Epplen, et al.
1999   DNA analyses support the hypothesis that infanticide is adaptive in langur monkeys. *Proceedings of the Royal Society of London Series B-Biological Sciences* 266:901–904.

Boserup, Ester
1965   *The Conditions of Agricultural Growth*. Chicago: Aldine.

Bove, F. J., and S. M. Busto
2003   Teotihuacan, militarism, and Pacific Guatemala. In: *The Maya and Teotihuacan: Reinterpreting Early Classic Interaction*, G. E. Braswell (ed.), pp. 45–79. Austin: University of Texas Press.

Brace, C. L., and A. Montagu
1977   *Human Evolution* (2nd Ed.). New York: Macmillan.

Brace, C. L., A. R. Nelson, N. Seguchi, et al.
2001   Old World sources of the first New World human inhabitants: A comparative craniofacial view. *Proceedings of the National Academy of Science* 98(4):10017–10022.

Brace, C. L., H. Nelson, and N. Korn
1979   *Atlas of Human Evolution* (2nd Ed.). New York: Holt, Rinehart & Winston.

Bradley, B., and D. Stanford
2004   The North Atlantic ice-edge corridor: A possible Palaeolithic route to the New World. *World Archaeology* 36(4): 459–478.

_____
2006   The Solutrean-Clovis connection: Reply to Straus, Meltzer and Goebel. *World Archaeology* 38(4): 704–714.

Bradley, D. G., and D. A. Magee
2006   Genetics and the origins of domestic cattle. In: *Documenting Domestication: New Genetic and Archaeological Paradigms*, M. A. Zeder, D. G. Bradley, E. Emshwiller, and B. D. Smith (eds.), pp. 317–328. Berkeley: University of California Press.

Braidwood, R. J.
1960   The agricultural revolution. *Scientific American* 203:131–148.

Braidwood, R. J., and B. Howe
1960   *Prehistoric Investigations in Iraqi Kurdistan*. Studies in Ancient Oriental Civilization, No. 31. Chicago: Oriental Institute.

Braswell, G. E. (ed.)
2003   *The Maya and Teotihuacan: Reinterpreting Early Classic Interaction*. Austin: University of Texas Press.

Braun, D. R, C. J. Norton, and J. W. K. Harris
2010   Africa and Asia: Comparisons of the earliest archaeological evidence. *In: Asian Paleoanthropology: From Africa to China and Beyond*, C. J. Norton and D. R. Braun (eds.), pp. 41–48. Dordrecht: Springer.

Breuer, T., M. Ndoundou-Hockemba, V. Fishlock, et al.
2005   First observations of tool use in wild gorillas. *PloS Biology* 3(11): e380. doi: 10.1371/journal.pbio.0030380

Briggs, A., J. M. Good, R. E. Green, et al.
2009   Targeted retrieval and analysis of five Neandertal mtDNA genomes. *Science* 325:318–320.

Bromage, T. G., and C. Dean
1985   Re-evaluation of the age at death of immature fossil hominids. *Nature* 317:525–527.

Brooks, A. S., L. Nevell, J. E. Yellen, and G. Hartman
2006   Projectile technologies of the African MSA: Implications for modern human origins. In: *Transitions before the Transition: Evolution and Stability in the Middle Paleolithic and Middle Stone Age*, E. Hovers and S. L. Kuhn (eds.), pp. 233–255. New York: Springer.

Brown, I.
1994   Recent trends in the archaeology of the southeastern United States. *Journal of Archaeological Research* 2(1): 45–111.

Brown, M. K., and T. W. Stanton (eds.)
2003   *Ancient Mesoamerican Warfare*. Walnut Creek, CA: Altamira Press.

Brown, P., T. Sutikna, M. K. Morwood, et al.
2004   A new small-bodied hominin from the Late Pleistocene of Flores, Indonesia. *Nature* 431:1055–1061.

Brubaker, L. B., P. M. Anderson, M. E. Edwards, and A. V. Lozhkin
2005   Beringia as a glacial refugium for boreal trees and shrubs: New perspectives from mapped pollen data. *Journal of Biogeography* 32(5): 833–848.

Bruhns, K. O.
1994   *Ancient South America*. Cambridge, UK: Cambridge University Press.

Bruhns, K. O., and N. L. Kelker
2007   Did the Olmec know how to write? *Science* 315:1365.

Brumm, A., G. M. Jensen, G. D. van den Bergh, et al.
2010   Hominins on Flores, Indonesia, by one million years ago. *Nature* 464:748–752.

Brunet, M., F. Guy, et al.
2002   A new hominid from the Upper Miocene of Chad, Central Africa. *Nature* 418:145–151.

Bruning, S. B.
2006   Complex legal legacies: The Native American Graves Protection and Repatriation Act, scientific study, and Kennewick Man. *American Antiquity* 71(3): 501–521.

Bryan, A. L., and R. Gruhn
2003   Some difficulties in modeling the original peopling of the Americas. *Quaternary International* 109–110:175–179.

Bryant, V. M.
2003   Invisible clues to New World plant domestication. *Science* 299:1029–1030.

Burger, R. L.
1992   *Chavín and the Origins of Andean Civilizations*. New York: Thames & Hudson.

———
2008   Chavín de Huántar and its sphere of influence. In: *The Handbook of South American Archaeology*, H. Silverman and W. H. Isbell (eds.), pp. 681–703. New York: Springer.

Butzer, K. W.
1984   Long-term Nile flood variation and political discontinuities in pharaonic Egypt. In: *From Hunters to Farmers*, J. D. Clark and S. A. Brandt (eds.), pp. 102–112. Berkeley and Los Angeles: University of California Press.

Cabanes, D., S. Weiner, and R. Shahack-Gross
2011   Stability of phytoliths in the archaeological record: A dissolution study of modern and fossil phytoliths. *Journal of Archaeological Science* 38:2480–2490.

Campbell, C. J.
2006   Lethal intragroup aggression by adult male spider monkeys (*Ateles geoffroyi*). *American Journal of Physical Anthropology* 68:1197–1201.

Cannon, M. D., and D. J. Meltzer
2004   Early Paleoindian foraging: Examining the faunal evidence for large mammal specialization and regional variability in prey choice. *Quaternary Science Reviews* 23:1955–1987.

Caramelli, D., C. Lalueza-Fox, S. Condemi, et al.
2006   A highly divergent mtDNA sequence in a Neandertal individual from Italy. *Current Biology* 16(16): R630–R632.

Caramelli, D., C. Lalueza-Fox, C. Vernesi, et al.
2003   Evidence for genetic discontinuity between Neandertals and 24,000-year-old anatomically modern humans. *Proceedings of the National Academy of Sciences* 100:6593–6597.

Carbonell, E., J. M. Bermúda de Castro, J. M. Pares, et al.
2008   The first hominin of Europe. *Nature* 452:465–469.

Carbonell, E., R. Sala Ramos, X. P. Rodríguez, et al.
2010   Early hominid dispersals: A technological hypothesis for "Out of Africa." *Quaternary International* 223–224:36–44.

Carter, H., and A. C. Mace
1923   *The Tomb of Tutankhamen*. London: Cassell.

Cartmill, M.
1972   Arboreal adaptations and the origin of the order Primates. In: *The Functional and Evolutionary Biology of Primates*, R. H. Tuttle (ed.), pp. 97–122. Chicago: Aldine-Atherton.

———
1992   New views on primate origins. *Evolutionary Anthropology* 1:105–111.

Casson, L.
2001   *Everyday Life in Ancient Egypt*. Baltimore: Johns Hopkins University Press.

Catto, N., and G. Catto
2004   Climate change, communities, and civilizations: Driving force, supporting player, or background noise? *Quaternary International* 123–125:7–10.

Centers for Disease Control
2009   www.cdc.gov/flu/about/disease

Chang, K.
1986   *The Archaeology of Ancient China* (4th Ed.). New Haven: Yale University Press.

_____
2000   Ancient China and its anthropological significance. In: *Peabody Museum Monographs 9*, M. Lamberg-Karlovsky (ed.), pp. 1–11. Cambridge, MA: Harvard University.

Chatters, J. C.
2001   *Ancient Encounters: Kennewick Man and the First Americans*. New York: Simon & Schuster.

_____
2004   Kennewick Man: A Paleoamerican skeleton from the northwestern U.S. In: *New Perspectives on the First Americans*, B. T. Lepper and R. Bonnichsen (eds.), pp. 129–135. College Station, TX: Center for the Study of First Americans.

Chauhan, P. R.
2010   The Indian subcontinent and "Out of Africa I." In: *Out of Africa I: The First Hominin Colonization of Eurasia*, J. G. Fleagle, J. J. Shea, F. E. Grine, et al. (eds.), pp. 145–164. Dordrecht: Springer, Netherlands.

Chen, F. C., and W.-H. Li
2001   Genomic divergences between humans and other hominoids and the effective population size of the common ancestor of humans and chimpanzees. *American Journal of Human Genetics* 68:444–456.

Cheng, Z., M. Ventura, X. She, et al.
2005   A Genome-wide comparison of recent chimpanzee and human segmental duplications. *Nature* 437:88–93.

Childe, V. G.
1929   *The Most Ancient East: The Oriental Prelude to European Prehistory*. New York: Knopf.

_____
1934   *New Light on the Most Ancient East*. London: Kegan Paul, Trench, Trubner.

_____
1950   The urban revolution. *Town Planning Review* 21(1): 3–17.

_____
1951   *Man Makes Himself* (Rev. Ed.). New York: New American Library.

Chimpanzee Sequencing and Analysis Consortium.
2005   Initial sequence of the chimpanzee genome and comparison with the human genome. *Nature* 437:69–87.

Ciochon, R. L., and E. A. Bettis
2009   Asian *Homo erectus* converges in time. *Nature* 458:153–154.

Ciochon, R. L., F. Huffman, et al.
2009   Rediscovery of the *Homo erectus* bed at Ngandong: Site formation of a Late Pleistocene hominin site in Asia. *American Journal of Physical Anthropology* (Supplement 48):110.

Cioffi-Revilla, C., and T. Landman
1999   Evolution of Maya polities in the ancient Mesoamerican system. *International Studies Quarterly* 43:559–598.

Clark, A. G., S. Glanowski, et al.
2003   Inferring nonneutral evolution from human-chimp-mouse orthologous gene trios. *Science* 302:1960–1963.

Clark, G.
1967   *The Stone Age Hunters*. New York: McGraw-Hill.

_____
1972   *Star Carr: A Case Study of Bioarchaeology*. Reading, MA: Addison-Wesley.

_____
1979   *Mesolithic Prelude*. Edinburgh: Edinburgh University Press.

Clottes, J.
2003   *Return to Chauvet Cave*. London: Thames & Hudson.

Coe, M. D.
1992   *Breaking the Maya Code*. New York: Thames & Hudson.

_____
1994   *Mexico: From the Olmecs to the Aztecs*. New York: Thames & Hudson.

_____
1999   *The Maya* (6th Ed.). New York: Thames & Hudson.

Cohen, M. N.
1977   *The Food Crisis in Prehistory*. New Haven, CT: Yale University Press.

_____
1989   *Health and the Rise of Civilization*. New Haven, CT: Yale University Press.

Cohen, M. N., and G. J. Armelagos (eds.)
1984   *Paleopathology at the Origins of Agriculture*. Orlando: Academic Press.

Coil, J., A. Korstanje, S. Archer, and C. A. Hastorf
2003   Laboratory goals and consideration for multiple micro-fossil extraction in archaeology. *Journal of Archaeological Science* 30:991–1008.

Colinvaux, P. A.
1979   *Why Big Fierce Animals Are Rare: An Ecologist's Perspective*. Princeton, NJ: Princeton University Press.

Collard, M., K. Edinborough, S. Shennan, and M. G. Thomas
2010   Radiocarbon evidence indicates that migrants introduced farming to Britain. *Journal of Archaeological Science* 37:866–870.

Colledge, S., and J. Conolly (eds.)
2007   *The Origins and Spread of Domestic Plants in Southwest Asia and Europe*. Publications of the

Institute of Archaeology, University College London. Walnut Creek, CA: Left Coast Press.

Colledge, S., and J. Conolly
2010   Reassessing the evidence for the cultivation of wild crops during the Younger Dryas at Tell Abu Hureyra, Syria. *Environmental Archaeology* 15:124–138.

Colwell, R. R.
1996   Global climate and infectious disease: The cholera paradigm. *Science* 274:2025–2031.

Conneller, C.
2004   Hunter-gatherers "on the move"? *Antiquity* 78(302):916–922.

Conroy, G. C.
1997   *Reconstructing Human Origins. A Modern Synthesis.* New York: W. W. Norton.

Cordell, L. S.
1998   *Prehistory of the Southwest* (2nd Ed.). Orlando, FL: Academic Press.

Covey, R. A.
2003   A processual study of Inka state formation. *Journal of Anthropological Archaeology* 22:333–357.

———
2008   The Inca empire. In: *The Handbook of South American Archaeology*, H. Silverman and W. H. Isbell (eds.), pp. 809–830. New York: Springer.

Cowgill, G. L.
2000   The Central Mexican Highlands from the rise of Teotihuacan to the decline of Tula. In: *The Cambridge History of the Native Peoples of the Americas, Vol. II: Mesoamerica, Part I*, R. E. W. Adams and M. J. MacLeod (eds.), pp. 250–317. Cambridge, UK: Cambridge University Press.

———
2004   Origins and development of urbanism: Archaeological perspectives. *Annual Review of Anthropology* 33:525–549.

Crown, P. L.
1991   Hohokam: Current views of prehistory and the regional system. In: *Chaco and Hohokam Prehistoric Regional Systems in the American Southwest*, P. L. Crown and W. J. Judge (eds.), pp. 135–157. Santa Fe: School of American Research Press.

Crutzen, P. J.
2002   Geology of mankind. *Nature* 415(6867): 23.

Cummings, M.
2000   *Human Heredity. Principles and Issues*, 5th ed. St. Paul, MN: Wadsworth/West.

Currat, M., G. Trabuchet, D. Rees, et al.
2002   Molecular analysis of the beta-globin gene cluster in the Niokholo Mandenka population reveals a recent origin of the beta(S) Senegal mutation. *American Journal of Human Genetics* 70:207–223.

Curtin, P. D.
2002   Overspecialization and remedies. In: *The Backbone of History: Health and Nutrition in the Western Hemisphere*, R. H. Steckel and J. C. Rose (eds.), pp. 603–608. New York: Cambridge University Press.

Curtin, R., and P. Dolhinow
1978   Primate social behavior in a changing world. *American Scientist* 66:468–475.

Cuzange, M. T., E. Delqué-Kolic, T. Goslar, et al.
2007   Radiocarbon intercomparison program for Chauvet Cave. *Radiocarbon* 49(2)339–347.

Cyphers, A., and A. Di Castro
2009   Early Olmec architecture and imagery. In: *The Art of Urbanism: How Mesoamerican Kingdoms Represented Themselves in Architecture and Imagery*, W. L. Fash and L. López Luján (eds.), pp. 21–51. Washington, DC: Dumbarton Oaks Research Library and Collection.

D'Azevedo, W. (ed.)
1986   *Handbook of North American Indians. Vol. 11: Great Basin.* Washington, DC: Smithsonian Institution Press.

Dalton, R.
2005   Scientists finally get their hands on Kennewick Man. *Nature* 436(7047): 10.

Darwin, C.
1859   *On the Origin of Species. A Facsimile of the First Edition.* Cambridge, MA: Harvard University Press (1964).

Darwin, F.
1950   *The Life and Letters of Charles Darwin.* New York: Henry Schuman.

Davies, N.
1983   *The Ancient Kingdoms of Mexico.* New York: Penguin.

Davis, L. G.
2011   The North American paleocoastal concept reconsidered. In: *Trekking the Shore: Changing Coastlines and the Antiquity of Coastal Settlement*, N. F. Bicho, J. A. Haws, and L. G. Davis (eds.), pp. 3–26. New York:

Davis, S., and F. R. Valla
1978   Evidence for domestication of the dog 12,000 years ago in the Natufian of Israel. *Nature* 276:608–610.

Day, M. H., and E. H. Wickens
1980   Laetoli Pliocene hominid footprints and bipedalism. *Nature* 286:385–387.

de la Torre, I.
2011   The origins of stone tool technology in Africa: A historical perspective. *Philosophical Transactions of the Royal Society B: Biological Sciences* 366(1567): 1028–1037.

de la Torre, I., and R. Mora
2005   Unmodified lithic material at Olduvai Bed I: Manuports or ecofacts? *Journal of Archaeological Science* 32(2): 273–285.

de Lumley, H., and M. de Lumley
1973   Pre-Neanderthal human remains from Arago Cave in southeastern France. *Yearbook of Physical Anthropology* 16:162–168.

de Waal, F.
1982   *Chimpanzee Politics*. London: Jonathan Cape.

_____
1987   Tension regulation and nonreproductive functions of sex in captive bonobos (*Pan paniscus*). *National Geographic Research* 3:318–335.

_____
1989   *Peacemaking Among Primates*. Cambridge, MA: Harvard University Press.

_____
1999   Cultural primatology comes of age. *Nature* 399:635–636.

_____
2007   With a little help from a friend. *PloS Biology* 5:1406–1408.

de Waal, F., and F. Lanting
1996   *Good Natured: The Origins of Right and Wrong in Humans and Other Animals*. Cambridge, MA: Harvard University Press.

_____
1997   *Bonobo: The Forgotten Ape*. Berkeley: University of California Press.

Dean, M., M. Carrington, C. Winkler, et al.
1996   Genetic restriction of HIV-1 infection and progression to AIDS by a deletion allele of the CKR5 structural gene. *Science* 273:1856–1862.

Dean, M. C., and B. H. Smith
2009   Growth and development of the Nariokotome youth, KNM-ER-15000. In: *The First Humans. Origin and Evolution of the Genus* Homo, F. E. Grine, J. J. Fleagle, and R. E. Leakey (eds.), pp. 101–120. New York: Springer.

del Carmen Rodriguez Martinez, M., P. Ortiz Ceballos, M. D. Coe, et al.
2006   Oldest writing in the New World. *Science* 313:1610–1614.

Delcourt, H. R. and P. A. Delcourt
1991   *Quaternary Ecology: A Paleoecological Perspective*. London: Chapman & Hall.

Delson, E., I. Tattersall, I., J. Van Couvering, and A. Brooks (eds.)
2000   *Encyclopedia of Human Evolution and Prehistory* (2nd Ed.). New York: Garland Publishing.

Demarrais, E., C. Gosden, and C. Renfrew
2005   *Rethinking Materiality: The Engagement of Mind with the Material World*. Cambridge, UK: McDonald Institute of Archaeological Research.

Demattè, P.
2010   The origins of Chinese writing: The Neolithic evidence. *Cambridge Archaeological Journal* 20:211–228.

Demuth, J. P., T. D. Bie, J. E. Stajich, et al.
2006   The evolution of mammalian gene families. *PloS ONE* 1(1): e85. doi: 10.1371/journal.pone.0000085

Desdemaines-Hugon, C.
2010   *Stepping-Stones: A Journey through the Ice Age Caves of the Dordogne*. New Haven: Yale University Press.

Desmond, A., and J. Moore
1991   *Darwin*. New York: Warner Books.

Diamond, J. M.
1987   The worst mistake in the history of the human race. *Discover* 8(5): 64–66.

_____
1989   The accidental conqueror. *Discover* 10(12): 71–76.

_____
1999   *Guns, Germs, and Steel: The Fates of Human Societies*. New York: W. W. Norton.

_____
2005   *Collapse: How Societies Choose to Fail or Succeed*. New York: Viking.

Diehl, R.
2004   *The Olmecs: America's First Civilization*. New York: Thames & Hudson.

Diehl, R. A., and M. D. Coe
1996   Olmec archaeology. In: *The Olmec World*, by M. D. Coe, R. A. Diehl, D. A. Freidel, et al., pp. 2–25. Princeton: The Art Museum, Princeton University.

Dillehay, T. D.
1989   *Monte Verde: A Late Pleistocene Settlement in Chile. Vol. 1: Paleoenvironment and Site Context*. Washington, DC: Smithsonian Institution Press.

_____
1997   *Monte Verde: A Late Pleistocene Settlement in Chile. Vol. 2: The Archaeological Content and Interpretation*. Washington, DC: Smithsonian Institution Press.

Dillehay, T. D., C. Ramírez, M. Pino, et al.
2008   Monte Verde: Seaweed, food, medicine, and the peopling of South America. *Science* 320(5877): 784–786.

DiPeso, C. C.
1974   *Casas Grandes, A Fallen Trading Center of the Gran Chichimeca*. Flagstaff: Northland Press.

Dirks, P. H. G. M., J. M. Kibii, B. F. Kuhn, et al.
2010   Geological setting and age of *Australopithecus sediba* from southern Africa. *Science* 328:205–208.

Dixon, E. J.
1999   *Bones, Boats, and Bison: Archaeology and the First Colonization of Western North America*. Albuquerque: University of New Mexico.

_____
2011   Late Pleistocene colonization of North America from Northeast Asia: New insights from large-scale paleogeographic reconstructions. *Quaternary International*, (in press, corrected proof). doi:10.1016/j.quaint.2011.02.027.

Domínguez-Rodrigo, M.
2002   Hunting and scavenging by early humans: The state of the debate. *Journal of World Prehistory* 16(1): 1–54.

Domínguez-Rodrigo, M., and T. R. Pickering
2003   Early hominid hunting and scavenging: A zooarchaeological review. *Evolutionary Anthropology* 12:275–282.

Dominy, N. J., and P. W. Lucas
2001   Ecological importance of trichromatic vision to primates. *Nature* 410:363–366.

Doran, D. M., and A. McNeilage
1998   Gorilla ecology and behavior. *Evolutionary Anthropology* 6:120–131.

Doran, G. H., D. N. Dickel, and L. A. Newsom
1990   A 7,290-year-old bottle gourd from the Windover site, Florida. *American Antiquity* 55:354–360.

Duarte, C., J. Mauricio, P. B. Pettitt, et al.
1999   The early Upper Paleolithic human skeleton from the Abrigo do Lagar Velho (Portugal) and modern human emergence in Iberia. *Proceedings of the National Academy of Sciences* 96:7604–7609.

Dunnell, R. C.
1982   Science, social science, and common sense: The agonizing dilemma of modern archaeology. *Journal of Anthropological Research* 38:1–25.

Durbin, R. M., et al. (The 1000 Genomes Project Consortium)
2010   A map of human genome variation from population scale sequencing. *Nature* 467:1061–1073.

Economist, The
2011   The Anthropocene: A man-made world. *The Economist* 399(8735): 81–83.

Edwards, M.
2000   Indus civilization: Clues to an ancient puzzle. *National Geographic* 197(6): 108–131.

Ehret, C.
1984   Historical/linguistic evidence for early African food production. In: *From Hunters to Farmers*, J. D. Clark and S. A. Brandt (eds.), pp. 26–35. Berkeley and Los Angeles: University of California Press.

Einwogerer, T., H. Friesinger, M. Handel, et al.
2006   Upper Palaeolithic infant burials. *Nature* 444(7117): 285.

Ellis, C. J., D. H. Carr, and T. J. Loebel
2011   The Younger Dryas and Late Pleistocene peoples of the Great Lakes region. *Quaternary International* 242(2): 534–545.

Emerson, T. E., and R. B. Lewis (eds.)
2000   *Cahokia and the Hinterlands*. Urbana: University of Illinois Press.

Enard, W., M. Przeworski, S. E. Fisher, et al.
2002   Molecular evolution of FOXP2, a gene involved in speech and language. *Nature* 418:869–872.

Erickson, D. L., B. D. Smith, A. C. Clarke, et al.
2005   An Asian origin for a 10,000-year-old domesticated plant in the Americas. *Proceedings of the National Academy of Sciences* 102(51): 18315–18320.

Erlandson, J. M.
1988   The role of shellfish in prehistoric economies: A protein perspective. *American Antiquity* 53:102–109.

_____
2002   Anatomically modern humans, maritime voyaging, and the Pleistocene colonization of the Americas. In: The First Americans, The Pleistocene Colonization of the New World, N. G. Jablonski (ed.), *Memoirs of the California Academy of Sciences*, 27:59–92.

_____
2010   Food for thought: The role of coastlines and aquatic resources in human evolution. In: *Human Brain Evolution: The Influence of Freshwater and Marine Food Resources*, S. C. Cunnane and K. M. Stewart (eds.), pp. 125–136. New York: Wiley.

Erlandson, J. M., and T. J. Braje
2011   From Asia to the Americas by boat? Paleogeography, paleoecology, and stemmed points of the Northwest Pacific. *Quaternary International* 239(1-2): 28–37.

Ezzo, J. A.
1993   Human adaptation at Grasshopper Pueblo, Arizona: Social and ecological perspectives. *International Monographs in Prehistory, Archaeological Series, 4*. Ann Arbor.

Fagan, B. M.
1993   Taming the aurochs. *Archaeology* 46(5): 14–17.

Falguères, C., J. J. Bahain, Y. Yokoyama, et al.
1999   Earliest humans in Europe: The age of TD6 Gran Dolina, Atapuerca, Spain. *Journal of Human Evolution* 37:343–352.

Falk, D., C. Hildebolt, K. Smith, et al.
2005   The brain of LB1, *Homo floresiensis*. *Science* 308:242–245.

_____
2008   LB1 did not have Laron Syndrome. *American Journal of Physical Anthropology, Supplement* 43:95 (abstract).

Falk, D., C. Hildebolt, K. Smith, et al.
2009   LM1's virtual endocast, microcephaly, and hominin brain evolution. *Journal of Human Evolution* 57:597–607.

Fedigan, L. M.
1983   Dominance and reproductive success in primates. *Yearbook of Physical Anthropology* 26:91–129.

Fiedel, S. J.
1999   Older than we thought: Implications of corrected dates for Paleoindians. *American Antiquity* 64(1): 95–116.

Fiedel, S. J., and G. Haynes
  2004   A premature burial: Comments on Grayson and Meltzer's "Requiem for Overkill." *Journal of Archaeological Science* 31:121–131.
Firestone, R. B., A. West, J. P. Kennett, et al.
  2007   Evidence for an extraterrestrial impact 12,900 years ago that contributed to the megafaunal extinctions and the Younger Dryas cooling. *Proceedings of the National Academy of Sciences* 104(41): 16016–16021.
Fischer, A. (ed.).
  1995   *Man and Sea in the Mesolithic: Coastal Settlement Above and Below Present Sea Level.* Oxford: Oxbow Books.
Fischer, A., M. Richards, J. Olsen, et al.
  2007   The composition of Mesolithic food. Evidence from the submerged settlement on the Argus Bank, Denmark. *Acta Archaeologica* 78(2): 163–178.
Fitzgerald, P.
  1978   *Ancient China.* Oxford: Elsevier Phaidon.
Flannery, K. V.
  1973   The origins of agriculture. *Annual Review of Anthropology* 2:217–310.

  1986   *Guila Naquitz: Archaic Foraging and Early Agriculture in Oaxaca, Mexico.* New York: Academic Press.
Flannery, K. V., and J. Marcus
  2000   Formative Mexican chiefdoms and the myth of the "mother culture." *Journal of Anthropological Archaeology* 19:1–37.
Fleagle, J.
  1983   Locomotor adaptations of Oligocene and Miocene hominoids and their phyletic implications. In: *New Interpretations of Ape and Human Ancestry,* R. L. Ciochon and R. S. Corruccini (eds.), pp. 301–324. New York: Plenum Press.

  1999   *Primate Adaptation and Evolution* (2nd Ed.). New York: Academic Press.
Fleischer, R. L., and H. R. Hart
  1972   Fission track dating: Techniques and problems. In: *Calibration of Hominoid Evolution: Recent Advances in Isotopic and Other Dating Methods Applicable to the Origin of Man,* W. W. Bishop and J. A. Miller (eds.), pp.135–170. New York: Wenner-Gren Foundation for Anthropological Research.
Foley, R. A.
  1991   How many hominid species should there be? *Journal of Human Evolution* 20:413–427.

  2002   Adaptive radiations and dispersals in hominin evolutionary ecology. *Evolutionary Anthropology* 11(Supplement 1): 32–37.

Food and Agriculture Organization of the United Nations.
  2010   Global Forest Resources Assessment 2010. http://www.fao.org/forestry/fra/fra2010/en/
Formicola, V., and A. P. Buzhilova
  2004   Double child burial from Sunghir (Russia): Pathology and inferences for Upper Paleolithic funerary practices. *American Journal of Physical Anthropology* 124:189–198.
Fragaszy, D., P. Izar, et al.
  2004   Wild capuchin monkeys (*Cebus libidinosus*) use anvils and stone pounding tools. *American Journal of Primatology* 64:359–366.
Franzen, J. L., P. D. Gingerich, et al.
  2009   Complete primate skeleton from the Early Eocene of Messel in Germany: Morphology and paleobiology. *PLoS ONE* 4:e5723.
Freundlich, J. C., H. Schwabedissen, and E. Wendt
  1980   Köln radiocarbon measurements II. *Radiocarbon* 22:68–81.
Friedman, F. D., et al. (eds.)
  1998   *Gifts of the Nile: Ancient Egyptian Faience.* New York: Thames & Hudson.
Fried, M. H.
  1967   *The Evolution of Political Society: An Essay in Political Anthropology.* New York: Random House.
Frisancho, A. R.
  1993   *Human Adaptation and Accommodation.* Ann Arbor: University of Michigan Press.
Frison, George C.
  1978   *Prehistoric Hunters of the High Plains.* New York: Academic Press.
Fritz, J. M., and G. Michell
  2003   *Hampi.* Bombay: India Book House.
Fuller, D. Q.
  2006   Agricultural origins and frontiers in South Asia: A working synthesis. *Journal of World Prehistory* 20:1–86.

  2010   An emerging paradigm shift in the origins of agriculture. *General Anthropology* 17:1–12.
Fuller, D. Q., N. Bolvin, T. Hoogervorst, and R. Allaby
  2011   Across the Indian Ocean: The prehistoric movement of plants and animals. *Antiquity* 85:544–558.
Fuller, D. Q, and L. Qin
  2009   Water management and labour in the origins and dispersal of Asian rice. *World Archaeology* 41:88–111.
Fuller, D. Q., L. Qin, and E. L. Harvey
  2009   An evolutionary model for Chinese rice domestication: Reassessing the data of the lower Yangtze region. In: *New Approaches to Prehistoric Agriculture,* Sung-Mo Ahn and June-Jeong Lee (eds.), pp. 313–345. Seoul: Sahoi Pyounguon.
Fuller, D. Q., Y.-I. Sato, C. Castillo, et al.
  2010   Consilience of genetics and archaeobotany in the entangled history of rice. *Archaeological and Anthropological Sciences* 2:115–131.

Fuller, D., R. Korisettar, P. C. Venkatasubbaiah, and
M. K. Jones
2004   Early plant domestications in southern India:
Some preliminary archaeobotanical results.
Vegetation History and Archaeobotany 13:115–129.

Gaffney, V., S. Fitch, and D. Smith
2009   *Europe's Lost World: The Rediscovery of Doggerland.*
York: Council for British Archaeology.

Gaillard, C., S. Mishra, M. Singh, et al.
2010   Lower and early Middle Pleistocene Acheulian in
the Indian sub-Continent. *Quaternary International*
223–224:234–241.

Galik, K., B. Senut, M. Pickford, et al.
2004   External and internal morphology of the BAR,
1002'00 *Orrorin tugenensis* femur. *Science*
305:1450–1453.

Garcia, T., G. Féraud, C. Falguères, et al.
2010   Earliest human remains in Eurasia: New ^{40}Ar/^{39}Ar
dating of the Dmanisi hominid-bearing levels,
Georgia. *Quaternary Geochronology* 5:443–451.

Gibbons, A.
2009   Celebrity fossil primate: Missing link or weak
link? *Science* 324: 1124–1125.

_____
2010   Tracing evolution's recent fingerprints. *Science*
329:740–742.

_____
2011   Skeletons present an exquisite paleo-puzzle.
Science 333:1370–1372.

Gibson, D., J. Glass, C. Lartique, et al.
2010   Creation of a bacterial cell controlled by a chemically synthesized genome. *Science* 329:52–56.

Gifford-Gonzalez, D., and O. Hanotte
2011   Domesticating animals in Africa: Implications of
genetic and archaeological findings. *Journal of
World Prehistory* 24:1–23.

Gilbert, M. T. P., D. L. Jenkins, A. Gotherstrom, et al.
2008   DNA from pre-Clovis human coprolites in
Oregon, North America. *Science* 320:786–789.

Gilbert, W. H., and B. Asfaw (eds.)
2008   *Homo erectus: Pleistocene Evidence from the Middle
Awash, Ethiopia.* Berkeley: University of California
Press.

Gilligan, I.
2010   The prehistoric development of clothing:
Archaeological implications of a thermal model.
Journal of Archaeological Method and Theory
17(1): 15–80.

Glassow, M. A.
1996   *Purisimeño Chumash Prehistory.* New York:
Harcourt Brace.

Goebel, T., M. R. Waters, and M. Dikova
2003   The archaeology of Ushki Lake, Kamchatka, and
the Pleistocene peopling of the Americas. *Science,*
301:501–505.

Goebel, T., M. R. Waters, and D. H. O'Rourke
2008   The Late Pleistocene dispersal of modern humans
in the Americas. *Science* 319:1497–1502.

Goodall, J.
1986   *The Chimpanzees of Gombe.* Cambridge, MA:
Harvard University Press.

Goren-Inbar, N. N. Alperson, M. E. Kislev, et al.
2004   Evidence of hominin control of fire at Gesher
Benot Ya'aqov, Israel. *Science* 304:725–727.

Gossett, T. F.
1963   *Race, the History of an Idea in America.* Dallas:
Southern Methodist University Press.

Gould, R. A.
1977   Puntutjarpa Rockshelter and the Australian
Desert Culture. *Anthropological Papers of the
American Museum of Natural History,* 54(1).

Gould, S. J.
1981   *The Mismeasure of Man.* New York: W.W. Norton.

_____
1985   Darwin at sea—and the virtues of port. In: *The
Flamingo's Smile. Reflections in Natural History,*
S. J. Gould (ed.), pp. 347–359. New York:
W.W. Norton.

_____
1987   *Time's Arrow, Time's Cycle.* Cambridge, MA:
Harvard University Press.

_____
1989   *Wonderful Life: The Burgess Shale and the Nature of
History.* New York: W.W. Norton.

Gramly, R. M.
1992   *Guide to the Palaeo-Indian Artifacts of North America*
(2nd Ed.). Buffalo, NY: Persimmon Press.

Grant, P. R.
1986   *Ecology and Evolution of Darwin's Finches.*
Princeton, NJ: Princeton University.

Grayson, D. K.
2004   Monte Verde, field archaeology, and the human
colonization of the Americas. In: *Entering America:
Northeast Asia and Beringia Before the Last Glacial
Maximum,* D. B. Madsen (ed.), pp. 379–387. Salt
Lake City: University of Utah Press.

Grayson, D. K., and F. Delpech
2003   Ungulates and the Middle-to-Upper Paleolithic
transition at Grotte XVI (Dordogne, France).
Journal of Archaeological Science 30:1633–1648.

Grayson, D. K., and D. J. Meltzer
2002   Clovis hunting and large mammal extinction: A
critical review of the evidence. *Journal of World
Prehistory* 16(4): 313–359.

_____
2003   A requiem for North American overkill. *Journal of
Archaeological Science* 30:585–593.

_____
2004   North American overkill continued? *Journal of
Archaeological Science* 31:133–136.

Green, R. E., J. Krause, et al.
2006   Analysis of one million base pairs of Neanderthal DNA. *Nature* 444:330–336.

Green, R. E., J. Krause, A. W. Briggs, et al.
2010   A draft sequence of the Neandertal genome. *Science* 328:710–722.

Green, T. J., B. Cochran, T. W. Fenton, et al.
1998   The Buhl burial: A Paleoindian woman from Southern Idaho. *American Antiquity* 43(4): 437–456.

Greene, J. C.
1981   *Science, Ideology, and World View.* Berkeley: University of California Press.

Greenwood, B., and T. Mutabingwa
2002   Malaria in 2000. *Nature* 415:670–672.

Gros-Louis, J., H. Perry, et al.
2003   Violent coalitionary attacks and intraspecific killing in wild White-faced Capuchin Monkeys (*Cebus capucinus*). *Primates* 44:341–346.

Grün, R., and C. B. Stringer
1991   ESR dating and the evolution of modern humans. *Archaeometry* 33:153–199.

Grün, R., C. B. Stringer, F. McDermott, et al.
2005   U-series and ESR analysis of bones and teeth relating to the human burials from Skhūl. *Journal of Human Evolution* 49:316–334.

Guidon, N., A.-M. Pessis, F. Porenti, et al.
1996   Nature and age of the deposits in Pedra Furada, Brazil: Reply to Meltzer, Adovasio, and Dillehay. *Antiquity* 70:408–421.

Haas, J., and W. Creamer
2004   Cultural transformations in the Central Andean Late Archaic. In: *Andean Archaeology,* H. Silverman (ed.), pp. 35–50. Malden, MA: Blackwell Publishing.

Haas, J., W. Creamer, and A. Ruiz
2004   Dating the late Archaic occupation of the Norte Chico region in Peru. *Nature* 432:1020–1023.

Haas, J., S. Pozorski, and T. Pozorski (eds.)
1987   *The Origins and Development of the Andean State.* New York: Cambridge University Press.

Haile-Selassie, Y., B. M. Latimer, M. Alene, et al.
2010   An early *Australopithecus afarensis* postcranium from Woranso-Mille, Ethiopia. *Proceedings of the National Academy of Sciences* 107(27): 12121–12126.

Haile-Selassie, Y., G. Suwa, and T. D. White
2004   Late Miocene teeth from Middle Awash, Ethiopia, and early hominid dental evolution. *Science* 303:1503–1505.

Hamilton, M. J., and B. Buchanan
2007   Spatial gradients in Clovis-age radiocarbon dates across North America suggest rapid colonization from the North. *Proceedings of the National Academy of Sciences* 104(40): 15625–15630.

Hanna, J. M.
1999   Climate, altitude, and blood pressure. *Human Biology,* 71:553–582.

Harlan, J. R.
1992   *Crops and Man* (2nd Ed.). Madison, WI: American Society of Agronomy and Crop Science Society of America.

Harlow, H. F.
1959   Love in infant monkeys. *Scientific American* 200:68–74.

Harlow, H. F., and M. K. Harlow
1961   A study of animal affection. *Natural History* 70:48–55.

Harris, E.
1989   *Principles of Archaeological Stratigraphy* (2nd Ed.). New York: Academic Press.

Harris, J. W. K., and S. Capaldo
1993   The earliest stone tools: Their implications for an understanding of the activities and behaviour of late Pliocene hominids. In: *The Use of Tools by Human and Nonhuman Primates*, A. Berthelet and J. Chavaillon (eds.), pp. 196–220. Oxford: Clarendon Press.

Harrison, R. J.
1985   The "Policultivo Ganadero," or secondary products revolution in Spanish agriculture, 5000–1000 B.C. *Proceedings of the Prehistoric Society* 51:75–102.

Hart, J. P., and C. M. Scarry
1999   The age of common beans (*Phaseolus vulgaris*) in the northeastern United States. *American Antiquity* 64(4): 653–658.

Haury, E. W.
1976   *The Hohokam, Desert Farmers and Craftsmen: Excavations at Snaketown, 1964–1965.* Tucson: University of Arizona Press.

Hawass, Z., and M. Lehner
1994   The Sphinx: Who built it, and why? *Archaeology* 47(5):30–41.

Haynes, C. V.
2005   Clovis, pre-Clovis, climate change and extinction. In: *Paleoamerican Origins: Beyond Clovis,* R. Bonnichsen, B. T. Lepper, D. Stanford, et al. (eds.), pp. 113–132. College Station. TX: Texas A&M University Press.

Haynes, G.
2009   Introduction to the volume. In: *American Megafaunal Extinctions at the End of the Pleistocene,* Gary Haynes (ed.), pp. 1–20. Dordrecht: Springer Netherlands.

Healan, D. M. (ed.)
1989   *Tula of the Toltecs.* Iowa City: University of Iowa Press.

Healan, D. M., and J. W. Stoutamire
1989   Surface survey of the Tula urban zone. In: *Tula of the Toltecs*, D. M. Healan (ed.), pp. 203–236. Iowa City: University of Iowa Press.

Henry, A. G., and D. R. Piperno
2008   Using plant microfossils from dental calculus to recover human diet: A case study from Tell

Al-Raqa'i, Syria. *Journal of Archaeological Science* 35:1943–1950.

Henry, D. O.
1989   *From Foraging to Agriculture: The Levant at the End of the Ice Age*. Philadelphia: University of Pennsylvania Press.

Henshilwood, C. S., F. d' Errico, and I. Watts
2009   Engraved ochres from the Middle Stone Age levels at Blombos Cave, South Africa. *Journal of Human Evolution* 57(1): 27–47.

Henzi, P., and L. Barrett
2003   Evolutionary ecology, sexual conflict, and behavioral differentiation among baboon populations. *Evolutionary Anthropology* 12:217–230.

Hetherington, R., J. V. Barrie, R. G. B. Reid, et al.
2003   Late Pleistocene coastal paleogeography of the Queen Charlotte Islands, British Columbia, Canada, and its implications for terrestrial biogeography and early postglacial human occupation. *Canadian Journal of Earth Science* 40:1755–1766.

Higham, C., and T. L.-D. Lu
1998   The origins and dispersal of rice cultivation. *Antiquity* 72:867–877.

Higham, T., C. B. Ramsey, I. Karavanic, et al.
2006   Revised direct radiocarbon dating of the Vindija G_1 Upper Paleolithic Neandertals. *Proceedings of the National Academy of Sciences* 103:553–557.

Higham, T., R. Jacobi, M. Julien, et al.
2010   Chronology of the Grotte du Renne (France) and implications for the context of ornaments and human remains within the Châtelperronian. *Proceedings of the National Academy of Sciences* 107(47): 20234–20239.

Hill, J. H.
2001   Proto-Uto-Aztecan: A community of cultivators in Central Mexico? *American Anthropologist* 103:913–934.

——
2010   New evidence for a Mesoamerican homeland for proto-Uto-Aztecan. *Proceedings of the National Academy of Sciences* 107(11): E33.

Hodder, I.
1990   *The Domestication of Europe*. Oxford: Blackwell.

Hodder, I. (ed.)
1996   *On the Surface: Çatalhöyük, 1993–95*. Monograph No 22. McDonald Institute Monographs and British Institute of Archaeology at Ankara.

Hoffman, M. A.
1991   *Egypt Before the Pharaohs* (Rev. Ed.). Austin: University of Texas Press.

Holloway, R. L.
1983   Cerebral brain endocast pattern of *Australopithecus afarensis* hominid. *Nature* 303:420–422.

——
1985   The poor brain of *Homo sapiens neanderthalensis*. In: *Ancestors, The Hard Evidence*, E. Delson (ed.), pp. 319–324. New York: Alan R. Liss.

Howell, J. H.
1987   Early farming in northwestern Europe. *Scientific American* 257(5): 118–126.

Hrdy, S. B.
1977   *The Langurs of Abu*. Cambridge, MA: Harvard University Press.

Hrdy, S. B., C. Janson, and C. van Schaik
1995   Infanticide: Let's not throw out the baby with the bath water. *Evolutionary Anthropology* 3:151–154.

Hudjashou Georgi, T. K., P. A. Underhill, et al.
2007   Revealing the prehistoric settlement of Australia by Y Chromosome and mtDNA Analysis. *Proceedings of the National Academy of Sciences* 104:8726–8730.

Huysecom, E., S. Ozainne, F. Raeli, et al.
2004   Ounjougou (Mali): A history of Holocene settlement at the southern edge of the Sahara. *Antiquity* 78(301): 579–593.

Iglesias Ponce de Léon, M.
2003   Problematical deposits and the problem of interaction: The material culture of Tikal during the Early Classic period. In: *The Maya and Teotihuacan: Reinterpreting Early Classic Interaction*, G. E. Braswell (ed.), pp. 167–198. Austin: University of Texas Press.

International Human Genome Sequencing Consortium
2001   Initial sequencing and analysis of the human genome. *Nature* 409:860–921.

Iriarte, J.
2009   Narrowing the gap: Exploring the diversity of early food-production economies in the Americas. *Current Anthropology* 50:677– 680.

Isaac, G.
1976   The activities of early African hominids: A review of archaeological evidence on the time span two and a half to one million years ago. In: *Human Origins: Louis Leakey and the East African Evidence*, G. Isaac and E. R. McCown (eds.), pp. 483–514. Menlo Park, CA: Benjamin.

Isbell, W. H., and A. Vranich
2004   Experiencing the cities of Wari and Tiwanaku. In: *Andean Archaeology*, H. Silverman (ed.), pp. 167–182. Malden, MA: Blackwell Publishing.

Isbell, W. H.
2008   Wari and Tiwanaku: International identities in the Central Andean Middle Horizon. In: *The Handbook of South American Archaeology*, H. Silverman and W. H. Isbell (eds.), pp. 731–759. New York: Springer.

Issar, A. S., and M. Zohar
2004   *Climate Change—Environment and Civilization in the Middle East*. Berlin: Springer-Verlag.

IUCN
2011   IUCN Red List of Threatened Species. Version
        1011.1. International Union for Conservation of
        Nature. http://www.iucnredlist.org/apps/
        redlist/details/159320

Jablonski, N. G.
1992   Sun, skin colour, and spina bifida: An exploration
        of the relationship between ultraviolet light and
        neural tube defects. *Proceedings of the Australian
        Society of Human Biology* 5:455–462.

Jablonski, N. G., and G. Chaplin
2000   The evolution of human skin coloration. *Journal of
        Human Evolution* 39:57–106.

_____
2002   Skin deep. *Scientific American* 287:74–81.

Jacob, T., E. Indriati, et al.
2006   Pygmoid Australomelonesian *Homo sapiens*
        skeletal remains from Liang Bua, Flores:
        Population affinities and pathological anomalies.
        Proceedings of the National Academy of Sciences
        103:13421–13426.

Jakobsson, M., S. W. Scholz, P. Scheet, et al.
2008   Genotype, haplotype and copy-number variation
        in worldwide human populations. *Nature*
        451:998–1003.

Jantz, R. L., and D. W. Owsley
2001   Variation among North American crania.
        American Journal of Physical Anthropology
        114:146–55.

Jarrige, J., and R. H. Meadow
1980   The antecedents of civilization in the Indus
        Valley. *Scientific American* 243(2): 122–133.

Jefferson, Thomas
1853   *Notes on the State of Virginia*. Richmond, VA:
        J. W. Randolph.

Jia, L., and W. Huang
1990   *The Story of Peking Man*. New York: Oxford
        University Press.

Jochim, M. A.
1976   *Hunting-Gathering Subsistence and Settlement: A
        Predictive Model*. New York: Academic Press.

_____
1998   *A Hunter-Gatherer Landscape: Southwest Germany
        in the Late Paleolithic and Mesolithic*. New York:
        Plenum Press.

Johnson, J. R., T. W. Stafford, G. J. West, et al.
2007   Before and after the Younger Dryas:
        Chronostratigraphic and paleoenvironmental
        research at Arlington Springs, Santa Rosa Island,
        California. *EOS Transactions, American Geophysical
        Union*, 88(25).

Jonaitas, A.
1988   *From the Land of the Totem Poles*. Seattle: University
        of Washington Press.

Jungers, W. L., W. E. H. Harcourt-Smith, R. E. Wunderlich,
        et al.
2009   The Foot of *Homo floresiensis*. *Nature* 459:81–84.

Kano, T.
1992   *The Last Ape. Pygmy Chimpanzee Behavior and
        Ecology*. Stanford, CA: Stanford University Press.

Kelly, R. L.
1995   *The Foraging Spectrum: Diversity in Hunter-Gatherer
        Lifeways*. Washington, DC: Smithsonian
        Institution Press.

_____
2003   Maybe we do know when people first came to
        North America; and what does it mean if we do?
        Quaternary International, 109–110:133–145.

Kembel, S. R., and J. W. Rick
2004   Building authority at Chavín de Huántar: Models
        of social organization and development in the
        Initial Period and Early Horizon. In: *Andean
        Archaeology*, H. Silverman (ed.), pp. 51–76.
        Malden, MA: Blackwell Publishing.

Kemp, B. M., A. Reséndez, J. A. R. Berrelleza, et al.
2005   An analysis of ancient Aztec mtDNA from
        Tlatelolco: Pre-Columbian relations and the
        spread of Uto-Aztecan. In: *Biomolecular
        Archaeology: Genetic Approaches to the Past*,
        D. M. Reed (ed.), pp. 22–46. Carbondale, IL:
        Center for Archaeological Investigations.

Kenoyer, J. M.
1998   *Ancient Cities of the Indus Valley Civilization*.
        Oxford: Oxford University Press.

_____
2008   Indus urbanism: New perspectives on its origin
        and character. In: *The Ancient City: New
        Perspectives on Urbanism in the Old and New World*,
        J. Marcus and J. A. Sabloff (eds.), pp. 183–208.
        Santa Fe: School for Advanced Research Press.

Kenyon, K. M.
1981   *Excavations at Jericho. Vol. 3*. Jerusalem: British
        School of Archaeology.

Kerr, R. A.
2008   Experts find no evidence for a mammoth-killer
        impact. *Science* 319(5868): 1331–1332.

Keynes, R.
2002   *Darwin, His Daughter and Human Evolution*. New
        York: Riverhead Books.

Kidder, T. R., A. L. Ortmann, and L. J. Arco
2008   Poverty Point and the archaeology of singularity.
        SAA Archaeological Record 8(5): 9–12.

King, B. J.
1994   *The Information Continuum*. Santa Fe: School of
        American Research.

_____
2004   *Dynamic Dance: Nonvocal Communication in the
        African Great Apes*. Cambridge, MA: Harvard
        University Press.

Klein, R. G.
1989/ *The Human Career. Human Biological and Cultural*
1999 *Origins* (2nd Ed.). Chicago: University of Chicago Press.

Kramer, A.
1993 Human taxonomic diversity in the Pleistocene: Does *Homo erectus* represent multiple hominid species? *American Journal of Physical Anthropology* 91:161–171.

Kramer, S. N.
1963 *The Sumerians: Their History, Culture, and Character.* Chicago: University of Chicago Press.

Krause, J., C. Lalueza-Fox, et al.
2007b The derived FOXP2 variant of modern humans was shared with Neandertals. *Current Biology* 17:1908–1912.

Krause, J., L. Orlando, D. Serre, et al.
2007a Neanderthals in central Asia and Siberia. *Nature* 449:902–904.

Krause, J., Q. Fu, J. M. Good, et al.
2010 The complete mitochondrial DNA genome of an unknown hominin from southern Siberia. *Nature* 464:894–896.

Krings, M., C. Capelli, et al.
2000 A view of Neandertal genetic diversity. *Nature Genetics* 26:144–146.

Krings, M., A. Stone, R. W. Schmitz, et al.
1997 Neandertal DNA sequences and the origin of modern humans. *Cell* 90(1): 19–30.

Kuijt, I., and B. Finlayson
2009 Evidence for food storage and predomestication granaries 11,000 years ago in the Jordan Valley. *Proceedings of the National Academy of Sciences* 106(27): 10966–10970.

Kulikov, E. E., A. B. Poltaraus, and I. A. Lebedeva
2004 DNA analysis of Sunghir remains: Problems and perspectives. Poster presentation. European Paleopathology Association Meetings, Durham, UK, August 2004.

Kuper, R., and S. Kröpelin
2006 Climate-controlled Holocene occupation in the Sahara: Motor of Africa's evolution. *Science* 313(5788): 803–807.

Kuzmin, Y. V.
2008 Siberia at the Last Glacial Maximum: Environment and archaeology. *Journal of Archaeological Research* 16(2): 163–221.

Kwak, M., J. A. Kami, and P. Gepts
2009 The putative Mesoamerican domestication center of *Phaseolus Vulgaris* is located in the Lerma-Santiago Basin of Mexico. *Crop Science* 49:554–563.

Lack, D.
1966 *Population Studies of Birds.* Oxford, UK: Clarendon.

Lahr, M. M., and R. A. Foley
1998 Towards a theory of modern human origins: Geography, demography, and diversity in recent human evolution. *Yearbook of Physical Anthropology.* 41:137–176.

Lalani, A. S., J. Masters, et al.
1999 Use of chemokine receptors by poxviruses. *Science* 286:1968–1971.

Lalueza-Fox, C., A. Rosas, A. Estalrrich, et al.
2011 Genetic evidence for patrilocal mating behavior among Neandertal groups. *Proceedings of the National Academy of Sciences,* 108:250–253.

Lamason, R. L., M-A. P. K. Mohideen, J. R. Mest, et al.
2005 SLC24A5, a putative cation exchanger, affects pigmentation in zebrafish and humans. *Science* 310:1782–1786.

Lamberg-Karlovsky, C. C., and J. A. Sabloff
1995 *Ancient Civilizations: The Near East and Mesoamerica.* Prospect Heights, IL: Waveland.

Larson, G.
2011 Genetics and domestication: Important questions for new answers. *Current Anthropology* 52(S4): S485–S495.

Lawler, A.
2007 Beyond the family feud. *Archaeology* 60(2): 20–25.

——— 2008 Indus collapse: The end or the beginning of an Asian culture? *Science* 320(5881):1281–1283.

——— 2009 Founding dynasty or myth? *Science* 325(5943): 934.

Leakey, Mary
1971 *Olduvai Gorge, Vol. 3: Excavations in Beds I and II, 1960–1963.* Cambridge: Cambridge University Press.

Leakey, M. D., and R. L. Hay
1979 Pliocene footprints in Laetolil beds at Laetoli, northern Tanzania. *Nature* 278:317–323.

Legge, A. J., and P. A. Rowley-Conwy
1987 Gazelle killing in Stone Age Syria. *Scientific American* 257(2): 88–95.

Lehner, M.
1997 *The Complete Pyramids.* New York: Thames & Hudson.

Lepre, C. J., and D. V. Kent
2010 New magnetostratigraphy for the Olduvai Subchron in the Koobi Fora Formation, northwest Kenya, with implications for early *Homo. Earth and Planetary Science Letters* 290:362–374.

Lerner, I. M., and W. J. Libby
1976 *Heredity, Evolution, and Society.* San Francisco: W. H. Freeman.

Lewis, R. B., and C. Stout (eds.)
1998 *Mississippian Towns and Sacred Spaces: Searching for an Architectural Grammar.* Tuscaloosa: University of Alabama Press.

Li, J. Z., Devin M. Absher, H. Tang, et al.
2008 Worldwide human relationships inferred from genome-wide patterns of variation. *Science* 319:1100–1104.

Li, T. Y., and D. A. Etler
  1992   New middle Pleistocene hominid crania from
          Yunxian in China. *Nature* 357:404–407.
Linnaeus, C.
  1758   *Systema Naturae*. Holmiae: Laurentii Salvii.
Liu, L.
  2009   State emergence in early China. *Annual Review of
          Anthropology* 38:217–232.
Liu, L., and H. Xu
  2007   Rethinking Erlitou: Legend, history and Chinese
          archaeology. *Antiquity* 81(314): 886–901.
Lohmueller, K. E., Amit R. Indap, S. Schmidt, et al.
  2008   Proportionally more deleterious genetic variation
          in European than in African populations. *Nature*
          451:994–997.
Lombard, M., and L. Phillipson
  2010   Indications of bow and stone-tipped arrow use
          64,000 years ago in Kwazulu-Natal, South Africa.
          Antiquity 84:635–648.
Lordkipandize, D., Tea Jashashuil, A. Vekua, et al.
  2007   Postcranial evidence from early *Homo* from
          Dmanisi, Georgia. *Nature* 449:305–310.
Lordkipandize, D., A. Vekua, R. Ferring, and P. Rightmire
  2006   A fourth hominid skull from Dmanisi, Georgia.
          The Anatomical Record: Part A 288:1146–1157.
Lovejoy, C. O., B. Latimer, G. Suwa, et al.
  2009a   Combining prehension and propulsion: The foot
          of *Ardipithecus ramidus*. *Science* 72e1–72e8.
Lovejoy, C. O., G. Suwa, S. W. Simpson, et al.
  2009b   The great divides: *Ardipithecus ramidus* reveals the
          postcrania of our last common ancestors with
          African great apes. *Science* 326:100–106.
Lowe, G. W.
  1989   The heartland Olmec: Evolution of material cul-
          ture. In: *Regional Perspectives on the Olmec*, R. J.
          Sharer and D. C. Grove (eds.), pp. 33–67.
          Cambridge: Cambridge University Press.
Loy, T. H., and E. J. Dixon
  1998   Blood residues on fluted points from Eastern
          Beringia. *American Antiquity* 63(1): 21–46.
Lucero, L. J.
  2003   The politics of ritual: The emergence of Classic
          Maya rulers. *Current Anthropology* 44(4): 523–558.
Lu, H., J. Zhang, K. Liu, et al.
  2009   Earliest domestication of common millet (*Panicum
          Miliaceum*) in East Asia extended to 10,000 years
          ago. *Proceedings of the National Academy of Sciences*
          106(18): 7367–7372.
Luo, Z., C. Yuan, Q. Meng, and Q. Ji
  2011   A Jurassic eutherian mammal and divergence of
          marsupials and placentals. *Nature* 476:442–445.
Lynch, T. F.
  1980   *Guitarrero Cave: Early Man in the Andes*. New York:
          Academic Press.

  1983   The Paleo-Indians. In: *Ancient South Americans*,
          J. D. Jennings (ed.), pp. 87–137. San Francisco:
          W. H. Freeman.

  1990   Glacial-age man in South America? A critical
          review. *American Antiquity* 55:12–36.
MacDonald, G.
  2011   Potential influence of the Pacific Ocean on the
          Indian summer monsoon and Harappan decline.
          Quaternary International 229(1–2): 140–148.
MacDougall, D.
  2009   *Nature's Clocks: How Scientists Measure the Age of
          Almost Everything*. Berkeley: University of
          California Press.
MacKinnon, J., and K. MacKinnon
  1980   The behavior of wild spectral tarsiers.
          International Journal of Primatology 1:361–379.
Malik, K.
  2007   Who owns knowledge? *Index on Censorship*
          36(3): 156–167.
Malm, T.
  1995   Excavating submerged Stone Age sites in
          Denmark—The Tybrind Vig example. In: *Man and
          Sea in the Mesolithic*, A. Fischer (ed.), pp. 385–396.
          Oxford: Oxbow Books.
Manning, K., R. Pelling, T. Higham, et al.
  2011   4500-year -old domesticated pearl millet
          (*Pennisetum Glaucum*) from the Tilemsi Valley,
          Mali: New insights into an alternative cereal
          domestication pathway. *Journal of Archaeological
          Science* 38:312–322.
Manson, J. H., and R. W. Wrangham
  1991   Intergroup aggression in chimpanzees and
          humans. *Current Anthropology* 32:369–390.
Marean, C. M.
  2010   When the sea saved humanity. *Scientific American*
          303 (August):54–61.
Marris, E.
  2006   Bushmeat surveyed in Western cities. Illegally
          hunted animals turn up in markets from New
          York to London. *News@Nature.com*. doi: 10.1038/
          news060626-10
Martin, P. S.
  1967   Prehistoric overkill. In: *Pleistocene Extinctions: The
          Search for a Cause*, P. S. Martin and H. E. Wright,
          Jr. (eds.), pp. 75–120. New Haven: Yale University
          Press.

  2005   *Twilight of the Mammoths: Ice Age Extinctions and
          the Rewilding of America*. Los Angeles: University
          of California Press.

Martin, R. D., A. M. MacLarnon, J. C. Phillips, and
  W. B. Dobyns
  2006   Flores hominid: New species or microcephalic
          dwarf? *The Anatomical Record: Part A* 288A:
          1123–1145.
Mayr, E.
  1970   *Population, Species, and Evolution.* Cambridge, MA:
          Harvard University Press.
McBrearty, S., and N. G. Jablonski
  2005   First fossil chimpanzee. *Nature* 437:105–108.
McBrinn, M. E.
  2010   Everything old is new again: Recent approaches
          to research on the Archaic period in the western
          United States. *Journal of Archaeological Research*
          18:289–329.
McDougall, I., F. H. Brown, and J. G. Fleagle
  2005   Stratigraphic placement and age of modern
          humans from Kibish, Ethiopia. *Nature*
          433:733–736.
McGhee, R.
  1996   *Ancient People of the Arctic.* Vancouver: University
          of British Columbia Press.
McGrew, W. C.
  1992   *Chimpanzee Material Culture. Implications for
          Human Evolution.* New York: Cambridge
          University Press.

  1998   Culture in nonhuman primates? *Annual Review of
          Anthropology* 27:301–328.
McHenry, H.
  1988   New estimates of body weight in early hominids
          and their significance to encephalization and
          megadontia in "robust" australopithecines. In:
          Evolutionary History of the Robust Australopithecines
          (Foundations of Human Behavior), F. E. Grine
          (ed.), pp. 133–148. Somerset, NJ: Aldine
          Transaction.

  1992   Body size and proportions in early hominids.
          American Journal of Physical Anthropology
          87:407–431.
McKusick, V. A. (with S. E. Antonarakis et al.)
  1998   *Mendelian Inheritance in Man.* (12th Ed.) Baltimore:
          Johns Hopkins University Press.
McNett, C. W.
  1985   *Shawnee Minisink: A Stratified Paleoindian-Archaic
          Site in the Upper Delaware Valley of Pennsylvania.*
          New York: Academic Press.
McPherron, S. P., Z. Alemseged, C. W. Marean, et al.
  2010   Evidence of stone-tool-assisted consumption of
          animal tissues before 3.39 million years ago at
          Dikika, Ethiopia. *Nature* 466:857–860.
Meehan, Betty
  1982   *Shell Bed to Shell Midden.* Canberra: Australian
          Institute of Aboriginal Studies.

Mellars, P.
  1989   Technological changes across the Middle-Upper
          Palaeolithic transition: Economic, social and cog-
          nitive perspectives. In: *The Human Revolution*,
          P. Mellars and C. Stringer (eds.), pp. 338–365.
          Princeton, NJ: Princeton University Press.

  2006   A new radiocarbon revolution and the dispersal
          of modern humans in Eurasia. *Nature*
          439:931–935.
Mellars, P., and P. Dark
  1999   *Star Carr in Context: New Archaeological and
          Palaeoecological Investigations at the Early Mesolithic
          Site of Star Carr, North Yorkshire.* McDonald
          Institute Monographs. London: David Brown.
Meltzer, D. J.
  1993a   Is there a Clovis adaptation? In: *From Kostenki to
          Clovis: Upper Paleolithic—Paleo-Indian Adaptations*,
          O. Soffer and D. Praslov (eds.), pp. 293–310. New
          York: Plenum Press.

  2004   On possibilities, prospecting, and patterns:
          Thinking about a pre-LGM human presence in
          the Americas. In: *Entering America: Northeast Asia
          and Beringia Before the Last Glacial Maximum*,
          D. B. Madsen (ed.), pp. 359–377. Salt Lake City:
          University of Utah Press.

  2006   *Folsom: New Archaeological Investigations of a Classic
          Paleoindian Bison Kill.* Berkeley: University of
          California Press.

  2009   *First Peoples in a New World: Colonizing Ice Age
          America.* Berkeley: University of California Press.
Meltzer, D., J. Adovasio, and T. D. Dillehay
  1994   On a Pleistocene human occupation at Pedra
          Furada, Brazil. *Antiquity* 68:695–714.
Meltzer, D. J., and V. T. Holliday
  2010   Would North American paleoindians have
          noticed Younger Dryas age climate changes?
          Journal of World Prehistory 23:1–41.
Merrill, W. L., R. J. Hard, J. B. Mabry, et al.
  2009   The diffusion of maize to the southwestern
          United States and its impact. *Proceedings of the
          National Academy of Sciences* 106(50): 21019–21026.

  2010   Reply to Hill and Brown: Maize and Uto-Aztecan
          cultural history. *Proceedings of the National
          Academy of Sciences* 107(11): E35–E36.
Mgeladze, A., D. Lordkipanidze, M. Moncel, et al.
  2011   Hominin occupations at the Dmanisi site,
          Georgia, southern Caucasus: Raw materials and
          technical behaviours of Europe's first hominins.
          Journal of Human Evolution 60:571–596.

Mihlbachler, M. C., C. A. Hemmings, and S. D. Webb
2000   Reevaluation of the Alexon bison kill site, Wacissa River, Jefferson County, Florida. *Current Research in the Pleistocene* 17:55–57.

Miller, A., and C. M. Barton
2008   Exploring the land: A comparison of land-use patterns in the Middle and Upper Paleolithic of the western Mediterranean. *Journal of Archaeological Science* 35:1427–1437.

Millon, R.
1988   The last years of Teotihuacán dominance. In: *The Collapse of Ancient States and Civilizations*, N. Yoffee and G. Cowgill (eds.), pp. 102–164. Tucson: University of Arizona Press.

Milner, G. R.
1998   *Cahokia Chiefdom: The Archaeology of a Mississippian Society*. Washington, DC: Smithsonian Institution Press.

Mitani, J. C., D. P. Watts, and S. J. Amsler
2010   Lethal intergroup aggression leads to territorial expansion in wild chimpanzees. *Current Biology* 20(12): R507–R508.

Molnar, S.
1983   *Human Variation. Races, Types, and Ethnic Groups* (2nd Ed.). Englewood Cliffs: Prentice-Hall.

Montet, P.
1981   *Everyday Life in Egypt in the Days of Ramesses the Great*. Philadelphia: University of Pennsylvania Press.

Moore, A. M. T.
1985   The development of Neolithic societies in the Near East. *Advances in World Archaeology* 4:1–69.

Moore, A. M. T., G. C. Hillman, and A. J. Legge
2000   *Village on the Euphrates: From Foraging to Farming at Abu Hureyra*. New York: Oxford University Press.

Moore, J. D., and C. J. Mackey
2008   The Chimú empire. In: *The Handbook of South American Archaeology*, H. Silverman and W. H. Isbell (eds.), pp. 783–807. New York: Springer.

Moore, L. G. and J. G. Regensteiner
1983   Adaptation to high altitude. *Annual Reviews of Anthropology*, 12:285–304.

Moore, L. G., S. Niermeyer, and S. Zamudio
1998   Human adaptation to high altitude: Regional and life-cycle perspectives. *Yearbook of Physical Anthropology* Suppl. 27:25–64.

Moratto, M. J.
1984   *California Archaeology*. New York: Academic Press.

Morwood, M. J., P. Brown, T. Jatmiko, et al.
2005   Further evidence for small-bodied hominins from the Late Pleistocene of Flores, Indonesia. *Nature* 437:1012–1017.

Morwood, M. J., R. P. Soejono, R. G. Roberts, et al.
2004   Archaeology and age of a new hominin from Flores in eastern Indonesia. *Nature* 431:1087–1091.

Moseley, M. E.
1975   *The Maritime Foundations of Andean Civilization*. Menlo Park: Cummings.

——
1992   *The Incas and Their Ancestors*. New York: Thames & Hudson.

Moseley, M. E., and K. Day (eds.)
1982   *Chan Chan: Andean Desert City*. Albuquerque: University of New Mexico Press.

Moura, A. C. A., and P. C. Lee
2004   Capuchin tool use in Caatinga dry forest. *Science* 306:1909.

Munro, N. D.
2004   Zooarchaeological measures of hunting pressure and occupation intensity in the Natufian: Implications for agricultural origins. *Current Anthropology* 45(supplement): S5–S33.

——
2009   Epipaleolithic subsistence intensification in the southern Levant: The faunal evidence. In: *The Evolution of Hominin Diets*, J.-J. Hublin and M. P. Richards (eds.), pp. 141–155. Dordrecht: Springer Netherlands.

Muttoni, G., G. Scardia, D. Kent, et al.
2009   Pleistocene magnetochronology of early hominin sites at Ceprano and Fontana Ranuccio, Italy. *Earth and Planetary Science Letters* 286:255–268.

Nadel, D.
2004   The Ohalo II brush huts and the dwelling structures of the Natufian and PPNA sites in the Jordan Valley. *Archaeology, Ethnology and Anthropology of Eurasia* 1(13): 34–48.

Napier, J.
1967   The antiquity of human walking. *Scientific American* 216:56–66.

Nentwig, W.
2007   Human environmental impact in the Paleolithic and Neolithic. In: *Handbook of Paleoanthropology*, W. Henke and I. Tattersall (eds.), pp. 1881–1900. Berlin: Springer.

Nevell, L., A. Gordon, and B. Wood
2007   *Homo floresiensis* and *Homo sapiens* size-adjusted cranial shape variations. *American Journal of Physical Anthropology, Supplement* 14:177–178 (abstract).

Neves, W. A., R. González-José, M. Hubbe, et al.
2004   Early Holocene human skeletal remains from Cerca Grande, Lagoa Santa, central Brazil, and the origins of the first Americans. *World Archaeology* 36(4): 479–501.

News in Brief
2007   Congolese government creates bonobo reserve. *Nature* 450:470. doi: 10.1038450470f

Nishida, T.
1991   Comments: Intergroup aggression in chimpanzees and humans by J. H. Manson and R. Wrangham. *Current Anthropology* 32:381–382.

Nishida, T., M. Hiraiwa-Hasegawa, T. Hasegawa, and Y. Takahata
1985   Group extinction and female transfer in wild chimpanzees in the Mahale National Park, Tanzania. *Zeitschrift Tierpsychologie—Journal of Comparative Ethology* 67:284–301.

Nishida, T., H. Takasaki, and Y. Takahata
1990   Demography and reproductive profiles. In: *The Chimpanzees of the Mahale Mountains*, T. Nishida (ed.), pp. 63–97. Tokyo: University of Tokyo Press.

Nishida, T., R. W. Wrangham, J. Goodall, and S. Uehara
1983   Local differences in plant-feeding habits of chimpanzees between the Mahale Mountains and Gombe National Park, Tanzania. *Journal of Human Evolution* 12:467–480.

Nissen, H. J.
1988   *The Early History of the Ancient Near East, 9000– 2000 B.C.* Chicago: University of Chicago Press.

———
2001   Cultural and political networks in the ancient Near East during the fourth and third millennia B.C. In: *Uruk Mesopotamia and Its Neighbors*, M. S. Rothman (ed.), pp. 149–179. Santa Fe: School of American Research Press.

Nowak, R. M.
1999   *Walker's Primates of the World*. Baltimore: Johns Hopkins University Press.

Nowell, A.
2006   From a Paleolithic art to Pleistocene visual cultures. *Journal of Archaeological Method and Theory* 13(4): 239–249.

Oates, J. F., M. Abedi-Lartey, W. S. McGraw, et al.
2000   Extinction of a West African red colobus monkey. *Conservation Biology* 14:1526–1532.

Oates, J. F., R. A. Bergl, J. Sunderland-Groves, and A. Dunn
2007   *Gorilla gorilla* ssp. Diehli. *2007 IUCN Red List of Threatened Species*.

O'Connell, J. F., K. Hawkes, K. D. Lupo, and N. G. Burton-Jones
2002   Male strategies and Plio-Pleistocene archaeology. *Journal of Human Evolution* 43:831–872.

Odell, G. H.
1998   Investigating correlates of sedentism and domestication in prehistoric North America. *American Antiquity* 63(4): 553–571.

Olsen, S. J.
1985   *Origins of the Domestic Dog: The Fossil Record*. Tucson: University of Arizona Press.

O'Rourke, D. H., and J. A. Raff
2010   The human genetic history of the Americas: The final frontier. *Current Biology* 20:R202–R207.

Ottoni, E. B., and P. Izar
2008   Capuchin monkey tool use: Overview and implications. *Evolutionary Anthropology* 17:171–178.

Ousley, S., R. Jantz, and D. Freid
2009   Understanding race and human variation: Why forensic anthropologists are good at identifying race. *American Journal of Physical Anthropology* 139:68–76.

Ovchinnikov, I. V., A. Gotherstrom, G. P. Romanova, et al.
2000   Molecular analysis of Neanderthal DNA from the northern Caucasus. *Nature* 404:490–493.

Owsley, D. W., and R. L. Jantz
2000   Biography in the bones. *Discovering Archaeology* 2(1): 56–58.

Padian, K., and L. M. Chiappe
1998   The origin of birds and their flight. *Scientific American* 278:38–47.

Palmer, S. K., L. G. Moore, D. Young, et al.
1999   Altered blood pressure course during normal pregnancy and increased preeclampsia at high altitude (3100 meters) in Colorado. *American Journal of Obstetrics and Gynecology* 180:1161–1168.

Pappu, S., Y. Gunnell, K. Akhilesh, et al.
2011   Early Pleistocene presence of Acheulian hominins in South India. *Science* 331(6024):1596–1599.

Parés, J. M., and A. Pérez-Gonzalez
1995   Paleomagnetic age for hominid fossils at Atapuerca archaeological site, Spain. *Science* 269:830–832.

Parpola, A.
1994   *Deciphering the Indus Script*. Cambridge: Cambridge University Press.

Pauketat, T. R., and R. P. Wright
2004   *Ancient Cahokia and the Mississippians*. Cambridge: Cambridge University Press.

Pearsall, D. M.
2000   *Paleoethnobotany: A Handbook of Procedures* (2nd Ed.). San Diego: Academic Press.

Peck, A., and C. Andrade-Watkins
1988   *Other People's Garbage*. Odyssey series, VHS video. Alexandria, VA: PBS Video.

Perlès, C.
2001   *The Early Neolithic in Greece*. Cambridge: Cambridge University Press.

Pettitt, P.
2008   Art and the Middle-to-Upper Paleolithic transition in Europe: Comments on the archaeological arguments for an early Upper Paleolithic antiquity of the Grotte Chauvet art. *Journal of Human Evolution* 55(5): 908–917.

———
2011   *The Palaeolithic Origins of Human Burial*. New York: Routledge.

Pettitt, P., and A. Pike
2007   Dating European Palaeolithic cave art: Progress, prospects, problems. *Journal of Archaeological Method and Theory* 14(1): 27–47.

Phillips, K. A.
1998   Tool use in wild capuchin monkeys (*Cebus albifrons trinitatis*). *American Journal of Primatology* 46:259–261.

Phillipson, D. W.
1984   Early food production in central and southern Africa. In: *From Hunter to Farmers*, J. D. Clark and S. A. Brandt (eds.), pp. 272–280. Berkeley and Los Angeles: University of California Press.

Pickering, R., P. H. G. M. Dirks, Z. Jinnah, et al.
2011   *Australopithecus sediba* at 1.977 Ma and implications for the origins of the genus *Homo*. *Science* 333:1421–1423.

Pickford, M., and B. Senut
2001   The geological and faunal context of late Miocene hominid remains from Lukeino, Kenya. *Comptes Rendus de l'Académie des Sciences, Ser. 11A, Earth and Planetary Science* 332:145–152.

Pinner, R. W., S. M. Teutsch, L. Simonson, et al.
1996   Trends in infectious diseases mortality in the United States. *Journal of the American Medical Association* 275:189–193.

Piperno, D. R.
2008   Identifying crop plants with phytoliths (and starch grains) in Central and South America: A review and an update of the evidence. *Quaternary International*. doi:10.1016/j.quaint.2007.11.011.

Piperno, D., and D. M. Pearsall
1998   *The Origins of Agriculture in the Lowland Neotropics*. San Diego: Academic Press.

Piperno, D. R., A. J. Ranere, I. Holst, et al.
2009   Starch grain and phytolith evidence for early ninth millennium BP maize from the Central Balsas River Valley, Mexico. *Proceedings of the National Academy of Sciences* 106(13): 5019–5024.

Piperno, D., and K. E. Stothert
2003   Phytolith evidence for early Holocene *Cucurbita* domestication in Southwest Ecuador. *Science* 299:1054–1057.

Piperno, D. R., E. Weiss, I. Holst, and D. Nadel
2004   Processing of wild cereal grains in the Upper Paleolithic revealed by starch grain analysis. *Nature* 430:670–673.

Pitblado, B. L.
2011   A tale of two migrations: Reconciling recent biological and archaeological evidence for the Pleistocene peopling of the Americas. *Journal of Archaeological Research* 19:327–375.

Pitulko, V. V.
2011   The Berelekh quest: A review of forty years of research in the mammoth graveyard in Northeast Siberia. *Geoarchaeology* 26:5–32.

Pitulko, V. V., P. A. Nikolsky, E. Yu. Girya, et al.
2004   The Yana RHS site: Humans in the Arctic before the Last Glacial Maximum. *Science* 303:52–56.

Plog, S.
1997   *Ancient People of the American Southwest*. New York: Thames & Hudson.

Plummer, T.
2004   Flaked stones and old bones: Biological and cultural evolution at the dawn of technology. *Yearbook of Physical Anthropology* 47:118–164.

Pohl, M. E. D., K. O. Pope, and C. von Nagy
2002   Olmec origins of Mesoamerican writing. *Science* 298:1984–1987.

Population Reference Bureau
2009   2009 World Population Data Sheet. http://www.prb.org/Publications/Datasheets/2009/2009wpds.aspx

Possehl, G. L.
1990   Revolution in the urban revolution: The emergence of Indus urbanization. *Annual Review of Anthropology* 19:261–282.

_____
1996   *Indus Age: The Writing System*. Philadelphia: University of Pennsylvania Press.

_____
2002   *The Indus Civilization: A Contemporary Perspective*. Walnut Creek, CA: Altamira Press.

Potts, R.
1988   *Early Hominid Activities at Olduvai*. New York: Aldine.

_____
1991   Why the Oldowan? Plio-Pleistocene toolmaking and the transport of resources. *Journal of Anthropological Research* 47:153–176.

_____
1993   Archeological interpretations of early hominid behavior and ecology. In: *The Origin and Evolution of Humans and Humanness*, D. T. Rasmussen (ed.), pp. 49–74. Boston: Jones and Bartlett.

Potts, R., and R. Teague
2010   Behavioral and environmental background to "Out-of-Africa I" and the arrival of *Homo erectus* in East Asia. In: *Out of Africa I: The First Hominin Colonization of Eurasia*, J. G. Fleagle, J. J. Shea, F. E. Grine, et al. (eds.), pp. 67–85. Dordrecht: Springer, Netherlands.

Powell, M. A.
1985   Salt, seed, and yields in Sumerian agriculture: A critique of the theory of progressive salinization. *Zeitschrift für Assyriologie und Vorderasiatische Archäologie* 75(1): 7–38.

Powis, T. G., W. J. Hurst, M. del Carmen Rodriguez, et al.
2007   Oldest chocolate in the New World. *Antiquity* 81(314). December. http://www.antiquity.ac.uk/ProjGall/powis/index.html.

Pozorski, S., and T. Pozorski
  1988   *Early Settlement and Subsistence in the Casma Valley,
          Peru.* Iowa City: University of Iowa Press.

_____
  2008   Early cultural complexity on the coast of Peru.
          In: *The Handbook of South American Archaeology,*
          H. Silverman and W. H. Isbell (eds.), pp. 607–631.
          New York: Springer.

Price, T. D.
  2009   Ancient farming in eastern North America.
          Proceedings of the National Academy of Sciences
          106(16): 6427–6428. doi:10.1073/pnas.0902617106.

Price, T. D., and O. Bar-Yosef
  2010   Traces of inequality at the origins of agriculture in
          the ancient Near East. In: *Pathways to Power: New
          Perspectives on the Emergence of Social Inequality,*
          T. D. Price and G. M. Feinman (eds.), pp. 147–168.
          New York: Springer.

Pringle, H.
  2009   A new look at the Mayas' end. *Science* 324(5926):
          454–456.

_____
  2011   Texas site confirms pre-Clovis settlement of the
          Americas. *Science* 331(6024):1512.

Proctor, R.
  1988   From anthropologie to rassenkunde. In: *Bones,
          Bodies, Behavior. History of Anthropology* (Vol. 5),
          W. J. Stocking, Jr. (ed.), pp. 138–179. Madison:
          University of Wisconsin Press.

Pruetz, J. D., and P. Bertolani
  2007   Savanna chimpanzees, *Pan troglodytes verus,* hunt
          with tools. *Current Biology* 17:412–417.

Pusey, A., J. Williams, and J. Goodall
  1997   The influence of dominance rank on the repro-
          ductive success of female chimpanzees. *Science*
          277:828–831.

Rak, Y., A. Ginzburg, and E. Geffen
  2007   Gorilla-like anatomy on *Australopithecus afarensis*
          mandibles suggests *Au. afarensis* link to robust
          australopiths. *Proceedings of the National Academy
          of Sciences* 104:6568–6572.

Ramos, P. A. S.
  1999   *The Cave of Altamira.* New York: Abrams.

Ranere, A. J., D. R. Piperno, I. Holst, et al.
  2009   The cultural and chronological context of early
          Holocene maize and squash domestication in the
          Central Balsas River Valley, Mexico. *Proceedings of
          the National Academy of Sciences* 106(13):
          5014–5018.

Rasmussen, M., Y. Li, S. Lindgreen, et al.
  2010   Ancient human genome sequence of an extinct
          Palaeo-Eskimo. *Nature* 463:757–762.

Rathje, W. L., and C. Murphy
  2001   *Rubbish!: The Archaeology of Garbage.* Tucson:
          University of Arizona Press.

Ray, H. P.
  2003   *The Archaeology of Seafaring in Ancient South Asia.*
          Cambridge: Cambridge University Press.

Redman, C. L.
  1978   *The Rise of Civilization.* San Francisco:
          W. H. Freeman.

Reef Water Quality Protection Plan Secretariat
  2011   *Great Barrier Reef, First Report Card, 2009 Baseline.*
          Brisbane, Australia: The State of Queensland.

Reich, D., R. E. Green, and M. Kircher
  2010   Genetic history of an archaic hominin group from
          Denisova Cave in Siberia. *Nature* 468:1053–1060.

Reimer, P. J., M. G. L. Baillie, E. Bard, et al.
  2009   IntCal09 and Marine09 radiocarbon age calibra-
          tion curves, 0-50,000 years cal BP. *Radiocarbon*
          51(4): 1111-1150.

Reinberg, S.
  2009   Swine flu has infected 1 in 6 Americans:CDC.
          U.S. News and World Reports. http://www.
          usnews.com/health [posted December 10, 2009].

Reinhard, K. I., and V. M. Bryant
  1992   Coprolite analysis. *Archaeological Method and
          Theory* 14:245–288.

Relethford, J. H.
  2001   *Genetics and the Search for Modern Human Origins.*
          New York: Wiley-Liss.

Renne, P. R., W. D. Sharp, et al.
  1997 ^{40}Ar/^{39}Ar dating into the historic realm:
          Calibration against Pliny the younger. *Science*
          277:1279–1280.

Rhesus Macaque Genome Sequencing and Analysis
          Consortium.
  2007   Evolutionary and biomedical insights from the
          rhesus macaque genome. *Science* 316:222–234.

Rhodes, E. J.
  2011   Optically stimulated luminescence dating of sedi-
          ments over the past 200,000 years. *Annual Review
          of Earth and Planetary Sciences* 39:461–488.

Richards, M. P., R. J. Schulting, and R. E. M. Hedges
  2003   Sharp shift in diet at onset of Neolithic. *Nature*
          425(6956): 366.

Richmond, B. G., and W. L. Jungers
  2008   *Orrorin tugenensis* femoral morphology and the
          evolution of hominin bipedalism. *Science*
          319:1662–1665.

Riddle, R. D., and C. J. Tabin
  1999   How limbs develop. *Scientific American* 280:74–79.

Ridley, M.
  1993   *Evolution.* Boston: Blackwell Scientific
          Publications.

Rightmire, G. P.
  1998   Human evolution in the Middle Pleistocene: The
          role of *Homo heidelbergensis. Evolutionary
          Anthropology* 6:218–227.

2004 Affinities of the Middle Pleistocene cranium from Dali and Jinniushan. *American Journal of Physical Anthropology,* Supplement 38:167 (abstract).

Rindos, D.
1984 *The Origins of Agriculture: An Evolutionary Perspective.* Orlando, FL: Academic Press.

Roaf, M.
1996 *Cultural Atlas of Mesopotamia and the Ancient Near East.* New York: Facts on File.

Robinson, W. J.
1990 Tree-ring studies of the Pueblo de Acoma. *Historical Archaeology* 24(3): 99–106.

Roebroeks, W., and P. Villa
2011 On the earliest evidence for habitual use of fire in Europe. *Proceedings of the National Academy of Sciences* 108:5209–5214.

Rogers, M. J, and S. Semaw
2009 From nothing to something: the appearance and context of the earliest archaeological record. In: *Sourcebook of Paleolithic Transitions,* M. Camps and P. R. Chauhan (eds.), pp. 155–171. New York: Springer.

Roosevelt, A. C., et al.
1996 Paleoindian cave dwellers in the Amazon: The peopling of the Americas. *Science* 272:373–384.

Rothschild, N. A.
1979 Mortuary behavior and social organization at Indian Knoll and Dickson Mounds. *American Antiquity* 44:658–675.

Rowe, M. W., and K. L. Steelman
2003 Comment on "Some Evidence of a Date of First Humans to Arrive in Brazil." *Journal of Archaeological Science* 30(10):1349–1351.

Rowley-Conwy, P.
2004 How the West was lost: A reconsideration of agricultural origins in Britain, Ireland, and southern Scandinavia. *Current Anthropology* 45(supplement): S83–S113.

2011 Westward ho! The spread of agriculturalism from central Europe to the Atlantic. *Current Anthropology* 52(S4): S431–S451.

Rudran, R.
1973 Adult male replacement in one-male troops of purple-faced langurs (*Presbytis senex senex*) and its effect on population structure. *Folia Primatologica* 19:166–192.

Ruff, C. B., and A. Walker
1993 The body size and shape of KNM-WT 15000. In: *The Nariokotome* Homo erectus *Skeleton,* A. Walker and R. E. Leakey (eds.), pp. 234–265. Cambridge, MA: Harvard University Press.

Sadr, K.
2003 The Neolithic of southern Africa. *Journal of African History* 44(2): 195–209.

Samson, M., F. Libert, B. J. Doranz, et al.
1996 Resistance to HIV-1 infection in Caucasian individuals bearing mutant alleles of the CCR-5 chemokine receptor gene. *Nature* 382:722–725.

Samuels, S. R. (ed.)
1991 *Ozette Archaeological Project Research Reports.* Pullman, WA: Washington State University.

Sanders, W. T., and J. Michels (eds.)
1977 *Teotihuacan and Kaminaljuyu: A Study in Prehistoric Culture Contact.* College Park: Pennsylvania State University Press.

Sanders, W. T., J. R. Parsons, and R. S. Santley
1979 *The Basin of Mexico: Ecological Processes in the Evolution of a Civilization.* New York: Academic Press.

Sandweiss, D. H., et al.
1996 Geoarchaeological evidence from Peru for a 5000 years B.P. onset of El Niño. *Science* 273:1531–1533.

Santos, G. M., M. I. Bird, F. Parenti, et al.
2003 A revised chronology of the lowest occupation layer of Pedra Furada Rock Shelter, Piaui, Brazil: The Pleistocene peopling of the Americas. *Quaternary Science Reviews* 22(21–22): 2303–2310.

Sarmiento, E. E.
2010 Comment on the paleobiology and classification of *Ardipithecus ramidus*. *Science* 328:1105-b.

Sarmiento, E. E., and J. F. Oates
2000 The Cross River gorilla: A distinct subspecies *Gorilla gorilla diehli* Matschie 1904. *American Museum Novitates* 3304:1–55.

Saunders, J. W.
2010 Middle Archaic and Watson Brake. In: *Archaeology of Louisiana,* M. A. Rees (ed.), pp. 62–76. Baton Rouge: Louisiana State University Press.

Savage-Rumbaugh, S., and R. Lewin
1994 *Kanzi: The Ape at the Brink of the Human Mind.* New York: Wiley.

Savage-Rumbaugh, S., K. McDonald, et al.
1986 Spontaneous symbol acquisition and communicative use by pygmy chimpanzees (*Pan paniscus*). *Journal of Experimental Psychology: General* 115:211–235.

Savard, M., M. Nesbitt, and M. Jones
2006 The role of wild grasses in subsistence and sedentism: New evidence from the northern Fertile Crescent. *World Archaeology* 38(2):179–196.

Savolainen, P.
2002 Genetic evidence for an East Asian origin of domestic dogs. *Science* 298:1610–1613.

Saxena, A., V. Prasad, I. B. Singh, M. S. Chauhan, and R. Hasan
2006 On the Holocene record of phytoliths of wild and cultivated rice from Ganga Plain: Evidence for rice-based agriculture. *Current Science* 90:1547–1552.

Schauber, A. D., and D. Falk
2008   Proportional dwarfism in foxes, mice, and humans: Implications for relative brain size in *Homo floresiensis. American Journal of Physical Anthropology, Supplement* 43:185 (abstract).

Schele, L., and D. Freidel
1990   *A Forest of Kings.* New York: William R. Morrow.

Schele, L., and M. E. Miller
1986   *The Blood of Kings: Dynasty and Ritual in Maya Art.* Fort Worth: Kimbell Art Museum.

Schmitz, R. W., D. Serre, G. Bonani, et al.
2002   The Neandertal type site revisited: Interdisciplinary investigations of skeletal remains from the Neander Valley, Germany. *Proceedings of the National Academy of Sciences* 99:13342–13347.

Schoeninger, M. J.
1981   The agricultural "revolution": Its effect on human diet in prehistoric Iran and Israel. *Paléorient* 7:73–92.

Schoeninger, M. J., M. J. Deniro, and H. Tauber
1983   Stable nitrogen isotope ratios of bone collagen reflect marine and terrestrial components of prehistoric human diet. *Science* 220:1381–1383.

Scriver, C. R.
2001   *The Metabolic and Molecular Bases of Inherited Disease.* New York: McGraw-Hill.

Semaw, S., M. J. Rogers, J. Quade, et al.
2003   2.6-million-year-old stone tools and associated bones from OGS-6 and OGS-7, Gona, Afar, Ethiopia. *Journal of Human Evolution* 45:169–177.

Semaw, S., M. Rogers, and D. Stout
2009   The Oldowan-Acheulian transition: Is there a "Developed Oldowan" artifact tradition? In: *Sourcebook of Paleolithic Transitions: Methods, Theories, and Interpretations,* M. Camps and P. R. Chauhan (eds.), pp.173–193. New York: Springer.

Senut, B., M. Pickford, D. Grommercy, et al.
2001   First hominid from the Miocene (Lukeino Formation, Kenya). *Comptes Rendus de l'Académie des Sciences, Ser. 11A, Earth and Planetary Science* 332:137–144.

Serre, D., A. Langaney, M. Chech, et al.
2004   No evidence of Neandertal mtDNA contribution to early modern humans. *Plos Biology* 2:313–317.

Seyfarth, R. M., D. L. Cheney, and P. Marler
1980a   Monkey responses to three different alarm calls. *Science* 210:801–803.

Seyfarth, R. M., D. L. Cheney, and P. Marler
1980b   Vervet monkey alarm calls: Semantic communication in a free-ranging primate. *Animal Behaviour* 28:1070–1094.

Shang, H., H. Tong, S. Zhang, et al.
2007   An early modern human from Tianyuan Cave, Zhoukoudian, China. *Proceedings of the National Academy of Sciences* 104:6573–6578.

Sharer, R. J.
1996   *Daily Life in Maya Civilization.* Westport, CT: Greenwood Press.

Shea, J. J.
2006   The origins of lithic projectile point technology: Evidence from Africa, the Levant, and Europe. *Journal of Archaeological Science* 33(6): 823–846.

———
2009   The impact of projectile weaponry on Late Pleistocene hominin evolution. In: *The Evolution of Hominin Diets,* J.-J. Hublin and M. P. Richards (eds.), pp. 189–199. Dordrecht: Springer Netherlands.

Shea, J. J., and M. L. Sisk
2010   Complex projectile technology and *Homo sapiens* dispersal into western Eurasia. *PaleoAnthropology* 2010:100–122.

Sheets, P. D.
2006   *The Cerén Site: An Ancient Village Buried by Volcanic Ash in Central America.* (2nd Ed.) Belmont, CA: Thomson Wadsworth.

Sheets, P. D. (ed.)
2002   *Before the Volcano Erupted: The Ancient Cerén Village in Central America.* Austin: University of Texas Press.

Shen, G., X. Gao, B. Gao, and D. E. Granger
2009   Age of Zhoukoudian *Homo erectus* with ^{26}Ar/^{10}Be burial dating. *Nature* 458:198–200.

Shubin, N., C. Tabin, and S. Carroll
1997   Fossils, genes, and the evolution of animal limbs. *Nature* 388:639–648.

Silk, J. B., S. C. Alberts, and J. Altman
2003   Social bonds of female baboons enhance infant survival. *Science* 302:1231–1234.

Silk, J. B., S. F. Brosman, J. Vonk, et al.
2005   Chimpanzees are indifferent to the welfare of unrelated group members. *Nature* 437:1357–1359.

Simpson, S. W., J. Quade, N. E. Levin, et al.
2008   A female *Homo erectus* pelvis from Gona, Ethiopia. *Science* 322:1089–1092.

Smith, A.
1992   Origins and spread of pastoralism in Africa. *Annual Review of Anthropology* 21:125–141.

Smith, A., P. Berens, C. Malherbe, and M. Guenther
2000   *The Bushmen of Southern Africa: A Foraging Society in Transition.* Athens: Ohio University Press.

Smith, B. D.
1992   *Rivers of Change: Essays on Early Agriculture in Eastern North America.* Washington, DC: Smithsonian Institution.

———
1997   Reconsidering the Ocampo caves and the era of incipient cultivation in Mesoamerica. *Latin American Antiquity* 8:342–383.

———
1999   *The Emergence of Agriculture* (2nd Ed.) New York: W. H. Freeman.

Smith, B. D., and R. A. Yarnell
2009   Initial formation of an indigenous crop complex in eastern North America at 3800 B.P. *Proceedings of the National Academy of Sciences* 106(16): 6561–6566.

Smith, F. H.
1984   Fossil hominids from the Upper Pleistocene of central Europe and the origin of modern Europeans. In: *The Origins of Modern Humans*, F. H. Smith and F. Spencer (eds.), pp. 187–209. New York: Alan R. Liss.

——   2002   Migrations, radiations and continuity: Patterns in the evolution of Late Pleistocene humans. In: *The Primate Fossil Record*, W. Hartwig (ed.), pp. 437–456. New York: Cambridge University Press.

Smith, F. H., A. B. Falsetti, and S. M. Donnelly
1989   Modern human origins. *Yearbook of Physical Anthropology* 32:35–68.

Smith, M. E.
2003   *The Aztecs* (2nd Ed.). Malden, MA: Blackwell Publishing.

——   2008   *Aztec City-State Capitals*. Gainesville: University Press of Florida.

Smith, P., O. Bar-Yosef, and A. Sillen
1984   Archaeological and skeletal evidence for dietary change during the Late Pleistocene/early Holocene in the Levant. In: *Paleopathology at the Origins of Agriculture*, M. N. Cohen and G. J. Armelagos (eds.), pp. 101–136. Orlando, FL: Academic Press.

Snow, C. P.
1965   *Two Cultures and the Scientific Revolution*. (2nd Ed.). Cambridge: Cambridge University Press.

Snow, D. R.
1980   *The Archaeology of New England*. New York: Academic Press.

——   2006   Sexual dimorphism in Upper Palaeolithic hand stencils. *Antiquity* 80(308): 390–404.

Soffer, O., J. M. Adovasio, D. C. Hyland, et al.
2000   The "Venus" figurines. *Current Anthropology* 41(4): 511–537.

Soffer, O., and N. D. Praslov (eds.)
1993   *From Kostenki to Clovis: Upper Paleolithic—Paleo-Indian Adaptations*. New York: Plenum Press.

Spencer, C. S., and E. M. Redmond
2004   Primary state formation in Mesoamerica. *Annual Review of Anthropology* 33:173–199.

Sponheimer, M., B. H. Passey, D. J. de Ruiter, et al.
2006   Isotopic evidence for dietary variability in the early hominin *Paranthropus robustus*. *Science* 314:980–982.

Spoor, F., M. G. Leakey, P. N. Gathago, et al.
2007   Implications of new early *Homo* fossils from Ileret, East of Lake Turkana, Kenya. *Nature* 448:688–691.

Stahl, P. W.
2008   Animal domestication in South America. In: *The Handbook of South American Archaeology*, H. Silverman and W. H. Isbell (eds.), pp. 121–130. New York: Springer.

Stanish, C.
2001   The origin of state societies in South America. *Annual Review of Anthropology* 30:41–64.

Starin, E. D.
1994   Philopatry and affiliation among red colobus. *Behaviour* 130:253–270.

Steckel, R. H., and J. C. Rose
2002   *The Backbone of History: Health and Nutrition in the Western Hemisphere*. New York: Cambridge University Press.

Steele, D. G.
2000   The Skeleton's Tale. *Discovering Archaeology* 2(1): 61–62.

Steele, D. G., and J. F. Powell
1999   Peopling of the Americas: A historical and comparative perspective. In: *Who Were the First Americans?*, R. Bonnichsen (ed.), pp. 97–126. Corvallis, OR: Center for the Study of the First Americans, Oregon State University.

Stein, B.
1994   *Vijayanagara*. Cambridge, UK: Cambridge University Press.

Steiper, M. E., and N. M. Young
2006   Primate molecular divergence dates. *Molecular Phylogenetics and Evolution* 41:384–394.

Steklis, H. D.
1985   Primate communication, comparative neurology, and the origin of language reexamined. *Journal of Human Evolution* 14:157–173.

Straus, L. G.
In press.   The emergence of modern-like forager capacities and behaviors in Africa and Europe: Abrupt or gradual, biological or demographic? *Quaternary International*, in press, corrected proof. doi:10.1016/j.quaint.2010.10. 002.

Strier, K. B.
2003   *Primate Behavioral Ecology*. Boston: Allyn and Bacon.

Stringer, C. B., and P. Andrews
1988   Genetic and fossil evidence for the origin of modern humans. *Science* 239:1263–1268.

Struhsaker, T. T.
1967   Auditory communication among vervet monkeys (*Cercopithecus aethiops*). In: *Social Communication Among Primates*, S. A. Altmann (ed.), pp. 281–324. Chicago: University of Chicago Press.

Struhsaker, T. T., and L. Leland
1987   Colobines: Infanticide by adult males. In: *Primate Societies*, B. Smuts, D. L. Cheney, R. M. Seyfarth, et al. (eds.), pp. 83–97. Chicago: University of Chicago Press.

Stutz, A. Jonas, N. D. Munro, and G. Bar-Oz
2009   Increasing the resolution of the broad spectrum revolution in the southern Levantine Epipaleolithic (19–12 Ka). *Journal of Human Evolution* 56:294–306.

Sumner, D. R., M. E. Morbeck, and J. Lobick
1989   Age-related bone loss in female Gombe chimpanzees. *American Journal of Physical Anthropology* 72:259.

Surovell, T. A., N. Waguespack, and P. J. Brantingham
2005   Global archaeological evidence for Proboscidean overkill. *Proceedings of the National Academy of Sciences* 102(17): 6231–6236.

Susman, R. L. (ed.)
1984   *The Pygmy Chimpanzee: Evolutionary Biology and Behavior.* New York: Plenum Press.

Susman, R. L., J. T. Stern, and W. L. Jungers
1985   Locomotor adaptations in the Hadar hominids. In: *Ancestors: The Hard Evidence*, E. Delson (ed.), pp. 184–192. New York: Alan R. Liss.

Sussman, R. W.
1991   Primate origins and the evolution of angiosperms. *American Journal of Primatology* 23:209–223.

Sussman, R. W., J. M. Cheverud, and T. Q. Bartlett
1995   Infant killing as an evolutionary strategy: Reality or myth? *Evolutionary Anthropology* 3:149–151.

Suwa, G., R. T. Kono, S. Katch, et al.
2007   A new species of great ape from the late Miocene epoch in Ethiopia. *Nature* 448:921–924.

Tamm, E., T. Kivisild, M. Reidla, et al.
2007   Beringian standstill and spread of Native American founders. *PLoS ONE* 2(9): e829.

Tattersall, I., E. Delson, and J. Van Couvering
1988   *Encyclopedia of Human Evolution and Prehistory.* New York: Garland Publishing.

Taylor, R. E., and M. J. Aitken
1997   *Chronometric Dating in Archaeology.* New York: Plenum Press.

Teresi, D.
2002   *Lost Discoveries. The Ancient Roots of Modern Science—from the Babylonians to the Maya.* New York: Simon & Schuster.

Texier, P.-J., G. Porraz, J. Parkington, et al.
2010   A Howiesons Poort tradition of engraving ostrich eggshell containers dated to 60,000 years ago at Diepkloof Rock Shelter, South Africa. *Proceedings of the National Academy of Sciences* 107(14): 6180–6185.

Thieme, H.
2005   The Lower Palaeolithic art of hunting. In: *The Hominid Individual in Context: Archaeological Investigations of Lower and Middle Palaeolithic Landscapes, Locales and Artefacts*, C. Gamble and M. Porr (eds.), pp. 115–132. New York: Routledge.

Thomas, D. H., J. O. Davis, D. K. Grayson, et al.
1983   The archaeology of Monitor Valley 2: Gatecliff Shelter. *Anthropological Papers* 59, Pt. 1. New York: American Museum of Natural History.

Tiemel, C., Y. Quan, and W. En
1994   Antiquity of *Homo sapiens* in China. *Nature* 368:55–56.

Tishkoff, S. A., F. A. Reed, et al.
2007   Convergent adaptation of human lactase persistence in Africa and Europe. *Nature Genetics* 39(1): 31–40.

Tocheri, M. W., Caley M. Orr, et al.
2007   The primitive wrist of *Homo floresiensis* and its implications for hominin evolution. *Science* 317:1743–1745.

Traverse, A.
2007   *Paleopalynology.* (2nd Ed.) Dordrecht: Springer, Netherlands.

Trigger, B. G.
2003   *Understanding Early Civilizations.* Cambridge, UK: Cambridge University Press.

Trinkaus, E.
2005   Early modern humans. *Annual Review of Anthropology* 34:207–230.

Trinkaus, E., S. Milota, R. Rodrigo, et al.
2003   Early modern human cranial remains from Pestera cu Oase, Romania. *Journal of Human Evolution* 45:245–253.

Trinkaus, E., and P. Shipman
1992   *The Neandertals.* New York: Alfred A. Knopf.

Turner, C. G., and J. A. Turner
1999   *Man Corn: Cannibalism and Violence in the American Southwest and Mexico.* Salt Lake City: University of Utah Press.

Van der Merwe, N. J.
1969   *The Carbon-14 Dating of Iron.* Chicago and London: University of Chicago Press.

Van Noten, F., and J. Raymaekers
1987   Early iron smelting in central Africa. *Scientific American* 258:84–91.

van Schaik, C. P., M. Ancrenaz, G. Bogen, et al.
2003   Orangutan cultures and the evolution of material culture. *Science* 299:102–105.

Vavilov, N. I.
1992   *The Origin and Geography of Cultivated Plants.* Cambridge, UK: Cambridge University Press.

Venter, J. C., M. D. Adams, E. W. Myers, et al.
2001   The sequence of the human genome. *Science* 291:1304–1351.

Verhoeven, M.
2004   Beyond boundaries: Nature, culture and a holistic approach to domestication in the Levant. *Journal of World History* 18(3): 179–281.

Vialet, A., L. Tianyuan, D. Grimaud-Herve, et al.
2005   Proposition de reconstitution du deuxième crâne d'*Homo erectus* de Yunxian (Chine). *Comptes rendus. Palévol* 4:265–274.

Vidale, M.
2010   Aspects of palace life at Mohenjo-Daro. *South Asian Studies* 26:59–76.

Vigilant, L., M. Hofreiter, H. Siedel, and C. Boesch
2001   Paternity and relatedness in wild chimpanzee communities. *Proceedings of the National Academy of Sciences* 98:12890–12895.

Vignaud, P., P. Duringer, H. MacKaye, et al.
2002   Geology and palaeontology of the Upper Miocene Toros-Menalla hominid locality, Chad. *Nature* 418:152–155.

Villa, P.
1983   *Terra Amata and the Middle Pleistocene Archaeological Record of Southern France.* University of California Publications in Anthropology, Vol. 13. Berkeley: University of California Press.

Visalberghi, E.
1990   Tool use in *Cebus*. *Folia Primatologica* 54:146–154.

Visalberghi, E. D. F., E. Ottoni, et al.
2007   Characteristics of hammer stones and anvils used by wild bearded capuchin monkeys (*Cebus libidinosus*) to crack open palm nuts. *American Journal of Physical Anthropology* 132:426–444.

Vogelsang, R.
1998   *Middle-Stone-Age-Fundstellen in Südwest-Namibia.* Cologne:Heinrich-Barth-Institut.

von Falkenhausen, L.
2008   Stages in the development of "Cities" in pre-imperial China. In: *The Ancient City: New Perspectives on Urbanism in the Old and New World,* J. Marcus and J. A Sabloff (eds.), pp. 209–228. Santa Fe: School for Advanced Research Press.

Wagner, D. P., and J. M. McAvoy
2004   Pedoarchaeology of Cactus Hill, a sandy Paleoindian site in southeastern Virginia, U.S.A. *Geoarchaeology: An International Journal* 19(4):297–322.

Wagner, G. A.
2007   Chronometric methods in paleoanthropology. In *Handbook of Paleoanthropology* 1, W. Henke and I. Tattersall (eds.), pp. 311–337.

Waguespack, N. M.
2007   Why we're still arguing about the Pleistocene occupation of the Americas. *Evolutionary Anthropology* 16(2): 63–74.

Walker, A.
1976   Remains attributable to *Australopithecus* from East Rudolf. In: *Earliest Man and Environments in the Lake Rudolf Basin,* Y. Coppens (ed.), pp. 484–489. Chicago: University of Chicago Press.

———
1991   The origin of the genus *Homo*. In: *Evolution of Life,* S. Osawa and T. Honjo (eds.), pp. 379–389. Tokyo: Springer-Verlag.

Walker, A., and R. E. Leakey
1993   *The Nariokotome* Homo erectus *Skeleton.* Cambridge, MA: Harvard University Press.

Walker, J., R. A. Cliff, and A. G. Latham
2006   U-Pb isoptoic age of the Stw 573 hominid from Sterkfontein, South Africa. *Science* 314:1592–1594.

Walker, R. B., and B. N. Driskell (eds.)
2007   *Foragers of the Terminal Pleistocene in North America.* Lincoln: University of Nebraska Press.

Walsh, P. D., K. A. Abernethy, M. Bermejo, et al.
2003   Catastrophic ape decline in western equatorial Africa. *Nature* 422:611–614.

Warneken, F., and M. Tomasello
2006   Altruistic helping in human infants and young chimpanzees. *Science* 311:1301–1303.

Warren W. C., L. W. Hillier, J. A. Marshall, et al.
2008   Genome analysis of the platypus reveals unique signatures of evolution. *Nature* 453:175–183.

Waters, M. R., S. L. Forman, T. A. Jennings, et al.
2011   The Buttermilk Creek Complex and the origins of Clovis at the Debra L. Friedkin Site, Texas. *Science* 331(6024): 1599–1603.

Waterston, R. H., K. Lindblad-Toh, E. Birney, et al. (Mouse Genome Sequencing Consortium)
2002   Initial sequencing and comparative analysis of the mouse genome. *Nature* 421:520–562.

Watkins, T.
2010   New light on Neolithic revolution in South-West Asia. *Antiquity* 84:621–634.

Watts, I.
2010   The pigments from Pinnacle Point Cave 13B, Western Cape, South Africa. *Journal of Human Evolution* 59(3-4): 392–411.

Webb, W. S.
1974   *Indian Knoll.* Knoxville: University of Tennessee Press.

Webster, D., A. Freter, and N. Gonlin
2000   *Copán: The Rise and Fall of an Ancient Maya Kingdom.* Belmont, CA: Thomson Wadsworth.

Weiner, S., Q. Xu, P. Goldberg, et al.
1998   Evidence for the use of fire at Zhoukoudian, China. *Science* 281:251–253.

Weiss, E., W. Wetterstrom, D. Nadel, and O. Bar-Yosef
2004a   The broad spectrum revisited: Evidence from plant remains. *Proceedings of the National Academy of Sciences* 101(26): 9551–9555.

Weiss, E., M. E. Kislev, O. Simchoni, and D. Nadel
2004b   Small-grained wild grasses as staple food at the 23,000-year-old site of Ohalo II, Israel. *Economic Botany* 58(supplement): S125–S134.

Weiss, U.
2002   Nature insight: Malaria. *Nature* 415:669.

Wendorf, F., and R. Schild
1989   *The Prehistory of Wadi Kubbaniya*. Dallas: Southern Methodist University.

1994   Are the early Holocene cattle in the eastern Sahara domestic or wild? *Evolutionary Anthropology* 3:118–128.

Wenke, R. J.
2009   *The Ancient Egyptian State: The Origins of Egyptian Culture (c. 8000–2000 BC)*. Cambridge, UK: Cambridge University Press.

Westergaard, G. C., and D. M. Fragaszy
1987   The manufacture and use of tools by capuchin monkeys (*Cebus apella*). *Journal of Comparative Psychology* 101:159–168.

West, F. H., and C. West (eds.)
1996   *American Beginnings: The Prehistory and Palaeoecology of Beringia*. Chicago: University of Chicago Press.

Westley, K., and J. Dix
2008   The Solutrean Atlantic hypothesis: A view from the ocean. *Journal of the North Atlantic* 1:85–98.

Wheat, J. B.
1972   The Olsen-Chubbuck site: A Paleo-Indian bison kill. *American Antiquity* 37:1–180.

White, T. D.
1986   Cut marks on the Bodo cranium: A case of prehistoric defleshing. *American Journal of Physical Anthropology* 69:503–509.

1992   *Prehistoric Cannibalism at Mancos SMTUMR-2346*. Princeton, NJ: Princeton University Press.

White, T. D., B. Asfaw, Y. Beyene, et al.
2009   *Ardipithecus ramidus* and the paleobiology of early hominids. *Science* 326:75–86.

White, T. D., B. Asfaw, D. DeGusta, et al.
2003   Pleistocene *Homo sapiens* from Middle Awash, Ethiopia. *Nature* 423:742–747.

White, T. D., G. WoldeGabriel, B. Asfaw, et al.
2006   Asa Issie, Aramis and the origin of *Australopithecus*. *Nature* 440:883–889.

Whiten, A., J. Goodall, W. C. McGrew, et al.
1999   Cultures in chimpanzees. *Nature* 399:682–685.

Whittle, A.
1985   *Neolithic Europe: A Survey*. Cambridge, UK: Cambridge University Press.

Wildman, D. E., M. Uddin, G. Liu, et al.
2003   Implications of natural selection in shaping 99.4% nonsynonymous DNA identity between humans and chimpanzees: Enlarging genus *Homo*. *Proceedings of the National Academy of Sciences* 100:7181–7188.

Williams, J. M.
1999   *Female Strategies and the Reasons for Territoriality in Chimpanzees. Lessons from Three Decades of Research at Gombe*. Unpublished Ph.D. Thesis, University of Minnesota.

Williams, M. A. J.
1984   Late Quaternary prehistoric environments of the Sahara. In: *From Hunter to Farmers*, J. D. Clark and S. A. Brandt (eds.), pp. 74–83. Berkeley and Los Angeles: University of California Press.

Willoughby, P. R.
2009   From the Middle to the Later Stone Age in Eastern Africa. In: *Sourcebook of Paleolithic Transitions*, M. Camps and P. Chauhan (eds.), pp. 301–314. New York: Springer.

Wilson, D. J.
1981   Of maize and men: A critique of the maritime hypothesis of state origins on the coast of Peru. *American Anthropologist* 83:931–940.

Winslow, D. L., and J. R. Wedding
1997   Spirit Cave Man. *American History* 32 (March/April): 74.

Wolpoff, M. H., J. Hawks, D. Frayer, and K. Hunley
2001   Modern human ancestry at the peripheries: A test of the replacement theory. *Science* 291:293–297.

Wolpoff, M. H., B. Senut, M. Pickford, and J. Hawks
2002   Paleoanthropology (communication arising): *Sahelanthropus* or '*Sahelpithecus*'? *Nature* 419:581–582.

Wolpoff, M. H., A. G. Thorne, et al.
1994   Multiregional evolutions: A world-wide source for modern human populations. In: *Origins of Anatomically Modern Humans*, M. H. Nitecki and D. V. Nitecki (eds.), pp. 175–199. New York: Plenum Press

Wong, K.
2009   Rethinking the hobbits of Indonesia. *Scientific American* 301 (November): 66–73.

Woo, J. K.
1966   The skull of Lantian Man. *Current Anthropology* 7:83–86.

Wood, B.
1991   *Koobi Fora Research Project IV: Hominid Cranial Remains from Koobi Fora*. Oxford: Clarendon Press.

2010   Reconstructing human evolution: Achievements, challenges, and opportunities. *Proceedings of the National Academy of Sciences* 107(Suppl. 2): 8902–8909.

Wood, B., and M. Collard
1999a   The human genus. *Science* 284:65–71.

1999b   The changing face of genus *Homo*. *Evolutionary Anthropology* 8:195–207.

Wood, B., and T. Harrison
2011   The evolutionary context of the first hominins. *Nature* 470:347–352.

Woolley, L.
1929   *Ur of the Chaldees*. London: Ernest Benn.

Wrangham, R., A. Clark, and G. Isabiryre-Basita
1992   Female social relationships and social organization of Kibale forest chimps. In: *Topics in*

Primatology, W. McGrew T. Nishida, P. Marler, et al. (eds.), pp. 81–98. Tokyo: Tokyo University Press.

Wrangham, R. W., and B. B. Smuts
1980   Sex differences in the behavioural ecology of chimpanzees in Gombe National Park, Tanzania. *Journal of Reproduction and Fertility* 28:13–31.

Wright, H. E.
1993   Environmental determinism in Near Eastern prehistory. *Current Anthropology* 34:458–469.

Wu, R., and X. Dong
1985   *Homo erectus* in China. In: *Palaeoanthropology and Palaeolithic Archaeology in the People's Republic of China*, R. Wu and J. W. Olsen (eds.), pp. 79–89. New York: Academic Press.

Wu, R., and J. W. Olsen (eds.)
1985   *Palaeoanthropology and Palaeolithic Archaeology in the People's Republic of China*. Orlando, FL: Academic Press.

Wu, X., and F. E. Poirier
1995   *Human Evolution in China*. New York: Oxford University Press.

Wuethrich, B.
1998   Geological analysis damps ancient Chinese fires. *Science* 281:165–166.

Yan, W.
1999   Neolithic settlements in China: Latest finds and research. *Journal of East Asian Archaeology* 1:131–147.

Yellen, J. E.
1980   *Archaeological Approaches to the Present*. New York: Academic Press.

Yi, X, Y. Liang, E. Huerta-Sanchez, et al.
2010   Sequencing of 50 human exomes reveals adaptation to high altitude. *Science* 329:75–78.

Yoffee, N.
2005   *Myths of the Archaic State: Evolution of the Earliest Cities, States, and Civilizations*. Cambridge, UK: Cambridge University Press.

Yokoyama, Y, C. Falguères, F. Sémah, et al.
2008   Gamma-ray spectrometric dating of late *Homo erectus* skulls from Ngandong and Sambungmacan, Central Java, Indonesia. *Journal of Human Evolution* 55:274–277.

Young, D.
1992   *The Discovery of Evolution*. Cambridge, UK: Natural History Museum Publications, Cambridge University Press.

Yudkin, J.
1969   Archaeology and the nutritionist. In: *The Domestication and Exploitation of Plants and Animals*, P. J. Ucko and G. W. Dimbleby (eds.), pp. 547–554. Chicago: Aldine.

Zazula, G. D., D. G. Froese, C. E. Schweger, et al.
2003   Ice-age steppe vegetation in East Beringia. *Nature* 423(6940): 603–603.

Zeder, M. A.
2008   Domestication and early agriculture in the Mediterranean Basin: Origins, diffusion, and impact. *Proceedings of the National Academy of Sciences* 105(33): 11597–11604.

Zhang, C., and H.-C. Hung
2008   The Neolithic of southern China–Origin, development, and dispersal. *Asian Perspectives* 47:299–329.

Zhang, F., S. L. Kearns, P. J. Orr, et al.
2010   Fossilized melanosomes and the colour of Cretaceous dinosaurs and birds. *Nature* 463:1075–1078.

Zhang, J. Z., Y. P. Zhang, et al.
2002   Adaptive evolution of a duplicated pancreatic ribonuclease gene in a leaf-eating monkey. *Nature Genetics* 30:411–415.

Zhao, Z.
2010   New data and new issues for the study of origin of rice agriculture in China. *Archaeological and Anthropological Sciences* 2:99–102.

Zhu, R. X., Z. S. An, R. Potts, et al.
2003   Magnetostratigraphic dating of early humans in China. *Earth Science Reviews* 61:341–359.

Index